RICHARD STRAUSS
Man, Musician, Enigma

Richard Strauss in 1925

RICHARD STRAUSS
Man, Musician, Enigma

MICHAEL KENNEDY

CAMBRIDGE
UNIVERSITY PRESS

PUBLISHED BY THE PRESS SYNDICATE OF THE UNIVERSITY OF CAMBRIDGE
The Pitt Building, Trumpington Street, Cambridge CB2 1RP, United Kingdom

CAMBRIDGE UNIVERSITY PRESS
The Edinburgh Building, Cambridge CB2 2RU, UK   http://www.cup.cam.ac.uk
40 West 20th Street, New York, NY 10011–4211, USA   http://www.cup.org
10 Stamford Road, Oakleigh, Melbourne 3166, Australia

© Cambridge University Press 1999

First published 1999

Printed in the United Kingdom at the University Press, Cambridge

Typeset in Minion 10.5/14 pt   [SE]

A catalogue record for this book is available from the British Library

Library of Congress cataloguing in publication data

Kennedy, Michael, 1926–
    Richard Strauss : man, musician, enigma / Michael
Kennedy.
        p.   cm.
    Includes bibliographical references and index.
    ISBN 0-521-58173-7
    1. Strauss, Richard, 1864–1949.   2. Composers –
Germany – Biography.   I. Title.
ML410.S93K46   1999
780'.92–dc21   98–35860   CIP   MN
[B]

ISBN 0 521 58173 7 hardback

For my friend Stephan Kohler,
in Straussian fellowship

CONTENTS

List of illustrations   *ix*
Preface   *xiii*
Acknowledgements   *xv*

PART I
1864–1898   *Youth in Munich*

1   The family   *3*
2   Wunderkind   *12*
3   Growing up   *27*
4   Meiningen   *37*
5   Third conductor   *46*
6   Dora and Weimar   *54*
7   First failure   *64*
8   Engagement   *77*
9   Pauline   *84*
10   The tone-poet   *101*

PART II
1898–1918   *The Berlin years*

11   At the Kaiser's court   *125*
12   Enter Hofmannsthal   *150*
13   The *Ariadne* crisis   *174*
14   Twentieth-century Offenbach   *189*

PART III
1918–1933   *Out of fashion*

15   Vienna   *205*
16   *Intermezzo*   *229*
17   *Helena*   *238*
18   *Arabella*   *247*
19   The gathering storm   *255*

PART IV
1933–1949   *The dark years*

20   Taking Walter's place   *269*
21   The Reich Chamber   *280*
22   Dismissal   *292*
23   Working with Gregor   *305*
24   Danae and Madeleine   *321*
25   After *Capriccio*   *334*
26   Eightieth birthday   *350*
27   *Metamorphosen*   *357*
28   'I am Richard Strauss . . .'   *363*
29   The exile   *368*
30   London   *375*
31   Last songs   *381*
32   Return to Garmisch   *387*

Appendix 1   Strauss as conductor and pianist   *401*
Appendix 2   Strauss and the gramophone   *406*

Notes   *409*
Select bibliography   *422*
Index   *427*

ILLUSTRATIONS

Richard Strauss in 1925 (property of the author) *frontispiece*

1 Strauss and his sister Johanna as children
   (Lebrecht Collection) *9*

2 Strauss aged about sixteen
   (Richard Strauss-Archiv, Garmisch) *21*

3 Strauss and his father, *c.* 1903
   (Lebrecht Collection) *25*

4 Dora Wihan
   (Richard Strauss-Archiv, Garmisch) *39*

5 Pauline de Ahna as Elsa in *Lohengrin*
   (Lebrecht Collection) *65*

6 Strauss and Pauline
   (Richard Strauss-Archiv, Garmisch) *87*

7 Strauss and 'Bubi' aged three
   (Richard Strauss-Archiv, Garmisch) *91*

8 At St Moritz: Strauss, Pauline and a friend, Herr Milch
   (Richard Strauss-Archiv, Garmisch) *107*

9 Rehearsing in the opera pit
   (Richard Strauss-Archiv, Garmisch) *131*

10 Strauss and Hugo von Hofmannsthal at Rodaun *153*

11 The Presentation of the Silver Rose: the autograph MS
    (Lebrecht Collection) *165*

12 The first singers of the Act III Trio in *Der Rosenkavalier*
    (Lebrecht Collection) *171*

13 The Strauss villa in Garmisch
    (Richard Strauss-Archiv, Garmisch) *197*

14   Father and son
      (Richard Strauss-Archiv, Garmisch)   *217*

15   Franz and Alice Strauss
      (Richard Strauss-Archiv, Garmisch)   *225*

16   Hans Knappertsbusch, Strauss and Eugen Papst playing Skat
      (Richard Strauss-Archiv, Garmisch)   *237*

17   Alice, Pauline and Richard Strauss
      (Richard Strauss-Archiv, Garmisch)   *249*

18   Strauss with grandsons Richard and Christian
      (Richard Strauss-Archiv, Garmisch)   *273*

19   Bayreuth 1934: Hans Tietjen, Winifred Wagner, Strauss and Emil
      Praetorius (Richard Strauss-Archiv, Garmisch)   *277*

20   Strauss with Joseph Gregor
      (Richard Strauss-Archiv, Garmisch)   *295*

21   Rehearsing the *Olympic Hymn*, Berlin, 1936
      (Richard Strauss-Archiv, Garmisch)   *313*

22   Symphonia domestica: Strauss with his son and grandsons
      (Richard Strauss-Archiv, Garmisch)   *315*

23   With Clemens Krauss at *Capriccio* rehearsal   *327*

24   With Viorica Ursuleac after the première of *Capriccio*, Munich
      1942 (Richard Strauss-Archiv, Garmisch)   *337*

25   With Alice in Vienna, 1943
      (Richard Strauss-Archiv, Garmisch)   *343*

26   With Baldur von Schirach and Gerhart Hauptmann
      (Richard Strauss-Archiv, Garmisch)   *348*

27   A Nazi 'Diktat' on Strauss's 80th birthday
      (property of the author)   *351*

28   With John de Lancie at Garmisch, 1945
      (Richard Strauss-Archiv, Garmisch)   *365*

29   In Garmisch, 1945
      (Richard Strauss-Archiv, Garmisch, copyright
      John de Lancie)   *367*

30   With Willi Schuh and Paul Sacher in Zürich, 1945
      (Richard Strauss-Archiv, Garmisch)   *370*

31 In the Theatre Royal, Drury Lane, October 1947
    (Hulton Deutsch Collection)   *377*
32 At Garmisch on his 85th birthday
    (Richard Strauss-Archiv, Garmisch)   *390*
33 At Garmisch 1949
    (Richard Strauss-Archiv, Garmisch)   *392*
34 Pauline at the funeral, 12 September 1949
    (Richard Strauss-Archiv, Garmisch)   *396*

PREFACE

My intention in writing this book was originally to expand upon my book on the composer in the Master Musicians series and to explain why I love the music of Richard Strauss so much, but that I understand why many people are either antipathetic to it or strongly hostile. But as I wrote, I decided that the first part of my intention was repetitive and boring and the second part negative and a waste of the reader's time. If people do not like Strauss's music, let *them* write a book to say why.

It then occurred to me that there is no detailed and extensive biography of Strauss in print written in English. The most recent was the translation of Kurt Wilhelm's splendid personal portrait, published in Britain in 1989. Norman Del Mar's three volumes contain much biography, but a generation has passed since Volume 3 was published; and admirable though Del Mar's achievement is, I take issue with most of his opinions both about the man and the music, especially the later music.

I also wanted to tackle fully the thorny subject of Strauss and the Third Reich. The only way to explain Strauss's position, I believe, is to set down the facts in perspective and in context. It is significant that in the latest large biography of Strauss to be published in German – Franzpeter Messmer's *Richard Strauss: Biographie eines Klangzauberers* – 481 pages of text are devoted to the life. Of these, 410 take the story up to 1933. The crucial and critical last sixteen years from 1933 to 1949 are dismissed in fifty-four pages. I have not gone so far as totally to reverse this disproportion, but the 1933–49 period occupies a substantial percentage of the book. I lived through the whole of the Nazi period, although I was a schoolchild when Hitler came to power, but I have vivid recollections of the years from 1933 to the Munich agreement of 1938 and know how different attitudes to the Nazis were up to the point where Hitler began his 'territorial demands'. I find insufferable the smug holier-than-thou attitude of people who know with such certainty exactly how honourably and courageously they would have behaved in Germany after 1933. Strauss was no hero; he was weak in many ways, immensely strong in others. He was centred almost exclusively on his family and on his work. He can be judged only against the full background of the time.

There is no shortage of superb books and monographs on Strauss's music so, while I have discussed the works, particularly the later operas which have been generally underrated until recent years, I have not gone into analytical detail. When we have Del Mar's volumes, William Mann's and Charles Osborne's books on the operas, the various Cambridge and ENO opera guides on individual operas and such marvellous monographs as Bryan Gilliam's *Elektra*, there is less need for another book in this field than there is, I believe, for a comprehensive biographical study. This I have attempted to provide as a tribute to his memory in the year of the fiftieth anniversary of his death. I shall not be alive when the bicentenary of his birth is celebrated in June 2064 but those who are will, I am convinced, reap the benefits of the further researches of Strauss scholarship. More will have emerged from the Garmisch archive and by then, I hope, there will be (in German and English) a complete edition of his vast correspondence. Also much needed is a critical edition of his works which will eradicate many of the textual errors in the printing of several of his scores and will take account of some of his unpublished revisions.

ACKNOWLEDGEMENTS

My first debt of gratitude is to the composer's grandsons, Richard Strauss and Dr Christian Strauss, for permission to quote from Strauss's letters and writing and for their hospitality in granting me access to the wonderful archive at Garmisch. I would also like to thank Dr Christian Strauss for his patience and frankness in answering my queries about his grandfather and father. I am deeply indebted to Stephan Kohler, director of the Richard-Strauss-Institut in Munich, for his generous help and advice, not only in many conversations about Strauss but in providing me with photocopies of material held by the Institut and for answering many questions. I have been helped with translations by Elizabeth Mortimer and Arthur Tennant, to both of whom I offer my heartfelt thanks as I do to Dr Delia Kühn for the many family reminiscences and other help. I am grateful for his assistance regarding the 1933–4 *Parsifal* to Dr Sven Friedrich, Director of the Richard-Wagner-Museum, Haus Wahnfried, Bayreuth. I very much appreciate help from Dr Günter Brosche, Director of the Music Collection of the Austrian National Library, Vienna. For permission to quote from his translation of *Intermezzo*, I am indebted to Mr Andrew Porter. To Joyce Bourne, who has typed the book, offered advice and had to endure my constant preoccupation with Strauss, my deepest gratitude.

No writer on Strauss can fail to acknowledge indebtedness to his predecessors. I have mentioned Norman Del Mar and other authors in the Preface. To their names I would add that of Kurt Wilhelm, whose *Richard Strauss persönlich* (1984) is indispensable (it is a pity it was insensitively cut for its English version). The first volume of Willi Schuh's unfinished official biography is the authoritative source for the early years. Also indispensable are Franz Trenner's catalogues of the works and of the Garmisch sketchbooks. A treasure trove is the collection of letters published as *Eine Welt in*

Briefen (which is long overdue for an English translation) and other volumes of Strauss's correspondence. The various monographs on Strauss's operas published by Cambridge University Press are a source of insight into the works' history and musical structure. For permission to quote from the Strauss-Hofmannsthal correspondence and from Willi Schuh's *Richard Strauss: a Chronicle of the Early Years, 1864-1898*, I acknowledge the kindness of Cambridge University Press.

PART I

1864–1898
Youth in Munich

1   The family

On the surface, life was good to Richard Strauss. He was successful, world-famous, rich and happily married for fifty-four years. Look a little below the surface and we see a different picture, that of a composer who was in tune with the times for only the early part of his career. For most of his life he found himself at odds with the direction music was taking. The world left him behind and he retreated from the world. Strauss the composer was strong, powerfully individual and passionate. Strauss the man was cool, aloof, easily complaisant, with a vein not so much of weakness as of haughty indifference which was to cause his name to be tainted (unfairly, as I intend to show). The exuberant, forceful, extrovert Strauss of his twenties and early thirties, obviously an artist in appearance and manner, became the reticent, understating bourgeois who could have been mistaken for a banker. This change was reflected even in his style of conducting. The life which began with a comet-like blaze of sensational excitement ended with a long sunset in which exile and the threat of disgrace cast lengthening tragic shadows. The musical parallel is exact: from the rush of strings and the ringing trumpet tone of *Don Juan* to a song in which death is awaited in a garden where summer is dying. The enigma of Richard Strauss, the why and the wherefore of the man and the musician, will perhaps never be solved. It can perhaps be explained.

In the opinion of the Canadian musician Glenn Gould, writing in 1962, Strauss was 'the greatest musical figure who has lived in this century'.[1] Yet a distinguished English critic, Rodney Milnes, writing in *The Times* in 1995, referred to the hypothesis that 'the court of posterity is still reserving judgment on Richard Strauss'. There has never been a consensus about Strauss. For as many who find his music enriching, exciting and satisfying, there are equally as many who find it shallow and meretricious. Regarded in his youth as the arch-fiend of modernism, in his later years he was written off as an extinct volcano, an arch-conservative living off his own fat, composing by numbers. Not only in his later years, either. When *Symphonia domestica* was first performed in London in 1905, Ernest Newman regretted that a composer of genius should ever have fallen so low. Progressives wrote him off after *Der Rosenkavalier*, regarding him as a traitor to the cause of advanced music which they thought he had espoused in *Elektra*. But it was, and is, impossible to write off Strauss. Like him or not, he is a giant figure in the music of his time, a time which stretched from before Wagner's death to four years after the end of the Second World War – from Brahms and Bruckner to Boulez and Messiaen. Throughout that long composing career – a total of seventy-eight years – he remained true to a belief in tonality as the cornerstone of musical craft. To quote Gould again: 'In him we have one of these rare, intense figures in whom the whole process of historical evolution is defied'.[2] He is accused of having betrayed modernity. But this is a criticism by those who equate modernity with the extravagance of the *avant-garde*. Let Strauss's own words refute the allegation: 'Modern? What does "modern" mean? Give the word a different significance! Have ideas like Beethoven's, write contrapuntally like Bach, orchestrate like Mozart and be genuine and true children of your own times, then you will be modern!'

That defiance is what I admire most in Strauss. Even though his music increases in popularity year by year, it is still largely misunderstood and underrated. The superficial judgments on him linger on. I see him as in many ways a tragic figure, symbolising the struggle to preserve beauty and style in Western European culture, a struggle that he lost, although not through any deficiency on his own part. His greatness has not yet been fully discovered and understood. This book is an attempt to advance that discovery and understanding.

There can be no real understanding of Strauss without acknowledgment of three fundamental strands in his personality: he was German and proud of it, steeped in love of and admiration for German art and culture; he was bourgeois and content to be so; and he regarded the family as the governing factor in life and morality. Overriding even these factors was his Nietzschean total absorption in art. Art was the reality in his life. The only purpose of life, he said, was 'to make art possible. Christianity had to be invented in order, after Phidias, to make possible the Colmar Altar, the Sistine Madonna, the

Missa solemnis and *Parsifal.*' Yet he never became pretentious, was never a poseur. He remained practical, down-to-earth and modest within a knowledge of his worth. His music is almost wholly autobiographical. As a subject for music, he told Romain Rolland, he found himself just as interesting as Napoléon or Alexander the Great. That was in 1902. In 1949, three months before he died, he wrote: 'Why don't people see what is new in my works, how in them, as is found otherwise only in Beethoven, the human being visibly plays a part in the work?'[3] Not only Beethoven, of course, but let that pass.

A comparison between Strauss and three of his contemporaries is pertinent. Of his relationship with Gustav Mahler (1860–1911) more will be said in some detail, but the chief difference between them is the absence from Strauss of any curiosity about the religious ethic in human life. Where Mahler agonised over the meaning of human existence, searched for a God and contemplated the possibilities of an after-life, Strauss had no interest in these subjects. True, he composed four movements of a Mass in D (o.Op. 31) in 1877, but solely as an exercise in setting a well-known text for unaccompanied choir. He shared a worship of Nature with Mahler, but even this was without the spiritual element which drove Mahler on. Strauss also lacked the immediate and intense pulling-power with an opera audience which Giacomo Puccini (1858–1924) enjoyed. Although several of Strauss's operas were sensational successes, they did not make so wide a general appeal as Puccini's and that is still the case. Perhaps he had most in common with Edward Elgar (1857–1934), not so much musically, although both were masters of colour and of binding their own experiences into their music, as in life-style. Both married the daughters of generals and seemed content to have their lives organised by them; both kept a distance between themselves and their colleagues; and both made conscious efforts not to appear 'artistic' in any flamboyant sense. Elgar could have been mistaken for a retired general or country squire, Strauss for a prosperous bank manager. But whereas Elgar was a prickly, uptight personality, Strauss was phlegmatic, at any rate outwardly. Of all of them, Strauss enjoyed the most congenial musical upbringing, pampered would not be too strong a word. Yet, like Elgar, he never attended a music college or conservatory.

Strauss's sister Johanna, three years younger almost to the day, has left an idyllic account of their childhood[4] which is no doubt accurate even if one suspects a view through rose-tinted glasses. The parentage is interesting. Their father was Franz Strauss, born illegitimate in 1822 to Johann Urban Strauss, a 22-year-old court usher's assistant, and the daughter of the master-watchman (town-musician) in Parkstein, Eastern Bavaria (they never married). Franz was brought up by uncles. His mother, Maria Kunigunda Walter, played several instruments and at the age of five Franz started to learn the violin and later the clarinet, guitar and all the brass instruments. He also sang rather well. His first job, at the age of fifteen, was guitarist in Munich to Duke Max, brother of King Ludwig I and father of Elisabeth ('Sissy') who became Empress of Austria. During these years of service at the ducal court at Schloss Possenhofens, he developed into a virtuoso on the horn (the unvalved *Waldhorn*) and wrote several works, including a concerto for the instrument. After ten years, in 1847, he joined the Bavarian Court Orchestra, the orchestra of the Court Opera in Munich, as principal horn. Four years later he married Elise Seiff, daughter of an army bandmaster. Their first-born, a son, died of tuberculosis aged ten months. During a cholera epidemic in 1854, Elise and their baby daughter, also ten months old, died. Like Verdi, Franz Strauss at the age of thirty-two had seen his family wiped out. The experience, coming after a hard childhood in which he had been virtually abandoned by his parents, left him embittered and inflexible. After two years he met the eighteen-year-old Josepha (Josephine) Pschorr, one of five daughters of the wealthy owner of the Pschorr brewery, which at that time was at 11 Neuhauserstrasse in the city. The brewery was founded by Josephine's grandfather, Joseph Pschorr, who died in 1841. His wife was heiress to another brewery family, the Hackers. Their son Georg succeeded him and he in turn was succeeded in 1867 by his only son Georg, Richard Strauss's uncle. An orchestral player's salary was insufficient to allow Franz Strauss to propose to a girl from a rich family; it was seven years before he did so. He was by then forty-two, she was twenty-five. They were married on 29 August 1863 and lived in a flat on the second floor of 2 Altheimereck, not far from the brewery, and there, on 11 June 1864, their first child Richard Georg was born.

Richard wrote[5] that his mother told him that from his earliest childhood he smiled at the sound of the horn and cried loudly when he heard the violin. His father practised diligently at home and his horn sounds through his son's music from the first works to the last. Scarcely any work by Strauss fails to include a memorable passage for the horn. In his reminiscences of his father, Strauss gives a fair assessment of Franz's musical taste and credo:

He would have considered it dishonourable ever to revise an artistic judgment, once he had accepted it as correct, and he remained inaccessible even in old age to any of my theories. His musical trinity was Mozart (above all), Haydn and Beethoven. To these were added Schubert, as song-writer, Weber and, at some distance, Mendelssohn and Spohr. To him Beethoven's later works, from the *finale* of the Seventh Symphony onward, were no longer 'pure' music (one could begin to scent in them that mephistophelian figure Richard Wagner). He approved of Schumann's piano compositions up to op.20; but his later compositions, because they were influenced by Mendelssohn and because of their rhythmic monotonies and repetition of phrases, were labelled 'Leipzig music' and were therefore valued less highly. . . Where music ceased to be an assembly of sounds and became, consciously, music as expression, my father followed only with mental reservations. He approved of *Tannhäuser* but *Lohengrin* was too sweet for his taste and he was incapable of appreciating the later Wagner.[6]

Indeed he was. Franz Strauss loathed Wagner and they clashed several times. Strauss was no ordinary horn-player. By virtue of his natural authority, he became what might today be called the orchestra's shop steward, its spokesman. In addition, he was so good a player, in spite of being an asthmatic, that there could be no question of his dismissal when he expressed himself vehemently. Wagner arrived in Munich in the year of Richard Strauss's birth, 1864. The court conductor was Franz Lachner, but within three years he had been replaced by Wagner's acolyte Hans von Bülow, who conducted the first performance of *Tristan und Isolde* and *Die Meistersinger von Nürnberg* in 1865 and 1868 respectively. During rehearsals of these operas Franz Strauss argued with Bülow and Wagner, but played the music so conscientiously and beautifully – he said Wagner's horn parts were really clarinet parts – that Bülow called him 'the Joachim of the Waldhorn' and Wagner remarked that he was 'an intolerable blighter, but when he plays his horn one cannot stay cross with him'.

Neither Wagner nor Franz emerges with much credit from some of the tales Richard Strauss told. As a favour to Hermann Levi, who became

Munich court conductor in 1872, Franz agreed to play in the Bayreuth orchestra for the world première of *Parsifal* in 1882. (The favour was in gratitude for Levi's having conducted the first performance of Richard's first symphony the previous year.) At a rehearsal Franz Strauss announced to the orchestra that he had arranged for a communal lunch, price one mark, in the Bürgerverein. Wagner interrupted, saying he had arranged for a communal lunch in the Festspielhaus restaurant. Strauss said that did not suit the players, they preferred to go home after the rehearsal and eat in the town. 'Then eat your sour gherkins where you please', the composer snapped. Strauss wrote from Bayreuth to his wife: 'You can have no conception of the idolatry that surrounds this drunken ruffian. There is no ridding me now of my conviction that the man is ill with immeasurable megalomania and delirium, because he drinks so much, and strong liquor at that, that he is permanently drunk. Recently he was so tight at a rehearsal that he almost fell into the pit.' Was this true? – other writers are silent on Wagner's drinking habits. When the news of his death in February 1883 was given to the Munich orchestra by Levi, all except Franz Strauss stood as a mark of respect.

The conductor Hans Richter once said: 'Franz Strauss's son may count himself lucky that he has not his father in the orchestra.'[7] But he had him at home and that was not easy. As the son laconically remarked: 'My father was very irascible; making music with him was always rather an anxious pleasure... But I learned how to play well when I accompanied him time and time again in Mozart's beautiful horn concertos and in Beethoven's horn sonata.'[8] The only occasion on which Richard lifted the curtain a little higher on his relationship with Franz was in March 1900 in Paris with Romain Rolland, who recorded in his diary for 9 March:

I ask him if his little boy (who is three) will be a musician. He hopes not; because he remembers the sorrow he caused his father and believes that of necessity his son, if he were to be a musician, when he is twenty would consider him a Philistine. He did as a matter of fact have to go through struggles with his family, with his father who was very musical, but of the old school . . . and understood nothing of his son's invention. Indeed, until he had achieved success he was always on the side of the critics against him, endlessly telling him: 'Can't you see? All that's absurd, it's not music'. And since he is afraid of being the same to his own son, he hopes he'll be a painter or sculptor.[9]

1 Strauss and his sister Johanna as children

Richard described Franz at home as 'extremely temperamental, quick-tempered and tyrannical'. The only words he ever uttered in public about the effect of this marriage on his mother were these:

My delicate mother required all her meekness and goodness to allow the relationship between my parents, sustained as it always was by genuine love and high esteem, to continue in undisturbed harmony. To what extent the very sensitive nerves of my mother suffered through all this, I cannot today decide. My mother had always to be so careful of her nerves that, although she had an artistic temperament, she was unable to read much and frequently had to pay for visits to the theatre and concerts with sleepless nights. She never uttered a cross word and she was happiest when she was allowed to spend the summer afternoons alone and quietly, busy with her embroidery in the beautiful garden of my uncle [Georg] Pschorr's villa.[10]

Some reading between the lines is required here. Strauss's sister Johanna, describing their mother as 'kindness in human shape', related how Josephine would try to act as peace-maker and mediator when father and son quarrelled over musical matters, as they obviously did very often, especially when Richard became a converted Wagnerian. The first signs of a crack-up appeared in April 1885, just before Richard's twenty-first birthday, when Josephine went into a nursing-home for treatment of a 'nervous disorder'. She was then just forty-seven and one may deduce that her ailment was partly menopausal. She was certainly a manic-depressive who convinced herself that her family was persecuting her. Given an overdose of morphine to calm her, she became ravingly insane. She was in the nursing-home for two months. Five months later she returned for five weeks more. There was then a remission for eight years, but between 1894 and 1909 she spent many periods in 'institutions' varying in duration between a month and nearly a year. In 1899 she spoke to Johanna about standing in her way and of 'removing herself so as not to damage Otto's career'. This was a reference to Lieutenant Otto Rauchenberger, the infantry officer Johanna had married on 8 July 1895.

How his mother's illness affected Strauss can be read in a letter he wrote to Johanna during their mother's first episode in 1885 in which he said that it was a waste of time trying to comfort 'Papa' who was 'becoming more and more unsociable. I think he feels that he's doing dear Mama a moral wrong of some kind if he allows himself to be distracted and doesn't sit all day brooding on our misfortune. Even though I'm forever preaching to him that on the contrary it's his duty to keep himself strong and fit by diverting and dispersing the dark thoughts for the sake of Mama and Hanna and me, it doesn't have any effect and I'm often at a complete loss to understand what has happened to the moral strength of which a man should possess more than a woman... I hope my resolution will hold out until you come home.'[11]

It is significant that when Josephine Strauss's illness recurred in 1894, Strauss shortly afterwards began to sketch his tone-poem *Don Quixote* which contains the most sympathetic and vivid musical illustration of mental delusion. Because of what had happened to his mother, Strauss deliberately cultivated a laconic, 'laid-back' and equable temperament, suppressing the tendency to choleric outbursts which he inherited from his father. He chose a wife of extremely volatile and explosive temperament through whom he could vicariously experience a side of his own nature which he suppressed with unusual if not invariable success. Perhaps it is also significant that in *Don Quixote* the horn, his father's instrument, is heard less prominently than in any of his major works. The most profound and illuminating of his orchestral masterpieces is haunted by the fate of his mother.

Strauss's letter to his sister gives us a bigger clue to his philosophy in later life than might at first be supposed. His mother's first bout of severe depression was the climax, clearly, of many years of domestic tension of which Strauss must have been sensitively aware. The duty 'to disperse dark thoughts' is a profoundly telling phrase and was something that he applied to himself. When it came to his own marriage, his principal aim was to live in comfort and security, albeit he chose a wife of extreme, but not neurotic, temperamental volatility. The image of himself that he presented to the world was of easy-going geniality. It was not a false image, but it hid a volcanic temperament that found expression in music. And it hid an inner fear of the 'dark thoughts' that haunted him, as we shall see.

If the tension at home exerted a major formative influence on Strauss's character, it also had its effect on his musical development and education. The next chapter will trace that development.

2 Wunderkind

The Strausses stayed at 2 Altheimereck for about a year. They moved into a larger flat on Sonnenstrasse at its junction with Schwanthalerstrasse. (By an extraordinary coincidence, this building many years later became the first headquarters of the Richard-Strauss-Institut.) Johanna was born there on 9 June 1867. In 1869 they moved again when a flat became available in the Pschorr-Haus at 3 Neuhauserstrasse. According to Johanna's memoirs, one of her brother's earliest musical experiences was being taken by his father to hear the band play for the midday changing of the guard on the Marienplatz. He remembered the tunes of the marches and asked Franz to play them on the horn.

Munich in 1864 had a population of only 150,000. It boasted seventeen theatres and the new Theater am Gärtnerplatz was under construction. The principal occupation of Bavarians was farming and they were conservative by nature. Folk-art flourished, hence the beautiful carvings and decorations in the churches, but there was a healthy scepticism towards local talent. The new buildings in Munich itself took Greece as a model because King Ludwig I, a lover of classical Greek art, rebuilt the city as a modern Athens before he died in 1848. Strauss's childhood and early youth was spent during the reign of Ludwig II, who preferred building castles and listening to Wagner's music to playing politics and waging war. As a member of the Court Orchestra, Franz Strauss was an employee of Ludwig and received from him the title of Kammermusiker and the Ludwig Medal for Learning and the Arts. He took part in the private performances which had an audience of one – Ludwig. During Ludwig's reign Bavaria became part of Bismarck's alliance of German states in 1871. In the Strauss household there was little interest in such matters – music was more important.

Richard began piano lessons in the autumn of 1868, when he was four.

They were given by his father's harpist colleague, August Tombo, and the boy made fast progress. Two years later he attended the cathedral school, which he enjoyed, and in 1872 started to learn the violin with Benno Walter, a cousin of Franz and leader of the Court Orchestra. 'I was always a bad pupil, because I did not enjoy practising, necessary though it was.'[1] In 1874 he entered the Ludwigsgymnasium (the Royal Grammar School) in Sendlingerstrasse. His form-master's report recorded his enjoyment of learning – 'very good work' – and his pleasant disposition: 'candour and good nature', 'unclouded merriment and high spirits'. The following year Strauss's mother was left 5,000 gulden by her Pschorr grandmother. She bought a Blüthner grand piano and treated Franz and herself to a holiday in Italy. The bequest also paid for several years of family holidays at Sillian in the Tyrol where the mountain air was good for Franz's asthma and Richard played the village organ. Another favourite holiday spot was Mindelheim, home of Josepha Strauss's sister Bertha, who was married to the district officer Carl Hörburger. Some of Richard's earliest compositions were dedicated to his Uncle Carl, who organised musical life in the town.

Richard began composing in 1870, when he was six. His first work was an introduction and trio for piano, *Schneider-Polka* (*Tailor Polka*), which he played while his father wrote it down. Next came a carol, *Weihnachtslied*, the words of which (by Schubart) were written beneath the notes by his mother. A *Panzenburg-Polka* for piano – 'Panzenburg' means 'paunch castle', a pile of empty beer barrels – composed in 1872 was orchestrated by Franz for an amateur orchestra, the Harbni, which he conducted. It was performed at a rehearsal in Georg Pschorr's house on the Bayerstrasse on 31 May. Franz said it sounded 'quite good'. Richard had by this time attended his first opera, Weber's *Der Freischütz*, 'trembling with excitement as he waited for the great moment when the curtain rose'.[2] He could already play the overture on the piano and he had often heard his father practising the horn solos for weeks before a performance. The second opera he attended, also in 1871, was Mozart's *Die Zauberflöte*. Strauss's first appearance as a conductor seems to have been on 23 February 1873 when an orchestration by Franz of the *Schneider-Polka* was performed at a concert in the Odeon promoted by Munich's Philharmonic Association.

Strauss's first *Lieder* were composed in 1871. On 21 August he completed a setting of Uhland's *Einkehr* and followed it with the same poet's *Winterreise*. Both were dedicated to his 'lieben Tante Johanna', wife of Georg Pschorr. She was a mezzo-soprano good enough, it is said, to have had a professional career if she had wanted one. She sang her nephew's first efforts for him. Strauss's first compositions for his father's principal instrument – for Franz also played both violin and viola – were two *Etudes* for horn, probably written in 1873.

Strauss did not have formal composition lessons until 1875. From then until 1880 he studied harmony, counterpoint and orchestration with Friedrich Wilhelm Meyer, one of the conductors of the Munich Court Orchestra. Strauss told his parents, when Meyer died in 1893, that 'he did more for my development than he himself probably knew'. He described his teacher as 'a simple man with a noble mind'.[3] A Concertante in C major for two violins, cello and piano (AV 157), composed in 1875, only came to light in 1995 when the score was found in Guernsey. Under Meyer's tuition Strauss in 1877 composed a *Serenade in G* for orchestra which was performed the following year in Munich at a concert by the Wilde Gung'l, an amateur orchestra which Franz Strauss conducted for twenty-one years from 1875 to 1896. It took its name from the Gung'l orchestra, a professional body established in Munich by Joseph Gung'l, and it gave public and private concerts, rehearsing in a tavern called *Drei Rosen*. The *Serenade* was the first work Strauss orchestrated himself. It sounds like Haydn and Mozart except that the scoring is weightier than theirs. It is impossible to identify the later Strauss in it, but were it to be passed off as a newly discovered symphony by, say, Weber, most people would be fooled.

Meyer made no attempt to divert Strauss's musical tastes from the path laid down by Franz. This meant that Richard was brought up mainly on a diet of Mozart, Beethoven, Schubert, Mendelssohn, Weber and Spohr. We can hear his youthful voice in a letter to his father written in the summer of 1878 after he had attended concerts given by conservatory students as part of their examinations:

In the last movement [Beethoven's Symphony No. 1] one of the violinists played B♭ instead of B♮ in the middle section, which set my teeth on edge. Next a Fräulein K. played the first movement of an [*sic*] A minor concerto by Schumann, which I didn't like very much, because it's not at all clear and the scoring is very thick. . . Then a

Fräulein Ch. played the very, very long and boring first movement of a piano concerto in B♭ minor by Rubinstein. It begins very dramatically and ends very dramatically, but the bit in between is *long* and very boring . . . Spohr's 8th Violin Concerto (Scena), played *very* well indeed by Herr. S. I was quite delighted by the magnificent composition, just as I was the first time I heard it, especially when I heard my favourite bit. The concerto has a quite unusual but very original character due especially to the recitative and the main theme of the last movement.[4]

But it was another violin concerto, Beethoven's, which enraptured him a few days later: 'This composition is, in my judgment', wrote the fourteen-year-old, 'one of the most beautiful there is. The simplicity and noblesse, the melody, the magnificent modulations and *what* scoring. I was completely transported. . . To be honest, when I heard it the first time it didn't really say anything to me, but yesterday I was quite carried away.'[5] The spell lasted. Romain Rolland, in his diary for 26 March 1906, recounts arriving with Strauss at the Théâtre du Chatelet in Paris for a rehearsal of *Symphonia domestica*. They heard Mischa Elman playing the slow movement of the Beethoven concerto. 'Strauss growls. I ask him "What's the matter?" – "Oh, nothing! That piece. I would like to have written it".'[6]

Strauss's youthful opinions on the music he heard are best sampled from his letters to his boyhood friend Ludwig Thuille. Three years older than Strauss, Thuille was brought up in a monastic orphanage. Josepha Strauss heard from a friend about the boy's musical gifts and thought he would be a good companion for Richard. She invited him to Munich, where Franz found a place for him in the School of Music. In 1877 Thuille went to Innsbruck to study, hence the correspondence between the boys. Writing from Munich on 5 October 1877,[7] Strauss refers to 'piano lessons, harmony lessons, violin lessons' and says he is now playing Czerny's *Schule der Fingerfertigkeit*, Field Nocturnes, Mendelssohn's D minor concerto and J. S. Bach's *Well-Tempered Clavier*. At this time he had heard Haydn's *The Creation* which 'made my heart leap up in my chest' and he went to an evening of string quartets – Haydn in C major, Mozart in E flat and Beethoven's Op. 135 – at which he could hardly decide which should be given pride of place – 'Haydn with his pleasantness, Mozart with his serious and yet so lovely and fresh composition, Beethoven with his deep seriousness and his gloom'. On New Year's Eve 1877 he took Thuille to task for suggesting that

Schubert was more recognised at that time than Mozart. 'In his own time Mozart was more recognised than now, since he is now no longer understood by most people. If you only knew what he composed in thirty-five years, you would be simply astonished and exclaim, That is not possible. . . So far as learning instrumental music is concerned, I can only give you *one* piece of good advice – not to learn it from a book, since this, as my father says, is the worst thing. So I advise you not to buy a book, since even my Papa only knows one by Hector Berlioz, who is a real scribbler and hack; instead ask for a table covering the range and best position of the various instruments that are used and learn the rest . . . from the scores of the great old masters.' A month later (26 January 1878): 'I am very eager to hear your opinion about the splendid *Symphonia Jovis* [*Jupiter* Symphony] of the master of masters. It is the most fantastic work I ever heard and I thought I was in heaven when those sounds reached my ears. *Musica, omnium artium pulcherrima, vivat!*' ['Long live music, most beautiful of all the arts']. Thuille, whose letters are lost, evidently put forward his own candidate and provoked this response (6 February 1878): 'the *Leonore* Overture [presumably No. 3], as wonderfully beautiful as it is, is *never* greater than the *Jupiter* Symphony. For me Beethoven is *never* greater than Mozart, the two of them are at the exact same level in their own way; Mozart is even more many-sided than Beethoven.'

At the end of March 1878, Strauss wrote: 'You shouldn't call Saint-Saëns a dolt or an ass; on the contrary he is a genius. Even if the *Marche héroïque* was not to your taste – as I can well imagine, for he has to make something for "his Parisians" that suits their taste! – I have heard very nice things by him, for example a very pretty piano quartet and a G minor piano concerto of his that he performed himself. This writer was very much praised *by my father*, which says a great deal in the case of a new composer.'

About a month later Strauss wrote his famous letter to Thuille in which he described his reactions to his first hearing of Wagner's *Siegfried*: 'I was bored stiff, I was quite frightfully bored, so horribly that I cannot even tell you. . . The last act is so boring you will die. The scene between Siegfried and Brünnhilde, all in adagio; I thought, Won't there ever be allegro; but no, this terrible howling and whining from a seventh down to a ninth, then back up again.' On the other hand, he considered Auber's *La muette de Portici* 'a very dramatic, extremely beautiful opera . . . I am learning little by little to appreciate Auber as an extraordinary fellow' and another favourite was Boieldieu's *La dame blanche* – 'such noble melodies, such magnificence and drama and such beautiful instrumentation!' In the autumn of 1878 came a sarcastic tirade against *Die Walküre* and a visit to another concert acquainted him with Schumann's Second Symphony, 'quite pretty' but with Schumann's 'inevitable tendency to ride his figures to death. . . When I said I thought the orchestration was quite tolerable, Papa declared that it was very clumsy, they were all blowing and bowing at the same time.'

At the same concert he heard Clara Schumann play Beethoven's G major piano concerto 'with a technique, an attack and an artistic interpretation the like of which I never heard before. Every note she struck was pure, every phrase she played corresponded to the overall artistic quality of the composition, so that there is probably no one else who would play this concerto the same way as Frau Schumann.' In his own piano-playing, he told Thuille, he was performing 'the B-minor concerto by Hummel (very beautiful but very difficult), while my teacher [Carl Niest from 1875] mainly pays attention to "finger position" in another sense of the word, not that my fingers are awkward or crooked but according to the principle "never the thumb on the highest note" (naturally with exceptions) and "breaking the habit of constantly using the pedal". I have also learned the thirty-two variations in C minor by Beethoven by heart.'

The letters give occasional glimpses of the Strausses at home. In the spring of 1879 he reports that 'Papa is still not quite back to feeling well again, and Mama unfortunately has been at the sofa, despite her impatience, as she always wants to be busy with housework.' Strauss's lifelong antipathy to religion began in his boyhood: it is clear that neither of his parents made any effort to instil any religious instruction or feeling into him. Replying to a remark by Thuille, he wrote in December 1878: 'Regarding the saying of twelve rosaries, I am unable to fulfil your request since, first of all, I don't know the rosary and, second, I have no particular desire to learn unintelligent blather.' We also learn from these letters that Strauss's health was precarious throughout 1879 even though he attended school, concerts and opera. He was in bed for seventeen days with 'an intestinal cold' in December 1877. A year later he told Thuille, 'My health is still not particularly good; I go to class, but I still have to watch my diet very carefully. On account of my wretched illness, which I wish were at the other end of the world, I have been prevented this whole time from taking lessons, which naturally makes me very sorry, and my parents would also rather spend money on lessons than on doctors and medicine.'

The other main subject in the correspondence was Strauss's progress with his compositions. His official Opus 1 in the catalogue of his works is the *Festmarsch* in E major for orchestra composed in 1876, dedicated to his uncle Georg Pschorr and first performed by Franz's Wilde Gung'l in the Centralsäle, Munich, on 26 March 1881. After initially declining it, Breitkopf & Härtel published it when Uncle Georg volunteered to pay the cost of printing. However, the first Strauss work to appear in print was the Little Gavotte in F major (o.Op. 57) for piano, written in the early part of 1879 and published that year in Munich under the title *Aus alter Zeit* (*In Olden Days*) in a Musical Picture Album collated by Lothar Meggendorfer.[8] (The numbering of Strauss's works sometimes causes confusion. He gave opus numbers to only eighty-six compositions. There are then 150 works without opus numbers which are given numbers from the Asow catalogue preceded by o.Op. After this, there is a further list numbered from AV151 to AV323 which also includes Strauss's arrangements of works by other composers.) By the time Strauss left school at the age of eighteen in 1882 he had written nearly 150 works including a symphony and five other orchestral works, forty-five piano pieces, a quantity of chamber music, fifty-nine *Lieder* with piano accompaniment and three orchestral *Lieder*. Many of these works were written for performance in the family circle of which, of course, Franz was the dominant figure. 'He had an infallible feeling for correct tempo', his son remembered years later.[9] 'He reproached his chief Hermann Levi with never getting into the right tempo before the third bar of a piece. He was very strict about rhythm. How many times did he bawl at me "You're hurrying like a Jew". . . He gave me a worthy preparation for the *haute école* of performance and interpretation of the classic master-works under Bülow. . . Under my father's strict tutelage I heard nothing but classical music until I was sixteen, and I owe it to this discipline that my love and adoration for the classical masters of music has remained untainted to this day.'

But there were other musicians, if not so eminent, in the family. Mention has already been made of Aunt Maria Johanna Pschorr (*née* Fischer-Dick) (1838–1918). Her sister Amalie married Anton von Knözinger, who became Bavarian Royal Auditor General. Their son Ludwig was a violinist and often played in string quartets with Richard. Another cousin, Carl Aschenbrenner, was the cellist in the quartet. In his old age he remembered that 'it was always a special pleasure to play a piano quartet, when Strauss would take the piano part. He was in his element then, when he could lead the ensemble from the piano, on which he was already a virtuoso. Frequently, when we had paused for a rest or after we had finished, Strauss would play us his latest composition or improvise freely.' In a letter to Thuille on 22 July 1879 Strauss mentions having written 'a comic wedding march with a church scene for the wedding of my cousin Linda Moralt, for piano and toy instruments (cuckoo, quail, cymbals, triangle, drum, rattle, nightingale), which I shall perform on the wedding day with my band, Hanna [his sister] and the four Pschorr boys; the whole thing is just a joke.' Another of Josepha's sisters had married a Moralt[10] and Linda was their daughter. The *Hochzeitmusik* was performed in Munich on 11 August 1879 when Linda married Jean Mayer. The autograph score has disappeared. One of his 'family' works, *Variationen über 'Das Dirndl is harb auf mi'*, for string trio, was published as recently as 1996. It was composed in March 1882 and performed in Munich on the 18th of that month. The title is what we should now call an 'in joke'. *Harbni* was the name of the orchestra comprising family and friends conducted by Franz Strauss. The work's introduction, seven variations and *finale* includes quotations from Wagner's *Ring* and is one of Strauss's first works to employ his favourite device of quotation.

Here are two more extracts from Strauss's letters to Thuille in 1879 which give an exuberant picture of the boy's vitality:

8 May: I'm composing very busily. (i) getting on with the scoring of my A minor overture.[11] (ii) I've re-written all three songs,[12] this time without any special modulations, *ergo* to Papa's satisfaction. (iii) I've composed 4 new piano pieces,[13] including 2 gavottes, the second of which is very pretty and original. (iv) I've written – wait for it – some variations for flute and piano[14] at the request of a pal. (v) I'm now working on the last movement of the sonata;[15] the 3-page-long development section has come out all right, and so the rest won't take much longer. Besides that I'm going to give it a shortish, melodic A♭ major Adagio, from which I'll lead straight

into a Scherzo. So you can see that I've had more than enough to do and still have. Besides that I'm busy doing counterpoint exercises; I'm already up to 4-part fugue now, the pinnacle towards which all counterpoint aspires.

22 July: I'm composing very busily. (1) I've written, perhaps I've already told you, a Romance in E♭ major for clarinet and orchestra,[16] which I'm very pleased with . . . (2) another new gavotte, No. IV in D major[17] with a bagpipe tune (musette) as trio; gavotte form suits me extraordinarily well for shorter piano pieces. . . (4) I've finished the A minor Overture at last; it makes a hellish din, I can tell you, but I think it'll be effective. Further, I've a quartet[18] in my head which will shortly burst the vessel where it now reposes and manifest itself on manuscript paper. But first I must alter the Horn Variations in E♭ major[19] that I composed last autumn and write them for *human* lungs and *human* lips, for they are almost unplayable as they are.

Strauss admired Thuille and respected his opinions. Replying to some criticisms of his E major piano sonata (o.Op. 38, composed autumn 1877), he wrote in December 1878: 'I'm very grateful to you for drawing my attention to this, and if I'd noticed this glaring mistake earlier I'd never have had the nerve to let you set eyes on such a clumsy piece of work, let alone dedicate it to you as something equal to your sonata, which is of a much higher standard than mine.' Thuille's teachers when he returned to the Royal School of Music, Munich, in 1879 were Joseph Rheinberger and Carl Bärmann. In October 1883 he joined the staff of the School and eventually succeeded Rheinberger as professor of counterpoint. Writing of his friend many years later, Strauss mentioned a violin sonata 'more mature than my own products of the same period' which 'aroused my special envy and competitiveness'. Strauss attributed to Rheinberger's influence that Thuille 'began to move in the direction of strict conservatism. . . Even my *Italy* [*Aus Italien*] made the strict contrapuntalist shake his head and later he often asked me how I could justify the construction of this chord or the other, or how I would explain this or that polyphonic line. I would simply reply: "I can't, I wrote it down because that's how it occurred to me." So towards the end of the century we became less close than we had been – I only know that Thuille was disturbed by the *Taillefer* battle music. I conducted his *Romantic Overture* in Berlin, but I also followed the composition of his charming symphony and piano concerto (unpublished) with interest. His opera *Lobetanz*, with a libretto by Bierbaum, was a success in several German

2 Strauss aged about sixteen

theatres.' When he was at Meiningen in 1886, Strauss conducted a symphony by Thuille, in Munich in 1897 the opera *Theuerdank* and, in Berlin some years later, a concert performance of an act from the opera *Gugeline*. Strauss does not mention that the librettos of *Lobetanz* and *Gugeline* were originally intended for him.

The elderly Strauss was not over-pleased when his letters to Thuille were published. He rebuked all writers who quote from them, as writers on Strauss must and always will, with this pronouncement: 'Unfortunately the callow correspondence that passed between us in those days (airy, empty-headed, impudent opinions about Richard Wagner, who was hardly known in those days, or at least not yet understood) still quite unnecessarily stalks the pages of biographical writing of all kinds.' He did not like to be reminded of his juvenile, father-inspired hostility to Wagner!

Thuille was useful as a safety-valve for Strauss when tensions at home were of high voltage. Although the Ludwigsgymnasium knew how talented a musician Richard was and gave him opportunities to perform and to write works for school concerts – a setting of a chorus from Sophocles' *Electra*, for example! – it provided no musical education. Richard wanted to leave and to join Thuille at the School of Music, but Franz said no. There were bitter arguments, but the parental view prevailed. Strauss conceded later that his father had been right: he told a friend in 1945 that it was at school that his passion for Ancient Greece began and was nurtured.

Signs of the mature Strauss in the instrumental and orchestral works written before 1880, when he was sixteen, are almost impossible to find. But in the songs we may easily perceive the stirrings of greatness, particularly where the gift of melody is involved and the response to the dramatic implications of the text. *Die Drossel* (1877, o.Op. 34) is a setting of Uhland, simple in concept but opening with a piano cadenza in which the arpeggiated motif represents the song of the thrush, *ad libitum*. From the same year comes *Lass ruh'n die Toten* (*Let the dead rest*, 1877, o.Op. 35), Strauss's only Chamisso setting, immediately remarkable for the bareness of the piano introduction and the use of rests. In a funereal C minor, the song evokes the poem's sombre thoughts with a chromatic intensity that foreshadows, for example, *Ruhe, meine Seele* of seventeen years later. The talent for tone-poetry and imitation of the sounds of nature discernible in *Die*

Drossel is evident in settings of Goethe's *Der Fischer* (1877, o.Op. 33) and Körner's *Spielmann und Zither* (1878, o.Op. 40). A fondness for employing extreme tonalities to evoke atmosphere such as one finds in *Elektra* is there in embryo in the Lenau setting *Nebel* (1878, o.Op. 47), where E flat minor characterises the darkness of the soul. His choice of texts and his care for finding the correct 'melodic form' to carry the words are also features of his early song-writing. At first, his sister recalled, he set whatever came to hand. As he matured, he became choosier ('I can't set that, it doesn't appeal to me!'). His youthful selection of poems probably reflects the Biedermeier fashion prevailing in Munich – Fallersleben, Gilm, Dehmel, for example. But Goethe, Lenau and Heine were also early enthusiasms. 'Recently, in Heine's *Buch der Lieder*', he wrote to Thuille, 'I found a sort of "supplement", a wonderful yet very sad song. I shan't tell you what it's called, otherwise you'll steal it from me. I shall also have a closer look at Lenau, who appeals to me greatly!' The Heine setting was *In Vaters Garten heimlich steht ein Blümelein*, composed in December 1879 (o.Op. 64). As for 'melodic form', Strauss's attitude was expressed years later to Max Marschalk: 'I work for a long time on melodies. It is a long journey from having the first idea to finally shaping everything melodically. It is not the beginning of the melody that is important, but its continuation, its development into a complete melodic form. A melody that seems to be born out of the moment is almost always the result of arduous effort. By the way, work is also a matter of talent!'

Strauss's juvenile songs end in 1879. About twenty songs composed between 1879 and 1884 and which belonged to Tante Johanna are lost (only their incipits and texts are known because they were seen by Strauss's first major biographer, Max Steinitzer). Perhaps the last boyhood song, though, was *Rote Rosen* (1883, o.Op. 76), dedicated as we shall see to a young love. This is a song of intrinsically Straussian beauty that points the way to *Morgen!* It sets the seal on an outpouring covering thirteen years from which we can justly claim Strauss as a *Wunderkind*.

The year 1881 saw the beginning of Strauss's fame as far as the general public was concerned. Four of his works were performed in Munich during March. On the 14th his String Quartet in A major, Op. 2 (November 1880) was performed in the Museumssaal by a quartet led by his teacher Benno Walter. The cellist was Hanuš Wihan, principal cellist of the Munich Court

Orchestra. The work is a typical product of a youth brought up on Haydn, Mozart and Mendelssohn, at its most promising in the *scherzo* where the straitjacket of strict sonata-form was not such a constricting influence on the boy's imagination. Two days later, in the same hall, Cornelia Meysenheim sang three Strauss *Lieder* – all settings of Emanuel Geibel, *Waldgesang: Die Liebe Saß als Nachtigall* (o.Op. 55); *O schneller mein Roß* (AV159); and *Die Lilien glühn in Düften* (AV160) (only *Waldgesang* survives). After this recital Strauss's relatives and friends gave him a gold signet ring, with his monogram RS inscribed on a black stone and a laurel wreath inscribed in gold letters 'Presented on the most memorable day of your life'. Strauss wore the ring until he gave it to his elder grandson Richard for his eighteenth birthday, 1 November 1945.

The *Festmarsch*, Op. 1, was played by the Wilde Gung'l, conducted by Franz Strauss, on the 26th. Four days later, on 30 March, Strauss's Symphony No. 1 in D minor (o.Op. 69), composed between 8 April and 12 June 1880, was performed by the Court Orchestra, conducted by Hermann Levi, in a Musical Academy concert in the Odeonssaal (destroyed in the Second World War). Franz, who had copied all the parts, played first horn. 'Father was naturally very nervous and worked up', Johanna recalled in her memoirs.[20] 'While Richard remained very calm and made no preparations. . . Richard in his Sunday suit was standing, as he always did, behind the first pillar on the left, by where the artists came in.' He returned to school next day as if nothing extraordinary had happened to him. One of his schoolmates was Max Steinitzer, who recalled in his 1911 biography that Richard behaved at school and in lessons 'just exactly as he had before'. Johanna said there was no great celebration at home – 'my parents wisely restrained themselves in praising him'. It is axiomatic to quote the review of the critic of the *Münchner Neueste Nachrichten* of 3 April 1881 who said that the symphony 'cannot lay claim to true originality, but it demonstrates throughout a fertile musical imagination, to which composition comes easily'. This was fair enough, but is not quite all there is to say. Since 1986 the public has had the advantage over earlier writers of being able to listen to a recording of the work. The 'remarkable skill in orchestration' also cited by the Munich critic is there for all to hear. The work owes massive debts to Mendelssohn and Weber but is far from mere plagiarism. It is a delight to hear. If it were to be

3 Strauss and his father, *c.* 1903

passed off as a recently discovered symphony by either of those composers, it would be cherished. So why not as early Strauss?

There is an inevitable parallel to be drawn between the relationship of Leopold Mozart and his son and Franz Strauss and his. But it cannot be pushed too far. While Leopold and Franz were both embittered men, Leopold exploited the executive virtuosity of Wolfgang and his sister. There was no question of Richard Strauss having a career as a pianist, good player though he was. It was obvious that composition was his sphere. Franz tried to keep his son from what he regarded as the malevolent influence of Wagner and there were terrible arguments about it, but eventually he capitulated. Where Franz differed from Leopold was in having no jealousy of his son. As we shall see, he was often severely critical of Richard's music and of his conducting, but the criticisms were offered in a conciliatory spirit, frequently with several injunctions not to take offence.

Apart from the performances of his music in 1881 this was the year in which Strauss began to revise his opinions about Wagner's music. The first dents in his armour of hostility came from hearing *Tannhäuser*, probably in 1877. He was impressed by the transformation from the Venusberg to the Wartburg valley. During the winter of 1880–1 he clandestinely studied the score of *Tristan* but made the mistake of playing a passage to a friend, probably Thuille. Franz overheard it, stormed in and forbade any more. But Richard was not cowed and began at this time to tell Franz: 'Remember, you sit in the middle of the orchestra. The overall effect is different.' Strauss's own recollection is:

At the age of seventeen I feverishly devoured the pages of the score of *Tristan* until my enthusiasm reached a pitch of intoxication which was dashed only when I went once again to a live performance, in the hope of reinforcing the impressions that my eye and inner ear had received from the page. Renewed disappointment and doubt, renewed resort to the score – until I realised that it was the discrepancy between a mediocre performance and the great composer's intentions, which I had read aright in the unsullied pages of the score, that prevented the work from sounding in the theatre as I had heard it inwardly. After that (in spite of my old uncle's [Georg Pschorr] warnings about the 'swindler of Bayreuth') I became a *complete Wagnerian*.[21]

In 1933 he wrote to the conductor Fritz Busch that 'even if only *one* person pays for a seat at *Tristan*, it must be performed for him because he must be the last surviving German'.

When Hermann Levi asked Franz to play in the orchestra at Bayreuth for the first performances of *Parsifal*, Franz took Richard to hear the dress rehearsal. It was a 'treat', to mark Richard's leaving school but he has left no comment on it. During his last year at the Ludwigsgymnasium, Richard began or completed his Violin Concerto, Op. 8, the *Stimmungsbilder*, Op. 9, for piano, and the Horn Concerto No. 1, Op. 11. In his final report his only 'very good' was for history. Latin and Greek were 'good', German and French 'nearly good', mathematics and physics 'middling'. But 'his conduct has been irreproachable throughout'.

3   Growing up

During the winter of 1882–3, Strauss attended lectures at Munich University, as his father wished. His subjects were philosophy, aesthetics, the history of art and Shakespeare. But the lectures – or the lecturers – bored him. He preferred to read and make his own choice of teachers. Thus he explored Goethe and the Greek classics, lifelong joys. He joined his father's Wilde Gung'l orchestra, playing in the first violins for three years until September 1885. Carl Aschenbrenner remembered how Strauss would irritate his father by 'still plucking or stroking his E string, which was almost never in tune' after Franz had raised his baton to start. 'The way Richard was unable to control his laughter made all of us laugh too and in the end pacified his scolding father.'

His first musical excitement after leaving school was the first performance on 27 November 1882 of his *Serenade* in E flat, Op. 7, for thirteen wind instruments, completed a year earlier. This was the first of many Dresden Strauss premières. It was given by the Tonkünstlerverein of Dresden (Musicians' Association) conducted by Franz Wüllner, who had conducted the world premières of *Das Rheingold* (1869) and *Die Walküre* (1870) in Munich. This was the first work by Strauss to be introduced outside Munich. It was soon to be followed by others. A few days later he left for his first visit to Vienna. Encouraged by Franz, he set out his stall beforehand. The object of the visit was the first performance of his Violin Concerto, which he had completed on 22 March, and he persuaded Max Kalbeck of the *Wiener Allgemeine Zeitung* to write a preliminary piece about composer and work. He wrote to Wilhelm Jahn, conductor at the Vienna Opera and of the Gesellschaft der Musikfreunde concerts, who made his box at the opera available to Strauss for *La traviata*. He called on Hans Richter, then chief conductor of the Opera and of the Philharmonic, and attended a Philharmonic concert.

The concerto was performed in the Bösendorfer rooms in the Herrengasse on 5 December by Benno Walter, with Strauss at the piano. 'The hall was reasonably full thanks to the complimentary tickets', he wrote home next day. 'My concerto was very well received: applause after the first F major trill, applause after each movement, two bows at the end. . . At least I didn't make a mess of the accompaniment.' The concerto was repeated two months later (8 February 1883) at a recital by Walter and Strauss in Munich. Walter also gave the first performance with orchestra in Cologne on 4 March 1890, when Wüllner conducted. Strauss conducted a performance in Leipzig on 17 February 1896 with Alfred Krasselt as soloist.

The year 1883 was the first Strauss had been able to devote wholly to composition. He completed the Horn Concerto he was writing for his father. Strauss's sister told the late Dennis Brain that she remembered her father using the high B flat crook while he struggled with the difficulties his son had devised; he regarded the many high B flats as too risky for public performance. When the concerto was first performed, in the horn and piano version, some time in 1888 at the Tonkünstlerverein, Munich, it was by one of Franz's pupils, Bruno Hoyer, with Richard as pianist. The concerto is for Waldhorn, the valveless natural horn, but Norman Del Mar, who was a horn-player, pointed out that the orchestral horn parts are written for the E flat crook but the solo part for the F horn which in 1883 was becoming standard. Some of the soloist's themes cannot be played on the Waldhorn. In June Strauss began a second symphony, starting with the slow movement, which was the last to be completed, and in the same month completed the *Romanze* in F for cello (o.Op. 75) which enjoyed a period of popularity and then disappeared from sight and sound for nearly a century. It was dedicated to Strauss's uncle, Anton von Knözinger, and was first performed (probably in Baden-Baden) on 15 February 1884 by Hanuš Wihan. Strauss also made a version with piano accompaniment for Wihan, shortening it to about one third of its original ten-minute duration. This version was inscribed to Ferdinand Böckmann, principal cellist of the Dresden Court Orchestra. It is a most attractive work in one richly melodic and flowing movement (*andante cantabile*). The abridged version was revived in Munich in October 1985 by Peter Wöpke and Wolfgang Sawallisch and the orchestral version in the Semperoper, Dresden, on 21 May 1986. The unabridged piano version has since been published and the orchestral version recorded.

The *Romanze* was composed shortly after Strauss had completed his Cello Sonata, Op. 6, in many ways the most mature and striking of his prentice works. Wihan, with Hildegard von Königsthal, gave the first performance of the sonata in Nuremberg on 8 December 1883. Ten days earlier, on 28 November, Levi had conducted another Strauss work, the *Concert Overture in C minor* (o.Op. 80), at the Odeonssaal. It was dedicated to him. Although never published, it had performances during 1884 in Augsburg, Innsbruck, Berlin and in Dresden, where it was probably the first Strauss work Ernst von Schuch conducted.

The first evidence of romance in Strauss's life occurred during his summer holiday in 1883 at Heilbrunn, Upper Bavaria. A Frankfurt family, the Speyers, were there too, the father a lawyer and son of a composer. There were two daughters and it was Lotti who attracted Strauss. Back in Munich on 11 September he composed a song, *Rote Rosen*, to a text by Karl Stieler, and sent it to her, with two other unidentified songs (probably *Die erwachte Rose* and *Begegnung*), on 19 October. The dedication was 'in deepest adoration'. The song, he wrote, was 'written specially for you alone, my dear Fräulein, a little verse for your album with my music a mere addition below the lines and in no way intended for even the smallest audience. . . I implore you not to be cross with me for *Rote Rosen*; because of the delightful memories it holds *for me*, I could not resist the impulse to set it to music for you, although I am afraid the text does not really lend itself to composition and so the result is not particularly felicitous. To a certain extent it applies so fittingly to you, and the ending to me, that at the first reading I was thrown into utter confusion.'[1]

The last verse reads: 'I feel the night, the night so cool and cloudless, but day and night have merged in one together. And your red rose suffuses all my dreaming of the fair garden where I found it blooming.' Lotti Speyer's reply (not written until 11 November) admitted that 'it was my very secret wish that you would dedicate a little song to me, and now it has been so beautifully granted. *Rote Rosen* is very beautiful, there is no question of "being cross with you". But the comparison you draw with the text is far too flattering to me . . . [and] has inspired your artistic imagination to conjure up something a little different. . . . Since September I have run often enough to our letter box to see if anything had come for me from Munich.' The song had its first public performance in New York on 30 November 1958 in a Carnegie Hall recital by Elisabeth Schwarzkopf.

As soon as the *Concert Overture* had been performed, Strauss – with his father's encouragement – left for an extended visit to Dresden and Berlin, armed with letters of introduction to conductors and composers. But first he went to Leipzig ('grubby and uninteresting') where he stayed with the Weis family, parents-in-law of Wihan. He played his *Concert Overture* to Karl Reinicke, conductor of the Gewandhaus concerts, and the first movement of his Second Symphony to Heinrich von Herzogenberg, the composer and friend of Brahms. He had finished the symphony's *finale* the previous evening (5 December). In Dresden he was profoundly impressed by his visit to the Gemäldergalerie. Strauss loved art galleries and visited them wherever he travelled. He knew by heart the contents of each and was extremely knowledgeable about paintings. In a letter to his mother (12 December) he outlined the gallery's contents and described Raphael's Sistine Madonna: 'The way the white halo gradually loses itself in the blue of the sky until it becomes a little denser in the heads of the cherubs, which I needed my opera-glasses to see properly – that is marvellous. The picture, and the overall impression it made on me, reminds me very vividly of the *pp* G major passage in the introduction to the *Consecration of the House*, the gentleness, softness and conciliatoriness [*Versöhnung*] accompanying the splendour of the design and the conception.'[2]

Because of measles in the Weis household, Strauss moved to the home of Ferdinand Böckmann and his wife Helene. Böckmann and Strauss performed the Cello Sonata at a 'practice evening' of the Tonkünstlerverein on 19 December. 'It got colossal applause', he reported, 'Böckmann was blissfully happy with it.' During rehearsals at home Strauss practised conducting with one of Helene Böckmann's wooden knitting needles, modelling himself on Ernst von Schuch. Frau Böckmann, in a memoir written many years later, said: 'My husband was in the middle of long and demanding rehearsals of Wagner at the time – he took the needle away from him with the words "My dear Richard, do just stop that! I've had Schuch fumbling about under my nose for three hours today and enough is enough!"'[3]

Incidentally, the Böckmanns were the great-grandparents of the Strauss biographer, scholar and opera producer Kurt Wilhelm. The Dresden Court Orchestra's principal horn-player, Oscar Franz, wrote to Franz Strauss to confirm that the 'wonderful sonata' had had a 'magnificent reception'. He added: 'It is indeed a splendid work. . . Your son is fundamentally whole-some by nature, and I hope it will be many a long day before he is sicklied o'er with the pale cast of thought. I . . . take the greatest pleasure in your son's success.' Whatever conductors may have thought about him, Franz's orches-tral colleagues obviously had respect and affection for him. In Dresden Strauss met the conductors Franz Wüllner, whom he found 'very good natured' and for whom he had 'a real affection', and Schuch, who was the more *galant* and smart. Both played major roles in Strauss's life.

He moved on to Berlin on 21 December. Letters of introduction from Levi opened many doors. From Botho von Hülsen, intendant of the Prussian court theatres, he received a free pass to operatic and theatrical per-formances. He was tremendously excited by Sardou's *Fedora*, calling the playwright 'the greatest dramatist since Shakespeare'(!). As usual, a stimu-lating dramatic experience found an outlet in composition. 'I got some relief by writing down there and then a tremendous introduction to my new piano variations with fugue in A minor [o.Op. 81/AV177]', he told his sister. (He completed this work – *14 Improvisationen und Fuge über ein Originalthema für pianoforte zu zwei Händen* – on his return to Munich. It is dedicated to Hans von Bülow but was never performed by him or pub-lished.) The adolescent response to Sardou may be excused, but that encounter with *Fedora* left its mark. *Fedora* is about a princess who tracks down the murderer of her fiancé after living with him for a time. The setting is high society in St Petersburg and Paris and in the background lurk revolu-tion and espionage. In 1916 Strauss wrote to his librettist Hugo von Hofmannsthal: 'As for a new opera . . . say a diplomatic intrigue in the setting of the Vienna Congress with a genuine highly aristocratic woman spy as the principal character – the beautiful wife of an ambassador as a traitor for the sake of love, exploited by a secret agent or some such rather amusing subject, and then add to it the famous session of the Congress when Napoleon's return is announced – you'll probably say: Trash. But then we musicians are known for our poor taste in aesthetic matters, and besides, if you were to do a thing like that it wouldn't be trash.'[4] In 1928 Strauss asked Hofmannsthal for 'at least a little Scribe, Sardou, or even Lortzing in Hofmannsthal garb!'[5] The poet declined gracefully, saying that 'it is after all perfectly true that from time to time I can do very well with an injection of Scribe and Sardou. I have, on the other hand, the gift – which these two never possessed – of kindling in the characters breath of life.'[6]

A new world of music awaited Strauss in Berlin. He heard Bülow play a concerto by Raff, 'dreadfully insipid' music but 'phenomenal' playing. The Joachim Quartet was a revelation – 'the greatest artistic pleasure I've yet experienced in quartet playing', he informed Johanna. 'The ensemble is magnificent, the purity of intonation and figuration, the clarity, the wonderful interpretation, the colossal calm of the adagio playing, the way Joachim subordinates himself when he has nothing special to play, he's just the top line, not the *primarius*, and then the colossal technique, a style of playing completely devoid of any kind of impropriety, a magnificent, noble tone, I was in seventh heaven.' The programme which precipitated this flood of adjectives was Beethoven's Op. 18, No. 6 (in B♭), a quartet by Herzogenberg and Schubert's C major quintet. He attended three performances of Brahms's Third Symphony (which had had its first performance under Richter in Vienna on 2 December). At first, as he wrote to Thuille, he did not understand it ('my head is still spinning') and thought it 'wretchedly' scored. After the next performances, however, it was 'one of the most beautiful, the most original and the freshest things Brahms has ever written. . . I'm beginning to get very attached to Brahms as a whole, he's always interesting and very often really beautiful as well.' At one of the concerts he heard Brahms as soloist in his D minor Piano Concerto, 'another very interesting piece.' He played it with beauty and drive.' He also heard a symphony by Scharwenka. He was bowled over by the playing of Eugen d'Albert and thought the Berlin Philharmonic not as good as Dresden's orchestra. Among the operas he heard were *Die Zauberflöte* and Auber's *Le domino noir*. He was a frequent visitor to the art galleries and was upset by the number of paintings of battle scenes in the Nationalgalerie – ironic, coming from the future composer of two of the noisiest and most graphic battle scenes in music! He met several artists and went to their homes, playing string quartets with Carl Becker and Anton von Werner and at the home of Emil Teschendorff. Other artists who entertained him were Ludwig Knaus and Paul Thumann and the sculptor Gustav Eberlein. He met Otto Lessmann, editor of the *Allgemeine Musikzeitung* and called on the publishers Bote & Bock. At the home of Hermann Klose, a coffee dealer whose family had moved to Berlin from Munich, he learned to play the card game Skat which was to remain a lifelong obsession.

Nor did he neglect his own compositions which he had brought with him. He completed his Second Symphony, Op. 12, on 25 January, having left the third (slow) movement to last, and the five piano pieces *Stimmungsbilder*, Op. 9, for two hands, during February.[7] News of all this was relayed by letter to Franz Strauss, who advised him: 'When you are doing something new, make sure that it is melodious and not too heavy, and that it's pianistic. Increasingly, it's my experience that only melodious music makes a lasting impression on musicians and amateurs, and melody is the most viable element in music.'[8] The Cello Sonata had a public and several private performances during his Berlin stay, but the most important events for him were the performances of the *Serenade* for thirteen wind instruments. Some were given by the orchestra of the Konzerthaus, conducted by Benjamin Bilse – 'much too slow, I thought they were all going to sleep', said the composer. On 27 February it was performed by the Meiningen Orchestra, which was visiting the Prussian capital. Its conductor, Hans von Bülow, rehearsed it, but at the concert sat in the audience while Franz Mannstädt conducted. Strauss had been apprehensive about meeting Bülow, knowing of the great man's clashes with his father. But, he wrote home, 'he was very amiable, very well-disposed, and very witty. . . Moreover he talked about you with the most colossal respect, you were the most refined musician, the most beautiful tone, magnificent phrasing and execution. "I learned a lot from him", he told me, "do write and tell him so".'[9] On 21 March, one of the court conductors, Robert Radecke, conducted the *Concert Overture* in C minor.

But it was not all work and no play. 'The social life here is marvellous, we've just no idea at home', he informed his parents; and to Lotti Speyer he wrote: 'Berlin hospitality is phenomenal, and in consequence I have an invitation of one kind or another almost every evening.' He went to several balls and 'danced till his legs gave way'. He told Thuille that 'in spite of never getting up before 11 (I seldom get to bed before 1.30, very often it's 3 or 4, and it was 7 after the Artists' Ball) and spending every evening in society or at the theatre or a concert, and paying calls most days or writing letters, I have not been idle.' His susceptibility to beautiful women was much in evidence. The eighteen-year-old daughter of the writer Friedrich Spielhagen was 'wonderfully pretty . . . with a delightful figure, perfectly beautiful throat and face, shining grey eyes' and 'with her you can go on talking all evening without running out of subjects. . . We talk about French plays, Spinoza, the existence of a Higher Being, then we poke fun at the other people there.' There was also a Hungarian soprano Fräulein Pollak, 'wonderfully pretty', whom he heard as Susanna in *Le nozze di Figaro*. Fräulein Schwarz, who lived with Fr. Pollak, had asked to see some of his songs. But he was most smitten with Grethe Begas, the young wife of a sculptor. He spent 'many agreeable evenings chatting with the amiable lady' and told Johanna she was 'a wonderfully beautiful woman who is very fond of flirting, expects it of you indeed, and will take pleasure in a compliment even if it's not quite as refined as it might be'. Writing to Thuille, he said she 'has locked me deep in her heart' and he is said to have composed some songs at her feet. In letters written to him after he left Berlin, Grethe (Gret for short) signed herself 'your foster-mama'. He left for home on 29 March 1884.

How did Bülow come to have the *Serenade* in the repertory of the Meiningen Orchestra? Strauss's Op. 2, his String Quartet in A major, had been published in 1881 by Eugen Spitzweg, son of Edmund Spitzweg[10] who had taken over the music publishing firm of Joseph Aibl. In the same year, Aibl published Strauss's Op. 3, the *Five Pieces* for piano, which Eugen sent to his friend Bülow. '*Do not care* for [them] . . . in the least', the great man replied. 'Fail to find any sign of youth in his invention. *Not a genius* in my most sincere belief, but at best a talent, with 60 per cent aimed to shock.' But he liked the *Serenade* enough to commission another piece for wind ensemble from Strauss. This was the *Suite* in B flat, Op. 4, completed in Munich in September 1884 and dedicated to Thuille. Bülow flummoxed Strauss by telling him late in October that the Meiningen Orchestra would perform it at the Odeonssaal, Munich, on 18 November and inviting him to conduct it. The orchestra would have spent some time on it before the tour began, but there was no possibility of rehearsal in the meantime! Strauss had never conducted in public before. He left a famous account of his début:

I fetched Bülow from his hotel: he was in an abominable mood. As we were going up the stairs in the Odeon he was fulminating against Munich, which had cast Wagner and him out, against old Perfall [Intendant of the Opera], called the Odeon a cross between a church and a stock exchange, in short he was as delightfully unbearable as only he could be. . . I conducted my piece through something of a haze; all I can remember now is that I didn't make a complete mess of it, but I simply couldn't say what it was actually like otherwise. Bülow didn't listen to my début, he was storming round and round the instrument room, chain-smoking. Just as I got back in there, my father came in by another door, deeply moved, to express his thanks. That was what Bülow had been waiting for. He pounced on my father like a ravening lion. 'You have nothing to thank me for', he yelled. 'I haven't forgotten the way you treated me here in this God-forsaken city. I did what I did today because your son has talent, not for your sweet sake.' Without another word my father left the room. . . Of course the effect of this scene was to completely ruin my début for me, but all of a sudden Bülow was in the best of tempers. He later made amends to my father, and my father did not harbour resentment against his son's benefactor.[11]

Next day Strauss was advised by Bülow to send the *Suite* to Brahms for his opinion. He sent the score via the Meiningen Orchestra's principal horn-player Gustav Leinhos, whom he had met in Berlin. Leinhos wrote on 15 December: 'When he gave me back your Suite, Herr Dr Brahms spoke very highly of your work, though he had looked in vain for the spring of melody which ought to be overflowing at your age.'

Strauss's other compositions after his return from Berlin included a Goethe setting, *Wandrers Sturmlied*, Op. 14, for chorus and orchestra, and a Piano Quartet in C minor, Op. 13. Both were heavily influenced by Brahms. The Piano Quartet was awarded first prize (300 marks) in a competition for a work in this form organised by the Berlin Tonkünstlerverein. (It was per-formed for the first time in Weimar on 8 December 1885 by Strauss and members of the Halíř Quartet.) A *Festmarsch* in D (o.Op. 84) was played by Franz Strauss's Wilde Gung'l on 8 January 1885. But the most important Strauss première at this time had occurred in New York on 13 December 1884 when Theodor Thomas conducted the Second Symphony at a New York Philharmonic Society concert. Thomas, born near Hanover in 1835, had lived in America since he was ten. A violinist and horn-player, he took up conducting in 1858 and formed his own orchestra in 1862. He was the New York Philharmonic's conductor from 1877 to 1891 when he became first conductor of the Chicago Symphony Orchestra. A friend of Franz Strauss, he visited him in the summer of 1884 and was shown Richard's new symphony. The work had its German première at a Gürzenich concert in Cologne conducted by Franz Wüllner. Strauss attended the rehearsals and was disingenuously delighted by his own music, as he usually was: 'It's immensely difficult but sounds colossal [a favourite adjective]', he wrote to his parents.[12] 'I was almost moved by the first movement. You should have seen them in the Scherzo, coming cropper after cropper [*wie sie durcheinander-purzelten*], it was hilarious. The Adagio sounds magical and the Finale is just as good. . . Papa will open his eyes wide when he hears how modern the Symphony sounds, and perhaps there's just a little bit too much counterpoint in it, but in compensation for that everything surges and pulsates so that it's a joy to hear it.' Most of the critics, except in Berlin, agreed with him. Another major performance followed on 4 March. This was of the Horn Concerto which had been published during 1884. Strauss's horn and piano arrangement, already performed in Munich, as has been related, is dedicated to his father, obviously its inspirer, but the published score was inscribed to Oscar Franz of the Dresden orchestra. But it was Gustav Leinhos who played it for the first time, in Meiningen. A month later came the first of Josephine Strauss's mental collapses. And there was another shadow over Strauss's life at this time. He was for the first time deeply in love – and with a married woman.

4 Meiningen

Richard Strauss first met Dora Wihan some time in 1883. Just when friendship turned to love cannot be discovered, but during 1884 seems likely. Wife of his father's colleague, the cellist Hanuš Wihan, Dora was four years older than Strauss, five years younger than her husband. She was a gifted pianist, good enough to play Strauss's Cello Sonata with her husband. She was very friendly with Johanna Strauss, and when Richard was in Leipzig he stayed, as we have seen, for a time with her parents, the Weis family. On the very day, 14 April 1885, their mother entered a nursing home, Strauss wrote to his sister: 'I saw your friend Dora yesterday and conveyed your greetings to her, but I cannot say that I am as pleased with her condition as I am, relatively, with Mama's. In our household the care of the sick is excellent (I have nothing but praise for Papa and myself), but at the Wihans it is as bad as ever. Frau Wihan will probably have to go to Bad Reichenhall, where her husband, out of jealousy, will not let her go alone.' There were, obviously, already strains in the Wihan marriage. In the recollections she wrote many years later, Johanna Strauss described Dora as 'like one of the family' in her relationship to the Strausses. 'Herr Wihan was insanely jealous over his pretty and already rather coquettish wife. I often witnessed scenes. For instance, she often asked me to spend the night with her, when her husband came in late from the opera and sometimes had had a drop to drink, so that she wasn't left alone. When Richard was with us we used to make music.'

Strauss wrote to his sister on 26 April 1885: 'At present I'm not in the very best of spirits and hope to be better disposed and brighter again in a few days' time perhaps. Your friend Dora is going to Reichenhall on Saturday next for four weeks with her mother. . . Hans is going to Russia at the beginning of May.' Johanna offered to return home, but Richard replied three days later: 'I'm afraid you can't share the thing that is oppressing me, even if you came home early.' The implication is that the oppression was caused by Dora's imminent departure. Whether part of Wihan's jealousy was caused by Strauss we do not know, but obviously Munich tongues wagged because in a letter to Richard in January of the following year, Franz Strauss wrote: 'Don't forget how people here have talked about you in connection with Dora W.' Richard was in Frankfurt when Wihan returned from Russia. Letters from home told him Hanuš and Dora were about to separate. Franz wrote in June 1885: 'Hanna has had a letter from Dresden, from Dora. She is quite well. Her dear ? husband joined her again in Dresden for a week, to her horror.' Richard replied: 'The news of Dora Wihan took me very much by surprise, but I was not amazed by it. I've seen it coming for a long time.' No doubt, but *was* it a surprise? He destroyed all Dora's letters and she his (with three exceptions, as we shall see), but it is extremely unlikely that he was not kept fully informed by her about what was going on. Johanna, one surmises, would have welcomed her friend as a sister-in-law; and when the divorce hearing took place, Strauss's mother, who also liked Dora very much, lent her a hat and veil to wear in court.

Along with this emotional turmoil came a request from Bülow, conveyed through Spitzweg. Would Strauss like to succeed Franz Mannstädt, who was moving to a post in Berlin, as assistant conductor in Meiningen of the ducal court orchestra? Strauss was overwhelmed and overjoyed. To receive such an offer from such a musician at the age of twenty-one! Leinhos, through whom some of the negotiations were conducted, assured Richard that the older orchestral players liked him and would work under him 'with plea-sure'. He would also be expected to conduct the choral society. The fee for the six and a half months from 1 October to 15 April would be 1,500 marks (about £75). As a preliminary, Strauss joined Bülow in Frankfurt to meet Princess Marie of Meiningen, sister of Duke Georg II who was to be Strauss's employer, and to attend Bülow's piano course at the Raff Conservatory. On 10 June he played his *14 Improvisationen und Fuge*, dedicated to Bülow, to the princess and its dedicatee. He met the conductor Fritz Steinbach and went to the opera to hear *Die Walküre* and 'a new opera by Massenet, *Hérodiade*, which is very charming in places, especially the ballet music, but doesn't amount to anything and has a rotten text'. This, we may presume, was Strauss's first encounter with a version of the Salome story. He went to

4 Dora Wihan

the theatre to see 'Heyse's latest tragedy *Don Juans Ende*, which is really capital'. This, too, was to have musical consequences. Strauss's appointment to Meiningen was confirmed by the Duke on 18 June. Thus he entered one of the smaller, most cultured and enterprising German courts, but where there was no opera house. Duke Georg was a passionate lover of drama and music. During his reign the duchy's theatre company and orchestra toured widely. He was responsible for the choice of programmes and guest artists and was closely involved with the management of the theatre. He had married an actress (Helene von Heldburg, stage name Ellen Franz) and was enthusiastic about what would today be called 'authenticity' in the presentation of plays. Strauss wrote in his memoirs of his youth:

My stay in Meiningen was all the more important to me because the theatre did not go on tour that winter and I had an opportunity to admire the wonderful performances of the classics, produced by Duke Georg, which excelled particularly in the careful handling of crowd scenes and the stylistic verisimilitude of the productions. . . An example of the Duke's working methods: on New Year's Eve the rehearsal went on till 9 o'clock, 10, and at last the clock struck midnight. The Duke stood up and everyone breathed a sigh of relief. The Duke: 'I wish the company a happy new year. The rehearsal will continue.' There was no eight-hour day then.[1]

Strauss wrote ecstatically to his father on 30 September describing his arrival at the station where Leinhos, Richard Mühlfeld (principal clarinet) and Anton Kirchhoff (principal oboe) were waiting to greet him. The first concert he attended, conducted by Bülow, was a Beethoven programme: *Egmont* overture, First and Seventh Symphonies and the 'Emperor' concerto played by Bülow's Frankfurt pupil Anna Haasters.

Strauss's first big occasion was on 18 October when he appeared as soloist, conductor and composer. He played Mozart's C minor Piano Concerto (K.491) with his own cadenza and conducted his Second Symphony. His friend Thuille was in the audience. Bülow's report to Spitzweg read: 'Strauss: homme d'or. Symphony *capital*. His playing – like his conducting début – positively breathtaking. If he wants to he can step into my shoes tomorrow, with H. H.'s [His Highness's] consent.' To Strauss himself Bülow wrote: 'You are one of those exceptional musicians who do not need to serve in the ranks first but have the right stuff to take on a higher command straightaway.' Bülow regarded the symphony as 'very important, original, formally mature'. It appealed to his conservative taste, but even today it sounds a good work, much less reliant on its classic models and with just a few hints of what lay only a few years ahead. It certainly deserves better than Brahms's comment 'Quite charming [*ganz hübsch*]'. Brahms added some advice: 'You should take a close look at Schubert's dances and practise inventing simple eight-bar melodies. There's too much thematic trifling in your symphony: all that piling up of a large number of themes on a triad, with only rhythmic contrast between them, has no value whatsoever.' Strauss said it was because of these remarks (heartily supported by Franz Strauss) that he had 'never disdained to incorporate a popular melody in my works' and realised that 'counterpoint is only justified when there is a poetic necessity forcing two or more themes to unite for a time'. In 1887 he warned the management of the Leipzig Gewandhaus Orchestra that 'because of its great difficulty and somewhat dense orchestration and its rich, somewhat too rich, contrapuntal work, the symphony makes a thoroughly unclear, confused, indeed perhaps even ugly impression in the first few rehearsals'.

Brahms had heard Strauss's symphony because he had arrived in Meiningen the previous day for rehearsals for the first performance of his own Fourth Symphony. Strauss told Franz that this was 'beyond all question a gigantic work, with a grandeur in its conception and invention, genius in its treatment of forms' and to his champion the conductor Wüllner he described it as 'one of the grandest creations in the whole field of orchestral music'. During his visit Brahms also conducted the *Academic Festival Overture*, with Bülow and Strauss playing in the percussion section. Neither had any idea how to count rests. 'In rehearsal', Strauss wrote, 'I was already out by bar 4 and I placed the full score on my music stand. Bülow would count vigorously for eight bars and then give up. . . I don't believe the percussion ever perpetrated so many wrong entries as when the two Kapellmeisters took part.'

Strauss learned the art of conducting at Meiningen by being allowed to take rehearsals. He rehearsed Mozart's *Requiem*, Brahms's Violin Concerto and *Serenade* in A and Schubert's *Unfinished* Symphony. Sometimes members of the Duke's family were present. On one occasion they asked for Wagner's overture to *Der fliegende Holländer*. 'With unexampled impudence, never having set eyes on the score before, I conducted a brisk and breezy performance of it at sight', he told Hermann Levi. 'It went very well.' The social life at Meiningen was also hectic and Strauss danced for hours with princesses and 'some jolly good actresses'. Princess Marie was reported as saying that 'this is certainly something very different from that Mannstädt fellow'. When Franz read about these activities, he warned his son: 'It's very agreeable of course to converse with cultivated, respectable and witty women, but a young artist, who belongs after all to the public, must make it his first concern that his reputation does not suffer from it.' Richard's reply was unabashed: 'You cannot reproach me if I express my pleasure at finding in this town of Meiningen, which has been accursed by the god Amor, the oasis of a few jolly actresses. You surely do not want that cheerful fellow you used to know, your son Richard, to return to Munich a philistine.' Besides, there was Dora.

At the end of November 1885, Bülow resigned from his Meiningen post after a petty quarrel over Brahms conducting the Fourth Symphony with another orchestra while at the same time conducting it during the Meiningen orchestra's tour. Bülow left, leaving Strauss in full charge. But he returned as a guest conductor at the end of January 1886 when he conducted Beethoven's *Eroica* Symphony. 'It was a performance such as I shall never hear a second time', Strauss wrote to his father.[2] 'I was so moved that after the last movement I cried like a child in the instrument room; I was alone with Bülow there and he put his arms round me and gave me a kiss that I shall never forget as long as I live.' Describing the concert to Levi as a 'huge triumph for Bülow' he added: 'But it did not lead to His Highness inviting our maestro to take up the intendancy again, which I believe would have met with no very great resistance from Bülow.' The loss of Bülow was a blow to Meiningen and it was rumoured that the Duke intended to reduce the orchestra from forty-nine to thirty-nine players. Strauss made overtures to Munich, where he knew a conducting post would become vacant in August 1886, and received encouragement from the intendant there, Carl von Perfall. If the Meiningen orchestra stayed at full complement, Strauss informed him, 'then I owe it to Herr von Bülow, whom I have to thank for so much and who has placed his trust in me, to remain here'. After Bülow's January concert, Strauss learned that the cut to thirty-nine players was definite; he was offered a three-year contract at a salary of 2,000 marks a year. Bülow advised him to accept the Munich post. Strauss would have preferred anywhere else because he wished 'to come to know the world somewhere else besides Munich', but on 1 February he took up Perfall's offer. King Ludwig II approved the appointment in April – a three-year contract from 1 August 1886 to 31 July 1889 at 2,000 marks for the first year, 2,400 for the second and third.

Meanwhile there was conducting to be done in Meiningen. He tackled works by Lachner, Rheinberger, Liszt and Tchaikovsky and, on 23 February 1886, the Symphony in F by his friend Thuille. The composer was unable to be there but Strauss told him of its warm reception and that the orchestra had liked it. Strauss also organised a series of chamber-music recitals. All these activities left him with little time for composition. But in October and November of 1885 he had added four *Lieder* to five settings of poems by Hermann von Gilm that he had composed in August in Steinach, on holiday, and in Munich. These songs, his Op. 10, include three which have remained among the most popular he wrote, *Zueignung*, *Die Nacht* and *Allerseelen*. The love-songs in the group were inspired by Dora. He showed six of the songs to Bülow's wife Marie while her husband was away on tour. She wrote to Bülow on 11 November: 'Yesterday Strauss brought me a song-cycle he has written with the intention of singing it to me, but he had to confine himself to playing it, while I followed the score, my sore throat worried him. Then I was "critical", i.e. I did not simply praise it but I also said which bits I didn't care for, which bits struck me as not having been really felt. The young man went away well pleased.' Well pleased enough to compose (or complete) three more settings. Of the six he played to Marie von Bülow on 10 November the latest, composed in Meiningen on 31 October, was *Allerseelen*. The next day he wrote *Die Verschwiegenen* and, on 12 November, *Die Zeitlose*. The ninth song, *Wer hat's getan?* was written on 13 November but was detached from the other eight and was not published and performed until 1974. Four of the songs (*Zueignung*, *Nichts*, *Die Georgine* and *Allerseelen*) were performed (presumably for the first time) at the second of Strauss's chamber-music recitals in Meiningen on 5 March 1886. Incidentally, when Franz wrote urging him to compose some more songs for his Aunt Johanna, Strauss replied that first he had to find 'some nice texts – sitting down and composing songs in cold blood, as I used to, is

something I can't do any more'. Between November 1885 and 24 February
1886 he composed the *Burleske* in D minor for piano and orchestra. This was
written for Bülow, who rejected it because it was 'unpianistic and had too
wide a stretch for him'. He expostulated to Strauss: 'A different position for
the hands in every bar? Do you think I'm going to sit down for four weeks
to learn a cross-grained piece like that?' Before he left Meiningen, he ran
through the *Burleske* with the orchestra, telling Bülow (7 April 1886) that
'the accompaniment, I suppose, is somewhat overloaded and the piano part
too detailed. I shall cut out some of the orchestral writing, then, given an
outstanding (!) pianist and a first-rate (!) conductor, perhaps the whole
thing will turn out not to be the unalloyed nonsense that I really took it for
after the first rehearsal. After the first run-through I was totally discouraged
and I've begun without delay to remodel the C minor Rhapsody for piano
and orchestra (with harp) which I've just begun.' The Rhapsody (AV213) was
eventually abandoned, the *Burleske* laid aside for the moment. At the Duke's
suggestion, Strauss set the *Bardengesang* from Kleist's *Die Hermann-
Schlacht* (AV181) for male voices and orchestra. This was performed in the
court theatre late in February 1886. It is lost and should not be confused with
the Klopstock setting under the same title composed as Op. 55 in 1906.

To mark his departure from Meiningen, Strauss dedicated his Piano
Quartet to Duke Georg 'in respect and gratitude'. The Duke's letter of thanks
said how sorry he was to see Strauss go and confessed that 'your achievements here have *thoroughly* cured me of my previous erroneous belief that
your youth made you unfitted as yet to be the sole director of my orchestra'.
The Duchess, who knew what an enthusiastic playgoer Strauss had been
during his stay, told him he had been 'the best *claqueur* we have had in the
theatre for a long time'. Strauss was awarded the Cross of Merit for Art and
Learning. This worried Franz Strauss: 'Don't forget, my dear son, to remain
simple, true and modest, this I beg you with a fearful heart. It is not that I
doubt your good sense . . . only I think a few words of warning will do no
harm.'[3]

Writing in 1909, Strauss acknowledged what he owed to Bülow:

The image of the works he rehearsed (all from memory) is lodged immovably in my
soul. . . There was never a trace of wilfulness, everything was a compelling necessity,
imposed by the form and content of the work itself. . . I must not forget the grace

with which he wielded his baton, the delightful manner in which he used to rehearse
– instruction often taking the form of an epigram. . . He was the wittiest compère
who ever lurked in the guise of a schoolmaster of genius. . . His anxious 'You have
only to learn to read the score of a Beethoven symphony *exactly* and you will already
have the interpretation too' would adorn the gates of any college even today. . .
Anyone who ever heard him playing Beethoven or conducting Wagner, who ever
attended his piano classes or witnessed him taking an orchestral rehearsal, must
regard him as the paragon of all the shining virtues of the interpretative musician. . .
Apart from what I owe to my father . . . such understanding of the art of interpretation as I can call my own I owe to my father's implacable enemy, Hans von Bülow.[4]

5   Third conductor

Strauss's tribute to Bülow was heartfelt, but at Meiningen also he encountered an individual who was to shape his future as a composer. This was Alexander Ritter, 'a very agreeable, cultivated man, his daughters are pillars of the choral society', as Strauss wrote to his father on 12 October 1885. Ritter was born in Narva, Estonia, in 1833 and married Wagner's niece Franziska in 1854. Bülow and he had been at school together. In 1856 Ritter went to Weimar to work with Liszt. He was for a while director of music in Stettin. After helping to run a music shop in Würzburg, he joined the Meiningen Orchestra in 1882 as a violinist. He was also a composer; his opera *Der faule Hans* had its first performance in Munich in October 1885, just after Strauss arrived in Meiningen.

Ritter at once took a liking to the young conductor thirty-one years his junior. He invited him to spend Christmas Eve at his home and began to talk to him about the aesthetic beliefs of Liszt and Wagner, both of whom he regarded almost as gods, and the philosophy of Schopenhauer. ('Do read Schopenhauer!' Strauss wrote to Thuille. 'The fellow is magnificent and hellishly good for sharpening up one's poor wits'). When the cuts were made in the Meiningen Orchestra, Ritter decided to apply for a job in the Munich Court Orchestra and was offered a place in the violas. So when Strauss moved to Munich, his mentor was there too. Strauss described Ritter's impact on him thus:

My upbringing had left me with some remaining prejudices against the works of Wagner and, in particular, of Liszt, and I hardly knew Wagner's writings at all. Ritter patiently introduced me to them and to Schopenhauer until I both knew and understood them. He demonstrated to me that the path onwards from Beethoven 'the musician of expression' (*Musik als Ausdruck* [Music as Expression] by Friedrich von Hausegger, as opposed to *Vom musikalisch Schönen* [The Beautiful in Music] by

Hanslick), led via Liszt who, like Wagner, had rightly recognised that sonata form had been extended to its utmost limits with Beethoven. . . New ideas must seek out new forms for themselves: the basic principle adopted by Liszt in his symphonic works, in which the poetic idea really did act simultaneously as the structural element, became thenceforward the guiding principle for my own symphonic works.[1]

Strauss left Meiningen on 10 April 1886. In the free time at his disposal until he started his new job on 1 August he took Brahms's advice and went to Italy where he visited Bologna, Florence, Rome, Naples, Capri, Amalfi and Sorrento. A visit to Venice was abandoned because of a cholera epidemic there. He was moved to tears by Raphael's St Cecilia in Bologna and said he did not understand Michelangelo enough. He climbed Vesuvius. His suitcase was stolen ('It might have been worse, there's no need to let it spoil our good temper'). He admired the elegant women in Rome ('more beautiful women in one spot than I have ever clapped eyes on before'). His sister had written to let him know that Dora Wihan was in Rome. 'I've seen nothing of her', he replied, 'I didn't know she was here.' Perhaps he was telling the truth; perhaps he was being discreet. He made friends with the painter Franz von Lenbach ('very witty in conversation and genial company') and he decided he would never become a convert to Italian music, 'it's such trash'. Verdi's *Aida* was 'dreadful Redskin music', Rossini's *Il barbiere di Siviglia* could only be enjoyed if the performance was exceptional but Verdi's *Requiem* had 'some very attractive and original things. I actually stayed till the end.' His strongest impression was of the beauty and splendour of nature in Italy and he began to sketch a symphonic fantasy about it which he completed on his return to Munich. He told Bülow that he was 'very content' to be sitting at his desk again because 'the one pleasure that persists, of which I shall never tire, is the work to which I have dedicated myself entirely'. He added: 'I've never fully believed in the idea that natural beauty acts as a stimulus, but in the ruins of Rome I learned better, the ideas came in flocks.' Before taking up his new duties, he visited Bayreuth where he was stirred by Felix Mottl's conducting of *Tristan und Isolde* (its first production in the Festspielhaus) and found *Parsifal*, conducted by Levi, difficult to comprehend.

He made his début as a conductor of opera on 1 October 1886 in

Boieldieu's *Jean de Paris*. The second opera he conducted, on 12 November, was Mozart's *Così fan tutte*, which in those days was so little regarded that it was automatically allotted to the third conductor. The tenor Heinrich Vogl, who sang Ferrando, gave Strauss advice about not conducting with 'too long an arm'. Vogl, Strauss recalled, 'liked to be sparing with his voice, loved fluid tempi and rightly felt that the long lever attached to the conductor's shoulder joint handicapped him'.[2] Other operas he conducted in his first two seasons were Rheinberger's *Des Thürmes Töchterlein*, Auber's *Le domino noir* and *La part du diable*, Delibes's *Le roi l'a dit*, Nicolai's *Die lustigen Weiber von Windsor*, Goldmark's *Die Königen von Saba*, Cherubini's *Les deux journées*, Lortzing's *Die beiden Schützen* and *Zar und Zimmermann*, Verdi's *Il trovatore* and *Un ballo in maschera*, Weber's *Der Freischütz*, Cornelius's *Der Barber von Bagdad*, Donizetti's *La favorite*, Kreutzer's *Das Nachtlager* and Flotow's *Martha*.

Strauss soon realised he had made a mistake accepting the Munich post. He frankly admitted, in his memoirs, that he was 'not a particularly good third conductor. Although I was adept at taking over at short notice . . . my lack of the routine, in which many less talented colleagues were vastly superior to me, my idiosyncratic insistence on "my own tempos", on occasion often hindered the smooth dispatch of operas in the approved manner. . . The operas I had to conduct in those days did not interest me sufficiently to study them properly.' During *Zar und Zimmermann* he beat two in a bar where the orchestra was used to four. The performance fell apart and he had to stop and start again. The incident haunted him for years. On another occasion a friend in the front row of the stalls saw him check his beat, lower his head and then, with a jerk, continue as though nothing had happened. She asked him later if he had felt ill. 'No', he explained, 'I was composing. A tune had suddenly occurred to me. The orchestra could manage without me for a bit.' He also had to conduct knowing that his critical father was playing first horn, 'not nearly as worried by the difficult solos in "Per pietà" [in *Così fan tutte*] as by the fear that his son would choose excessively modern (i.e. extremely fast) tempos'.

The one bright feature of this Munich period was the relationship with Ritter. Strauss and he met nearly every evening in Leibenfrost's wine parlour. They were often joined by Thuille, himself a convert to the 'new music', and Siegmund von Hausegger, a composer who was later to marry Ritter's daughter. Occasionally they were joined by Franz Strauss, who was certainly not there to join in adulation of Liszt and Wagner but shared Ritter's dislike of Levi. Ritter and Strauss *père* were anti-semitic, largely because of Levi, and between them they turned Richard against the man who had conducted some of his youthful works. For instance, Strauss wrote to Bülow in December 1887 that Levi's interpretation of Beethoven's Ninth Symphony was 'the most demeaning, the most abominable, account of a piece of music I have ever heard'. Another unedifying example of the young Strauss's tendency to trim his sails to another's opinion occurred in 1887 when he went to Leipzig to conduct his F minor Symphony on 13 October. There, probably through Max Steinitzer, he met Gustav Mahler, then second conductor at the Stadttheater. Mahler played him the first act of his version of Weber's uncompleted opera *Die drei Pintos*. In a letter to Bülow, Strauss (describing Mahler as 'a new, very delightful acquaintance. . .a highly intelligent musician and conductor') said the arrangement was 'a masterpiece'. On this recommendation, Bülow studied the vocal score and replied to Strauss in vehement terms. His reaction had shown 'acute lack of judgment', the work was 'infamous, antiquated rubbish'. Strauss recanted. To be fair to him, as he pointed out, he had heard only Act I ('which in conception is almost entirely by Weber and which still does not seem so bad to me, so my lack of judgment must indeed be chronic') but he had now seen Acts II and III in rehearsal in Munich 'and completely understand your horror, they really are extremely mediocre and tedious. . . I most deeply regret that you, revered master, have been the innocent victim of my youthful rashness.'

Like many fanatics, Ritter could attribute nothing good to any of his opponents. Brahms was an object of revulsion to him and he weaned Strauss away from his Brahms enthusiasm. Max Steinitzer said that Ritter often 'sounded more like a tub-thumping party man than a musician weighing composers' merits and demerits'. He turned the impressionable young Strauss's opinions round so that Richard could write to the Dresden composer Jean Louis Nicodé that Brahms's Second Symphony was 'really badly and aridly scored' and by 1889 was calling Brahms a 'canting, abstemious Temperance-Leaguer'.[3] For the rest of his life, Strauss had a poor opinion of Brahms, but in the years 1884 and 1885 he was heavily under the

Brahms influence. Having developed in his adolescence in the tradition of Mendelssohn and Schumann, he moved towards Brahms as a representative of the same classical German tradition, based on the forms of symphony, sonata and concerto. The genius of the *Burleske* is that it shows Strauss using parody as an act of homage. The *scherzo* of Brahms's B flat Piano Concerto is an obvious model for certain passages in the *Burleske*, just as *Gesang der Parzen* and *Nänie* are the models for *Wandrers Sturmlied*. A spell of Brahms-worship was a necessary stage in Strauss's development, whatever he may later have thought of 'leathery Johannes' as a composer.

Strauss's disillusionment with Munich was compensated by the growing number of requests for him to conduct his own music. He conducted his Second Symphony in Frankfurt on 7 January 1887, Leipzig on 17 October 1887, Mannheim on 10 January 1888 and Cologne in June 1889. (Bülow, who admired the work greatly, conducted it in Hamburg and Bremen.) But the biggest thrill was an invitation to conduct the symphony in Milan on 8 and 11 December 1887, his first dual success outside Germany. He was given six rehearsals and made the best of them. 'I am the lion of the hour', he wrote home, 'everyone in raptures.' The orchestra gave him an inscribed silver baton. The adulation pleased him especially because, as he wrote sarcastically, he was 'far from spoiled by recognition and benevolence in my beloved home-town'. Nevertheless it was in Munich, on 2 March 1887, that he conducted the Court Orchestra in the first performance of his symphonic fantasy *Aus Italien*. His father had been practising the horn solos for days and there was a tense atmosphere in the hall before the performance – the orchestra had greeted the last movement with laughter at rehearsal. The first three movements were applauded but the *finale*, *Neapolitanisches Volksleben*, was hissed and catcalled. Strauss was delighted. He wrote to Lotti Speyer: 'Of course I found it all tremendous fun. . . The opposition have pronounced me half-mad, talk about my going astray and all that sort of rubbish. I felt immensely proud; the first work to have met with the opposition of the multitude – that proves it must be of some significance.'

Aus Italien, Strauss wrote, 'consists of *sensations evoked by* the sight and the wonderful natural beauties of Rome and Naples, *not descriptions of* them. . . *Expression* is our art.' It seems unbelievable today that this attractive piece, a halfway house between his youthful classicism and the originality of the tone-poems, could excite controversy. In later life he called it, accurately, 'a timid experiment'. When it was first performed in Boston conducted by Wilhelm Gericke in the 1888–9 season, a critic reported that 'the auditors [listeners] marched out by platoons during the pauses between the movements, and some of the bolder ones made a dash for the door during the performance'.[4] Where *Aus Italien* showed most daring was in the brash and colourful *finale*, an evocation of the colourful bustle of Naples. Its main theme was what Strauss believed was 'a well-known Neapolitan folk-song' but was in fact a popular song, *Funiculì, funiculà*, by Luigi Denza (1846–1922), a Neapolitan who composed it in 1880 to mark the opening of Naples funicular railway. Strauss's treatment of it is witty and by no means vulgar. *Aus Italien* was dedicated to Bülow, who wrote to Ritter on 30 December 1887: 'Is age making such a reactionary of me? The author is a genius, but I find he has gone to the utmost limit of what is musically possible (within the bounds of beauty) and has often, indeed, gone beyond the limit without any really pressing need for it. A wonderful, enviable mistake, the prodigality of the ideas, the abundance of associations, only.' Strauss conducted further performances in Cologne and Frankfurt.

In his letter to Lotti he mentioned that he was working on an orchestral work to be called *Macbeth* and on a violin sonata. The latter, in E flat, Op. 18, was completed on 1 November 1887 and dedicated to his cousin Robert Pschorr. It had its first performance in Elberfeld on 3 October 1888 by Robert Heckmann and Julius Buths. Ten days later it was played in Munich, this time with Strauss as pianist. Strauss also wrote a number of songs at this period. His Op. 15, four settings of Count von Schack and one of Michelangelo, was composed in November-December 1886, Op. 17 (six Schack settings) between December 1886 and April 1887 and Op. 19 (six more Schack settings) in January-February 1888. In March 1888 he wrote his four Felix Dahn settings *Mädchenblumen* in which girls are hymned through their botanical equivalents. Offering them to Spitzweg for publication he called them 'complicated and experimental' and unlikely to be a success – only too true. He then sent 'these extremely ungrateful songs' to the Berlin publisher Adolph Fürstner who accepted them for a fee of 800 marks, which was 300 marks more than Spitzweg had paid for *Aus Italien*.

Part of Strauss's uneasiness in Munich was attributable to the intendant

of the Court Opera, Baron Carl von Perfall, a composer of marked conservative tendency who regarded any Bülow protégé with suspicion. He criticised Strauss's conducting, especially his tempos and any unusual nuances
of phrasing. Strauss was infuriated by an episode in the summer of 1888
which came to a head just after he had returned from Bologna, where he
heard Martucci conduct *Tristan* ('I have never been made so acutely aware
of how much marvellous *bel canto* there is in *Tristan*'). Because Levi was ill,
he had been asked by Perfall in March to take the rehearsals for the world
première of Wagner's *Die Feen*, an enterprise about which he had doubts,
for, as he told Bülow, 'Wagner is present in *Die Feen* all right, but he's still
wearing boy's bootees, Herculean though they are!'[5] Nevertheless, it was a
prestigious occasion. He described what happened next in a furious letter to
Bülow written on 17 June:

> By not so much as a word was it ever hinted to me that if Levi was not back in time
> I should *not* conduct the work. I've been immensely conscientious and I've
> rehearsed it really well. Now Levi's leave has been extended to 15 August and today
> Perfall reveals to me that he has transferred the direction of *Feen* to my superior in
> rank (Hofkapellmeister) and seniority (in art!!), Fischer. Imagine it! *Final* rehearsals
> start tomorrow, the performance is fixed for the 29th [August]. . . Fischer, he said,
> was my superior in routine, which is the most important thing in the theatre. Can
> you believe your ears? Yet there was no fuss a few weeks ago when I conducted
> Zöllner's *Faust* (which is very difficult and had been rehearsed by Levi in an extra-
> ordinarily slipshod way) with one little rehearsal, and *Freischütz* (which I've never
> done before) *without* a rehearsal of any kind. . . Then he lectured me about my pre-
> sumption in making such claims at my age. It's all more than I can stand. . . I've now
> at last realised that this is not the soil to nourish a musical life which is to give any
> kind of joy. I'm not capable, on my own, of pulling the cart out of the mud that
> everything here is stuck in. The whole place is a waste land, a swamp, a beery swamp.

In his memoirs written many years later, Strauss described Franz Fischer
as 'one of the most untalented musicians I have ever met . . . a real malefac-
tor in the pit'. He wrote then that he 'handed in his resignation', but matters
did not move that fast. 'I have to admit', he told Bülow in the same letter,
'that I do not have the means to give up the post here, badly paid as it is,
without something to take its place.' Both Bülow and Spitzweg advised him
to wait until his contract expired on 31 July 1889. Meanwhile Bülow made

some moves. He was a friend and former colleague of Hans Bronsart von Schellendorf, who had become intendant of Weimar Opera in 1887. The director of music there was Eduard Lassen, who had been Hofkapellmeister since 1858. Bronsart wrote to Strauss, suggesting a meeting, on 25 August 1888, but formal negotiations were not held until January to March 1889. Strauss outlined to Bronsart his dissatisfaction with Munich and his hopes for Weimar:

Fresh from the school of Bülow, I came here primarily as a new broom to initiate some good *expressive* orchestral playing, in which I was, however, only partially successful and then only after fighting every inch of the way; the reason for this was my position as *No. 3* which meant that I lacked all authority and not only could *not* count on the backing of my chief but could also be sure of the inveterate opposition of my two colleagues, who simply follow other principles such as are more comfortable for all concerned. . . These experiences have convinced me that . . . I must insist in Weimar on a full and varied share of the work . . . on co-ordination with Lassen and also on the title and rank of a Hofkapellmeister.

When his appointment was confirmed it was only as Kapellmeister and his salary of 2,100 marks was less than he received in Munich (it was raised to 3,000 in January 1890). Even so, he was so anxious to leave Munich that he accepted these conditions. His last weeks there were soured by the sudden pensioning-off in June of his father. Franz learned of it from a letter pinned to the orchestra's notice-board. A side-effect of this shabby act was that it intensified the anti-semitism of both father and son, who blamed not only Perfall (who was chiefly responsible) but Levi. Richard was away conducting *Aus Italien* in Wiesbaden and wrote to Franz: 'Now dear Papa use your retirement to take a good rest and look after your health and strength, so that we shall have you with us in good health as our loving and beloved father for a long time to come. I wish you that with all my heart! . . . Think of me with the old love and affection.'

His departure for Weimar and the conclusion of his father's professional career marked the real end of Strauss's apprenticeship. It has been related in some detail because it set the pattern for the rest of his life.

6   Dora and Weimar

Where, all this time, was Dora Wihan? She left Munich permanently in 1887, perhaps earlier. She went to America and on return became a lady's companion and piano teacher at Lixouri on the Greek island of Kefallinía until 1891. Strauss wrote regularly to her there and she to him. Strauss, against his normal custom, destroyed her letters. She kept his until she died on 31 January 1938, when she asked her sister to burn them. His photograph, inscribed 'To his beloved and only one, R.', stood on her piano until she died. But three letters from her to him and one from him to her have survived. He wrote lengthily to her on 9 April 1889 from Munich in reply to a letter which had given him sorrow. 'The fact is that your letter, putting off the prospect of seeing you, my sweet Dora, again for the foreseeable future, has upset and distressed me deeply. God, what wooden expressions those are for what I really feel. Do you want me to console you? How pray? I can't quote "Meister, 's ist nicht so gefährlich"[1] at you, or say that time heals all wounds, because it is precisely "time" which is dealing the wounds, heavens, I'm even cracking jokes about it – in one word, it's abhorrent!!!!' He then told her of his delight at leaving his Munich post and of how much he owed to Ritter. 'Imagine, I've even joined the Lisztians now; in short, a more progressive standpoint than the one I now hold is hardly conceivable. And yet, with the clarity that has come to me, I feel so well – but it's impossible to write about things like this. There's nothing for it – you will have to come and see me; would you know me when you saw me?. . . I'm going to Bayreuth as an assistant, piano rehearsals and so on. Recently I made Frau Wagner's acquaintance. She took a great interest in me, I even had the honour of going to *Freischütz* with her. . . My God, I've got so much to tell you! And you won't come!!! By the time you do I shall have forgotten everything.'

Next he told her – 'a deadly secret' – that he was going to Weimar. 'I have the *highest* hopes! Bronsart is a capital fellow, a man of honour from tip to toe (just like Perfall) and very progressive (just like Perfall), while Lassen is old and tired and looking forward to being relieved of some of his burden (just like Fischer).' The parenthetical observations were, of course, heavily sarcastic and indicated how fully Strauss had kept her informed in their letters of his feelings about his employer and superior. 'Oh, yes', he continued, 'Strauss the artist is doing very well! But may no happiness be complete?! On the way back from Berlin I stopped in Meiningen. Steinbach had already rehearsed my *Macbeth*, so I got them to play it for me four times. It sounds horrid, but I think it impresses thinking people, even in its present state. . . In the text of my opera I've finished (at any rate until the next revision) the first act and the second act as far as the end of the big love-scene. . . I've also finished the sketch of a new tone-poem (probable title: *Tod und Verklärung*) and shall probably start the full score after Easter. . . You really mustn't leave me alone for so long – my God, I have hoped for two years, only to close the book of my hopes at the end of that term with the words "It just isn't possible". Oh dear, I don't want to become sentimental, but if my new orchestral piece contains more dissonances than your little ears can stand, you will have no right to complain! Farewell now, stay fond of me.'

This letter leaves no doubt that he resented her enforced absence from Munich. The meeting with Cosima Wagner to which he referred was in March 1889. He had gone to Bayreuth in the summer of 1888, hearing *Die Meistersinger* conducted by Richter and *Parsifal* by Felix Mottl. On the recommendation of Bülow to Julius Kniese, Cosima's musical adviser, he was invited to Bayreuth as a musical assistant for the 1889 festival, rehearsing the choir for the Grail scenes. Cosima invited him to dine at Wahnfried and after the festival went through the scores of *Tannhäuser* and *Lohengrin* with him, since these were the first Wagner operas he was to conduct in Weimar. Meanwhile his own creative life was far from inactive. On his second visit to Italy in the spring of 1888, when he heard *Tristan und Isolde* in Bologna, inspiration had come to him as he stood in the cloister of Sant'Antonio, Padua. In his sketchbook he wrote the principal theme of the tone-poem *Don Juan*, with, surely, thoughts of Dora. He already had a completed tone-poem on his desk. Composition of *Macbeth* began probably in the spring of 1887. He had evidently completed it by January 1888 when he wrote to Carl Horbürger that it was 'a completely new path.' He sent it to Bülow who was critical of its ending with a triumphal march for Macduff. Strauss revised it, but both Bülow and Franz Strauss were shocked by the dissonance. 'The greatest music can be written without experimentation', Franz wrote, 'with great and noble ideas simply attired, without grand instrumental brilliance, and then it is understood at all times and by all people.' He implored his son to rid *Macbeth* of its 'rolls of excess instrumental fat'. This had some effect, in that Strauss revised the scoring during the winter of 1890–1, telling his sister that he was thoroughly enjoying himself: 'as there wasn't enough brass in it, I am adding a part for bass trumpet, which is rendering capital service.' He had been dissatisfied with *Macbeth* at the first performance at Weimar on 13 October 1890. 'In many places too many inner parts prevent the principal themes from standing out as clearly as I would wish.' The revised version was performed in Berlin on 29 February 1892 to enthusiastic acclaim. Bülow was now converted to it 'in spite of all its acerbities and the monstrosities of its material'. Although the first of the tone-poems to be written, *Macbeth* was the third to be performed: *Don Juan* had its first performance at Weimar on 11 November 1889 and *Tod und Verklärung* at Eisenach on 21 June 1890. Strauss conducted on both occasions. Also at the Eisenach concert, Eugen d'Albert gave the first performance of the *Burleske* Strauss had written four years earlier in Meiningen. What of the opera Strauss mentioned to Dora? Ritter encouraged him to think about one and Strauss found a subject in a feuilleton article in the Vienna *Neue freie Presse* about 'secret artistic-cum-religious orders, which were founded in Austria to combat the worldliness of Minnesang'. Every true Wagnerian, Ritter pointed out, should write his own libretto and Strauss began his early in 1888. It was completed, after interruptions and revisions, in October 1890. He gave it the ultra-Wagnerian title *Guntram*.

The first of the surviving letters from Dora to Strauss was sent to him in Weimar in October 1889. He had written to her for her birthday and she had asked his sister for his new address. 'You want to know which birthday it is? Oh, do not ask, it is dreadful how old I have grown here [Lixouri]: the 29th! Isn't that awful? But in this country, where Methuselahs are nothing rare, it's regarded as the prime of life. . . Well, friendly fate will bring us together somewhere, especially if we take "chance" by the arm to help it along, isn't that so? If you didn't go to Milan until the spring, it would be by no means impossible for me to meet you there and then travel on with you. I would like so dreadfully to go to Venice for a few days, tell me, Richard, would you go there with me? I've promised myself that little detour as a reward for sticking it out in my exile for nearly three years! . . . Farewell, my old beloved friend and accept another thousand deeply felt greetings from your Dora.'

The Italy meetings did not materialise. In the second letter to survive, dated 25 April 1890, there is more formality. She drops the intimate 'du' for the standard 'sie'. The 'deeply felt' (*innig*) greetings at the end become 'cordial' (*herzlich*). She ends: 'According to what Hanna tells me, they do not expect you in Munich until July; I shall have left Europe again long before then, and so I must look forward to other years!' In 1891, when Strauss was again working at the Bayreuth Festival, he wrote to his sister 'I have not yet been able to get a ticket for Dora for 27 or 30 August, at the moment the only one reserved is for the first performance. So if you don't hear anything further, Dora will have to come on the 19th.' We do not know if she did. She wrote to Strauss 'on an impulse' from Dresden in March 1893 after hearing of his illness and reading his old letters: 'My dear friend, will you be very, very surprised if a sign of life from me surfaces after such a long time?. . . Inner condition: recognizing the truth of the old saying that the greatest human happiness is the power of memory. Do not be afraid, dear friend, I am certainly not going to become sentimental, but the outcome was that I had to write you a few words, even though it is only a friendly greeting dispatched to the far south [Egypt] to tell you *how glad* I am that you are now fully recovered. Are you very angry with me now, at this unexpected invasion of your retreat from the world? Then punish me and never reply to your old friend (now truly *old*) Dora.'

The double reference to 'old' seems to indicate she knew their relationship was now in the past – the Marschallin and Octavian! They met for the last time in January 1911 in Dresden before the première of *Der Rosenkavalier*. Johanna arranged a meeting with Strauss and his wife Pauline. Brother later wrote to sister: '[Pauline] was very put out in Dresden by the fact that you were always in the company of your friend D.W., whose constant presence even in the most intimate family circle was bound to be burdensome to Pauline. Since you obviously had no consideration for her, you have no reason to be surprised that Pauline, who is very sensitive in these matters, proved somewhat withdrawn.' Johanna did not much like Pauline; and Pauline must have been well aware of Dora's place in her Richard's past.

Which brings Pauline into the narrative. She has been there, although as yet not in a major role, since the summer of 1887 when Strauss went to Feldafing on Lake Starnberg to stay at his Aunt Johanna Pschorr's villa. The neighbours were Major General Adolf de Ahna and his wife Maria. The general had a post in the Bavarian War Ministry and was an enthusiastic amateur baritone, good enough to sing some of Sachs's arias in *Die Meistersinger*. They had a daughter, Pauline Maria, born in Ingolstadt on 4 February 1863. She studied singing at Munich School of Music and also had lessons from Strauss's schoolfriend and biographer Max Steinitzer. While Strauss was at Feldafing, Steinitzer told him he was having musical difficulties with his pupil and asked him to stand in for him with her occasionally. 'I assured him that the family are wild about his works and would certainly be glad to receive him. Strauss agrees, everyone is thrilled, and after the very first lesson with Pauline, Strauss tells me: "She is much more talented than you think, we have only got to bring her gifts out".' Strauss sent her for acting lessons from Ritter's wife Franziska and coached her in the roles of Agathe (*Der Freischütz*), Elsa (*Lohengrin*) and Gounod's Marguerite (*Faust*).

At this stage Strauss had no interest in Pauline beyond her vocal technique. Dora was the love of his life. And the next woman to fascinate him, though not in any amatory way, was Cosima Wagner. He took up his duties in Weimar on 8 September 1889 and his first important engagement was a revival of *Lohengrin* on 5 October. The theatre was small and oil-lit, its equipment out of date. The orchestra, too, was small – only six first violins, for instance. But Strauss threw himself energetically into rehearsals for *Lohengrin*, turning 'half the theatre upside down', as he said. He reported to Cosima on 'preparations on a scale quite unprecedented for this place, with two five-hour orchestral rehearsals, one blocking rehearsal and a whole series of piano rehearsals on stage for soloists and chorus. The dress rehearsal was immensely successful, while the performance itself gave me only partial satisfaction. . . None of the entrances went right, they sang out into the audience, ignored the Master's stage directions! The stage director is a totally incompetent, elderly, bass-singing theatrical hack.' Cosima attended one of the later performances, after which Strauss wrote to his sister: 'a *brilliant* success. Colossal praise from Frau W., who was quite enchanted and said that only in Karlsruhe[2] (among all opera houses) had she been so profoundly impressed. . . All the tempos wonderful, the modulations of them had been sensitive and unobtrusive, there was great breadth in the performance, the orchestra had been finely shaded and discreet. . . In short, she was full of praise, quite moved and even kissed me.'

One may pardon the young Strauss's gushing adulation for the widow of the composer to whose work he was now an ardent, proselytizing convert. He played her his *Don Juan* and some of his *Lieder* and, at her request, Bülow's *Nirwana*, a work Strauss often conducted and of which Cosima had a very high opinion, as well she might since it contains remarkable anticipations of *Tristan und Isolde*. 'I was frightfully interested in her perfectly correct judgement of Bülow, of whom we talked a great deal', Strauss informed his sister. (Cosima on the subject of her cuckolded first husband's music must indeed have been interesting.) 'She mentioned Papa several times in the most amiable fashion, how wonderfully he played. She regards his opposition in the most just of lights. She understands very well, she says, how difficult it was in those days for the gentlemen of the Munich orchestra to be fair about something so completely new. . . She swept me off my feet.' Unfortunately, no comment by Franz Strauss on this letter, if Johanna showed it to him, is recorded. Flattered though he was by this favour from the châtelaine of Bayreuth, Strauss displayed total artistic integrity in his approach to staging Wagner. He adored *Lohengrin* all his life; it had first been performed, under Liszt, in Weimar and for its hundredth performance there on 11 May 1891 Strauss insisted on new sets and costumes. Told that this would cost too much, he offered 1,000 marks from his own pocket. (He could not afford this large sum but intended to borrow it from his father.) If that was not accepted, then he would refuse to conduct and would resign. The bluff worked and the Grand Duke of Saxe-Weimar-Eisenach paid up.

Strauss's fanaticism as a Wagner partisan led to his first conflicts with the Weimar intendant, Bronsart. These began over *Tannhäuser* in March 1890.

He conducted it almost uncut and consulted Cosima in minute detail over how the singers should act. The performances, he told her, had been better than the rehearsals had led him to expect, 'except for the idiocies in the staging and the frightful performance by the Elisabeth'. But his pupil, the tenor Heinrich Zeller, had been 'amazing'. Strauss informed Bronsart that he wanted full control of Wagner productions. The intendant replied that there could be no question of the producer being subordinate to the conductor – yes, even over 100 years ago the producer was taking control! The conductor could advise, not instruct. He did not want Weimar to be an extension of Bayreuth. 'Some modification of your ultra-radical views would be altogether desirable', he told Strauss.

Every good musician who had a close association with Wagner has a better and more reliable knowledge of the performance of his operas than the Master's unmusical widow. . . You, my dear Strauss, sometimes select tempos (let me remind you of the end of the *Tannhäuser* overture among many other instances) which notoriously contradict Wagner's known intentions. . . You must learn to control yourself at least enough, even when you are excited, to stop using at every moment turns of phrase which you would condemn severely in the mouth of another person. You *must* learn to respect individualities in your dealings with *your* artists at least enough, even though they are working under your general direction, to acknowledge their entitlement to a certain degree of independent artistic judgement, and you must not call it 'style-less' every time somebody feels differently from you about a matter. . . If your temperament . . . is so immoderate that you cannot control it, then you have no future in circumstances which rest on subordination.

Bronsart later stressed that he was not out of sympathy with Strauss. On the contrary his goodwill and sympathy had increased during their association. Strauss had 'an artistic ability more promising than any I have ever dared to dream of', but he was alarmed since he had recognized that 'the extreme artistic opinions you have made your own, even if you have adopted them from an alien source, have taken deeper root than I believed before we knew each other'.

Bronsart later followed these admonitions with more: 'You often conduct Wagner in such a manner that I don't understand why you don't introduce other instruments, other harmonies, etc.' He warned Strauss that he must adapt his artistic endeavours to Bronsart's views – 'it is essential if you want to keep your post'. But, he added, he regarded Strauss's 'extreme tendencies' as 'the symptoms of a certain *Sturm und Drang* phase which natures of genius customarily go through in order to work off an excess of vigour'. The battle for Wagner had been won, Bronsart reminded him. Fanaticism belonged to the past. Strauss seems not to have resented these sensible criticisms and probably learned from them. 'For my part', he told Franz, 'everything shall be done so that we do get on all right together.'

On Strauss's behalf it should be said that, although subordinate to the ageing Lassen, he was determined that Weimar should become an important opera centre. Whereas he had had no artistic control in Munich, now he wanted it all. He was made angry by incompetence in artistic matters and by backstairs intrigues. He threatened to throw his baton at the chorus for wrong entries and he threatened to bring the curtain down if Wolfram left the stage during Elisabeth's prayer in *Tannhäuser*. He worked incessantly, taking on guest engagements elsewhere which involved overnight train journeys to be back in Weimar for morning rehearsals. Soon, he was to pay for it.

Spiritually he was intoxicated by his good relations with Bayreuth. Wagner's son Siegfried had gone to Weimar for *Tannhäuser*. He asked Strauss's advice on music he had written. Strauss told Thuille of a conversation with Siegfried about Berlioz. Siegfried appears to have been lukewarm, but Strauss was enthusiastic. He told Cosima (letter of 26 November 1889) that the *Requiem* was 'the richest creation of this unique genius', but she poured a little cold water. The *Requiem* had horrified her, but *Béatrice et Bénédict* had restored her faith. Strauss, too, loved Berlioz's last opera, and Cosima recommended *Les nuits d'été* to him. In December 1890 he went to Karlsruhe for Mottl's performance of *Les Troyens* – 'a mixture of stupefying nonsense and spine-tingling genius', was his verdict, conveyed to his father. Dido's love scene was music 'of such fabulous beauty and magical sound that I forgot the entire nonsense on the stage'.[3] Especially he noted the 'fabulous orchestral refinement'.

While composing *Macbeth*, Strauss told his uncle Carl Horbürger in a letter dated 11 January 1888 that it was 'a kind of' symphonic-poem, 'but not after Liszt'. Although Liszt's symphonic-poems inspired Strauss by their blend of poetic idea and musical structure, his own polyphonic methods were in direct contrast. Nevertheless he was a faithful interpreter of Liszt's music. At Weimar in the summer of 1890 he conducted an all-Liszt programme, describing her father to Cosima in a letter of 15 August 1890 as 'surely the most many-sided and various of all symphonists from the aspect of musical expression'.[4] Some weeks later he conducted *A Faust Symphony* and told Thuille that it had confirmed his belief that Liszt 'is the only symphonist, the one who had to come after Beethoven and represents a gigantic advance on him. Everything else is drivel, pure and simple.' He had the grace to add later in the letter: 'Oh well, perhaps my enthusiasm is making me talk utter nonsense; at all events, it was glorious! . . . I worked up such energy and passion and rhythm that the theatre shook and then I swayed about and stormed so much in *Mephisto* that it gave me the father and mother of a stitch.' This description of his youthful conducting style is confirmed by Arthur Johnstone, the *Manchester Guardian* critic, writing in May 1902 about Strauss's conducting of the same work in Düsseldorf. Johnstone mentions 'fantastic gestures' which worked up the audience 'into a sort of phosphorescent fever'. The laconic Strauss of the minimal gestures came later. So did the Strauss who could more level-headedly appreciate the importance of Liszt. Asked by the *Allgemeine Musikzeitung* in 1911, Liszt centenary year, wherein lay Liszt's decisive significance in the development of German music, he replied: 'Franz Liszt was the first creative genius of the nineteenth century, before Richard Wagner, *to understand Beethoven correctly*.'

Perhaps as a result of his upbringing by his father, Strauss at this stage of his life was easily swayed by others in his views. Although brimmingly self-confident about his own music – and free of self-pity if it failed – he was much less sure of his opinions on others, as can be deduced from his *volte-face* over Mahler's *Die drei Pintos*. Cosima and Ritter encouraged him to believe that German art was unarguably superior to all other; thus success for Gounod's *Faust* in Germany was 'one of the greatest blots of shame', Mascagni's *Cavalleria rusticana* was 'a *pot-pourri* of the very worst, crass operatic effects'. Even in the case of a devout Wagnerian like Chabrier, Cosima's scorn influenced Strauss against, one suspects, his better musical judgment. Free of their influence when he went as court conductor in Berlin in 1898, one of the first premières he conducted there was of the fragment (only one act) of Chabrier's last opera *Briséis* in January 1899. 'Very free, highly seasoned French music', he wrote to his parents on 29 December 1898, 'it'll sound charming but won't be much of a success.' The sensuous and erotic fervour in the score of *Briséis* anticipates *Salome*, and Strauss may well have subconsciously remembered the French work when working on his first operatic masterpiece.

7　First failure

When *Tod und Verklärung* had its first Vienna performance on 15 January 1895, conducted by Hans Richter, the critic Eduard Hanslick wrote that the nature of Strauss's talent 'is really such as to point him in the direction of music drama'. This comment was made after Strauss's first opera, *Guntram*, had been performed but is none the less perceptive. Strauss did not begin to compose the music of *Guntram* until 1892. His first foray into operatic composition had been two years earlier when, in September 1890, he completed his new version of Gluck's *Iphigénie en Tauride*, modelling it on Wagner's version of *Iphigénie en Aulide*. 'My revision', he told the publisher Adolph Fürstner in April 1891, 'consists of a completely new translation, actually a new text in parts (with some elements taken from Goethe's play), especially in the first act, in which the order of the scenes has been entirely changed, and the last act, for which I have composed a new ending, as well as changes in the scoring, to bring it into line with modern requirements at least to some extent etc etc.' He had, he claimed, 'given new life to a beautiful work' and hoped it would be performed at Weimar in the 1891–2 season. But it did not reach the Weimar stage until 9 June 1900, six years after Strauss left, when Rudolf Krzyzanowski conducted it. Neither then nor since has much interest been shown in it, but it has documentary importance as Strauss's first stage music.

Back into Strauss's life in Weimar in the spring of 1890 came his singing pupil Pauline de Ahna. He persuaded the Weimar Intendant, Bronsart, to let her make her stage début on 22 May as Pamina in *Die Zauberflöte*. 'Her success exceeded all expectations', he told his sister. A five-year contract from 1 July followed. Her teacher since her lessons with Strauss had been Ritter's wife Franziska and she now moved on to Emilie Merian-Genast. Strauss coached her in interpretation. The roles she sang at Weimar show

5 Pauline de Ahna as Elsa in *Lohengrin* at Weimar, 1891

how hard she worked – and was worked. In the 1890–1 season they included Pamina, Anna in Marschner's *Hans Heiling*, Eva in *Die Meistersinger*, Elvira in *Don Giovanni*, Elsa in *Lohengrin* – her favourite – and Elisabeth in *Tannhäuser*. She also sang in concerts, on one occasion singing Isolde's *Liebestod*. Her Elsa, Strauss told his parents on 14 February 1891, was 'simply fabulous, in particular magnificently acted'. She was invited to sing it with Mottl conducting at Karlsruhe three months later. In 1891–2 her roles included Thomas's Mignon, the Queen in Ritter's *Der faule Hans*, Agathe in *Der Freischütz*, Leonore in *Fidelio*, Constance in Cherubini's *Les deux journées*, the Countess in *Le nozze di Figaro*, Fricka in *Die Walküre*, Charlotte in Massenet's *Werther* and Venus in *Tannhäuser*. In *Don Giovanni* she sang during its run both Donna Anna ('well sung but sugary', was her own verdict) and Elvira ('too dainty and much too fluting, too lovable and German in expression and acting – not a Spanish woman thirsting for revenge').

After hearing Pauline as St Elisabeth in Liszt's oratorio in 1890, Cosima engaged her for 1891 at Bayreuth as a Flower Maiden in *Parsifal* and the Shepherd Boy in *Tannhäuser*. But she also sang Elisabeth in the latter, alternating with Elisa Wiborg. Strauss was at Bayreuth too, as répétiteur and 'musical assistant'. His ambition to conduct there had been dashed by an attack of pneumonia in May 1891 when for six days his life was in danger. Cosima visited him during his convalescence at Feldafing and walked in the garden with Franz Strauss! On 1 July he went to Bayreuth, stayed in Wahnfried and met Romain Rolland for the first time. His relationship with Pauline at this time was that of master-and-pupil and had undergone a minor upheaval just before his illness when she had made mistakes during one of Lassen's works while the composer was conducting. 'You are now so set on going your own way that my presence and the influence it inevitably exercises could only seem a burden to you', Strauss wrote. 'I regret therefore that I must gratefully decline your kind invitation both today and in the future.' But the breach was healed and in January 1892 he allied himself with her when Bronsart refused to cast her as Elisabeth in a revival of *Tannhäuser* because he feared another soprano would leave the company. Strauss advised Pauline to resign, which she did, only to discover, as Strauss told his father, that 'I overestimated the Grand Duke's regard for Fräulein de Ahna.

Things blew up in our faces last Sunday and Bronsart, without a word of warning, engaged a first-rate, ultra-dramatic singer.' Pauline withdrew her resignation and Franz Strauss admonished his son: 'Why will you always try to go head first through a brick wall?' Franz took Pauline's side during another quarrel. 'Put things straight again', he advised Richard. 'Fräulein de Ahna seems to be rather given to over-exciting herself, and a man of good breeding can always allow some latitude to a lady of that kind without lowering himself. Besides, I am sure she is the singer who will come closest to realizing your intentions.' This seems to indicate that Strauss already had her in mind for his opera *Guntram*.

Strauss's preoccupation during his illness was with *Tristan und Isolde*, which he was to conduct in Weimar in January 1892. 'Dying is probably not so bad', he wrote to Arthur Seidl, 'but I would like to conduct *Tristan* first.' He had conducted the Prelude to Act 1 at a Weimar concert in 1891 when Hermann Levi had written to him that he had 'not heard it so beautifully played since 1871 (under Wagner)'. There was no pit in Weimar and Strauss worked out in detail the dynamic nuances necessary to allow the singers to be heard. He gave the work uncut, a rare event then, and had at least seventeen orchestral rehearsals which enabled him to claim that the score 'acquired something intimate like chamber music'. After the first performance on 17 January 1892 he told Cosima that, within the limitations of the means at his disposal, it was 'an excellent performance of this glorious work. . . Now I've conducted *Tristan* for the first time, and it was the most wonderful day of my life!'[1] Tristan was sung by Strauss's pupil Heinrich Zeller, Isolde by Virginia Naumann-Gungl. (When the production was revived two seasons later, on 13 January 1894, Pauline sang Isolde – 'too early, of course, but somehow because of her youth and great acting a particularly charming performance', Strauss wrote in his memoirs.)[2] Among the congratulatory letters Strauss received was one from Bülow signed 'your old admirer who sincerely holds you in high esteem'. Throughout his life Strauss revered *Tristan* and *Lohengrin* above all other music and, in Wagner's *oeuvre*, preferred them to *Der Ring des Nibelungen*. Writing to Joseph Gregor, one of his librettists, in 1935 he said: '*Tristan* does not, as you believe, represent the "dazzling resurrection" of romanticism, but the end of all romanticism, as it brings into focus the longing of the entire 19th century, longing which is finally released in the *Tag- und Nachtsgespräch* and in Isolde's *Liebestod*. . . *Tristan* is the ultimate conclusion of Schiller and Goethe and the highest fulfilment of a development of the theatre stretching over 2,000 years.'

In spite of the *Tristan* triumph, Strauss still felt frustrated in Weimar. He wanted Bronsart to make him Hofkapellmeister, but Bronsart would not offend the older and senior Lassen. Visits to other centres as guest conductor kept Strauss from boiling over, but it was Bayreuth, where he had never conducted, on which he set his heart. However, during 1892 he had a major altercation with Cosima because she did not invite his two pupils, Pauline and Zeller, back to the festival that year. Zeller was replaced as Tannhäuser by Max Alvary, whom Strauss described as 'that miserable ham-actor'. Another soprano was chosen to alternate with Wiborg as Elisabeth instead of Pauline, 'of whose great gifts I grow continually more convinced, in spite of everything'. But Cosima would not budge. As far as his own conducting was concerned, she offered him the rehearsals of *Die Meistersinger* for Hans Richter and the last two performances. Strauss was furious – two performances 'after the great Hans Richter has had the pleasure of ruining all that I have built up in those rehearsals!' He was even blunter in a letter to his sister: 'I'm not going to make myself available just to take the *Meistersinger* rehearsals for that lazy blighter Richter.'[3] He assured Cosima he was not acting from wounded vanity ('I'm a stranger to that') but because he knew he would achieve nothing as a stopgap. Eventually Strauss agreed to her offer after she had promised him Mottl's *Tristan* if Hermann Levi's illness compelled him to drop out of *Parsifal*. In the event, however, Strauss had pleurisy in June and was ill again with bronchitis in July. His doctors told him he must spend the following winter in the sunshine. Bayreuth was out of the question.

At this juncture, it is appropriate to consider Strauss's reputation generally, not only in Weimar. The Weimar years were the leanest in his life for composition – 'the theatre and cards, as well as my fiancée, claimed almost all my attention', he wrote in his memoirs.[4] In December 1889 he wrote a quartet for male-voice choir on a Swedish text, *Utan svafvel och fosfor* (o.Op. 88), for a charity event; in January 1890 he completed the Dahn settings, *Schlichte Weisen*, Op. 21, dedicated to his sister, with the fifth song *Die*

Frauen sind oft fromm und still; later that year he made his *Iphigénie en Tauride* version; in the spring of 1891 he composed a *Fanfare* (o.Op. 88A) for a gala performance of Wilhelm Iffland's play *Die Jäger* (the *finale* quotes the main theme of the *finale* of Beethoven's Ninth Symphony); in December 1891 he wrote two settings of Lenau, Op. 26, for Zeller; and for the golden wedding of the Grand Duke and Grand Duchess in October 1892 he wrote four orchestral movements (o.Op. 89) to accompany *tableaux vivants* on historical events (the third was published in 1930 under the title *Kampf und Sieg*). The Op. 27 songs for Pauline were composed in 1894. But it should not be overlooked that throughout 1889–92 he was writing the libretto of *Guntram* and in 1892–3 wrote the music.

Apart from operas and concerts in Weimar, Strauss was a regular guest conductor in Leipzig, Berlin, Frankfurt, Cologne and Dresden. In the last-named in January 1890 he attended (but did not conduct) the second performance of his *Don Juan*. The orchestra, he told his father, was 'indisputably the best at the moment'. His association with it was to give him lifelong pleasure. He returned to Munich as a guest conductor on seven occasions and in January 1891 refused the offer of a two-year engagement as conductor of the New York Symphony Orchestra. Some of his weekly schedules, involving much travelling, explain why his health suffered. He conducted both *Macbeth* and *Tod und Verklärung* in Berlin and *Don Juan* in several cities. He was delighted when a Cologne critic called him 'the outstanding living composer' and at Leipzig in March 1892 'young enthusiasts accompanied me to the station and cheered as the train pulled out, one even kissed my hand. In short, my fame is advancing by leaps and bounds', he proudly reported to his mother.[5]

While in Berlin in March 1892, Strauss met the socialist writer John Henry Mackay (1864–1933), a Scotsman by birth who lived most of his life in Germany. He was later to set four of his poems. Mackay's novel *Die Anarchisten* (1891) caused a stir and Strauss read it avidly. Mackay was also the biographer of the Berlin philosopher Max Stirner, whose *Der Einzige und sein Eigentum* (*The Individual and his Property*) was an exposition of unrestrained egoism. Although Strauss never finished the book – he regarded it as 'a curiosity' – it inspired him to draft two scenarios for a *Don Juan* opera in the first of which incest is part of the plot. At the age of twenty-eight, he examined his own personality in a letter to the composer Eugen Lindner. He wrote of how application of his ethical principles was often put at risk through 'the most remarkable obstacles, even in my own breast' which 'with the help of my distinctly overwrought nerves, often encourage the most extraordinary blossoming of paradox or, if you want it in plain language, *nonsense*. One of those obstacles is a devil of opposition, who means well but has three powerful enemies in the world, and he goes crazy at the sight of them; those three enemies are hypocrisy, the impudence of dilettantes, and philistinism. I do not believe that there are many people who make a more honest and sincere attempt to do justice to everything that is beautiful, or that at least *is produced by serious artistic endeavour*, and to *exercise and express* that judgment, as long as I find myself in the company of *honest, truthful artistic understanding.*'[6]

We are now approaching the end of Strauss's musical adolescence. Its climax was the completion, production and failure of his first opera *Guntram*. The first version of the libretto occupied him from August 1887 to 17 March 1892. He set the opera in thirteenth-century Germany: Guntram and his mentor Friedhold are troubadours in a clandestine band of *Minnesinger* called the Champions of Love. They have been sent to help refugees from the tyranny of Duke Robert. Guntram prevents a woman from drowning herself and discovers she is Freihild, the duke's wife, who has been forbidden by her husband to help the poor. Guntram falls in love with her. Her father, the Old Duke, and Duke Robert invite him to their court to a feast where Guntram sings of the blessings of peace, hoping to convert Duke Robert. A messenger boy brings news of an invasion. The duke pours scorn on Guntram, they fight and the duke is killed. The Old Duke imprisons Guntram but Freihild vows to free him. In his cell, Guntram agonises whether his deed was justified. Freihild comes to free him, and pours out her love. Guntram agrees to submit to trial by the brotherhood, is cast out and then renounces Freihild. In the second version, the brotherhood plays no part and after his renunciation Guntram leaves to seek solitude. Finally Strauss made Guntram renounce the brotherhood by refusing to stand trial. He then walks out of Freihild's life to expiate his guilt in solitude, far away.

Strauss circulated the libretto among his friends Ritter, Thuille, Friedrich Rösch and his father. Franz had many criticisms, summed up in the words

'You must take great care not to get into the atmosphere of *Parsifal* or *Tannhäuser*.' He urged his son to compose melodious music ('of course you will turn up your nose at my opinion'). Strauss began his convalescent trip to Greece, Egypt and Sicily on 4 November 1892. It was paid for by his uncle Georg Pschorr with a gift of 5,000 marks. Within a fortnight he was revising the libretto of Act 3 of *Guntram*. When the new version reached the devoutly Roman Catholic Ritter, he was horrified. On 17 January 1893 he wrote to Strauss urging him to burn the new Act 3, which had 'ruined the opera and robbed it of any kind of tragedy'. Obviously, Strauss had been under various literary influences. All this, ridiculous as it may seem today, because Guntram now acted voluntarily instead of submitting to the brotherhood's judgment: 'I carry my law in my own heart. I am my own judge.' Strauss refused to alter anything and denied the 'influences' with which he had only a 'nodding acquaintance': 'I didn't get to the end when I was reading Stirner. . . I've never read Nietzsche's *Beyond Good and Evil*; for the last four months I've studied only Wagner, Goethe and Schopenhauer. . . . Each one of us is the only person who knows *what* he is. But what he does with himself after he has recognised himself is his business. . . Here, too, please do not confuse me with my dramatic figure! *I* am not giving up art, and I'm not Guntram either! . . . The deuce, I'm sure that *I* wouldn't have renounced the beautiful Freihild.'

Although he had composed some of the music in Weimar, he settled to the task in earnest in March 1892 and completed the prelude to Act 1 by 24 March. The first scene was composed 'at one go' on 8 April. It was 'simple and tuneful', he told Franz. The short score of Act 2 was completed in Weimar on 19 October. Revision of the libretto of Act 3 followed. He began to compose Act 3 in Cairo on 1 December and completed it there on Christmas Eve, writing on the manuscript 'Deo gratias! Und dem heiligen Wagner.' He began orchestrating Act 1 on 29 December. This took him until 27 February 1893, in Luxor. It had turned out 'very refined'. Act 2 was completed in full score on 4 June, Act 3 on 5 September in Marquartstein. The opera was dedicated 'to my beloved parents'. His father was concerned about the size of the orchestra. Strauss responded: 'One must have a specific size of orchestra in mind in order to be able to score at all, and then the only correct size is the one I specify. . . But don't worry, dear Papa, the score will be very delicate, even if the horn players have to blow a high C every now and again. Horns and trumpets (the latter, like all the brass, are being used more gently) are my weakness. That comes of having so great an artist on the horn for a father.'[7]

While in Palermo in May 1893 he played through Act 3 and decided that, while 'admittedly hyper-*Tristan*-ish, it's the most advanced in the precision of expression, the richest and most impressive in the melodic invention, and altogether by far the best thing I've ever written. Of course there'll be a dashed lot of head-shaking, but I'm really quite exceptionally pleased with Act 3. . . Hold tight to your seats, my friends!'

He returned to Weimar in October 1893 thoroughly depressed with a place where he had to rehearse *Der Freischütz* with four second violins. While in Florence on his homeward journey from Egypt, Strauss had met Hermann Levi and discussed the approach Levi had made to Franz Strauss asking whether Richard would leave Weimar to become Hofkapellmeister in Munich on an equal footing with Levi. But it emerged that Mottl and Weingartner were also being considered for Munich and Strauss was kept in suspense for months. In addition, Munich offered the world première of *Guntram* but kept postponing the date. Karlsruhe then did likewise but its principal tenor decided he could not cope with the role and Mahler failed in his attempts to persuade the Hamburg management to let him stage the world première there. So Strauss had to settle for Weimar, which he knew was unsuitable for the work. He had already released Guntram's Peace Narration for performance and this had been sung in Heidelberg and Karlsruhe in January 1894 by Emil Gerhäuser. Another opera world première planned for Munich was that of Humperdinck's *Hänsel und Gretel*, but the illness of a singer caused postponement, so the already arranged Weimar performance on 23 December 1893, conducted by Strauss, became the world première. Pauline de Ahna was to have sung Hänsel but injured her foot and the Gretel learned the role in three days and took over until Pauline rejoined the cast on 7 January. Strauss had been friendly with Humperdinck since the 1880s and loved this opera which he described as 'a masterpiece of the highest quality . . . original, new and so authentically German'.[8]

Over the previous year, Strauss's relationship with Pauline had warmed to love. They became secretly engaged during March 1894. The news was made public on 10 May, the day of the *Guntram* première. By now Strauss's Munich appointment had been approved and his resignation from Weimar was gazetted on 13 April. Some idea of the difficulties he faced rehearsing *Guntram* can be gauged from the fact that the score asks for sixty-two string players and Weimar provided twenty-one. In his memoirs, Strauss wrote that the score 'was not in any way suitable for the existing circumstances and bears witness to my hair-raising naiveté in those days. . . My poor valiant pupil Heinrich Zeller went through agonies with his insanely demanding role – at the time somebody calculated that the part had so-and-so many bars more than that of Tristan – each rehearsal made him hoarser and hoarser and at the first performance he had a struggle to last out to the end. My fiancée knew her part faultlessly and her performance was vocally and dramatically outstanding. The audience applauded her tumultuously after the second act.'[9]

The reviews were cool. Another performance was given in Weimar on 1 June as part of the congress of the Allgemeiner Deutscher Musikverein. The Munich performance materialised on 16 November 1895. It was a disaster. The principal soprano and tenor, Milka Ternina and Heinrich Vogl, refused their roles. The orchestra, led by Benno Walter, Strauss's cousin and violin teacher, went on strike and sent a deputation to Perfall, the Intendant, asking him to relieve them of 'this scourge of God'. Max Mikorey, the tenor who took over Guntram, had lapses of memory during the performance even though the role was cut and said afterwards he wanted an increase in his pension before he would sing it again. The critics were savage, praising only Pauline's Freihild. There were no more performances. Just why *Guntram* received only one Munich performance is unclear. According to Strauss's diary, Possart had promised to put it on once a month 'whatever the circumstances' and Mikorey had agreed to sing without a pension increase. The long review of the performance in the *Münchner Neueste Nachrichten*, which Strauss blamed for the work's failure, ended by pointing out that 'the applause, which was rather restrained after the first act, reached a climax after the second. After the second and third acts the composer and the singers took repeated curtain calls.' So there was no public hostility. The review, written by Oskar Merz, reads today as a judicious piece of criticism, fair and perceptive. His conclusion that 'individual parts of Strauss's opera might be effective in the concert-hall' is incontrovertible, as is his opinion, on the evidence of this opera, that *Guntram* was 'an uncommonly complex *orchestral work*' but there was a chance that 'when [Strauss] has improved his understanding of the essence and requirements of opera... he will at some future date use that technique rightly in the service of the theatre, should heaven send him a good operatic subject in an apt form'.

Guntram was revived, heavily cut, in Frankfurt in 1900 and in Prague in 1910. The next performance was a broadcast on Strauss's seventieth birthday in June 1934 conducted by Hans Rosbaud. A month later Strauss made his own cuts – but did not revise any of the score – and this version was first performed in Weimar on 29 October 1940 conducted by Paul Sixt and in Berlin on 13 June 1942 conducted by Robert Heger. Strauss described the 1940 performance as 'magnificent' and said: 'The second half of the second act and the whole of the third act made a strong impression and even I had to confess that, compared with all the operas which had been written apart from mine in the past forty years, the work was still "viable".'[10] Hearing *Guntram* today it is difficult to comprehend the furore its 'difficulty' caused. Its libretto is a handicap. Strauss, writing to his librettist Joseph Gregor in 1945, said: 'The text is no masterpiece (even the language leaves something to be desired) but it provided the 'prentice Wagnerian, sloughing his skin in the process of gaining independence, with the opportunity to write a great deal of fresh, tuneful, sappy music.' No one now cares much about the decision by Guntram in Act 3 which so upset Ritter, but contemporary critics were much exercised by it. Even so, Max Hasse, writing in the *Münchner Neueste Nachrichten* after the Weimar première, conceded that 'the music transfigures the last scene of decision to such a pitch that at the moment of listening to it one simply believes and only later turns to critical deliberations. The musical language of Richard Strauss speaks altogether with a convincing power.' It was already a mature language, for *Guntram*, although a first opera, is not a prentice piece. For all its Wagnerian echoes, and there are plenty, it is thoroughly Straussian, as the preludes to Acts 1 and 3 testify. There is even the first operatic example of self-quotation when, while Guntram is thinking of his youth, the solo violin quotes the appropriate theme from *Tod und Verklärung*. The arias for Guntram and Freihild are fiery and lyrical but no one would claim that the opera could hold the stage today. The best of its music is worth preserving, however, and for that reason the existence of a recording is welcome.

The failure of *Guntram* wounded Strauss deeply – he never completely got over it – and proved that he was vulnerable. As quotations from his letters have shown the reader already, he lacked the quality of self-criticism. When he heard his music he was as excited and thrilled as a child. He never liked it to be cut unless he cut it himself, and throughout his life he toler- ated weak passages which a composer harder on himself would have identified and deleted. *Guntram* was his first real setback and it hurt, par- ticularly the actions of the Munich orchestra. He moved into his house in Garmisch in June 1908, thirteen years after these events and when he had the triumph of *Salome* under his belt. Yet in the garden he erected a tombstone with the inscription: 'Here rests the honourable and virtuous youth Guntram, singer of love songs who by the symphony orchestra of his own father was cruelly stricken down. Rest in peace!' *Guntram* also cost Strauss the close friendship of Siegfried Wagner, who said that the opera had betrayed Wagnerian principles. Cosima, too, was unenthusiastic. 'It is unbe- lievable', Strauss said, 'how *Guntram* has made me enemies. But one can only write as one's heart dictates.' He had his revenge when he met Siegfried in Berlin where Strauss was staying at the luxurious Hotel Adlon. 'Is your business making such good profits, then?', Siegfried asked. 'Yes', was the reply, 'and it's my own business, not my father's.'

When the score was published, Strauss in January 1895 sent a copy to Verdi 'as a token of my respect and admiration for the undoubted master of Italian opera. As I can find no words to describe the deep impression made upon me by the extraordinary beauty of *Falstaff* and have no other means of expressing my gratitude for the enjoyment it has brought me, I beg you to accept this score, at the very least.' Verdi replied circumspectly, saying he had not yet had time to read the score, 'but from dipping into it here and there I have seen that *Guntram* is the work of a very expert hand'.

The production of *Guntram* ended Strauss's Weimar years. He summed up this period thus: 'On the whole, people were very nice to me (Bronsart, Lassen, the Court); but I recklessly squandered some of the goodwill they bore me, by my youthful energy and love of exaggeration, so that people were not sorry to see Pauline and me leave.' On the other hand, one of the young singers in the company, Marie Schoder – who later married the leader of the Weimar orchestra and as Marie Gutheil-Schoder became a member of Mahler's Vienna Opera and a marvellous exponent of Strauss roles – wrote many years later that Strauss 'kept intellectual and musical Weimar on tenterhooks with the inspiring achievements of his fiery genius. . . My God, what evenings those were in the Opera House in our beloved Weimar. . . Even though I was only a slip of a girl my sensitive heart warmed to that fiery spirit which kindled my own ardour too in many an hour of the most intensive study.'

8   Engagement

Before going into more detail about Strauss's engagement to Pauline, we need to return to his winter of convalescence in Egypt and elsewhere. On the journey out he spent a few days on the island of Vido, off Corfu, where he drafted a new opera scenario, *Das erhabenes Leid der Könige* (*The Sublime Suffering of Kings*), about the ancient Germans. The hero was Hermann, leader of German resistance to Roman rule in the time of Augustus. Strauss visited Olympia on 16 November, writing in his travel diary: 'The free sense of beauty, the religion of nature, pure visual perception – Olympia! Philosophical world-transcending sublimity, profoundest inwardness – Bayreuth!' He had got it bad! From 16 to 25 November he was in Athens. The Parthenon moved him to tears. His lifelong love affair with Greek art began in earnest there. On arrival in Egypt he confessed he was beginning to 'feel a little surfeited with all this sight-seeing. . . I have been reading Aeschylus, Sophocles, Plato, and now luxuriate in *Wilhelm Meister*; dear God, there's so much in that book.' In Luxor he again began to read Schopenhauer, filling his diary with excerpts from *The World as Will and Idea* – 'that gigantic edifice of speculative thought'. But he had 'modest reservations' about the philosopher, particularly regarding sex. '"The ecstasy of the act of genera-tion is the delusion practised by the species on the individual; after the act, the delusion vanishes!" Yes, for the beast, or for those humans who are only beasts and make no use of their gift of human reason. But for the human being who loves with full consciousness, this consciousness is so over-powering and lasting that the consciousness of the enjoyment, the physical *as well as the psychic*, endures (in the man as well).' Later he wrote: '*Consciousness* of the affirmation of the will is our ultimate goal – so far. What is to come, who knows! I affirm consciously, that is my happiness!'[1]

At this time he wrote another, and very curious, opera scenario, *Der*

Reichstag zu Mainz. The characters are identified by initials such as A., B., P. and S. The S. stands for a young Russian pianist, Sonja von Schéhafzoff, whom Strauss knew in Meiningen. Alexander Ritter at fifty-nine fell passionately in love with her. Sonja is also thought to have had a *tendresse* for Strauss. The scenario clearly indicates that Sonja, Strauss and Ritter are involved, as is Pauline. Its interest lies in its being an early indication of Strauss's inclination to bring autobiography into his work. It is the first pointer to *Ein Heldenleben, Symphonia Domestica, Feuersnot, Intermezzo* and others.

Early in April he sailed to Sicily and worked on the orchestration of Act 2 of *Guntram* in Taormina, which remained one of his favourite holiday places. For pleasure he read Goethe's *Italian Journey.* He felt completely restored to health, 'of body and soul', and he was longing to hear a Beethoven quartet again and to conduct. He spent two weeks in Ramacca as guest of Bülow's daughter and son-in-law, Count and Countess Gravina, playing piano duets with the Countess. He arrived back in Munich on 15 July and spent the rest of the summer in the family retreat of Marquartstein. Then began, in Weimar, the long and tedious negotiations with Levi over the Munich Opera post and in particular the conductorship of the eight Academy Concerts, which Strauss particularly coveted. No one, Levi pointed out, could transfer them to him because the orchestra elected the conductor. 'The minute your contract has been ratified, I shall resign as conductor of the Academy and recommend you as my successor. There is not the least doubt that the orchestra will elect you, but you cannot be given a contractual assurance of the concerts.' In October 1894 Strauss became the Academy conductor. In the summer of 1894, before taking up his new post, he conducted three performances of *Tristan* and one of *Die Meistersinger* in Munich and fulfilled his ambition to conduct at Bayreuth. He conducted his first *Tannhäuser* there on 22 July, with Pauline as Elisabeth. Cosima, who had heard reports of the difficulty of *Guntram,* slyly greeted him with '*Ei, ei,* such a modernist and yet conducts *Tannhäuser* so well.'

Two deaths in 1894 robbed Strauss of men who had signally helped his career. His uncle Georg Pschorr, husband of Johanna, died in June. Pschorr had paid for Strauss's Egyptian winter. 'I'm so grateful to our good, kind uncle', he had written to his sister from Luxor, 'truly, it moves me to tears.'

In December 1893 he wrote two pieces for piano quartet (AV 182), *Arabian Dance* and *Little Love Song*, which he dedicated to his uncle in gratitude for his holiday. Hans von Bülow died in Cairo on 12 February. He and Strauss had grown apart since Strauss's conversion to Wagner and aversion to Brahms. But Bülow remained convinced of Strauss's gifts as a composer, even when he could not admire some of his music. After Strauss had conducted *Macbeth* at a Berlin Philharmonic concert on 29 February 1892, Bülow wrote to his wife: 'You know, *Macbeth* is mad and benumbing for the most part, but *in summo gradu* it's a work of genius.' When Strauss recovered from his illness in 1891, Bülow wrote to Spitzweg: 'Thank God Strauss is safe! That one has a great future, he deserves to live.' Strauss himself assured Bülow in 1892 that, in spite of the change in his artistic philosophy, 'nothing, nothing on this earth ever was or will be capable of slaying or even diminishing my unbounded love, respect and profoundest gratitude'. Strauss called on him in Hamburg in January 1894 when Bülow was already ill. He wrote to his father: 'He is very despondent and weak. . . He was very nice and gave the impression only of a man totally destroyed by pain!'

Two days after Bülow's death, Strauss was asked to alter the programme of his scheduled Hamburg Philharmonic programme on the 26th to 'take account of' the sad news. Strauss proposed *Héroïde funèbre* or *Orpheus* by Liszt, *Nirwana* by Bülow, Beethoven's *Eroica*, and the preludes to *Tristan* and *Die Meistersinger*. The programme was rejected and Strauss refused to conduct, despite pleas from Cosima and Bülow's daughter Daniela Thode. He also refused to conduct Brahms's *Requiem* in Hamburg in Bülow's memory. According to Joachim, he told the authorities 'I don't conduct music for dilettantes', meaning the people who had rejected the *Eroica*. Strauss paid tribute to Bülow for the rest of his life through his conducting of the *Prelude* to Act I of *Tristan*. He wrote in his diary: 'My performance of the *Tristan* prelude (ebb and flow) is yet another thing that I owe to teaching given me by Bülow by word of mouth.'[2] All who heard Strauss's conducting of the Prelude agree that it suggested the drawing in and letting out of a single breath.

Strauss's 'utter dissatisfaction' – his words to Humperdinck – with his post at Weimar in his last year there was mitigated by the friendship of his two vocal pupils 'de Ahnchen' and 'Zellerlein'. He became secretly engaged to Pauline de Ahna late in March 1894, having asked her parents for her hand on 22 March. The secrecy can only have been because Strauss did not want anyone in the Weimar company to think he was favouring his fiancée, but his sister wrote to him on 5 April saying it was impossible to keep the matter secret: the news was 'causing astonishment' everywhere. There are many anecdotes about the engagement, some involving an unlikely challenge to a duel from Strauss to another singer, but probably the only true story is that told by Strauss in his memoirs. During a rehearsal of *Guntram*, Strauss corrected Zeller, singing the title-role, many times. When it came to Freihild's Act 3 aria, which Pauline knew perfectly well, she stopped singing and asked Strauss: '"Why don't you stop me?" "Because you know your part."' Strauss continued: 'With the words "I want to be stopped", she threw the vocal score which was in her hands at that moment, aiming it at my head, but to general hilarity it landed on the desk of the second violin Gutheil.'[3] The significance of this anecdote is that it shows that much of Pauline's eccentric behaviour was a cover for her insecurity and also that she had a prima donna's temperament. When she gave up the stage, she became a housewife prima donna assoluta! In later years she would inform people – such as Otto Strasser of the Vienna Philharmonic Orchestra – that her parents had opposed her marriage because she, a general's daughter, 'wanted to marry a horn-player's son'. She must often have said it – many heard her and Strauss himself put these words into Christine's mouth in *Intermezzo*, the opera based on their marriage for which he wrote the libretto in 1916–18. The reality was very different. Her parents were delighted with the match. It was Pauline herself who, as soon as she was engaged, began to have misgivings. Mainly these arose from a conflict between her career and marriage, secondarily because she doubted if she would make a good wife. We tend to forget that Pauline was a deeply serious musician for whom her singing was all-important. The greatest factor binding the Strausses' long marriage was a mutual and passionate devotion to music.

On 24 March 1894, two days after her parents had said 'yes', she wrote, very formally and in desperation, to 'mein lieber Herr Strauss'. It was all suddenly descending on her like a shower-bath, she wrote. 'I beg you for God's sake not to rejoice so excessively, you know better than anyone how many faults I have, and I tell you in all honesty that in spite of the happiness I feel,

I am sometimes terribly afraid. Will I be capable of being what you want and what you deserve?' Then she came to the real point. 'May I not first fulfil my guest engagement in Hamburg, so that I shall at least have a triumph to show off proudly to my respected teacher? . . . You should not overestimate me, and your parents and Hanna know my moods too; O God, and now I am suddenly supposed to turn into a model housewife, so that you do not feel disappointed. Dear friend, I am afraid that it will fail. . . Won't all the conducting you will be doing this summer be too much of a strain for you? O God, I am so worried and concerned. Will your parents like me, and Hanna, if she only knew how I have tried to dissuade you from everything. My dear friend, we really don't need to marry so soon; if each of us could first get accustomed to finding all the happiness we can in our careers, you in M[unich] and I in Hamburg. Please bring my contract with you; forgive this letter, but the two feelings – my happiness and my fear of a new life – weigh on me so that I am only half capable of reasoning. Please allow me at least to sing a lot more parts here . . . the greatest happiness is our art, dear friend, do not forget that. I can't write any more today. Please do not hold any of it against me.' The letter is signed 'Sincerely yours, Pauline de Ahna', and has a postscript raising a technical point about the role of Freihild.

Everything about this letter points to the conclusion that, even though her parents approved of Strauss's intentions, Pauline's inclination was to say 'No'. On the day she wrote to Strauss, her father wrote to her saying that 'if you and he were of one mind about your wishes and desires, then we could only say "yes" and give "our blessing", for we know of nothing in the whole business that does not give us cause for joy. . . When I reflect on the uncertain, worrying future that you will now escape, by marrying a husband of good artistic repute, an interesting man and one devoted to you, I can only rejoice yet again with my whole heart that your destiny has taken this turn. . . Picture yourself, on the one hand as an artist more or less at the mercy of the directorial whims and tyranny of Pollini [the Hamburg Intendant] and on the other as the wife of a respected man who, although he has known all your good and your less good aspects for years, nonetheless loves you with his whole heart and is devoted to you.' Next day the de Ahnas received a letter similar in vein to what Pauline had written to Strauss. Pauline's sister Mädi went on the offensive. Strauss, she reminded Pauline, has expressly said she could continue with her career or give it up, as she wished. For Pauline to say, as she apparently had, that she was too much of an egoist to make a loyal wife was nonsense – remember the summer of 1892 in Reichenhall and Marquartstein, Mädi said, when the fact that she was in love was transparently obvious. 'Everyone's patience wears out in the end, and it might happen with Strauss, too, if you keep him in suspense for eternity; people get tired of that sort of thing, my dear Pauline.'

General de Ahna pointed out some practicalities in a letter written on 25 March. 'If you really might – as you say you may – turn Strauss down, it would be impossible for him to enter your house again because of the mortification, he certainly wouldn't do so and you would be unable to ask him or expect him to teach you and help you from that moment on. . . In any case, no one would believe that you had turned him down, it would generally be assumed that Str. had not wished to keep up his friendship with you after leaving Weimar.' The crisis continued until April. Strauss's attitude, typically humorous and low-key, can be gauged from another letter to Pauline from her father in which he repeats Strauss's assurance that she can continue her career and adds that he had said that 'if you come under an unfamiliar director in Hamburg it will make you properly appreciate being conducted by him at last'. Pauline sent more letters to Mädi, who described them as 'crazy'. 'Give up this eternal struggling with your fiancé', she urged, 'in the long run it's bound to annoy him seriously if he sees that all the love and respect he has for you never gets any other response than your *rather dull* refrain: being an opera singer is the most important thing for me! You can combine the two so easily, so enjoy the period of your betrothal wholeheartedly, and be a little "incarnate poetry" (as Count Wedell called your Isolde) off-stage as well.' Mädi understood her sister well, as other parts of this wise letter (9 April) reveal: 'when the boorish words are out, you always regret them at once. . . It will be all right if you have a little row now and again – I think Strauss quite enjoys some variety – as long as you don't do it in front of a third person. . . If Johanna comes, promise us that you will be calm and equable, of course it wouldn't do if you exaggerate things, don't ever let her hear of a serious disagreement with Strauss, his family think the world of him, quite rightly, and from other quarters too we hear nothing but praise for his talent and for his artistic reputation in the world at large.'

General de Ahna added an exasperated postscript: 'I am tired of having my old age soured by you. At your age [31] . . . one ought to know what one wants and not promise *today* to be a good and loyal wife and suddenly declare tomorrow that one has changed one's mind. . . If you want to make yourself unhappy and cast a shadow over whole families, then do so, but thereafter I wash my hands of you.'[4]

Whatever self-examination Pauline experienced in the next month, she agreed to the official announcement of their engagement on the day of the *Guntram* première, 10 May. After their summer in Bayreuth, they were married in Marquartstein on 10 September. The ceremony, according to the Catholic rites, was in Grassau parish office. The honeymoon was spent in Italy. On return to Munich they moved into a flat at Hildegardstrasse 2/I in the suburb of Schwabing and in March 1896 to one in Herzog-Rudolf-Strasse 8/III in the same district. Strauss's wedding gift to 'meiner geliebten Pauline' was the four songs of his Op. 27, each a masterpiece: *Ruhe, meine Seele!*, *Cäcilie*, *Heimliche Aufforderung* and *Morgen!* All except *Cäcilie*, which was composed the day before the wedding, had been written in Weimar between 17 and 22 May.

9 Pauline

Strauss's marriage to Pauline was the most important step in his life. It lasted until his death fifty-five years less two days later. So much has been written about their relationship solely from the viewpoint of her temperamental nature that an impression is given of a knockabout music-hall act. This side of her existed and many (not all) of the anecdotes are true. But it was a more complex relationship and deserves to be examined at some length. It was firmly based on a mutual passion for music: Strauss never asked or expected her to give up her career to be a housewife. The first creative fruit of their union was Strauss's happiest and wittiest tone-poem, *Till Eulenspiegels lustige Streiche*. While in Weimar he had written the draft text for a one-act opera about the struggle between Till Eulenspiegel and the philistines of Schilda, a bastion of petty bourgeoisie. This was later developed into his second opera *Feuersnot*. It is unlikely any music was composed for the *Till* opera, but Strauss began to compose the tone-poem at some time in 1894, completing it on 6 May 1895. In sketchbooks for it there are facetious comments in Pauline's handwriting: 'Horrid composing', 'Mad', 'Dreadful mess'. One can imagine the newly-weds chaffing each other at the piano. Rehearsals for the Munich première of *Guntram* prevented Strauss conducting the first performance of the tone-poem in Cologne on 5 November. To Franz Wüllner, who took his place and asked for elucidation of the work's 'programme', he sent the telegram: 'Analysis impossible for me. All wit spent in notes.' He did not provide his description of the *lustige Streiche* until a year later and even then made no comment on the enchanting epilogue with its subtle allusion to Wagner's *Siegfried Idyll*. The work was a major success, in spite of Eduard Hanslick's grudging review. Fifty years later, in 1944, Strauss wrote out a new autograph copy of *Till* 'for my beloved children and grandchildren: to dear old Till, in honour of his 50th birthday'. While doing so, he made many small corrections and added some optional ornamentation in the 'street ditty' Till whistles before his trial, noting that 'the curlicues are a witty improvisation by the clarinets in my beloved Berlin Staatskapelle!' This score has never been published and only one or two conductors have troubled to inspect it. So the revisions remain ignored and largely unknown.

While Strauss and Pauline were on holiday in Cortina d'Ampezzo in the summer of 1895, he sketched two acts of a setting of Goethe's *Lila* and contemplated a new tone-poem, writing in his diary the words 'Contemplation, Experience, Recognition, Worship, Doubting, Despair'. These tell us that *Also sprach Zarathustra* was taking shape. *Lila*, conceived by Goethe as a *Singspiel*, was a favourite of Strauss's and he had set some of the numbers when he was fourteen. Getting stuck with his new venture, he sought the aid of Cosima Wagner about aspects of Goethe's plot which baffled him. She provided detailed suggestions but by then Strauss had cooled off about the project, probably because the *Zarathustra* tone-poem was proving more urgent. This coincided with a cooling-off in his relationship with Bayreuth, where the sycophancy surrounding Cosima repelled him. He had once been considered as a prospective son-in-law by Cosima, who would have liked him to marry Eva! We do not know what precipitated the entry in his diary on 11 January 1896: 'Momentous conversation with Siegfried Wagner, unspoken but nonetheless irrevocable separation from Wahnfried-Bayreuth. Only indirectly my fault.' Siegfried was jealous of Strauss's success as composer and conductor. The Bayreuth 'party-line' on *Guntram*, *Till Eulenspiegel* and a tone-poem based on Nietzsche was one of disapproval. Nevertheless, Pauline was still invited to sing in Liszt at a Bayreuth concert, Cosima dined with Richard and Pauline in Munich and Richard was still welcome at Wahnfried.

Strauss's increasing regret that he had accepted the Munich post was fuelled by disgruntlement with Possart's behaviour over a contract for Pauline. On 8 February 1896 Strauss wrote in his diary: 'He promised my wife a guest contract from 1 January 1896 (6,000 marks, 40 appearances). He doesn't make a move.' The contract was eventually signed on 6 March but it provided for only twenty guest appearances. Meanwhile Strauss had applied to be director of opera at Mannheim and in December 1896 sought Mottl's post in Karlsruhe. By this time he had been appointed chief conductor at Munich from 1 October, when Levi retired. This had been preceded by a major row with Possart, who had tried to get Pauline's twenty-appearance contract annulled. 'Ugly scenes over *Guntram* etc. In short – dirty rotten trickery.' Matters were no easier on the home front, where Strauss's parents and Pauline were at daggers drawn during the summer holiday at Marquartstein. 'Stop seeing each other', was Strauss's advice. He reproached his parents for not taking into consideration 'the idiosyncrasies' of Pauline's nature.

What were those idiosyncrasies? No one would call Pauline a feminist in the sense the word is understood today, but she believed that being a woman did not automatically mean she should take second place. We have seen that her hesitation over marriage was because she feared she might have to give up her singing career. When she sang St Elisabeth in Liszt's oratorio – her favourite part – at Bayreuth, Strauss saluted her in his letter wishing her good luck as 'my dear comrade in life and art!!' She had a prima donna's temperament, flying off the handle without warning and then calming down again equally unexpectedly. Strauss was – except once – unperturbed by it and said he 'needed' this kind of stimulation. He knew how to cope with her. Writing to her from Frankfurt after some fracas, he mentioned her 'adorable contrition' and went on 'You really ought not to make so much of these things. Since I know you so very well, and also know for certain that you are very fond of me, "scenes" like this are never going to be able to shake my trust in you. The only thing is that I'm often distressed for you, because your nerves are not strong enough to help you stand up to these bursts of feeling. . . So calm down, my sweet darling . . . my love for you is always the same. So there's nothing to forgive.'

She did not always accompany him on his conducting tours, so he wrote to her nearly every day. The letters describe the cities he visited, their art and architecture, and go into detail about rehearsals and the music he was conducting. And there would be more intimate passages, as this on 20 September 1899: 'So, my dear Bauxerl, now it's 10 o'clock in the evening. . . now I intend to read a little Treitschke and then crawl into bed around 10.30. It's nice when things are different! Good night, my dear, dear Bauxerl. Baby has long been sleeping the sleep of the – little egoist! God, how much longer

6 Strauss and Pauline

am I to be without the two of you! . . . Are you singing a lot? And properly – for a long time and with *full* voice? Write me a long letter soon!!' She did not like the responsibilities of running their house when he was away – paying the bills, making decisions. She had not been brought up for a domestic life, she was a singer, an artist, and she resented being 'the little woman'. But the idea that she regarded his music as, to quote Norman Del Mar, 'plebeian, vulgar stuff, entirely derivative and undistinguished' is rubbish.[1] This totally distorted view has been propagated, especially by Alma Mahler, whose book[2] about her husband contains much invective against Pauline. Just how untrustworthy was her memory is shown by her reference to the Vienna première of Strauss's second opera, *Feuersnot*, in

1902 when Mahler was director of the Vienna Court Opera. Mahler, says Alma, did not conduct it 'because he had an aversion to the work'. In fact, Mahler conducted three performances – the fourth was cancelled because both critics and public hated the work – and conducted a revival in 1905. Strauss had at one stage offered to conduct, but Mahler dissuaded him saying that 'if you take this difficult work over with one rehearsal, our players might be disconcerted'.[3] Strauss thanked him for 'the incomparably beautiful rendition' and referred to 'the magical sound of the orchestra'. Alma's description says that Pauline shared a box 'with us [her and Mahler]' and 'raged the whole time: no one could like this botched piece of work . . . there was not an original note in it, everything was stolen from Wagner, from many others'. When Strauss read Alma's books in 1946, he wrote against this passage: 'Totally unbelievable! At any rate entirely fabricated, or at least it is a mystery on which misunderstanding this whole story is based. The more so as my wife particularly liked *Feuersnot*.' Probably Pauline – or Strauss, who of course shared the box, not Mahler – was trying to explain to Alma that there were *quotations* from Wagner and others in *Feuersnot*. Against another scurrilous anti-Strauss incident in Alma's book, Strauss wrote: 'I don't pretend to understand such things.'

Pauline's real attitude is illustrated by incidents affecting people closer to her and Strauss than the vicious and mendacious Alma Mahler. In 1948 Strauss and his publisher Ernst Roth had been unable to remember the title of one of Strauss's songs, although they could recall the first line. When Roth related this to Pauline later in the day, she said: 'It's called *Befreit*, a lovely song.' She then sang it quietly to herself. Roth commented: 'Half a century is a long time to keep something in your head if you don't think anything of it.'[4] Manfred Mautner Markhof, a close friend, called at Garmisch for tea one day. He and Pauline discussed the Recognition Scene in *Elektra*. 'Yes', she said, 'only the Elektras usually act it wrongly. They fall on their brother's neck, like a girl finding her lover again. I'll show you how it ought to be.' She then walked slowly toward Mautner Markhof, humming the melody. When she reached him, she put her arms round him cautiously, let herself sink against him and was embracing his knees by the end of the scene. She was seventy-nine years old. Mautner Markhof helped her to her feet and saw that tears were running down her cheeks, so moved was she by her husband's music.[5]

For at least ten years Pauline and Richard gave *Liederabende* throughout Europe and elsewhere. (The birth of their son, Franz, in 1897 caused her retirement from the opera stage.) Strauss either accompanied at the piano or conducted; it is no coincidence that between 1894 and 1906 he composed eighty-one songs, several with orchestral accompaniment. Not all were written for Pauline – Hans Giessen and Ludwig Wüllner were favourite male interpreters – but many were. She occasionally sang a Wagner extract in recitals, but on the whole she devoted herself solely to her husband's music. How good a singer was she? First, here is Strauss's opinion, written in 1910: 'The model interpreter of my songs. Her performance is distinguished in equal measure by the most subtle penetration of the poetic content, impeccable taste in shaping the melody, refinement and grace.'[6] In 1947, in Lugano, he again paid tribute to her 'thoroughly poetic interpretation' and continued: 'Her excellent breathing technique stood her in good stead, particularly in Pamina's aria [*Ach, ich fühl's*], Agathe's A♭ major cavatina [*Der Freischütz*] and in Elisabeth's Prayer (at Bayreuth) which I have never since heard sung with such poetry as by Pauline. Similarly *Traum durch die Dämmerung*, *Morgen!*, *Freundliche Vision*, with a completely even tone and poetic interpretation. . . What a shame that she turned too early to the wonderful career of an excellent, model housewife and mother!'

At her Vienna début in January 1900, Eduard Hanslick, after making mincemeat of *Ein Heldenleben* on its première in the city, wrote that

the singing of Frau Strauss-de Ahna, Richard's graceful wife, shone out like a ray of bright, warm sunlight over this battlefield. . . Frau de Ahna's excellently trained, rich, sweet soprano voice did our hearts good! Richard Strauss proved an incomparable accompanist, and his wife's performance earned enthusiastic applause. We may surely call her his better and more beautiful half.

How Pauline loved to quote that last sentence! It found its way into the libretto of *Intermezzo*, to her delight. A favourite item in her repertory was the *Drei Mutterlieder*, comprising Strauss's *Meinem Kinde* (Op. 37, No. 3), *Wiegenlied* (Op. 41, No. 1) and *Muttertändelei* (Op. 43, No. 2). Strauss orchestrated them for her and they gave the first performance of these versions in Elbersfeld on 8 July 1900.

During their tour of the United States from February to April 1904, they gave thirty-five concerts and recitals. In Philadelphia, Pauline felt faint and momentarily left the platform. Asked the reason for her indisposition, Strauss replied 'Hunger' and added that he had said to her 'Wiener Schnitzel with spaghetti, right after the concert, my dear. You must know that's her favourite dish.' In Boston, a critic complained that her voice 'seemed forced and thin' in Symphony Hall, while another wrote that 'whatever her vocal methods, her readings are infused with warmth and artistic conviction. We must assume that Madame Strauss sings her husband's songs exactly as he wishes them to be sung.' Elena Gerhardt, writing in 1924, said Pauline had 'a delightful lyrical soprano voice', while Alexander Dillmann referred to her 'bell-like silver voice, to which is added an expression, a rapture which forces everyone momentarily into its power and under its spell'. Her platform manner, as might have been expected, was sometimes bizarre. She would often cover the piano postlude to a song by flourishing a scarf or fan and bowing deeply. She also wore extravagant hats. She had to contend with her husband's eccentricities at the piano. He often looked as if he was bored with his own music and would play transitional passages between songs, as Alfred Orel described after an Elisabeth Schumann recital in the 1920s: 'It was always passages from his operas with which he made the transition, and specifically passages which were musically closely related to the song in question, but revealed that close relationship only now in the way he played them.'[7]

Pauline's last year before the public was 1905. After that, her only verified appearance was in a Strauss programme in Munich on 10 January 1908 when she sang five songs with orchestra. She never made a recording.

Reviews of her recitals often refer to cancellations through illness. She had suffered during the birth of their son on 12 April 1897. A month earlier, the doctor had predicted twins. Strauss was in Stuttgart on tour with Possart, for whom he had written the melodrama *Enoch Arden* (Tennyson) which they performed together on many occasions while it enjoyed a vogue (Strauss called it a 'worthless' piece, but gave it an opus number). He wrote in his diary: 'Hallelujah. A giant boy just arrived safely. Pauline well. God be praised and thanked! My dear Paula in the gravest danger, but all has turned out well!' He returned home (in Berlin) four days later, being met at the station by his sister who described the 'terrible danger' Pauline and the child

7 Strauss and his son, 'Bubi', aged three

had been through. The boy had been baptised 'Richard' but, as Strauss told his parents, 'I shall overrule the emergency baptism and will call him *Franz Alexander*, as he was born on the anniversary of Ritter's death!' He was known as 'Bubi'.

When the Strausses settled into their home in Garmisch in June 1908,

Pauline more than ever devoted herself to her husband's well-being. Her main aim was to enable him to concentrate on his work and she kept the house spotless, provided regular meals and insisted – remembering his pneumonia – that they went for a walk every day. While waiting for her to join him one day in 1895 (when they lived in Munich), he used the twenty minutes to compose *Traum durch die Dämmerung*. She refused to put him on a pedestal and her sharp tongue never offended him. 'It's what I need', he said. It was also what she needed, a reminder that she was a personality in her own right who liked to move into the centre of the stage at times. However many times it is quoted, Strauss's remark to Romain Rolland in 1900 about the Hero's Consort in *Ein Heldenleben* remains a vital and essential key to their relationship:

It's my wife I wanted to portray. She is very complex, very much a woman, a little depraved, something of a flirt, never twice alike, every minute different to what she was the minute before.[8]

Equally true is Lotte Lehmann's description of one of her visits to Garmisch. '"Believe me, Lotte"', he said to me the day I was leaving, "the whole world's admiration interests me a great deal less than a single one of Pauline's fits of rage."' Lehmann continued

I often caught a glance or a smile passing between her and her husband, touching in its love and happiness, and I began to sense something of the profound affection between these two human beings, a tie so elemental in strength that none of Pauline's shrewish truculence could ever trouble it seriously. In fact, I rather suspect that they were always putting on a kind of act for their own benefit as well as for that of outsiders.[9]

Karl Böhm, the conductor, who became a friend of the Strausses in the 1930s, remembered an occasion when Pauline was ill and he visited her. 'As Strauss slowly climbed up to the third floor he said "Believe me, I really needed my wife. I actually have a lethargic temperament and if it were not for Pauline, I shouldn't have done it all."' Another time, in Garmisch, Böhm remembered Strauss saying 'I'd like a Fachinger' and Pauline retorted 'Get it yourself.' 'When I went to move the table back to stand up, she said "No, stay where you are, he can climb over the bench and get it for himself." And then, when he was outside, she said to me: "It does him good to move about, you know." A small event, but one that helps to explain a lot in vindication of her.'[10]

If Strauss returned late from a conducting tour, or even from abroad, Pauline would not always wait up to greet him. He was liable to find a note: 'Your milk is on the side-table. Goodnight.' It is often said that she would order him into his study each morning with the words 'Richard, go and compose!' Is it not more likely that what she really said was 'Now, Richard, off you go and compose', with the unspoken implication 'Keep out of my way while I see to the house'? Friends who invited them to dinner lived in terror of her attempting to lure servants to work for her! She even inspected other people's houses to see if they met with her standards of cleanliness. Callers at Garmisch were asked to pull a pair of slippers (provided) over their shoes before walking on the parquet floor. But, as her grandson Dr Christian Strauss told me:

In those days the Zöppritzstrasse [the road in which the Strauss villa stands] was not made up and was muddy and the Bavarian people still wore shoes with nails in them, so she quite understandably did not want her parquet floor ruined by nails. You have to look at these things in the context of the time.

Their letters tell the true story. In September 1897 Strauss was offered the directorship of Hamburg Opera, in succession to Mahler, by the Intendant there, Bernhard Pollini. Strauss wrote to her in Marquartstein, where she was recovering from the birth of Bubi, that he would refuse the offer if Pollini 'won't have you any more than Possart will'. She implored him

to give *no* consideration at all to my engagement, but if *you* will be happier in Munich with 12,000 marks, then we'll stay in Munich, dearest! If you want to go to Hamburg because of the way they try to hold you back in Munich – darling – then go to Hamburg, *without* trying to push through my engagement immediately. . . I cried all day today, without any reason really, I am just taking everything hard and my nerves leave much to be desired, dearest good Richard. You and Bubi are all my happiness . . . let us take care to earn a lot of money, so that you can soon live *your own life*. You will be here on the 10th, I am so looking forward to it, I weep for sheer longing for you . . . I love you with the utmost love. Paula.

Strauss's reply to 'my beloved, sweet, charming wife' ended: 'I love *you* more than I can say; I think you already know that, so words are in any case superfluous.' That was in 1897. In 1930, thirty-six years after their wedding, he wrote: 'I don't know if it's the same for you – my inner belonging to you grows greater all the time, I think of you and the children [Franz, his wife Alice, and their first son] all day long. I am wholly happy only with you. With our family!'

Today it is felt necessary to enter the bedroom of every subject of a biography. We know nothing of the Strausses' sex life. Only the music can tell us their secrets: the love music in *Ein Heldenleben* and *Symphonia Domestica*, the descriptions of intercourse in the preludes to Act I of *Der Rosenkavalier* and Act III of *Arabella*, the tenderness of the 'Träumerei' interlude in *Intermezzo*, the rapture of the love duet in Act II of *Arabella*. And much more. Strauss, a reticent man often regarded by others as cold and aloof, transferred his intimate feelings into his music. The passages mentioned above are clearly not just feats of imagination. Elisabeth Schumann hinted at repressions when she reported Pauline as saying to her 'What does one do with a man who, when he begins to get sensual, starts composing?!'[11] But Pauline may have been deliberately misleading Schumann: she knew her amorous history and proclivities and she kept sopranos away from Richard. There has never been any suggestion or evidence that Strauss was unfaithful. Some have tried to imply a romance with Elisabeth Schumann when they toured America in 1921, but not only was the soprano passionately in love with her husband – a friend of Strauss, the conductor Carl Alwin – at this time, but Strauss's son accompanied his father on the trip. (It was on this tour, in Washington, that Strauss was talking to his son and Mme Schumann about the Jews when he turned to Franz to say: 'Just you try and find a man like Alwin among the Christians.') The beautiful Maria Jeritza was also a friend of Strauss – his last song, *Malven*, was 'a last rose' for her in 1948 – but that was as far as it went.

Rather delightfully, Pauline was intensely jealous where her Richard was concerned. When she was eighty, she told the wife of producer Rudolf Hartmann: 'I would still scratch the eyes out of any hussy who was after my Richard.' After a performance of *Elektra* in Berlin in the 1930s conducted by Wilhelm Furtwängler, the soprano Viorica Ursuleac, who had sung Chrysothemis, was asked to join the Strausses for dinner in their hotel suite. Pauline, secretly annoyed, turned the tables by talking incessantly about the attractiveness of Furtwängler. Strauss grew angry and left the room. 'I only wanted to make him jealous', Pauline sobbed. Next day Strauss met Ursuleac and said: 'She's always playacting and I always fall for it.' The outstanding example of Pauline's jealousy occurred in the spring of 1902 just before Strauss left for England to conduct his works in London and elsewhere. One morning she opened a letter addressed to Strauss and read: 'Dear Herr Strauss, I expected to see you yesterday in the Union Bar, but in vain, alas. I am writing therefore to ask if you will be so kind as to let me have a few tickets for Monday and Wednesday of this week. With my best thanks in anticipation, yours sincerely, Mieze Mücke. Lüneburgerstrasse 5, ground floor right.'[12] Not exactly a love missive, but Pauline was outraged. She fumed inwardly for a week, let Strauss depart for England and then sent him a telegram saying she wanted a divorce. She consulted their lawyer, Friedrich Rösch, a close friend of Strauss, and set about closing their Berlin house, withdrew 2,000 marks in gold from the bank, and returned Strauss's letters unopened. Richard was flabbergasted but on 26 May wrote to Pauline from the Isle of Wight with touching humour but some asperity:

My dear Pauxerl. This business . . . is so stupid! Now: you get the precious document on Whit Monday and spend a week harbouring fearful resentment against your adulterous spouse while I sail off to England in blissful ignorance of the storm brewing at my back. . . The first act of your revenge is to draw my beautiful money out of the bank. I wish I knew what you intend to do with full 2,000 marks. There were no bills waiting to be paid and that one dress from Gerson's can hardly cost 1,500 marks. . . I have never been in the Union Bar, don't even know where it is, any more than I know who Mücke is. . . You could have thought that out for yourself, instead of demanding grand statements from me and simultaneously sending back my letters. . . However, as that is you all over, and as you still do not know what you have in me, and *never will know*, I must ask you to seek out the proof and the explanation you want yourself in Berlin, as I am not in a good position to do it on Wight.

Now: either precious Mme Mücke has confused me with someone else – after all, Berlin also boasts Edmund von Strauss [conductor at the Berlin Opera], Oscar Straus, etc – or someone has played a stupid and unnecessary joke on us. I am asking Rösch to check the address of the said Mücke. . . If she exists, he can ask her who the letter was intended for. If it then emerges that the letter was not meant for me, Rösch can box the lady's ears with it, three times if he will, and send me a short telegram, four words long: Mücke settled and explained.

It's a beautiful afternoon and it's been quite spoilt for me, instead of going for a stroll in God's wonderful nature. Yesterday I had already begun composing something really nice [*Symphonia Domestica*] and had to waste my time on a letter clearing myself. You really could spare me things like this. . . I will send the authorisation for the 2,000 marks to the bank at once. The best thing would be if you took it straight back and left the bills for me, which I can then settle on 11 June (in celebration of my birthday). For today, loving greetings and kisses from the adulterer to yourself and Bubi. . . Still, for the time being, your Richard.[13]

In spite of its good humour, hurt and fear are lurking behind the words of this letter. When Strauss turned this episode into his opera *Intermezzo* nearly twenty years later, the music after 'Storch' [Strauss's name in the opera] receives the telegram is full of anguish and tension. He wrote to Hofmannsthal on 22 January 1927: 'Harmless and insignificant as the incidents which prompted this piece may be, they nevertheless result, when all is said and done, in the most difficult psychological conflicts that can disturb the human heart. And this is brought out only by the music.'[14] Rösch soon solved the mystery. The visitor to the Union Bar was Josef Stransky, the Czech conductor who was to succeed Mahler in New York in 1911 and was in 1902 visiting Berlin with an Italian company. With two colleagues, he spoke about opera to Mücke, who asked for a ticket. She was told that 'Herr Strausky', as she heard the name, would send her one. Nothing arrived, so she looked up Strausky in the telephone directory. She could not find him, but settled for 'Strauss, Richard, Kapellmeister' at Joachimsthalerstrasse 17.

Why did Pauline fly off the handle in so ridiculous and spectacular a manner on this occasion? The answer can only be that she was of an extremely jealous disposition and that it was her nature to react in extremes. When Strauss in 1916 first contemplated making an opera from the incident, he approached the playwright Hermann Bahr for a libretto and sent him a detailed description of his relationship with Pauline. This is so important it must be quoted substantially:

He is a lover of order, like her, though it is partly her influence that he became so. He plans everything very carefully, can always find time for anything, while in fact he works very hard and yet regards himself as not at all hardworking. She thinks he is a kind of absent-minded professor, remote from the world. . . That is just her fantasy: she can interrupt his work at any time, he will go for walks and outings with her whenever she wants. She thinks she is hard at work all day long because, in her very vivid imagination, she attributes to herself all the work done at her command by servants and others. . . She is very pedantic in her love of order and passion for cleanliness. In her heart, too, she loves seemliness and purity, and rigorously deplores moral shortcomings in others, unless mitigated by some cause for fellow-feeling. In such cases she can be very tolerant. . .

One of the favourite subjects the couple argue about is that she, because of her pedantry, can only ever see one way to reach a goal, whereas he will weigh all the possibilities and choose the most convenient and time-saving. She will not acknowledge the help he gives in his quiet way, because she thinks he is no use in practical matters. . . She, though she possesses practical gifts, creates confusion because of her superabundant imagination and over-lively temperament. . . She has the habit often of not listening when people say things to her, and often forgets that she has been asked a question, what it was, or what she answered. . . Her vivid imagination, jumping rapidly from one thing to some other diametrically different thing, often leads her to assume another person already knows what she is talking about. But she is so fidgety and quick that the other person would have to be a mind-reader to know what she means by 'this doings' or 'that thingy'. . . She doesn't trust him not to muddle things, or pay something twice, or allow the tradesmen to take advantage of his good nature. . . Yet bills and receipts cause her enormous trouble and are only mastered after enormous expenditure of effort. . . The idea that her husband takes up all her time is another thing that exists solely in her imagination. He spends most of his time quietly on his own working. Because she has the feeling that she is always doing things for him, she longs to be left on her own, but no sooner has he gone away than she experiences great longing for him.[15]

Bahr declined to write the libretto and Strauss wrote his own. Compare the above with these extracts from *Intermezzo* in which Robert and Christine Storch are Richard and Pauline Strauss. Their maid Anna retains her real name.

> *Christine*: I have to supervise everything and be sure that everything's right. When you're here, why! the telephone never stops ringing.
> *Robert*: Why don't you leave the servants to answer?
> *C.*: And who would do the housework then?
> *R.*: I know, don't tell me: it all falls on you!
> *C.*: Well, on whom if not me? . . .
> *R.*: I would pay the bills gladly -

C.: – and you'd pay them twice over . . .

R.: Does thinking seem such a hard, strenuous labour?

C.: The hardest of all. For me at least – exhausting!

R.: That's where I beg to differ. And only thinking that's fruitful, the artist's or the scholar's, the true creator's – that is real thinking. . . For me, work is a pleasure.

C.: Working is never a pleasure.

R.: Then give it up! No need for you to do it! . . .

C.: . . . I come right out with what I'm feeling. He's so crafty, he can control himself, conceal things. That only makes me still angrier. I cannot find the words that I want then, and that's why we have terrible quarrels.

Anna: The master knows what lies behind them, that *gnä' Frau* loves him -

C.: Yes, but that's no way to win an argument – for I put myself in the wrong. All he wants is a quiet life, so he lets me have my way and I, I always, I become a monster!

In a later scene, when Robert is playing Skat with his cronies in Vienna:

Commercial Counsellor: If I had a wife like her, I should soon be in a madhouse! . . . At the very thought of her I begin to tremble.

R.: All the same, for me she makes the perfect wife. . . She's what I need. I need someone who's fiery and lively around me. Everyone's possessed of two natures; the difference is this, there are some who only show their *good* side, while she, she is really one of those gentle, shy, tender creatures but rough on the outside. I've met with many and they're the best kind. You think she's a hedgehog, all spiny and prickly.[16]

Hard as it is to believe, it is said that Pauline had no idea that she was represented so faithfully in *Intermezzo* until the curtain rose in Dresden on 4 November 1924. She was furious, chiefly because she resented her private life being exposed to the public and because Anna was included. (Anna Glossner made her own strong protest to Strauss.) When the soprano Barbara Kemp asked her 'Did you enjoy it?' Pauline replied 'Better than you did!' When Lotte Lehmann, who sang Christine, told her it was really 'a compliment', she replied: 'I don't give a damn.' Driving back to Garmisch next day, their chauffeur Theodor Martin overheard the tremendous protestation by Pauline to Strauss throughout the journey. A thunderstorm was raging, but the storm in the car was worse. But after two days, Pauline was mollified when Strauss pointed out what a beautiful reconciliation he had composed. Not Anna, however. She went home for two days and had to be enticed back.

There are marital relationships which thrive on a neurotic vitality unconnected with their sexual life. Their satisfaction derives from a constant state of siege. They bicker, they belittle each other and they do it in public. It provides them with equilibrium. Such were the Strausses. A family who knew them well, and to whom I have spoken, remember musical evenings at Garmisch when Pauline said to Strauss: 'Oh, you sing your own rubbish, I'm not bothering tonight.' Even so, one may doubt whether, as Norman Del Mar states, Pauline really refused to walk back to their hotel with Strauss after the première of *Die Frau ohne Schatten* because she regarded it as 'the most stupid rubbish he had ever written'. In the first place, the evidence for the anecdote is unsubstantiated and in the second she attended rehearsals and must in any case have known the music while it was being composed. Perhaps she was baffled by the libretto and regarded it as pretentious; and perhaps she was taken aback by the portrait of herself which emerged in the character of the Dyer's Wife. She knew that this was intentional because when Hofmannsthal first proposed the idea for the opera in 1911, he told Strauss that 'for one of the women, your wife might well, in all discretion, be taken as a model . . . a bizarre woman, with a very beautiful soul *au fond*; strange, moody, domineering and yet at the same time likeable'.[17] Strauss must have mentioned this to Pauline, for when he went to Vienna a fortnight later to discuss the project further with his librettist, he wrote to her: 'You'll be enchanted by it. . . Regarding the portrait of yourself, you need have no worry. He has adopted a few very general features, culled from fleeting remarks I have passed, with happy results. No one will recognise you in this, have no fear. In any case your wish is our command.' He was, perhaps, being less than frank. The abrasive element in the Dyer's Wife reflected the behaviour noted – and one has to presume accurately – by Ida Dehmel, widow of the poet Richard Dehmel, in her diary on 22 March 1905:

I spent only one hour in the company of Frau Strauss de Ahna, in Pankow, Parkstrasse 25, where she was on a visit with her husband. Kessler and Hofmannsthal were there. In that short time, and in front of total strangers, she managed to utter so many ignorant, tactless and crude indiscretions that it was the absolute lowest anyone could have experienced from a woman. 'Yes, men', she said, 'the main thing is to keep a tight rein on them.' At the same time she made a gesture of reining in a horse, while making whipping motions with the other. When she heard the other men praise Strauss for his *Zarathustra* and *Eulenspiegel* she screamed in a fury: 'You're only encouraging him to write more stuff like that, and being played everywhere, too! Who likes it? I don't. Can't see anything in it!'

One suspects that this was just Pauline at her most ostentatiously perverse. But what caused such behaviour? Probably an inferiority complex and a suppressed resentment that she had given up her fame and career. Perhaps also a ferocious over-compensation for shyness. She was no beauty and was, for example, always reluctant to be photographed. But whatever others thought about their relationship, they themselves were snugly secure. Here is part of a letter from Strauss, written on 27 November 1897 before she joined him for a *Liederabend*:

You leave on Monday at 11.30 and you get to Brussels at 6 p.m. Don't forget the music and *Tannhäuser* etc. Bring one dress and one hat too many rather than too few, so that you are quite smart and dashing, only bring immaculate boots and buy everything else you need (gloves, etc), because things are dearer in Brussels than in Munich. . . I am looking forward to seeing you enormously and to our splendid joint enterprise. Do be sensible, don't catch cold, have coffee, rolls and everything else brought to you in the compartment by the sleeping-car attendant (tip 2 marks).

The letter shows how protective of Pauline he was. Even before the Mücke episode, she occasionally blasted off at him in a letter. To one of these he replied from Liège in December 1896: 'Have just received your wrathful missive – ah, that's my old, cutting little woman again, signed "Bi" this time too, that always portends something of a tempest! It doesn't matter, my dear Bauxerl, I've had so many dulcet letters by now that I can perfectly well sustain the occasional one that modulates into the minor.' Can it be doubted that the case of his highly-strung mother was in his mind at these times?

10 The tone-poet

Lortzing's *Der Waffenschmied* was the first work Strauss conducted on his return to Munich. This was on 20 October 1894. He followed it with *Tristan* and *Die Meistersinger* (which he had conducted there in the summer), Weber's *Oberon*, Mozart's *Die Zauberflöte* and Ignaz Brüll's *Das goldene Kreuz*. In the first part of 1895 he conducted *Carmen*, *Hänsel und Gretel*, *Martha*, *Il trovatore*, Maillart's *Les dragons de Villars* and Kreutzer's *Das Nachtlager von Granada*. He sought Cosima's advice for a new production of *Rienzi* (22 May). Pauline's first Munich appearance under his baton was as Elisabeth in *Tannhäuser* on 23 June. At a Munich Wagner festival in the summer he conducted three performances each of the four operas listed above.

In November 1894 Strauss also took over the Munich Musical Academy symphony concerts. His inaugural programme included Beethoven's Seventh Symphony and in his second he conducted Liszt's *Faust Symphony* and some Haydn. He also introduced the preludes to Acts 1 and 2 of *Guntram* which were 'received with tempestuous approval', according to one Munich critic. These had been published, with Strauss's own concert endings, earlier in the year. Strauss's appetite for work can be gauged from the fact that he had been appointed conductor of the Berlin Philharmonic in succession to Bülow and had ten concerts with the orchestra in 1894–5. He ended his first concert with Beethoven's Seventh; the programme included Brahms's Violin Concerto and the prelude to Act 2 of Schillings's new opera *Ingwelde*. Among the composers whose music he conducted in this Berlin season were Liszt, Wagner, Anton Rubinstein, Schubert, Johann Strauss (*Perpetuum mobile*), Rameau, Berlioz, Dvořák, Mozart, Mendelssohn, Schumann, Smetana, Tchaikovsky and Weber. He conducted four extracts from *Guntram* at the last concert of the season. He was not invited back for a second season, being replaced by Nikisch, and after two seasons he was replaced as conductor of the Musical Academy by Mottl and Max Erdmannsdörfer.

He received the notice of his removal from the Munich Academy post while Pauline and he were on holiday in Florence in October 1896. '*Auch gut*' was his only comment. A few days later, on the 11th, he wrote in his diary: 'First idea for an orchestral piece: Don Quichotte, mad, free variations on a knightly theme.' This makes an excellent cue for quoting Strauss's illuminating reply in 1895 to a questionnaire from the author Friedrich von Hausegger relating to the nature of artistic creation:

Complete isolation is the best thing, for my production at all events. The 'ideas' in the afternoon – two hours after lunch or later – at the start of a walk, or after a long walk in the beauties of nature. . . I have no doubt that an 'inner' working of the imagination, of which I am not conscious, makes the principal contribution to my creativity. . . For example, four bars of a beautiful melody come to me suddenly. . . I've no idea of how or whence they have come to me, I sit down at the piano and try to work them out further according to their thematic character and whatever else their development seems to require – in a short time these four bars evolve into an 18-bar melody, which seems to match my expressive need well and happily and which I estimate will make a 32-bar period in order to be fully evolved and complete. After I have got the first 18 bars relatively quickly . . . all of a sudden the 18th bar won't go on as I want. I try three, four, five ways to develop it – it's no use – I sense that the natural production, if I may call it that, is over. As soon as I realise that, I don't attempt to go on, but I keep good hold of what I have and impress it on my mind.

A few days later, just as the first idea came to me, so all of a sudden what seems to be the right continuation of it occurs to me. So my imagination must have been working on it inwardly. . . I composed most between my eighth and 18th years. The fact that I am now getting slower and slower is due to my growing self-criticism, which has been intensified by my cultural betterment in general. . . My professional colleagues often accuse me of displaying a colossally well-developed orchestral technique, sumptuous polyphony, skilful new forms in my works, while there is something seriously wrong with my musical 'invention'. But if I have discovered all these new colours in the orchestra, then that must have been preceded . . . by the need to express something with these 'new colours' that could not be said in the old colours – if that is not the case, then one simply does not come upon these new colours. . . If I am always being accused of being too difficult, too complicated – the deuce! – I can't express it any more simply, and I struggle for the greatest simplicity possible; there's no struggle for originality in a real artist. What makes my style of musical expression often appear over-refined, rhythmically over-subtle, rich, is probably a taste that has been refined by my abundant knowledge of the entire literature and my great experience of everything to do with the orchestra; this makes me prone to regard as trivial, commonplace, over-familiar and therefore not needing to be trotted out again, things which still appear to others, not merely the lay public, as highly 'modern' and belonging to the 20th century. . . While reading Schopenhauer or Nietzsche or some history book, I will get an uncontrollable urge to go to the piano. Before long a quite distinct melody appears. The pre-condition is neither a particular mood . . . nor exterior impressions. . . The intellect alone is engaged.[1]

Strauss also told Hausegger about the composing of his songs:

I will have had no desire to compose for a month. Suddenly one evening I will pick up a volume of poetry, leaf through it carelessly; then a poem will strike me, and a musical idea for it will come to me, often before I've finished reading it properly: I sit down; the song is finished in 10 minutes. . . If I should happen, at a time when the vessel is full to the brim, so to speak, on a poem whose content is even only roughly appropriate, the opus is there in a jiffy. If the poem, all too often alas, does not present itself, then the urge to produce something is still satisfied, and any poem that strikes me as in the least suitable gets set to music, but then it's slow work, a lot of artifice goes into it, the melody flows dourly.[2]

As already related, Strauss wrote *Traum durch die Dämmerung* in twenty minutes. In 1918, while at Bad Ischl, Strauss told Max Marschalk: 'While waiting for you just now, I picked up Arnim and read the little poem *Der Stern* and while I was reading the musical inspiration came to me. I wrote the song down at once and if you like I will play it to you.' Over forty years later, Strauss added a postscript to the above: 'If I get stuck at a particular point when I am composing in the evening, and no profitable further working seems possible, rack my brains as I may, I close my piano or my sketchbook, go to bed and the next morning when I wake up *the continuation is there.*'

Another of Strauss's methods of working, when he was composing a large-scale piece such as *Ein Heldenleben* and *Don Quixote*, was to write in his sketchbooks, alongside themes and their development, descriptions of individual episodes. For example, 'Don Q. continues to maintain his convincing charm, Sancho reluctant, wants to leave him, then Don Q. unfolds his vision of peace to him, when S. again expresses his doubts after this, Don Q. becomes enraged, whereupon S. holds his tongue and goes to bed; then cello solo, vigil, lament.' Later: 'Barcarole Var.8 etc., after this nothing but fast and short D minor variations. . . Don Q. cured from madness. Death and conclusion. Seized by trembling, death approaches, last, *swift* battle, ends on pedal point memory.' The notes for *Ein Heldenleben* are more detailed. Here are a few: 'As adagio the longing for peace, after the battle with the world. Flight into solitude, the idyll . . . (a) after the love-scene, the envious and the critical cease to be heard. He remains immersed in D♭ major. (b) war-cry B♭ major; he bestirs himself and looks and sinks back into G♭ major (accompanied by the war-cry, trumpets *con sordini* – doubt, disgust) . . . Close battle in C major, tremolo E, then let the delicate works of the arts take shape, *pp*, all solos . . . Intensify embrace, victorious jubilation, love theme into first theme, extend this and into B major.' Colour also had a role in Strauss's creative psyche. While writing *Also sprach Zarathustra* he noted: 'Passion theme in A♭ (brass, dark blue).' When reading a libretto, as in the case of *Salome, Ariadne auf Naxos, Intermezzo* and others, he would jot a musical idea in the margin – the words immediately suggested the appropriate setting.

The loss of two conductorships was a blow to Strauss's pride. But it is probable at this date that he had not matured as a symphonic conductor. In October 1897, when he visited Amsterdam to conduct the Concertgebouw Orchestra in two programmes, audiences were small and the reception cool. The Dutch composer and critic Alphons Diepenbrock wrote to a friend: 'His success. . .was only middling. . . The orchestra's opinion is that he "Can't conduct".'[3] Strauss wrote to Pauline that his *Tod und Verklärung* had been 'a gigantic success' and that it was a 'real pleasure' to conduct the orchestra. (He was staying in the same hotel as Sarah Bernhardt and told Pauline 'she is still handsome, but the whole hotel has reeked of her perfume since yesterday'.) Notwithstanding the Dutch players' opinion, a contributory factor in Strauss's removal from the Munich post was his insistence on championing new works besides his own. His own were usually well received, but the public was (and has remained) unenthusiastic about Schillings, Ritter and Rezniček, all of whom Strauss programmed.

However, he was increasingly in demand as guest conductor of his own (and others') works. Thus he visited Berlin, Frankfurt (to conduct the first performance of *Zarathustra*), Brussels, Liège, Düsseldorf, Budapest, Heidelberg, Hamburg, Barcelona (where *Don Juan* was encored), Paris, Moscow, Zürich and Madrid. In Madrid, where Pauline accompanied him, he was shown the Tiepolos in the Royal Palace by the Queen. At the Prado he was profoundly impressed by 'some glorious Velazquez' of which, as he wrote to his father, 'we have absolutely no conception at home'. His first visit to London was in 1897. On 7 December, in the Queen's Hall, he conducted the English première of *Tod und Verklärung* after some Mozart and Wagner. Of particular importance to Strauss were the concerts given by the Liszt-Verein in Leipzig.

During his second season, 1895–6, at Munich Opera, Strauss conducted (besides *Guntram*) Heinrich Zöllner's *Der Überfall*, Gluck's *Iphigenia in Aulis*, Cornelius's *Der Barbier von Bagdad* and Adolphe Adam's *La poupée de Nuremberg*. Most memorable for him was Possart's new production in the Residenztheater of *Don Giovanni* for which Strauss had a large number of rehearsals. In his remaining seasons the new German works he conducted were his friend Ludwig Thuille's *Theuerdank* (he was objective enough to write to his parents: 'I conveyed Thuille's *Theuerdank* to the churchyard where he will probably be interred for good'), Schillings's *Ingwelde* and Siegmund von Hausegger's *Zinnober*. In 1897 he conducted new productions of Mozart's *Die Entführung aus dem Serail* and *Così fan tutte*. Strauss's love of *Così* – also Mahler's – did much to reinstate it in public affection. His improvisation of the continuo in the *secco* recitatives was especially witty and attractive. Otto Klemperer had 'an unforgettable memory of the [Mozart] performances he conducted at the old Residenz theatre in Munich. They were enchanting. He accompanied the recitative himself on a harpsichord and made delightful little decorations.'[4] Klemperer errs here in remembering a harpsichord. Most German opera houses after Mahler's time used a small upright piano for recitatives and this was certainly what Strauss played in Munich. (In the first Glyndebourne seasons – 1934 and 1935 – Fritz Busch used an upright.) While in Munich Strauss conducted 121 performances of operas by Mozart (seventy-five) and Wagner (forty-six). The Mozart performances, as he wrote years later, were 'among the truly wonderful memories of my life'.[5]

Otherwise, he was becoming disillusioned with Munich. He wrote to Pauline from Amsterdam in October 1897: 'Whenever one is abroad, one realises how provincial Munich is and what boorish fools its inhabitants are.' He was angry over the delays and deceit concerning a contract for Pauline. Even though he had been appointed Hofkapellmeister in 1896 when Levi retired, he never felt he had the full support of the management and he believed his success as a composer was resented. He knew, too, that Perfall and Possart were continually trying to lure Mottl from Karlsruhe. In March 1898 the violinist Carl Halíř, who had led the orchestra in Weimar and was now leader of the Berlin Royal Court Opera orchestra, wrote to tell him that Felix Weingartner was about to give up all his opera work in Berlin. Strauss asked Halíř to make further inquiries and thus learned that the artistic director of the Prussian royal theatres, Georg Henry Pierson, would offer a contract if Strauss made a move. When Strauss went to Berlin the following month for a performance of his melodrama *Enoch Arden*, he agreed terms for a ten-year contract as First Conductor of the Berlin Royal Opera, jointly with Karl Muck, from 1 November 1898 at a salary of 18,000 marks, with pensions guaranteed for him and his widow. By coincidence, at this very moment he was offered the conductorship of the New York Metropolitan at an annual income of 42,000 marks. He refused and explained to his mother (who was about to be readmitted to the institution where she was treated for her mental ailment) that 'I shall still be able to graze in American pastures ten years from now, while at the moment it's more important to make myself still better known in Europe. [So much for Strauss the avaricious money-accumulator]. . . . Ah, the joy of being able at last to throw the stick back at the feet of that brew in Munich, who have treated me really shamefully.' Since April 1897 he had been sketching a symphonic poem *Held und Welt* (*Hero and World*) with *Don Quixote* 'as satyr play to accompany it'. *Don Quixote* was completed on 29 December 1897. With the Berlin contract signed, he resumed serious work on what by July 1898 he was calling *Heldenleben* and completed the sketch at Marquartstein on 30 July, the day Bismarck died. He began the orchestration on 2 August and finished it on 1 December, by which time he had moved to Berlin. His final months at the Munich Opera, between July and October 1898, were mainly devoted to Mozart and Wagner, but his last official performance was *Fidelio* on 18

8 At St Moritz: Strauss, Pauline and a friend, Herr Milch

October. He wrote to Pauline, who had from 1 October rented 'a wonderful flat' in the Berlin suburb of Charlottenburg at Knesebeckstrasse 30 ('nine rooms with warm air-heating, 2800 marks')[6]: 'Tomorrow, *Fidelio* for the last time! Then *finis*! Off and away – into your arms!' He was crowned with six laurel wreaths after this performance and ruefully noted that 'I'm beginning to be extremely popular here now – *too late!*'

As if composing *Heldenleben*, conducting operas and his own works and moving to Berlin were not enough, Strauss in the summer of 1898 was deeply concerned in a matter for which he is still given too little credit – the campaign for composers' copyrights and performing rights. Strauss is frequently the object of sneers because he was concerned about his royalties and was a stickler about contracts. His critics do not explain why a composer should be any less interested in making money than a business-man, industrialist, politician or even journalist. He remembered his father's early deprivation; he read of the financial struggles of Mozart and Schubert; and, as a family man before all else – as cannot be too often emphasised – he was fearful throughout his life that he would not leave enough money for his heirs' comfort. As he once told Pauline: 'One can never know how long one will remain fashionable or when one will be overtaken and knocked out of the running by someone luckier or more gifted.' But he was not selfish: he was concerned about the remuneration of *all* his fellow-composers.

The German copyright act of 1870 extended copyright for an author's life-time and for thirty years after death. But there were anomalies and vague-ness concerning music. Strauss decided to try to obtain improvements, and had two allies, the composer 'Hans Sommer' (H. F. A. Zincke, 1837–1922) whom he had met in Weimar, and his schoolfriend the lawyer and composer Friedrich Rösch (1862–1925). In July 1898 they wrote to 160 composers asking for their support in a campaign to reform the copyright laws. They had 119 replies and at a conference in Leipzig in September their proposals for submission to the Reichstag were unanimously approved. This confer-ence also led to the foundation of a composers' association, the *Genossenschaft deutscher Tonsetzer* (*GDT*) (League of German Composers) which had a membership of 250 by November. This association was opposed to the policy of the *Allgemeiner deutscher Musikverein*, which had decided to support establishment of an Institute (*Anstalt*) for Musical Performance Rights by the Association of German Publishers and Retailers, because of the *Anstalt's* policy on royalties for non-stage works. New German copyright laws were passed in 1901 but did not clarify whether per-formance rights under protection belonged to the composer or publisher. The *GDT* established its own performing right *Anstalt* on 14 January 1903. Among the changes Strauss and his friends achieved were protection of a work's melodic content and control of permission for reprints in collections and anthologies (particularly significant in the case of songs). Strauss had long been connected with the *Allgemeiner deutscher Musikverein*, but he declined election to its committee in 1898 and only agreed to become its president in 1901 after an almost total change of its committee membership. Composers' rights were of concern to Strauss for the rest of his life and took up a lot of his time and energy. Sometimes his colleagues' attitudes drove him to distraction. 'If I had learned any other trade', he said, 'God knows I would switch horses to get away from this bunch!'

Strauss's high principles in this matter were immediately apparent in the publication of *Ein Heldenleben* for which he had asked 10,000 marks.[7] On 22 November 1898 he wrote to his friend, the publisher Eugen Spitzweg, head of the firm of Joseph Aibl:

It is with great regret that I learn of your refusal to take *Heldenleben*, because, as I have said before, it is absolutely impossible for me to give the performance rights of my works to the publisher in the future. This is the cardinal point in our whole movement, and as instigator I cannot set a bad example.

Publishing rights to the publisher.

Creator's rights to the creator.

There's no other way from this day forward. You have written a long screed about the percentages we want to claim all for ourselves. I can assure you, not for the first time, that we composers have completely renounced all demands for percentages and claim no percentages for ourselves at all, and we even dispute the right of publishers to claim percentages for works of which they have not expressly bought the performance rights. Are you coming to *Don Quixote*?

In his letters to Spitzweg up to 1904, Strauss asked increasingly higher prices for his works, but their chief disagreement was over the provision of performing materials for *Guntram* to Angelo Neumann, director of Prague's New German Theatre. Strauss wanted them to be sent for 500 marks rather than the usual 1,000 and, when Spitzweg refused, he asked that they should be sent free of charge. He conducted the performance in 1901 – clearly, he was more interested in assuring a performance of his ill-fated opera than in making money from it. He once asked Spitzweg to lend scores and parts free of charge to the Kaim Orchestra in Munich for two programmes of his music; and he furiously attacked him over difficulties in providing the scores for a performance of his Op. 34 *Zwei Gesänge* by Berlin Philharmonic Chorus: 'Don't you know that a performance by this choir is of the greatest importance for us both? If you only knew how many complaints there are on all sides, how difficult you are making dissemination and acquisition of my music for concert promoters and the public. You forget that as a business-man and publisher, along with your *rights* you have certain *obligations*.'

Once the *GDT*'s performing-right society was incorporated in 1903, Strauss immediately invited Mahler to join. Since 1897 Mahler had been a member of the Austrian *Gesellschaft der Autoren, Komponister und Musikverleger*, of which Strauss disapproved because of the connection with publishers, but he resigned at the end of 1903 and joined *GDT* in spite of a warning from his Vienna publisher that the high fees demanded by the *GDT* would harm the number of performances of his works. The reverse occurred.

Whatever frustrations Strauss endured in his operatic work in Munich between 1894 and 1898, they did not affect his creativity as they had in Weimar. In those four years he composed four major tone-poems, toyed with ideas for operas and ballets, wrote thirty-two songs, orchestrated five songs and composed the two great unaccompanied Op. 34 choral songs, *Der Abend* and *Hymne*. Strauss's reputation as an orchestral composer is chiefly founded on his tone-poems. It is not the purpose of this book to analyse and examine the tone-poems in detail: this has been done excellently elsewhere and the works are now so well known and so frequently performed and recorded that further exposition could only be superfluous where, say, *Don Juan* and *Till Eulenspiegel* are concerned. The former, it is true, still exercises musicologists, who are uncertain about exactly what its structural design is – free sonata or free rondo.[8] While one might jocularly say that *Macbeth* often sounds as if it might be Strauss, *Don Juan* put down a marker as the unmistakable work of a composer of genius. Its near-perfect scoring, its energy and lyricism and sense of novelty, still powerful after over a century, ensure its secure place in the symphony orchestra's repertory. *Tod und Verklärung*, too, has at long last left behind the odium with which many commentators once surrounded it because of the so-called 'banality' of the *Verklärung* section. It is now highly regarded both for its musical content and its unusual form – Strauss himself pointed out that it 'makes the main theme its point of culmination and does not state it until the middle'. Much depends, too, on the conductor's approach to the work's final section – no one who heard Dimitri Mitropoulos conduct it could ever take seriously a criticism of the music as banal. If this work is the dark-Alberich in Strauss, *Till Eulenspiegel* is the light-Alberich. Musical humour of this vintage and quality had not been heard in German music for many a long year. Again, the rondo form was the perfect vessel for the content, and time has in no way dimmed or diminished the pyrotechnical brilliance of the whole enterprise.

More needs to be said about *Also sprach Zarathustra*, if only because it gives the lie to the impression of Strauss as a non-intellectual musician, even something of a philistine. Strauss was incontrovertibly an intellectual by any standard of measurement, but he was never an intellectual with his head in the clouds. He liked people to think he was non-intellectual just as Ralph Vaughan Williams liked to pretend he knew nothing about orchestral technique and Elgar pretended he knew nothing about double counterpoint. It was a pose in all cases. In his twenties (and before) Strauss read Goethe, Shakespeare and Schopenhauer. Karl Böhm wrote that 'sometimes it was quite impossible to follow Strauss in every topic of his conversation: one had to be as well up in literature as in music to be able to hold one's own with him. He was as at home in German literature as no other musician. . . he knew *Faust* by heart. He was equally familiar with Russian literature.'[9] During composition of *Guntram*, as we have seen, Strauss explored Nietzsche. He was interested in the writings of the radical and anarchistic John Henry Mackay (who wrote the poem *Morgen!*). During the 1890s, as John Williamson has pointed out, Strauss was 'remarkably open to libertarian, individualistic ideas'.[10] As he had shown by his alteration of the third act of *Guntram*, Strauss was concerned with the self-justification of the individual and this chimed in with Nietzsche's rejection of Christianity, of which Strauss approved. Strauss described *Also sprach Zarathustra* as a tone-poem 'freely after Nietzsche'. This has led to controversy and argument over whether he meant that the music was 'about' Nietzsche and his ideas or 'about' Richard Strauss, using Nietzsche's book as a peg on which to hang musical ideas generated by a reading of it. Strauss was no believer in democracy, but danger lies here in regarding Nietzsche's concept of a Superman as a proto-Nazi Aryan hero. Nietzsche saw the Superman, to quote Williamson, as 'the revaluer of morality through the Will to Power, as the incarnation of the central Nietzschean idea of Eternal Recurrence.' The Superman in *Zarathustra* is the yea-saying individual who replaces the values of a herd-like religion. Strauss depicted this life-affirmation by using the waltz not as a bourgeois relaxation but as the expression of excited energy, as he was to use it again in *Salome* and *Elektra*. Whether his intention was fulfilled in the music, listeners must decide for themselves. Some may find the solo violin's waltzing too suggestive of ballrooms rather than a cosmic dance. There is in any case no reason to believe that Strauss subscribed to a Superman philosophy. The poetic visions of the poem, he said in 1946 in a letter to Martin Hürlimann, afforded him 'much aesthetic enjoyment'.

The truth about *Zarathustra* can probably only be answered, pusillanimous as it may seem, by the reply that it is 'about' both Nietzsche *and* Strauss. But we should also assume that Strauss meant what he said when, at the time of the first Berlin performance, conducted by Nikisch on 30 November 1896, he wrote that he had not intended to write 'philosophical music. . . I meant rather to convey in music an idea of the evolution of the human race from its origin, through the various phases of development, religious as well as scientific, up to Nietzsche's idea of the *Übermensch*. The whole symphonic poem is intended as my homage to the genius of Nietzsche.' Yet, as we shall see, the most Nietzschean of his works was to be *Eine Alpensinfonie*.

Although *Macbeth* and *Don Juan* were only loosely programmatic compared with the realistic representation of *Till*, the significance of *Zarathustra* is that it was about abstract ideas. He told his French friend Romain Rolland that 'in his mind, he really did want to express, right up to the end of the symphony [*sic*], the hero's inability to satisfy himself, either with religion or science or humour, when confronted with the enigma of nature'.[11] But Strauss gave *Zarathustra* a dramatic theme by opposing Nature (tonality of C) to Man (tonality of B). The work's harmonic scheme is complex, *avant-garde* for its date and in advance of anything Strauss had already attempted. Dissonance is unresolved – the undermining of tonality is anticipated and foretold. C and B both organise and destabilise. Strauss told Dr Anton Berger in Frankfurt in 1927: 'I only wanted to show that it is impossible to bring B minor and C major together. The entire piece demonstrates all possible attempts, but it does not work. That is everything!'[12] Chromatic side-slips, a favourite Strauss procedure, occur throughout and particularly in *Von der Hinterweltlern* (*Of the Backworldsmen*). The orchestra was the largest Strauss had yet used and he scored for it with a distinctiveness of colour and, in the use of divided strings, unsurpassed virtuosity which give the work the character of a concerto for orchestra. Today its attraction as a showpiece for virtuoso orchestras has overtaken its Nietzschean overtones where the public is concerned – aided by Stanley Kubrick's inspired use of its dramatic opening in his film *2001 – A Space Odyssey*. And Strauss himself knew how good it was. After the final rehearsal at Frankfurt for the first performance on 27 November 1896, he wrote to Pauline:

Zarathustra is glorious – by far the most important of all my pieces, the most perfect in form, the richest in content and the most individual in character. . . The Passion theme is overwhelming, the Fugue spine-chilling, the Dance Song simply delightful. I'm enormously happy and very sorry that you can't hear it. The climaxes are immense and scored!!! Faultlessly scored – and the beautiful concert hall helps. Orchestra is excellent – in short, I'm a fine fellow, after all, and feel just a little pleased with myself, and I shan't allow the population of Munich to spoil the feeling.

The fate of the work in Munich is worth relating. Strauss refused to grant rights for a performance at the Academy Concerts in 1897 – not surprisingly, since he had been removed from the conductorship. The work was first played in his native city in a transcription for eight hands at two pianos and in one for two pianos. Strauss offered to conduct a performance on 17 March 1899, but Perfall rejected him and gave it to Franz Fischer. The first time the composer conducted *Zarathustra* in Munich was on 16 March 1900.

For his next tone-poem Strauss again found the perfect form and format: variations. But why did he pick on Don Quixote as the subject? Because, I believe, his mother's continuing illness haunted his imagination and he knew from her condition – and perhaps even from Pauline's highly-strung temperament – how narrow was the line between sanity and derangement. True, the adventures of Don Quixote provided marvellous opportunities for Strauss's genius as a storyteller and graphic illustrator and he seized them marvellously. The almost casual beginning of the work, with three themes in rapid succession depicting the chivalrous, *galant* and delusional aspects of Quixote's character, is an anticipation of Strauss's method in several later works – *Symphonia Domestica*, *Intermezzo* and *Arabella* among them. The celebrated depiction of the sheep (flutter-tonguing woodwind and brass), the flight through the air (wind machine, flutter-tonguing flutes, harp glissandi), the priests (two bassoons) are as vivid as woodcut illustrations in a volume of Cervantes and are balanced by the poetic melody for Dulcinea, the use of harmonic side-slips to represent Quixote's madness, if that is what it is, and the great impassioned vision of a world of chivalry in Variation III in which Strauss's orchestral mastery reaches heights of eloquence he rarely approached again. The use of several instruments to represent Don Quixote and Sancho Panza, not just solo cello and solo viola, is another example of Strauss's flexibility in his portraiture. As a composition it is the highwater mark of his skill. He himself shied away from illuminating comment on it. He wrote somewhere about having taken 'variation form *ad absurdum* and showered tragic persiflage upon it' and at another time said *Don Quixote* was 'the battle of *one* theme against a nullity'. Not very helpful.

In *Don Quixote* Strauss achieved what he only rarely achieved – what any composer only rarely achieves – namely, a perfect fusion of the creative idea with the method and means of expression. On one level, it is a virtuoso translation of a favourite piece of literature into music; on another, deeper, level, it is the soul of Richard Strauss laid bare as he rarely laid it bare. We hear in the dream of chivalry, in Quixote's vigil over his armour and in the pouring-out of his feelings for Dulcinea, the Strauss who feared to look too closely into his own nature and was able to divert that inner gaze by a superhuman effort at 'dispersing the dark thoughts', the phrase he had used in his letter to his sister in 1885 when he was so disturbed by his father's lack of 'moral strength' over his mother's illness. Music was Strauss's means of escape, as we shall see when we reach the darkest period of his life, and in much of his music he wore a mask. Occasionally he let it slip. In *Don Quixote* he ripped it away for those with ears to hear beyond the sheer versatility, cleverness and poetry of the score. That is why it is the greatest of his orchestral works, perhaps of all his works.

Its companion-piece, *Ein Heldenleben*, has been as much misunderstood as *Don Quixote* has been (by many) underrated. Like *Don Quixote*, it is an allegory about the fundamentals of human nature and existence and reflects Strauss's preoccupation at this period of his life with the Nietzschean ideology of an individual's right to self-determination in the face of a hostile world. The framework of the tone-poem is 'individual – love – struggle –

withdrawal into solitude', the four movements of a symphony. What *Ein Heldenleben* is not is a musical depiction of Kaiser Wilhelm II's militaristic ambitions for Germany. This canard was begun by Strauss's French friend Romain Rolland who in his diary for 22 January 1898 – before he had heard *Ein Heldenleben* – wrote of 'Neroism in the air'.[13] The American historian Barbara W. Tuchman in her book *The Proud Tower* expatiated on this theory by pigeon-holing Strauss as the musical counterpart of the Kaiser. She took her cue from Rolland who, on 1 March 1900, described Strauss as 'the typical artist of the new German empire, the powerful reflection of that heroic pride which is on the verge of becoming delirious, of that contemptuous Nietzscheism, of that egotistical and practical idealism which makes a cult of power and disdains weakness'.[14] But Rolland was shrewd enough to notice 'certain dispositions which I had not seen clearly before, and which strictly speaking belong more to the people of Munich, the South Germans: an elemental vein of the clownish humour, paradoxical and satirical, of a spoilt child, or of Till Eulenspiegel'.[15] The real Strauss revealed himself to Rolland a few evenings later (9 March) when, in a carriage together going to the Vaudeville, he said: 'I am not a hero; I haven't got the necessary strength; I am not cut out for battle; I prefer to withdraw, to be quiet, to have peace. I haven't enough genius. I lack the strength of health and willpower. I don't want to over-strain myself. At the moment I need to create gentle, happy music. No more heroic things.'[16] Within the next decade he was to compose *Salome* and *Elektra*!

Even if, as Strauss told his father, it is 'only partly true' that the Hero of *Ein Heldenleben* is Strauss himself, it is true that Hero in the context of this work is a synonym for Artist and that the work, with its wit and humour which are so often overlooked, is the autobiography of a *Kapellmeister* who was still stung by the failure of his first opera and who, as is often quoted, saw no reason why he should not write about himself. This, by people lacking a sense of humour, is interpreted as megalomania. (Conductors have contributed to this distortion. Tempi have become slower. Strauss's 1941 and 1944 recordings both last under forty minutes.) In the tone-poem the principal subject – designated by Strauss in his sketches as 'heroic strength' rather than 'the Hero' – is introduced by eight bars in which there is no counterpoint. Polyphony begins after this introduction with other themes criss-crossing as in the opening of *Don Quixote*. Just as there is structural novelty in *Tod und Verklärung*, so there is in *Ein Heldenleben*, which starts with a development section. Strauss's notebooks describe it as the 'primary unfolding of abilities' (*primäre Entfaltung der Fähigkeiten*) culminating in the six great shouts of defiance, the 'challenge to the world' (*grosse Herausforderung an die Welt*). Between each challenge is a pause, 'composed' as carefully as any in Bruckner.

Writing to his father shortly after the Berlin première of *Ein Heldenleben* (22 March 1899), Strauss referred to some of the critics as having 'spat poison and gall, mainly because they thought from the analyses that the nasty description of the "Moaners and Adversaries" was aimed at them'. Although there can be no doubt that he had the press critics in mind, the 'adversaries' also included philistines generally, all those 'cheeky uneducated laymen who pronounce judgments on the most sublime works of art as if they were equal to their creators'. The motif in this section which is scored for two tubas recurs throughout the work to represent, in Strauss's words from his sketches, 'the absolute indolence of the world' (*absolute Indolenz dieser Welt*). Its parallel fifths mock the strict academicism of musical pedants among teachers. But everyone in 1899 noticed that the motif fitted the name 'Dok-tor Döh-ring', the Munich critic Theodor Döhring, who did not approve of programme-music. In a sketchbook, the tuba theme originally had the rhythm ♩ ♪ ♩ which fits 'Dok-tor Döh-ring' better than the final version in the full score. Döhring seems to have been an amiable chap, for after Strauss had conducted *Ein Heldenleben* in Munich on 19 October 1899, the critic mentioned that he had been told that the motif was 'directed personally at the author. It is nice of Strauss that he does not put this into the voices of the evil moaners but treated it more like an old grizzly bear. From his own point of view, Strauss is perfectly entitled to count him [i.e. Döhring] among the Philistines insofar as Philistines are taken to be those who are not always able or willing to follow the matadors of the new art on their bold paths – and who do not praise the things they cannot like in their innermost hearts.'

Another controversial section of *Ein Heldenleben* is the Battle, regarded when the work was new as the apex of cacophony and dissonance. But that phase has passed. The word 'Battle', however, and the trumpets and drums of war have inevitably been linked with militarism. Strauss meant it as an allegory: this battlefield is of the spirit, of inner conflicts. Much of the sound and fury is, incidentally, governed by a 3/4 beat, another witty touch as Strauss again brings the waltz into serious matters. The battle is followed by the 'Works of Peace', over thirty quotations from Strauss's works. More self-glorification, more megalomania! But what would have been said if he had quoted *other* composers' works at this point? The Artist's Life must reflect his own creativity, and the section is one of the most beautiful, dreamlike and intricate in the work. Autobiography is ever-present: the wooing motif from the third section of *Ein Heldenleben* (*The Hero's Companion*) is counterpointed by a theme from *Guntram*, a reminiscence of Strauss's engagement to Pauline during rehearsals for the opera. The last section is entitled The Hero's Flight from the World and Fulfilment. Plainly, this did not apply to Strauss himself in any literal way. With his schedule, he had no hope of retreating from the world. The sketchbook notes say: 'He is over-come with revulsion, he pulls right back into the idyll, now only wanting to live on his own reflections, desires and the quiet, contemplative resolution of his very own personality.' He then described the 'fulfilment' as 'the expression of the psyche of the man grown old'. This has been taken to refer to his father, who noticeably mellowed in old age after his fiery years. The work originally ended quietly with the violin and horn billing and cooing until the music faded away. Supposedly ribbed by a close friend (Friedrich Rösch) that he could only compose quiet endings, Strauss added the five bars of swelling brass opulence which at the end of his life he ruefully mocked as 'state funeral'. Two conductors have recorded (1996) the first ending. Its poetic effect is in keeping with Strauss's original concept of the work.

Finally, it should be emphasised that Strauss composed *Ein Heldenleben* in Munich, completing the sketch on holiday in Marquartstein on 30 July 1898, when he wrote in his diary: 'Evening, 10 o'clock, the great Bismarck has been dismissed!' Willi Schuh, in his Strauss biography, interprets this as a reference to Bismarck's dismissal as chancellor by the Kaiser.[17] That event occurred in 1890. He died on 30 July 1898 and it was this to which Strauss was referring – dismissed from life! Strauss began the orchestration on 2 August and completed it after his move to Berlin. It is in no respect a work of his Berlin period. Everything about it was inspired by his experiences as composer and conductor in his native city.

The songs Strauss wrote during his second spell in Munich contain several of his masterpieces in the genre. Almost all of them are regularly included in recitals today. For years his *Lieder* have been under-rated, but the tide has turned and at last they are rightly classified among the greatest of their kind. Only now, when so many more of them are known and have been recorded, can the width of their emotional range be fully appreciated. They contain in microcosm the essence of Strauss. There is no doubt that he used the *Lied*, with its constricted space, as a testing-ground for his operatic creations. In the *Lied* he could blend voice and character, tone and emotional meaning, into a compressed unit, trying out techniques (sometimes radical) which would be useful for him when applied to a larger context. 'Sentimentality and parody are the sensations to which my talent reacts most strongly and most fruitfully', he once told Hofmannsthal, and both are to be found in his songs. Rolland was easily misled by the sentimental aspect of Strauss's *Lieder*. 'Rather weak, in the manner of Gounod', he wrote on 20 May 1899.[18] 'The Germans are in ecstasies. When this terrible hero wishes to lay bare his amorous heart, he's a child, a little trite and very sentimental. Madame S. plays to the public, displays her bosom and her smile.' But to Hans Hotter, Strauss once said, 'Actually, I like my songs best.' It is a strange statement and perhaps should be taken with two pinches of salt, but it is significant in that he perhaps felt that, in the smaller space of the *Lied*, he had achieved greater artistic success, had hit the bull's-eye more regularly. His attitude to song-writing was cogently expressed in the 1930s in a letter to his librettist Joseph Gregor. 'A perfect Goethe poem doesn't need any music; precisely in the case of Goethe, music weakens and flattens out the word. A Mozart string quartet says everything profound with more beauty of sentiment than any words. . . Many songs owe their origin to the circumstance that the composer looks for a poem which will match a fine melodic idea and the poetically musical atmosphere – Brahmsian songs! If he *can't* find a poem you get a Song *without* Words (Mendelssohn). Or the *modern* Lied: the verse gives birth to the vocal melody – not as happens so often, even in Schubert, that the melody is poured over the verse without getting the cadence of the poem quite right!'

In contrast to several of his contemporaries, Strauss went to living poets for many of his texts. The poets of his Op. 27, his wedding-present to Pauline, were contemporaries – Mackay, Karl Henckell and Heinrich Hart. When he moved to Munich, he set three poems by Otto Julius Bierbaum (1865–1910), founder and editor of a progressive periodical dealing with literature and the arts, as his Op. 29. They included *Traum durch die Dämmerung*, one of his most popular songs from the start, and the impressively dark and brooding *Nachtgang*. Later, *Jung Hexenlied* became one of Pauline's party-pieces, and *Freundliche Vision* followed in Berlin. The first Strauss setting of poetry by Richard Dehmel (1863–1920), a Nietzschean, was *Stiller Gang*, for voice, piano and optional viola obbligato. Bierbaum sent the poem to Strauss in December 1895 and ten days later the song was composed. Dehmel objected to the setting of *Mein Auge* (Op. 37, No. 4, 1898) because he regarded his poem as immature ('my innards are churning at the very thought of it'). Strauss set ten Dehmel poems for voice and piano and one, the elaborate and compelling *Notturno*, for voice, violin and orchestra. *Befreit* (Op. 39, No. 4, 1898) is among Strauss's finest songs, an impassioned outpouring from the depths of his heart, yet Dehmel thought it 'a little too soft for the poem.' Dehmel also regarded the setting of *Der Arbeitsmann* (Op. 39, No. 3, 1898) as 'too convulsive, he simply hasn't got the measure of it'. It is not surprising that Dehmel regarded Strauss as 'basically a disguised naturalist with romantic impulses. That is no commendation in my view, romanticism is *behind* us.' Dehmel went on to be a significant influence in the music of Arnold Schoenberg (*Verklärte Nacht* and many songs).

Dehmel, an epileptic, was friends with August Strindberg, Detlev von Liliencron and Otto Erich Hartleben. He was a socialist believer in workers' poetry and was an advocate of free love: his poems contain erotic language which shocked his contemporaries. If it seems strange to find Strauss in this company, it is because he identified with Dehmel's struggle against a hostile opposition. After all, during his Munich years, he felt himself to be in the same boat and although he had no socialist beliefs which led him to set *Der Arbeitsmann* and Henckell's *Das Lied des Steinklopfers*, their texts echo his rebellious feelings about established and conventional opinion. Nevertheless the Dehmel settings which drew the most Straussian music are the more lyrical *Mein Auge*, *Waldseligkeit* and *Wiegenlied*. Dehmel, like

Henckell and even more like Bierbaum (whose wife ran off with the conductor Oskar Fried) were protagonists of the *Jugendstil* (Art Nouveau) style to which Strauss's music of this period belongs. Two of his songs were published during 1896 in the movement's magazine *Jugend* which first appeared at Christmas 1895. One of them, *Wenn. . .* (Op. 31, No. 2, 1895), to words by Carl Busse, begins in D♭ major and ends a semitone higher in D major. Where the key-change occurs, Strauss inserted a footnote advising singers 'who intend to perform this work in public before the end of the nineteenth century to sing it transposed down by one note from this point onwards, so that the piece concludes in the key in which it began'.

Just as Strauss's relationship with Dehmel cooled (although they kept in touch until 1910), so his with Bierbaum ended abruptly in November 1903 after the poet had turned music critic for a performance of Strauss's *Taillefer*, a setting of Uhland's ballad. 'What does he know about setting Uhland?' Strauss asked his parents.[19] 'Can I help it if the piece is performed with too small a choir, which was inaudible, in too small a room, where it made a gigantic noise?. . . Could none of my "friends" in Munich take the trouble to explain this to that amateur Bierbaum. Or – wouldn't they?' The poet whom he set over the longest period (1894–1906) was another socialist, Henckell. His first setting, *Ruhe, meine Seele* (Op. 27, No. 1, 1894), delighted the poet, who described the music in a letter to Strauss as 'shivering so lightly, with hardly a wave breaking'. Only *Das Lied des Steinklopfers* was a 'protest' song; all the other Henckell songs are lyrical, such as *Ich trage meine Minne* (Op. 32, No. 1, 1896), *Liebeshymnus* (Op. 32, No. 3), the delightful *Kling!* (Op. 48, No. 3, 1900) and *Winterweihe* and *Winterliebe* (Op. 48, Nos. 4 and 5). In his Munich period Strauss set only two poems by Emanuel von Bodman (1874–1946), the first one of his most magnificent, the operatic *Gesang der Apollopriesterin* (Op. 33, No. 2, 1896) for voice and orchestra. Among his settings at this period of non-contemporary poets were his magnificent *Zwei Gesänge*, Op. 34, for an unaccompanied chorus of sixteen voices. *Der Abend* (Schiller) and *Hymne* ('Jakob! Dein verlorner Sohn') (Rückert), completed respectively on 16 March and 7 May 1897, are the vocal equivalents of his tone-poems in their variety of tone-colour and intricacy of polyphony. Also in May 1897 he set another *Hymne*, to words by Schiller, for women's chorus, wind band and orchestra for the opening of the

Sezession Exhibition in Munich on 1 June 1897, when he conducted. There is scarcely a song composed by Strauss between 1894 and 1898 which is not worth deep study for each represents an aspect of his art parallel to the extraordinary accomplishment of his orchestral works. Taken together, they form an illuminating preparation for his achievements in opera.

PART II

1898–1918
The Berlin years

11 At the Kaiser's court

The years from 1900 to 1914 were Strauss's years of glory. If we are to understand the tragedy of his later years, we must savour to the full what he was, and what he meant to music, in the first decade and a half of the twentieth century.

In spite of the failure of *Guntram*, Strauss's interest in the stage was not dampened. We have seen that he toyed with several ideas for operas. He also received suggestions for several ballets. Although he considered them he wrote only a small amount of music for them. He told Max Steinitzer that part of the difficulty was that a composer could not guarantee exact matching of theme and gesture, but the lack of real dramatic substance in the scenarios submitted to him must have been a determining factor. Otto Bierbaum offered him *Pan im Busch* in May 1895 (it was later set by Mottl) and *Der rote Stern* a year later. In 1896, too, Frank Wedekind offered him a 'great spectacular ballet'. Strauss sketched some music for *Die Flöhe oder der Schmerzenstanz*, but abandoned it quickly. In 1898 Dehmel tried to interest him in a 'dance-play', *Lucifer*, but in vain. However, he began to sketch music for a ballet, *Der Kometentanz*, suggested to him in 1896 by the writer Paul Scheerbart (1863–1915). He mentioned it in a letter to Mahler dated 22 April 1900: 'I am writing a one- or two-act burlesque ballet: *Kometentanz*, an astral pantomime – naturally something departing wholly from the usual hopping-about. . . Would you accept the ballet for the Vienna Opera, have the first performance and use some nice scenery? On the strength of my honest face? . . . It will be ready to be performed about autumn 1901. . . Naturally, I only performed your songs[1] so that you would be all the more sure to accept my ballet! That's the way I am! Well known for it!' Mahler replied: 'Your ballet is accepted *in advance*!'[2] (It is noticeable how much more relaxed their relationship was before Alma came on the scene.) Strauss mentioned this ballet to Rolland in March 1900, telling him that the *maître de ballet* in Berlin had rejected it as 'not serious'. From Rolland we learn something about the scenario:

A King, a tyrant, surrounded by his women, his jesters, his ministers, his poets, his scholars, wants to be put amongst the stars. No one can carry out his wish. The poet declares that only poets have a place there. The magician can make the stars come down to earth and they do in fact appear; but the King cannot join in their dance. The tyrant becomes frenzied and threatens everyone; but he suddenly disappears into the ground, together with his court; and the stars rise slowly into the sky, carrying away the jester, the poet, and the magician – art, humour and knowledge – in their sacred dance. And the ballet finishes in the infinite space in which worlds disappear.[3]

During their time together in March 1900, Strauss and Rolland also discussed Watteau's painting *L'Embarquement pour Cythère*, which Strauss described as a *Märchen-malerei* (fairy-tale painting). This led to his devising an elaborate ballet, *Die Insel Kythere*, the scenario of which he wrote in the summer, and he began to compose the music in the September. The characters ranged from pilgrims, Moors, Chinese and *commedia dell'arte* figures to Venus, Adonis, Diana and Amor. Ten numbers were projected for Act 1, four for the four scenes of Act 2 and sketches exist for eleven numbers of Act 3. Although he abandoned the scheme, he did not waste the music: he used two themes in *Feuersnot*, a minuet and gavotte found their way into *Le bourgeois gentilhomme*, another theme went towards the ballet *Josephs Legende* and another became Ariadne's 'Bald aber naht ein Bote' in 'Es gibt ein Reich' (F.S. p. 124, cue no. 62). It was this ballet which diverted him from what might have become his first collaboration with Hugo von Hofmannsthal. They had first met on 23 March 1899 in the Berlin suburb of Pankow when Hofmannsthal and Count Harry Kessler visited Dehmel. Present besides the Strausses was Paul Scheerbart. Later the two men met again in Paris, where Hofmannsthal mentioned a ballet he was writing, *Der Triumph der Zeit*, 'in three acts with some parts predominantly in the nature of a pantomime and others designed rather for the introduction of dances'.[4] In November 1900 Hofmannsthal sent the scenario to Strauss, who returned it and said he liked it but added that *Kythere* was preoccupying him and he then had work for at least three years.

On 2 May 1898, during his last spell in Munich, Strauss began but soon abandoned a 'Spring Symphony'. In February 1899, his first winter in Berlin, he sketched a one-act opera libretto *Ekke und Schnittlein* which his father said was too frivolous. This too was abandoned after two months. But another contemplated project was to lead to something tremendous some years later. Early in 1900 he had the idea for a symphonic-poem *Künstler-Tragödie (Artist's Tragedy)*. In a letter to his parents on 28 January 1900 he wrote: 'Deep in my bosom slumbers a symphonic-poem which is to begin with a sunrise in Switzerland. So far only the idea (love tragedy of an artist) and a few themes exist.'[5] He began the composition sketch in earnest on 3 July. Later he called it 'Love tragedy of an artist / in memory of Karl Stauffer'. This refers to Karl Stauffer-Bern, a Swiss-born artist who moved to Berlin in 1880 at the age of twenty-three and won celebrity as a portrait-painter. On holiday in Switzerland he was befriended by a wealthy couple, Emil and Lydia Welti, who lent him money when he ran into a bad patch. Stauffer and Lydia had an affair which ended in prosecution, prison, mental asylum and betrayal. Both committed suicide in 1896. A book was written about Stauffer which Strauss read on his move to Berlin. He was moved by Stauffer's obsession with work and planned a two-part symphonic-poem, first dealing with Stauffer and Lydia, then their tragedy. The work opened with Stauffer's happy childhood in the Swiss Alps but progressed no further. The opening was taken up eleven years later for *Eine Alpensinfonie*.

Strauss's first assignments as opera conductor in Berlin in November 1898 were *Tristan* (5th), *Carmen* (8th), *Hänsel und Gretel* (11th), *Die lustige Weiber von Windsor* (12th), *La muette de Portici* (13th) and *Fidelio* (15th). Berlin was what today we might call a 'swinging' city. It was prosperous and expansionist. The arts thrived there. It was wealthy and go-ahead. The Kaiser's determination that Germany should be the most respected and feared nation in Europe throbbed through Berlin. No greater contrast to conservative, provincial Munich could be imagined – except that the Court Opera was ultra-conservative. This reflected the Kaiser's taste. He regarded himself as musical and even wrote pieces for male voice choir. But his opinions on music were not those of a seer. In no respect was Strauss a Wilhelmine Berliner, *pace* Barbara Tuchman.

It is fortunate that we have Rolland's diaries, for they tell us the truth about Strauss's opinion of Berlin and his employer. The concert audience there, he said, comprised connoisseurs; the opera audiences were pleasure-seekers, 'nothing but bankers and shopkeepers'. His first interview with the Kaiser began with Wilhelm II barking: 'You're yet another of these modern musicians!' The Kaiser had heard Schillings's *Ingwelde* – 'execrable, no melody. And you are one of the worst.' Modern music was worth nothing. 'I like *Freischütz* better.' So do I, Strauss replied. Then: 'Verdi's *Falstaff* is detestable.' 'But, your majesty, Verdi is eighty years old and it's splendid, after having created *Il Trovatore* and *Aida,* to renew oneself at the age of eighty, to create a work like *Falstaff,* which has genius in it.' 'I hope that when you're eighty, you'll write better music.' The Kaiser later described Strauss to the conductor Ernst von Schuch as 'a serpent I've harboured in my bosom'. Strauss's view of the Emperor was that he wanted to impose his will every-where, but when he encountered resistance he withdrew in silence, which was more dangerous than his despotism. His inability or unwillingness to understand modern art of any kind was because he was surrounded by aca-demic cliques. The Kaiser occasionally wrote music. When someone joked about it, Strauss commented: 'One should never make fun of the composi-tions of crowned heads because one never knows *who* has composed them.' Strauss hated Berlin's 'moral hypocrisy – why shouldn't one have the right to say whatever one likes when one knows it's true?' And he detested the extension and augmentation of censorship in Berlin, with its redoubling of puritanism. He cited the removal of a Böcklin picture from a shop-window because it was considered 'indecent' – 'it's the Middle Ages. Fortunately, in music you can say everything, no one understands you.' Bach's Mass in B minor was so free, audacious and independent in each of its parts – 'how fortunate those words are there, to mislead people! Without that, to be logical, one should not allow it to be performed.' He could foresee (jocu-larly) the return of heretics being burned at the stake in Berlin – they had already made Siegmund and Sieglinde cousins, not brother and sister! This typical Bavarian once said he would like Berlin 'if it wasn't so full of Prussians'. His enthusiasm for Nietzsche won him no friends in the culture-reactionary court circles.

From Rolland we can draw the most vivid pictures of Strauss at this point of his career.[6] They liked each other, but Rolland was a fearlessly objective observer. They had first met at Wahnfried in 1891. In January 1898, Rolland attended a Lamoureux concert in Paris conducted by Strauss: 'a young man, tall and thin, curly hair, with a tonsure which begins at the crown of the head, a fair moustache, pale eyes and face. Less the head of a musician than that of any provincial Squireen. . . It was enough to see him at the end of the Beethoven symphony [Fifth], his great body twisted askew as if struck by both hemiplegia and St Vitus's Dance at the same time, his fists clenched and contorted, knock-kneed, tapping with his foot on the dais, to feel the malady hidden beneath the power and the military stiffness.' In April 1899 Rolland visited Strauss at his Charlottenburg flat – 'furnished with some taste – a large rough sketch for some German picture, interesting (nude man and woman). . . Very pale eyes; the moustache so fair as to be almost white. Speaks French with difficulty, but sufficiently. Tall, but holds himself with extreme lassitude. Childish and involuntary shyness in his smile and gestures, but one feels underneath a pride which is cold, self-willed, indifferent or contemptuous of the majority of things and people.'

In Düsseldorf a month later Rolland heard Strauss conduct *Ein Heldenleben* and noted 'something childish in his physiognomy, and something sickly in his thinness, his baldness, his round back, the worn-out and anaemic expression of his face'. Then in Paris, March 1900: 'He is younger in the face than last year. A face without a wrinkle, unblemished and clear, like that of a child. A big, shiny forehead, pale eyes, a fine nose, frizzy hair; the lower part of the face is slightly twisted; the mouth often makes an ugly pout, from irony or from displeasure. Very tall and with broad shoulders; but his hands attract one's attention, delicate, long, well-kept, and with something rather sickly and aristocratic about them which doesn't correspond to the rest of the individual, who is plebeian on the whole and rough and ready. He behaves very badly at table, sits by his plate with his knees crossed, lifts his plate near to his chin in order to eat, stuffs himself with sweets like a baby, etc.' In March 1906 Strauss conducted *Symphonia Domestica* in Paris. Rolland was present: 'He seems to become more and more untidy as the years go by. He conducts with his whole body – arms, head and behind together; at moments he seems to dance on his knees; he crouches down; he makes tense and pulsating movements, like electric vibrations, with his hands. . .he always looks bored, sulky, half-asleep – but lets nothing escape him. . . The impression he gives is pale, uncertain, eternally youngish, a little inconsistent. But when seeing him close to, at the concert, conducting his orchestra, I was struck by the *other* Strauss: his face is ageing, hardening, shrinking; it is acquiring and retaining an intense seriousness.'

During the 1900 visit to Paris, Rolland took Strauss round the Louvre and was impressed by his taste in art. 'We go through the Dieulafry galleries, which he greatly admires. He sings the praises of slavery, talks of Cheops, who decreed that the whole nation should spend sixty years building his pyramid, and says that his wife considers that to be a very good thing. Needless to add that he is not a great supporter of socialism, in which he does not believe. . . In the evening he comes to dinner. . . This time he is completely unaffected and calm and really likeable (although Clothilde [Mme. Rolland] – but not I – was shocked by the rather boorish lack of ceremony of his manners).'

On arrival in Berlin, Strauss did his best to bring some fresh air into the repertoire of the Court Opera. Towards the end of his first season (1898–9) he conducted *Die Fledermaus* (8 May 1899), its Berlin première, and on 14 January 1899 he introduced (as related in an earlier chapter) the only complete act of Chabrier's *Briséis*. Other new or unfamiliar operas he conducted were Fernand Le Borne's *Mudarra* (18 April 1899) with a cast including Emmy Destinn, Auber's *Das eherne Pferd* (5 May 1900), with Paul Knüpfer in the cast, Meyerbeer's *Robert le Diable* (26 April 1902), Weber's *Euryanthe* (18 December 1902), Schillings's *Der Pfeifertag* (17 September 1902), Bernhard Scholz's *Anno 1757* (18 January 1903), Hans Sommer's *Rübezahl* (15 February 1905), Humperdinck's *Heirat wider Willen* with Destinn (14 April 1905), Auber's *Der schwarze Domino* with Geraldine Farrar (28 October 1905), and the original *Leonore* of Beethoven (20 November 1905). In addition, of course, there were many performances of Mozart, including a new production of *Così fan tutte* (7 March 1905), and of Wagner.

Berlin gave him considerable freedom to conduct his own works elsewhere and he enjoyed the concerts he conducted in Berlin with the Tonkünstler-Orchester at which he championed new works, an example being the revised version of Sibelius's Violin Concerto on 19 October 1905 when Carl Halíř, the orchestra's leader, was soloist. Other contemporary

9 Rehearsing in the opera pit

composers whose music he conducted included Bischoff, Brecher, Bruckner, Bruneau, Chabrier, Elgar, Hausegger, Huber, D'Indy, Mahler, Mascagni, Pfitzner, Reger, Reznićek, Ritter, Schillings, Carl von Schirach (a theatrical director in Weimar whose son Baldur was to play a significant part in Strauss's old age), Stanford, Thuille – and himself. His views on the new works he conducted were expressed thus: 'Let time be the judge! No matter if a man is over-praised – it is better for twenty to be regarded too highly than for one to have the way barred to him. The main thing is that a man has the will and ability to do something.' In an article called 'Is There a Progressive Party in Music?', written in 1907, Strauss urged listeners to beware of 'fashionable catchphrases' like 'leader of the modernists'. He continued: 'In view of the fact, repeatedly confirmed by history, that a great artistic figure is accepted instinctively by the general public almost as a fact of nature, although they may not form any clear idea of his aims, the activities of any small group of experts forming what might be described as a progressive party are not of decisive importance. . . One should only beware of becoming confused by the fact that the same broad public gives as much tumultuous applause to things which are effortlessly pleasing, easily understandable and even banal as it gives to works which are artistically significant, novel and ahead of their time.' This, too, was the peak period of the partnership between Pauline and himself at concerts and recitals. In his Berlin period from November 1898 he wrote forty-two songs up to 1906 when Pauline retired, after which he wrote no *Lieder* until 1918. Several earlier songs were also orchestrated during this time.

Thus we can see that while Strauss was settling into his new post in Berlin, his creative endeavours were directed solely to *Lieder* and to toying with ideas for a ballet. But he hankered after a second opera, as his abortive attempts at various libretti have shown. Just before he left Munich in 1898 he met the satirist Ernst von Wolzogen, founder of the *Überbrettl* movement (cabarets in which political songs were the principal feature). Wolzogen soon realised how hurt Strauss had been by the failure of *Guntram* and how ready he was for revenge on bourgeois philistine opinions.

In a collection of Dutch medieval legends Strauss found an ideal vehicle called *The Extinguished Fires of Audenaarde*. This story tells of a young man who seeks help from a magician to win the love of a girl who has rejected him. She had promised him a night of love and to reach her he was pulled up the side of her house in a basket. Half-way up, he was left suspended for the whole of a winter's night and was jeered by the townspeople when lowered in the morning. The magician's plan is to extinguish all the fires in the town, letting it be known that they can only be re-lit from the flame which will spring from the girl's anus when she has been exhibited nude in the market square. Wolzogen was impressed, but realised it could not be staged as it stood. After hearing *Also sprach Zarathustra* hissed in Munich in 1899, he suggested to Strauss that they could set it in Munich, make the hero into the magician's apprentice and make the girl sacrifice her virginity to re-light the fires. Moreover, it will be known that the old magician, who never appears, had once been hounded out of Munich. Thus they could establish a parallel between Wagner and Strauss while at the same time having some fun at Wahnfried's expense, since they both disliked the deification of Wagner by Cosima. Strauss began to sketch the music in October 1900. Two months later the sketch was finished and orchestration occupied him from 1 January to 22 May 1901. The latter date was Wagner's birthday and Strauss inscribed the last page of the score blasphemously: 'Completed on the birthday and to the greater glory of the "Almighty!"'.

The score (and libretto) of *Feuersnot*, as the one-act opera was named by Wolzogen, is full of witty quotations and allusions (to *Die Meistersinger*, *Tristan* and *Parsifal* among others). Strauss quotes Munich folk-tunes, uses a children's chorus and develops the first signs of the light conversational style which he was to continue to perfect for the next forty years. Textures are often also light and airy, perhaps the influence (not for the last time) of Humperdinck's *Hänsel und Gretel*. A big waltz tune has an important function. Perhaps its satirical topicality is no longer pungent after nearly a hundred years, but it is such a delightful work – a favourite of Sir Thomas Beecham, who conducted its first and only English performances in 1910 – that its overshadowing by its two one-act successors is a pity. Its central feature is the monologue by the young magician Kunrad (Strauss) in which he harangues the people of Munich and, because the everlasting fire has failed him, asks how he is to show that he is the true apprentice of his master. Fine as this is, the greatest part of the score is the final love scene, an example of true Straussian radiance, often performed as a separate orchestral item.

Strauss described *Feuersnot* as 'a little intermezzo against the theatre . . . to wreak some vengeance on my dear native city'.[7] While calling it a 'by no means perfect work (especially in the all too unequal handling of the orchestra)', he suggested that 'it still introduces into the nature of the old opera a new subjective style at just the very beginning of the century. It is in its way a sort of upbeat.' Strauss was still talking and writing about *Feuersnot* to the end of his life. Clearly it had a special importance for him and one can hear, as one listens to it, that it was as seminal for him as *Manon Lescaut* was for Puccini. One can hear in it so much of what was to follow. Even parts of *Die Frau ohne Schatten* have their origins there. He went on raiding the score for the next forty years, irrespective of whether he was conscious of doing so. In *Feuersnot*, Strauss the opera composer stepped fully armed on to the stage. It has wit, charm and eloquence, all facets of his art which he continued to explore; and they all refer back to this underrated and productive score.

Unfortunately for Strauss in the year 1901, the libretto included passages which were bawdy and referred explicitly to what today we should call 'bonking'. Whereas Verdi encountered censorship trouble over politics in his operas, Strauss up to 1914 was to have the same trouble because of sexual and religious bigotry. His own employers in Berlin soon learned of the contents of the libretto of *Feuersnot* and let it be known that the opera's première could not be staged there. So we find Strauss writing to Georg Henry Pierson, artistic director of the Berlin Court Opera, on 11 April 1901 (before he had completed scoring the work), renouncing a Berlin Court Opera première for any of his dramatic works. And he kept his vow. He gave the *Feuersnot* première to Ernst von Schuch at Dresden, but not without some bickering over price:

So 1500 marks is still too much! O this theatre! To hell with all opera composing! . . . Perhaps I should send you something more for nothing? Say a fire-engine? So as to put out the Need-of-money-fire? . . . I find 1500 marks really not too much. Let Fürstner do as he likes, anyway. If it doesn't come off, then I can traipse off to Vienna, where Mahler will do anything if only I will give him the première. I shall change my name to Riccardo Straussino and have my works published by Sonzogno, then you'd agree to everything.[8]

Even in Dresden, alterations to the text were requested which Strauss refused to countenance. He wrote to Schuch on 17 November 1901, four days before the first performance: 'To deduct from the opera its mordant sharpness is to achieve a success through misunderstanding. This I would gladly forfeit: better a huge flop, in which case you will at least have thrown in the faces of that pack of philistines a few thorough coarsenesses and beneficial impertinences.'[9]

The Dresden first performance was a success: Strauss was so pleased that he gave the first performances of eight of his next eleven operas to Dresden. He conducted *Feuersnot* in Frankfurt on 3 December. He had been bluffing Schuch about Vienna. Although Mahler wanted to perform *Feuersnot*, he told Strauss he was not interested in a 'race' with other opera houses and in any case the libretto ran into censorship troubles. Its Vienna première, which Mahler conducted, was on 29 January 1902. The critical reception there was almost universally hostile, Hanslick writing of 'melodies like iron filings' and Max Graf in *Die Musik* (1 March 1902) referring to 'salvo after salvo from right to left, conservatives and radicals'. The fourth scheduled performance was cancelled, although Mahler slotted in another performance on 19 April. The Berlin première was delayed (through a singer's illness) until 28 October, when Emmy Destinn sang the role of Diemut. But after seven performances it was withdrawn because of objections by the Kaiserin. As Wolzogen wrily commented: 'After giving birth to seven children, she probably didn't have a high opinion of "Fa-la-la".' To his credit, Count von Hochberg, the Intendant, immediately resigned. The ban was then lifted and the resignation withdrawn.

Even if he complained grumpily to his parents, Strauss gloried in the publicity and notoriety aroused by the furore over *Feuersnot*, the sheep in *Don Quixote* and the battle in *Ein Heldenleben*. Wolzogen tried to interest him in a new libretto based on Cervantes with the failure-guaranteeing title of *Coabbradibosimpur oder Die bösen Buben von Sevilla*. Strauss mislaid it (it surfaced among his effects). He was already contemplating his next operatic subject. A young Viennese writer, Anton Lindner, whose poem *Hochzeitlich Lied* Strauss had set in March 1898 as Op. 37/6, sent him Hedwig Lachmann's prose translation of Oscar Wilde's play *Salomé* (written in

French in 1891) and offered to convert it into a verse libretto. Strauss asked for some sample scenes, but was unimpressed. He had already decided that Lachmann's version had possibilities and his copy, now in the Garmisch archive, shows that against the first line – 'Wie schön ist die Prinzessin Salome heute Nacht!' – he noted the introductory key of C sharp minor and inserted bar-lines as though the vocal rhythm had already come to him as he read. So when in November 1902 he attended a performance of Max Reinhardt's production of the play at the Kleines Theater, Berlin, with Gertrud Eysoldt in the title-role, and Heinrich Grünfeld remarked 'Surely you could make an opera of this?', he truthfully replied 'I am already busy composing it.' But it was not until 27 July 1903, on holiday in the de Ahna villa at Marquartstein, that he really got down to it, composing on an upright piano in the 'ironing room' on the ground floor and writing on the ironing table.

It would be true to say that the libretto for *Salome* is in effect Strauss's own. He saw the play's operatic potential and ruthlessly adapted it for his own purposes, cutting it nearly in half. Textual details distracting from the main thrust of the plot were eliminated, as were secondary characters, some of whose dialogue was reallocated elsewhere. Many of Wilde's flowery phrases, written for their effectiveness when spoken, were deleted and the lengthy debates on religious and moral issues were shortened. Changes were made in the order and choice of words so that they became more singable. Some other deletions were made in order to strengthen Strauss's view of his heroine as an innocent virgin. Thus her complaint in her first entry that 'it is strange that the husband [Herod] of my mother looks at me like that' continues in Wilde, but not in the opera, 'I know now what it means. In truth, yes, I know it.' It was perhaps prudishness, or knowledge that the opera would have a hard time with court censors, that led him to delete Wilde's lines (in Salome's final aria): 'I was a virgin and you deflowered me. I was chaste and you filled my veins with fire.'

Meanwhile, there were other preoccupations. In the spring of 1902 he went to England on a conducting tour. A particularly far-sighted summing-up of him was written by the critic of the *Manchester Guardian*, Arthur Johnstone, who was to die aged forty-three only two years later. Strauss, he said, 'seems to have an irritating effect on all critics, except a certain very small minority. . . He is enigmatic, Sphinx-like, a complex personality not to be conveniently catalogued. . . Those who assert that Strauss is a mere eccentric will sooner or later find themselves in the wrong. He has in a few cases played tricks on the public, but he is nevertheless a master-composer, in the full and simple sense of those words – a master-composer just as Mozart was.' Giving himself a brief holiday on the Isle of Wight, he began a new work on 2 May, heading the sketchbook 'Idea for a domestic scherzo with a double fugue on three subjects: "My home" (a symphonic self – and family – portrait; a little equanimity and a lot of humour). F major: Papa returns from travel, weary, B major: Mama, D major: Bubi, a mixture, but more like his Papa. Country walk for all three, cosy family supper. Mama puts Bubi to bed. Papa et Mama seuls: scène d'amour. Le matin: Bubi yells, joyful waking. . . Richard spends all afternoon working on a melody which was finally finished in the scene in the evening (doing and watching).' So began *Symphonia Domestica*, ironically to be interrupted by the threat of divorce over the Mieze Mücke misunderstanding (see chapter nine). This attractive subject pushed aside the stirrings of *Salome*. The composition-sketch was completed, aptly, the following June at Sandown when Pauline and Bubi joined him on the Isle of Wight while he recovered from a mild illness after conducting the first Strauss Festival in London in June 1903.[10] Orchestration was completed on 31 December 1903. (The Isle of Wight seems to have had a beneficial effect on Strauss. In his sketchbooks used there one finds waltz themes which later found their way into *Der Rosenkavalier*, *Intermezzo*, *Arabella* and *Capriccio*.)

On return from the 1902 visit to England, he began (on 13 July at Marquartstein) to sketch a choral work, a setting of Uhland's ballad *Taillefer* for soprano, tenor and bass soloists, chorus and orchestra. This was his offering to the University of Heidelberg where the Philosophy Faculty was to confer an honorary doctorate on him on 26 October 1903. He conducted the first performance of *Taillefer* in the Town Hall, Heidelberg, that evening. The honour gave him enormous pleasure and ever thereafter he signed his name 'Dr Richard Strauss'. In Britain this was considered a *nouveau-riche* gesture – imagine Vaughan Williams always signing himself 'Dr Ralph Vaughan Williams' – but to Strauss it was a sign that he counted in academic estimation. In 1900 the Prussian Royal Academy had refused to elect him as a member, although it recanted in 1909 when, with typical humour, Strauss informed his proposers that there must be some mistake 'unless, without my noticing it, all my disreputable fifths have turned overnight into meritorious sixths'. On hearing he had been elected he wrote again: 'Please forget the bad joke in my last letter. As an academician, one must cease making jokes and conduct oneself with the dignity and decorum befitting that high distinction. I shall devote all the summer to the study of proper behaviour.' *Taillefer* breaks no new ground, but it is excitingly, if pompously, written for a huge orchestra (145 players) and chorus, and its subject-matter (the Battle of Hastings) may well in this case have appealed to bombastic Wilhelmine sentiments at that period of naval expansion. Odd as it may seem, Mahler was '*especially* fond' of it (as he wrote to Strauss in March 1906).

Early in 1904, Strauss obtained leave of absence from Berlin to make his first visit to the United States, arranged by the piano firm of Steinway. Pauline accompanied him as soprano soloist and recitalist. He was awaited as the most talked-about composer of the day and he reserved the first performance of *Symphonia Domestica* for the visit. They sailed in the liner *Moltke*, arriving in New York on 24 February. Three days later a Strauss Festival opened in Carnegie Hall organised by Hermann Hans Wetzler (1870–1943), a conductor and composer who had settled in New York in 1892 and in 1903 had founded the Wetzler symphony concerts. The *Musical Courier* reported that the opening concert, at which Wetzler conducted *Also sprach Zarathustra* and Strauss *Ein Heldenleben*, was attended by 'everybody who counts in the culture of our metropolis. There were princes of finance, dictators of society, queens of opera, autocrats of the baton, lords and ladies of the piano and violin, and all the rest.' The writer described Strauss as 'the one great musical spirit which has made for something new since Wagner laid down his pen, the one pioneer who has tried to penetrate into the blue of unexplained heights'. He ended his long notice 'Vivat Richard Strauss, Imperator!' Also in this first concert David Bispham sang three Strauss *Lieder*, an adventurous choice, too: *Die Ulme zu Hirsau, Nachtgang* and *Das Lied des Steinklopfers*.

The Strausses gave their first New York recital on 1 March and went on to Philadelphia (4 and 5 March) and Boston (7 and 8 March). At the Boston concerts, Strauss conducted the Philadelphia Orchestra. The local critic was almost lost for words in admiration of the composer's interpretation of *Till Eulenspiegel* and *Tod und Verklärung*. Strauss returned to Boston on 19 April to conduct Boston's own orchestra in *Don Quixote* and *Don Juan*. Writing to his father next day he called it 'one of the greatest orchestras in the world'. He told Roland Tenschert in 1942 that this was the first time he had heard *Don Quixote* properly performed. 'I then said to myself: "that's the way it should sound". If each part does not come through, it's just chaos. It's just that everything is thematic as in a string quartet by Haydn.' The fourth and last concert of the New York Strauss Festival on 12 March included the first performance of *Domestica*, conducted by Strauss. There had been over a dozen rehearsals, all but the last two taken by Wetzler. (Strauss described the orchestra as a 'band of anarchists', but was pleased with it.) The work was received with such acclamation that two further performances on 16 and 18 April were arranged in Wanamaker's department store, where a whole floor was cleared and converted into a concert hall. This association of art and commerce caused a horrified reaction in Germany ('prostitution of art'), as did Strauss's comment: 'Earning money for his wife and child is no disgrace, even for an artist!' Today, we can only smile. Strauss did not conduct *Symphonia Domestica* in Berlin until 8 January 1905. He conducted it in Dresden on 8 March and in London on 1 April. Mahler had conducted it in Vienna on 23 November 1904.

From then until today, *Symphonia Domestica* has been a stumbling-block for those not fully committed to Strauss. While his critics acknowledge that music could be autobiographical, it seemed to them that autobiography so undisguised was 'tasteless'. A man describing making love to his wife, bathing their baby, quarrelling – this was embarrassing invasion of privacy. Similar objections were to be made to the opera *Intermezzo*. To Strauss, the family was the centre of his existence as man and musician and it was as natural to him as breathing to depict his family life in musical terms. But just as Till Eulenspiegel's exploits are of secondary importance to the brilliance of Strauss's musical invention, so there are features of *Symphonia Domestica* which are of far greater importance than its programme. In its quicksilver introduction, where the themes are introduced so casually and lightly, we hear a prefiguring of the operatic conversational style of

Intermezzo, Arabella and *Capriccio*. This is Strauss at his most light-fingered and buoyant, the music shaping itself naturally and (almost) without manipulation. Its structure is interesting, too. The first part is a sonata exposition, in the style of Liszt's B minor pianoforte sonata and Schoenberg's First Chamber Symphony where the constituent elements are recapitulated and developed in the *finale*. The subject of the work, too, far from being tasteless, was ahead of its time. Strauss here writes symphonic music – it is the only work he called a symphonic-poem instead of a tone-poem – about ordinary people. The *verismo* of the Italian opera composers was banishing gods and goddesses from opera and Strauss himself would introduce the telephone into an opera in 1924. In *Symphonia Domestica* the chimes of the household clock play an important structural as well as emotional role. It is a work that takes us close to his inner being, normally so well disguised.

After Strauss conducted *Domestica* in Paris on 25 March 1906, Rolland wrote: 'Whatever one may think of the first part . . . the end burns with joy, one can't resist it; I really think there's been nothing like it in symphonic music since Beethoven.' He had heard a performance in Strasbourg in 1905 and wrote to Strauss on 29 May: 'It seemed to me the most perfect and the most unified work of art you have written since *Tod und Verklärung*, with a quite different richness of life and art. . . The finale is full of joy and breadth such as you have rarely attained. . . What's the use of the programme, which diminishes the work and makes it puerile?. . . It's a regular symphony. . . Let music keep its mystery.' Strauss replied non-committedly: 'Perhaps you are right so far as the programme of *Domestica* is concerned; you agree entirely with G. Mahler, who completely condemns the principle of programme music.'

Strauss's reply to Rolland was written on 5 July 1905. A fortnight earlier, on 20 June, he had completed *Salome*, three weeks after the death of his father, aged eighty-three. Richard had played some of the score to the old man, who had commented: 'O God, what nervous music. It's like having your trousers full of maybugs.' This was the work which was to give Strauss worldwide fame far greater than he had hitherto experienced and it is the work which, in my opinion, is the apex of his pre-1914 period, notwithstanding the greater popularity of *Der Rosenkavalier*. More even than

Elektra with its moments of atonal harmony, *Salome* seems to me to be the most influential score Strauss ever wrote. It changed the nature of opera. It put Freudian psychology on the stage without knowing it. It summed up the *fin-de-siècle* era of decadence in the arts in a consuming yet detached analysis. And it exists in two versions, German and French. This extremely important fact has been overlooked in virtually all the many books written about Strauss. He himself never referred to the French version, as if he had forgotten about it because he realised it had no practical future. But its existence is another pointer to the compelling fascination the subject had for him; and it began with the letter to Rolland of 5 July in which he referred to completing *Salome* and added: 'Wilde originally wrote *Salomé* in French, and it is his original text which I want to use for my composition. I cannot entrust this work to a translator, but I wish to preserve Wilde's original, word for word.' Rolland advised him on the stresses and accentuation in French in great detail over the next weeks until Strauss completed the transcription in mid-September. He then read and corrected the vocal score, a task which took him until November. So we know Strauss was working on the French text and consequent adjustments to the music between July and September 1905 and that he completed the Dance of the Seven Veils on 30 August. This disposes of the theory, by those who regard the Dance as inferior to the rest of the opera, that it suffered because Strauss left it to the last when the white-hot inspiration of the rest of the work had cooled. I have no doubt he left it to the last because it was a detached orchestral interlude which he could compose quickly and fluently. Even so, it was written while the opera was fully occupying his mind and pen.

As Strauss worked on the French version his adaptation became more than a translation aimed at the commercial advantages of performance at the Opéra-Comique but 'a real French opera' in its own right, as he wrote to Rolland, 'a quite special French edition of my opera which does not give the impression of being a translation but of being a real setting of the original'. That was in September 1905. Two months later, thanking Rolland for his trouble, Strauss wrote: 'You will only get an idea of the full extent of my work when you have the German edition and can compare how I have modified the rhythm and melody to fit the character of the French language.' He was justified in his claim, for the two versions differ in many subtle respects

and the French version does sound like a French opera. It was first performed in March 1907 in a private performance at the Petit-Théâtre conducted by Walter Staram with a French cast. (It is curious that Rolland made
no mention of this in his diary.) Later in the month (the 24th) it was performed at the Théâtre de la Monnaie in Brussels. There was a performance
in New York at Oscar Hammerstein's Manhattan Opera two years later when
Mary Garden sang Salomé, having studied the role with Strauss. After that,
it disappeared until 1989 and a subsequent recording. Strauss had been over-
optimistic in thinking that singers and players would learn two versions of
the opera. When Strauss conducted *Salome* in Paris on 5 May 1907 it was
with the German text. In 1909 he approved a free re-translation into French
of Lachmann's libretto, adapted to fit the German vocal line. But if Strauss's
original plan proved impracticable, the existence of the French version is an
important consideration in his attitude to his opera.

Nothing else in Strauss's career matched the furore caused by *Salome*. The
clashes with the cast before the first performance in Dresden on 9 December
1905, when the first Salome (Marie Wittich) went on strike because 'I'm a
decent woman', are well documented – the delays she caused led to Strauss
threatening to place the première elsewhere. But Schuch brought off a fine
performance which the public vociferously acclaimed. Only the critics had
reservations. Other opera houses clamoured for the work. Mahler wanted
to produce it in Vienna, but the censor obstructed it 'for religious and moral
reasons'. (It is said that the main objector was Emperor Franz Josef's daughter Archduchess Valerie.) Mahler was prepared to resign over the matter –
and it may have been one of the straws which eventually broke the camel's
back in May 1907 – but Strauss wrote to him on 15 March 1906: 'For heaven's
sake do not let *Salome* give rise to a question of confidence! We need an artist
of your determination, your genius and your outlook too badly for you to
put anything at stake on *Salome's* account. In the end we shall attain our
ends without this!'[11] Strauss had been a little hurt that Mahler did not attend
the Dresden première – 'Where were you on the 9th? I missed you *very
much*' – and Mahler first heard the opera, which he regarded as a major masterpiece, in Graz in May 1906, when Puccini also attended. The following
morning at breakfast in their hotel, Strauss went up to Mahler's table and
reproached Mahler for taking everything, e.g. the [Vienna] Opera, too seri-

ously: 'he should look after himself better. No one would give him anything for wearing himself out. A pigsty that would not even put on *Salome* – no, it was not worth it!'[12]

In that Graz audience, too, was an unemployed man named Adolf Hitler. In 1939 the Nazis banned *Salome* in Graz, whereupon Strauss wrote to his relative, the conductor Rudolf Moralt: 'The idea that *Salome* is supposed to be a Jewish ballad is very humorous. The Reichskanzler himself told my son in Bayreuth that *Salome* was one of his first operatic experiences and that he raised the money to pay for his fare to go to the first performance in Graz by begging from his relatives. Literally!!'

In Berlin the opera waited almost exactly a year for its première there on 5 December 1906. Objections came from the Empress and other members of the royal family. Eventually Hülsen, the Intendant, suggested the anachronistic appearance of the Star of Bethlehem in the night sky (the events of the opera occur while Christ is a grown man) and all was well. Fifty performances followed in twelve months and Strauss was overwhelmed by Destinn's performance of the title-role, which she later sang with him in Paris. In London the censor (the Lord Chamberlain) required some altera-tions in the German text which were ignored during performance and, as the conductor Thomas Beecham remarked, went unnoticed. After one per-formance at the New York Metropolitan in 1907, the daughter of the financier J. Pierpont Morgan secured cancellation of the rest of the run and the opera disappeared from that theatre until 1934 (the Vienna Opera House did not hear it until 1918). Strauss conducted *Salome* in Turin at the end of 1906, but the first Italian performance had already been given in Milan, con-ducted by Toscanini. Strauss was there and wrote to Pauline that the con-ductor had 'with the aid of a mercilessly raging orchestra, simply butchered the singers and the drama (*à la* Mottl). It is a miracle it was nevertheless a success.'

But nowhere was there so much intrigue as for the first Paris performance of the German version in May 1907. Rolland noted the previous November that two cliques were wooing him, as a friend of Strauss, to influence the composer to favour their choice for the title-role, one of whom was the mis-tress of the production's financial backer. Strauss was not to be swayed: he brought Destinn. He arrived in Paris feeling unwell – 'trouble with my heart', he told Rolland. He was none too pleased with the orchestra at rehearsals and was disappointed that there were only three or four curtain-calls on the first night. Someone told him that the French President intended to confer the Légion d'Honneur on him. 'I have well deserved it', he replied. According to the journal of André Gide, although he said the remark might be apocryphal, Pauline was so upset by the relatively cool reception that she said to a neighbour at the opera: 'Well then, it's time to come back here with bayonets.'[13] Gabriel Astruc, the impresario responsible for taking *Salome* to Paris, hoped for ten performances, but only six were given. In a letter to Strauss's German-born English friend and financier Sir Edgar Speyer, written on 20 June 1907, Astruc said: 'I can confide in you that M. Strauss and his wife took up such an attitude *vis-à-vis* the members of the orchestra that it was impossible to give the projected number of per-formances.'[14] Strauss had said to Rolland on arrival in Paris: 'The smallest town in Germany has a concert hall, an orchestra, choirs, organs better than you have in Paris.'

Nevertheless, the reception accorded to Strauss on this occasion, the fuss made of him, is more indicative than anything that happened in his own country of the position he now held in the world of music. Not only did the President (Armand Fallières) go to the Théâtre du Châtelet for the première, but most of the Government and all the Parisian 'smart set'. In the audience were Jean de Reszke, Baron Henri de Rothschild, Otto H. Kahn, Sir Edgar Speyer, Gabriel Fauré, Albert Carré, Arthur Rubinstein, Camille Erlanger and others. Some French commentators criticised Fallières for this attention to Strauss because he had not similarly patronised French artists. But Joëlle Caullier, in her superb and illuminating study of the impact of German con-ductors on the French imagination between 1890 and 1914, points out that 'in 1907, the first Moroccan crisis had just been surmounted, coming close to war, and a good number of men were looking for ways of reviving the idea of a *rapprochement*, at least economic, between France and Germany. It is perhaps in the perspective of this *rapprochement* that one must place Fallières's gesture in conspicuously attending the *Salome* première with nearly all the government.'[15]

A week after the Paris première, Rolland found Strauss 'very nice, very good-natured . . . not a second of posing, not a premeditated gesture. . . He complains of his heart and of excessive tiredness. He doesn't lose much love over Paris, of which he has surely seen the worst sides. He again goes back over the story of the intrigues which surrounded *Salome*, that the part should be given to such and such a soprano because she was so-and-so's mistress. Then he complains about the anarchy in France: "I don't want to say anything about the Colonne orchestra", he said, "it played well". Thereupon he starts railing against republics, which he can't bear: France, America.' While in Paris he heard Dukas's *Ariane et Barbe-Bleue* and liked it. He defended Berlioz against French critics of the composer ('he has genius, too much genius, what does it matter?') and was indignant that none of Berlioz's operas was performed in France. To a Frenchman who said Saint-Saëns was a greater musician, Strauss replied: 'Yes, he writes better, but he has nothing to say.' When he attended a performance of Debussy's *Pelléas et Mélisande* he was baffled, even though he knew the score because he had studied it at Rolland's behest while working on his French *Salomé*. 'Is it always like this? Nothing more? There's nothing, no music. The harmonics are very subtle, there are good orchestral effects, it's in very good taste; but that's nothing at all. I consider it no more than Maeterlinck's drama, by itself, without music.' Ravel considered *Salome* 'stupendous', the most outstanding European work in the previous fifteen years. He always said he learned much from Strauss's scores. 'Strauss is the liberator who has been able to extend the liberties taken by Berlioz, and he has given the wind instruments a new importance, new at least for the time when he was writing. . . It's only his irresistible comic sense which sometimes saves his tunes from an excessively facile sentimentality.'[16]

The French critic Jean Marnold voiced to Strauss a frequent criticism of *Salome*, that the music for Jochanaan was 'commonplace'. Strauss, interestingly, at first denied it but then said: 'I didn't want to treat him too seriously. You know, Jochanaan is an imbecile. I have no sympathy at all for that type of man. In the first place I would have liked him to be a bit grotesque.' Nearly thirty years later, on 5 May 1935, Strauss wrote to Stefan Zweig: 'I tried to compose the good Jochanaan more or less as a clown; a preacher in the desert, especially one who feeds on locusts, seems infinitely comical to me. Only because I had already caricatured the five Jews and poked fun at Father Herodes did I feel that I had to follow the law of contrast and write a pedantic-Philistine motif for four horns to characterise Jochanaan.'[17] His dislike of religion and its adherents never wavered. Strauss's son Franz noticed that if conductors sentimentalised Jochanaan's description of Christ on the Sea of Galilee, Strauss would stamp his foot and urge them to speed up. Yet – another part of the enigma – the music for Jochanaan can sound impressive. Strauss was too much the natural dramatist, *au fond*, to damage a characterisation because of his prejudices, whatever he may have said. He was austere in his approach to *Salome*. His interpretation was powerful but the power was obtained with minimum effect. He objected to 'dramatics' in Salome's dance – 'no flirting with Herod, no playing to Jochanaan's cistern', he told the producer Erich Engel in 1930, 'only a moment's pause beside the cistern on the final trill. The dance should be purely oriental, as serious and measured as possible, and thoroughly decent, as if it was being done on a prayer-mat. Only with the C sharp minor should there be a pacing movement and the last 2/4 bar should have a slight orgiastic emphasis. I have only once seen the dance done really aristocratically and stylishly, by Frau [Marie] Gutheil-Schoder.' Not many of today's producers would satisfy him!

Strauss's search for an ideal Salome was life-long and perhaps he only found her towards the end with Ljuba Welitsch and Maria Cebotari. Writing to Stefan Zweig on 28 June 1935 after Cebotari's success as Aminta in *Die schweigsame Frau*, he described her as 'a dream come true' and added: 'How long did I have to wait with *Salome* – and am still waiting!'[18] What he admired in Gutheil-Schoder was her ability to combine childish naiveté with overpowering sensuality. Her voice lacked the warmth of Barbara Kemp and Maria Jeritza, but they had other drawbacks. While conducting *Don Giovanni* and *Die Zauberflöte* in Switzerland in 1917 with Elisabeth Schumann as Zerlina and Papagena, he had the idea that she could sing Salome – she had youth and childish charm and could also suggest a latent sensuality. Instead of the sixteen-year-old princess with the voice of Isolde, he suddenly wanted a light, capricious Salome. The soprano understandably protested that she could not sing such a dramatic role, but Strauss insisted that her voice coincided with his idea of the character. He offered to transpose anything that was in too low a key and, as he would be the conductor, he guaranteed to 'damp down' the orchestra. The experiment was never tried, but it remains a tantalising prospect, in line with Strauss's injunction that *Elektra* (and by implication *Salome*) should be conducted 'like fairy-music by Mendelssohn'. Herbert von Karajan remembered that Strauss once complained to him: 'Nowadays all the heavy voices are singing Salome. It's all gone out of control. I *don't* want this!' His ideal at that time, the conductor said, was Cebotari.[19]

Queasiness about *Salome* remains even in these permissive, liberal times. This can only be a tribute, however unwilling, to the potency of the music which, after nearly a century, has lost little or nothing of its power to shock. If the listener is proof against shock, he is liable to question whether *Salome* is art or kitsch. That, certainly, is a matter of taste. But it is a waste of time to inquire into the 'morality' or otherwise of *Salome*. This was of no interest to Strauss. He was a supreme story-teller, delighting in the mixture of good and bad and enjoying his virtuosic skill in raising Wilde's often tawdry imagery to the level of genius. Those who argue that Strauss coarsened Wilde by the use of Lachmann's translation should listen to the French version in which the music sounds often more refined, if less pungent and powerful. The opera is a study in obsession right from the start when the clarinet's roulade precedes Narraboth's declaration of obsession with Salome. After that it never lets up – Salome's obsession with Jochanaan, Jochanaan's obsession with hatred of Herodias, the Jews' with religious dogma, Herod's with Salome, Herodias's with revenge and finally Salome's with the severed head. And, let us never forget, Strauss's obsession with Pauline, for it is she who is there at the root of the opera, her capriciousness in Salome, her sharp edges in Herodias. The vocal line of each character depicts his or her personality: Salome's wheedling seductiveness and final crazed *Liebestod*, Jochanaan's ranting alternating with sanctimony, Herod's neurotic imaginings. *Salome*, for the first time in the history of opera, explored the mental pathology of the characters, much of this being achieved by the 105–strong orchestra which, like a stream of consciousness, tells us what is in the characters' hearts and minds before they know it themselves. *Salome* represents the period in Strauss's career when he could accurately be described as a man of his time (probably by accident). At the turn of the century the *femme fatale*, the sexually aware woman, obsessed writers and artists. One has only to think of Wedekind's *Erdgeist*, Gorky's *Nachtaysl*,

Zola's *Nana*, the poetry of Dehmel and Altenberg, the paintings and draw-
ings of Schiele, Klimt and Beardsley. Wilde's *Salomé* was part of this trend.

Hofmannsthal described *Salome* as Strauss's 'most beautiful and dis-
tinctive work' and amplified this by noting that 'in all its splendid impetu-
ous novelty, [*Salome*] was the irresistible upsurge and triumph of a *new*
composer'. The poet, as usual, was perceptive. The sheer beauty of the score
is often overlooked – much of it sounds (or should sound) light, transparent and subtly coloured. But neither can one overlook Rolland's perceptiv-
ity. Were it not for 'the magic of the instrumental richness', he thought the
music would be 'on the cold side'. Stravinsky thought Strauss could charm
and delight (as in *Der Rosenkavalier*) but could not move listeners 'because
he was never committed. He didn't give a damn.'[20] We come here to the
central factor in the enigma of Richard Strauss. Was there, as Hans Keller
said, a 'hole in the heart'?

How and why listeners are moved by certain music must remain a
mystery, deeply subjective. Those who are not moved by Strauss are those
who miss the element of spirituality in his music. An anti-religious composer, there is nothing of the spiritual in him. Nor was he much interested
in the conflicts of love and patriotic duty such as one finds in Verdi's operas.
One will not find in Strauss the ability to pierce the heart with the sudden
welling-up of nostalgic emotion one finds in the slow movements of
Dvořák's 'American' quartet and Cello Concerto. There is no immense quest
for 'the meaning of life' as there is in Mahler's symphonies. (Strauss once
remarked: 'Mahler is always seeking redemption. I don't know what I'm
supposed to be redeemed from.') Compared with Mahler and Dvořák,
Strauss was a detached artist, observing his characters either in his tone-
poems or his operas with a cool, Mozartian eye. Yet, like Mozart, he understood the human heart. One *is* moved by the Marschallin's fear of old age,
one *is* moved by Salome's descent into madness while she cradles the severed
head, one *is* moved by Elektra's recognition of the brother she believed dead.
Romain Rolland feared in 1907 that Strauss 'had been caught by the mirage
of German decadent literature. . . The difference between them and you is
the difference between an artist who is great (or famous) at *one* time (a
fashion) and one who is (who should be) great for *all* time. Of course one
must be of one's own time and reflect the passions of one's time. But after

all, isn't Shakespeare also of our time? . . . I mention Shakespeare to you, because I was thinking of him while listening to your *Salome*. In it you have spent a force of frenzied passion capable of following *King Lear*! And I was saying to myself "Why isn't it *King Lear*? What a *King Lear* Strauss could write! One would never have seen the like".'[21] Strauss told Rolland this letter had given him great pleasure. 'I am the sort of man to whom one can say everything, and who listens with pleasure to all comments, who is grateful for them when they are sincere and thoughtful and come from someone in whom one has entire confidence. You are right. The text of *Salome* is not good. I took it because I hadn't anything else and because I had something to say. What was I to do? I can't write my libretti like Wagner.'[22]

It is a major misjudgment to delude oneself with a belief that Strauss's music did not come from his heart for all his apparent nonchalant attitude towards composition. It came easily to him; he could compose anywhere – in hotels, gardens, trains. Ideas came to him on walks or even when playing cards. His sketchbook never left his side. Once a work gripped him, he would work far into the night. He *enjoyed* composing, and he was not always as self-critical as he might have been. He made light of it, but he was a profoundly serious artist. As Mahler observed of *Salome*, 'deeply at work in it . . . is a live volcano, a subterranean fire.' The subterranean fire gave us the greatest of Strauss – and *Salome* was the first great volcanic eruption.

12　Enter Hofmannsthal

Strauss was overworking in 1907. It was nothing for him to rehearse at the opera in Berlin in the morning, conduct or rehearse a symphony concert in the afternoon and conduct an opera in the evening. Next morning he would be on the train to another engagement. Some years earlier his father had warned him against 'assaulting your health in order to earn enough money to be able to live from your savings later, so as to do nothing but compose. Do you imagine that anyone can create anything of the spirit when the body is enfeebled?' Strauss replied that hard work never killed anyone. But on returning from Paris in May 1907, he conducted *Die Meistersinger* in Berlin and caught a night train to Cologne for a morning rehearsal of a concert. In the afternoon he collapsed and myocardial insufficiency was diagnosed. He went to the spa at Bad Neuheim and he began to think about a quieter life. Perhaps it was for physical rather than overtly psychological reasons that, around this period of his life, Strauss lost the decisiveness which one finds in his letters to his parents and in his dealings with the opera houses where he was first engaged. In its place come signs of weakness, failure of nerve, unwillingness to meet unpleasant truths head on and, also, a growing inner loneliness. He had told Rolland at the start of the century 'I am no hero, I am weak.' Increasingly, this manifested itself. He was known for his easy-going, phlegmatic attitudes, but these were not easily assumed. Every now and then a choleric temper, inherited from his father, would erupt fero-ciously. Colleagues knew that if Strauss suddenly went red in the face, they should beware.

Although the Kaiser never heard *Salome*, he remarked that it would do Strauss a great deal of harm. Strauss's comment has become famous: 'The harm it did me enabled me to build my villa in Garmisch.' He and Pauline had long wanted to return to Bavaria and for Strauss to concentrate on composition while still working as a guest conductor. They engaged an architect, Seidl, and planned the beautiful house at Zöppritzstrasse 42, Garmisch, in which they were to live for most of the next forty years.

The three-storey house, large but not overpoweringly so, stands in spacious gardens in the shadow of the Bavarian Alps. From his study window Strauss could see the Zugspitze and the Wettersteingebirge. It is a typical Art Nouveau villa, creamy-white in colour, with a pinkish roof and green-and-white shutters. Extra rooms were added in the 1920s. The interior is homely and comfortable yet with a certain grandeur. Books and mementos abound, and there are some fine paintings. Strauss also had a collection of local South German paintings on glass, some of which hang on the wall of the staircase. Also on this wall and on an upstairs landing are some deer's heads, trophies of the hunting enthusiasm of Strauss's son and daughter-in-law, an enthusiasm he did not share. While clearly the home of a rich and discriminating artist, it is also very much a family home.

Strauss had been working on a fourth opera since 1906. This was *Elektra*. Hugo von Hofmannsthal had begun to write his version of Sophocles's *Electra* in 1901. It turned out to be a very Viennese *fin-de-siècle* piece of work, influenced by Nietzsche's dark view of Ancient Greece, by Freud's *Interpretation of Dreams* (it is thought that Hofmannsthal did not read this book until 1904, but he knew of Freud's ideas) and by the obsession with the *femme fatale* which was in the air at that time – Wilde's *Salomé* and Sardou's *Tosca* in literature, for example, Klimt's *Judith* and Corinth's *Salome* in painting. Hofmannsthal showed an Electra living in squalor in the courtyard of the palace of Mycenae, planning a dreadful revenge on her mother Klytämnestra, Queen of Thebes, who had murdered her husband Agamemnon, Electra's father, by killing him with an axe in his bath and was now living with her fellow-conspirator Aegisthus. She awaits, too, the return of her brother Orestes who will do 'the deed' – the murder of Klytämnestra and Aegisthus – with the axe she has buried in the ground. When Orestes comes, she forgets to give him the axe but her feeling of triumph as the murders occur is so great that she dies, exhausted and spent, after her ritual dance. Where does Freud come in? Repressed sexuality, for one example. Because of her sacrifice of everything to the desire to avenge Agamemnon, Electra has killed her own sexual desires. 'Do you think', she asks Orestes, in the play but not in the opera, 'when I rejoiced in my body that his sighs and groans did not penetrate to my bedside? The dead are jealous; and he sent me hate, hollow-eyed hate, as a bridegroom.' Her sister Chrysothemis, on the other hand, who lives in the palace, yearns for marriage and children. She would like to forget everything from the past. 'Forget?' Electra retaliates. 'I am not a beast, I cannot forget.' The importance of dreams comes into the play, too. Klytämnestra asks Electra if she knows a remedy for the horrific nightmares which are destroying her. The sacrifice of a woman's life, your own, Electra replies, and describes in hideous detail how Orestes will kill Klytämnestra. 'Then you will dream no more, then I need dream no more.'

Hofmannsthal's play had its première in Berlin on 4 October 1903. It was produced by the thirty-year-old Max Reinhardt at the Kleines Theater with Gertrud Eysoldt as Electra. It is not known exactly when Strauss saw *Electra*, but it was probably at one of three performances between 21 October and 7 November 1905 when the play was revived at the Deutsches Theater. Some time later Strauss and Hofmannsthal met and Strauss mentioned his intention of setting *Electra* to music. On 7 March 1906, Hofmannsthal inquired if the composer was still interested. Strauss replied that he was 'as keen as ever' and had already cut the play (by about a third) into shape for a libretto. But he thought he ought to wait a few years because the subject was so similar to *Salome* and he needed to move further away from the style of that opera. As he put it in some recollections written in 1942, 'at first I was put off by the idea that both subjects were very similar in psychological content, so that I doubted whether I should have the power to exhaust this subject also. But . . . *Elektra* became even more intense in the unity of structure and in the force of its climaxes.'[1] Some of Strauss's doubts arose from his lifelong desire for contrast between one work and the next. Thus we find *Till Eulenspiegel* followed by *Also sprach Zarathustra*, *Guntram* by *Feuersnot*, *Symphonia Domestica* by *Salome*, *Elektra* by *Der Rosenkavalier*. Hofmannsthal, alarmed, protested that the subjects were not at all similar: *Salome* was 'a torrid mixture of purple and violet' while *Electra* was 'a mixture of dark and bright.' Strauss was not convinced and suggested some other subjects. But Hofmannsthal was nothing if not persistent and arranged a meeting in Vienna on 8 May 1906 at which he persuaded Strauss to go ahead. Apart from a few preliminary sketches, the music was begun in

10 With Hugo von Hofmannsthal at Rodaun, 1912

earnest while Strauss was on holiday at Marquartstein in June 1906. By December he had written enough to be able to play parts of it to Hofmannsthal, who wrote to a friend 'I think it will be very good.'

This holiday immediately followed the festival of the Allgemeiner Deutscher Musikverein at Essen where Mahler's Sixth Symphony had its first performance on 27 May. A young conductor, Klaus Pringsheim, was present and has remembered how, after a rehearsal, Strauss remarked, in his nonchalant way, that the movement (presumably finale) was 'over-scored –

the Strauss of the *Salome* score. . . The word made Mahler thoughtful (because Strauss had said it). He kept coming back to it, talked much about his relationship to Strauss. . . He spoke not of himself but of the other, whom he had never failed to recognise, asked without envy, without bitterness, almost humbly, reverently, what might be the reason why everything came so easily to that other and so painfully to himself; and one felt the antithesis between the blond conqueror and the dark, fate-burdened man.'[2] In another description of the same episode Pringsheim quoted Mahler as saying that 'Strauss needs only a few rehearsals, yet the music always "sounds right", whereas he, Mahler, toils with the orchestra in countless rehearsals to bring out everything as he wants it – but when could he really say after a performance that nothing was lacking?'[3] Even Alma Mahler, no admirer of Strauss, said that although Mahler was surrounded by admirers, including Mengelberg, at Essen 'the only one who still mattered for him was Strauss. Beside him all the rest were more or less insignificant.' It was after one of the Essen rehearsals that, according to Alma, Strauss unfeelingly burst in on Mahler, who was in an agitated state, to tell him he would need to conduct a funeral march or something of the sort before the Sixth because the local mayor had died. If this occurred, it was surely a practical forewarning such as one professional conductor would give to another who was his friend. In his copy of Alma's book, which he read in Switzerland in 1946, Strauss wrote in the margin: 'I don't pretend to understand such things.' He called the book 'the inferiority complexes of a loose woman' (*Minderwertigkeitskomplexe eines liederlichen Weibes*).

Progress on *Elektra* was slow in 1907 because of Strauss's involvement with the Garmisch house, productions of *Salome* and his many guest-conducting engagements which in this year cut into his holiday. He also had his duties at the Berlin Court Opera (sixty operas a season). He orchestrated in the winter months. By 7 October 1907 he had reached the Recognition Scene between Elektra and Orestes. At this point he suffered a 'creative block' and began to score what he had already composed. Probably at this point he was again thrown by the similarities between *Salome* and *Elektra*, 'the tremendous increase in musical tension to the very end: in *Elektra*, after the Recognition Scene, which could only be completely realised in music, the release in the dance – in *Salome*, after the dance (the heart of the plot) the dreadful apotheosis of the end'.[4] By Christmas Day he had scored up to Klytämnestra's entrance.

Although the two men collaborated during composition of *Elektra*, it is not technically a collaboration. As will be seen, Hofmannsthal contributed some extra lines at Strauss's request, but the libretto is strictly Strauss's work, a skilful reduction of the play. Before continuing with the history of the opera's composition, it is worthwhile looking in some detail at what Strauss did to the original play. He used his copy of the fifth edition, published in 1904, and, as was his custom, made musical annotations in the margin. These were either themes or indications of orchestration. His cuts were made for two main reasons, to speed up the action and condense it for musical purposes and to simplify some of Hofmannsthal's psychological implications which he felt could not be put across to an opera audience. He also made one very significant change. Throughout the play Hofmannsthal never uses the name Agamemnon. The king is an un-named presence: Electra refers always to *Vater*. Strauss knew this would confuse an opera audience and ensures that in her first monologue Elektra names him six times – and the opera begins with the orchestra playing a fortissimo D minor motif of four notes which obviously declaims 'Agamemnon'.

Strauss left the opening scene – a virtuoso 'conversational' prologue, giving the audience the information they need – and Elektra's first monologue almost uncut. Four of the five serving-maids describe Elektra's behaviour, how at the same hour each day she 'wails for her father, making all the walls resound'; how, if they go too close to her, she spits at them and calls them flies and bluebottles; how she screams at them that she is nurturing a vulture in her body; and how a food-bowl is put for her with the dogs and how Aegisthus strikes her. Only the fifth maid speaks up for her – 'Is she not a King's daughter?. . . Not one of you is worthy to breathe the same air as she breathes' – and she is taken into the house and beaten up. Elektra appears alone, at the same hour of the day as Agamemnon was murdered. She describes his murder and how she, Chrysothemis and Orestes, will avenge him. Then they will dance around his grave and over his murderers' bodies. 'I will raise my knees high, step by step.' The sopranos who sing Elektra are thus faced by Strauss with a long and testing aria on their entrance, with no 'warming-up' in brief exchanges such as he allowed Salome. And, at the reference to the dancing, we hear for the first time the heavy waltz rhythm of the cathartic, trance-like dance which precedes Elektra's death in the final scene.

The next scene, between Elektra and Chrysothemis, was cut by half by Strauss. He fashioned it so that it concentrated on Chrysothemis, the dweller in the present, the 'now', as opposed to Elektra's preoccupation with past and future. Chrysothemis has come to warn Elektra that 'they' are planning to lock her away in a tower. Who are 'they', Elektra asks. Do you mean the two women, 'my mother and that other woman, that weakling Aegisthus, he who performs heroic deeds only in bed?' She advises her sister not to prowl around listening to what people are saying but to 'sit at the door like me and wish for death and judgement to fall on her and on him'. No, Chrysothemis says, she cannot live like that. She blames Elektra's hatred for their being kept in 'this prison'. She wants to have children, even by a peasant. She envies the serving-maids when she sees them pregnant. What is the point of living as she does – 'our father is dead, our brother is not coming back'. In the play, Electra has much more to say. When Chrysothemis tells her that Klytämnestra has had a dream about Orestes, Electra replies that it is she who sends this nightmare to her mother: 'I visited this dream upon her.' She then describes how Orestes will come and kill Klytämnestra with the axe. Strauss, with his flair for what would work best in opera, transferred this speech to the next scene, her confrontation with Klytämnestra, when she tells her mother directly that it is she who sends her the bad dreams.

Klytämnestra is one of the juiciest roles Strauss created. It is short, but contraltos or mezzo-sopranos will ever be grateful to him for the chances it gives them to make audiences' flesh creep. However, it has to be said that the first singer of the role, Ernestine Schumann-Heink, disliked the opera. It was 'a horrible din', she declared. 'We were all mad women.' Strauss thought she was miscast. But quite apart from the music, which singing-actress could resist the stage-direction's description of the queen on her entrance? – 'in the dazzling torchlight her wan and bloated face seems more pale against her scarlet robes. She is leaning both on her confidante and on an ivory stick, encrusted with jewels... The queen is completely covered in precious stones and charms. Her arms are covered in bracelets, her fingers with rings. Her eyelids are exceptionally large and it seems to cause her considerable effort to keep them open.' Strauss himself had something to say about how the role should be enacted. This was written later in his life and in some degree contradicts the stage direction: 'Klytämnestra should be shown not as a weather-beaten elderly witch but as a handsome, proud woman of about fifty whose disintegration is not a physical but a spiritual affair.'

Hofmannsthal's Klytämnestra differs in several important respects from Sophocles' Clytemnestra. In the Greek play her dream is not the major event it is in the Austrian. She believes that her murder of Agamemnon was justified: she was avenging the killing by Agamemnon of her first daughter, Iphigenia. She is not sent nearly mad by nightmares about her son Orestes but is genuinely upset by the (false) news of his death. Hofmannsthal converted her into a case-book study from Freud, a decadent woman who has deliberately shut out the memory of the murder of her husband. In the play, but not in the opera, she says: 'First it was to come, then it was past – in between I did nothing.' Strauss's cuts in this, the fourth, scene amount to about forty per cent of Hofmannsthal's original. He reconstructs it so that it can become virtually a second monologue for Elektra into which he inserts her vision of Orestes murdering Klytämnestra and Aegisthus that, in the play, Elektra relates to Chrysothemis. To balance this insertion, Strauss cut twenty-four lines from Elektra's taunting of Klytämnestra where he no doubt felt that Hofmannsthal was justified in repeating himself but it would be difficult for a composer to do so. Throughout the opera, his aim was always to tauten the action and increase the tension.

In June 1908, Strauss sent the score orchestrated up to the Recognition Scene to the publisher Fürstner, who had bought the rights to the opera for 100,000 marks. From April 1907 to the early part of 1908, Strauss was also much occupied with the building of the Garmisch house. He and Pauline moved in in June 1908 and on the 21st Strauss, after a nine-months hiatus, began to compose the Recognition Scene. He asked Hofmannsthal for additional text for 'a great moment of repose' for Elektra after her *Es rührt sich niemand. O lass deine Augen mich sehn . . . !* ('No one is stirring. O let my eyes gaze at you . . . !' F.S. p. 272, three bars before cue no. 149a). The poet provided eight lines within three days, his first piece of creative work for Strauss as librettist. The scene was finished by 6 July.

The Recognition Scene contains the most lyrical music in the opera. Elektra's happiness at the thought of Orestes 'doing the deed' – a waltz again – is crowned when Orestes and his tutor are invited into the palace to deliver their message. Klytämnestra's dying screams are heard as Aegisthus returns from the fields. Elektra greets him and, taunting him, leads him towards his doom in the palace by torchlight to a waltz which is a very obvious anticipation of *Der Rosenkavalier*. When Chrysothemis runs from the palace describing the scene of carnage, Elektra says to her: 'Can I not hear it? Not hear the music? It comes from me.' From this point, the opera goes to its conclusion in a great waltz-sequence as Elektra revels in her triumph. 'I must lead the dance.' It is her dance of death. At this point Strauss asked Hofmannsthal for some extra lines for a duet between the sisters as they exult together. But apart from Chrysothemis's cries of 'Orest' as she hammers on the palace door, the orchestra has the last word for thirty-nine bars, something Strauss did not emulate until *Daphne* thirty years later.

The letters from Strauss to Hofmannsthal about *Elektra*, although few in number, ideally illustrate the relationship between the two men which was to continue for another twenty years. Although Hofmannsthal was a playwright, Strauss was the more practical man of the theatre. He was mystified by the lay-out of the scene for the killing of Klytämnestra and Aegisthus:

Surely Orestes is *in* the house. Surely the front door in the middle is shut. Chrysothemis and the serving maids hurried off on p.88 *into the house on the left*. On page 91 [after the murder of Aegisthus] they are 'rushing out madly.' Out of where? The left or through the middle? Page 93: Chrysothemis comes running out. Out of which way? Through the courtyard gate on the right? What for? Surely Orestes is in the centre of the house! Why does Chrysothemis run back in on p.94? Why is she at the end beating at the front door? Surely because it is barred? Do please answer my questions in detail.[5]

The composition sketch was finished by 20 August and the full score on 22 September. To Ernst von Schuch, who was to conduct the first performance on 25 January 1909, Strauss wrote: 'The end is quite juicy.'[6] In his memoir on *Elektra*, he was 'almost tempted to say' that the opera 'is to *Salome* what the flawless and stylistically more uniform *Lohengrin* is to the inspired first venture of *Tannhäuser*. Both operas are unique in my life's works; in them I penetrated to the uttermost limits of harmony, psychological polyphony (Klytämnestra's dream) and of the receptivity of modern ears.'[7] The Wagner parallel seems unnecessarily harsh; although *Elektra* is now generally regarded as the greater work, the sheer colour, drama, novelty and intensity of *Salome* set it apart. The theory that after *Elektra* Strauss shied away from 'modernity' and retreated into a cosy world free from atonality is rubbish. One cannot call *Der Rosenkavalier* a turning-back because *Elektra* was not the apex of some steadily planned creative development in Strauss's style. It was another example of the contrast he needed and required. Strauss was not systematically evolving towards an *avant-garde* style, as Schoenberg did. His style was flexible according to the expressive demands of the subjects he chose – and the more contrast there was (as in his *Lieder*), the better he liked it. So in *Elektra*, he found the gruesome music to illustrate Klytämnestra's nightmares just as he had found the appropriate music for the adventures of Till Eulenspiegel and Don Quixote and for Salome as she leans over the cistern to hear what is happening to Jochanaan. In many respects, *Salome* is a more progressive score than *Elektra*, which is structurally nearer to a number opera. The Klytämnestra music sounds atonal or whole-tone, but is in fact tonal, as analysis of the chords can prove. By a paradox, the *avant-garde* is also conventional. Even before she describes her nightmare, the sensitive ear will notice several contrasting stylistic influences: anticipations of *Der Rosenkavalier*, echoes of *Das Rheingold*, even a bit of Delius-like chromaticism.

Elektra involved Strauss in no really radical change of style or method beyond what had served him so well in *Ein Heldenleben*. Klytämnestra's nightmare aria, though, is a special case, one of the most extraordinary pieces Strauss wrote. Beginning with the metallic clanking and rattling of the ornaments with which Klytämnestra bedecks her wracked body, the music becomes bitonal and atonal as she recounts her dream that her bone-marrow is melting and that 'something' crawls over her as she tries to sleep. Strauss's genius as an illustrative orchestrator can match every exotic overtone in Hofmannsthal's text (although in cutting the play, Strauss deleted many of the overtly sexual lines, as he had also done in *Salome*). But the music is not merely graphic virtuosity; it comes from the depths of Strauss's psyche and his torment, so well disguised by his own outward nonchalance, that his mother was mentally unstable.

The scenes between Klytämnestra and Elektra and the two scenes between Chrysothemis and Elektra are the first of many superb confrontations between two women singers in Strauss's operas. In the first scene for the sisters, the normal sensual desires of woman for man are expressed but in the second there appears the unnatural quasi-lesbian attitude of Elektra towards her sister. Arabella and Zdenka, loving sisters, are psychologically not worlds removed from their hating classical ancestors; Elektra's monologues of obsession with blood and revenge are savage forerunners of the Marschallin's musings on the passage of time in *Der Rosenkavalier* and Countess Madeleine's reverie on words and music in *Capriccio*. Yet they are all sisters under Strauss's skin. Even in a score that is whip-lashed and blood-soaked, the wit in Strauss surfaces irresistibly. As Elektra taunts Aegisthus and lights his way to death, she does so to a pre-run of the music with which Octavian-Mariandel teases Ochs. Elsewhere, too, there are anticipations of the waltz rhythms of *Der Rosenkavalier*. Elektra's crippled, stilted dance of death, foreshadowed in her first aria, is a waltz every bit as savagely distorted as Ravel's climax to *La Valse*. Few composers have known themselves and what they wanted to do more clearly than Strauss. He saw all that the topically Freudian text of Hofmannsthal's play offered him and he had the technical and psychological armoury with which to meet its challenge. With *Salome* and *Elektra* he had done all that he felt was in him to do for emotional cripples: it was for others to probe more analytically. With the interval of a third he drew the family tree of Agamemnon's tragic clan; with a rising fourth he imprinted Elektra's recognition of her brother indelibly on the history of opera; with the tension between C minor and C major in almost every scene in the opera, he delineated the murdered Agamemnon and the atonement for his murder; and with chords of E flat minor and C major he brought down the curtain on his one implacable tragedy. In reflecting upon the harmonic relationships in *Elektra* we need again to quote Glenn Gould: 'Through all of Strauss's works there runs one prevalent ambition, the desire to find new ways in which the vocabulary of key-signature tonality can be augmented without at the same time being allowed to deteriorate into a state of chromatic immobility.'[8]

Today we no longer react to the music of this great opera with the expressions of horror that greeted it in 1909 – 'barbaric dissonance', 'the nadir of ugliness', etc. But its power to grip us and to rivet us to our seats with appalled fascination is undiminished. And we recognise the now familiar Strauss elements: three superb parts for women's voices, a fine baritone role and, above all, an orchestral score of astonishing virtuosity and brilliance. Much of the sound may be blood and iron, but there are also *scherzo*-like episodes when the texture becomes like chamber-music – 'fairy music by Mendelssohn', as Strauss said. The orchestra is the largest Strauss used in an opera, with over sixty strings balanced by over forty woodwind and brass which include bass oboe, E flat clarinet, two basset horns, eight horns (four doubling Wagner tubas), bass trumpet and contrabass trombone. The twenty-four violins and eighteen violas are each divided into three sections, but six violas are asked to double on violin. Strings and horns are the prominent sound, but listen for the marvellous use of the Wagner tubas when Klytämnestra makes her entry – they suggest a wounded animal. In a work lasting less than two hours, it is deplorable that the habit of making cuts in certain scenes has become a tradition. Strauss disapproved. He calculated the effects in *Elektra* exactly, and the structure is harmed by cuts. 'Unity of structure' is what had attracted him to the play.

Next time Strauss ventured into Greek mythology it would be to entangle it with the *commedia dell'arte*. His ears pricked up in February 1909 when Hofmannsthal casually let slip that he had been drafting a scenario for an opera which 'contains two big parts, one for baritone and another for a graceful girl dressed up as a man. . . Period: the old Vienna under the Empress Marie Theresa.' The world of *Der Rosenkavalier* was evolving; and the point about *Elektra* is that Strauss did not need to travel very far to enter it. Both operas, if the truth be told, belong to the Vienna of 1900. The point, sometimes overlooked, about *Der Rosenkavalier* is that it was the first libretto Hofmannsthal wrote specifically for Strauss to set to music. With this 'comedy for music', the great partnership – comparable with Mozart and da Ponte and Verdi and Piave – began. Fortunately most of their collaboration was conducted by mail, so the fascinating relationship between them can be studied in depth. Their personalities were markedly different. Hofmannsthal, ten years younger than Strauss, was moody, insecure, priggish, introverted, a loner. Sometimes, as he wrote in 1909, his work could be held up for two or three weeks by what he called 'a slight but most deplorable nervous depression'. Strauss was self-confident, practical, good-natured and level-headed. Some writers have suggested that two such contrasted men did not really like each other. Many expressions of affection and respect in their letters contradict such a theory. They met comparatively rarely, but this was not because of animosity nor because, as is sometimes said, Hofmannsthal disliked Pauline and therefore refused to stay at Garmisch. He needed solitude and distance – 'space', as today's vogue-word has it – and preferred staying in a hotel to being a house-guest. In their correspondence they maintained for over twenty years a formality unthinkable today – it was always 'Dear Dr Strauss' and 'Dear Herr von Hofmannsthal' – just occasionally 'My dear Friend' or 'Dear Poet' from Strauss. 'Richard' and 'Hugo' – never! It was Strauss who realised the potential in their partnership. In his first letter about *Elektra*, written in Berlin on 11 March 1906, he asked for 'first refusal' on anything 'composable' that Hofmannsthal might write, adding: 'Your manner has so much in common with mine; *we were born for one another* [my italics] and are certain to do fine things together if you remain faithful to me.'[9] Hofmannsthal's attitude is epitomised in a letter to his friend Count Harry Kessler written after the première of *Elektra* in 1909:

I hope I shall be able to exert a certain influence on him. In this unusual relationship, it is my duty to guide him in a certain sense. I have more understanding of art than he has, or perhaps it is a question of a more elevated, a better taste. He may well be my superior in energy or in actual talent, but that is beside the point.

Strauss in 1945 said that Hofmannsthal had 'educated my often not wholly unexceptionable taste', but the poet misjudged the musician, perhaps because he did not know him all that well. Strauss's knowledge of paintings and of literature from Goethe to many modern writers was the equal of Hofmannsthal's, but he did not parade it.

When the news leaked out that Strauss's next opera after the scandals of *Salome* and *Elektra* was to be a comedy set in eighteenth-century Vienna, opera houses queued to include it in their repertories. The first performance of *Der Rosenkavalier* in Dresden on 26 January 1911 was one of the great operatic evenings of the sunset period before the First World War. So many people wanted to attend the fifty Dresden and thirty-seven Vienna performances during 1911 that special trains were run. In the Munich carnival, nineteen Knights of the Rose, dressed in silver silk, rode in procession. Cigarettes and champagne were named *Rosenkavalier*. Still today a train of that name crosses part of Europe daily.

Most accounts of the genesis of *Der Rosenkavalier* begin with Hofmannsthal's letter to Strauss dated 11 February 1909 in which he mentions an 'entirely original scenario' and adds that 'Count Kessler with whom I discussed it is delighted with it.' Kessler (1868–1937) was a German diplomat, scholar, journalist and director of the Cranach-Presse in Weimar. Hofmannsthal was staying with him in Weimar in February 1909. The discovery in 1988 of Kessler's diaries for the period 1906–9 reveals the large part he played in planning the plot of *Der Rosenkavalier*. Kessler told Hofmannsthal of the operetta *L'ingénu libertin* (1907) by the French composer Claude Terrasse (1867–1923) for which the librettist Louis Artus had borrowed episodes from Louvet de Couvray's novel *Les aventures de Chevalier de Faublas* written in 1781. Kessler outlined a scenario based partly on Molière's *Monsieur de Pourceaugnac* about a self-important provincial who goes to Paris for a young wife, Sophie. 'He felt that was something he could do for Strauss', Kessler wrote. 'The money such a comedy could earn for him and Strauss would enable him to pay for his children's education.' On 12 February he and Hofmannsthal worked all day on the script – 'Hofmannsthal's and my work fits together so well that it is sometimes difficult to tell it apart.' Next day they went to Berlin where Hofmannsthal gave Strauss the scenario.

Entries over the next few days pinpoint familiar aspects of the plot of *Der Rosenkavalier*. For example, 'in the first act P. [Pourceaugnac, who became Ochs] can give the notary his instructions while on the right side the Marquise has her hair set and a flautist plays a languishing tune'. There is also this important earlier diary entry on 11 February: '[Hofmannsthal] has found a reason why Faublas is dispatched to Sophie as a bride-messenger to announce – according to ancient Viennese custom – the visit of the bridegroom and present her with a silver rose. This would start the second act, a beautiful and delicate contrast to the coarse Pourceaugnac.' There is little doubt that Hofmannsthal himself invented this 'ancient custom', although he probably borrowed the idea from some noble family's coat of arms. He changed Faublas into Octavian.

Strauss's enthusiastic response to the first scene of the *Rosenkavalier* libretto is well known: 'It'll set itself to music like oil and melted butter: I'm hatching it out already. You're da Ponte and Scribe rolled into one' (21 April 1909). A month later: 'My work is flowing along like the Loisach: I am composing everything – neck and crop' (including, at one point, a stage direction!). Part of the reason for Strauss's relaxation at this time was that he had been granted a year's sabbatical in 1908–9 from the Berlin Court Opera. He had been promoted to General Music Director in 1908. Although he was conducting at festivals and in concert-halls, he was enjoying a year's relief from the strain of conducting operas month after month. He returned to his Berlin duties in October 1909 and on the 24th conducted the 25th performance of *Elektra* in the city (Leo Blech had conducted the first Berlin performance on 15 February). His first appearance as conductor at the Vienna Opera, on 19 June 1910, was with *Elektra*.

The shape of things to come (frequently) showed itself in July 1909 when Strauss told Hofmannsthal that 'as it stands I can't possibly use the second act. It is not well planned and is flat . . . too much on one level.' He suggested changes to the action after Ochs's entrance which Hofmannsthal accepted without demur. Most of what amuses and delights audiences was devised by Strauss. 'Your criticism was definitely most helpful and beneficial', Hofmannsthal wrote. Strauss explained: 'My criticism is intended to spur you on, not to discourage you.' To Kessler, Hofmannsthal confessed regarding these changes that 'I was dismayed at first, but then I came more and more to accept them. The act has certainly gained a great deal from them. . . I am very grateful to Strauss for this. . . Given the accuracy of his instinct, I can be sure that it is essentially right.' But when Strauss first played part of Act 1 to him, Hofmannsthal was annoyed by the fortissimo accompanying Ochs's description of the girls on his farm falling back on the hay when he touches them. He wrote to Kessler: 'He is such an incredibly unrefined person, he has such a frightful bent towards triviality and kitsch. . . An extraordinarily mixed character, but vulgarity rises in him as easily as groundwater.'

Hofmannsthal would not write and Strauss would not compose during the winter, so the *Rosenkavalier* correspondence ceases between September 1909 and March 1910. Strauss said he would start to orchestrate Acts 1 and 2

11 The Presentation of the Silver Rose: a page of the autograph MS of Act 2, *Der Rosenkavalier*

in Berlin on 1 October – 'tedious task!' His next letter, 2 May 1910, signalled beginning of composition of Act 3. A fortnight later his mother died, aged seventy-two. His next letter to his librettist discloses misgivings about the plot of Act 3 after the Marschallin's arrival at the inn – 'too broad, too scattered, everything in orderly succession instead of one thing bursting on top of another'. Here, too, Hofmannsthal was co-operative. At the last minute he began to worry that after Ochs's final exit, interest waned and there were longueurs. He proposed cuts. Strauss reminded him: 'It is at the conclusion that a musician, if he has any ideas at all, can achieve his best and supreme effects – so you may safely leave this for me to judge.' He was as good as his word, for the final section of the opera includes the great Trio – its theme a slowed-down version of the waltz which accompanies Mariandel's 'Nein, nein, I trink kein Wein' in the inn – and the duet for Sophie and Octavian which Strauss composed *before* Hofmannsthal wrote the words for it ('something Mozartian', was Hofmannsthal's description, 'a turning-away from Wagner's intolerable erotic screaming'). The poet had raised no real objections to the toning-down of Ochs's boasts of his amorous activities in the hay requested by the Dresden Intendant, Count von Seebach, when he was sent the libretto (he also decreed that the Marschallin and Octavian must be *out* of bed at the beginning of the opera). Strauss made some of the alterations in the libretto but allowed the original to stand in the piano and full score – 'our purpose is not to weaken our comedy but simply to bluff those people who read the libretto *in advance* with malicious intent!'

Part of the enormous success of *Der Rosenkavalier* – Strauss always spelt it *Rosencavalier* – was attributable to Alfred Roller's marvellous sets and costumes, which were retained beyond the Second World War. For the Dresden première, the bass for whom the part of Ochs was written – Richard Mayr – was not released by Vienna Court Opera and the local producer, Georg Toller, was unable to cope with the stage action. Max Reinhardt took over anonymously – he had been invited there by Strauss, who naively could not imagine why Toller was furious. He wrote to the conductor Schuch in November 1910: 'I couldn't possibly have foreseen that so intelligent a man as Toller would not have been simply delighted to have been helped by a Reinhardt. Even today I would be ready to learn like a schoolboy from you or Mahler or anybody else without a thought of being knocked off my pedestal.'[10] The opera's effectiveness as a 'comedy for music' owes almost everything to Strauss's understanding and knowledge of the theatre and of what would work on the opera stage. Early in planning of the work, he pointed out that audiences would wonder how on earth, in Act 3, the Marschallin of all people would turn up out of the blue at an inn in the seedier part of Vienna. He, not the librettist, inserted a stage direction during the confrontation between Ochs and the Police Commissioner instructing Ochs's bastard son Leopold (a mute role) to run off through the centre door. He returns just after the Marschallin arrives and receives a nod of approval from Ochs. (Even so, this detail often escapes notice unless the producer makes it obvious.)

Although *Der Rosenkavalier* is not Strauss's greatest opera, there is no doubt that it is the best loved. Nothing is likely to displace it as the public's favourite. It has a good plot, it is both touching and funny, it has glorious tunes, it has characters who come to vivid life and enter one's life like old friends, it is (or should be) a visual delight and it has a wonderful libretto. Yet it is, on fuller inspection, flawed. Its plot has loose ends. It also, as Strauss admitted, has longueurs, notably in the middle of Act 3. Hofmannsthal, for his part, was always dissatisfied with the way Strauss had set parts of the text – 'in the wrong style altogether', he complained. The burlesque chorus of Faninal's servants in Act 2, for example, was written 'to be rattled off in burlesque fashion, i.e. in the transparent Offenbach style; what you did was to smother it with *heavy* music and so to destroy utterly the purpose of the words, the deliberate pastiche of an operetta. The fun of this passage has ceased to exist. . . Similarly at the end of Act 1. Out of the footmen who turn up one after the other [when the Marschallin has sent them to call Octavian back], uttering their brief messages with pronounced Bohemian accent, you have made a sort of brief chorus of huntsmen, which always strikes one as quite terrible at this juncture. The exit of the Baron in Act 3 offends, I feel, no less gravely against the style of the whole work.'[11] That was written in June 1916 – it rankled!

Some of the greatest singers of the twentieth century have given extra life and credibility to the roles of the Marschallin, Octavian, Sophie and Ochs: something of their personalities seems to linger in the music as a perpetual challenge to their successors. Yet all the other parts are as sharply and vividly drawn. Where in music is there a more accurate description of *nouveau riche* pomposity than in Faninal? The Italian conspirators, Valzacchi and Annina, are given music of Rossinian sparkle and gaiety as they whisper, wheedle and change sides as easily as they change key. Sophie's duenna, fussing, excitable, maternal; the landlord of the inn; the lawyer – all are characterised with the surest touch. The opera's music is a wonderfully unified composite of its several models – Wagner and Mozart obviously, but also Johann Strauss. The use of the waltz – a dance still banned at the Kaiser's stuffy court when the opera was written – is at once tribute to *Die Fledermaus* and smack in the eye for *Die lustige Witwe* of Lehár, of whose music and its success Strauss was contemptuous and perhaps a bit jealous. Strauss showed in *Der Rosenkavalier* that a comic opera could be written in an advanced musical idiom. The waltz, as has often been pointed out, is an anachronism in *Der Rosenkavalier*. But the whole opera is an anachronism. The Vienna of the 1740s is a Vienna invented by Hofmannsthal and is in reality a post-Freudian Vienna (equivalent of Edwardian London). The music glances at the eighteenth century but belongs essentially to the twentieth. Yet, paradoxically, attempts by producers to update the opera to the time of composition or to move it into the nineteenth century fail. To succeed, it needs a pastiche eighteenth-century setting for Strauss's Bavarian parody of Vienna. The work must not be coarsened. 'Viennese comedy, not Berlin farce', Strauss said in his memoirs, but in one respect he always risked the farcical element gaining the upper hand through the contradictory nature of the characterisation of Baron Ochs, whom he mod-elled on Verdi's Falstaff. He visualised him as 'a handsome country Don Juan, almost 35 years old, a nobleman (though somewhat coarsened by country life) who can behave himself correctly enough in the Marschallin's salon'. What, by pinching her maid's bottom? The trouble is that Ochs's music runs counter to Strauss's idealised view of him. Strauss advised Schuch before the first performance: 'Light, flowing tempi, without com-pelling the singers to rattle off the text. In a word, Mozart not Lehár.' Strauss also remarked 'Sentimentality and parody are my line of country' and the best performances of *Der Rosenkavalier* are those in which the essential ele-ments of lightness and parody are paramount. The *Tristan* quotation in the erotic introduction to Act 1 and in the first scene sounds this parodistic note at the start. This love will not end in a *Liebestod* but in living to love another day, when the tears have dried.

It is a mistake to regard *Der Rosenkavalier* as whipped cream and *Sachertorte*. It is a hard-iced cake – harmonically sometimes more advanced than *Elektra*. Something is wrong if it sounds too luscious. There is a citric tang in the harmony, an acerbity in some of the string-writing, disillusion in the celesta's chime. Hofmannsthal may have been dewy-eyed about love at first sight, but Strauss was more cynical. The coldness Rolland found in *Salome* and the detachment in *Elektra* are there in *Der Rosenkavalier*. As an example: at the end of the Presentation of the Rose in Act 2, everyone's favourite bit of Strauss when the raptures of the young love of Octavian and Sophie fill the theatre from gallery to stalls, the E flat clarinet interjects a phrase heard earlier in association with Octavian's sexual intercourse with the Marschallin and the same phrase, slightly varied, accompanies the subsequent primly proper conversation between Octavian and Sophie. Strauss is telling us, I believe, that Octavian is just as much a roué, though still in embryo, as Ochs. His love for Sophie will not last (the celesta tells us that). There is more, too, to the Marschallin than the *grande dame* whose looks are beginning to fade. She is capable of ruthless cruelty – in her treatment of Octavian when he returns in Act 1 and in her crushing rebukes to Ochs in Act 3. (She has, after all, given his recital of his amours in Act 1 tacit approval. She is certainly not shocked.) Yet she melts our hearts in the Trio, that marvellous vocal setpiece which – paradoxically, like the other great setpieces in the opera such as the Presentation and the three Sophie-Octavian duets – is still conceived instrumentally, the voices another strand in the orchestral texture. The legend in the Strauss family is that when Strauss was working on the Trio at the piano, searching for a way to continue what he had started, Pauline called from another room 'Go on, go on.' 'Isn't it getting too long?', he replied. 'No!' she answered. 'Go on, go on!'

Within a month of the Dresden performance, *Der Rosenkavalier* was staged in Nuremberg, Munich (1 February 1911), Basle and Hamburg. There followed Milan, Prague, Vienna and Cologne (where Strauss first conducted it, on 17 June). The London première, conducted by Beecham, was on 29 January 1913 and the New York Metropolitan première on 9 December 1913, conducted by Alfred Hertz. It did not reach Paris until 1927, a proposed 1915 production having been cancelled. The Vienna critics disliked the work intensely ('cheap, low-class wit') but it had thirty-seven performances there in eight months. The Milan première was conducted by Tullio Serafin. The waltzes were hissed and booed because the Scala audience tolerated them only in ballet and fights broke out in the audience. Berlin, where Strauss had given up his post as general music director in 1911 to become a regular guest conductor, heard it first on 14 November 1911. Hülsen, the Intendant, had at first told Strauss 'That's not the text for you' but was eventually won over after he had insisted on some bowdlerisation. Neither Hofmannsthal nor Strauss minded much, as long as the opera was performed. It was such a success that the Kaiser attended a performance, the only Strauss opera he heard. He remarked 'That's no music for me!'

Strauss, writing to Hofmannsthal in July 1911, promised 'very beautiful décor' in Berlin, but when the poet saw it he complained about 'the insult of the crude blue curtain on to which a painter, practised in lavatory decoration, has daubed figures *from the work itself* – this, translated into your sphere, is like a player-piano strumming the principal passages of your music in the theatre-bar or in the cloakroom while people are taking off their hats and coats.' He thought the Berlin production 'pervaded with the most thick-skulled barrack-room spirit' and that its 'drill-sergeant thoroughness and vast expense of money' had trampled out all subtle charm and flattened all emphasis 'to drab monotony'. The Berlin performances were uncut. Strauss had been furious to learn that, as soon as he had left Dresden, Schuch began cutting the opera, something for which he was notorious. The composer wrote an angry letter threatening legal action if the cuts were not restored except for those he had sanctioned. In another letter he pointed out to Schuch that he had overlooked a good long cut in Act 3 where the action was delayed for several minutes. He meant the Trio. Schuch was not amused. (In a letter to Franz Schalk in September 1921, Strauss described Schuch as 'a greatly talented conductor, but in other respects a very modest subaltern of a Kapellmeister'.)

The 'intelligentsia's' attitude to *Der Rosenkavalier* is summed up by a quotation from a letter to Hofmannsthal from Thomas Mann, written after the Munich première, conducted by Felix Mottl. Mann and Strauss did not like each other. The novelist described the composer as 'the sort of person

12 The first singers of the Act III Trio in *Der Rosenkavalier*, Dresden 1911: (L to R) Minnie Nast (Sophie), Eva von der Osten (Octavian), Margarethe Siems (Marschallin)

you might meet in a skittle-alley, who happened to have talent' and Strauss regarded Mann as 'a boring patrician'. Mann told Hofmannsthal he had read the libretto beforehand with delight in its 'grace and delicacy'. He went on:

But what in God's name do you really feel about the way Strauss has loaded and stretched your airy structure? A charming joke weighed down by four hours of din! ... Where is Vienna, where is the 18th century in this music? Hardly in the waltzes. They are anachronistic, and put the stamp of operetta on the entire work. Would that it were one. But it is the most prestigious type of music drama – and as Strauss has not the slightest comprehension of Wagner's skill in not burying the declamation in the gigantic orchestra, not a word can be heard.

The last point may well have been true, because Mottl was notorious for allowing the orchestra to 'drown' singers.

Of more musical importance is the opinion of musicians younger than Strauss. In the audience at some of the Vienna performances of *Der Rosenkavalier* was Anton von Webern, then aged twenty-seven. He wrote to his friend and mentor Arnold Schoenberg (aged thirty-six) that Strauss's opera 'pleases me less and less. I am inclined to pass the harshest judgment on it, but on the other hand there does indeed exist with Strauss such an immense virtuosity in everything which Pfitzner and Reger, for instance, do not possess. At any rate, he certainly amounts to more than they.'[12] (Webern himself in 1910 had composed his own radical *4 Pieces*, Op. 7, and the *2 Songs*, Op. 8, worlds away from Strauss.) Webern in the summer of 1911 had organised financial aid for Schoenberg, who had left Vienna and his teaching commitments to escape from the rabid anti-Semitic behaviour of a neighbour. His leaflet appealing for donors had forty-eight signatories, including Strauss. Since *Der Rosenkavalier* and Schoenberg's *Six Little Pieces*, Op. 19, both belong to 1911 and this is the year when Strauss's 'retreat' from modernity is charted, this is the moment to examine the relationship between the two composers.

Schoenberg was living in Berlin in 1901 when he was engaged by Ernst von Wolzogen, librettist of *Feuersnot*, as conductor-composer at his satirical cabaret *Überbrettl*, performed in a house in the Alexanderplatz. Wolzogen, we may safely suppose, gave Schoenberg an introduction to Strauss, who obtained him a teaching post at the Stern Conservatory and promised to look at the score of the tone-poem *Pelleas und Melisande*. He also gave him

work copying the parts of his own enormous choral work *Taillefer* and recommended him to other composers for similar work. Schoenberg was twice
awarded scholarships of 1,000 marks a year by the Liszt Foundation, of
which Strauss was a trustee. Strauss described Schoenberg's music as 'a bit
overcharged at present' but as having 'great talent and gifts'. In 1903
Schoenberg left for Vienna but kept in touch with Strauss. He hoped Strauss
might conduct one of his works at his Berlin concerts, but Strauss said the
'madly conservative' audience would not accept them. Offered the *Five
Orchestral Pieces*, Op. 16, in 1909, he found them incomprehensible but told
Schoenberg: 'I have courage, but your pieces are such daring experiments in
colour and sound that for the moment I dare not introduce them to the
more than conservative Berlin public.'[13] They last met at a Berlin concert
conducted by Strauss in February 1912. Schoenberg and Webern went to see
Strauss at the end. 'He was very friendly', Schoenberg wrote in his diary, 'but
I was clumsy. I was embarrassed like a 15-year-old schoolboy.' By this date
Strauss knew the direction in which Schoenberg was moving, but this did
not prevent him supporting the younger man, for 'one never knows what
posterity will think about it'. He became a trustee of the Mahler Foundation,
established after his friend's death in May 1911, and agreed on three occasions that 3,000 kronen should be paid to Schoenberg. But in a letter to
Mahler's widow Alma, he wrote: 'The only person who can help poor
Schoenberg now is a psychiatrist . . . I think he'd do better to shovel snow
instead of scribbling on music-paper.'[14] It was an injudicious remark and
even less judicious to write it to the feline Alma, who immediately relayed it
to Schoenberg. When invited to 'write something' for Strauss's fiftieth birthday in 1914, Schoenberg refused. He quoted Strauss's remarks and added:

It seems to me that the opinion I myself and indeed everyone else who knows these
remarks is bound to have of Herr Strauss as a man (for here is envy of a 'competi-
tor') and as an artist (for the expressions he uses are as banal as a cheap song) is not
suitable for general publication. . . He is no longer of the slightest artistic interest to
me, and whatever I may once have learnt from him, I am thankful to say I misunderstood. . . I cannot refrain from mentioning that since I have understood Mahler (and
I cannot grasp how anyone can do otherwise) I have inwardly rejected Strauss.[15]

But, as will be seen later, Schoenberg defended Strauss in 1946 from accusations of Nazism.

13   The *Ariadne* crisis

After *Der Rosenkavalier*, Strauss never enjoyed an overwhelming triumph. Its worldwide success was such that it would always have been a hard act to follow. But although he remained the leading figure in German music and the appearance of every new work he wrote was a major event, the zenith had been reached. Ironically his next opera was to be a radical advance on anything he had attempted and is one of his greatest achievements. Yet *Ariadne auf Naxos* did not at first interest him and he wrote it more from a sense of obligation than from inspired enthusiasm. The most frequent criticism of Strauss is that after *Elektra* he retreated into the cosy rococo world of *Der Rosenkavalier* and ceased to be a 'progressive' composer. This is to take a very simplistic view of modernism. In fact Strauss's time-travelling into the eighteenth century in *Der Rosenkavalier* and into the *commedia dell'arte* in *Ariadne auf Naxos* was a move ahead of the pack. Stravinsky, Prokofiev, even Schoenberg and, in England, Vaughan Williams (with his Violin Concerto) all wrote works which looked back to a baroque era. And all the Strauss operas after *Ariadne* are distinguished by their originality of concept and, in many respects, execution.

Before the première of *Der Rosenkavalier*, Strauss was badgering Hofmannsthal for work for the summer. He hankered after *Semiramis*, but Hofmannsthal was hostile to the idea. A letter from Garmisch on 17 March 1911 mentions Strauss's anxiety to hear about 'the little Molière piece.' In his reply, Hofmannsthal referred to 'the 30-minute opera for small chamber orchestra which is as good as complete in my head; it is called *Ariadne auf Naxos* and is a combination of heroic mythological figures in 18th century costumes with hooped skirts and ostrich feathers and, interwoven into it, characters from the *commedia dell'arte*.' He also outlined the plot of what was to become *Die Frau ohne Schatten*, 'a magic fairy-tale with two men confronting two women and for one of the women your wife might well, in all discretion, be taken as a model. . . Anyway, she is a *bizarre* woman with a very beautiful soul *au fond*, strange, moody, domineering and yet at the same time likeable.' (From that, no one could deduce that Hofmannsthal disliked Pauline. He obviously understood her.)

By mid-May Strauss was getting impatient. He had even been in touch with the Italian poet Gabriele d'Annunzio, hoping for a libretto on 'an entirely modern subject, very intimate and psychologically extremely nervous'. Nothing came of it, but Hofmannsthal was alarmed when news of it reached him. To give himself work, therefore, Strauss was, as he put it, 'torturing myself with a symphony – a job, when all's said and done, that amuses me even less than chasing maybugs'. He had taken up the sketches made in 1902 of his *Artist's Tragedy*, based on the 'love-tragedy' in the life of the artist Karl Stauffer (see chapter eleven). These sketches are headed: *The Antichrist: An Alpine Symphony*. The connection with the *Artist's Tragedy* can be deduced from Strauss's customary commentary. Thus he noted the artist's 'child-like religious feelings towards the power of nature', but this matures into 'initial independent thinking and first attempts, then transition to fugato in G minor'. *The Antichrist* is a reference to Nietzsche's book of that name written in 1888. Its stance appealed to Strauss, who was confirmed in his assumptions by another book, Leopold von Ranke's *German History during the Reformation*. Christianity, Strauss noted, was only capable of being prolific 'for a certain time', which was why the German nation could only gain renewed vigour by being liberated from Christianity. These thoughts were confided to his diary on 19 May 1911, the day after the death of Gustav Mahler, an event which deeply upset him. He was unable to work for days and would scarcely speak. 'The Jew Mahler could still be uplifted by Christianity', he wrote. 'The hero Richard Wagner descended to it again as an old man, under the influence of Schopenhauer. Are we really once again as we were at the time of the political union of Charles V and the Pope? Wilhelm II and Pius X? I will call my *Alpine Symphony* the Antichrist, because in it there is moral purification by means of one's own strength, liberation through work, worship of glorious eternal nature.' These ideas – human creativity and Nature – are essentially Nietzschean. But how do they link with *Eine Alpensinfonie*? Also in the sketchbooks of this date is the plan for a four-movement work headed *The Alps*, which it can be presumed was shorthand for *The Antichrist: An Alpine Symphony*. The movements are outlined in some detail: I. Night: Sunrise/ascent: woods (hunt)/waterfall (alpine fairy)/flowery meadows (shepherds)/glacier. Thunderstorm/descent and calm. . . II. Country joy and dance. III. Dreams and ghosts (after Goya). IV. Liberation through work: artistic creativity.

Clearly, the fourth movement is the Antichrist idea and III probably became the section named *Vision*, the most unsettling music in the work, which immediately follows the arrival on the summit. Perhaps unwilling to confess too much in public, Strauss dropped *The Antichrist* from the title and concentrated the work into the one-movement form of I, thus retaining his original starting-point for the *Artist's Tragedy*. The climbing of a mountain acts as a simile for a man's journey through life. It was, though, too much to expect that the average member of a concert audience would search for the philosophical basis of the music he was hearing presented by an orchestra of at least 123 players and a title which invited a pictorial response. There is, of course, no contradicting that Strauss's orchestration is so graphic that the symphony can be accepted solely as a description of mountaineering, with its dangers, elation and natural beauty. 'I have finally learned to orchestrate!' he declared at rehearsals of the work and undoubtedly the work represents a high-water mark of his genius in this respect. Such movements as the waterfall, the mists obscuring the sun and the beginning and end of the work which depict night ('as though the eye had to get used to the dark', Strauss said) are miracles of illustration in music. Those unsympathetic to Strauss jibed at the symphony as 'a tourist's guide to a day in the mountains', and the easy melodic flow of the music encourages a superficial response. These critics overlook, or miss, the archlike symphonic development, as elaborate as anything he had previously attempted. In their anxiety to label the work as 'bombastic naiveté' (or some such phrase), they overlook that 'On the summit', far from being the work's towering climax, uses less than half the orchestra, and is only a short-lived triumph, subsiding into a tender oboe solo over tremolando strings, which is followed by the veiled mystery of the 'Vision' section. Another Strauss paradox – all is not what it seems. In recent years, when performances and recordings have increased in number, there has been more chance and hence more readiness to listen for this masterpiece's deeper meaning and hidden significance. Far more than *Also sprach Zarathustra*, it is Strauss's most Nietzschean composition. He laid it aside in 1911, completed it on 8 February 1915 and conducted the first performance in Berlin on 28 October 1915 with the Dresden Court Opera Orchestra to whom, with the Dresden Intendant Count Nikolaus Seebach, it is dedicated. He wrote to Hofmannsthal: 'You must hear the *Alpine Symphony*. It is really quite a good piece!'

In mid-May 1911 Hofmannsthal let Strauss know that progress on *Die Frau ohne Schatten* would be slow. But he now reverted to his 'little Molière piece'. Hofmannsthal wanted to write something as a thank-offering to Max Reinhardt for his help in the production of *Der Rosenkavalier*. His first idea was to provide a short operatic work to be performed as an intermezzo or *Divertissement* in a Molière play which Hofmannsthal would himself adapt for the Berlin stage. Such musical *intermèdes*, in Molière's day, were performed between the acts or at the beginning or end of the action. Initially, Hofmannsthal decided to adapt *La Comtesse d'Escarbagnas*. But on a visit to Paris he had seen *Le bourgeois gentilhomme* and had realised that, for the Turkish entertainment M. Jourdain (the *bourgeois gentilhomme*) plans for his guests after a sumptuous dinner-party, he could substitute the opera *Ariadne auf Naxos*. He would jettison the sub-plot of the play and the opera would be performed in Jourdain's presence and be punctuated by brief remarks from him and other spectators. He sent Strauss a draft libretto on 19 May. The composer replied next day. Shocked by Mahler's death, he could muster only tepid enthusiasm: 'The first half is very nice. . . For the dances . . . one could write some pleasant salon music. I shall enjoy the thing very much and I am sure I can bring off something striking.' Two days later he sent Hofmannsthal his requirements for set numbers. He showed most interest in a 'great coloratura aria' for Zerbinetta, leader of the *commedia dell'arte* troupe and a character taken from Molière's *Les Fourberies de Scapin*. She should be sung by someone like Selma Kurz, Frieda Hempel or Luisa Tetrazzini. This horrified Hofmannsthal. The fee for one such star, he said, would swallow half of Reinhardt's gross takings each night. By this time Strauss had sketched most of the incidental music for the Molière play and hoped to have the opera ready by 1 July. He had in mind an orchestra of twenty players (eventually increased to thirty-seven). Yet he was still not much interested by the project. 'You probably know my predilection for hymns in Schiller's manner and flourishes à la Rückert. Things like that excite me to formal orgies and these must do the trick where the action itself leaves me cold. Soaring oratory can drug me sufficiently to keep on writing music through a passage of no interest.' Was ever composer so honest about his abilities or so percipient about his own limitations?

Hofmannsthal was beginning to be displeased. He was only undertaking this work as a favour and a service to Strauss and Reinhardt, he said. But the squall passed and Strauss the practical asked on 10 June how Hofmannsthal proposed to effect the transition from play to opera. There would be a linking-scene in prose, the librettist replied, in which the Dancing Master and Composer talk about the public and the critics while the stage is being set for the opera and the singers are making-up and trying out their parts. It was not until five weeks later that he had the idea of Jourdain sending his footman with the instruction that the comedians' entertainment and the opera should be performed simultaneously, causing immediate friction between the opera singers and the harlequinade led by Zerbinetta. In the meantime, the completed *Ariadne* libretto was received by Strauss on 14 July. 'I like it well enough', he wrote. Hofmannsthal, on holiday at Aussee in the Salzkammergut, was piqued by this cool reception. He wrote a long letter explaining the 'meaning of this little poetic work'. It was about fidelity, like *Elektra*. Ariadne/Elektra was opposed by Zerbinetta/Chrysothemis. Zerbinetta could belong to any man, Ariadne to only one. Ariadne gives herself to Bacchus, believing him to be Death but he is both Death and Life at once. To Zerbinetta, he is just a new lover to replace the old one. Bacchus had been wounded by his affair with Circe, but the impact on him of Ariadne's love, even though she mistakes his identity, 'I need not expound further to an artist such as you.'

Strauss's reply was masterly. It was, he said, a beautiful letter. Now he understood the piece because the action was described so wonderfully that 'a superficial musician like myself' could now tumble to it. But if that was the case, what about the audiences and the critics? Shouldn't the piece itself be as clear as Hofmannsthal's explanation? Anyway, perhaps he was out of sorts. He had been alone in Garmisch for four weeks, Pauline being away, and had not touched a cigarette for all that time – 'let the devil be cheerful in such circumstances!' Hofmannsthal, who seems to have had no or very little sense of humour, was mollified, but pointed out that the critics had not understood the libretti of *Elektra* and *Der Rosenkavalier*: 'the essence of poetic meaning comes to be understood only very gradually.'

The contrasts between the two men are brightly illuminated by these exchanges. For all his slightly priggish attitudes, Hofmannsthal was afraid of losing Strauss. 'I like you very much indeed, I enjoy working for you, and I owe you much that is beautiful, agreeable and good', he began one of his letters. What brought their relationship to a crisis-point was not so much the genesis of *Ariadne* as Strauss's early realisation that Reinhardt's Berlin theatre would be totally unsuitable for the production of the play and opera. For one thing, its pit was inadequate for even thirty-seven musicians. In November 1911 Strauss told Hofmannsthal he would discuss with Reinhardt whether he was in a position to stage *Ariadne* at all: 'I still don't see where he's to get his orchestra and singers from.' This frightened Hofmannsthal. 'Wild horses will not get me to carry out this adaptation of Molière and the introductory scene unless Reinhardt is to produce it. . . A world première of this work at some Court theatre or other would mean a complete flop.' Six weeks later he confided to Strauss how much it meant to him that Reinhardt should produce it in the Deutsches Theater, Berlin. His letter requires ample quotation:

Remember how much is at stake between the two of us who have been brought together by something higher, perhaps, than mere accident. . . You would be doing a grave injustice to the work *and to me* if, without absolute and compelling necessity (such as cannot emerge for several months), you were to take away the original première . . . from the one theatre for which, and for the special qualities of which, I have devised and executed it in every detail. This 'opera', with its subtle stylistic make-up, with its profound meaning hidden beneath the playful action, framed as it is by the Molière piece, a fact itself symbolic in intention (for Jourdain stands for the public), is a conception of the most fragile, the most uncommensurable kind. It is one of my most personal works and one I cherish most highly. It . . . can only exist, or come into being, where a theatrical genius of a superior order knows how to weld the parts together. . . That in this case *you* should find it possible to disregard everything that matters to me . . . to force me into a theatre where I could not appear without a sense of debasement, this *does* touch me; the mere thought that you on your part should entertain such a possibility does hurt me, and hurts me more than just momentarily. Here I find myself misunderstood and injured by you at the most vulnerable point in our relationship as artists. . . How in such circumstances am I to devote myself to the task of writing out another project of a similar kind? How am I to write a single line of *Die Frau ohne Schatten* if, over this affair, you not only upset my own relations with Max Reinhardt. . .but face me with the certain prospect of having to abandon altogether every hope of Reinhardt's assistance in the preparation of this future work, subtle and allergic to all routine as it is bound to be. . . What can stimulate me again and again is the prospect of the beauty which will be called into being by a union of our two arts. . . But . . . the painful memory of the spectacle offered at the Dresden and Berlin productions of *Elektra* . . . is one thing I have repeatedly had to suppress by force, otherwise I might have stopped working in the middle of the second act of *Rosenkavalier* . . . *I beg of you, do not inflict on me this injury*; do not injure us both, do not injure our relationship! If you now estrange me from yourself, you can find in Germany and abroad men of talent and rank who will write libretti for you, but it won't be the same. . . The subtly conceived exiguity of this play . . . will be lost, meaningless, a tattered rag in incompetent hands. Only in Reinhardt's, yours and mine, can it grow into a singing flower, the incarnation of dance. . . Everyone concerned must stake his life, the impossible must become possible . . . I will go with you through anything, my dear Dr Strauss, but never let me see you, in matters of art, choose the most convenient alternative in preference to the higher, the richer possibilities; it would not be like you. It would be acting against your own anarchic nature as a genuine artist. As soon as this were to happen, you would cut yourself loose from me for ever; for I am meant to associate myself with what is best in your character, and not to do convenient business with you.[1]

Well might Strauss have remembered that Hofmannsthal had once written to him regarding *Ariadne* that 'when two men like us set out to produce a "trifle" like this, it has to become a very serious trifle'. The start of the letter in which he must have replied to Hofmannsthal's outpouring is missing. But in the section that survives he remarks that 'surely it's not my fault' that the Deutsches Theater was not an opera house. He had written to Reinhardt to say that *Ariadne* could not be done in that theatre. 'This fact is unalterable', he told his librettist, 'and we've *got* to reconcile ourselves to it.' There was no question of dropping Reinhardt himself, but 'where with Reinhardt and an operatic cast with whom I wouldn't risk failure?' Later he reminded Hofmannsthal that 'art comes first and all other considerations come afterwards!' *Touché!* What Hofmannsthal did not know was that Pauline had been moved to put her thoughts on the matter on paper. She was totally opposed to the Deutsches Theater and told her husband: 'Your things demand the best, the very best, people at every level, an elegant theatre with room to breathe in it and good resources for sets and costumes. . . Producing this little opera in his [Reinhardt's] place is madness. It's good enough for a Busoni, but not for a Richard Strauss. Please listen to me, you will be grateful. I have always given you *good advice!*'[2] (This, incidentally, scarcely sounds like the woman who is supposed to have gone round saying how much she disliked her husband's music.)

Dresden was considered but was also rejected. Strauss then heard about the new theatre in Stuttgart seating 800 where the Intendant was his old friend Max von Schillings and offered it the première. Hofmannsthal was unenthusiastic. 'Whoever is going to see it in Stuttgart, that most God-forsaken spot on earth?' But Reinhardt agreed and signed a contract on 6 February 1912. Strauss meanwhile (27 January) had invited Emmy Destinn to sing Ariadne, writing to her as 'unforgettable, unsurpassable Salome' and declaring that 'you've never had a greater admirer of your art than me'. She accepted, so Strauss told Hofmannsthal on 6 February, but later she withdrew and the part went to a young Czech soprano Mizzi (Maria) Jeritza. Strauss resumed work on the incidental music and the opera in April 1912 and completed the score on 22 July. It was now his turn to worry about the production. He was not impressed by the work of Ernst Stern, Reinhardt's stage designer at the Deutsches Theater who was designing *Ariadne*. 'For God's sake see to it that Stern doesn't produce any trashy effects', he warned Hofmannsthal. 'I'm still in favour of Roller, who is a much more solid and thorough worker. With Stern everything looks *dashed off quickly for cheapness*. Please keep at him.' Strauss was at first delighted with rehearsals at Stuttgart, but as the performance drew nearer, the troubles began. The Stuttgart actors and singers were disgruntled because of the number of leading roles cast from the Berlin theatres; the workshops sulked because Reinhardt brought props and costumes from Berlin; and Strauss lost his temper at the dress rehearsal because Schillings had arranged for a performance of *Undine* in the main theatre which drew away the senior technical staff. On the first night, 25 October 1912, the play lasted well over two hours and the King of Württemberg then held a reception lasting fifty minutes before the opera (eighty-five minutes) began. By then the audience was tired. It was not a success. As Strauss came to recognise, most of the playgoing public did not want the opera and vice versa. Economically and practically, too, the difficulties were almost insuperable.

Yet when *Ariadne I*, as we may call the 1912 version, is performed (with the play judiciously cut), it is an enchanting entertainment and certainly the most innovatory of all the collaborations between Strauss and Hofmannsthal. It opened up a new path in music, embracing neo-classicism before Stravinsky and others did so in the 1920s. In the wit and stylishness of the music for the play and in the time-travelling music of the opera – from eighteenth-century pastiche to neo-Wagnerism – it represents not a retreating Strauss but a composer looking ahead for different challenges. It is part of the enigma of Strauss that he should have been so lukewarm about the whole idea, yet wrote some of his finest music for it. Most people today know the revised version of 1916 in which the linking scene was converted into a sung Prologue. But many of those who have heard the first version agree with Sir Thomas Beecham in preferring it to its successor. They are really two different works, the 1912 version being lighter and more quizzical. In the first version, the rivalry and bickering in the linking scene between the prima donna who is to sing Ariadne and Zerbinetta is carried over into the opera, while Jourdain makes philistine comments during the opera. Zerbinetta has a lengthy aria, cut in 1916, in which she tries to prepare Ariadne for the truth about Bacchus, extolling him in extravagant language. Her coloratura aria, *Grossmächtige Prinzessin*, is nearly eighty bars longer, a tone higher and demands high F sharps. At the end, the comedians creep back on the stage, Zerbinetta recapitulates some of her big aria, the dance music returns and the troupe laughs its way off the stage, leaving Jourdain (who has been asleep) to make his final wry comments. The last music to be heard is his theme from the overture to the play.

Knowing how Strauss liked to have a new work in prospect while he finished the composition on which he was working, Hofmannsthal tried in March 1912 to interest him in a ballet score for *Orestes and the Furies* for Serge Diaghilev's Ballets Russes which were the talk of Europe. He hoped it would appeal to the composer's 'mastery over the dark, savage side of life' which had given rise to *Salome* and *Elektra*. Strauss was not interested, but three months later he jumped at Hofmannsthal's next Diaghilev ballet proposal, a scenario written in collaboration with Count Kessler on Joseph and Potiphar's wife, 'the boyish part of Joseph of course for Nijinsky, the most extraordinary personality on the stage today'. Just after sending the scenario to Garmisch, Hofmannsthal informed Strauss that *Die Frau ohne Schatten* had now 'taken a powerful hold on my mind'. Strauss replied that he was not making progress with *Joseph*: 'The chaste Joseph himself isn't at all up my street, and if a thing bores me I find it difficult to set to music. This God-seeker Joseph – he's going to be a hell of an effort! Maybe there's a pious tune for good-boy Joseph lying about in some atavistic recess of my appendix.' This was just before Strauss left for the Stuttgart rehearsals of *Ariadne*. Hofmannsthal said he would find a chaste Joseph a bore too: 'I cannot believe that you should be incapable of finding some bridge between this boy Joseph and the recollection of your own adolescence; whether there was a Potiphar's wife or not, there must have been something lofty, radiant, hardly attainable above you, waiting to be taken by force – this is the meaning of Joseph's dance.' Strauss made enough progress to play some of the score to Hofmannsthal, Kessler and Nijinsky on 12 December 1912. The librettist was 'perturbed' and wrote next day to express his – and their – concern about the style of the first two Joseph themes ('not the incomparable third theme, that of union with God'). Apparently the themes were too Mozartian, too eighteenth-century. Nijinsky 'implores you to write the most unrestrained, the least dance-like music in the world, to put down pure Strauss for this leaping towards God which is a struggle for God. To be taken by you beyond all bounds of convention is what he longs for.' It was in this letter that Hofmannsthal let slip his basic attitude to their collaboration: 'In every task before us, the final criterion can only be sensitivity in the matter of style, and of this I must consider myself guardian and keeper for the two of us.'

Strauss laid aside *Joseph* (which was now called *Josephs Legende*) to write the *Festliches Präludium* for the opening of the new Vienna Konzerthaus on 19 October 1913. He completed it on 11th May, scored for the largest orchestra he ever employed (over 150 players) with a large part for organ. It is a huge rhapsody in salute to the Viennese nineteenth-century musical tradition and contains allusions to Weber, Beethoven and Brahms. Its extravagant scoring makes it a rarity, but it is more than just a piece of occasional bombast. It is a composition of some complexity, the work of a supreme craftsman. His remark to Hofmannsthal that he was inspired by 'flourishes *à la* Rückert' is amply confirmed by the Rückert setting, the *Deutsche Motette*, which he wrote in 1913, completing it on 22 June, for the Berlin Court Opera chorus and its chorus master Hugo Rüdel, who gave the first performance in the Berlin Philharmonie on 2 December 1913. With a range of four octaves, it is probably the most challenging tonal choral work ever written. The voices are divided into twenty-three parts (sixteen chorus lines and seven soloists) with a dynamic range from *pp* to *ff*. Rückert's text is in the form of a Persian 'ghasel' in which there is a rhyme in the first two lines (*gegangen, befangen*) and thereafter in every subsequent even-numbered line (*zugegangen, ausgegangen*). In addition, the refrain line *o wach in mir* ('watch in me') occurs at the end of the rhyming lines. This structural discipline in no way inhibited Strauss. Instead it appears to have spurred him to ecstatic imaginative flights. The ground-plan of the *Motette* is an opening section with antiphonal effects followed by a polyphonic middle episode reaching a climax in which the two sections are combined. In a long coda, the chief themes are nostalgically reviewed in music which shows Strauss at his most luxuriant, characteristic and masterful. It is a choral equivalent of the *Alpensinfonie* in its glowing melodic splendour.

The *Ariadne* crisis dragged on through 1913. Hofmannsthal was disgusted by the 'unbelievable degree of antagonism' the work had encountered from 'the scribbling race'. Strauss's first suggestion for revision was that they should provide *secco* recitatives in the prose scene linking play and opera and to jettison the Molière play. Hofmannsthal decided (9 January 1913) to re-write the scene as a Prologue, to convert M. Jourdain into a rich Viennese patron of the arts and to enlarge the role for the young Composer. It would take place in a hall of the patron's house where dressing-rooms had been improvised. Both men attended performances throughout Germany of *Ariadne I*. Some enchanted them, some appalled them – and always it was the performance and direction of the Molière that offended them. By early in June Hofmannsthal had written the Prologue – he now regarded the first version of *Ariadne* as 'a lost cause' – which he sent to Strauss. The response from Strauss was frigid – 'not to my liking at all. Indeed, it contains some things which are downright distasteful to me – the Composer, for instance: to set him to music will be rather tedious. . . I can't accept as justified your wish to have this second version regarded as the only valid and definitive one. To me, its first version is still the right one.' He was infuriated in December 1913 by the critics' warm reception for Wolf-Ferrari's comic opera *Der Liebhaber als Artz*, based on Molière's *Le médecin malgré lui*. 'Must one really take all this nonsense lying down?' he asked. He praised Hofmannsthal's distillation of Molière and continued: 'Doesn't it make you sick to read how the audience for Wolf-Ferrari was kept deliciously amused throughout the whole evening, whereas during our short Molière, in which you have really only retained what is amusing and typical, they were bored to tears and could scarcely wait for the opera to begin?' He wanted Hofmannsthal to persuade another writer, such as Arthur Schnitzler, to 'explode the myth of the boring *Bourgeois*'. Not my line, Hofmannsthal replied. After seeing a good Munich production of *Ariadne* on 2 January 1914 he decided Strauss was right – 'we shall change nothing, not one thing. And you are right too that it must remain in small theatres.' This was conducted by Bruno Walter, who had become music director in Munich in 1913. This was his first new production and he went to Garmisch where Strauss played the work through to him. 'I am still conscious of the pleasure the composer's cool and perfect piano performance of the rather artificial but masterly work gave me', Walter wrote in his memoirs. 'His playing was as lucid and objective as his written music on the desk before us, but in spite of its uniform coolness it still left the impression of latent agitation.'

Strauss completed the score of *Josephs Legende* on 2 February 1914, having once again raided his discarded ballet *Kythere*. Three weeks later he wrote a short cantata for male voice choir to Hofmannsthal's words to mark the twentieth anniversary of Count von Seebach's appointment as Dresden Intendant. Then, at last, Hofmannsthal sent him the libretto for Act 1 of *Die Frau ohne Schatten*. (At the end of March the previous year they had met in Verona and driven in an open car to Rome and from Rome to Garmisch. En route they discussed the plot of the opera.) Strauss wrote to his librettist on 4 April 1914: 'The first act is simply wonderful: so compact and homogeneous that I cannot yet think of even a comma being deleted or altered. My problem now will be to find a new simple style which will make it possible to present your beautiful poetry to the listeners in its full purity and clarity. . . Let me congratulate you on your beautiful and perfect achievement.' Nevertheless he began to make suggestions for alterations to the text and wrote (20 April): 'I am now generally getting into the style and melodic character and shall easily finish the first act during the early summer.' On 6 May he went to Paris to begin rehearsals of *Josephs Legende*. Nijinsky had split with Diaghilev in 1913 and Joseph was now to be danced by Leonide Massine, with Marie Kuznetsova as Potiphar's Wife. Michael Fokine was the choreographer, José-Maria Sert the designer, Léon Bakst the costume-designer. Rehearsals were fraught. Ballets based on Schumann's *Papillons* and Rimsky-Korsakov's *Scheherazade* were in the same programme. Both were to be conducted by Pierre Monteux. *Josephs Legende* was conducted by Strauss. Time was severely restricted and Strauss had a low opinion of French orchestral musicians after his experiences with *Salome*. Stravinsky was at the rehearsals and admired Strauss's conducting, but 'his manner towards the orchestra was not admirable and the musicians heartily detested him, but every corrective mark he made was exact: his ears and his musicianship were impregnable'.[3] The reason for Strauss's annoyance was valid enough: the Paris orchestras were bedevilled by the 'deputy' system whereby a player could send a substitute if he was giving a private lesson or had a more lucrative engagement. In six rehearsals of a difficult new score, no progress was made – at the last rehearsal the principal flautist made bad mistakes, but he had not been at any previous rehearsals. Strauss in his memoirs admitted he was 'very impatient' and that the Berlin Intendant Hülsen, who was present, 'saw the world war breaking out even then'. Sert set a story told in the Book of Genesis in a sixteenth-century Venetian style modelled on Veronese. The ballet looked sumptuous. Lydia Sokolova, who danced in it as a slave-girl, recalled that 'the costumes were magnificent, particularly those of Potiphar's wife. She moved about on high gilded clogs, attended by servants, two of whom had a couple of honey-coloured wolfhounds on white leads. Nearly everything in the ballet was some shade of gold, except for Massine's white tunic.'[4] The first performance, at the Opéra, was on 14 May. Rolland was there and described Strauss as looking 'considerably aged, thickened, heavier and red-faced'. Sitting in front of

Rolland was d'Annunzio, who booed when the curtain fell. 'His girl friend Ida Rubinstein must have quarrelled with Strauss; she was to have interpreted the part of Potiphar's wife and withdrew at the last moment.' A good reason, but perhaps d'Annunzio was also thinking of Strauss's refusal of a libretto he had offered!

After spending his fiftieth birthday in Garmisch, Strauss went to London for the première there of *Josephs Legende*, conducted by Thomas Beecham at the Theatre Royal, Drury Lane, on 23 June. (While in England he was made an honorary Doctor of Music of Oxford University.) Writing to Hofmannsthal on his return, he described the occasion as 'a great success in spite of the fact that most of the press was hostile and even the most sophisticated Englishwomen found the piece indecent. The production had been improved in many respects, but the main thing, Joseph's dance, still inadequate and hence boring. Orchestra magnificent, all performances sold out.' In London, Potiphar's Wife was danced by Tamara Karsavina and Maria Carmu in turn.

Beecham, who had conducted the London premières of *Feuersnot*, *Salome*, *Elektra*, *Der Rosenkavalier* and *Ariadne auf Naxos* (in a translation of the Molière play by Somerset Maugham), wrote that in his opinion Strauss showed no talent for this kind of thing: 'in spite of a few vivid and picturesque moments, the piece went with a heavy and plodding gait.'[5] That, I fear, is as good a summing-up as one could find. It would be pleasing to claim that *Josephs Legende* is a neglected masterpiece, but it is not. One of the enigmas of Strauss is that his obsession for work – perhaps inherited from his father – led him to compose works in which he was not particularly interested while he waited for Hofmannsthal to send him the work he really wanted. If Hofmannsthal had finished Act 1 of *Die Frau ohne Schatten* a year sooner, I doubt if *Josephs Legende* would have been composed. Yet one is bound to add that nor was he much interested by the idea of *Ariadne*, which turned into a masterpiece, and still less by the Prologue to the second version, which is one of the best things he ever did. He composed *Eine Alpensinfonie* to keep himself occupied, but that had a long gestation and sprang from deep-rooted necessity. No doubt he was flattered by the idea of composing for Diaghilev, along with up-and-comers like Stravinsky and Ravel, especially when the original plan was that Nijinsky should dance, produce and be choreographer. But the scenario was so alien to his sympathies, as he quickly recognised, that he could do no more than compose a workmanlike score, glitteringly orchestrated, but empty of real inspiration.

He returned from England to plunge back into composing *Die Frau ohne Schatten*. His son Franz recalled that he played every new passage to Pauline. 'I can still remember how the Watchmen's call at the end of Act 1 came into being. I was already in bed and I heard the music rising from below. He played it with such rapt emotion – I have never heard it performed more beautifully since.'[6] Strauss was thrilled by the second act libretto: 'wonderful . . . superbly magnificent. . . You've never written anything more beautiful and compact in your life. . . I only hope my music will be worthy of your fine poetry. At present I am still far from satisfied with myself.' Curiously, in view of the fact that she was based on Pauline, he found that the character of the Dyer's Wife 'has not yet quite translated itself into music, whereas Barak is right up my street'. At this juncture the Strausses went on holiday to the Dolomites. While they were there, the First World War began and they had to hurry home to Garmisch through the Brenner Pass while it was choc-a-bloc with Austrian troop transports. Strauss completed the short score of Act 1 on 20 August, writing on the manuscript: 'the day of the victory at Saarburg. Hail to our brave troops. Hail to our great German fatherland.'

14   Twentieth-century Offenbach

That inscription on the manuscript of *Die Frau ohne Schatten* reveals Strauss as a German patriot, rejoicing in a military victory. But Strauss the German artist soon surfaced. In late September 1914, when the war had lasted for two months, he wrote to Max Reger saying he would gladly conduct Reger's *Patriotic Overture*. He then added: 'To think that the Duke of Meiningen has thrown out his old and famous orchestra on to the street: whoever heard of such a thing – *that* is German vandalism! How are we innocent citizens to summon up enthusiasm for all the fearful sacrifices this war demands of us if the Kaiser's own sister [Duchess of Meiningen] sets an example like that!' A few weeks earlier he had refused to sign a chauvinistic manifesto issued by German artists and intellectuals. He said he would happily renounce his Oxford doctorate if, in exchange, the British would hand over or sink a dreadnought, but declarations about matters concerning war and politics were not fitting for an artist, who must give his attention to his creations and to his work; it was the business of those who make it their living or career. Richard Specht, writing in the Budapest *Pester Lloyd* on 12 September 1914 said that Strauss had voluntarily kept away 'from all manifestos, declarations, interviews, printed opinions, vocal fanfares and particularly from any injurious appraisal of enemy conduct'.

Hofmannsthal, at the age of forty, was called up before Austria declared war because he had joined the army as a volunteer in 1895. He was now sent to Pisino, Istria, with the territorial reserves. Strauss was relieved to hear (writing on 8 October) that he was 'no longer at the front but in safety at a quiet post'. He had reported that he had sketched 'the first four changes of scene of Act ii. . . The text is really brilliant, goes into music with marvellous ease, stimulates me all the time, and is so short and concise: my dear Scribe, you've really pulled off your masterpiece here.' He then added:

Amidst all the unpleasant things which this war brings with it – except the brilliant feats of our army – hard work is the only salvation. Otherwise the incompetence of our diplomacy, our press, the Kaiser's apologetic telegram to Wilson and all the other undignified acts that are being committed would be enough to drive a man to distraction. And how are the artists treated? The Kaiser reduces the salaries at the Court Theatre, the Duchess of Meiningen turfs her orchestra out into the street, Reinhardt stages Shakespeare, the Frankfurt theatre performs *Carmen, Mignon, The Tales of Hoffmann* – who will ever understand this German nation, this mixture of mediocrity and genius, of heroism and obsequiousness?. . . We're bound to win, of course – but afterwards, Heaven knows, everything will be bungled again!

A certain amount of chauvinism there, perhaps, and again Strauss's belief that art was the most important element in human affairs. He began the short score of Act 2 on 27 October 1914 and completed it on 8 April 1915. In the 1914–15 winter he also completed the full score of *Eine Alpensinfonie* on 8 February in Berlin. He was particularly thrilled by Marie Gutheil-Schoder's Elektra in Berlin – 'unbelievably magnificent. . .an experience'.

Hofmannsthal was able only to work on the libretto of Act 3 when he could get to Rodaun. In addition, he was anxious about the health of his father (who died in December 1915). He was also depressed by the war. But Strauss was 'full of energy. Why are you letting your spirits droop? You may rely on Germany. . . But as for politics: I think we'll view them from a long way off and leave them to those concerned with them. Only hard work can console us.' He was now (April 1915) beginning to worry about the first two acts. He had let the Intendants in Dresden and Berlin read them and 'both displayed total incomprehension. . . Everything tells me that the subject and its theme are difficult to understand and that everything must be done to make it as clear as possible.' When he received the text of Act 3 ('magnificent'), he found it too sketchy. He asked for more lines and was concerned that the character of the Empress 'doesn't touch us closely enough on the human plane'. There followed pages of very practical criticisms of the plot and text. The two men discussed these at a meeting in Vienna on 25 April just before Hofmannsthal was due to be posted to Cracow in Poland. (After two months he was released because of poor eyesight.) Strauss played what he had composed to his collaborator, who was so impressed that he made much less fuss than usual about acceding to Strauss's requests.

Hofmannsthal also dissuaded Strauss from his proposed ban on performances of their operas in Munich. Strauss said he had allowed himself to be 'pacified with excuses and tricked with empty promises' by the Intendant, Baron Franckenstein, and the conductor Bruno Walter, for three years. 'I would now require . . . some definite written guarantees about the upkeep of my works in my native city, or else I shall not enter the Munich Hoftheater so long as its present directors are in office.' Don't do this, Hofmannsthal urged, you can't win – 'the artist has always, always the worst of it against officials, public authorities or business men.' Strauss was fidgety at this time, too, because his son Franz had volunteered for the army at the age of seventeen. He was, however, rejected as unfit. His father wrote to him (22 November 1914): 'It is a quite unexpected stroke of luck for you and for us that . . . you will be spared from risking life and limb in this dreadful war – although I know that it is against your honourable and courageous will. Now, it is to be hoped, you will feel a double spur as you strike out along the path which leads by way of scientific study of the fine arts to a noble, cultural end.'

In Berlin on 28 October 1915 he conducted the first performance of *Eine Alpensinfonie* and the first Vienna performance on 5 December. Hofmannsthal went to Berlin on 7 January to hear him conduct a Beethoven concert. The subject of the revision of *Ariadne* was raised and on the 17th they met again. They decided to attend a performance and then to discuss it with Reinhardt. 'I am now full of hope that this hapless child will be rehabilitated', Hofmannsthal wrote. 'After all, quite a lot was wrong with the work itself.' From this we may infer that Strauss had agreed to look again at the libretto of the Prologue sent to him in 1913. Pauline also seems to have expressed her views, for on 18 February 1916 Hofmannsthal wrote a long letter to her explaining his position on *Ariadne*. It seems from this, too, that Strauss was already considering Vienna for the première of *Die Frau ohne Schatten*. 'Nowhere will the libretto meet with so little goodwill, with so much preconceived incomprehension as in Vienna', the Vienna-born poet warned her.

Amazingly, when one remembers Strauss's initial dislike for the Prologue, he composed the music for it with remarkable speed. He completed the full score of Act 2 of *Die Frau ohne Schatten* on 4 May and began the short score of the Prologue immediately, completing it on 27 May. He had meanwhile appalled Hofmannsthal by – on the suggestion of his fellow-conductor in Berlin, Leo Blech – making the role of the Composer a trouser-role for a soprano (or high mezzo-soprano) 'since the tenors are so terrible'. The librettist thought it 'odious' and smacking a little of operetta. 'Oh Lord, if only I could bring home to you completely the essence, the spiritual meaning of these characters.' Once again, he sighed, they differed over the conception of a character as they had over Zerbinetta. He felt 'quite faint in mind and body' over it. Strauss replied sharply. 'Why do you always get so bitterly angry if for once we don't understand each other straight away?' He would give way on some points Hofmannsthal had raised, but not on the Composer. Some decision on cuts had to be made, there was argument over how the Opera should now end, but Strauss was able to complete the full score on 19 June. He removed one of Zerbinetta's arias altogether, cut her big aria and transposed it down a tone for much of its course. It is obvious from his letters that he knew he had done something good with the Prologue. 'The little love scene between Zerbinetta and the Composer has turned out particularly pretty! . . . it is one of my very best ideas. The whole thing is, in my opinion, rather well organised.' He judged truly. The hustle and bustle of backstage preparations before a performance, the panic over changes to the score by the rich patron's instructions, the bickering and self-interest of the Prima Donna and the Tenor who are to sing Ariadne and Bacchus, this was the world in which Strauss thrived and which he knew at first-hand from his experiences with the casts of *Guntram* and with court opera Intendants. Add to this the Composer, susceptible to the charm of Zerbinetta even though she comes from a different musical world, suddenly inventing a new melody ('Du, Venus' Sohn') and at the end giving radiance to the whole piece with his glorious outburst of 'Musik ist eine heilige Kunst' ('Music is a holy art'), and the result was a masterpiece in which Strauss further developed the conversational style, somewhere between recitative and aria, which was his major contribution to the art of opera. 'Du, Venus' Sohn' is sung in *Le bourgeois gentilhomme* and its tune occurs in the Overture. Strauss knew it was too good a melody to waste and made sure he incorporated it into the Prologue. The removal of Jourdain and the fact that the 'richest man in Vienna' never appears in the Prologue made the opera seem more detached from the preceding horse-play. This is particularly marked at the end, when Zerbinetta is allowed only one short ironic comment and the elevated mood of the love duet prevails. It becomes a heavier piece.

The first performance of *Ariadne II* was in Vienna on 4 October 1916, conducted by Franz Schalk. The Ariadne was again Jeritza. The Composer was sung by the 28-year-old Lotte Lehmann in her first Vienna season. She had a major success. Strauss had written the role for one of his Berlin singers, Lola Artôt de Padilla, who had been his Berlin Octavian and sang the Composer at the first Berlin performance on 1 November. The second version was cautiously received but, after performances in Dresden, Leipzig, Düsseldorf and other cities, gradually replaced the original version. It did not reach London until 1924 and America (Philadelphia) until 1928.

Composing the Prologue changed the course of Strauss's creative development. What is more, he knew it at once. A few days before finishing it, he wrote (18 May 1916) to Hofmannsthal: 'Do write me a libretto again some time with "a lot of love"! That always gives me the best ideas: Act 1 and end of Act 3 *Rosenkavalier*, *Salome* – here's a case in point.' A week later he was floating suggestions for a new opera: 'either an entirely modern, absolutely realistic domestic and character comedy . . . or some amusing piece of love and intrigue . . . say a diplomatic intrigue in the setting of the Vienna Congress with a genuinely highly aristocratic woman spy as the principal character – the beautiful wife of an ambassador as a traitor for the sake of love, exploited by a secret agent or some such rather amusing subject. . . You'll probably say: Trash! But then we musicians are known for our poor taste in aesthetic matters, and besides, if you were to do a thing like that it wouldn't be trash.' Predictably, Hofmannsthal found these ideas 'truly horrid' and could not resist adding: 'You have every reason to be grateful to me for bringing you (as now once again with *Die Frau ohne Schatten*) that element which is sure to bewilder people and to provoke a certain amount of antagonism, for you have already too many followers, you are already all too obviously the hero of the day, all too universally accepted.' Strauss's reply was one of the most important he wrote. He knew 'only too well' what he wanted:

When you've heard the new Vorspiel . . . you'll understand what I mean and will realise that I have a definite talent for operetta. And since my tragic vein is more or less exhausted, and since tragedy in the theatre, after this war, strikes me at present as rather idiotic and childish, I should like to apply this irrepressible talent of mine – after all, I'm the only composer nowadays with some real humour and a sense of fun and a marked gift for parody. Indeed, I feel downright called upon to become the Offenbach of the 20th century, and you will and must be my poet. What I have in mind with my impromptu suggestions, which you resent so much, is a political-satirical parody of the most trenchant kind. Why shouldn't you be able to write that? . . . Sentimentality and parody are the sensations to which my talent responds most forcefully and productively. . . What *Rosenkavalier* lacks in compactness you have learned in the meantime (as shown by the superb brevity and balanced structure of *Fr. o. Sch*) and what it lacks in lightness I have learned in *Ariadne*. Long live the political-satirical-parodistic operetta!

This spurred Hofmannsthal to a sour reply (which he did not send, but retained) complaining about all the Offenbach-like bits of *Rosenkavalier* which Strauss had, in his view, botched. Strauss now (18 July 1916) reverted to Act 3 of *Die Frau ohne Schatten*. He had been troubled for some time about the crucial scene when the Empress sees her husband turned to stone. She is told he will return to life only if she agrees to accept the shadow of the Dyer's Wife. After an intense struggle she cries 'I will not' – and is saved, as is her husband. 'I am as determined as ever', Strauss wrote, 'to treat the whole passage . . . as a spoken passage.' The result – although it is often cut – was a memorable operatic moment. Strauss referred to it years later: '*Die Frau ohne Schatten*, a child of sorrow, was completed in the midst of trouble and worries during the war when, owing to the kindness and consideration shown by a Bavarian, Major Distler, my son, whose heart had not kept pace with his rapid growth, was saved from being prematurely called up. . . The Bavarian M.O. had the good sense to declare him unfit. These wartime worries may be responsible for a certain nervous irritation in the score, especially halfway through the third act, which was to "explode" in melodrama.'[1]

That may be, but Strauss's difficulties with Act 3 of *Die Frau ohne Schatten* stemmed from the Prologue to *Ariadne* because there he had found a way ahead, slipped into the style and found it difficult to recapture the zest for

Hofmannsthal's mystical-mythical fantasy fairy-tale. What is more, Hofmannsthal sensed it. He wrote from Aussee on 24 July: 'The music for the Vorspiel is as enchanting in recollection as anything could be: like fireworks in a beautiful park one enchanted, all too fleeting summer night. What remains in my ear of the scenes from the third act (of *Die Frau ohne Schatten*) with the exception of the first scene [which Strauss composed in May and June 1915, i.e. *before* he wrote the *Ariadne* Prologue] leaves me, I cannot help it, somewhat oppressed and gloomy, my dear Dr Strauss.' The reply from Garmisch must have perturbed the librettist: 'I entirely share your opinion that the Vorspiel marks the peculiar new road we must follow', Strauss wrote,

and my own inclination is for realistic comedy with really interesting people – either like *Rosenkavalier* with its splendid Marschallin, or with a burlesque, satirical content. . . But to change the style in *Frau ohne Schatten*, a style that pleases you and at which we must both aim – that's quite impossible. . . The trouble is the subject itself with its romanticism and its symbols. Characters like the Emperor and Empress, and also the Nurse, can't be filled with red corpuscles in the same way as a Marschallin, an Octavian, or an Ochs. No matter how I rack my brain – and I'm toiling really hard, sifting and sifting – my heart's only half in it, and once the head has to do the major part of the work you get a breath of academic chill (what my wife very rightly calls note-spinning) which no bellows can ever kindle into a real fire. Well, I have now sketched out the whole end of the opera . . . and it's got verve and a great upward sweep – but my wife finds it cold and misses the heart-touching flame-kindling melodic texture of the *Rosenkavalier* trio. I'm willing to believe her, and I keep probing and searching. . . I shall make every effort to shape Act 3 in line with your intentions, but let's make up our minds that *Frau ohne Schatten* shall be the last romantic opera.

This was abdication with a vengeance; and when he had completed the short score of Act 3 in September 1916 he said he had 'become so uncertain that I no longer know what's successful and what's bad'. And he urged Hofmannsthal to give him Offenbach-like libretti 'peopled by human beings à la Hofmannsthal instead of puppets. . . I have now definitely stripped off the Wagnerian musical armour.' There was a further distraction from *Die Frau ohne Schatten* in that Strauss had already begun to think about a 'modern, completely realistic opera' in the new style. Hofmannsthal knew that he himself could not promise what Strauss wanted in this line and took it upon himself to ask Hermann Bahr if he could think of something and write the libretto. Bahr was a journalist, critic, playwright and former manager of the Deutsches Theater in Berlin with Reinhardt. He was also married to the soprano Anna von Mildenburg, once Mahler's mistress in Hamburg, a great Wagnerian singer and a particularly fine interpreter of the role of Klytämnestra. In 1910 Bahr had a success with his play *Das Konzert* about the marital troubles of a musician. Perhaps this reminded Strauss of his Mieze Mücke incident of 1902 when Pauline had threatened divorce; at any rate he decided in 1916 that this would make a good operatic subject and asked Bahr to write the libretto. Strauss gave him full details of how he wanted each character to be defined, in particular Baron Lummer, with whom the wife in the opera becomes mildly involved. (He was also based on a real person in whom Pauline had been interested: 'a shy young man of few words', Strauss said, 'whose character as an adventurer emerged only when he half-shamefacedly tried to get money from my wife; until then he had been extremely modest and had aroused her sympathy.' A visitor to Garmisch after Strauss died was told by Franz Strauss: 'That's the chair "Baron Lummer" sat in.') Bahr took six months until the summer of 1917 to tell Strauss that it would be best if Strauss wrote it himself. Undeterred, Strauss sketched the dialogue of the first two scenes and sent them to Bahr with a scenario (written the previous autumn) urging him to reconsider. But Bahr remained adamant and Strauss wrote the text during a week in a Munich clinic in July 1917.

Strauss's work-load as a conductor was still phenomenal. He conducted many concerts in Berlin and his duties at the Berlin Court Opera were still heavy – twenty-seven appearances in 1912–13, eighteen in 1913–14, thirty-two in 1914–15, twenty-seven in 1915–16, twenty-five in 1916–17, and twenty-three in 1918–19. These were mainly Mozart and Wagner, but also included *Aida*, *Carmen* and *Il barbiere di Siviglia*. In January 1917 he conducted *Der Rosenkavalier* in The Hague and Amsterdam, supervised a Strauss Week in Mannheim and then took *Ariadne II* and *Elektra* to Switzerland with casts including Marie Gutheil-Schoder (as the Composer and Elektra), Anna von Mildenburg, Maria Jeritza and Karl Oestvig. While in Zürich, Strauss invited Romain Rolland to *Ariadne*. His old friend was ill and did not attend.

13 The Strauss villa, Zöppritzstrasse 42, Garmisch

On return to Garmisch, Strauss wrote to him about an article by Rolland which the writer had sent him: 'I see with satisfaction to what an extent we are agreed on so many questions of a purely humane kind, or questions of principle, in our affection for our respective countries, and in our admiration for our courageous armies in the battlefield. Moreover, it is precisely we artists who should firmly keep our gaze fixed on all that is beautiful and noble and who should put ourselves at the service of truth.' He then remarked on reports he had heard of maltreatment of German prisoners of war by the French. 'I have always wished that men like you could, by personal investigation in enemy territory, ensure the continuation of their work of justice and of truth on a more solid and convincing basis. *Wouldn't you like to do this?. . .* It would be possible for me to invite you to Garmisch this spring and there to offer you an opportunity to gain various impressions of our nations at war.' This extraordinary suggestion provoked Rolland to write in his diary: 'How little those poor Germans suspect what the state of mind is in Europe! Reverse the situation: a German invited to France, it would be like one of Napoleon's soldiers in besieged Saragossa!'

Strauss conducted in Scandinavia in February 1917, returned to Berlin, and in mid-May returned to Switzerland to conduct Mozart with an opera company including Barbara Kemp, Paul Knüpfer (his Berlin Ochs), the tenor Robert Hutt and the 29-year-old soprano Elisabeth Schumann who had sung Sophie in Hamburg in 1911 and at the New York Met in 1914. On the Swiss tour she sang Zerlina in *Don Giovanni* and Papagena in *Die Zauberflöte*. This was her first encounter with Strauss and she was impressed by 'his intellectual face, his open features, his vigorous yet polished gestures' which 'communicated the whole essence of the man and conveyed a sense of his greatness as an artist and as a man. I was charmed by his impulsive kindliness.'[2] Strauss was charmed by her artistry and personality and invited her to visit him where he was staying in Zürich at the home of the Reiff family, patrons of the arts, and to sing some of his *Lieder* to him, beginning with *Blauer Sommer*. It was then, as I have already written in an earlier chapter, that he suggested she should sing Salome. This did not happen, but there was a more significant result of this meeting. Strauss had composed no *Lieder* since 1906, mainly because he was immersed in writing operas, very largely because Pauline retired from the concert-platform that year, and also because he was embroiled in a wrangle with publishers about copyright and performing rights. Ever since he had written songs as a boy for his Aunt Johanna, Strauss had liked to be inspired by a particular voice. Schumann re-kindled his desire to compose songs and in February 1918 he began to set six poems by Clemens Brentano, joint compiler of *Des Knaben Wunderhorn*, with Schumann in mind. Yet only one or two of the songs of Op. 68 were suitable for her and it has never been discovered that she sang the whole cycle. Perhaps significantly, the first to be composed, No. 4, *Als mir dein Lied erklang*, was inscribed 'Meiner Pauline'. The other five were composed between 6 and 21 February in the order Nos. 2, 3, 1 and 5. The sixth song was completed on 4 May. Nos. 1 and 5 were first sung, in Vienna on 12 October 1918, by Franz Steiner. No. 6 was sung first on 29 September in Dresden by Mary Grasenick. When Strauss toured the United States in the autumn of 1921, Schumann, Claire Dux, Elena Gerhardt and George Meader sang with him in orchestral concerts and piano recitals. Schumann included only two of the Brentano cycle, No. 2 *Ich wollt ein Sträußlein binden* and No. 3 *Säusle, liebe Myrthe!* These are the most immediately enticing of the set, which as a whole reflects the vocal writing in *Ariadne auf Naxos*, notably *Als mir dein Lied erklang*, with its long and glorious cantilena. The most remarkable song is No. 6, *Lied der Frauen wenn die Männer im Kriege sind* (Song of the Women when the Men are at War), a *Lied* that needs a heroic soprano to cope with its tempestuous opening and its nobly majestic ending.

To return to 1917, Strauss's work in the summer was, first of all, completion of the full score of Act 3 of *Die Frau ohne Schatten* on 24 June. He then found himself enmeshed yet again with the Molière-Hofmannsthal *Le bourgeois gentilhomme*. In the summer of 1916, just after Strauss had completed the Prologue, Hofmannsthal – spurred by a remark by Hermann Bahr that Strauss's incidental music for the Molière was the finest thing he had done – wrote to the composer: 'Please do not rashly waste these pieces of music; I am sure I shall succeed in inventing a second delicate action for this comedy.' So off they went again, with Hofmannsthal expanding his version to three acts and Strauss criticising the libretto to the extent that at one point Hofmannsthal wrote: 'Your proposals I consider, if you will forgive me, beneath discussion. They demonstrate to me that your taste and mine are miles apart, at least as concerns possibilities of this kind. Pray let me have in due course your decision whether I am free to dispose otherwise of this Molière adaptation, of which I do not intend to alter one iota.' And so on in a subsequent letter. But he calmed down and Strauss composed extra music, some of it incorporating themes from the original score by Lully, between 26 July and 11 October. He completed the orchestration at Christmas 1917, having a few days earlier conducted the 100th Dresden performance of *Der Rosenkavalier*. The first performance of *Le bourgeois gentilhomme* was produced by Reinhardt in the Deutsches Theater, Berlin, on 9 April 1918. It was a flop and was withdrawn after thirty-one performances. Hofmannsthal, on 8 July, reverted to his dislike of Zerbinetta's aria in *Ariadne* and asked for 'entirely new music'. About *Le bourgeois gentilhomme* he said it had been his 'mistake' to return to it 'in order to rescue those enchanting fragments of incidental music'. Now there was the paradoxical result that 'the interposition of your music . . . has turned a Molière play . . . into a definite failure.' Should they not now make an opera of it or find some other solution? No, said Strauss, enough was enough and that went for Zerbinetta too. He was already composing 'my little domestic opera', as he called it to Hofmannsthal on 12 June 1918. (He had sent the draft libretto to Hofmannsthal, who said he would 'do my best' to read it although he lacked all sympathy for 'the genre of realism'.) Strauss preserved his Molière incidental music by arranging a nine-movement Suite. He conducted its first performance in Vienna on 31 January 1920.

Strauss made no effort to have *Die Frau ohne Schatten* staged while the war continued, although he had discussions with Dresden. He realised that in wartime conditions it would not be adequately produced. The war impinged on him when he travelled, as he wrote to Pauline on 9 December 1917: 'My darling . . . I'm not one to complain, but eight hours from Berlin to Bielefeld in an unheated train – that came close to getting even me down. No restaurant car, nothing hot to eat or drink. . . Trains full of the wounded, trains loaded with whole fleets of aircraft or with ambulances that have been shot to pieces – appalling!' He complained bitterly in the summer of 1918, however, when the Garmisch regional government removed the copper lightning conductor from his house and replaced it with an inferior one. If the state forcibly requisitioned a citizen's property, he said, it should pay the costs the citizen incurred. But bureaucracy ruled otherwise. An irritation of a different kind also surfaced again at this time. The Berlin publishers Bote & Bock had had an option on his next songs since 1903. Strauss tried several times to extricate himself from the contract but they held him to it and pressed him hard at the end of 1917. (Publishers as a whole had never forgiven Strauss for his campaign on copyright and performing rights.) The

Till Eulenspiegel in him thought of a way round. He asked the theatre critic Alfred Kerr to write him some verses lampooning the music publishers; twelve were provided by March 1918. Strauss composed four of the songs while he was conducting in Amsterdam that month and the rest at home in Garmisch in less than a week in May. He called the cycle *Krämerspiegel* (Shopkeeper's Mirror), Op. 66. Kerr's poems were full of puns and allusions. Bock (goat) munches flowers symbolising music. Bote (messenger) goes to the Rosenkavalier. Breitkopf & Härtel receive savage treatment, and so do several other firms. The texts are witty (and libellous) and so is the music, full of quotations from Strauss's tone-poems and operas. The long piano prelude to the eighth song, re-stated at the end of the twelfth song, twenty-three years later became the glorious Moonlight Music in *Capriccio*. Strauss sent the songs to Bote & Bock, who refused them as scurrilous and sued for breach of contract. The court ordered Strauss to provide 'proper songs', whereupon he composed six of his most recondite *Lieder* (Op. 67) which, although they are innovative and among the most challenging he wrote, could never be called popular or easily saleable. Three are settings of mad Ophelia's nonsense rhymes in *Hamlet* and three are from the 'Book of Ill-Humour' from Goethe's *Westöstlicher Divan*, poems written when Goethe was elderly and disillusioned by wars in Europe, which no doubt was Strauss's mood, too, in the spring of 1918. The Ophelia songs continue Strauss's musical reflections on madness which began in *Don Quixote* when they were related to his fears about his mother's mental health. *Krämerspiegel* was not published until 1921 and then only in a private edition limited to 120 copies, illustrated by Michael Fingesten. The publisher was Paul Cassirer, to whom Strauss wrote on 10 March 1921: 'At least there is a man who, even though a publisher himself, has the necessary humour to assess this work correctly.' The cycle was published by Boosey & Hawkes in 1959. Strauss dedicated it to his friend and lawyer Friedrich Rösch 'in merry humour'. A private first performance was given by Sigrid Johanson, accompanied by Michael Raucheisen, at Kerr's invitation in a friend's home between 1918 and 1920. Other performances were given in the Logenhaussaal, Dresden, by Mary Grasenick on 26 June 1919 and in the Hotel Kaiserhof, Berlin, on 1 November 1925 by Johanson and Raucheisen (in 1925 Sigrid Johanson was the first Marie in Berg's *Wozzeck*).

For his own publisher, Fürstner, who was excluded from mockery in *Krämerspiegel* (except in so far as he was included among publishers in general) Strauss composed his Op. 69, *Fünf kleine Lieder*, in the third week of June. Three are settings of Achim von Arnim and two of Heine. Each is dedicated to a woman friend of the Strausses, the third (*Einerlei*) to Mizzi von Grab, mother of his future daughter-in-law. Best-known of the set is the last, *Schlechtes Wetter*, which ends with a waltz. As related earlier, the first, *Der Stern*, was composed while Strauss was awaiting a visit from Max Marschalk. He told him: 'Just now . . . I took up my copy of Achim von Arnim and read the little poem "Stern" and, as I read, the musical inspiration came to me. I wrote the song down on the spot.' In this summer, too, he orchestrated five of his earlier songs, *Des Dichters Abendgang*, *Waldseligkeit*, *Winterweihe*, *Winterliebe* and *Freundliche Vision*. On 19 December he orchestrated *Der Arbeitsmann* and dedicated it to the bass Fritz Stein, although Ernst Kraus gave the first performance of this version, with the Berlin Philharmonic, conducted by Strauss, on 20 April 1919. The score then vanished and emerged in a London saleroom in 1986.

PART III

1918–1933
Out of fashion

15   Vienna

As the war neared its end in November 1918, Strauss continued to fulfil conducting engagements. In Coburg for *Der Rosenkavalier*, this great German patriot squared up to the prospect of his country's defeat. He wrote to Pauline:

Things are starting to be really desolate. The war is over, definitely over! But what is to come may be worse. . . It's a scandal that we have to live through times like these. They say we shall all have diligently to learn new ways now. I shan't make the effort to do so until the situation has become a little clearer. . . I am still holding my head high in the belief that Germany is too 'diligent' to fall into such a complete decline – in spite of all the nonsense the worthy government has instituted. Bismarck's dream has suffered a rude awakening, at all events, and 200 years of Prussiandom are at an end. Let's hope that it will be replaced by better times. I don't believe it will – but there's nothing we can do about historical facts. Please don't upset yourself unnecessarily. . . We are going to need all our nerve now to steer our little ship safely on its way. We will think over everything calmly, although I wouldn't know what else to do, even now, other than carry on as usual for as long as possible, according to plan, for as long as theatres and concerts keep going and pay fees. If you love me, then there isn't much the world can do to harm us.

There we see the true Strauss, the man whose world centred on his family and his work. He was the archetypal bourgeois, admirable in his loyalty to his lifelong ideals. Steering their 'little ship' safely on its way was proving difficult. In May 1918 he had quarrelled with the Berlin Intendant, Hülsen, and was increasingly unhappy and insecure in his relationship with the court opera. Later in the summer, feelers were put out towards him from the Vienna Court Opera, where Baron Leopold von Andrian-Werburg had become manager in July. He was a childhood friend of Hofmannsthal, who came to hear of the approaches and on 1 August wrote to Strauss an extraordinary letter declaring himself an opponent of his appointment because 'you would put your own personal convenience, and above all the egoism of the creative musician, before the uphill struggle for the ultimate higher welfare of that institution'. He said he did not believe Strauss would be willing to throw himself wholeheartedly into building up the repertoire.

I believe, when it came to engaging artists, making enemies, friends, etc. etc., in short in handling the whole policy of the theatre, the advantage to your own works would be uppermost in your mind. . .The great danger of your life, to which you surrender and from which you try to escape in almost periodic cycles, is a neglect of all the higher standards of intellectual existence. . . I wish you well, better than most people have done in your life. You have not looked for many friends, and have not had many.[1]

Strauss accepted this insulting letter 'without offence'. Yes, his composing was his principal interest but he restricted it to the summer. 'I have resolved to devote five winter months for the next ten years or so to my work as a conductor.' In Vienna, in an advisory capacity, he would undertake each month a completely new production of an outstanding masterpiece and would also support new works.

It has been my devoutest wish for the past thirty years to assume the *de facto* supreme direction of a big Court Opera House on the artistic side. It was denied me: either because I was always regarded as the opposite of the so popular routine official, or because as too independent an artistic personality, as a composer of some reputation, I was not credited with sufficient interest in the routine running of a theatre and its everyday requirement, such as a purely reproductive artist would have. During twenty years' work in Berlin, under the utterly autocratic Count Hülsen, a man inaccessible to all influence, I finally gave up any attempt to have a say in the management of that institution and have thus become the kind of person you are now judging so severely. What still keeps me in Berlin is my duty not to withdraw the father's loving hand from my own works at Germany's premier artistic institution, and a delight in a magnificently disciplined orchestra.[2]

What occurred in the meantime we do not know, but a month later Hofmannsthal was advocating Strauss's move to Vienna, although at this stage there was no talk of his being director of the opera. In December he wrote: 'I *want* you here.' Strauss had been to Vienna in October when *Salome* was at last performed at the Vienna Court Opera, with Maria Jeritza in the title-role and Franz Schalk conducting. Quite probably a firm offer was made to him at this time. But in Berlin Hülsen had retired and Dr Georg Droescher was elected by the staff of the opera house to succeed him. Strauss agreed to take over temporary directorship of the State Opera, as it was now called after the Armistice, but he soon discovered that Droescher was no easier to work with than Hülsen. He refused to conduct in Berlin as a sub-ordinate to Droescher but, as he told Hofmannsthal on 7 January 1919, 'It has emerged that, while Droescher is sole Director, I have a special position *directly under the Ministry*, can conduct and produce whatever I want and whenever I want to, and have a decisive say in all matters of importance.' He had been a court conductor since 1885, the last great composer to act in that capacity. Now he was discovering that civil servants and workers' councils had replaced emperors and aristocratic intendants. In June 1919, to Strauss's surprise, Max von Schillings was appointed director of Berlin State Opera. 'Today', he told Hofmannsthal, 'on the motion of Mme [Barbara] Kemp, its leading singer, . . . [the staff of Berlin Opernhaus] elects Max Schillings. This, one would think, has now definitely reduced the Artists' Self-Government *ad absurdum*. . . I suppose my closer connections with the Berlin Opera will now have to come to an end.' (Schillings married Kemp four years later.) He fulfilled the rest of his Berlin opera commitments, which included his first *Parsifal*, and he conducted the concerts of the State Opera Orchestra until 1920 when he was succeeded by Wilhelm Furtwängler.

Germany was in a state of unrest and in the major cities such as Berlin and Munich there was fighting between Government troops and the 'Spartacists', as the revolutionary German Communist Party was then known. In March 1919 he wrote from Berlin to Pauline in Garmisch:

I've just come back from the theatre where it should have been *Fidelio* but wasn't, as the lights went out. There was a lot of shooting today, the government troops won at Alexanderplatz and did a thorough clear-out of the Spartacists. . . I wonder if I am really so very necessary as Rösch thinks I am for the organization he is setting up so energetically to unite the associations of independent artists and the various musicians' bodies. . . With these matters to think about, which are very important for the future of the arts, it is best to forget the whole idiotic revolution and enjoy the inner satisfaction of working selflessly for a good cause.

This was a reference to further efforts to improve economic conditions for musicians and to ensure that, under the new post-imperial régime, the work of the *Genossenschaft deutscher Tonsetzer* was continued. Strauss himself, though by no means poor, could not yet afford to give up conducting so as to concentrate on composition. Most of his savings, which on the advice of the London-based financier Edgar Speyer (dedicatee of *Salome* and owner of a Frankfurt banking firm) he had deposited in London, had been sequestrated (and were never returned) and the 6,000 gold francs which was his fee from Diaghilev for *Josephs Legende* had never been paid because of the war. Strauss's biggest fright from the Spartacists came when his son Franz was about to travel from Garmisch to Heidelberg to begin his university course at the end of April 1919. Journeys were taking hours in bad conditions. 'Why on earth did you leave home? Garmisch seems to be quiet still, and now that Starnberg has been "taken" by the Government troops today, the danger that the beaten Spartacists would fall back on Garmisch has more or less disappeared. My head often feels as thick as a melon, but I won't give in to things. Only worry about my family can get to me, such as overcame me yesterday when I heard about your sudden departure.'

He had also become involved in another good cause. In August 1917 he joined the artists' council of the Salzburg Festival Society which had been formed, largely through the enthusiasm of Hofmannsthal, to make Salzburg a leading artistic centre. Other members besides Hofmannsthal and Strauss were Reinhardt (who in 1918 bought the Schloss Leopoldskron in Salzburg), Franz Schalk and Alfred Roller. The idea of promoting the music of Mozart appealed strongly to Strauss. To launch such a scheme at this time required amazing courage and foresight. After 1918 in Europe, there were food shortages, roaring inflation and transport chaos. To raise money for an arts festival and a new concert hall must have seemed madness, and not surprisingly political factions in Salzburg itself and in Vienna made the whole enterprise exceedingly risky. When he went to the United States in 1921, Strauss raised several thousand dollars for the festival and encouraged the foundation of an American committee of friends of the festival. He had been less successful some months earlier on his visit to South America. But, as he told Hofmannsthal, 'what is Salzburg to a Brazilian or, even worse, to a German living in Brazil?' He expressed his ideals for Salzburg in 1920:

The Salzburg Festspielhaus . . . is to be a symbol, full of the light of truth and the reflection of culture. . . All Europe will know that our future lies in art, and especially in music. . . In these days when the gods of the mind are far fewer than those of material things, and when egoism, envy, hatred and mistrust seem to rule the world, he who supports our proposals will be doing a good work, and contributing substantially toward the revival of brotherliness and love of our neighbour.

In the 1922 festival Strauss conducted *Don Giovanni* and *Così fan tutte*, the casts including Alfred Jerger, Richard Tauber, Richard Mayr, Lotte Schöne and Elisabeth Schumann. In the same year he was elected president of the Festival Society, but because of the bureaucratic and financial squabbles he lost interest and resigned in 1924, a year in which no festival was held, but remained on the artistic council. The first of his operas to be performed there was *Ariadne auf Naxos* in 1926. He conducted one of the three performances. It was not until 1929 that *Der Rosenkavalier*, with legendary casts, began its association with the festival.

Before returning to the Vienna negotiations is the moment to consider Strauss's position as a composer at this time. In 1919 he was fifty-five, his position as Germany's greatest living composer unchallenged. His international reputation was enormous. Although the operas of Franz Schreker enjoyed a boom (they were wittily described by Otto Klemperer as 'typical inflation music'), Pfitzner had a success with *Palestrina* in 1917 and the prodigious talent of Erich Korngold was the talk of the dinner-tables, Strauss's supremacy was virtually unassailable. His relationship with Pfitzner is worth a digression. There had been tension between them since March 1900 when a work by Pfitzner was sandwiched between two Strauss tone-poems in Berlin. The Strauss works were a hit with public and critics, Pfitzner's not. They respected rather than admired each other's music and conducted it. Strauss recommended Pfitzner for the post of chief conductor in Strasbourg which he held from 1908 to 1918. Pfitzner could not bear to hear his work disparaged, whereas Strauss could mock himself and his music. It was after the première of *Palestrina* in 1917 that Pfitzner told Strauss how difficult he had found the second act. Strauss replied: 'Why did you write it, then, if you found it so difficult?' Pfitzner was not amused. Strauss introduced Pfitzner's operas into the Vienna repertory, but his attitude to their composer is epitomised in a letter he wrote to Schalk in March 1919: 'The good fellow is so prickly and so idealistic. We want to do everything we can for him and for his works but not have him in the vicinity. Why do people always say "Strauss and Pfitzner". They could say Pfitzner all on his own so far as I'm concerned – greatest composer of all time – since Beethoven, that is. What little I am, I want to be alone, not in company. The eternal labelling by the press: modernism. For my part, I want to have nothing to do with it. If only they would leave me alone, unshorn, away from the herd.' He was only too aware of the changing climate – Stravinsky, Hindemith, Weill, Berg, Webern and of course Schoenberg – and he had no particular interest in it. He did not want to follow their path. In his rejection of the post-1918 *avant-garde*, he must often have reminded himself of his father. But because he did not follow the younger set does not mean that he did not want to strike out along a new path in his own work. He could not interest Hofmannsthal in the kind of work he wanted, so he turned to his *Krämerspiegel* collaborator, Alfred Kerr:

I should like to play the musical Aristophanes of today's Grand Operetta – known as The Revolution. In *Singspiel* form, like the *opéras comiques* of Auber. On the one hand, the state of the theatre today, with workers' soviets and works' committee, prima donnas' plots, tenors' ambitions, General Intendants of the old régime proffering their resignations, could provide the milieu of one plot – and the political operetta: National Assembly, Old Comrades' associations, party politics, while the people starve, a souteneur as Minister of Education and Culture, a burglar as Minister of War, a murderer as Minister of Justice, could form the background of the other comic scene.

Kerr began what Strauss years later described to Stefan Zweig as 'a saucy operetta', based on Wieland's *Peregrinus Proteus*. But nothing came of it. The years 1919 and 1920 are a blank in the catalogue of Strauss's works; in 1921 he composed only – some only! – the *Drei Hymnen*, Op. 71, to texts by Hölderlin with accompaniment for large orchestra, songs which anticipate the richness of the *Vier letzte Lieder* of twenty-seven years later and constitute a major work, sadly underrated and neglected. Part of the explanation is that he was composing the opera *Intermezzo* and that the Vienna Opera and travels abroad ate into his time. The first performance of Op. 71 was given in Berlin on 4 November 1921 by Barbara Kemp, with Gustav Brecher conducting.

Strauss agreed in October 1918 to go to Vienna a year hence. Hofmannsthal now supported the idea and claimed he always had. It was not an auspicious time. Black market, inflation, fuel shortages, poverty – none of the splendour and grandeur of Mahler's day. Reports that Strauss had obtained an inordinately high salary (it was 80,000 kronen) for five months' work circulated among the singers and staff and led to a strong movement opposing his appointment – the 'Revolt against Richard Strauss', as Richard Specht called it. In April 1919 Strauss sent a telegram to a Viennese official, his friend Ludwig Karpath: 'Accustomed to setting artistic goals above everything, apathetic by nature against personal insults, I will not let go of my artistic dream Vienna-Salzburg, but I cannot do without the support of colleagues and friends.' The 'personal insults' had come from the retired director of the Opera, Hans Gregor, who wrote in the *Wiener Journal*: 'What does this composer's name have to do with the position of director of the former Court Opera? How will, for instance, the opera develop which is directed by a man who looks down with disdain on certain Viennese favourites (such as Puccini)... Strauss is everything other than a philanthropist; he has a heart only for himself, is an egoist and considers every matter from this point of view.' The matter was ended when an open telegram assuring him how much he was wanted and needed in Vienna was signed by, among many others, Julius Bittner, Alma Gropius-Mahler, Selma Kurz, Hofmannsthal, Max Kalbeck, Ludwig Karpath, Eusebius Mandyczewski, Ferdinand Löwe, Alfred Roller, Georg Szell, Richard Specht, Paul Stefan, Arthur Schnitzler, Jakob Wassermann, Egon Wellesz and Stefan Zweig. So Strauss took up his duties.

Schalk greeted him, with the whole company present, and Strauss pledged to strive with all the influence he possessed to improve and safe-guard their 'social status' and 'to bring about the fulfilment of your demands, especially the claims of those who now have to contend with hardship: orchestra, chorus, ballet and stage staff'. He participated in a festival to mark the opera house's fiftieth anniversary. He conducted *Fidelio*, *Tristan und Isolde*, *Die Zauberflöte*, *Der Rosenkavalier* and *Ariadne auf Naxos*. (Incidentally, three Puccini operas were performed during the festival.) Although it is always said that Strauss and Franz Schalk were co-directors, this was not the intention. Speaking to Roland Tenschert in 1944,

Strauss emphasised that 'it had not been a co-directorate as he himself had been chosen as head. Because he was unable to be in Vienna for the whole opera season owing to his guest appearances, he had himself suggested that he should be given one of the house artists as deputy for the time he would be absent. He had himself mentioned Franz Schalk as being a conductor who had served the opera for many years.'[3] This is confirmed in Franz Grasberger's authoritative *Richard Strauss und die Wiener Oper*, where Andrian refers to Strauss in October 1918 as *künstlerischen Oberleiter der Hofoper*.

Strauss encountered another typical Viennese controversy before he took over. He had persuaded the soprano Elisabeth Schumann to leave Hamburg and to join the Vienna company. He also discussed with her husband, the conductor Carl Alwin, the possibility of his also going to Vienna. This led to an article by Max Graf in the *Neues Wiener Journal* accusing Strauss of being 'a true happy-go-lucky South German' who would exercise nepotism for a friend who was a mediocre conductor compared with some young Austrians. Strauss, Graf continued, could play Skat with Alwin while Pauline could gossip with Elisabeth. This drew a furious response from Pauline, who wrote to the *Journal* pointing out that she had only once spoken to Elisabeth Schumann and that Strauss had never played Skat with Alwin. 'My husband is at least as able as the writer of the article to judge the qualities of a conductor. . . If my husband is annoyed by inaccurate press reports before he has even arrived, *he may well leave Vienna in disgust*.' Alwin could not play Skat.

As a kind of dowry Strauss gave Vienna the world première of *Die Frau ohne Schatten* on 10 October 1919. He had withheld the work from the stage during the war, but now realised he had released it too early. The Vienna first performance was splendid, with Jeritza as the Empress, Lotte Lehmann as the Dyer's Wife, Lucie Weidt as the Nurse, Richard Mayr as Barak and Karl Aagard-Oestvig as the Emperor, but 'its way over the German stage was fraught with misfortune. In Vienna itself, owing to the strain imposed by the vocal parts and to the difficulties over the sets [by Roller], the opera had to be withdrawn more often than it was performed.'[4] The Dresden première was a disaster. 'It was a serious blunder to entrust this opera, difficult as it was to cast and produce, to medium and even small theatres immediately after the war', Strauss wrote. Both he and Hofmannsthal had been disappointed with Roller's Vienna designs. Strauss said Roller 'approached the piece with far too much resignation and gave up the "magic tricks" from the start. The music alone can't do everything and certainly not *this* kind of thing: one might as well write an oratorio and have done with the stage altogether!'

From the start, too, the critics misunderstood the opera and were baffled by its symbolism. The libretto was regarded as incomprehensible, but throughout his life Strauss defended it and praised its conciseness – one has only to look at a page of the text to see what he meant. To anyone acquainted with *Die Zauberflöte*, with its motifs of trial and purification, *Die Frau ohne Schatten* should present few problems. It is a fairy-tale and also a hymn to marriage and its fulfilment by children, as well as a quest for humanity and love. A woman without a shadow is infertile. The half-spirit, half-human Empress, daughter of Keikobad, ruler of the spirit world, has not conceived after nearly a year of marriage and spirit law decrees that the human who takes a spirit bride must make her pregnant within a year or be turned to stone – she must gain a shadow. In company with the evil and ambivalent Nurse, perhaps the most interesting character in the opera, the Empress descends to the world of mortals as represented by the poor home of Barak the Dyer and his shrewish wife. They too are childless because the wife is refusing her husband intercourse. The Nurse bribes the wife to sell her shadow. But when the Empress realises that this would destroy Barak, whose desire for children rules his life, she refuses to drink from the fountain of the Waters of Life. If she were to do so, Barak's wife's shadow would be hers and the Emperor, who has by now been turned to stone, would be saved. Her refusal is what makes her human, she gains a shadow of her own, the couples are reunited and the voices of their unborn children are heard.

Some regard this opera as Strauss's greatest; and if one hears and sees a great performance, it is easy to be tempted into agreement. Yet it remains a problem work, veering towards pretentiousness and with passages where one can be conscious of Strauss's difficulty in sustaining interest in the characters. There is no doubt that by composing the Prologue to *Ariadne* in his vein of parody and sentimentality *before* completing Act 3 of *Die Frau ohne Schatten*, he lost the impetus for the bigger work. Nevertheless, the best parts of the work are very great – Barak's music, the orchestral interlude describing Barak's character, the Emperor's aria, the falcon music, the Empress's melodrama. If one wishes to isolate a passage where the usually objective Strauss bares his soul and reveals loneliness and vulnerability as if afraid to look too deeply into his heart for fear of what he might find, but does so on this occasion, then it is the Emperor's aria in Act 2 ('lead me to the desolate rocky cleft where neither man nor beast can hear my lament!'). And there is the sheer virtuosity of the orchestral score, best described by the opera's first conductor, Schalk, in an essay he wrote in 1919 for the Vienna *Blätter des Operntheaters*. He wrote:

The musicians, even those familiar with the Strauss works, were forced to realise after the first rehearsals that the manner of execution which they had used until then was not adequate. They had to find a much more delicate art of playing, a more differentiated dynamic, a complete command of the middle voices which let one hear even the most hidden tones. The score does not include any unimportant voices, no polyphony in the old sense, rather a counterpoint of the whole, often even thematic complexes of harmony. A polyrhythmic structure of a great boldness is the necessary result.

One of the violinists in the Dresden première, Arthur Tröber, has recalled that the dress rehearsal there had to be abandoned at midnight because of technical difficulties. 'The music and words bewildered us. . . It was said this was more a subject for the gynaecological ward than for the stage. It was several years before we could relate to this opera, which was so beloved by Strauss.'[5]

Strauss rarely revised a work after publication unless he made extensive changes as in *Ariadne auf Naxos* and *Die ägyptische Helena*, but he made an exception in the case of Act 3 of *Die Frau ohne Schatten*. When Clemens Krauss was conducting a new Munich production in 1939 he wrote to Strauss on 8 September, more than a month after the first night, asking for 'a new version of the two passages for the Guardian of the Threshold (with less orchestra). It really is a pity one cannot understand the text in these passages. You once said they should be composed again?!' Strauss replied: 'You are absolutely right. . . The passage has been annoying me for long enough!' He thereupon revised and reduced the scoring of both passages, sending them to Krauss headed 'Prima le parole dopa la musica'. He wanted conductors to regard the new instrumentation as binding. Strauss's manuscript was reproduced on two pages of No. 2 of the *Richard Strauss-Blätter* of the International Richard Strauss Society in 1971, with details of the revisions.[6]

Hofmannsthal recognised that in this work he had placed a 'gigantic burden' on Strauss's shoulders 'although it is true that he carried it up the very steep mountain as if it were child's play'. Time had overtaken them both. They had first contemplated *Die Frau ohne Schatten* in 1911. Eight years later, the world had changed for ever. Their opera belonged to the pre-1914 world. It was totally unsuited to the war-weary, defeated and sleazy Germany and Austria of 1919. It was emphatically not the opera to introduce in a Vienna where at least 200,000 children were near to starvation, 130,000 men were out of work, people died in the streets from hunger or revolution-ary bullets and the streets and parks were piled with uncollected refuse.

But Strauss was never one to take too much notice of the world around him. The profiteers might be in the boxes at the opera, but he went on as if the audience was composed of connoisseurs. In his second year in Vienna, the State Opera acquired the Redoutensaal in the Hofburg as a second opera stage. Roller converted the room into an exquisite theatre at a cost which infuriated the press. But it was a success not only as the ideal place to stage such operas as *Le nozze di Figaro* and *Don Pasquale*, but as a home for ballet, where the dancers included Tilly Losch. It was for the ballet company in the Redoutensaal that Strauss orchestrated eight keyboard pieces by François Couperin as the *Tanzsuite* which was first danced there on 17 February 1923, conducted by a musician who was to play a major part in Strauss's life henceforward, Clemens Krauss. When Boieldieu's *Jean de Paris* was revived in the Redoutensaal, Strauss, who conducted it, re-worked the Princess's coloratura aria especially for Selma Kurz. He conducted all Wagner's operas except *Parsifal* in new productions, several devised by himself, and the stan-dard Mozart operas including *Così fan tutte* in which he accompanied the recitatives on the piano, improvising them and often bringing in sly allu-sions to his own works.

The financial position of the Vienna State Opera was so bad when Strauss and Schalk took over that in the late summer of 1920 they took the Vienna Philharmonic to South America to raise dollars. Strauss was accompanied by his son. When the ship took on coal at the Cape Verde Islands, the decks became filthy. Back at sea, Strauss wrote to Pauline, 'there began a whole-sale swabbing down that it would have done your heart good to see, scrub-bing of all the decks, roofs and cabins, spring-cleaning of our persons and changing of clothes.' The voyage, he told her, was 'good for composition: I have already filled a sketchbook with melodies and themes'. And he read Goethe. The concerts in Rio were given to almost empty halls as the result of rivalry between two impresarios. Rio was in any case more interested in the fourteen-day visit of King Albert of the Belgians. Strauss noted (as he told Pauline) 'an outlay on flags and soldiery such as Wilhelm in his day could not have outdone. At home we are getting rid of that junk, here the swindle is flourishing.' However, the tour ended successfully, with invita-tions to the Vienna Opera to visit Brazil at Brazilian expense. While in Rio he attended a performance of *Der Rosenkavalier* conducted by Tullio Serafin, with Claudia Muzio 'as an extremely elegant and charming Marschallin' and wrote to Hofmannsthal to tell him. Curiously, earlier in 1920, Hofmannsthal had sent him a scenario called *Danae, oder die Vernunftheirat* (*Danae, or the Marriage of Convenience*) which 'continues exactly the line *Rosenkavalier, Ariadne-Vorspiel, Bürger als Edelmann.* It asks for light, nimble-witted music, such as only you can write, and only at this stage in your life. The subject is early mythological antiquity, flippantly treated.' It was what Strauss had been asking him for, but for some reason the preoccupied composer never mentioned it, perhaps never read it, and it was not until 1936, as we shall see, that he became interested in what was to become *Die Liebe der Danae*.

Strauss's absences from Vienna undoubtedly undermined his authority there. He toured Hungary and Romania in 1921 and attended the first Donaueschingen festival of contemporary music, of which he was honorary chairman. It was there, after hearing Hindemith's 'cheeky, mad but very tal-ented' second string quartet, that he asked the young composer why he wrote atonally when he had such talent. Hindemith replied: 'Herr Doktor, you make your music and I'll make mine.' The music Strauss was writing was very different. During August and September he sketched out in short score a ballet to his own scenario, *Schlagobers* (*Whipped Cream*). Schalk was annoyed by Strauss's decision to tour the United States in the autumn of 1921 and demanded an explanation. 'I am not going for pleasure', Strauss replied.

14 Father and son

'After England confiscated the chief part of my capital, having no pension to look forward to from any quarter, I have only the royalties from my works to fall back on if anything happened to me that stopped me conducting. Even operatic successes are unreliable – if the royalties fail, which I hope will not happen for a while yet, I shall be a beggar and shall leave my family in "poverty and shame". I must free myself from this worry, if I am to work in peace again.' This was the guiding principle behind all Strauss's actions – his family was paramount. Snide comments are continually made about Strauss and money, but he saw no reason why an artist should not be recompensed for his work the same as any other craftsman or businessman. Starving in a garret may be romantic (it isn't), but there is a snobbish view that for a composer to be rich is somehow immoral! Strauss was quite open about his intentions: 'I shall conduct until I have one or two million saved up, then I shall stop.' Strauss's dream, never fulfilled, was to live in Italy where, in the sunshine and warmth, he would do nothing but compose. Ernst Roth, who was Strauss's publisher in his last years, said of him:

He had no business sense at all. His contracts were drafted by his lawyers and he trusted their advice implicitly. In investing his money, he relied on the counsel of experts, which was not always good. His houses in Garmisch and Vienna were not speculative investments, he built them for himself and never parted with them. After *Salome*, he sold his publishing rights for large sums and retained the performing and mechanical rights for himself. He did not bargain. He was invariably correct and reliable in all his dealings and had absolute confidence in his partners. It would never have crossed his mind to check accounts or have them checked by accountants. His music earned big money for concert-promoters, opera-houses, conductors and singers. His were box-office successes and Strauss, who was no hypocrite, felt entitled to his fair share, said so and demanded it.

To Gustav and Alma Mahler, this was a vulgar, bourgeois attitude.

Strauss sailed for the United States on 19 October 1921 in the White Star liner *Adriatic* with his son Franz and Elisabeth Schumann. (Schumann was the choice of the tour's American organisers. Originally the baritone Franz Steiner had been engaged.) He was fêted there with civic receptions and press conferences. Besides accompanying Schumann in recitals, he conducted the Philadelphia and other orchestras in his works. He told journalists that his favourites among his symphonic poems were 'those that show me and my opinions most clearly: *Zarathustra, Quixote, Domestica*' and he said he found jazz 'very interesting, especially the rhythms'. To Pauline, he reported on 'the filthy American food' and that apart from New York, 'which is really fabulous, staying in the land of universal mechanisation is deadly boring. All the hotels are overheated even when the weather is mild.' But he 'let it all flow over me patiently, for the good of our dear country, and am looking forward to seeing you again'. In her diary of the tour, Elisabeth Schumann relates that Strauss brought her Pauline's letters to him to read – 'tender lines, quite different from the way she speaks!' In Detroit, at their recital, she noted that he played some of his own songs by heart. 'He is not a good "by-heart" player and something quite wonderful happened with *All' mein' Gedanken*. By the third bar he had forgotten the accompaniment and he composed a completely new song. I kept up with him, the words fitted perfectly, nobody in the audience suspected a thing and when we reached the end safe and sound, I looked to the right out of the corner of my eye. All I saw was his mouth stretching from ear to ear in one huge grin. . . Later I begged him to write down the new version, but he said "Oh, I've already totally forgotten it".' During the tour a Strauss recital was broadcast for the first time. He sailed for home on 4 January 1922, returning by way of England, where he conducted the Hallé in Manchester on the 21st, and told Schalk that 'after this horrendous and exhausting tour, I look forward to rational activity at my desk and some stimulating work in the theatre.'

But what awaited him was a deteriorating relationship with Schalk who, perhaps understandably, wanted to be regarded as the director. He had been at the Vienna Opera since Mahler's day and most of the daily administrative problems came to his desk. But he took a long time to come to decisions. Strauss was quick to make up his mind and was a bold planner. This caused friction which came to a head in June after he had returned from his first post-war visit to London, where Elgar and Bernard Shaw welcomed him warmly. Schalk, who knew the plight of the opera house's finances, resented Strauss giving permission to star singers to perform at other theatres in his operas. Strauss did his best to keep the peace. 'It seems I have used the wrong tone in trying to be clear and have unwittingly affronted you, which I did not intend', he wrote.

Once for all I could not ask for a better colleague with whom I could harmonise so artistically. We must try to bridge the small differences between us: Upper and Lower Danube. You know how much I love Austria, but a shot of Boche-blood into your perhaps somewhat too persistent *Gemütlichkeit* would certainly do no harm. I am convinced you can unhesitatingly trust my leadership. . . Let's concentrate on quality and perfection, the only argument with which we can justify our directorship. Drop a work even after the dress rehearsal if it has not reached the degree of perfection which it should. I am rather unhappy that my operas are only performed in Vienna when I am present. It does not look good and is compromising for me in reality. As long as I remain a kind of pseudo-director in Vienna I would propose that you perform my operas little or not at all. Then there are more chances for the others.[7]

Hofmannsthal acted as go-between and Strauss became conciliatory. His librettist wrote to him (4 September 1922): 'Now that you have gained so fine and intelligent a victory over yourself, let me say this: you would have had the worst of it in any case; the real victim would have been this fine unique institution and that means the eventual sufferer you yourself – as a composer.'

Both Strauss and Schalk were strongly criticised for their directorship. Paul Bekker was Vienna correspondent of *The Musical Times* in which in February 1922 he complained that the State Opera was 'gradually assuming the character of a place of merely superficial amusement for the wealthy classes and for the *nouveaux riches* whose taste is all too often heeded by the management'. The company ensemble was disorganised 'owing to a strong preference on the part of the directors for "guest" singers whose mission is sensationalism while some of the finest artists of the theatre are enjoying involuntary leave'. Bekker also complained that, apart from Strauss, the only contemporary composers performed were Puccini and Erich Korngold. The latter, now twenty-five, had had a major success throughout Germany and Austria since 1920 with his opera *Die tote Stadt*. But one of the Vienna Opera's – and Strauss's – most savage opponents was Korngold's father Julius, music critic of the *Neue Freie Presse* and co-librettist with his son of *Die tote Stadt* (although this was a well-kept secret). Bekker told readers of *The Musical Times* in August 1922 that Julius Korngold's sole consideration in his reviews was not how artists sang, played or conducted but what their attitude was towards Erich. Matters came to a head when Erich wrote to the directors to complain that his opera's success was being affected by holidays and the unannounced appearances of substitute singers. Strauss and Schalk summoned him to their office and laid into him about the connection of Julius's reviews to performances of Erich's works. They told him he could no longer conduct his own operas because of his father's attitude. Erich responded by asking for the popular and money-making *Die tote Stadt* to be withdrawn from the repertory. Strauss, who had helped to promote Korngold's career since his *Wunderkind* years, told him not to be childish and refused. So the situation arose where Korngold could attend other and less competent conductors' rehearsals of *Die tote Stadt*, at one of which a singer called out 'Why isn't Korngold conducting?' and Erich shouted back: 'Because my father writes bad reviews of the opera's directors. Let's make a resolution. Korngold shall conduct!' Called again before Strauss, he explained that he had been pained by the rehearsal and would prefer that his work was not done at all. In a moment of inspiration, he quoted from the

Prologue to Strauss's *Ariadne auf Naxos*, when the young Composer, faced with the prospect of an appalling presentation of his opera, says: 'Lieber ins Feuer!' ('Rather throw it in the fire!'). Strauss was disarmed: he immediately reinstated Korngold.

Meanwhile, what of Strauss as composer? He was still at work on scoring *Intermezzo*; and he must have discussed future plans with Hofmannsthal. They had not collaborated since 1917. The poet had been thrilled by the Vienna première of *Josephs Legende* ('the most beautiful sets I have seen on the stage for years ... and why on earth this never-ending denigration? I ask myself: is there anything better, or even as good in this genre?'). He ends this letter, written on 21 March 1922: 'Now for *Helena* which, together with *Rosenkavalier* and *Ariadne*, is to become for me a third work certain of enduring for many years to come.' This was the first mention of what was to become *Die ägyptische Helena*. During the summer Strauss worked on the orchestration of his ballet *Schlagobers*, completing it on 16 September and writing to Hofmannsthal on the 12th: 'I feel like doing another *Rosenkavalier* just now.' It was not until 1 April 1923 that Hofmannsthal next mentioned *Helena* when he referred to 'the little light opera' and the 'light, gay, airy piece'.

Strauss planned *Schlagobers* as a tribute to Vienna, a city he liked ('People are deceitful everywhere', he said, 'but in Vienna they're so pleasant about it') and where he was hoping to settle, using Garmisch as a summer residence. He and Pauline lived in a flat in the Mozartplatz but she wanted a garden and something bigger. Strauss consulted the Minister of Works about a site where he could build and was offered one in the former private garden of Archduke Franz Ferdinand at the Belvedere in the Jacquingasse. He paid for it with dollars he had earned in America and some assistance from the Jewish industrialist Emanuel von Grab, whom he had known since 1907 and at whose home in the country he had often stayed, playing Skat with his host. Now, to his pleasure, his son Franz was showing interest in Grab's daughter Alice. The lease of the Belvedere house and grounds was to belong to Strauss and his heirs for sixty years. He paid for the lease by giving the autograph score of *Der Rosenkavalier* to the Austrian National Library and that of *Schlagobers* to the City Library. Some years later, he agreed to conduct one hundred performances at the State Opera over five years and in addition gave the score of *Die ägyptische Helena* to the National Library.

Strauss said: 'In the end, with 60,000 dollars' worth of manuscripts and 200,000 schillings' worth of conducting, I paid handsomely for my building site. I probably paid too much.' The Strauss 'palace' at the Belvedere was seized upon by his opponents in Vienna, who also objected to his absences, his salary and the performances of his own works. His supporters like Carl Alwin made matters worse by their over-exuberant counter-attacks. It was the kind of situation beloved by Viennese intriguers.

With the Austrian economic situation, particularly inflation, growing worse, Strauss and Schalk sailed in the summer of 1923 to South America with the State Opera company and the Vienna Philharmonic Orchestra to tour Argentina, Uruguay and Brazil. On 12 July Strauss reported to Hofmannsthal the success of *Salome* and *Elektra* in Buenos Aires. There, on 21 August, he completed *Intermezzo*. In Rio de Janeiro, there were ten performances of *Elektra* and, while there, Strauss received a letter from his son saying that he and Alice wanted to marry. He telegraphed his delighted approval. At concerts, works by Bruckner, Mahler, Korngold, Pfitzner, Schillings and Franz Schmidt were included in the programmes. Sailing home, Strauss wrote to Hofmannsthal on 8 September: 'I hope to find *Helena* at Garmisch, preferably with entertaining ballet interludes; a few delightful elf or spirit choruses would also be most welcome. I . . . would like to have some pleasant work to do at Garmisch during the autumn. Best of all, a second *Rosenkavalier* without its mistakes and *longueurs*. You'll just *have to write that for me some day*. I haven't spoken my last word yet in that genre. Something delicate, amusing and warm-hearted!' But the *Helena* libretto was not ready. Hofmannsthal had 'the whole piece worked out in my head'. The music, he advised the composer, would have to be 'easy-flowing, on occasion as nearly conversational as the Vorspiel to *Ariadne*. . . The more lightheartedly you can handle this, the better it will be; there is, in any case, no German artist who does not become more heavy-handed over whatever he does than he ought to be.' Prophetic words! As for the second *Rosenkavalier*, 'I feel I shall get it one day. I have some notion of a plot. . . The best way you can encourage and animate me is by getting to work on *Helena* with a rapid, easy hand. Tell yourself that you mean to handle it as if it were to be merely an operetta – it's bound to be by Richard Strauss in the end. Over *Die Frau ohne Schatten* we both became too heavy-handed.'

If no *Helena* awaited him, the crisis at the Opera remained. The financial outlook was grim. Official refusal to provide a rehearsal stage and a store for scenery infuriated Strauss, who suggested to Schalk that it would perhaps be better 'if I did not come at all this winter, until the worst depression is past, so that the treasury can avoid having to pay my salary. Not that I do not want to come, but if it is a relief for the poor state purse I am willing to make the sacrifice. . . It is a farce. One speaks of the bankruptcy of the opera. . . I am not going to sit around a third year and let myself be insulted by the press. I do not want to leave only because of the obnoxious Mr [Julius] Korngold, but there must be a purpose for me to stay.' Strauss agreed that Schalk should conduct operas by Pfitzner, Schreker, Bittner and Korngold but pointed out that, like his own *Die Frau ohne Schatten,* their works were poorly attended. 'The important principal function of the State Opera', he told his colleague, 'is to give the most exemplary performances possible of the classic repertory. . . Why the novelties? If we are honest, we must admit that outside of the composer and his clique, no one takes any real delight in them. . . Besides that, it is difficult today to persuade the first-rate singers to learn and sing the usually very taxing roles in the new operas. . . I am working for a theatre based on quality.'

He was cheered in October by the arrival of the first section of the libretto for *Die ägyptische Helena.* He was at once enthusiastic and keen at first that there should be spoken dialogue. 'Please continue in that splendid style of the first few scenes', he told Hofmannsthal. Two days later he received the completion of Act 1. He wrote to his librettist on 23 October: 'The end of Act 1 is very beautiful. . . So far I've sketched out about a third: most of it virtually sets itself to music. . . But more than ever I'm in favour of spoken dialogue. . . I hope to have basically sketched out the first act by the end of November. It's coming on unbelievably fast and is giving me no end of pleasure. But the work would be in vain if Act 2 were not to come off equally well or to contain the necessary climax.' On 5 November he wrote that he had 'got as far as the return of Menelaus and can seriously report that everything so far is wonderful'. But on 26 December he pointed out 'the fundamental mistake of Act 1 as a drama to be set to music' and sent a list of suggested structural changes. The opera was not to be such plain sailing as he had thought.

The year 1924 was a watershed for Strauss. He would be sixty in June and he was the senior figure in German music. But he had not had an indisputable public success since *Der Rosenkavalier* in 1911. He who had been in tune with the times in the first decade of the century was now passed by, not that he really cared. In Czechoslovakia, Janáček, ten years older than Strauss, was writing operas which, although they had to wait many years before they were publicly acclaimed, blended tradition, nationalism and innovation in ideal proportions. Four major Schoenberg works had first performances in 1924. Berg's *Wozzeck* was completed and would be performed in 1925. With *Les Noces* in 1923, Stravinsky had revolutionised rhythm. None of this remotely interested Strauss, who regarded the *avant-garde* experiments with as much distaste as his father had regarded Wagner. His birthday occasioned a long article in the *Zeitschrift für Musik* by the 21-year-old Marxist intellectual philosopher Theodor Adorno, who had studied composition with Alban Berg. Much of it would have qualified for *Private Eye*'s Pseuds' Corner if it had existed then:

The talk about Strauss's superficiality is irresponsible; the entire depth of his music consists in the fact that its whole world is nothing but surface, that it floats loose on the surface of the world instead of letting go of an admittedly fragmentary reality of external things in the fruitless chase after that inner reality which is, by itself, quite unreal. And just as Strauss, by virtue of his concrete-musical vision, escaped the fate of throwing process-without-end into the soul and winding up in lyrical form-anarchy, so he was also charmed against the temptation of empty forms, which give the appearance of objectivity and yet possess, at best, the objectivity of the machine.

Heaven help us! Compare the tribute of Gerhart Hauptmann:

A child of the imperial era, he is nevertheless sounder than that age, and even during the war when sickliness was rife his art remained as healthy as ever. None of the questioning and morbidity of Dostoievsky or Strindberg is contained in it or can permeate it. It is free from Catholic mysticism, since Strauss's eye and art delight in the wonders of the world that can be seen, heard and felt.

Strauss began 1924 with a composition which was close to his heart, the *Hochzeitspräludium* (o.Op. 108) for two harmoniums written for the wedding of Franz and Alice on 15 January, when it was played by Carl Alwin and Rudolf Friedel. Anxiety soon followed, for on their honeymoon Franz

15 Franz and Alice Strauss

contracted typhoid in Egypt and for a time was very seriously ill. Another occasion which meant much to Strauss was Hofmannsthal's fiftieth birthday on 1 February. 'Anything I could tell you in words would be banal in comparison with what, as the composer of your wonderful poetry, I have already said to you in music', he wrote. He was able to tell his collaborator of the 'sensational success' of *Ariadne* the previous week in Amsterdam. He went to Brussels and to Rome (to conduct *Salome*) at the end of January and on return wrote a short Fanfare for the Vienna Philharmonic ball on 4 March – 'once I've settled in the Belvedere', he told Hofmannsthal, 'no hard currency in the world will make me leave my botanical garden in the winter.' In his sketchbooks of this date he noted a plan for 'a last tone-poem: Beast (War) – martyr (suffering) – Man (work)'.

He inaugurated his sixtieth birthday celebrations by conducting the first performance of *Schlagobers* in Vienna on 9 May. It was a ghastly flop. Let the radical writer Karl Kraus be quoted as a sample of the critical reception. He referred to Strauss as 'quite certainly more of a stock company than a genius. . . There has not been a nastier desolation of the spirit even of the ballet or a more thoroughgoing degradation of theatre to a level of a pre-school than this *Schlagobers*, in which the droll old master, ever the joker, comes to terms in his own fashion with the social question.'[8] A gay and witty confection set in a confectioner's shop, with characters like Princess Pralinée, Prince Cocoa and Mlle Marianne Chartreuse, was not the dish of whipped cream to set before starving, bankrupt Vienna. Strauss's friend Romain Rolland was in Vienna and attended the second performance. He found the music 'highly agreeable' and concluded that the critics' 'righteous indignation' stemmed from personal motives. 'The cabal has given its orders. Strauss has caused too many wounds to self-esteem, even among his adherents. They are taking their revenge.' Rolland, percipient as ever, called to see Strauss, whose reaction to the reviews of *Schlagobers* was 'People always expect ideas from me, big things. Haven't I the right, after all, to write what music I please? I cannot bear the tragedy of the present time. I want to create joy. I need it.' Rolland found him, in the Mozartplatz flat, 'surrounded by a circle of ladies and boring society people'. He was preoccupied by 'nationalist follies, by our threatened European Civilisation. Civilisation, for him, is concentrated in Europe, a little Europe, three or four nations. And they are destroying themselves! He doesn't understand. He never has a smile on his face. No sudden bursts of gaiety, of fire, of unconscious "ragamuffin-ery", as there used to be in the past.' Listening to *Schlagobers* today one hears only the music, not a social question, and one wonders why this delightful score has had so bad a press. It is not top-drawer Strauss, but it is superior in invention to *Josephs Legende* and its transparent, light and fanciful scoring continues the vein of *Le bourgeois gentilhomme* and, although no one in May 1924 yet knew it, of *Intermezzo*. It was not music for its time but for any time. There was a plan in 1943 for a film of *Schlagobers*. When he read the scenario Strauss refused to allow the music to be used. 'Unworthy rubbish', he exclaimed. 'By comparison my harmless unassuming *Schlagobers* plot is pure Goethe!'

All Strauss's operas except *Guntram* were performed in Vienna during the birthday celebrations and he conducted several of his tone-poems. At the last of the concerts Rolland heard him conduct *Don Quixote* and 'the prodigious' *Symphonia Domestica*, adding: 'Strauss grows animated while conducting it . . . [and] becomes the young Strauss once more, laughs with the timpani, takes pleasure with the joy he is unleashing.' Just before the actual anniversary, 11 June, he received a heart-warming letter from Hofmannsthal. 'Everything connecting us is dear, most dear, to me, and for my part I wish to see no end to this connection.' He reminded Strauss of his belief that 'the individual can produce nothing of lasting value unless it be linked to tradition' and that he had learned more 'from the features of the older, still living works of literature' than from any '"demands of our time" which might seem to be in the air'. This attitude had earned him nothing but criticism from his contemporaries, but 'the only person who always recognised whatever there was, received it with real joy, received it productively and translated it into higher reality, was you'. Strauss was touched to the heart and vowed to make *Helena* 'a particularly fine composition'.

As the 1924–5 season at the Vienna Opera approached, the matter arose of renewing Strauss's contract after five years. He stipulated that Schalk should be retired after the 1924–5 season and was sure that the Ministry of Culture would agree. Schalk meanwhile had negotiated a new contract which contained a clause giving him sole responsibility for making decisions when Strauss was away. Schalk dealt all year round with the Ministry officials and had their support; they too had read Karl Kraus's gibes that 'a beggar state spends billions, while the city gives the master a piece of property on which to construct a castle in Vienna's most elegant park. All this and a week-long celebration of enthusiasm in the ideal expectation that the creator of a musical world that has the Will to Tourism written all over its face should remain with us for a few months of the year in full non-connection to the institution with which he has been entrusted.'[9] Strauss underestimated Schalk and forgot that he was German and Schalk was Austrian. Both Franz and Alice warned him that he could not run the opera house in an authoritarian manner on a long rein. Nor could he totally override economic considerations in the name of artistic excellence. He returned from his summer holiday to Vienna in September to conduct the first performance on the 20th of the 'festive spectacular' which he and Hofmannsthal had adapted from Beethoven's *Die Ruinen von Athen* into which they incorporated parts of the *Prometheus* ballet music. Strauss had concocted a *mélange* of themes from the Third and Fifth Symphonies to accompany the speech in the melodrama of the Stranger. On 1 October he conducted the Vienna première of *Der Bürger als Edelmann*. Neither event was well received. Strauss wrote to Hofmannsthal that he was 'furious beyond words' at this 'impertinence' of the 'stupid drivel' written about '"the rather feeble" Beethoven! who can still crush that pack of scribes with his little finger!'

Then, having moved into the mansion in the Jacquingasse, he left for Dresden to supervise rehearsals for the first performance of *Intermezzo*. While he was there, two emissaries arrived from Vienna, Dr Ernst Kosak, a Ministry official, and Ludwig Karpath, the Ministry's adviser on national theatres and a friend of Strauss (who had dedicated *Schlagobers* to him). They had come to tell Strauss of Schalk's new contract and to insist upon his agreement to the clause about sole responsibility. The argument went on for several days until Kosak said that he was empowered to accept Strauss's resignation if he offered it. 'Then you can have it at once', Strauss retorted, aware that he had effectively been dismissed. Pauline's comment was: 'He should be congratulated for getting rid of this heavy burden. My family and I are happy it's turned out like this. Now we can move into our beautiful Vienna house and live in and with the Vienna society. What my husband needs for his living he can earn in four weeks and then he can compose in peace.'

That was still their dream and, at the age of sixty, Strauss might have been forgiven for thinking it was near to realisation. Little did he suspect what lay ahead.

16   *Intermezzo*

The gestation of *Intermezzo* – 'a bourgeois comedy with symphonic interludes' – had been lengthy, over five years. This opera's origins in the misunderstanding over Mieze Mücke in 1902 and in Pauline's mild flirtation
with 'Baron Lummer' have been related in chapter nine. The first night
audience was left in no doubt of the autobiographical connection because
the baritone Josef Correck, who sang Robert Storch, was made up to look as
much like Strauss as possible and Lotte Lehmann, who created the role of
Christine, knew Pauline well and had studied her mannerisms. The world
première, conducted by Fritz Busch, was in the intimate Schauspielhaus of
the Dresden State Theatres. Lehmann sang only in the first performance, her
role being taken over thereafter by the local Dresden soprano Grete Nikisch.
Although it was apparently well received, *Intermezzo* was slow to enter the
repertory after the expected initial interest. Its second performance, on 6
November, was at Erfurt, followed by Hamburg and Karlsruhe before the
end of 1924. On 28 March 1925, Georg Szell conducted its first performance
in Berlin, where there were forty-two performances over the next ten years.
It was introduced to Munich on 21 May 1926 by Hans Knappertsbusch. The
first Vienna performance, with Lehmann and Alfred Jerger and conducted
by Strauss, was on 15 January 1927. *Intermezzo* did not reach the United
States until 1963 in a concert performance and until 1977 on the stage (by
students). Britain first heard it, from a visiting company, at the 1965
Edinburgh Festival; the first home-grown production was John Cox's at
Glyndebourne in 1974. It has still not been staged in London nor at a
Salzburg Festival. It was in Munich, at the little Cuvilliés theatre from 1964,
that regular attention began to be paid to it in a production with Hermann
Prey and Hanni Steffek. During Clemens Krauss's great Munich régime,
1937–43, when Strauss was in the forefront of his repertory (although he

ignored *Elektra*), a new production of *Intermezzo* by Rudolf Hartmann was planned. Krauss, who was a great Strauss conductor and a close friend of the composer, seemed to consider that he had a mission to persuade Strauss to revise and re-shape his operas. He did so with *Arabella* and *Die ägyptische Helena*, but with *Intermezzo* he got nowhere. He wanted to convert it from two acts to three and to delete the scene when Christine says good-night to her little son. Strauss dug his heels in. Perhaps Puccini might have altered the structure (he must have been thinking of the revisions to *Madama Butterfly*), but he was not Puccini.

The belief that *Intermezzo* is in some way 'distasteful' because it deals with a slice of Strauss's real life evidently dies hard. Norman Del Mar's treatment of it is a ripe display of English puritanism. In truth, the fact that it is a piece of unalloyed autobiography and that it belongs to the stream of Strauss's consciousness that led to *Ein Heldenleben* and *Symphonia Domestica* is what makes it so successful an opera, one of the three greatest he composed. Undoubtedly it was as a result of composing the Prologue to *Ariadne auf Naxos*, even though he had initially been reluctant to do so, that led him to the fluent, conversational style of *Intermezzo* and left him struggling to cope with the high-flown symbolism provided by Hofmannsthal for Act 3 of *Die Frau ohne Schatten*. Nevertheless, just as he regarded *Don Quixote* as the 'satyr-play' to *Ein Heldenleben*, so *Intermezzo* is the satyr-play to *Die Frau ohne Schatten*. In Strauss's sketchbook for *Intermezzo*, the theme of the Unborn Children in the earlier opera becomes the central theme of reconciliation in *Intermezzo*. The sponger Baron Lummer is wittily given a motif derived from the Shadow theme of *Die Frau ohne Schatten* and Christine's quarrelsome motif has links with the corresponding theme of the Dyer's Wife. That Lotte Lehmann created the roles of the Dyer's Wife and Christine confirms the interrelationships between the operas for they are both, in different ways, about Strauss's marriage. In *Intermezzo* Strauss was composing what he composed best, his family and professional life, because they meant most to him – he loved the backstage chaos of the opera house and the sporadic domestic chaos of Garmisch, and in the Prologue and in *Intermezzo* he could put them into music. In *Intermezzo* he could revel in his conducting (quotations from operas), in his Skat playing (the other players in Act 2 are all recognisable friends of Strauss, like the *Kammersänger* who was based on the Berlin bass Paul Knüpfer and the *Kommerzienrat* based on Willy Levin) and in quarrels and making-up with his wife. There is no more tender and touching episode in all Strauss than the orchestral interlude which accompanies Christine's fireside reverie.

The irony about *Intermezzo* is that it appeared in 1924 when Strauss had generally been written off by influential critics in Germany, Britain and America as no longer a composer holding out any progressive interest. He belonged to the past. Yet *Intermezzo* is in so many respects an innovative opera and a commentary on bourgeois culture in the early years of the Weimar Republic. The autobiographical surface element in *Intermezzo* occupied minds so much that they missed its deeper implications, although they were noted by two other composers, Hindemith, whose *Neues vom Tage* (1929) is deeply influenced by *Intermezzo*, and Schoenberg, whose *Von Heute auf Morgen* (1930) is based on the marital life of Franz Schreker. *Intermezzo* is unmistakably a *Zeitoper*, a work of its time, putting on to the opera stage episodes which had never been there before – Christine checking Robert's grocery list for his train trip, answering and making telephone calls, tobogganing, dancing at a Grundlsee restaurant, visiting a divorce lawyer; Robert discussing opera rehearsals, playing Skat, walking in the rain in the Prater. Although it should not be exaggerated, for Strauss detested the cinema and hardly ever visited one, there is a use of cinematic technique in the thirteen short scenes. Films flourished in Weimar Germany, where the industry was the largest in Europe and was having an adverse effect on opera attendances. During the period in 1916–17 when Strauss was contemplating collaboration on *Intermezzo* with Hermann Bahr, he sent some sketches of scenes which he suggested were '*fast nur Kinobilder*' ('almost like cinema pictures'). A decade later Berg was to use film itself in Act 2 of *Lulu*. Once again Strauss had pointed a way, as he had done in *Elektra*. He was no extinct volcano. The importance of *Intermezzo* lay in his ability to invent a new type of opera and yet to compose it in the harmonic style which had served him for decades. (The waltzes in the Grundlsee scene come from a sketchbook of 1902–3.) Bryan Gilliam has pointed out[1] the parallel in the tonal structure of the second version of *Ariadne auf Naxos* – opening in every-day C major and ending in F sharp major, Strauss's 'dream key' in which he had also composed Don Quixote's dream of his knightly deeds, the Presentation of the Rose, the Empress's first aria in *Die Frau ohne Schatten* and Daphne's metamorphosis. (The key of D flat major Strauss reserved for the sublimities of the *Rosenkavalier* Trio, the Act 3 duet between Barak and his Wife, and the end of *Capriccio*.)

But if we wish to understand the real significance of *Intermezzo* for Strauss, then it will be found in the long preface to the full score in which he expatiated on his use of secco recitative and on the relative importance of words and music. Here are some extracts from this major statement of intent, significantly attached to this particular opera:

I have always lavished the greatest possible attention on meaningful declamation and on ensuring that the dialogue is taken at a lively pace, and have pursued this aim with growing success from one work to the next. . . In *Salome* and *Elektra* I took steps to prevent the dialogue from being drowned by the symphony orchestra. Unfortunately, even here the dialogue will still be found to be too encumbered by instrumental polyphony unless exceptional care be taken to observe my precise dynamic markings and thus to invest the orchestral writing with the translucency that I took for granted when writing the work, and that I know from perfect performances is capable of being achieved.

(Conductors reading this are allowed to smile ruefully here.)

Strauss then confessed that his attempt to score for the orchestra in *Ariadne* and *Die Frau ohne Schatten* in order to ensure clarity of the dialogue, especially in the Nurse's scenes, had not been completely successful.

The fault may lie either in my own lack of ability, so that even this light and diaphanous orchestration is still too polyphonically textured, with too many restless figurations . . . or it may be due to faulty diction on the part of the average opera singer or, again, to the regrettably far too palatal intonation of our German singers and to their tendency to force their voices on our large stages. Orchestral polyphony, no matter how delicately coloured or how softly it is played, is the death of the spoken word on stage, and the Devil himself is to blame for the fact that we Germans are exposed to counterpoint from our earliest infancy.

He then draws attention to the need for 'meticulous execution' of his orchestral dynamics. (At rehearsals Strauss would often be heard to say 'Speak forte and sing piano', 'Piano in making music is soft not holding back; forte is not loud but firm and strong. Both are relative.') He continues in the preface:

It was in the first act [Prologue] of *Ariadne* . . . that I successfully essayed the vocal style that has now been taken to its logical conclusion in *Intermezzo*. In none of my other works, however, is the dialogue of greater importance than it is in this bourgeois comedy, which offers so few opportunities for a proper cantilena to develop. The symphonic element has been so carefully and repeatedly worked and polished that it is often merely hinted at. . . It is generally only in the longer orchestral interludes that the lyrical element and the account of the characters' psychological lives are more fully developed. . . I would ask the conductor, when rehearsing *Intermezzo*, to pay the greatest possible attention to all the delicate transitions from the purely spoken to the sung and half-spoken word, to all the subtle turns in the conversation where prose vacillates between *recitativo secco* and *accompagnato* and finally extends to so-called *bel canto*, where absolute clarity may sometimes be sacrificed to sheer beauty of sound. . . In turning away from the tried-and-tested themes of the traditional opera libretto, with its concentration on love and murder, and by trespassing all too temerariously on 'real life', this new work represents a new departure in music drama, a direction that others may perhaps pursue with greater talent and felicity than I.

Extraordinarily, one of the first people to appreciate *Intermezzo* was Schoenberg, who had no liking for Strauss. Writing to Webern on 3 May 1926 he confesses that, to his great surprise, he had found it 'not at all unlikable', meaning principally the libretto which impressed him as the work of 'a very genial, warm person – a consequence not of his art but of his personality – it convincingly reveals a side of his personality that has actually captivated me'. The music was 'weak in invention and containing all too many sequences', but he might like it better after repeated hearings. Twenty years later, in an essay on Strauss and Furtwängler, he declared that 'works like *Salome, Elektra, Intermezzo* and others will not perish'. Not many in 1946 would have included *Intermezzo*. Hofmannsthal attended the Vienna première and wrote to Strauss two days later that as yet he lacked the right perspective to comment on it. 'I was startled by the high seriousness of the approach; I had imagined the whole thing far more like a comedy and the importance of the symphonic interludes not so weighty. . . As comedy, the penultimate scene, where the wife is alone with the servant girl, seems to me particularly successful; as a serious scene the last one is perhaps especially fine.' Nearly two years later, however, Hofmannsthal told Strauss that he thought the reason why *Intermezzo* had not achieved popular success was the libretto. It offered 'a character sketch rather than a plot' and the Baron Lummer episode failed because 'the librettist has trivialized this young man's character'. In a reply on 1 November 1928, Strauss said this was a little unfair. 'The fact that the critics and the public don't understand what it is meant to be and what it is ought not to speak against it in our eyes. Of course it has little "action"; on the contrary, the action is trivialized from the outset (as you quite rightly observe of the figure of the Baron) and treated ironically. But then, what are these so-called dramatic plots? They've remained the same for two thousand years: murder and destruction, the intrigue of mean minds against the hero, betrothal after overcoming obstacles, or separation – surely all this is not very interesting and has, moreover, been seen heaven knows how many times before. On the other hand – as Goethe said when he advised everybody to write their memoirs – each individual is unique in his way and will never occur again. And that is why I consider an attractive and consistent character portrait as in *Intermezzo* more interesting than any so-called plot. Some day perhaps some people with more highly developed stage sense will share my taste and appreciate *Intermezzo* more than today's cinema generation.' Time has proved him right.

Since it plays an important part in *Intermezzo*, now would seem the right place to say something about Strauss and Skat. It is a card-game played mainly in Germany and Austria, having evolved in Thuringia between 1810 and 1820 from a game called 'Sheep's Head'. It requires much skill and the money stakes can be high. Three usually play, but a fourth or fifth player can take part. Hands are played quickly so a game can be started, stopped after a few minutes and resumed. This makes it ideal for theatrical folk, who can play during rehearsals or even performances. It resembles Bridge in using trumps and the calling of a contract, and Poker in its need for quick decisions and bluff. Strauss's passion for Skat had a serious underlying cause. He once confessed that there was not a moment in the day when he was not thinking of music in some way or another. He was almost tormented by it. Playing Skat was the only time he escaped from music. The need increased as he grew older. He told Hans Hotter: 'For me, everything sounds. Only at my age its transformation into the notes on paper does not always work as it did; so many of the melodies I have already written. It can be frustrating to feel the thing you want to do and not be able to do it. The only thing which does not "sound" for me is cards. It's a great relief.'[2]

Strauss's love of cards began in boyhood in games with Thuille. He had taken up Skat by the time he left Berlin in 1884. One of his Skat cronies in later years was the tenor Franz Klarwein, son of the owner of Garmisch station restaurant. He described Strauss as 'a very good player, flexible and ready to take risks. Like a mathematical genius, he knew what cards the other player had after three or four tricks. He was a master bluffer and when he bluffed you made mistakes. That was his great strength. He often won, even when we had all the trumps.' Klarwein said that Pauline would some-times break up the games at Garmisch. Strauss 'would become angry when he played badly, because of his mistakes, but would take the winnings out of the safe when Pauline wasn't looking and give them to the others'. After the dress rehearsal for the première of *Capriccio* in Munich in 1942 he invited Klarwein and Hotter, both singing in the opera, to come to the Hotel Vierjahreszeiten at 4 p.m. for Skat. They played until 11.30. The two singers wanted to go to bed but Strauss was losing and wanted to continue the game. So they let him win. Strauss's son Franz played regularly, also Emanuel von Grab (Franz's future father-in-law), the chauffeur Theodor Martin, the industrialist Manfred Mautner Markhof, Friedrich von Schuch (son of the Dresden conductor) and the conductors Karl Böhm, Hans Knappertsbusch and Fritz Busch. For his friend Willy Levin he wrote a 'Skatkanon' for four male voices on New Year's Eve 1903. The words were 'Scat spielen wir fröh-lich bei Willy Levin. O weh, alles ist hin, nie wieder spiel ich bei Willy Levin' (We play skat happily at Willy Levin's, O dear, all is there, never again will I play at Willy Levin's). He also had Skat-playing companions in the orches-tras, choruses and administrations of opera houses throughout Germany. 'Are we playing tonight?' he asked Heinz Tietjen in Vienna on one occasion. 'Oh yes, your *Schlagobers*', was the reply. 'I don't mean that. I mean, are we playing Skat?'

After a performance of *Intermezzo* in Munich conducted by Hans Knappertsbusch in 1925, Strauss wrote '10 Golden Rules for the Album of a Young Conductor'.[3] Their cynical practicality has amused most musicians

(Nos. 3 and 4 are often quoted), but Norman Del Mar found them 'distasteful' and 'despite an occasional note of practical wisdom' lacking in integrity.[4] Rather a severe judgment on a joke. The rules are:

1. Remember you are not making music for your own pleasure but to please your listeners.
2. You should not perspire when conducting: only the audience should get warm.
3. Conduct *Salome* and *Elektra* as if they were by Mendelssohn: fairy music.
4. Never look encouragingly at the brass, except with a short glance to give an important cue.
5. But never let the horns and woodwind out of your sight. If you can hear them at all, they are still too loud.
6. If you think the brass is not blowing hard enough, tone it down another notch or two.
7. It's not enough if you yourself can hear every word the soloist sings, when you know the text by heart. The audience must be able to follow without effort. If they can't hear the words they will go to sleep.
8. Always accompany a singer in such a manner that he can sing without straining.
9. If you think you have reached the utmost prestissimo, double the pace.*
10. If you follow these rules carefully you will, with your fine gifts and great accomplishments, always be the darling of your listeners.

*Today (1948) I should like to amend this: go twice as slowly (addressed to conductors of Mozart!).

Strauss admitted that he broke Rule 2: 'I perspire only in Beethoven's C minor Symphony, the Ninth and the *Eroica*. And of course in *Tristan* and Act 1 of *Walküre*.' Speaking to Dr Anton Berger in Frankfurt am Main on 29 May 1927, Strauss said of the C minor Symphony: 'It's said that in the first movement, fate is knocking at the door. Nonsense, this movement is an outburst of fury of Beethoven, a "*Götz von Berlichingen*"!' The reference to *Götz von Berlichingen* is to one of Goethe's earliest and most celebrated plays, *Götz von Berlichingen mit der eisernen Hand* (*Götz von Berlichingen with the Iron Hand*). It is about a feudal baron in the Peasants' Revolt. In Act 3 Götz is besieged in his castle by imperial troops. One of them calls for his surrender and Götz replies: 'Vor Ihre Kaiserliche Majestät hab ich, wie immer, schuldigen Respekt. Er aber, sag's ihm, er kann mich am Arsch lecken . . .!'

16 Hans Knappertsbusch, Strauss and Eugen Papst playing Skat

('I have all due respect for his imperial majesty. Even so, he can lick my arse . . .!'). This passage is known in Germany as 'the Götz quotation'. *Leck mich am Arsch* ('lick my arse') can be implied as an obscene retort simply by use of the word 'Götz'; a musician wishing to use it might simply hum the opening of Beethoven's Fifth Symphony, of which the coarse phrase is the verbal equivalent in dactylic rhythm. In the eleventh song of the cycle *Krämerspiegel*, in which Strauss lampooned the publishers, the singer's last two lines are: 'Der lässt ein Wort erklingen / wie Götz von Berlichingen' ('He lets the word ring out like Götz von Berlichingen'). This is introduced and accompanied by the pianist's repetition of the opening of the Fifth Symphony. Strauss knew that the allusion would be fully understood and appreciated.

17 *Helena*

The cinematic aspects of *Intermezzo* have been mentioned. Perhaps Strauss sought to defeat the new medium by giving some of it to the old medium of opera. But a closer encounter awaited him through the project for a film version of *Der Rosenkavalier*. This would, of course, be a silent film, with music provided 'live' by an orchestra in the cinema and no singers. Hofmannsthal and Strauss were approached towards the end of 1924 by the Austrian film company Pan-Film. The director of the film was to be Robert Wiene, who in 1919 had made the bizarre *The Cabinet of Dr Caligari*, following international success with *Raskolnikov*, a version of Dostoevsky's *Crime and Punishment*. The authors apparently stipulated certain conditions which the film company accepted. Writing to Strauss on New Year's Day 1925, Hofmannsthal reassured him that the film would not cause the opera to suffer, but would act as a fillip for it. His scenario for the film 'is treated in the manner of a novel: it introduces the characters or, for those who know them, tells something new of these old acquaintances. Nowhere (not even in the final scene) are the events of the opera exactly repeated – *not in a single scene.*' A 'great deal of money' was to be invested in the film and a 'substantial profit' expected. Strauss was lukewarm, although he agreed to re-arrange the music for a fee of 10,000 dollars. Most of the score was taken from the opera, but Strauss composed a military march in F major for scenes set in the camp of the Feldmarschall. He also used a military march in E major, composed in 1905 and dedicated to the Kaiser, the *Brandenburgsche Mars*, also of 1905, the third movement from his 1892 music for the Grand Duke of Weimar's golden wedding and a movement from his Couperin *Tanzsuite*. It is believed that he delegated the task of condensing the film score to Carl Alwin and Otto Singer. A version for a twelve-piece salon orchestra exists, but whether it was Strauss's work is unknown.

The scenario was virtually a new work, with several new scenes and considerable divergence from the original. Ochs's castle is shown, with the baron being dressed by his servant and prepared for his visit to the Marschallin in Vienna. The Feldmarschall, never seen nor heard in the opera, has a large role. We see the Marschallin's convent girlhood and her first meeting with the Feldmarschall. He leaves her on their wedding day to command the Emperor's army. Warned of the Octavian situation, he returns to Vienna just when his wife is giving a masked ball in the garden of their palace. The Feldmarschall and Octavian fight a duel. All ends, like *Figaro*, in reconciliation, but the film's final sequences have been lost. The film was made between June and August 1925 in Vienna and at the Schönbrunner Film Studios. The décor was by Alfred Roller, designer of the opera's first production. A leading French actress, Huguette Duflos, played the Marschallin, with Jaque Catelain as Octavian and Elly Félicie Berger as Sophie. The Ochs was Michael Bohnen, who had sung the role several times on stage and gives by far the most convincing performance.

Strauss alarmed Hofmannsthal by at first refusing to conduct at the film's first showing at the Dresden Opera House on 10 January 1926, but he relented. He also visited London for the première there, staying at the Carlton Hotel in the Haymarket and conducting at the Tivoli in the Strand on 12 April. Next morning, he recorded a suite of music from the film in the Queen's Hall.

He filled the winters with journeys to conduct his own works – in Berlin, Leipzig, Turin, Amsterdam and elsewhere. He visited London again in November 1926 when he conducted *Eine Alpensinfonie* in Queen's Hall (the BBC Wireless Orchestra combined with the Covent Garden orchestra). This was the occasion when the thunder-machine toppled over. In the same month he conducted the Hallé in Manchester. One city remained closed to him: Paris. Visits by German musicians had still to be officially approved. A request by the soprano Germaine Lubin that Strauss should be invited to conduct *Der Rosenkavalier* and *Ariadne auf Naxos* was refused in 1924. Although it was noted that he had not signed the German intellectuals' manifesto in 1914, there was still rancour over the way he had treated French orchestral players in 1906. A further request, initiated by the conductor Gabriel Pierné in 1927, evoked a Ministry decision that the visit could be allowed provided that it was regarded as private. Strauss did not go. It was not until December 1929 that approval for an official visit was given and, at a Strauss festival in the Théâtre des Champs-Elysées, he conducted *Der Rosenkavalier* on 29 October 1930 and *Salome* on 5 November. (The intended Paris première of *Der Rosenkavalier* in January 1915 had been cancelled. It was first performed there in February 1927. *Elektra*'s Paris première was not until 25 February 1932.)

After the Op. 71 Hölderlin settings, Strauss wrote only two songs between 1921 and 1928. Both were settings of Goethe poems from the *Westöstlicher Divan*. The first, *Erschaffen und Beleben* (*Creation and Animation*), was composed in Vienna in December 1922 for the Berlin Opera bass Michael Bohnen (who was to be Ochs in the *Rosenkavalier* film), but Strauss re-dedicated it in 1945 to Hans Hotter. It is a drinking-song, with amusing descriptive passages in the accompaniment. Perhaps both Bohnen and Hotter found it too difficult, for it was not published until 1951 and not performed until February 1952. The second Goethe song was written in Garmisch on Strauss's sixty-first birthday in 1925. *Durch allen Schall und Klang* was a contribution to a book of offerings by friends to mark Romain Rolland's sixtieth birthday on 29 January 1926. The song (which was not performed until April 1953) was dedicated to Rolland as 'the great poet and highly honoured friend, the heroic fighter against all evil powers working for the downfall of Europe, with expressions of truest sympathy and sincerest admiration'. Rolland was deeply touched. Strauss's friendship, he told the composer in reply, 'has been one of the greatest gifts vouchsafed to me by destiny. And that across so many ruins of empires – and friendships – our own should remain pure and steadfast, I am proud.'

The early part of 1926 found Hofmannsthal still cutting and adjusting the libretto of Act 2 of *Die ägyptische Helena*. In March Strauss invited him to Jacquingasse to hear a play-through of Act 1. Strauss asked Elisabeth Schumann to sing the aria *Ein Feuer brennt, ein Tisch ist gedeckt* (*A fire is lit, a table laid*) and gave her the manuscript inscribed 'To the first Helena, Elisabeth, in memory of March 27, 1926.' Hofmannsthal wrote next day: 'I am more delighted with this *Helena* music than, I believe, about any of your other compositions ever, and I feel I am right in this, even though I altogether lack the words to express myself properly. . . The after-glow of the music is wholly enchanting; everything so light and transparent, for all its high noble seriousness.' Strauss left for Greece in May 'to get a few beautiful tunes for Act 2 – even though my biographer, Herr Specht, considers it old-fashioned that nowadays I have *only* the ambition to "make beautiful music".' A year later, with the music still unfinished, Strauss alarmed Hofmannsthal (as he had done in *Ariadne auf Naxos*) with his intention to make the role of Da-ud, the sheikh's son, a trouser-role for a mezzo. This time, however, he capitulated: 'Of course, you are right, but just think of the tenors at small opera houses! I know them. I have now written Da-ud as a tenor, but am at the same time setting out an arrangement to indicate how the part can be sung, at a pinch, by a mezzo-soprano.' The Greek visit was not, in fact, a composition holiday. He went at the invitation of the Greek Government which wanted to build a Strauss Festival Theatre and a Strauss Conservatory. Funds were available and Strauss was asked to choose a site, supervise the building and direct the festival. He was accompanied by Michael Rosenauer, who had designed his Vienna house. They chose a site on the Museion hill, near the Acropolis. As happens all too often, political squabbles killed the project.

Strauss's restless imagination now toyed with two other projects. Hearing *Die Meistersinger* again gave him 'the urge to write a work of this type some day – unfortunately, needless to say, at a respectful distance. But nevertheless some really German piece.' That was in June 1927. A fortnight later he wrote again to Hofmannsthal: 'Now after *Helena* I should like to write a little one-act opera – either gay or sad – a kind of curtain-raiser for *Feuersnot*. The other day I read Turgenev's fine novel *Smoke*. Stripped of all accessory matter, this story contains an operatic text.' A few weeks later Strauss enlarged upon his *Meistersinger* project: 'As I've said before, what I'd like best of all, time and again, would be to put myself to music – but unfortunately I can't put myself into poetry. Your beautiful letter about *Meistersinger* gave me indeed much pleasure, but it failed to touch upon the very thing that I wanted to express in that work – no matter whether in the age of the Minnesingers or the baroque period of Karl Theodor of Mannheim – it was the autobiographical element that would have attracted me in particular: I myself ("the cosmopolitan"), between Puccini and Pfitzner, add three original female characters who tangle the threads of envy and jealousy even more, the whole thing in an attractive historical setting.'[1] Hofmannsthal killed off the idea with one sentence: 'I can think of no subject which would appeal to me less than this.' The full score of *Helena* was completed on 8 October 1927. It had taken Strauss longer than usual. As in *Elektra*, he had come to a halt (in June 1925) at the entrance of Sheikh Altair. 'I want to give the whole thing the pure, sublimated style of Goethe's *Iphigenie*, and it is therefore particularly difficult to find, for this entrance of the sons of the desert, the kind of music that still sounds sufficiently characteristic to the ears of 1925 without degenerating into the so-called realism of *Salome* or even the eccentricities of today's modernists.'

Although the relative failure of *Die ägyptische Helena* is sometimes attributed to the libretto, there is no evidence that Strauss was dissatisfied with it. In Act 1 he had even repeated the slip he had made in *Der Rosenkavalier*: he set one of the stage directions to music. In an interview before the first performance, he said: 'I consider it to be one of the most attractive ideas in Hofmannsthal's text that Helen is not satisfied to regain her husband's love with the aid of the potion of oblivion and of a story cleverly constructed by the nymph Aithra, but that she should, after renewed tragic doubts and experiences, insist, in the second act, on winning through on her own strength, in spite of and without the aid of magic potions, solely by the divine power of beauty and by her own dynamic nature.'[2] With the opera completed, now began the comedy of casting it for the première in Dresden. It was written with magnificent voices in mind: Maria Jeritza, as beautiful physically as she was sensational vocally, should be Helen. The tenor role of Menelaus was conceived for Richard Tauber. The exquisite lyric soprano Lotte Schöne was thought of as Aithra. But none of these three sang in Dresden on 6 June 1928. Dresden could not afford Jeritza's exorbitant fee. She wanted the role but behaved abominably. Strauss used his influence to obtain her a fee at Dresden higher than the highest allowed by the Deutscher Bühnenverein (Association of German Theatres). When news of this leaked out, the Association threatened to boycott all Strauss's stage works throughout Germany. His riposte was to threaten a première in Vienna where Jeritza was a member of the company. There was outrage in Dresden. All right, Strauss said, the première shall be in Dresden, with Vienna and Jeritza the next day. Now Jeritza rebelled: she would not sing at all if she did not sing in the world première. Strauss pleaded with her: 'You see things from afar and do not know the exasperation I have been caused in the past eight weeks over this tiresome and at bottom utterly stupid question of the première. Legally, of course, I am in the right. But do you know what has happened? The Saxon Ministry of Culture got on to the German ambassador in Vienna to work on the Austrian ministries to desist from giving the world première in Vienna!'

Strauss had already accepted that a Vienna première with Jeritza was an impossibility and was prepared to accede to Dresden's suggestion that Helena should be sung by Elisabeth Rethberg. 'I don't believe we'll find anybody better in the circumstances', he told Hofmannsthal. 'I hope you agree.' This unleashed a tirade from the librettist. 'You want me to write something new for you', he replied, 'and at the same time you inflict on me what I consider more loathsome than anything else that could happen.' And so on.[3] Before receiving this, Strauss had remained cool and good-tempered ('I fear we shall see a good many non-Helens yet and hope the piece will prevail, just as in its time *Salome* prevailed in spite of Auntie Wittich'). Hofmannsthal cooled down – 'Forgive me, but this is after all truly a matter of life and death.' (It wasn't.) When Strauss received Hofmannsthal's original letter, he replied with an uncharacteristic touch of venom:

Why do you always turn so poisonous the moment artistic questions have to be discussed in a businesslike manner and you don't share my opinion? To accuse me immediately of not understanding you is neither polite nor just. If I may say so, I think I understood you a good deal sooner than many other people, otherwise I wouldn't have put your books to music against the advice of the 'most competent' people – among whom theatre managers and critics are as a rule included, *though not by me. . .* You are still doing me an injustice if you think me indifferent to the fate of my operas on the stage! Why else am I constantly travelling about among big and small theatres, to keep an eye on things both good and bad . . .? After all, my operas (even *Salome* and *Rosenkavalier*) at first had but slight success and a terrible press.' [This was not true of those two operas!][4]

Hofmannsthal asked him 'to expunge the whole thing from your memory'.

It was fixed that the first performance should be in Dresden, with Rethberg, on 6 June 1928, with Vienna following on 11 June, Strauss's sixty-fourth birthday. Jeritza then gave an interview in March. She backtracked on several issues and said she had not learned the part. Strauss wrote to his son: 'I have the feeling, after that interview, that she wants to get out of it. . . If she claims she does not yet know Act 1, at least, I am sure she is lying!' Rehearsals in Dresden were stormy. Fritz Busch, the conductor, was ill and missed many of them. The producer Otto Erhardt did not really believe in the opera and was driven wild by Pauline's interference. He was heard on one occasion to mutter Herod's last words in *Salome*: 'Man töte dieses Weib!' Strauss had played the opera to Busch at Garmisch. Busch told him he found Da-ud's aria cheap. Strauss repeated this criticism to Pauline with enjoyment and added: 'That's what's wanted for the servant girls. The general public would not go to *Tannhäuser* if it didn't contain "O du mein holder Abendstern" or to *Die Walküre* without "Wintersturme". Well, well, that's what they want.' (Years earlier, on 5 March 1905, he had written to Mahler: 'Your Fifth Symphony again gave me great pleasure in the full rehearsal, a pleasure only slightly dimmed by the little Adagietto. But as this was what pleased the audience most, you are getting what you deserve.')[5]

The conductor Leo Wurmser was on the Dresden music staff and took a major part in preparing the opera when Busch was away ill. At the first rehearsals Pauline, from the front row of the stalls, demanded horses, which had not been provided. At the end of Act 1, she complained there was not enough thunder. Strauss asked Erhardt for more, and in an aside muttered: 'Wives are always all for thunder!' During the final dress rehearsal Strauss asked Busch to let him conduct Act 1. Wurmser wrote years later: 'It was like a different opera; one big broad line from beginning to end, the right tempi and rubatos, co-operation with the singers and many of the 4/4 passages beaten in 2. Busch sat in the stalls following the score and I sat beside him, trying tactfully to point out what Strauss did differently.'[6] The opera was well received in Dresden, but better followed in Vienna five days later. Strauss described it to Pauline as 'the greatest triumph of my life. . . At the end the enthusiasm was beyond bounds, for Jeritza, too, whose triumph was undisputed.' But Rethberg had sung 'Zweite Brautnacht', Helen's big Act 2 aria, much better, he thought.

After the initial burst (with performances in Berlin, Frankfurt, Stettin, Lübeck, Magdeburg and Nuremberg), enthusiasm for the opera waned. The New York critics savaged it (with Jeritza) in the autumn of 1928. Strauss was a 'burnt-out case'. In Vienna it suffered from performances by second-rate casts. When Jeritza was away, the role of Helen could not be adequately filled. It became the least known of Strauss's mature operas and was not staged in Britain until June 1997, when the general reaction could be summed up as 'Why were we told this was a bad opera?' Contrary to expectation, no one was mystified by Hofmannsthal's treatment of the contradictory myths about Helen, the most beautiful woman in the world, daughter of Leda and the god Zeus and wife of Menelaus. The Trojan War was caused by Paris's abduction of Helen. Writing in 1928, Hofmannsthal explained how his imagination had been stimulated by thoughts of how 'the night when the Greeks entered the burning city of Troy, Menelaus must have found his wife in one of the burning mansions and carried her out of the city between the collapsing walls. This woman, his beloved abducted wife, the most beautiful woman in the world, had been the cause of these terrible ten years of war, of this plain littered with dead, and of this fire. She was also Paris's widow and the friend of the ten or twelve other of Priam's sons who were now all either dead or lay dying. She was thus also the widow of these ten or twelve young princes! What a situation for a husband to face!' But how did Helen and Menelaus come together again? Hofmannsthal did some research and based his libretto on the surviving versions of the legend. In Book 4 of the *Odyssey*, Telemachus, son of Odysseus, arrives in Sparta searching for his father. There he discovers Helen and Menelaus, living happily together. How, after all that had occurred? Hofmannsthal wrote: 'How modern this is! How close to the story-telling of our own time! But involuntarily one asks oneself, what has happened in the meantime? What can have happened that this marriage reverted once more to a life of peace and companionship in the sunlight?'

One theory, exploited by Euripides in *Helen*, was that Paris did not abduct Helen but a phantom likeness of her created by the gods in order to cause the war. Meanwhile the real Helen was spirited away by Hermes to Egypt. Hofmannsthal concluded that 'only magic' could have solved the mystery. In the opera, which opens on an island off the Egyptian coast in the palace of the sea-god Poseidon, Menelaus is intent on killing Helen in retribution for the slaughter she had caused. Hofmannsthal duly introduces magic potions. These are administered by Poseidon's mistress, the sorceress Aithra, who also owns an Omniscient Sea-Shell (Mussel) which tells her what is happening elsewhere in the world. In Act 2, Sheikh Altair and his son Da-ud arrive in the desert where Helen and Menelaus are living. Both fall in love with Helen. The drugged Menelaus kills Da-ud in the mistaken belief he is Paris. What attracted Hofmannsthal to the subject were his favourite themes of marriage, fidelity, reconciliation. Sorcery, we discover, is powerless in the realm of true human emotion. No reconciliation can be based on deceit. The Egyptian and Trojan Helens become one woman for Menelaus, who forgives and believes in the strength of his marriage. Some have discerned a political agenda in *Helena*, the reconciliation of Europe after the First World War. It is a feasible theory, but more important is that Menelaus, having seen both sides of Helen, the phantom and the real, accepts the real woman with all her faults. Act 1 is about enchantment, Act 2 about disenchantment.

Hofmannsthal regarded it as his finest libretto because, as he told his friend Max Rychner, 'it meets the requirements for being performed on an operatic stage; in its rhythm it tends towards song, and aria-like parts alternate with declamatory passages (which Strauss handles with such power).'[7] Strauss realised that the original intention of an operetta-like work with spoken dialogue could not be sustained into Act 2 and he converted the work into a romantic opera, with some of his most elaborate and richly ornate orchestration. In doing so he wrote his *bel canto* opera, much of it derived from the song-like style of Act 3 of *Die Frau ohne Schatten*, but less portentous. The melodic flow, with the voices pre-eminent more than in his previous operas, is sustained through a series of arias and ensembles without let or hindrance, showing how much Strauss had learned from *Intermezzo* so that he could merge his conversational style into what one might call 'romantic baroque'. The radiant lyricism of much of the score was to be equally incandescent, although in a different context, in his next opera, *Arabella*.

18　*Arabella*

With Franz Strauss's marriage (in a Catholic ceremony) to Alice von Grab, the Strauss family circle was both strengthened and tightened. Strauss was delighted by the union; he adored Alice and in correspondence, as with Hofmannsthal, always referred to the couple as 'my children'. His relief when Franz recovered from the typhus he contracted on honeymoon had a musical result in the concerto he wrote for the pianist Paul Wittgenstein who had lost his right arm during the First World War and commissioned a series of works for left hand only from several composers, among them Ravel, Franz Schmidt, Prokofiev, Korngold and Britten. The Strauss work, sketched in the second half of 1924 and completed in January 1925, was called *Parergon zur Symphonia Domestica* because he based it on the Child's theme from the symphony. But here it is presented in F sharp minor in fevered harmonies (as advanced as anything in *Elektra*) with a C sharp on muted brass stabbing at it like a recurring pain. The atmosphere of gloom and anxiety persists even through stormy episodes for soloist and orchestra until the crisis passes and C sharp is converted by the bassoon into F major, followed by a clarinet theme expressing relief. Thereafter all is *scherzando*. Wittgenstein gave the first performance, with Fritz Busch conducting, in Dresden on 6 October 1925. During 1926 Strauss wrote a second piece for Wittgenstein, the *Panathenäenzug* in four sections like Liszt's B minor sonata. This was first performed at a Berlin Philharmonic concert on 16 January 1928 by Wittgenstein, with Bruno Walter conducting.

Alongside his work on the last part of *Die ägyptische Helena*, Strauss composed four romantic and unjustly neglected settings of Eichendorff, *Die Tageszeiten,* for male chorus and orchestra. The orchestral description of the different times of day is sheer Strauss magic to the extent that the chorus tends to have a subsidiary role. The work derived from a request by Viktor

Keldorfer, conductor of the Schubert Society (*Schubertbund*) of Vienna, when the choir serenaded Strauss outside his Mozartplatz home in Vienna on 1 May 1924. Keldorfer suggested Eichendorff as a poet. Nothing happened for three years. Then Keldorfer was summoned to Garmisch and handed the song-cycle, which had its first performance in Vienna on 21 July 1928.

It was on 1 October 1927 that Hofmannsthal, writing from Bad Aussee, gave Strauss the first hint of their next collaboration. He had been looking at an unfinished comedy, *The Cabby as Count*, and 'it occurred to me for the first time that the whole thing had a touch of *Rosenkavalier* about it' – a Vienna setting, an attractive woman as the central figure.[1] Nothing more was said and over the next weeks the Jeritza crisis occupied both men – and Strauss was thrilled by the arrival of his first grandson, Richard, born on 1 November. But on 13 November, Hofmannsthal returned to the subject. He was '*wholly* engrossed' in a new dramatic work. 'I have been able to combine several features of this cabbies' world with elements from another projected comedy and hope . . . to have invented the scenario for a three-act comic opera, indeed almost an operetta.' Two days later, 'the characters of this new comedy for music are cutting their capers under my very nose, almost too obviously' – especially the baritone role, 'the most remarkable character in the piece, from a semi-alien world (Croatia), half buffo and yet a grand fellow capable of deep feelings, wild and gentle, almost daemonic'. Hofmannsthal told Strauss the plot, at that stage, in Vienna on 16 December. Strauss was worried about the Croatian. Victory for *Der Rosenkavalier*, he reminded his collaborator, was ensured by the Marschallin. The new piece lacked an interesting female character. Hofmannsthal agreed, but pointed out that the opera was to be called *Arabella* and she, not the Croatian (Mandryka), was the principal character. Strauss meanwhile had borrowed from the library the four volumes of Franjo Z. Kuhač's collection of Southern Slav folk-songs and threatened 'a colossal ballet for our second act' and 'enchanting songs for our Croatian'.[2] Hofmannsthal was horrified – everything must be authentic and there could be no question of a Croatian dance at a Vienna cabbies' ball.

He now disclosed to Strauss that one of the chief elements in the plot derived from a short story he had written in 1909, *Lucidor, Characters from an Unwritten Comedy* (first published in 1910 in *Neue Freie Presse*). In it a widow lives in a Vienna hotel with two daughters, Arabella and Lucile. The

17 Alice with Pauline and Richard Strauss

latter is dressed as a boy (Lucidor) because this helps the family fortunes and Arabella's chance of a good marriage. Lucidor's love for one of Arabella's admirers 'grows' in proportion to the increasingly unkind treatment he receives from Arabella until finally, to console the unhappy man, she grants him an assignation – 'in the name of her sister, in a completely dark room, speaking only in a whisper'. (This happens night after night in the story.) In revising the plot in 1927 Hofmannsthal provided Arabella with 'a most unlikely suitor out of the blue' – the Croatian Mandryka. One cannot admire too strongly the instinct that led Hofmannsthal to combine *Lucidor* with those elements of *The Cabby as Count* which provided the opera with such a strong flavour of local colour as the Cabbies' Ball. This was an annual event in Vienna after 1787, one of the highlights of the Carnival, held in the 1860s at the Sperl Hotel in the Leopoldstadt district. Two classes dominated, the cab drivers and their families and the aristocracy who turned up in evening dress with decorations but without women. (Hofmannsthal's Countess Waldner would not have been allowed in.) A young girl was chosen as carnival queen and the occasion was presided over by a feminine mascot known as the Fiakermilli. One of the most famous was Emilie Turecek (1846–99), a Viennese folk-singer who was patron of the ball for several years. Hofmannsthal captured the Vienna of 1860, very different from that of *Der Rosenkavalier*. It was a Vienna nearer to their own day – 'more ordinary, less glamorous, more vulgar'. Three years earlier, Emperor Franz Josef had ordered the demolition of the city walls and the construction of the Ringstrasse, with its opera house, stock exchange, town hall, parliament and other great buildings. This was to be the Vienna of the artist Hans Makart. It was a Vienna living beyond its means, a nervous, febrile city and society. Strauss reflects this in the music which opens the opera. On one level it depicts the Fortune-Teller and her cards and the anxious fussiness of Arabella's mother; on another it tells of insubstantiality and unrest. Arabella herself was described by Hofmannsthal in one of his letters as like Shaw's St Joan in her consciousness of her strength, and it is only when she enters to her serene oboe melody that the music attains the warmth and compassion which will dominate it to the end.

 Strauss's response to the libretto of Act 1 was cool: 'I am trying hard to discover what it lacks for being set to music.' Later he realised it was Arabella herself who worried him. She was not sufficiently interesting 'and almost unattractive'. As late as November 1928 he admitted to Hofmannsthal that he had tried to compose the start of Act 1 'but the thing doesn't even begin to come to music and, to be perfectly frank, the characters don't interest me in the least, above all Arabella, who does not experience the slightest psychological conflict throughout the three acts. She doesn't love Matteo from the start; as for her flirtation with the three Counts . . . I think you probably overrate its poetical effect. That she should easily switch from the building contractor [a character later excised] to that wealthy paragon of virtue Mandryka is as natural as it is uninteresting.' He wanted 'a new motive' that would lend her interest in Mandryka 'a truly moral significance'.[3] Eventually Hofmannsthal supplied this by imbuing her with the romantic intuition that she would know Mr Right, *der Richtige*, when he came along. Strauss eliminated several characters including a gypsy fiddler ('too like Lehár'), the building contractor and a Jew. He insisted that Mandryka's faith in Arabella must somehow be shaken and that he should 'hurl himself into the vortex of the ball and, under the influence of champagne, have a real love scene – possibly with Fiakermilli'. Hofmannsthal was uncharacteristically phlegmatic in his acceptance of these strictures. He wrote Acts 2 and 3, with changes suggested by Strauss, and left Act 1 on the side until 29 December 1928, when he had lunch at Jacquingasse and read the whole libretto to Strauss and Pauline. Strauss liked Acts 2 and 3 and Hofmannsthal agreed to re-write Act 1. This took him until July 1929. 'Could a little more lyricism be fitted into *Arabella*?', Strauss had begged. 'The *aria*, after all, is the soul of opera.' On 6 July Strauss accepted Act 1 'with one exception'. This was that 'Arabella must at all costs conclude the first act with a longish aria, soliloquy, contemplation, if only for dramatic reasons'.[4] Four days later Hofmannsthal sent the text of Arabella's 'Mein Elemer.' On 14 July Strauss sent a telegram from Garmisch: 'First act excellent. Many thanks and congratulations.' Hofmannsthal never opened the telegram. It arrived at Rodaun on 15 July. He was about to leave the house for the funeral of his son Franz, who had committed suicide two days earlier, when he had a stroke, collapsed and died.

As a tribute to his collaborator Strauss began to compose the music almost at once and had nearly completed the composition-sketch of Act 1 by 30 July 1930. The full score was finished on 12 October 1932. Hofmannsthal believed that Act 3 was 'the best thing I have ever written for the stage'. It has become almost *de rigueur* to regard the libretto of *Arabella* as superior to the music. I do not believe that *Arabella* would have steadily increased in popularity, as it has, on the strength of the text. The music, perfectly fitted to a disarming text, is what has carried this opera to success. It is Strauss's mastery, through the peculiar charm and magic of his music, that persuades listeners not to care a jot about whether the plot is credible. Those who find weaknesses in the music point to Strauss's apparent lack of sympathy with the characters. But he often showed reluctance for a new enterprise. He had been scathing about the Prologue to *Ariadne auf Naxos*, yet he composed a masterpiece. It has also been customary to patronise Strauss over *Arabella*, to suggest (as Norman Del Mar does) that here at last was the sort of unintellectual subject he could understand, something ordinary and prosaic and not too demanding. What nonsense! There are, in any case, no *ordinary* characters in Strauss operas, least of all in *Arabella* ('What a bunch!', wrote William Mann), once he had finished with them. The idea that he was always intellectually outgunned by Hofmannsthal cannot be sustained. He wrote not once but several times that he had no difficulty in understanding the librettos of *Die Frau ohne Schatten* and *Die ägyptische Helena*. He regarded them as wonderful – and why should he not have done, he who read Goethe from end to end and was steeped in the classics of literature? When he applied the brakes to some of Hofmannsthal's loftiest exegeses, it was not because he could not follow them but because he doubted if they could be put over to an opera-house audience. That was his primary consideration. Mourning for his friend as he worked in his study in Garmisch, Strauss perhaps perceived how cunningly Hofmannsthal had provided him with a libretto which allowed him to develop further the melodic conversational recitative style of *Intermezzo* and still to divert from it into those captivating arias which finally endear Arabella to us, even if we have already lost our hearts to her sister Zdenka. Strauss also perceived that the libretto was socially more critical and sharp than it appears on the surface. The 'Vienna, city of my dreams' was shown as a city where, below the surface, there was sleaze and discontent. It is an opera, dramatically and musically, that is full of ironies. When we are told that Arabella has been to an opera, a quotation in the orchestra tells us she had heard *Lohengrin*. But there is more to it than just a neat allusion to amuse Strauss – *Lohengrin* is also an opera about a woman waiting for the right man to come along.

Although it is sometimes said that Strauss set the text of Acts 2 and 3 exactly as the poet left them, in fact he made dozens of small alterations. The setting of the text marries words and music effortlessly and fluently in a mosaic of subtleties. And there are the great, elevating set-pieces – Arabella's duet with Zdenka in Act 1; Arabella's aria to end this act; her Act 2 duet with Mandryka, one of the most sublime love-duets ever written; Mandryka's autobiographical aria in Act 1; Arabella's Act 3 loving tribute to Zdenka (sometimes unforgivably cut); and the final staircase duet of reconciliation when an exalted tenderness, unique in Strauss, enters the music. In spite of his misgivings, Strauss breathed life and love into the mysterious Arabella and the not-so-simple Mandryka. He fashioned an unforgettable secondary role in Zdenka; he captured the quirks and oddities of the girls' parents, the Waldners. There remains the contentious figure of the Fiakermilli. Clemens Krauss, who conducted the première, always disliked this character and did his best, or worst, to persuade Strauss to alter it. In 1939 he and the Munich producer Rudolf Hartmann talked him into cutting some of her part at the end of Act 2 and to run the last two acts together (a mistake). Three years later, for a Salzburg Festival performance, Krauss wanted more changes but Strauss would only agree to an extra couplet (written by Hartmann and Krauss) being added to the couplet she sings in her first appearance. Strauss set it to music (the autograph is in the Music Department of the Austrian National Library) but, as a recording of the Salzburg performance proves, it was not used, probably because the soprano who had learned it was taken ill a few days before the first night. It still awaits performance. Perhaps Strauss believed that one day, with the right singer and the right production, her yodelling would seem less like an ill-judged caricature of Zerbinetta. I have heard him proved right. Finally, there is the orchestral score, a wonderful, kaleidoscopic symphonic web, with melodic and harmonic details integrated into a grand design. Anyone who believes this is backward-looking Strauss has not listened closely. The scoring is masterly, every effect telling. Glowing, picturesque, restrained, timpani the only percussion, it is like chamber music in its clarity and luminosity. The colours coruscate, the waltzes insinuate; and over it all gleam the rays of a perennial romanticism, perhaps the last of its kind. Strauss ultimately composed an opera in which a poetic, romantic, compassionate and – unfashionable word – loving view of human nature is paramount. In the words of his friend Ludwig Karpath, *Arabella* is an opera that makes one feel good inside.

19   The gathering storm

With the completion of *Die ägyptische Helena* in October 1927 and the absence of any new libretto from Hofmannsthal to occupy him, Strauss's desk was empty. He wrote *Die Tageszeiten* at the end of the year. The only music he composed in 1928 – between 14 August and 24 September – was five songs for voice and piano, *Gesänge des Orients*. This was his Op. 77, the last songs to which he attached an opus number. They are settings of free poetic renderings of writings by Hafiz (Shams-ud-den Mohammed), the thirteenth-century Persian poet whose *Divan* (collection of short poems) was the inspiration of Goethe's *Westöstlicher Divan*. In this case the adaptations were by Hans Bethge, from whose *Die chinesische Flöte* (1908) Mahler had extracted the texts of *Das Lied von der Erde*. Strauss selected four Hafiz and one anonymous poem. Although among his least-known songs, they are of extraordinary beauty, continuing the long cantabile vocal style of *Helena*. They are dedicated to Elisabeth Schumann and her husband Carl Alwin but, like the Brentano songs, they were unsuited to Schumann's voice. They were first sung by the Hungarian tenor Koloman von Pataky, accompanied by Strauss, in Berlin on 5 June 1929.

After 1924 Strauss and Hofmannsthal kept a wary eye on what was happening at the Vienna Opera. Hofmannsthal was open about his self-interest. When Strauss resigned, he wrote to him imploring him to keep his relationship with the authorities there 'tolerable'. It was important that their operas should remain in the repertory. 'I do not think you care very much about these things', he wrote, adding perceptively 'or indeed about almost anything (apart from your productive work).' In June 1926 Franz Schneiderhan was appointed general director of the Austrian State Theatres, to Strauss's approval. 'We shall just have to see he doesn't take any final decisions until he's heard me out in detail about requirements of the Vienna

Opera', he wrote to Hofmannsthal. 'A re-engagement of [Felix] Weingartner, even as a guest conductor, would be a bad thing.' Strauss was manoeuvring towards the appointment of Clemens Krauss as director. He admired Krauss's work at Frankfurt since 1924 and Krauss was due in July 1926 to conduct *Ariadne auf Naxos* at the Salzburg Festival, the first Strauss opera to be performed there. At the end of 1928, Schalk was dismissed from the directorship in Vienna and Krauss was appointed in his place, joining his former Frankfurt colleague, the Austrian producer Lothar Wallerstein who had been in Vienna since 1926. Strauss had sent a telegram to Krauss: 'I implore you to accept without delay. Trust yourself and me. This is the decisive moment.' Strauss himself had returned to the Vienna Opera as guest conductor of *Elektra* on 7 December 1926, following it with the Vienna première of *Intermezzo* on 15 January 1927. A student in the city at this date was Herbert von Karajan, who recalled later that he had never felt so drawn to any other interpretation of Mozart that he had heard since Strauss's. He was at the *Elektra* rehearsal. 'Strauss arrived, played the opening bars fortissimo and broke off. "Is there anybody here who doesn't already know the piece?" No. "In that case the rehearsal is over".' Strauss was also lenient towards singers of his music where textual accuracy was concerned. If they sang his roles with dramatic conviction, he was always prepared to overlook a cavalier attitude towards the actual notes.

Hofmannsthal's death – for three years he had suffered from arterio-sclerosis – was a savage blow to Strauss. In spite of their clashes of opinion while collaborating, their friendship was based on mutual respect. Hofmannsthal regarded himself as intellectually superior, but it is doubtful if Strauss was much worried by this. 'Thanks be to the noble, unforgettable man', he wrote in his diary for 15 July 1929, and he wrote to Hofmannsthal's widow Gerty: 'No musician ever found such a helper and supporter. No one will ever replace him for me or the world of music.' Pauline was deeply concerned about the effect of the news. As a diversion she threw one of her famous tantrums, made Strauss work and forbade him to attend the funeral (Franz Strauss went in his place). Perhaps she was right, for on the day after the librettist died, Strauss called unexpectedly on his neighbours Elisabeth Schumann and Carl Alwin. He read the text of *Arabella* to them, frequently stopping when overcome by tears. Schumann related how he had 'wept long and unrestrainedly, tears forced from the very depths of his soul'. He had in any case not been well earlier in the year and during 1929 completed only three short works, two settings for bass and piano of poems by Rückert (neither song being performed until August 1964) and the patriotic *Austria* for male voice choir and orchestra, an anthem written for Strauss by Anton Wildgans. A pencil sketch of the start of Act 1 of *Arabella* bears the dates 22 July–22 September 1929, indicating that he began to compose the music exactly a week after Hofmannsthal's death. By 30 July 1930 he had completed the short score of Act 1 having told Karpath that 'Hofmannsthal's glorious text composes as smoothly as butter!'[1] During 1930 he also worked on his edition of Mozart's *Idomeneo*, completing it on 30 September. This had been proposed to him before Hofmannsthal's death by Krauss and Wallerstein to mark the 150th anniversary of the first performance. There is no case for believing that *Idomeneo* held up work on *Arabella*. Strauss told Krauss in June 1929 that he would begin serious work on it the following spring, as he did. Wallerstein translated Varesco's libretto into German prose and Strauss took a knife to the 'interminable recitatives'. *Idomeneo* was largely unknown at this date, a historical curiosity. But Strauss knew and loved it. He told the stage director and opera Intendant Bruno von Niessen in 1932 that 'individual numbers such as the "Zeffiretti" aria [Ilia's 'Zeffiretti lusinghieri'] and the famous E flat quartet were favourite pieces of my early youth'. He had, he said, 'undertaken the task to win *Idomeneo* back for the German stage... If we succeed, I will personally answer for my impiety to the divine Mozart if I ever get to heaven.'[2] What he had to answer for was the elimination of Elettra, rival to Ilia for Prince Idamante's love and her conversion into Ismene, a priestess of Poseidon, determined that Idamante should not marry a Trojan slave. One Elettra in opera was enough for Strauss! He included the extra arias Mozart had written for the Vienna performance in 1786 and omitted Elettra's 'Idol mio', Idamante's 'No, la morte' and Idomeneo's 'Torna la pace'. Arbace was shorn of both his arias (as he often is) and became a baritone. Idamante was assigned to a soprano (as he often is). Strauss added two numbers: an orchestral *Interludio* after the chorus 'Corriamo, fuggiamo', its middle section quoting from 'Torna la pace', and a quartet for Idamante, Idomeneo, Ilia and the High Priest (bass) inserted in the final scene before the chorus 'Scenda Amor'. The quartet was based on Idomeneo's recitative 'Popoli, a voi l'ultima legge' and Ilia's 'Se il padre perdei'. Almost every aria was cut, either by a bar or two or by as many as forty bars. The orchestration remained almost exactly Mozart's except for the deletion of the keyboard continuo.

Strauss conducted the first performance on 16 April 1931. A performance in Magdeburg followed a few days later. It was staged in Berlin in November 1932. The public reaction was favourable, but the critics were generally hostile. 'Mozart with whipped cream' was an obvious verdict (Berlin). In his revision of Köchel's catalogue, Alfred Einstein called it 'a gross act of mutilation'. Strauss's response (to Niessen) was 'Let the critics say what they will, I know my Mozart better than those gentlemen do and at any rate I love him more ardently than they!'[3] A writer in the *Dresdner Nachrichten* said that 'one constantly recognises when it is Mozart's turn to speak and when Strauss's'. Those inimical to Strauss consider that his edition of *Idomeneo* was a public relations exercise to demonstrate that it was his turn to speak – with no very great success with his last three operas and now deprived of Hofmannsthal, he needed to project himself as the standard-bearer of German-Austrian culture, winning back the German stage for himself by linking himself to Mozart, posing as Idamante-Strauss inheriting the throne of Idomeneo-Mozart. This is to take a very low view of Strauss's integrity. Today, when *Idomeneo* has been fully restored to the repertory, there may seem no place for Strauss's 'pre-authentic' labour of love. But it has dramatic qualities, and the juxtaposition of Mozart and romanticism is piquant in itself. It has not been performed since Strauss conducted it in Vienna in December 1941.[4] It is time it was heard again.

In October 1930, after completing *Idomeneo*, Strauss left Garmisch to conduct his music in Paris and Brussels. The previous month there had been elections in Germany, where unemployment had reached over three million in the summer and membership of Adolf Hitler's National Socialist (Nazi) party had risen from half a million to nearly two million. Allied troops had left the Rhineland in July and now there was talk of restoring Germany's eastern frontier. Nationalism was in the air. Twenty-four parties contested the election. The Nazis, who had twelve members in the Reichstag, were expected to win fifty seats. The British Ambassador in Germany was impressed by their campaign. 'The movement is new and vigorous and obviously appeals to youth.' He added that there was 'much rowdyism' among Nazi supporters, leading to bloodshed. The Nazis emerged as the second largest party with 107 seats. Over six million had voted for them. The party celebrated with attacks on Jews and known Communists. France observed all this and became very nervous. Strauss wrote from Paris to his son Franz: 'There had been fears of nationalist demonstrations, but in the end my concert went well and everyone is being fearfully nice to me. In general, ever since those stupid Hitler elections, the atmosphere here has been grim; people spoke of nothing else but the war that Germany is supposed to want to start at any moment.'

Strauss was an adherent of the Paneuropa movement to promote European unity and was hoping to discuss it with Aristide Briand, the French Foreign Minister. He wrote to Pauline: 'As old Clemenceau assured me, I am wholly "*admis*" here, so that's the most important objective achieved. My symphonic poems are played at every French concert, so I can take my leave with no further worries.' From Brussels he informed her that 'here, too, the ambassador hailed me as the most effective ambassador of peace'. These letters to Pauline (he always wrote to her every day when he was away from home) also contain touchingly intimate passages: 'I don't know if it's the same for you – my inner belonging to you grows greater all the time. I think of you and the children all day long. I am wholly happy only with you. With our family! . . . The director of the [Brussels] Conservatoire still remembers exactly how beautifully you sang my songs here – and how you argued my own view, that Bavaria and Austria are the most beautiful places to be, and nowhere is the air as good as in Garmisch, and nowhere is so beautiful as in my own house with my beloved Pauxerl, who is now most tenderly embraced by her own faithful R.' There is another charming anecdote concerning a time when Strauss went to stay at the Vienna house with Franz and Alice. After three days he said: 'You are both very kind and take so much trouble, but I'm so bored! I must go home to Mama.'

He returned to Garmisch to work on *Arabella* and to prepare for the *Idomeneo* première. He assured Krauss on 17 October 1931 that he was working 'fluently' on *Arabella* and that Act 3 was almost ready in sketch form (he finished the sketch on 26 November). He then told Otto Erhardt 'Don't ask me when the score will be ready! The times are not ripe for such a work as this: I shan't be in too much of a hurry over it.' One reason for this sudden hesitancy may have been a visit he had had in the summer from Anton Kippenberg, director of the publishers Insel-Verlag. Kippenberg mentioned that one of his authors was Stefan Zweig, the fifty-year-old Austrian novelist and biographer then at the height of his popularity. 'Ask him if he has an opera libretto for me', said Strauss. On 29 October Zweig, who lived in Salzburg, sent Strauss No. 31 of fifty privately printed facsimiles of one of Mozart's slightly indecent letters to his cousin. (Zweig was a noted collector of writers' and musicians' autographs.) He added: 'I have been wondering whether I might visit you and present a musical project to you.' Strauss was delighted and tried at once to interest him in his pet project of an opera about 'the woman adventurer, the grande dame as a spy, a play of intrigue'. But Zweig was no more interested in this than Hofmannsthal had been. The two men met on 20 November in the Hotel Vierjahreszeiten in Munich, where Strauss was to conduct *Elektra*. They decided on a comedy based on Ben Jonson's *Epicoene, or the Silent Woman*, Strauss making it clear that he could not begin work on it until the summer of 1932 at the earliest. Zweig's impression of Strauss gives us a vivid portrait:

Difficulties do not menace him but rather serve to amuse his creative mastery. . . When his eyes light up, one feels that something daemonic lies deep down in this extraordinary person who at first arouses something like distrust, by his punctuality, by his methodical ways, his respectability, his artisanship, his seeming nerveless-ness at work, just as his face first impresses as almost banal with its fat, child-like cheeks, the rather ordinary roundness of features and the hesitantly retreating brow. But only one glance into his eyes, these bright, blue, highly radiant eyes, and one instantly feels some particular magic power behind this bourgeois mask. They are perhaps the most wideawake eyes I have ever seen in a musician, not daemonic but in some way clairvoyant, the eyes of a man cognizant of the full significance of his task.[5]

Early in February 1932 Strauss told Fritz Busch, whom he had chosen to conduct the première of *Arabella*, that he had orchestrated the first one hundred pages. Act 1 was finished on 6 March, Act 2 on 6 June and Act 3 on 12 October. This was contrary to his usual pattern of composing in the summer and scoring in the winter. During this period he conducted in Florence, Genoa and Milan in April and two performances of *Fidelio* at the

Salzburg Festival in August. He visited Zürich in November for a Strauss festival at which he conducted *Die Frau ohne Schatten* and was the pianist with the Hungarian violinist Stefi Geyer in his early Violin Sonata. In December 1932 he conducted in Strasbourg. Strauss wrote to Erhardt in July 1932 to say he had temporarily put off the *Arabella* première. 'I have become somewhat wearied by the effort of it all and would like to interrupt it with a new work. . . Secondly, the financial circumstances (neither the publisher, the theatre nor the public has any money) have now become so difficult that I believe it would be foolish to squander a big work in the uncertainty of the present times.'

That uncertainty was the political situation in Germany. The Nazis continued to prosper in local elections and their stormtroops (Brownshirts) killed their rivals and women and children in the streets. The Chancellor, Dr Brüning, ordered the Brownshirts to be disbanded but had difficulty in holding a majority in the Reichstag. He resigned and was replaced on 30 May by Count Franz von Papen who dissolved the Reichstag and reversed the ban on Brownshirts. Bavaria insisted on keeping the ban but was overruled by Papen. A general election followed on 31 July. The Nazis won 230 seats, voted for by 13.5 million. They were the largest single party but could not command an absolute Reichstag majority. Papen did not invite them to join the government and Hitler intensified street violence. On 13 August Papen offered Hitler the post of Vice-Chancellor. The reply was Chancellor or nothing. In September, after a clever procedural move by its president, Hermann Goering, the Reichstag was again dissolved and new elections were called for November 1932. In these the Nazis lost ground, winning only 197 seats and securing only thirty-three per cent of the vote. Papen again offered Hitler a post which was again refused. Unable to command a majority in the Reichstag, he resigned. The German President, Hindenburg, who had already refused to have Hitler as Chancellor, now was compelled to ask Hitler to form a government. Hitler said that he would only rule without the Reichstag and through a 'presidential cabinet'. Hindenburg said this meant dictatorship and asked General von Schleicher, a former Defence Minister, to be Chancellor and try to form a government. Early in 1933 Papen met Hitler in Cologne and suggested they should co-operate against Schleicher and be joint Chancellors. Hitler replied that he would only join a government of which he was unrestricted Chancellor. On 28 January Schleicher, unable to command a majority, asked Hindenburg to dissolve the Reichstag. When this was refused he resigned and Hindenburg had no alternative but to appoint Hitler as Chancellor on 30 January. Reichstag or not, majority or not, Germany was now ruled by a dictator.

This was the background, distant though it may have seemed, for the next year of Strauss's life. A date for the *Arabella* première in Dresden had been fixed: 1 July 1933. Other houses were clamouring for it. Furtwängler was to conduct it in Berlin, Hans Knappertsbusch in Munich and Krauss in Vienna, so its general circulation was restricted until after 1 October. In Dresden Busch was to conduct, Josef Gielen was producer and Leonhard Fanto designer. Discussions about casting were held by Strauss with Busch and the Dresden Intendant Alfred Reucker, joint dedicatees of the opera. Meanwhile, in June 1932, Zweig had sent Strauss a draft synopsis of *The Silent Woman*, to be known as *Die schweigsame Frau*. Strauss was delighted: 'It is enchanting – a born comic opera – a comedy equal to the best of its kind – more suitable for music than even *Figaro* and the *Barber of Seville*. Let me ask you urgently to complete the first act as soon as your other important tasks permit. I can't wait to work on it intensively.' He filled in time in September by compiling an eight-movement Suite from *Schlagobers* (he conducted the first performance in Mannheim on 8 November). He received the first act libretto of *Die schweigsame Frau* in October. At this time in Dresden, Nazi Brownshirts were beginning to stir up trouble for Fritz Busch who, although not Jewish, was an outspoken critic of the stormtroopers' activities and was accused of favouring Jews and taking too much leave. In February 1933 Strauss went to Dresden to read the first two acts of *Die schweigsame Frau* to Reucker, Busch and Fanto ('they responded with great enthusiasm'). A fortnight later, on 7 March, a demonstration against Busch was organised by the Brownshirts. He was deprived of his post in favour of his assistant, Hermann Kutzschbach, and then ordered into the pit to conduct *Rigoletto* for an audience containing Nazis who jeered him. The next day Reucker, also non-Jewish, was dismissed and replaced by Dr Paul Adolph.

At a February meeting in Berlin, Strauss had told Busch and Heinz Tietjen, the Intendant of Prussian state theatres, that *Arabella* would only be released for Dresden if the dedicatees were in control. If, because of the Nazis, Busch refused to conduct, another venue would have to be found. 'When Strauss said this', Busch wrote in his autobiography, 'there is no doubt that he was sincere.'[6] A letter from Strauss to Krauss on 27 March insists that without Busch and Reucker, the July première was off. But that same letter gives away that something was going on behind the scenes involving Tietjen, an accomplished wheeler-dealer, who had been told by the Nazis to solve the problem so that the bad publicity involved in the withdrawal of a new opera by one of the world's leading composers could be avoided. 'Some friendly advice', Strauss wrote, 'don't commit yourself to Dresden in any way! Should the administration there, who apparently aren't always *au fait* with developments in Berlin, approach you directly with an invitation, use me as an excuse, as one whose "agreement in principle you must first secure". In this way the Dresden affair can be stalled until Tietjen gives the go-ahead.' Krauss received this letter on the day the Nazi party proclaimed a boycott of Jews from 1 April. From it we may deduce that some sort of pressure was being put on Strauss, not least the Dresden opera management's insistence upon the legal terms of their contract, and this meant abandoning Busch. Writing to Fanto on 4 April, Strauss still regarded 1 July as impossible. If Krauss was to conduct, he would have to join the Dresden opera team, which was impossible because of his Vienna commitments. 'So far we have found neither a Mandryka, an Elemer nor a Waldner. . . Thus July is impossible. . . Whether I can honour my pledge for a Dresden première in the autumn must depend . . . on the composition of the new musical administration in Dresden.' But by 20 April, some agreement between Strauss and Dresden, as well as with Vienna regarding Krauss, had been reached. In spite of the composer's misgivings, 1 July was to be the date of the first performance. The role of Arabella was offered to the soprano Viorica Ursuleac, under contract to Dresden. She was also Krauss's mistress (they married after 1945) and often sang as a guest in Vienna. The Viennese baritone Alfred Jerger was chosen as Mandryka for Dresden and Vienna. In view of the shortage of time for preparation, Strauss asked that the Dresden soprano Eva von der Osten, the creator of Octavian in *Der Rosenkavalier* in 1911, should act as an advisory stage director. Her husband, the bass Friedrich Platschke, was to sing Arabella's father, Count Waldner. Busch, by the way, was much admired as a conductor by both Hitler and Goering. The latter, who was running the opera in Berlin (to Goebbels's chagrin), wanted him as conductor of the Preussische Staatsoper. Busch went straight from Dresden to Berlin to meet Goering on three occasions. He would have liked the post, but Furtwängler had the last word and Hitler backed him against Goering. Hitler, for his part, tried to make the Dresden Nazis change their minds about Busch but, amazing as it may seem, he got nowhere. Eventually Busch found his way to Buenos Aires and Glyndebourne, but still received offers (which he refused) from Germany to conduct there.[7]

Strauss attended all the rehearsals of *Arabella*. Ursuleac has described what she called a unique experience: 'The theatre was simply closed for three weeks and rehearsals went on from early morning until late into the night. Everyone, right down to the meanest stagehand, was inspired by the work, an unforgettable period and its success was fabulous.'[8] A Strauss première still caused intense excitement and was a major social as well as artistic event. The Dresden periodical *Das schöne Sachsen* reported: 'For weeks people in musical circles have talked of nothing else. In Dresden no effort was spared to ensure that the day of the première would become a festival for Richard Strauss and his music.'[9] Despite increased prices, every ticket was sold and some people had travelled thousands of miles to be there. As the curtain rose on Act 3, 'all present felt after a few moments that in the dramatically practical, picturesque atmosphere of the hotel vestibule all the best and most spiritual theatrical ingredients had been assembled. . . The work ended with a storm of approval such as had seldom been demonstrated in the history of operatic first performance.' Strauss told Karpath a few days later, 'Krauss conducted so well that, according to the old Viennese tradition, it must be about time to get rid of him!' How taken aback Strauss was is shown in a letter he wrote to Zweig in January 1934:

Confidentially – I was not expecting too much of *Arabella*. I worked hard on it and now this enormous success, hardly less, so far, than that of *Rosenkavalier*. It is strange. The public is inscrutable. Despite all one knows about the art, one knows least what one is really capable of doing. . . What suits me best, South German bourgeois that I am, are sentimental jobs; but such bull's-eyes as the *Arabella* duet and the *Rosenkavalier* trio don't happen every day. Must one become seventy years old to recognise that one's greatest strength lies in creating kitsch?

The Vienna and Berlin premières of *Arabella* were on the same evening in October 1933. Ursuleac sang in Berlin with Furtwängler. In Vienna Lotte Lehmann was Arabella. Her mother died that evening, but she still sang radiantly, although Ursuleac deputised for her in the next four performances. Ursuleac sang the role in London in May 1934 and all over Europe. Strauss first conducted it in Amsterdam on 20 November 1934. Ursuleac was taken aback by his very fast tempo at rehearsal of the final scene when Arabella descends the hotel staircase with a glass of water to offer Mandryka. 'Herr Doktor', she remonstrated, 'if you conduct at the same pace this evening I shall have to gallop down the stairs. . . It's such a shame when the music is so beautiful.' He growled in reply 'Oh, those six-four chords.' In the evening he took the scene 'with poetic breadth'. She thanked him next day in the Rijksmuseum. 'You've only yourself to blame', he said and gave her a ring. 'There, that's for your Arabella.'[10] At the Budapest première in January 1935 the young répétiteur was Georg Solti, later a distinguished interpreter of the opera. Fritz Busch conducted it in Buenos Aires.

Although *Arabella* was a big success in Germany and Austria, it was not well received in Britain and America (Paris did not stage it until 1981!). This has been attributed to the political situation, but I doubt it. Most of the London and New York critics regarded it as inferior to *Der Rosenkavalier*, Strauss repeating himself. Ernest Newman admitted he had 'sadly misjudged' the opera in 1934 and in 1953 wrote of 'the rare delicacy of much of the psychological and musical line-drawing, the quiet art with which what is in large part essentially a conversation piece was worked out'.[11] Bull's-eye!

PART IV

1933–1949
The dark years

20   Taking Walter's place

To try to interpret 1933 from a distance of sixty-five years later is a frustrating task. With the sanctimonious piety of hindsight available to us in the
1990s, we can put our hands on our hearts and swear that we would never
have lived under the Nazi régime, never have worked for it in any way. But
we now know what happened. It requires an immense exercise of the historical imagination to understand the national and international climate of
1933. Although some far-seeing people knew immediately that Hitler's
accession to power would eventually mean war, many more, especially
among Germans, were convinced that the Nazis were a nightmare which
would soon pass. They would bankrupt the country and that would be the
end of them. But millions of young Germans were unemployed and they
saw only hope in Nazi policies. Germany had been crushed by the Versailles
Treaty, the governments of the Weimar Republic in the 1920s had been
futile, inflation had risen to astronomical proportions. By appealing to
nationalist fervour, Hitler convinced millions that Germany had a great
future. But what about the fanatical anti-Jewish ravings and actions which
accompanied all the other propaganda? What about the violence in the
streets, the smashing of Jewish shop windows? Germany was accustomed to
anti-Semitism in one form or another, either virulent (from fanatics) or
casual and thoughtless. Lord Esher, private secretary to King Edward VII,
recounted in his memoirs a conversation between Kaiser Wilhelm II and the
British Foreign Secretary, Sir Edward Grey, in 1907: 'Grey had two long talks
with him. At the first he declaimed violently against Jews. "There are far too
many of them in my country. They want stamping out. If I did not restrain
my people, there would be Jew-baiting".'[1] Another very important difference
between 1933 and today is that no one in 1933 was bombarded with news
bulletins every half-hour for twenty-four hours a day. Even on the wireless

(radio), news was infrequent. There was no television, only cinema news-reels. People relied on the newspapers, and not everybody read them.

Richard Strauss grew up accustomed to anti-Semitic remarks from his father. But these were no more malevolent than an Englishman exclaiming 'the bloody Scots' or 'the ruddy Welsh'. Strauss had many Jewish friends and there is nothing in any of his letters or other writings to indicate any anti-Semitic feelings. Indeed, in letters to Strauss in September and October 1893, Siegfried Wagner remarked that Strauss 'obviously' had no anti-Semitic sentiments because he refused to agree with Siegfried's vitriolic abuse of Hermann Levi. After the Second World War, Strauss refused to defend himself in public from accusations of anti-Semitism because he regarded it as beneath his dignity to do so. The conductor Otto Klemperer told of a visit to Garmisch for tea in 1932 when Strauss, Pauline and Alice entertained him. 'Naturally the talk turned to the theme of the day, the Nazis, who were obvi-ously coming to power. Strauss said "But tell me, what will happen to the German theatres and opera houses if the Jews leave?" Frau Strauss turned to me, "Herr Doktor, if the Nazis give you any trouble, just you come to me. I'll show those gentlemen who's who". Strauss looked at her in surprise. "That would be just the right moment to stand up for a Jew!" The shame-lessness was so naked one couldn't be angry.'[2] Shameless perhaps, disin-genuous certainly. It was the sort of remark his father might have made, not to be judged in the light of knowledge of the Holocaust. And it was made in the presence of his beloved daughter-in-law who was Jewish. It has been stressed several times in this book that the epicentre of Strauss's life was his family, closely followed by his music. Also he was a proud German – a Bavarian who disliked Prussians – but conscious that he was part of the German/Austrian culture which was a mainspring of his being: Goethe, Schiller, Beethoven, Mozart, Schubert and Wagner. So when it is asked why, in 1933, he did not leave Germany like many others, the answer is that he saw no reason to uproot his family and himself from the home they loved nor to abandon hope for keeping the flame of German culture alive. Besides, he had despised the Weimar Republic and its ineffectuality. He is known to have said to Hofmannsthal and Count Kessler in 1928 that Germany needed a dictator (he was not the only German to have that idea) – and, of course, he meant a dictator who would implement his (Strauss's) views on how

Germany's musical life should be organised. Strauss is often derided as an 'opportunist', but although he described himself (to Rolland) as 'weak', he believed he had a patriotic responsibility. Those non-Jews who left Germany did so because they could not breathe freely under such a vile system. Strauss never put his feelings on the subject into words, but he would have subscribed to what Furtwängler said in 1945: 'All those who became emigrants or demanded that one should emigrate, have relieved Hitler of having to prove one thing: his claim that he was the true representative of the German nation. They thought that one *had* to leave a Nazi Germany, but this is wrong. Germany never was a Nazi Germany but a Germany subjugated by the Nazis.'

Arnold Schoenberg, writing in 1946 as 'not a friend of Richard Strauss', said: 'I do not believe that he was a Nazi, just as little as W. Furtwängler. They were both Deutsch-Nationale – Nationalistic Germans, they both loved Germany, German culture and art, landscape, language and its citizens, their co-nationals. They both will raise their glass if a toast is brought to Germany "Hoch Deutschland" and though they estimated French and Italian music and paintings highly, they consider everything German as superior.'[3] Herbert von Karajan's opinion was that to Strauss 'the Nazis were a bunch of Hottentots'.[4]

Strauss said to his family in 1933: 'I made music under the Kaiser and under Ebert[5] – I'll survive under this one as well.' He was the last great composer who had been a court composer – at Weimar under a duke, in Berlin under a Kaiser who disliked his music but left him alone. He knew how to handle these people – and they came and went. But he must also have known that 'this one' was different and that there was likely to be a growing and serious threat to Jews. That meant Alice and her two sons (her second, Christian, was born in 1932). He knew in 1933 that he must be prepared to compromise with the régime to protect his beloved family, whatever it cost. As we shall see, it cost him his reputation as far as many people were concerned, but the person who paid the highest price was Alice, who had virtually to forget that she was Jewish and to suppress whatever she felt about the situation, especially when many of her relatives disappeared into a concentration camp. She knew that she would be considered – as she was – the most unpopular Jew in Germany because she had sold her birthright for a mess of potage. The uncharitable, like Klemperer, had another explanation for Strauss's conduct: 'Why didn't he leave? He was Richard Strauss, famous throughout the whole world, and if he had left Germany, then people would have realised that the outlook there was black. But no, he stayed. And why? Because in Germany there were 56 opera houses and in America only two – New York and San Francisco. He said it himself, "That would have reduced my income".' Yes, the income from his music was extremely important to him. At nearly seventy, he wanted to leave his family well provided for. And, it may be said, the world knew the outlook was black in Germany. Thomas Mann and others left, but it made no difference even if they were regarded with admiration. If Shostakovich had left Russia, what difference would it have made to Stalin? Strauss's not unnatural interest in his royalties – and he had fought for years on behalf of his fellow-composers in this respect – was a part of his total absorption in music. His own operas were his livelihood and provided for his family. Nothing else was more important to him. Another explanation of Strauss's conduct which is often advanced can be dismissed out of hand – that he was naïvely apolitical. As many quotations from letters in this book will have shown, he was well informed about German and foreign affairs. From Bismarck to Hitler, he knew what was going on. He admired Romain Rolland's involvement in world affairs and was himself an early advocate of European union.

Germany and Strauss received early warning of what the Nazis' Jewish policy involved. The conductor Bruno Walter, Jewish-born, was in America when Hitler came to power. He returned to Germany in March 1933 to resume his duties as conductor of the Leipzig Gewandhaus Orchestra. A director of the Gewandhaus told him that the police wanted to stop his concert. Walter offered to resign but was urged to stand his ground. Arriving for rehearsal next morning he found the hall locked and a poster saying the concert had been cancelled. He returned to Berlin where he was to conduct a 'Bruno Walter concert' in a series organised by the Jewish impresario Louise Wolff. She told him that Goebbels's Propaganda Ministry, while not banning the concert, had let her know that if it took place the hall would be wrecked. As substitute conductor, the name of Strauss, who was in Berlin to conduct *Elektra*, was suggested. At first, Strauss emphatically refused to conduct the concert, but Louise Wolff sent her daughter, Dr Lili Brandenburg, to see Dr Julius Kopsch, a Berlin jurist, composer and conductor, who was a member

18 With his grandsons Richard and Christian

of the Nazi party, to ask him to persuade Strauss to conduct, otherwise the orchestra would suffer a serious financial loss. Mrs Wolff added that it was Bruno Walter's specific and personal wish that Strauss should take over, this being his last request before leaving Berlin. Strauss thereupon agreed to conduct provided that his fee of 1,500 marks was given to the orchestra, who were to have been paid by Walter.[6] Why Walter did not disclose that it had been his request, thus relieving Strauss of much odium at the time, is hard to fathom. Equally, why did Strauss himself never mention it? There was always ill-feeling between the two, dating back to the dissatisfaction felt by Strauss and Hofmannsthal at the way their operas were staged during Walter's régime in Munich. At a concert in Zürich in 1946, Strauss saw Mrs Wolff's surviving daughter, Edith Stargardt-Wolff, and called out to her: 'You know, don't you, I never wanted to conduct then.'

As a result of this affair, Wilhelm Furtwängler wrote to Goebbels to say that 'men like Walter, Klemperer, Reinhardt etc. must have their artistic say in Germany'. Goebbels's reply was that music and politics could not be separated and that it was a national duty to eradicate 'foreign', by which he meant Jewish, elements to open the way for artists who had been ignored or suppressed during the Weimar Republic years.

Strauss made his comments on the Walter affair in his private notebook in an entry beginning: 'Now I might examine the price I had to pay for not keeping away, from the beginning, from the National Socialist movement.' He described his action as 'to do a favour to the Philharmonic Orchestra and upon the urging of Kopsch and Rasch [Hugo Rasch, music editor of the Hitler-supporting *Völkischer Beobachter* but a friend of some years' standing]'. By substituting for 'that mean and lousy scoundrel' Walter he

started a storm against me by the foreign and especially the Jewish Viennese press, which did more damage to me in the eyes of all decent people than the German Government can ever compensate me for. I was slandered as a servile, selfish anti-Semite, whereas in truth I have always stressed at every opportunity to all the people that count here (much to my disadvantage) that I consider the Streicher-Goebbels Jew-baiting as a disgrace to German honour, as evidence of incompetence – the basest weapon of untalented, lazy mediocrity against a higher intelligence and greater talent. I openly testify here that I have received so much support, so much self-sacrificing friendship, so much generous help and intellectual inspiration from

Jews that it would be a crime not to acknowledge it with all gratitude. True, I had adversaries in the Jewish press . . . but my worst and most malicious enemies were 'Aryans' – I merely need to mention the names of Perfall, Oscar Merz (*Münchner Neueste Nachrichten*), Theodor Döhring (*Der Sammler*), Felix Mottl, Franz Schalk, Weingartner and the whole party press: *Völkischer Beobachter* and the rest.

He did not mention that he had a Jewish publisher and that Hofmannsthal was part-Jewish.

While he was in Berlin at this time, it seems probable that some high party officials contacted him. They needed him to give their régime an air of respectability; he needed them to protect his family. He wrote to Kippenberg on 29 March: 'I have brought back from Berlin great impressions and real hopes for the future of German Art once the first throes of the revolutionary storm have subsided.'[7] This letter is important in view of what was to follow in November of that year.

After the completion of *Arabella*, Strauss's principal musical preoccupation in the closing weeks of 1932 was revision of *Die ägyptische Helena* in collaboration with Lothar Wallerstein and Clemens Krauss, who wished to stage it at the 1933 Salzburg Festival. Act 1 was left largely untouched but considerable changes were made in Act 2, involving the provision of extra and substitute lines of text by Wallerstein. Some juggling of the action was sanctioned by Strauss, who completed the task on 15 January 1933. Krauss was not fully satisfied and put forward further proposals, but Strauss would not budge. This 'Vienna version' had two performances in Salzburg on 14 and 24 August, together with one performance of *Die Frau ohne Schatten* which thrilled Strauss. After the 1926 *Ariadne*, Krauss in 1929 began the series of Strauss operas in Salzburg which were a feature of the festival, especially *Der Rosenkavalier*, performed each year from 1929 to 1935 with Lotte Lehmann or Ursuleac as the Marschallin, Adele Kern as Sophie, Richard Mayr and Fritz Krenn as Ochs and a succession of illustrious Octavians – dream casts! (After Krauss left Vienna for Munich, there was a gap in 1936 and *Der Rosenkavalier* returned from 1937 to 1941, excluding 1940, conducted either by Knappertsbusch or Karl Böhm and with Lehmann, Rethberg, Hilde and Anny Konetzni as the Marschallin.) A second revision of *Helena*, at Berlin in 1935 and Munich in 1937, was undertaken by Krauss and Rudolf Hartmann, but this mainly affected the location of the opening of Act 1, which was moved from a room in Aithra's palace to a terrace in front of the palace with the sea as background, and necessitated dividing the act into two parts. Publication of the full score in 1996 in the Complete Edition of the Stage Works reverted to the 1928 original.

In September 1933 he orchestrated four of his songs – *Frühlingsfeier* (Op. 56, no. 5), *Mein Auge* (Op. 37, no. 4), *Befreit* (Op. 39, no. 4) and *Lied der Frauen* (Op. 68, no. 6) – for Ursuleac. (It was to be seven years before he orchestrated the previous five songs of Op. 68.) He conducted the first performances with her in Berlin on 13 October. This was done in the aftermath of another furore when, in July, he returned to Bayreuth for the first time since 1894 to conduct five performances of *Parsifal* – 22 and 31 July, 2, 10 and 19 August – in place of Toscanini who, the previous May, had informed Winifred Wagner that 'the sorrowful events which have wounded my feelings as a man and as an artist' had undergone no change. In other words, he would not conduct there while the Nazis ruled Germany. Heinz Tietjen, who was general manager of Bayreuth, had anticipated Toscanini's withdrawal and, amazing as it may seem, had approached Fritz Busch even though the Dresden demonstrations against Busch had already begun. Strauss was then invited and he accepted. Since he already knew what odium he had incurred by substituting for Walter, there is no reason to doubt Strauss's honesty when he wrote to Zweig on 17 June 1935: 'Who has told you that I have exposed myself *so far politically?* . . . because I stood in for that other "non-Aryan" Toscanini – that I did for the sake of Bayreuth. It had nothing to do with politics.' To him it had not, but he should have realised how it would be interpreted by others. But Wagner was a god to him, Bayreuth holy ground. He had no reason to feel behoven to the Wagner family. There had been coolness since his quarrel with Siegfried in 1896. Cosima had described *Salome* as an obscenity. But they were both dead and in any case it was Wagner and Wagner's music which held Strauss in thrall. He had always had a particular passion for *Parsifal* and had argued against its release after 1913 for 'prostitution in every provincial opera house, no matter how small'. He believed it should be performed only at Bayreuth, as Wagner had wished. This may now seem a lunatic, restrictive belief, but it was genuinely held and it is an indication of his opinion about Bayreuth and this above all operas. While there in 1933, he met Hitler, patron of the festival, and suggested that

19 Bayreuth 1934: Heinz Tietjen, Winifred Wagner, Strauss and Emil Preetorius

the new government should subsidise Bayreuth by levying a one per cent royalty on every Wagner performance in Germany. Hitler said there was no legal precedent. Hitler gave a reception at Wahnfried. Alice Strauss wanted to refuse the invitation, but Winifred Wagner insisted on her attendance on the grounds she would make herself a laughing-stock. Hitler, although knowing she was Jewish, kissed her hand when they met. But he had already been persuaded by Winifred to permit Jewish singers – among them Emanuel List and Alexander Kipnis – to sing at this festival. In the event, Strauss's conducting of *Parsifal* also caused a musical scandal. His timing was four hours eight minutes compared with Toscanini's four hours forty-eight minutes in 1931. Ernest Newman, in his *Sunday Times* review, described Strauss as 'merely second-rate' and unworthy of the orchestra. But the legend of Strauss's 'fast' *Parsifal* can only be sustained in comparison with Toscanini (who took twenty minutes longer on Act 1 alone). Levi's timing in 1882 was four hours four minutes, four minutes quicker than Strauss, while Furtwängler was four minutes slower at four hours twelve minutes in 1936. The real speed merchants were Clemens Krauss (1953) at three hours forty-four minutes and Pierre Boulez (1970) at three hours thirty-nine minutes. An undated timing for Strauss of three hours fifty-six minutes is still seventeen minutes slower than Boulez.

Winifred Wagner sent Strauss a page of Wagner's autograph sketches for *Lohengrin*. Thanking her, on 23 September, he wrote: 'My modest help for Bayreuth was only a respectful repayment of the great debt of gratitude stored up in my heart for all that the great master gave to the world and to me in particular. It is really I who should thank you for the opportunity, in the evening of my life, to conduct his sublime work once more, in that sacred place: it was a high honour and satisfaction for me.' The production in 1933 was the original 1882 staging, and was nearly falling to bits. Late in 1933, Winifred, Tietjen and the designer Emil Preetorius decided to re-stage *Parsifal* in 1934. This caused uproar and the Wagner old guard, headed by Wagner's daughters Eva and Daniela, organised a petition seeking to preserve the original sets. The thousand signatories included Toscanini and Strauss – and Ernest Newman. Hitler favoured a new production and asked that Alfred Roller should design it. The result differed little from the previous staging. Strauss conducted some of the 1934 performances. He never returned to Bayreuth.

Strauss's worship of Wagner's music had led him to sign the letter of protest, organised by Hans Knappertsbusch, which was published in the *Münchner Neueste Nachrichten* of 16 April 1933. This was a violent reply to Thomas Mann's lecture on Wagner, first given at Munich University on 10 February 1933 to mark the fiftieth anniversary of the composer's death, in which he gave a warning of the Nazis' appropriation of Wagner 'for an unholy alliance of *Macht* and *Kultur*'. The lecture was later repeated in Amsterdam, Paris and Brussels. What enraged Strauss and other Wagnerians was Mann's description – among much high praise – of Wagner's genius as 'an amalgam of dilettante accomplishments' and 'the dried-flower arrangements of bourgeois vulgarity'. Knappertsbusch, who was then music director of the Bavarian State Opera, wrote: 'Whoever dares publicly to belittle the man who like few others has represented the power of German *Geist* to the world will have something coming to him.' He approached leading figures in Munich's artistic society, including Strauss, to sign the protest, in addition to some leading pro-Wagnerian Nazis.

21   The Reich Chamber

What of progress with *Die schweigsame Frau*? A letter from Zweig dated 13 April 1933 says he is delighted that Strauss's work was proceeding well. He added: 'Politics pass, the arts live on, hence we should strive for that which is permanent and leave propaganda to those who find it fulfilling and satisfying. History shows that it is in times of unrest when artists work with the greatest concentration; and so I am happy for every hour in which you turn words into music, which lifts you above time for the benefit and inspiration of later generations.' This, be it remembered, was from a Jewish writer living in Austria.

Since the Nazis took control, Dr Josef Goebbels had been engaged in a power struggle with Alfred Rosenberg, the head of the Reich's foreign affairs department, for the control of cultural activities in the Reich. Rosenberg, a fanatical anti-Semite who founded the Fighting League for German Culture in 1929, was the epitome of reactionary ideas, Goebbels less ideologically hidebound. Goebbels was the victor because he was the shrewder politician. He could usually, but not always, rely on Hitler's support. But Hitler's attitudes on music were unpredictable. He knew more about it and had better taste than most of his associates. He kept sole control of Bayreuth's financing and gave his own money to promoting Bruckner. His attitude to Strauss was that of a hero-worshipper: he had attended the Graz première of *Salome* in 1906 and regarded Strauss as a successor to Wagner. So although Strauss was to earn the scorn of Goebbels and prove to be an embarrassment to the Nazi régime, Hitler was always loath to move against one of Germany's great men because of the odium it would bring on his régime. Once Rosenberg had been vanquished, Goebbels was able to set up the Reich Chamber of Culture, with seven inner chambers of which music was one, with fine art, theatre, literature, the press, radio and cinema. Each inner chamber had its president, vice-president and business manager. The Reich Chamber of Culture was founded on 1 November 1933 and its inaugural meeting was on 15 November, when Strauss conducted his *Festliches Präludium*. Goebbels appointed Strauss and Furtwängler, neither a member of the Nazi party, as president and vice-president of the Music Chamber, no doubt in the belief and expectation that their names lent credibility to the organisation. There is nothing to be gained by any apologist for Strauss in pretending that he accepted the post under some kind of duress. Strauss said and wrote several times that he was not asked if he wanted the post, but this is not true. Goebbels offered him the post in a telegram sent on 10 November 1933.[1] Whether Strauss did not receive it, we do not know. But it was sent. In his private memorandum of 1935 Strauss said that he took the presidency – although he says he was not consulted about the membership of the pre-sidial council – 'because I hoped that I would be able to do some good and prevent worse misfortune if from now onwards German musical life was going to be, as it was said, "reorganised" by amateurs and ignorant place-seekers'. In his opening address to the Reich Culture Chamber on 15 November he sent to Hitler and Goebbels 'the heartfelt thanks of the whole German musical fraternity' for the prospect of a renewed intimacy between music and the people such as had existed in the sixteenth century. He saw that in this presidential post he had the power to achieve his lifelong ambition to alter and extend German thirty-year copyright laws to guarantee composers a more secure income, and when Germany agreed to conform to the Berne convention of a fifty-year period of copyright protection, he had won his case at last. But he had to struggle to gain this victory. Strauss asked Hitler for the copyright extension at Bayreuth in 1934. Hitler ordered the Propaganda Ministry to act, but Goebbels tried to work it so that the royalties from the extra twenty years were paid into a special Ministry fund. Strauss pointed out that the Nazis had pressed for the fifty-year period before they came to power and Goebbels was unable to argue against Hitler on that point. Strauss's ally in helping to overcome Goebbels's objections was the Bavarian Justice Minister, Dr Hans Frank. Opportunism, cry the Strauss-denigrators, he was just interested in his own bank account. His record in fighting for his fellow-composers refutes this cheap charge.

Strauss's enthusiasm for his task led him to do what many composers have done in similar circumstances – he wrote a song, *Das Bächlein*, on 3 December 1933 and dedicated it to Goebbels 'in remembrance of 15 November 1933'. The text of the poem, once falsely attributed to Goethe, is about a stream and ends with the lines

Der mich gerufen aus dem Stein
der, denk ich, wird mein Führer sein
(He who has summoned me from the stone
He, I believe, will be my leader)

There is no evidence that the song was performed in its original form during Strauss's lifetime, but its existence has been used in evidence against him, particularly because of the triple repetition in the setting of the words 'mein Führer'. But Strauss was never one to resist an allusion or a play on words and this must have seemed irresistible. It is a delightful song, in any case. When a complete edition of his songs was contemplated during the war, Strauss ordered the dedication to be suppressed. He had by then, in April 1935, orchestrated it and dedicated this version to Viorica Ursuleac 'from the thankful composer of *Helena*'. She gave the first performance seven years later in Berlin.

Strauss was not alone in thinking that the new regime might benefit the arts. Most professionals in the German arts world welcomed the proposed changes – after the chaos and cuts of the Weimar Republic, things could only improve. Asked after the war why he had accepted the post of vice-president, Furtwängler replied: 'Because I hoped in those days that on an official basis I would achieve more than I would ever have been able to achieve as a private person. At that time many people in Germany believed that the Nazis would only be able to establish themselves totally when all decent persons had shirked their responsibility.'[2] In choosing such major international figures as president and vice-president of the Music Chamber, the Nazis probably intended to demonstrate that they would leave the administration of musical affairs in the hands of musicians. Strauss also saw the opportunity to ride some of his favourite hobby-horses. One was the reservation of *Parsifal* for Bayreuth. Another was his campaign against 'the abysmal quality of programmes' played by spa orchestras (to which he listened when he went for his annual 'cures'). He hoped the Music Chamber would recommend 'entertainment music of decent quality' for spa bands and that a stop be put to 'the murder' of such items as Siegfried's Funeral March by orchestras of sixteen players. They should play the Strausses (Johann and Josef), Mozart, Schubert and 'charming French and Italian pieces'. Laudable, no doubt, but hopeless. Who would stop playing the waltz from *The Merry Widow* (Strauss wanted to exclude 'the worst rubbish from Viennese operetta') and give the public only Mozart divertimentos and Schubert dances? (He wrote disparagingly to Joseph Gregor about 'Frau Alphonse Rothschild in Vienna who saw one of the silliest operettas 32 times in one winter. My chauffeur and Anna the housekeeper prefer *Die Meistersinger* to *The Merry Widow* if they get the choice.') He was on surer ground in his belief that 'exploitation of works of art is theft of the nation's spiritual wealth and must be punishable as such'. By this he meant arrangements by unscrupulous publishers. He liked to say: 'As long as something like *Lilac Time* is possible, no one can say that composers have any real protection.' This is the moment to examine Strauss's attitude to other composers whose music he rather loftily, if not snobbishly, dismissed as beneath notice. He admired the music of Johann Strauss II but had contempt for Lehár, whose compositional technique he regarded as fallible. There was also, perhaps, a tinge of jealousy. Lehár's operettas made money and filled the theatres, including the Vienna Opera, when more serious works were struggling to find audiences. *The Merry Widow*, 'born' within a few days of *Salome*, might just possibly have had an influence on the waltzes which run through *Der Rosenkavalier* and there is a resemblance between Count Danilo and Mandryka. Near the end of his life, Strauss said to his daughter-in-law: 'I was unjust to Lehár. I have always been too unconciliatory.' Puccini was another box-office rival nearer to home. Strauss claimed never to have sat through one of his operas to the end. When Clemens Krauss extolled the beauty of *La bohème*, Strauss replied ironically: '*Jaja*, very beautiful, all melody, all melody!' He said to Viorica Ursuleac: 'Everyone thinks I'm hostile to Puccini. It isn't true. But I can't listen to his operas because if I do I can't get the melodies out of my head afterwards. And I can't write Puccinian Strauss.'

Strauss also thought that foreign works had too large a share of the repertory. 'The operas of Verdi and Puccini are less trouble and less demanding than our German works, which are significantly more taxing for both per-formers and listeners. . . Germany, with its universality and greatness of heart, affords generous hospitality to meritorious works of art from abroad, but it must be done in proportion, more or less, to the hospitality shown by foreign countries. . . The foreign repertory should occupy a third, or perhaps once in a while, as an exception, half the scheduled programme, and that is still a considerably higher percentage than foreign countries afford to us.' He had a point, but he ignored public taste. (The five most popular opera composers in Germany from 1932 to 1940 were, in order, Wagner, Verdi, Puccini, Mozart and Lortzing. The most popular individual operas in that period were *Carmen, Der Freischütz* and *Der fliegende Holländer*. The only Strauss opera included – and it came last – was *Der Rosenkavalier*, which survived in spite of its half-Jewish librettist. No Mozart opera reached the first fifteen. On the other hand, both from 1919 to 1933 and from 1933 to 1945, Strauss was easily the most performed composer of orchestral music by living composers.) Before we condemn Strauss's views as nationalist and chauvinist, we do well to remember the complaints made to the BBC in 1940 by ten British composers (including Vaughan Williams, Bantock, Ethel Smyth, John Ireland and Constant Lambert) that 'British composers should be allotted a far bigger share of broadcasting time' and that 'of every 22 hours of serious music provided today eighteen are given over to the foreigner! It is inconceivable that any fair-minded listener will consider this to be an adequate recognition of native music at such time as the present.'[3]

Another of Strauss's projects as president of the Reich Music Chamber was education, which he believed was the most important factor in achiev-ing a higher degree of receptivity to music. He objected to the 'mindless' bawling of patriotic and hiking songs by schools and the Hitler Youth associations. He wanted all pupils to be taught harmony and theory, an instrument and music appreciation – and they must be taught by music teachers, not amateur music-lovers who normally taught mathematics. But he wrote an essay in 1933, 'Contemporary Remarks on Musical Education' (*Zeitgemässe Glossen für Erziehung zur Musik*), in which he praised the Nazi propaganda and cultural ministries as the most eminent in the world. This passage was deleted – without any indication – by Willi Schuh when the essay was included in all his editions of Strauss's *Betrachtungen und Erinnerungen* (1949, 1957, 1981) and it does not appear in the English version published in 1953. In the euphoria of 1933, when Strauss believed that copyright and other problems which had concerned him for years would be solved by the new régime, his praise would be intended as flattery to help him get his way.

A second presidency came Strauss's way at the start of 1934, that of the newly formed Permanent Council for International Cooperation among Composers. This was founded at Strauss's instigation by composers from many nations to break down national barriers and promote the performance and exchange of music. A festival was planned for Vichy in September 1935. Strauss regarded it as of prime importance: 'the first step towards smoothing the way abroad for those of our composers who have not yet been performed in other countries'.

It did not take long before Strauss awoke to the dangers inherent in his appointment. On 13 December 1933, less than a month after the inauguration of the Music Chamber, he wrote to his vice-president, Furtwängler: 'A cultural warden in Frankfurt has objected to a performance of Debussy's *Nocturnes*. Minister Goebbels told me recently to report directly to him any instances of a provincial caesar exceeding his powers, but I think that is scarcely necessary, as you have ultimate responsibility for concert programmes. Please write and tell Councillor Spiess that nothing stands in the way of a performance of *Nocturnes*, any more than that of any of the symphonies of Mahler.' He was appalled by the commissioning of new incidental music for *A Midsummer Night's Dream* to replace Mendelssohn's. He himself had been asked and had vehemently refused. In July 1934, an article appeared in *Der Stürmer*, edited by the fanatically anti-Jewish Julius Streicher, headed 'Richard Strauss and the Jews – we don't want to believe it'. It announced that Strauss was working on a new opera with a Jewish librettist and attacked the Dresden Intendant, Paul Adolph, for agreeing to stage the piece – it was 'improper' in the Germany of today for an opera text to be written by a Jew. As for Strauss, if it was true that he was collaborating with a Jew, that could give no cause for pleasure: 'therefore, for the time being, we cannot believe it'. Strauss was told he could not conduct *Fidelio* at the 1934 Salzburg Festival because of differences between the German and

Austrian governments following the assassination by two Nazis of the Austrian Chancellor Dr Dollfuss on 25 July. He was allowed to go only a few days before Krauss conducted *Elektra* on 17 August. He took a bow and walked and talked with Stefan Zweig and Bruno Walter (who does not seem to have borne any grudge). Living in Garmisch, not Berlin, he did not oversee the day-to-day work of the Music Chamber nor was he consulted about some of its decrees. In the autumn of 1934 he wrote to Julius Kopsch, who had also helped him in the copyright imbroglio with Goebbels: 'I cannot possibly be in Berlin on the 16th October. In any case, nothing will come of the meetings. I hear that the paragraph concerning Aryans is to be tightened up and *Carmen* banned! In any event I, as a creative artist, do not wish to take an active part in any further foolishness of this kind. . . My time is too precious for me to waste it by associating myself with this amateurish nonsense. My extensive and serious reform proposals have been turned down by Goebbels.' He was already realising he was trapped.

He was busy completing the full score of *Die schweigsame Frau*. Act 1 had been finished on 19 January 1934 and Act 2 took him until 24 August. In March he went with Pauline to the French Riviera, stayed in Juan les Pins and conducted *Arabella* in Monte Carlo. He kept in touch with Zweig, who was in London in May for the première there of *Arabella*, describing the audience's response as 'rising to quite un-English enthusiasm'. On 11 June Strauss celebrated his seventieth birthday. He was given the Freedom of the City of Dresden, there were Strauss weeks in Dresden, Berlin, Munich and Vienna. President Hindenburg awarded him the Eagle Shield of the German Reich, Goebbels gave him a bust of Gluck and Hitler gave him a photograph inscribed 'To the great composer Richard Strauss, in sincere admiration'. On 10 July Strauss completed a revision (mainly cuts) of his first opera, *Guntram*, for a concert performance on Berlin Radio conducted by Hans Rosbaud. (This version was first staged at Weimar, conducted by Paul Sixt, on 29 October 1940. In 1942 it was performed in Berlin, when the Jewish Alice Strauss found herself in a box at the opera house with Goebbels.)

The first signs of a stormcloud were visible in May 1934, as Strauss – without realising the full significance – reported to Zweig on 25 May: 'Can you imagine, the Ministry of Propaganda inquired the other day if it was true I am setting to music a text by Arnold Zweig [1887–1968, dramatist and novelist]. My son put things straight at once. . . I then asked Goebbels whether there are any "political objections" against you, to which he answered no. Well, we won't have any troubles with Morosus . . .[4] All efforts to relax the stipulation against the Jews here are frustrated by the answer: impossible as long as the outside world continues its lying propaganda against Hitler.' With their first collaboration nearly complete, Strauss was already thinking about their next. In August 1934, just after Pauline had had an operation, Zweig suggested a one-act opera, *24 October 1648*, set in the last year of the Thirty Years' War. This eventually became *Friedenstag*. He wanted, he said, to combine three elements: 'the tragic, the heroic, and the humane, ending in a hymn to international conciliation and to the grace of creativeness, but I would like to leave out emperors and kings and make everything anonymous'. The plot was of a besieged fortress. The commander can no longer hold it but has vowed never to surrender. He gives his men the chance to leave or to stay with him when he blows it up. His wife guesses his intention and stays with him. Just before the fuse is lit, there is a cannonshot, followed by bells. It is peace. The enemy commander appears. The two men glower at each other but eventually embrace. 'I do not mind *at all*', Zweig wrote, 'if you pass this plan on to someone else . . . to save you all cursed political bother.' Strauss was pleased and was also captivated by the translation of a Casti libretto, *Prima la musica, poi le parole* ('First the music, then the words'). As far as the 1648 opera was concerned, he wanted to introduce a love affair between the commander's wife and one of the officers, with the commander shooting himself. 'A bit too operatic in the unfortunate sense of the word', Zweig replied. Meanwhile Strauss reported (21 September) that Hitler had approved the performance of *Die schweigsame Frau* in Dresden, having read the libretto. He had raised the matter with Goebbels at Bayreuth in July when he told him that 'the whole affair was a big disgrace'.

One of Zweig's letters to Strauss from London in October 1934 is of particular interest because of its reference to one of the most frequently repeated anecdotes concerning Strauss at this period. Toscanini is supposed to have said: 'To Strauss the composer I take off my hat. To Strauss the man I put it on again.' Zweig wrote: 'A foreign newspaper tells a stupid story about Toscanini having made sarcastic and derogatory remarks about you at a party held in my honour here in London. How *stupidly* this episode is *invented* (it appeared under the headline "Toscanini's hat shop") is evident by the fact that I *never* saw Toscanini in London; he has not been here for a year and, of course, he never made a comment like that. Unfortunately, there are always people inclined to draw persons who are a thousand times superior to them into a smear campaign. Now, I do not want you to be annoyed about Toscanini if you hear about this idiotic fabrication; as far as I know he *never* made such a silly joke, certainly not in my presence, since he knows my devotion to you.' Not evidence that Toscanini never uttered the quip, but at least an identification of the source of a remark which is still in circulation. If Strauss made any comment, it has not survived.

After his November visit to Amsterdam to conduct *Arabella*, Strauss returned to Garmisch to settle down to a chore he knew he could not escape. As he told Zweig on 21 December, 'I kill the boredom of the Advent season by composing an Olympic hymn for the proletarians – I, of all people, who hate and despise sports. Well, Idleness is the Root of all Evil.' The hymn was commissioned by the National Olympic Committee, not by the government. The Berlin Olympic Games were to open on 1 August 1936 so Strauss was getting a distasteful task out of the way in good time. He set a poem by Robert Lubahn for mixed chorus and large orchestra and arranged it also for piano, for male chorus and for voice and piano. But he let fly with his views on sport to the president of the National Olympic Committee, whose reply filled five indignant pages. In due course, Strauss (by then in disgrace) conducted the work in the Olympic Stadium, but was ordered by Hitler not to conduct at a rehearsal at which Hitler was present. During the winter Olympics at Garmisch in 1936 no one from the Nazi party nor from the government visited Strauss, although foreign diplomats called at his home.

During November and December 1934 the first major politico-musical crisis of the Nazi régime arose over Paul Hindemith. Since its success of the previous March, when Furtwängler conducted the first performance in Berlin, his Symphony *Mathis der Maler*, based on material from the opera of that name on which he was still working, had been performed throughout Germany and commercially recorded. He was on the council of the Reich Music Chamber and thus had the support of Goebbels, but he was regarded with enmity, because of his association with Jews, by Goebbels's rival Rosenberg, who encouraged the editor of Rosenberg's mouthpiece *Die Musik* to launch a partially successful campaign for a boycott of Hindemith's music. Whether Goebbels or Rosenberg would have prevailed was rendered irrelevant when Furtwängler intervened with an article defending Hindemith which appeared in the *Deutsche Allgemeine Zeitung* of 25 November. Furtwängler's aim was to ensure that Hitler would approve the world première of the opera *Mathis der Maler* in Berlin in 1935. But Furtwängler ended his article with a warning about the danger of political denunciation being applied to matters of art. This was taken as an attack on Nazi cultural policy and Goebbels had no alternative but to close ranks with Rosenberg. On 6 December Furtwängler was forced to resign as vice-president of the Music Chamber and as conductor of the Berlin Philharmonic and Staatsoper. For most of 1935, Hindemith's music was under a cloud. He himself visited England and accepted a post in Turkey. But by 1936 he had rehabilitated himself, although *Mathis der Maler* had to wait for its première in Zürich in May 1938.

Strauss's involvement in this affair arose from a speech made by Goebbels on 6 December, the day Furtwängler was stripped of his posts. Goebbels mentioned neither Furtwängler nor Hindemith by name, but attacked atonality as musical bankruptcy. Strauss was in Holland, but his son Franz, knowing his father's views on atonal compositions, drafted a telegram of congratulations to Goebbels, gained approval for its wording from Strauss, and sent it. Sure enough, it was published in a newspaper on 11 December. Strauss really seemed to believe that he was going to be able to purge German musical life of the elements he disliked and which he believed were bad for it. He was now almost as hostile to the latest developments in music as his father had been to Wagner, Mahler, Bruckner and even his own son's music. It was not an admirable attitude, but it was governed by musical taste, not political consideration. Zweig, observing all this from England and America, asked Strauss if the première of *Die schweigsame Frau* should not be postponed 'in order to avoid any connection with the events in the musical world (Furtwängler and so on). . . The world première of an opera by Richard Strauss must be an *event* of the highest artistic significance, not *an affair.*' Strauss replied that, as Hitler and Goebbels had approved it, there was nothing to do or postpone.

This is the point at which to examine the role played by Strauss's son Franz, who has been described in a book on music in the Third Reich as 'an ardent Nazi who loved to show off the accoutrements of his party status'.[5] He was at no time a party member nor a member of any Nazi organisation nor was he ever required to undergo deNazification proceedings.[6] Franz was spoiled and over-protected at home. He had wanted to study medicine, but his father did not approve. He found it hard to defy his father's forceful personality and became in effect Strauss's manager, his wife Alice acting as secretary and archivist. He saw the miserable results of the Weimar Republic, the enormous national debt and unemployment. He was impressed, from 1930 to 1937, by the strong man Hitler. He was caught up in the euphoria of the time, as were many others, not all of them Germans. Very few had read *Mein Kampf.* As the anti-Jewish laws became more rigorous between 1936 and 1938 and his own family became affected, he was cured of his youthful idealism. Faced with the brutal reality of persecution and the threat to the life of his wife and sons, he came down to earth with a bump. After 1937, as his son Christian said to me, 'one kept one's head low and hoped to survive the period with as low a profile as possible'. Soon Franz was to see his son Richard excluded from high school and it required a begging letter from Richard Strauss before the young Richard could receive an education which would familiarise him with Goethe and Schiller. During all the years from 1936 Franz was loyal and courageous in defence of his wife and children.

Ironically, in February 1935 Strauss was to experience his own first chill wind of official disapproval. The Nazis' ideal German composer was Hans Pfitzner, of whom a new biography was published that month written by the pro-Nazi critic Walther Abendroth. In a chapter on *Palestrina*, Abendroth damned the whole school of modern German composers, among whom he obviously included Strauss because he deplored the development of programme-music. One inflammatory passage read: 'Whoever feels the exalted virility of Hans Pfitzner's musical language to be ascetic thereby proves only one thing: that their corrupted ears seek here in vain the feminine voluptuousness and torpor of sounds padded with fat to which they are accustomed from other influences.' This was clearly aimed at Strauss and provoked a defensive reply in the Leipzig *Allgemeine Musikzeitung* by Peter Raabe, another Nazi. In gratitude for this support, Strauss set a short Goethe poem,

Zugemessne Rhythmnen, from the 'Book of Hafiz' on which he had already drawn. He dedicated it to Raabe with a punning reference to Abendroth's name and quoting Abendroth's words: 'Ein im Abendrot des feminenen 19 Jahrhunderts auf klanglichen Fettpolstern duseldner Programmusiker' ('In the sunset of the 19th century from a maker of programme-music padded with fat'). The poem says that whereas a talented poet may like established forms and rhythms, these soon become 'hollow masks without blood or meaning' and he must create new forms in their place. In the music, Strauss quotes the melody of the *finale* of Brahms's First Symphony to represent talent. He then quotes Arabella's 'Richtige' theme and the Ideology theme from *Tod und Verklärung* as new forms and ends with a piano postlude based on the opening phrase of *Die Meistersinger*. It was a private joke between Strauss and Raabe, has never been performed and was not published until 1954 (in the *Richard Strauss Jahrbuch*). It was composed in Garmisch on 25 February 1935. The previous day he had set Rückert's poem for eight-part unaccompanied choir, *Die Göttin im Putzzimmer* (*The Goddess in the Boudoir*), one of his most delightful choral pieces. He had begun it a few weeks earlier as a song for bass and piano but switched to a choral setting. The text is an allegory about artistic creation, a favourite subject especially when allied to confusion and bustle as in the Prologue of *Ariadne auf Naxos*. 'What disorder in the household! What a riot of erotica', the poem begins and Strauss finds intricate counterpoint to describe the 'little shelves, cupboards full of powder-puffs. . . What formidable enchantress must this be to order chaos into harmony?' The muse of creativity, of course; and at the word *plötzlich* (suddenly), as the goddess stands dressed 'in colourful frippery' and 'all things around her come to life', the music of chaos lengthens into long lyrical lines of block harmony. The magical ending is a clue to Strauss's essential integrity where artistic matters were concerned as he salutes the muse and Love – 'both of you turn . . . into a raiment of celestial light'. In this little masterpiece, we hear the first pre-echoes of *Daphne* and *Capriccio*. It was not performed until 2 March 1952 when Krauss conducted the Vienna State Opera Chorus.

22   Dismissal

On 20 February 1935 Strauss wrote to Zweig:

For the future – should I have the good fortune to receive one or several new librettos from you, let us agree that nobody will ever know about it or about my setting them to music. Once the score is finished, it will go into a safe that will be opened only when we both consider the time propitious. This being so, will you take the opportunity to write something new for me – possibly for my estate?[1]

Has there ever been a stranger request from one great artist to another? Was Strauss in touch with reality? Did he really think such a bizarre arrangement could work? Is it not further proof that he really believed he could 'buck the system'? Zweig had no illusions. His reply on 23 February was masterly:

Sometimes I have the feeling that you are not fully aware – and this does you honour – of the historical greatness of your position, that you think too modestly of yourself. Everything you do is destined to be of historical significance. One day, your letters, your decisions, will belong to all mankind, like those of Wagner and Brahms. For this reason it seems inappropriate to me that something in your life, in your art, should be done in secrecy. Even if I were to refrain from ever mentioning that I am writing something for you, later it would come out that I had done so secretly. And this, I feel, would be beneath you. A Richard Strauss is privileged to take in public what is his right; he must not seek refuge in secrecy. . . I am aware of the difficulties that would confront a new work if I were to write the text: it would be considered a provocation. And to work together secretly seems to me beneath your rank, as I said. I will be happy, however, to assist with advice anyone who might work for you. . . I will co-operate with anybody whom you care to name, without credit or reward.[2]

Strauss would not give up. Three days later he wrote: 'If you abandon me, too, I'll have to lead from now on the life of an ailing, unemployed retiree.

Believe me, there is no poet who could write a usable libretto for me, even if you generously and unselfishly were to "co-operate". He had told Goebbels and Goering, he said, that he had spent fifty years searching for librettists.

To find *Salome* was a stroke of luck, *Elektra* introduced me to the incomparable Hofmannsthal, but after his death I thought I would have to resign myself forever. Then by chance (is that the right word?) I found you. And I will not give up on you just because we happen to have an anti-Semitic government. I am confident this government would place no obstacles in the way of a second Zweig opera and would not feel challenged by it if I were to talk about it with Dr Goebbels, who is very cordial with me. But why now raise unnecessary questions that will have taken care of themselves in two or three years?[3]

So he repeated his request for a secret collaboration. This letter shows that Strauss still believed he could manipulate the Nazis as he had previous rulers such as the Kaiser's court. He did not realise he was being 'used' by Goebbels and he did not know that Goebbels had written in his diary: 'Unfortunately we still need him, but one day we shall have our own music and then we shall have no further need of this decadent neurotic.' Strauss also clearly believed that the Nazis would not retain power for long.

Zweig ignored Strauss's request when he replied on 14 March with a suggestion that Strauss should consider an opera on the Spanish tragi-comedy *Celestina*. But Strauss returned to the subject on 2 April when he had to tell Zweig that a second collaboration with him would not be accept-able: 'I consider it honourable to let the Minister [Goebbels] (but no one else) know that I will continue to compose Zweig texts as I cannot find another librettist, but only in secret; that nobody will know about this . . . and that I will work only for my desk drawer, for my pleasure, for my estate.'[4] Could gullibility and naiveté go further? What must Goebbels have thought on having this secret confided to him? Strauss's next letter contained a grain of interest in *Celestina* if many changes were made. Zweig was delighted and added: 'I will jot down a few things which you then could pass on to some-body to work on. I repeat that, because of my admiration for you, I gladly and without reward will advise anybody, and anonymously will assist anybody who can produce a usable text for you. . . In the meantime, the performance of *Die schweigsame Frau* will disclose the attitude of public opinion towards my collaboration.'[5]

Strauss was still obstinate:

> Your generous offer to help another librettist is very kind – you know as well as I do that there is no one else. . . Please stay with me and work with me. . . No one will hear about it – in any case, I am protected on all fronts as far as Dr Goebbels is concerned. . . Whatever you 'jot down' for me will never be 'passed on to somebody to work on' because it is not so much the material that matters, but the kind of person who does this 'working on'. You know that yourself. So let's forget it.[6]

Zweig's response was severely practical. He asked Strauss to write on the piano score and full score of *Die schweigsame Frau* the dates on which he had started and finished the opera. 'That would easily head off much fatuous argument, because it would be evident . . . that you started the opera long before the changes in politics. It will save us silly talk and conjecture.' Strauss complied by writing 'Started October 1, 1932, completed October 20, 1934' on the autograph score. The overture (potpourri) is dated 'January 17, 1935'. He then tried to interest Zweig in a project he had also tried on Hofmannsthal – *Semiramis* – asking him to examine which aspects 'can be made relevant to our contemporary thinking. Audiences nowadays won't go along even with Helena and Menelaus and they, heaven knows, are modern enough.' Zweig suggested that he could write the libretto in collaboration with a contemporary playwright, Lernet-Holenia. Strauss read 'with indignation' two of Lernet-Holenia's 'so-called comedies' and commented: 'You cannot seriously believe that a man capable of publishing such silly, tasteless and witless stuff could write a libretto for me? . . . No, dear Herr Zweig, this will not do. If you desert me now. . . I have no choice left but to retire.' He plugged away about *Semiramis* ('I would love to compose one more grand opera, with ballet, pageant march, battle music and so on').[7]

Zweig's reply, sent to Strauss at Kissingen where he was taking a cure at a sanatorium, repeated that he could not help in a 'full working capacity'. But he suggested Joseph Gregor, 'the greatest theatre expert', who was 'one of my intimate friends'. With Gregor, he said, 'I could discuss in detail the plan and execution of each scene. . . I believe he could be your best collaborator, and you could know that I, bound to him in friendship and to you in admira-

20 Strauss with Joseph Gregor

tion, would participate in his work with true devotion.' Strauss capitulated, more or less. 'If you think you can work with that splendid man Gregor, I am of course in full agreement.' Gregor, born in 1888, had entered Vienna University as a philosophy student in 1907 and also became a private pupil of the composer Robert Fuchs and the musicologist Guido Adler. He became a 'production student' at the Court Opera in 1910, met Max Reinhardt and assisted him in Berlin in a production of *Faust*. After war service, he joined the staff of the Austrian National Library in 1918. He began to organise the library's theatre bureau and was its director from 1922 to 1953, building up a remarkable archive. He was a novelist and playwright, but his finest literary work was his *Weltgeschichte des Theaters* (1933), a book Strauss admired.

Zweig had a long talk with Gregor about *Semiramis* in the spring of 1935 and Gregor wrote 'a very cordial letter' to Strauss who told Zweig: 'I am not so sure about Gregor as I am about my proved and tested Zweig.' So he asked Zweig for 'active participation' in *Semiramis* and that he should not forget *1648* and what he called *Dopa la musica*. Meanwhile Zweig suggested a

Mexican subject about 'a legendary figure revered as a saint'. This brought a rebuke from Bad Kissingen: 'Perhaps you are not aware how passionate an anti-Christ I am, and that the real Saviour will be as obnoxious to me as the white one will probably be uninteresting. . . No, such a passive prophet battling with the high priests, and at the end the awful Cortez: I don't think that's my dish. . . If I have to choose, I'd rather take that monster Semiramis, who has at least some air of grandeur as a general and ruler. I do not always need to compose the Sweet Vienna Girl.'[8] By 17 May, Strauss had received Gregor's *Semiramis* libretto. He wrote to Zweig: 'You must have read Gregor's foetus by now. Any critique is superfluous. A philologist's childish fairy-tale. If *you* are not able to forge a "grand opera" for me from Calderón's work, I'll just have to forget it. But how am I to tell dear Gregor? Now what? Please don't *you* forsake me! . . . Once and for all, please stop urging new poets on me.'[9]

Zweig also told Gregor that his libretto was 'not viable'. And he told Strauss firmly and finally that he could not work for him 'fully and openly' although, he repeated, he would always offer advice.

But the official measures, instead of becoming milder and more conciliatory, have only grown harsher. Some of those measures cannot but offend one's sense of honour; what one sincerely hoped and felt obliged to hope proved to be erroneous. You will discover yourself, I fear, that the cultural development will more and more go to the side of extremists. . . As an individual one cannot resist the will or insanity of a whole world; enough bitterness and hatred. This alone has become a sort of accomplishment these days, and is almost harder than writing books.[10]

He had recently been told by his publisher, Insel Verlag, that because he was Jewish they could no longer (after thirty years) continue to work with him.

Strauss replied: 'Your letter is very painful for me. I can understand that you have misgivings. But your misgivings cannot be greater than mine. Neither of us can follow a path different from that prescribed by our artistic conscience. Only one command exists for us: to be creative for the good of mankind.'[11] A week later, on 28 May, he left Garmisch for Munich where he conducted *Feuersnot* and *Arabella* and attended rehearsals of *Die Frau ohne Schatten*, which Knappertsbusch was to conduct. On 2 June he met Zweig in Bregenz and they discussed the *1648* opera and 'two one-act plays'.

On 12 June he arrived at the Hotel Bellevue, Dresden, to supervise rehearsals of *Die schweigsame Frau*. Next day he wrote to Pauline with all the exuberant naiveté he had always shown when he heard one of his scores come to life for the first time: 'Beloved! The opera is magnificent: both the work and its execution . . . it is already running smoothly on the stage and in the orchestra. . . The text non plus ultra: as I've said before, it's the best comic opera since Beaumarchais. . . I hope Rosenberg and a few others like him will burst. One has to provide one's own compensation for all the nonsense that goes on in the world around one. You have nothing to worry about: nobody can raise any objections to *this* opera. Perhaps it has too much wit and humour for the present age! . . . It will be a shame if you won't come up before the performance itself. If possible, come to the dress rehearsal.' Karl Böhm, who conducted, recalled how Strauss insisted that 'Everybody must understand Zweig's words.' Böhm remonstrated: 'Herr Doktor, look at the score! How is Cebotari to get her words out through that?' Then Strauss took the score back to his hotel, crossed out doublings, turned a *mf* into a *p* 'and then the words could be understood word for word'.[12] Awaiting him in Dresden was a letter from Zweig about *Semiramis*. Strauss was irate: 'Your collaboration with good Gregor makes my skin crawl. Why do you insist on saddling me with an erudite philologist? My librettist is Zweig: he needs no collaborators – as you could have convinced yourself yesterday after the rehearsal of the first act. Your libretto is simply first-rate, the act finales terrific. . . The Silent One will be on the radio on July 8, unabridged.'

Zweig wrote back on 15 June, but his letter has not been preserved. It precipitated a violent reply on the 17th from Strauss:

Your letter of the 15th drives me to despair! This Jewish obstinacy! Enough to make a man anti-Semitic! This racial pride, this feeling of solidarity! Do you believe I am ever, in any of my actions, guided by the thought that I am 'German' (perhaps, *qui le sait*)? Do you suppose that Mozart was consciously 'Aryan' when he composed? I recognise only two types of people: those who have talent and those who have none. The 'People' [*Volk*] only exist for me when they become the audience. Whether they are Chinese, Bavarians, New Zealanders or Berliners matters nothing to me provided they have paid in full at the box office. Now please stop plaguing me with that good Gregor.[13]

He then mentioned the Walter and Toscanini *affaires* (as quoted in an earlier chapter) answering the question 'Who told you I have exposed myself politically?' and made his remark about 'going through the mime' of being president of the Music Chamber. He ended with a postscript: 'The show here will be terrific. Everyone is wildly enthusiastic. And with all this you ask me to forgo you? Never ever.'

This letter was addressed to Zweig in Zürich. It was removed from the Hotel Bellevue postbox by a member of the Saxony Gestapo who sent it to the governor of Saxony, Martin Mutschmann. For several days, as we shall see, no further action was taken. But in Berlin on 20 June, a confidential memorandum about *Die schweigsame Frau* was sent by the Office for the Cultivation of Art to all district supervisors of the Nazi Cultural Unit. It stated that 'like almost all Strauss's works, it has been published by the Jewish music publisher Fürstner, the text is by the Austrian Jew Stefan Zweig who, furthermore, according to the foreign press, has placed his share of the royalties at the disposal of Jewish "charities". The vocal score is the work of the Jew Felix Wolfes. The general intendant of the Dresden State Opera, Councillor Adolph, is married to a woman wholly of Jewish parentage... The National Socialist Cultural Unit has good cause to distance itself from this work.' Strauss wrote again to Zweig on 22 June to tell him how good the opera was – if Zweig could see it, he would 'drop all race worries and political misgivings with which you, incomprehensibly to me, unnecessarily weigh down your artist's mind'. He had nothing but praise for the cast, headed by Friedrich Plaschke as Morosus and Maria Cebotari as Aminta, the production by Josef Gielen, the conducting of Karl Böhm and the sets and costumes by Leonhard Fanto. 'Dr Goebbels, who will be here with his wife on Monday, will give a government subsidy for this. As you can see, the wicked Third Reich has its good side too. . . There is still silence about Hitler's attending. At any rate, the opera is magnificent, truly an entirely perfect, mature masterpiece; it would be a pity if I were to scuttle composing now.' Receiving this, Zweig wrote to Gregor on 24 June, the day of the première: 'Although he is enthusiastic about the rehearsals, very powerful opposition to the performance has built up, even at the eleventh hour. The good man will soon find out that whoever meddles in politics ends up squatting among nettles. . . A mighty conflict must be taking place behind the brownshirted scenes.'[14]

Although Zweig could not then have known it, a 'mighty conflict' had occurred on 22 June, the day of the dress rehearsal. Friedrich von Schuch, son of Ernst von Schuch who conducted the premières of *Feuersnot*, *Salome*, *Elektra* and *Der Rosenkavalier*, was administrative head of the Saxon state theatres, under Paul Adolph, the Intendant. Adolph had decided that Zweig's name should be omitted from the printed programme. The opera was described in the score as 'freely adapted from Ben Jonson by Stefan Zweig. Music by Richard Strauss'. Adolph altered it to 'From the English of Ben Jonson' but did not tell Strauss, although warned by others, notably Fanto, that he ought to do so. On the afternoon of the 22nd Strauss was playing Skat in the Hotel Bellevue with Schuch, Fanto and the Dresden-based tenor Tino Pattiera. 'Suddenly, to the surprise of his partners, Strauss said out of the blue: "I want to see the programme".'[15] We do not know who had put him up to this, although suspicion must fall on Fanto. (Fanto was almost certainly Jewish, but he had told the Nazis he was a foundling and knew nothing about his parents.) Adolph was telephoned and reluctantly agreed to show Strauss the printer's proof. When this arrived, 'Strauss got his well-known flushed face and declared: "You can do this, but I will leave tomorrow and the show can take place without me". Then, by his own hand, he restored the official wording. The next day a meeting took place in the Staatskanzlei at which neither Strauss nor I was present. The result was compliance with Strauss's wishes.' Adolph was dismissed some days later.

The performance was a success. At a party afterwards in the Hotel Bellevue the only government representative was Ernst Hanfstaengel, a friend of Hitler from early days. He was a Bavarian and became chief of the foreign press department of the party. He was rich, had been educated at Harvard and spent ten years in the United States. He was a good pianist and something of a clown. In the mid-1930s he was under a cloud because his views were considered too moderate and he had made some frank comments about leading Nazis. At the Dresden party, according to Böhm, Hanfstaengel 'made a speech about the qualities of *Die schweigsame Frau* – including the text – and berated the government to such a degree that I said to my wife afterwards "In a week he'll be either in a concentration camp or in Switzerland". A short time after that he was, indeed, in Switzerland.'[16] (In

1937 he fled to England and spent the war in the United States as an adviser on the Third Reich to President Roosevelt.)

Another result was that neither Hitler nor Goebbels attended the world première on 24th June – 'either on purpose', Strauss wrote in a private memorandum on the events, 'or, as was announced, prevented from flying by a storm in Hamburg. State Commissioner Hinkel then gave a good warm talk at the City Hall. It is a sad time when an artist of my eminence has to ask a brat of a minister what he may set to music and what he may have performed. . . I almost envy my friend Stefan Zweig, persecuted for his race, who now refuses to work with me in public or in secret because, he says, he does not want to have any "special privileges" in the Third Reich. To be honest, I don't understand this Jewish solidarity and regret that the "artist" Zweig cannot rise above "political fashions". If we do not preserve artistic freedom ourselves, how can we expect it from soap-box orators in taverns? With *Die schweigsame Frau* my life's work definitely seems to have come to an end. Otherwise I might have been able to create other works not entirely without merit.'

This mood of self-pity, blended with an apparent lack of appreciation of the dangers lurking for Jews, was atypical of Strauss. He wrote those words on 3 July. The chronology of the Dresden Affair after the first performance is of some importance and has not previously been clearly set out. Strauss returned to Garmisch on 27 June as we know from his letter to Zweig dated the 28th: 'Back last night at 12.30 a.m., returning from Dresden by car. The second performance despite tropical heat, not a subscription performance, astonishingly well attended; this time the second act was better received than the first, very successful. . . My, what odd ideas you have! Why should I become popular at any price, that is, tied to the rabble and performed in every low-class theatre? For a year I've tried hard at the Propaganda Ministry to put an end to all those flea-bitten opera houses which massacre *Lohengrin* with an orchestra of thirty and a chorus of fifteen.' He wanted large and medium-sized opera houses to be enabled 'to present the masterpieces of our German literature in the manner the composer desires. This is to be done through increased grants which are to be tied to definite standards of the repertory and production guidelines of the highest artistic quality, through larger orchestras, expanded ensembles, increased budgets for sets,

and so on.' As far as his own work was concerned, 'I don't compose for provincial stages with orchestra of fewer than fifty players or for travelling
shows. . . The difficulties of the *Schweigsame* cannot be reduced below my
own directives. Let them work hard, and those who are too lazy had better
keep their hands off and play operettas. I have never had the talent to write
what can be performed easily: that is the special gift of inferior musicians.'
He again asked Zweig for *1648* and the comedy *Prima la musica*, 'but without
Gregor whose collaboration I strictly refuse. . . Texts invented by Zweig, I
will compose only under the name of Zweig. What happens thereafter let be
my worry, please.'

At some point after 26 June, the date of the second performance,
Mutschmann, the governor of Saxony, sent the intercepted letter (17 June)
from Strauss to Zweig directly to Hitler and added: 'The world première of
Die schweigsame Frau took place before a full house, including 500 invited
guests. The second performance was so sparsely attended that the management issued free tickets; the third performance was cancelled, purportedly
because of illness of the principal actress.' Presumably he meant Cebotari. If
this was so – and no records seem to have survived – this cancellation obviously was not connected with any ban on the work, since Mutschmann did
not send the intercepted letter until after the proposed third performance.
Zweig, writing to Gregor on 4 July, guessed the way things were going.
'Adolph appears to have left our friend in the lurch', he wrote. 'Even already,
it would appear, the performances have been abandoned. It would not surprise me if S. threw the whole thing back at them, for they are working
against him with all manner of spitefulness, ill repaying him for compromising himself for them before the entire world.'

On 6 July Strauss went to the little town of Berchtesgaden to meet Gregor
on the 7th. The same day, the 6th, as he related in a private memorandum
written on 10 July, 'Ministerial Counsellor [Otto von] Keudell, commissioned by State Secretary Funk, called on me and demanded that I resign as
president of the Reich Music Chamber for reasons of "ill-health". I did so at
once.' Keudell had with him a copy of Strauss's letter to Zweig. 'I did not
know that I, the president of the Reich Music Chamber, was under direct
state police surveillance, nor that I, after a life of creating eminent works,
"recognised in the whole world" was not considered above criticism as "a

good German". Yet the unheard-of has happened: Herr Minister Goebbels dismissed me without even asking for an explanation of the sequestered letter.'

Still nothing was done to prevent performances of *Die schweigsame Frau*. The performance on 8 July was to be broadcast and we know that it was because Zweig hoped to hear it but found that because of Nazi jamming it could only be received in Saxony. After this, it was banned from the stage in the Third Reich. It would seem, therefore, that it was banned after the fourth scheduled performance, of which three were given. It will be noticed that Karl Böhm kept his head below the parapet throughout all this. He was a Nazi supporter, although never a party member, but on this occasion evidently decided that discretion was the better part of valour. The opera was later performed in Graz, Milan, Zürich, Prague and Rome. In Vienna there were two 'mini-scale' private performances, on 15 December 1935 and 10 January 1936, under the auspices of the Vienna Richard Strauss Society. Zweig did not attend any of these performances. He wrote to his wife two days after the première:

By now I have a general idea what happened in Dresden. People agree on only one point, that the city was in the grip of an African heat wave. . . As for the opera, one thing is certain, it is *very* much too long, secondly it is an atrociously difficult work and so the very opposite of my original conception of it – not a light opera, but loaded with all the *raffinements* and really oppressive because it is too replete. Single passages are said to be outstanding and the first act well rounded. Then it gets to be tiring, like *Arabella* and *Die ägyptische Helena*. His technique remains intact, but the dynamic isn't there.[17]

This, of course, was based on hearsay.

Strauss, in his notes on the history of *Die schweigsame Frau*, recalls how he was able to set the libretto 'lock, stock and barrel, without the slightest further change. None of my earlier operas was so easy to compose, or gave me such light-hearted pleasure.' Zweig, in *Die Welt von Gestern* (*The World of Yesterday*) said how amazed he was by Strauss's knowledge of the theatre. 'I have never known anyone who knew how to maintain such a detached and unwavering objectivity with regard to himself. . . He knew that as an art form, opera was finished. Wagner was such an enormous mountain that nobody could ever surpass him. "But", he added, with a broad Bavarian laugh, "I have helped myself by making a detour round him."' There were all the signs of a collaboration perhaps equal to that with Hofmannsthal, but with less tension, and that was probably why Strauss was so reluctant to lose the chance to continue it.

Die schweigsame Frau is another slice of Garmisch home life – lovable old man with a noisy, quarrelsome wife. Strauss also saw in Zweig's libretto – which is good but not quite as good as the composer made out – chances to re-explore the farcical aspects of *Der Rosenkavalier* and the *parlando* style of the *Ariadne* Prologue. In the eighteenth-century London of *Die schweigsame Frau* we meet again a company of singers and actors. The principal soprano, Aminta, is another Zerbinetta. The plot to trick the rich old retired admiral, Sir Morosus, who abominates noise since his hearing was damaged, into a mock marriage with a silent woman (who turns into a virago) has echoes of Ochs – and, of course, of Don Pasquale. It is strange and rather touching to find Strauss paying homage to Italian comic opera, a genre about which he had often been scathing. But he adored Verdi's *Falstaff* and his potpourri overture is an admiring sidelong glance at Rossini – when the curtain rises the first male character we encounter is a barber! The libretto (which diverges in many ways from the Jonson play) also provides many opportunities for Strauss's favourite game of quotations – from himself, Verdi, Monteverdi, Mozart, Wagner, Weber, and others, including the Fitzwilliam Virginal Book. Yet, although he was revisiting old territory, Strauss injected a sparkling freshness into the score and, after all, he had never before attempted a comic opera in traditional form. Although the opera is too long – but need not be as savagely cut as Karl Böhm's post-war performances, one of which is available on CD – it has wit and charm. Its highlights include the Act 1 duet for Morosus's nephew Henry and his wife Aminta, who later disguises herself as the 'silent woman Timidia', the septet in the same act, the sextet in Act 2, and the nonet in Act 3, remarkable ensembles all; the graceful minuet which opens Act 2 and the poetic curtain to Act 2 when Morosus falls asleep off-stage on a low D flat while Aminta, on-stage with Henry, sings a top D flat. The comic interplay between the actresses Isotta and Carlotta can be very funny, as John Cox's Glyndebourne production showed; the 'noise' scene in Act 2, with bells, banging doors and exploding ammunition is a *tour de force*; and the opera ends, after Morosus (like

Falstaff) has seen the joke against himself, with a cosy epilogue in which Morosus-Strauss sings contentedly 'How beautiful music is, but how really beautiful when it is over. How beautiful is life, but only when one is no fool and knows how to live it.' An orchestra of ninety-five players is used but treated for much of the time like a chamber orchestra. Not all the melodic invention is at Strauss's highest level, but it is a comic opera which deserves to hold the stage – and can when sympathetically produced. Paul Henry Láng's remark that Strauss's 'apparent commonplace can conceal qualities that are not commonplace at all' is especially true when applied to *Die schweigsame Frau*, about which Láng also pointed out that the ensembles are 'devilishly difficult – so difficult that only the most extraordinary virtuosity can do justice to them'.[18] Today most companies can provide that virtuosity. Obvious throughout the opera is how much Strauss enjoyed composing it. It is ironic that such a light-hearted, life-enhancing piece should have been produced under such dark and menacing shadows. When it was produced at Dresden in 1946, Strauss wrote to the conductor Joseph Keilberth: 'So now, after 10 [11] years the honourable Sir Morosus has been liberated from the concentration camp of the Reich Theatre Chamber and been brought back to his birthplace, where twelve [11] years ago I had great trouble getting the name of the librettist on the programme.' It was too late for Zweig, who committed suicide together with his wife in Brazil in February 1942 at the age of sixty. He left a note hoping that friends 'might see the dawn. Being too impatient, I go before them.'

23   Working with Gregor

Strauss's dismissal from the presidency of the Reich Music Chamber upset him only insofar as he suddenly felt himself to be exposed. He had sided with a Jew; how might this affect Alice and her children now that he was in disgrace? With this fear at the forefront of his mind, he wrote at once to Hitler to explain that the 'improvised sentences' in his letter to Zweig of 17 June had been dashed off 'in a moment of ill-humour'. They did not represent his view of the world nor his true conviction. 'My whole life belongs to German music and to a tireless effort to elevate German culture. I have never been active politically nor even expressed myself in politics. Therefore I believe that I will find understanding from you, the great architect of German social life. . . I will devote the few years still granted to me only to the purest and most ideal goals. . . I beg you, my Führer, most humbly to receive me for a personal discussion.' It was a shaming grovel, one cannot pretend anything else. The old man was clearly terrified. Hitler ignored his request.

In his private memorandum on these events, Strauss admitted that his efforts as president to improve German musical life had been useless. He was never consulted about appointments of conductors and intendants. His budgetary plans were ignored. 'My office was never anything more than a meaningless label, bringing me nothing but hostility and abuse from abroad without giving me the satisfaction of being able to put into effect any decisive measures for German theatre and German music. All my appeals to the German cultural conscience vanished without trace. They are continually reorganizing, but nothing actually happens.' He was replaced by Peter Raabe, a party member, who took a more active role, attended many more meetings of the Music Chamber and influenced its decrees. But it was Hans Hinkel of the Propaganda Ministry, not Raabe, who in September 1935 issued the first list of compositions officially banned by the Third Reich.

Gradually Goebbels diminished the power of the Music Chamber after he had quarrelled with Raabe over compositions selected for the festival of the Allgemeiner Deutscher Musikverein in June 1936. The Chamber became a rubber-stamp for Ministry decisions. Raabe, to his credit, totally dissociated himself from the 1938 Entartete Musik (Degenerate Music) exhibition and refused to visit it.

It is probable that Strauss would have resigned his presidency during 1935 because of the frustrations he felt. But it is equally probable that, if the letter to Zweig had not presented an excuse, Goebbels would have sacked him anyway. Goebbels had realised by now that he had made a mistake in giving the post to a man who was too autocratic in many respects – he would not have agreed to the edict against Jewish composers nor the proscription of Hindemith – and who was also not ruthless enough to implement Goebbels's instructions. Strauss had advised him, for example, that there should be no ostracism of Hindemith from the Reich Music Chamber.

At least Strauss's sense of humour did not desert him during this crisis. On 12 December 1935 he was sent a bureaucratic questionnaire to establish his *bona fide* as a composer. He had all the answers typed except that to the last section which required the names of two composers who would give references about his professionalism. In his own hand Strauss wrote: 'Mozart and Rich. Wagner'.

Strauss's cure for all ills was work, but in July 1935 he had none on hand. During August he wrote the first two of three settings of Rückert which he had promised to Eugen Papst, conductor of the Cologne Male Voice Choral Society. A third was added in October. They were first sung, by the dedicatees, on 5 April 1936, when each song was encored. The work, *Drei Männerchöre* (o.Op. 123), is a near-masterpiece. The first two songs obviously refer to Strauss's personal predicament. Here are the 'dark thoughts' which had haunted him since the time of his mother's illness. In the light-hearted third song, they are dispersed. Strauss's male chorus compositions, little known, are worth exploration. Strauss's meeting with Gregor at Berchtesgaden on 7 July, engineered by Zweig, was intended to establish a basis for some kind of working relationship. Gregor took six sketches of librettos of which Strauss took away three. Two were to become *Friedenstag (1648)* and *Daphne*. There is controversy over the identity of the third:

Gregor said it was *Die Liebe der Danae*; Strauss denied it. Probably it was *Semiramis*. Strauss was anxious to press on with *24 October 1648*, as it was still called, and invited Gregor to stay at Garmisch from 30 July so that they could begin work. From there Gregor wrote to Zweig: 'That work in Garmisch was very difficult was, naturally enough, by no means the fault of the old gentleman himself, who is absolutely upright in nature and whom, as a result of this personal contact, I treasure and respect more than ever. The problems, on the contrary, stemmed more from those who surrounded him.' Evidently he had clashed with Pauline or with Franz and Alice. Zweig advised him to 'keep a few notes because we really must always recognize the master as an historical figure and it is, to a certain extent, our duty to preserve our impressions of him'.

By the time Gregor returned to Vienna on 15 August he had completed the first drafts of the librettos of what became *Friedenstag* and *Daphne*. He immediately began to revise the former and sent a new version to Strauss, who acknowledged it on 24 August as 'a great step forward'. Before further progress could be made, Strauss went to Vichy in September for the first festival of the Permanent Council for International Co-operation among Composers. Strauss had worked hard preparing the festival, in which Jewish composers were included, notably Paul Dukas, who had died a few months earlier. Strauss conducted his opera *Ariane et Barbe-bleue* and the tone-poem *L'apprenti-sorcier*. The German ambassador to France withdrew from the festival. Strauss wrote home to Pauline: 'Civilised France is a real rest-cure.'

Strauss disliked working with Gregor from the start. He resented Zweig's withdrawal, but insisted that everything he queried in the libretto should be referred to Zweig. On 6 October he wrote to Gregor:

I have newly worked through the second half of *Friedenstag* [as it had now become]. I don't believe I shall ever be able to find music for it, there are no real people; the Commander and his wife – it all goes on stilts. The whole scene from the entry of the Holsteiner [the enemy commander] is faulty in construction, the conversation between the two commanders is completely undramatic. Thus would two school-masters converse on the theme of the Thirty Years' War.

He made most of the same points to Zweig on 31 October:

I have not found the music I expect of myself. The whole subject is, after all, a bit too commonplace – soldiers, war, famine, medieval heroism, dying together – it isn't quite my field, with the best of goodwill. Our friend doubtless is very gifted but he lacks the higher creative power and ideas that stray a bit from the beaten track. This is particularly noticeable in his *Daphne*, whose appealing basic idea is not worked out at all. Lots of words, schoolmarm banalities, no concentration on one focus, no gripping human conflict. . . I am posting this letter from Tyrol and am asking that you had also better not write to me across the German border because all mail is being opened. Please sign your name as Henry Morosus; I will sign as Robert Storch [the character of Strauss himself in *Intermezzo*].

On 20 November Strauss told Gregor that he was 'diligently at work'. On 13 January 1936 the composition sketch was complete. The full score was finished on 16 June. The six-month gap before the orchestration was finished is explained by a long foreign tour by Strauss. In February he went to conduct *Arabella* in Genoa and to Milan for the Italian première of *Die schweigsame Frau*. He planned to go from there to Antwerp, where some of his operas were to be performed at the Royal Flemish Opera. He was to go by car along the Riviera to Monte Carlo and then northwards through Eastern France. Before Strauss left Milan, Hitler reoccupied the Rhineland on 7 March in defiance of the Treaty of Versailles. French politicians urged military action, the generals pleaded for restraint. War talk was everywhere. Anti-German feeling in Belgium ran high and the Antwerp authorities wanted to cancel the Strauss season: the opening performance of *Ariadne auf Naxos* was indeed cancelled. But no one could contact Strauss, who wondered why French soldiers along the Maginot Line had stared in astonishment at his Munich number-plate. He arrived in Antwerp in total ignorance that there was a European crisis.[1] The mayor of Antwerp, Camille Huysmans, decided that the festival should go ahead. As Strauss wrote to Pauline: '*Ariadne*. . . is going to be done today [25 March] after all, since I scored a wild success on Monday with *Salome*, every ticket sold. A fabulous dinner for fifty on Sunday, at the house of the richest man in Antwerp; the entire crème of the city came afterwards. I accompanied some of my songs. On Tuesday a formal reception at the city hall, with the mayor making a speech in *German*, an unheard-of event!'

The reception was given by Huysmans and the city council. Strauss was the only German between the two World Wars to be inscribed in the Golden Book of the city. Strauss's improvised reply to Huysmans's speech referred to the humanity required of every good European. 'Just as Goethe created the concept of world literature, we should believe that the hour will come when music will unite the great minds of the world.' He elaborated to Pauline:

It is no exaggeration to say I have *made* this success a German one entirely on my own, through my work, my conducting and my presence here. The newspapers are raving. I'd like to see any other German artist do what I have done – at a time like this, in a foreign country in a hostile mood. Really I deserve the Goldest Medal of the Propaganda Ministry. Here I am, after fifty years, still risking my neck as the pioneer of German music!

But the Propaganda Ministry ensured that the German press carried no reports of the disgraced composer's success. While in Belgium, Strauss went to see the paintings by Memling and Van Eyck in the galleries in Ghent and Bruges, examining the pictures in detail for a long while. In a dark hour in Vienna in 1944 he was to say to a friend: 'Belgium 1936! That was a world worth living in.'

The other draft libretto Gregor gave to Strauss in July 1935 was *Daphne*. Although he professed to be 'greatly pleased' by it (letter of 15 September), ten days later he told poor Gregor that the more often he read it, the less it pleased him. 'You still always get intoxicated with your own ideas', Strauss told him. Karl Böhm was at Garmisch when Gregor was working on the text. He and Strauss sat outside in deckchairs while the libretto was brought down page by page from Gregor, who was working in Strauss's study, by Franz Strauss. 'Strauss read them and then passed them over to me', Böhm recalled. 'And then occurred something almost incredible that enabled me virtually to experience the creative act myself. The pages already had in the margin – let me repeat, after being read only once – details of the rhythm and usually the key and, when more persons were concerned, even precise indication of the musical form. Strauss needed hardly more time for this creative process than I did to read the text.'[2]

Strauss's criticisms of the draft libretto soon began. Gregor based it on the Greek myth of Apollo pursuing the nymph Daphne, daughter of Peneios and Gaea. Daphne was saved by Gaea who spirited her away to Crete and caused a laurel-tree to spring up in her place from whose leaves Apollo wove a wreath for his forehead as consolation. Apollo, who had coveted Daphne for a long time, had arranged the murder of his rival Leukippos by advising the mountain nymphs to bathe naked so that they could be sure only women were present. As a result Leukippos was soon discovered and torn to pieces by the nymphs. In the opera Leukippos's love for Daphne is not returned, for she has no sexual feelings. Apollo comes to the village disguised as a cowherd. He woos Daphne but she recoils from his passionate kiss. Leukippos goes to the Dionysian feast disguised as a girl at the suggestion of Daphne's maids. He dances with Daphne, but Apollo gives his disguise away and kills him. Daphne refuses to go with Apollo and Apollo asks Zeus to grant Daphne her wish. In the moonlight, she is transformed into a laurel.

'The image of the swineherd Zeus is not good', Strauss objected on 15 September, 'an abortive Wotan.' Ten days later: 'It completely lacks a grand confrontation between Apollo, Leukippos and Daphne. . . This must be a *Kleistisch szene*, dark and mysterious. . . The catastrophe must be much more violent, without the schoolmasterly, ideological banalities of the completely superfluous Zeus. In short, the whole thing as evolving, in a not particularly well imitated Homeric style, will not attract a hundred people into a theatre.' Poor Gregor. He was hurt and did not reply for a fortnight. Strauss knew he had gone too far and pointed out that his strictures did not mean he did not think a 'pleasant single-act work' could not be created, but 'the surgeon's knife does smart when he works without an anaesthetic'. Gregor was too much in awe of Strauss to stand up to his often patronising and bullying criticisms. Whereas Hofmannsthal knew that argument spurred Strauss to a positive creative response, Gregor was fearful of the consequences of confrontation. In his last letter to Zweig, on 31 October, Strauss bemoaned Gregor's inadequacies and made a last vain plea: 'Won't *you*, even now, write a new work for me?'

While Strauss composed *Friedenstag*, Gregor re-worked *Daphne* in collaboration with Zweig. Strauss and Gregor met in Munich on 11 December; more revisions followed. The first scene was much changed and now included Zweig's suggestion of a long opening monologue for Daphne.

By mid-January the text was approved and Strauss, his interest now fully aroused, began a detailed critical examination of the text: 'Tiny, superfluous words used to fill out a line should be omitted, also subordinate clauses which begin with "in which" and "during" – do you get my drift? I beg you not to be annoyed.' In January 1936 Strauss began to sketch *Daphne* and in the first part of February played through *Friedenstag* to Gregor, who wrote ecstatically, describing the finale as 'even simpler, more monumental and more climactic' than the finale of Beethoven's Ninth. Strauss said nothing. From mid-February to 7 April 1936 Strauss was in Italy (where *Arabella* was to be produced by Lothar Wallerstein in Milan) – he liked to leave Germany at this period as often as he could. During his absence he kept in close touch with Gregor, but he had now begun to discuss the opera with Clemens Krauss and Wallerstein, much to Gregor's annoyance, expressed in a letter to Zweig in April: 'I have already made a new version on the basis of discussions between him and Wallerstein – suddenly everything is to be re-worked yet again on the advice of Clemens Krauss.' Gregor nearly had to suspend work on *Daphne* because of financial problems – a book he was also writing promised more immediate monetary rewards. Hearing this, Strauss gave him an advance against royalties, as he had already done for *Friedenstag*. Strauss was constantly revising the text of Daphne's first aria. He was increasingly concerned about the psychological symbolism of *Daphne*. It was beginning to take on an autobiographical meaning for him. As he pondered Daphne's withdrawal from the darkness of a human world she does not understand towards the Apollonian light, he realised that this was his own position *vis-à-vis* the Nazis. He was increasingly withdrawing from the world into a private idyll at Garmisch where only composition mattered. One has only to visit the Strauss villa in Garmisch to appreciate how cut off from the outside world one can feel there. 'The world looks very different, Dr Strauss, from the way you imagine it in your study in Garmisch', Goebbels once said to him. He saw himself increasingly as the last guardian and exponent of the great German artistic tradition, continuing the German admiration for Ancient Greece and his own reverence for Goethe and Nietzsche. In March 1936 he asked Gregor 'Could not Daphne represent the human embodiment of nature itself, touched upon by the two divinities Apollo and Dionysus, the contrasting elements of art? She has a premonition of them but cannot comprehend them; only through death does she become a symbol of the eternal work of art. She can rise again as the perfect laurel tree?' As this Nietzschean symbolism intensified, Strauss saw the role of Daphne's father Peneios as another musical portrait of himself – his daughter represents his ideal of artistic fulfilment, the sign-manual of a lifetime's devotion to art. How Hofmannsthal would have enjoyed this!

At the beginning of April, the influence of Krauss magnified. Strauss wrote to Gregor: 'I am of the opinion, as also is Clemens Krauss . . . that Leukippos's female disguise ought not to be altered. . . Now, the final confrontation between Daphne, Apollo and Leukippos – his death. . . She is betrayed by both of them, by "brother" Apollo and by "sister" Leukippos! She can no longer live, since the Dionysian drink has made her untrue to her own nature. There the god discovers, to his own purification and to her fulfilment, the wonder of the laurel-tree transformation! How does that please you?' It seemed that all was now plain sailing. Daphne's metamorphosis would occur before a choral finale and a big aria from Peneios. The letters to Gregor ceased in mid-April. The full score of *Friedenstag* was completed on 16 June and dedicated to 'my friends Viorica Ursuleac and Clemens Krauss'. He was now ready to work uninterruptedly on the short score of *Daphne*. In August there was the bore of conducting the *Olympic Hymn* in Berlin. In November he went to London where on the 5th he was presented by Sir Hugh Allen, director of the Royal College of Music, with the Gold Medal of the Royal Philharmonic Society before Adrian Boult conducted *Also sprach Zarathustra*. Next evening, Strauss conducted the Dresden State Opera in *Ariadne auf Naxos* at Covent Garden. He also conducted the Dresden orchestra in a concert of Mozart and Strauss. Arthur Tröber, a violinist in the orchestra and later its director, recalled that 'for some unknown reason there was some catastrophic wobbling in Mozart's G minor Symphony. Here, too, the composer, like us, got flustered, as could be seen from his gestures. However, the English applauded all the same with almost southern enthusiasm. Richard Strauss would seem to have been distracted or absent-minded during this London visit since at a reception given by the German Ambassador [Ribbentrop], he made a charming speech about the orchestra members and then proposed the toast "to his beloved

21 Rehearsing the *Olympic Hymn*, in the Olympic Stadium, Berlin, 1936

Vienna Philharmonic". A colleague promptly called out "We are the Dresdeners!" Grins all round.'[3]

While in London Strauss renewed acquaintance with Berta Geissmar, who had been Furtwängler's secretary in Berlin and was now acting in the same capacity for Beecham. She was highly critical of Strauss's role after 1933 and, at her meeting with him at Covent Garden, intended to say so. 'Yet I refrained', she wrote. 'I must admit it, I was entirely bewitched by his fabulous charm.'[4] One does not often read of this quality in Strauss, but its abundance must have also affected Elisabeth Schumann, Maria Jeritza and Viorica Ursuleac.

In the spring of 1937, Strauss told Krauss that he could not make progress with the end of *Daphne*. Krauss replied: 'I told him that the idea of bringing people on to the stage to sing to the tree after the transformation was absurd. The moment people are brought together with the transformed tree, it has nothing to do with Daphne but is just a theatrical device.' Krauss's solution was relayed to Gregor by Strauss on 12 May:

We are both agreed that after Apollo's farewell song, other than Daphne no one should appear on the stage – no Peneios, no solo voices, no chorus. In short, no oratorio. . . In the course of Apollo's last outpouring Daphne, in astonishment, raises her gaze slowly from Leukippos's corpse and, as the god takes his leave, wants to follow him but is halted after only a few steps, standing as if rooted to the spot. Now, in full view, in the moonlight, the miracle of transformation is slowly worked upon her – but *with the orchestra alone*. . . Right at the end, when the tree stands complete, she should sing without words – only as a nature sound, eight more bars of laurel motif!

Gregor complained to Zweig on 28 May: 'I took great pains to convince Strauss that the conclusion of *Daphne* was much better as we had planned it. His objections are always the same: "Who sings that? Surely just the male and female choruses!"' It had always been Gregor's idea that *Friedenstag* and *Daphne* belonged together, to be performed on the same evening as a double bill. Strauss, in their correspondence, never commented on this, presumably realising that the idea was impracticable. Both works were to end with choral apotheoses, but Krauss's idea ended that link.

With *Daphne* mapped out although not fully composed, Strauss began in the summer of 1936 to think of his next opera. Gregor revived the ideas of

22 Symphonia domestica: Strauss with his son Franz and grandsons
     Richard and Christian

Semiramis and *Celestina*. Strauss would not contemplate *Semiramis* with
Gregor and *Celestina* ended tragically. 'After *Daphne* I should really like to
do something cheerful! I've had enough of tragedy.' As always, the desire and
need for contrast. At this point a letter arrived from his friend the Swiss
critic and musicologist Willi Schuh. It will be remembered that in April 1920
Hofmannsthal sent Strauss the outline of 'a light piece in three acts, closely
related to operetta', called *Danae, oder die Vernunftheirat* (*Danae, or the
Marriage of Convenience*). Strauss was busy at the time with *Intermezzo* and
the Vienna Opera. He put it in a drawer where it remained until 1933 when
the publisher of Hofmannsthal's collected works asked for it to print in a
periodical called *Corona*. It was this magazine which Schuh sent to him.
Strauss was delighted and asked Gregor to read it. As it happened, Gregor
had offered Strauss a *Danae* scenario at the beginning of their collaboration
but Strauss did not remember it. Gregor still pressed the claims of *Celestina*
but Strauss wanted the Hofmannsthal *Danae*. Gregor worked into it some
of his own scenario, but Strauss instantly identified it and rejected it – too
heavy, too scholastic, too grotesque. 'Once again you want to go too deep,

but the subject isn't suited to it.' Auber's *Fra Diavolo*, light and airy – that should be Gregor's model. And on another occasion Strauss took Gregor to see Correggio's 'Danae' in the Villa Borghese. 'It's just this lightness, this joy, that I'm searching for', he said.

The year 1937 saw Strauss weeks in Frankfurt and Munich. Krauss was now Generalmusikdirektor of the Munich Opera, much to Strauss's pleasure, with Rudolf Hartmann as chief producer. In 1937 Krauss conducted *Der Rosenkavalier*, *Salome* and *Ariadne auf Naxos*. Casts included such singers as Ursuleac, Hans Hotter, Hildegarde Ranczak, Ludwig Weber, Georg Hann, Adele Kern, Julius Patzak and Torsten Ralf. Strauss had hoped to go to Paris, a city he loved, in September 1937 for the World Fair, but he was ill during the late summer. From October 1937 to April 1938 he spent in Italy except for one interruption when he received the news from Alice that his grandson Richard, then eleven, had been beaten up by boys in his school in Garmisch because of his Jewish blood. Despite the débâcle of July 1935, Strauss was still of use to the Nazis, who wheeled him out as the great figure of German music for the opening night of the Olympic Games in 1936. He felt able, therefore, to write to certain party officials about Richard and eventually to Hitler. It was decreed that both Richard and his six-year-old brother Christian should be regarded as Aryans but would not be eligible for party membership, military service or public office. Their grandfather, at whatever cost in the cat-and-mouse game the Nazis were playing with him, had won them safety. But it was an uneasy truce. During the *Kristallnacht* pogrom of 9–10 November 1938, the Garmisch Nazis planned to arrest Alice, but she was away. (She was hidden in the Düsseldorf clinic of the gynaecologist Professor Dr Fritz Lönne, a close friend of the family.) Richard and Christian were again beaten up and taken to the square in Garmisch where they were compelled to spit at Jews rounded up there. On her return, Alice was placed under curfew and her personal papers were confiscated. In addition, there was a grim clue to what the Nazis really thought of Strauss when in 1938 an official book called *Men of Germany, 200 Pictures and Biographies* was published in Berlin. Those included were figures prominent in German life up to the end of the 1914–18 War. Strauss was omitted.

Strauss completed the short score of *Daphne* in Taormina, Sicily, on 9

November 1937 and the full score on Christmas Eve. A few weeks later he played it to Gregor on an inadequate hotel piano. Again Gregor gushed extravagant praise about the ending. 'Come on', the embarrassed Strauss said, 'it's only the *Walküre* Magic Fire music with different notes.' On his return to Germany, perhaps out of gratitude or under compulsion, he conducted his own music at the first Reichsmusiktage, organised by the Propaganda Ministry, in Düsseldorf on 28 May. Earlier in the month, in Garmisch, he composed another work (o.Op. 124) for unaccompanied male voice chorus for the Vienna Schubert Society's golden jubilee. This was a setting of a poem, *Durch Einsamkeiten, durch waldwild Geheg* (*Through Loneliness, through Wild Woods*), by Anton Wildgans and like two of the Rückert poems he had set in 1935, it spoke of a longing for death: 'A ferryman waited for me who rowed my boat well to a quiet country, always avoided and still always longed for: to peace.' Strange words to set for a jubilee celebration.

On 14 March 1938 Hitler drove into Vienna amid scenes of exultant enthusiasm. The *Anschluss* had been achieved and within four days anti-Jewish laws were enforced. Gregor was not Jewish, but he was aware that the Nazis knew of his friendship with Zweig. His post at the Nationalbibliothek was now under threat. The Nazis kept him on tenterhooks about his admission to the Reich Writers' Chamber – if he was excluded, his books would not be published. A list of possible successors to his job was circulated. On 27 June 1938 he wrote to Strauss for help:

You can imagine how desperate I am today. For long months this 'sword of Damocles' has been hanging over me. I thought from Dr Drewes's [Dr Heinz Drewes, Minister of Culture in the Third Reich] last letter that everything had been sorted out, but I now see that nothing has changed... From Berlin they throw books at me that appeared many years ago! In my great, great anxiety, I beg you once again, respected Herr Doktor, to take up my cause... Forgive me for burdening you with my sorrows, but it is terribly important to me, otherwise I would not bother you. Please accept, for whatever you are able to do, the thanks of a miserable and abject fellow being.

Whether Strauss pulled strings is not known, but Gregor was admitted to membership of the Writers' Chamber in the spring of 1939.

Clemens Krauss persuaded Strauss to award him the first performance of

Friedenstag. If ever there was a proclamation of a composer's faith in a conductor, this was it because it meant that, for the first time in his life, Strauss had allowed one of his operas to be premièred in Munich, something he had vowed never to let happen after the city's treatment of *Guntram.* The performance, when *Friedenstag* was coupled with Beethoven's *Die Geschöpfe des Prometheus,* was on 24 July 1938, with Hotter as the Commandant, Ursuleac as Maria and Ludwig Weber as the Holstein commander. The tenor role of the Piedmont soldier who sings most movingly of his homesickness was taken by Peter Anders. What a strange work to set before a German audience in 1938. If the Nazis had known that it was to a great extent the work of Zweig, it would surely have been banned. Anti-Strauss factions still maintain that the opera was propaganda for the Nazis, a theory impossible to take seriously when one considers that the plot was Zweig's idea. True, the Nazis might admire a commandant who obeys orders from on high to the last letter and prefers death to the dishonour of surrender, but that is only one aspect of the opera. Its message is overtly anti-war and pro-peaceful reconciliation. When it was performed in Dresden in 1995, Zweig's name was given equal prominence with Gregor's in the programme credits.

Friedenstag is Strauss's most austere opera, with only one important female role. It is unique among his operas for its bleakness of mood. There is no doubt of the sincerity of the music in spite of Strauss's inner conviction that militarism and anti-militarism were not his 'dish'. The two most lyrical episodes are the Piedmontese youth's Italian folk-song and Maria's big aria. The most impressive episodes are the gloomy and despairing opening choruses, with a funeral-march ground bass reminiscent of Mahler's Sixth Symphony, and the gaunt music to which the starving townspeople sing their wails for 'Hunger' and 'Bread'. The Commandant's aria in which he recalls the Battle of Magdeburg and asks two soldiers if they will die with him is also remarkably effective in its use of a popular style. Strauss's keen dramatic sense is evident in the scene when the fortress awaits a renewed assault but instead the peace bells ring. When the Holsteiner troops arrive, they do so to a brutal march with the Lutheran chorale *Ein' feste Burg* as its bass – surely intended by Strauss as a condemnation of religion's part in mankind's wars. But hovering behind *Friedenstag* is the giant shadow of Beethoven's *Fidelio.* A loving wife, a prisoners' (townspeople's) chorus, the bugle-call at the crucial moment, the final C major hymn to peace and comradeship – the resemblances are too many to be coincidental. Strauss could not rise to Beethoven's heights of ecstasy in the final chorus, which is rhetoric rather than oratory or evangelism. Nevertheless, *Friedenstag* has virtues of its own and, although in the second rank of Strauss operas, is far from negligible and further tribute to his versatility. After Munich, it was performed in 1938 in Dresden, Graz, Breslau, Kassel, Magdeburg, Karlsruhe, Oldenburg and Königsberg, the last-named staging it on Christmas Day. In 1939 it had premières in fourteen cities, including Berlin (8 March) and Vienna (10 June). The Vienna occasion marked Strauss's seventy-fifth birthday and was attended by Hitler, which indicates that Strauss was no longer *persona non grata* as far as he was concerned. Hitler had a long talk with Hotter, asking him if the role of Scarpia in *Tosca* was now too high for him ('that G flat in Act 2?'). He said it was his wish to give Munich a new opera house. In January 1940 *Friedenstag* had its Rostock and Venice premières on the same day. Thereafter it disappeared from the repertory in Germany and Austria until Graz in 1950, but was performed in Paris and Brussels in 1949. At a Vienna reception for his birthday, Strauss sought his first favour from the newly-appointed Governor of Vienna, Baldur von Schirach. The Nazis had arrested Strauss's close friend, the industrialist Manfred Mautner Markhof. Strauss said to Schirach that all he wanted for his birthday was Mautner Markhof's release – 'the arrest can only be an error, in any case.' The wish was granted.

Gregor's ideal of a double bill of *Friedenstag* and *Daphne* was realised in Dresden on 15 October 1938 when *Daphne* had its first performance conducted by Karl Böhm to whom it was dedicated. Just before Christmas 1937, Böhm received a postcard from Strauss showing a photograph of Bernini's statue of Daphne. The composer wrote 'I am getting on well with *Daphne*. Would it give you some little pleasure if I were to dedicate it to you as a Christmas gift?' Böhm replied: 'What a silly question!' At the Dresden dress rehearsal Pauline kissed Böhm, saying 'You're not getting a second kiss now, you're too sweaty.' *Daphne* was her favourite among her husband's operas. Böhm said he would never again conduct the two operas in one evening. Even so, during the 1938–9 season in Germany and Austria, the double bill was performed nineteen times. The role of Daphne was created by

Margarete Teschemacher (wearing a costume based on Botticelli's *La Primavera*, in accordance with Strauss's wish), that of Apollo by Torsten Ralf.

Daphne emphatically belongs in the front rank of Strauss operas. As with the Prologue to *Ariadne auf Naxos*, he was distinctly unenthusiastic about it at first, but as he worked on, the subject gripped him. It marks a new development in his style, the beginning of what has been described as his 'Indian Summer' (although the germ of *Daphne* – its pastoral opening oboe theme – can be traced back to *Die Göttin im Putzzimmer*). We have seen its significance for him in his isolated position during the 1930s, its Nietzschean overtones and, of course, the attraction of a Greek mythological subject. But the reason for the slow and steady growth of appreciation of *Daphne* is the lyrical beauty of the music, the stream of melody allotted to the soprano singing the title-role (the vocal line as fully flexible as if written for an instrument), the silvery harmonies which give the work its translucent texture, the fine writing for both the tenors (Leukippos and Apollo). It is, like *Salome* and *Elektra*, near to being a vocal tone-poem, designed in an imposing arch-like structure. There are the big vocal set-pieces – the feast of Dionysus, the Apollo-Daphne love duet culminating in the mysterious dark harmonies of their kiss, Daphne's lament for Leukippos – but the final F sharp major transformation scene belongs to the orchestra and is an example of the pellucid instrumental scoring which was to dominate the works of the last decade of his life. It sounds effortless and fluent, but the conductor Oskar Suitner thought that the difficulty of the orchestral writing in detail and ensemble went far beyond that of all Strauss's operas. *Daphne* is the first obvious product of the ageing, troubled Strauss's desire to escape inwardly into a pursuit of the ideal work of art and let the world go hang.

24   Danae and Madeleine

Throughout 1938 Strauss and Gregor worked on the text of what was at this point called *Midas and Danae*. As usual, Strauss played a major part in fixing the plot of what Hofmannsthal had offered him as a kind of operetta – just as he had *Die ägyptische Helena*! The opera in its final form opens with King Pollux warding off his creditors by pointing out that a rich suitor is being sought for his daughter Danae. King Midas of Lydia, the richest man in the world, has shown interest and is on his way. Danae has dreamed of being embraced like a lover by a shower of gold and is only interested in a suitor who brings her the gold of her dreams. Midas arrives, but calls himself Chrysopher, telling her he has come to prepare her for Midas's arrival. They go to the harbour to await him – Jupiter in disguise. Danae recognises him as the lover of her dream. Four queens, who are decorating Danae's marriage-bed, recognise Jupiter – he has previously made love to each of them under a different disguise. He now finds them middle-aged and worries that Danae may be attracted to Midas/Chrysopher. He warns Midas he will return him to his former life as a donkey-driver if he attempts to win Danae. The four queens tell Danae about their former intimacy with Jupiter and advise her to aim for Chrysopher. But Chrysopher tells her he is really Midas and proves it by turning the contents of her room to gold. They embrace, there is a clap of thunder and Danae is turned into a gold statue. Jupiter asks the statue to choose between Midas and him. She chooses Midas and is restored to life. She and Midas are next seen in the desert. He no longer has the golden touch and explains to Danae how Jupiter has taken his place when her father's emissaries arrived in Lydia with her portrait. Danae is moved, forgets her passion for gold and remembers that she has chosen poverty with Midas rather than luxury with Jupiter. Mercury appears to Jupiter to tell him that everyone on Olympus, especially his wife Juno, is laughing at his failure to seduce Danae. Jupiter says farewell to the four queens. Pollux and his creditors are all angry with Jupiter for various reasons and Mercury suggests he should placate them with a shower of gold and then track down Midas and Danae. In the last scene in Midas's hut, Danae sings of her happiness. Jupiter arrives to try to make her discontented but acknowledges defeat.

Strauss had rejected Gregor's first scenario early in 1937 as 'nowhere near light enough for me. . . Why in the case of Danae, who is poor and so much in love with gold, does Jupiter *not come straightforwardly to her in the form of the gold-giving Midas*, just as he came to his other sweethearts as bull, swan, etc? It must be clearly stated that Jupiter, in all other matters the almighty, is so hellishly frightened only of his stronger spouse Hera (just like Wotan) that he comes to his beloved ones so transformed that Hera doesn't at once notice.' And so on. 'It has lost all the effect of Hofmannsthal's simple fable, that is the fact that Danae is cured of her excessive love of gold and in the end is content with the poor donkey-driver.' Everything Gregor suggested was slapped down. It was all too heavy. 'Listen to Caruso's recording of the aria from Donizetti's *L'elisir d'amore* [Una furtiva lagrima]', he was exhorted. 'I love that piece. That is what *Danae* must be like!' Originally the opera was to be in two acts. Then Clemens Krauss pointed out that the Act 2 finale was not a satisfactory ending. The opera, he said, 'is concerned with a completely unsuccessful adventure of Jupiter, and one cannot conclude . . . by making him return to Olympus, his thunder having been stolen – that would make the god cut a ridiculous figure'. So the third act in Midas's hut was invented and partly explains why the character of the music changes so markedly in this more lyrical act. In June 1938 Strauss began fully to compose the opening scene. As he worked on, he found more and more problems. 'The relationship between Jupiter and Midas is utterly unclear. . . How can Jupiter make a visible appearance as Jupiter-Midas at the end of Act 1, because all the world can see that he is Jupiter and *not* Midas?' Problems in the last act were solved by Clemens Krauss. When Gregor wrote it in accordance with Krauss's changes, Strauss rejected his draft completely. The dialogue was too lofty, and he never wanted to read the word *Geliebter* (Beloved) again. Gregor was so upset that he could not work for weeks and did not attend the first performance of

Daphne. But Strauss poured soothing oil and a new final scene was written. He was by now thoroughly interested in the character of Jupiter who, after being satirically treated in the first two acts, was now becoming a benevolent self-portrait and a further symbol of Strauss's attitude to his own artistic position in Nazi Germany. 'For the end of the opera', he wrote, 'I need a beautiful long farewell speech by Jove, like that of Hans Sachs at the end of *Meistersinger.* Contents: joyful resignation.' Two months later: 'Now, he is returning to his own proper sphere of activity, once again to direct the affairs of the world which he has created in all its beauty, and to rejoice that he has succeeded in fashioning *one jewel* in the hearts of men which cannot even enter into his own dreams, and before which all, all his might, all the magic of gold, is powerless. . . The phrase "Sich ich liebe" can stay in the same way as – if you remember – Salome's refrain "Ich will den Kopf des Jochanaan!" Things like that always work well in opera! You need not restrict yourself for space. If it contains genuine wisdom and beautiful poetry, then however much more there is of it, I will still be able to cope! And in a posthumous work everything is allowed.' Strauss was convinced that *Die Liebe der Danae* – the title was suggested by Ursuleac – would never be performed in his lifetime and, as we will see, did as much as he could to keep it from the stage. With the libretto finally sorted out, he continued the work of composition. He had the grace to write to Gregor: 'Heartfelt thanks and congratulations. All your trouble has been splendidly rewarded. I am very happy.'

With the dawn of 1939 his first task, on 3 January, three days before he completed the short-score of Act 1 of *Danae,* was to complete a four-minute Occasional Waltz (*Gelegenheitswalzer*) called *München* (o.Op. 125) which he had been asked by the city council to write for a short film about Munich's cultural heritage. After the film had been shot, its public showing was forbidden on orders from Hitler and Goebbels, who planned some monumental new buildings for Munich, including a redevelopment of the Nationaltheater, and did not want its cultural past to be glorified in advance. Strauss seems not to have been informed of this, nor of the decision by Munich's mayor to authorise a private showing at the film studios on 24 May when Carl Ehrenberg conducted an augmented chamber orchestra in Strauss's waltz. The waltz had its first public performance in Munich on 14

March 1940 conducted by Oswald Kabasta. Strauss must have been unaware of this, too, because when he gave the manuscript to the Bavarian Municipal Library in 1949 he described it as 'neither published nor performed'. More will be heard of it later.

The short-score of Act 2 of *Danae* was completed on 2 February, Act 3 on 21 March. As his seventy-fifth birthday in June approached, the musicians of Germany prepared to celebrate it. Festival weeks were held in Berlin (where a young conductor named Herbert von Karajan conducted *Salome*), Munich and Dresden. It was perhaps at this time, during a Dresden rehearsal of *Elektra* conducted by Böhm, that Strauss gripped Frau Böhm's hand in the Recognition Scene and would not let go. She asked him at the end what was wrong and he replied: 'I had quite forgotten that I wrote it.'[1] But the chief celebration was reserved for Vienna, away from the political centre of the Reich. Otto Strasser, manager of the Vienna Philharmonic and formerly one of its players, in his memoirs described the birthday concert which Strauss conducted. It began with the suite from *Le bourgeois gentilhomme*. This was the occasion when Strauss remarked that he had 'written it with the left hand, so to speak'. Then Strauss's eleven-year-old grandson Richard played the flute in an arrangement of the final duet from *Der Rosenkavalier*. 'Lovely', his grandfather commented, 'but no sense of rhythm, just like most flautists.' The final work was the *Symphonia Domestica*. Both Strasser and Böhm have described how Strauss turned and looked at his wife and son in their box when their themes were first played. Strasser described what happened after the tumultuous ovation at the end: 'When I met him at the exit from the platform, he suddenly threw the baton away, stumbled into the artists' room, sat down, visibly distressed and muttered: "Now it's all over" and began to cry bitterly. I was moved and at the same time had no idea what to do. He was a man who took such joy in life: was he thinking of the end at this moment of moments? After a while his son arrived and put his arms round his father, who was growing calmer, and all was well again.' It was rare for Strauss to let the mask drop and it is significant that this was caused by *Domestica*, the most personal of his orchestral works. What was 'all over'? The world in which they had lived so cosily and in such insulated isolation, perhaps.

But next day he was his old self again, off to Dresden to conduct *Arabella*.

Work was still the great antidote and although he was still orchestrating *Die Liebe der Danae* (Act 1 was finished on 7 September 1939 while he was at a Swiss spa at Baden, near Zürich), he was already badgering Gregor over his next project. After the conclusion of work on *Daphne*, Gregor besieged Strauss with scenarios for future work – operas and ballets. All were rejected. Then Strauss remembered the last suggestion Zweig had made to him, the Abbé Giambattista Casti's libretto *Prima la musica e poi le parole*. Gregor could see nothing in it. Zweig had come across it in the British Museum. It had been set to music by Salieri and performed at Schönbrunn in 1786 in a double bill with Mozart's *Der Schauspieldirektor*. Its slight plot concerns a composer and a poet who are ordered by their patron, a Count, to produce words and music for a scene for two singers, one of whom is the patron's mistress. Strauss's idea, which he told Zweig, was 'a sort of discourse set in dialogue' on the old question: is the music or the text more important in opera? He had discussed this subject with Clemens Krauss during rehearsals of *Arabella* in 1933 and it had lodged in his memory. By 1935 Zweig had decided he could not continue open collaboration with Strauss and, at a meeting with Gregor in June of that year, worked out a scenario for Gregor to present to the composer: 'A group of comedians come upon a feudal castle. They fall headlong into a delicate situation. A poet and a musician both sue for the hand of the châtelaine; she herself does not know which to choose.' Gregor quickly wrote a scenario based on this plot in the summer of 1935 and sent it to Garmisch, where it aroused no response beyond irritation that it was not by Zweig. It lay neglected for four years until March 1939 when Strauss resurrected the idea. Gregor wrote a new version. 'Nothing like what I had in mind', Strauss replied. So it went on for six months, Gregor growing more despondent, Strauss more choleric. Strauss showed Gregor's latest draft to Krauss, who was scathing in his criticism. Strauss found it 'too lyrical and poetic'. He wanted 'intellectual theatre, dry wit. Really I don't want to write any more operas but I'd like to make something really special out of the Casti, give it a dramaturgic treatment, a theatrical fugue (even good old Verdi resorted to a fugue at the end of *Falstaff*!). Think of Beethoven's quartet fugue [original finale of Op. 130] – these are the sort of things old men amuse themselves with.' In October 1939 Strauss sent Gregor his detailed synopsis, which contained most of the features of *Capriccio* as we now know it. Five days later he spent a day at Garmisch discussing the project with Krauss and Rudolf Hartmann, after which Krauss wrote a scenario. Strauss, Gregor and Krauss then each wrote a section of the dialogue for the first scene. If the idea was to prove that Gregor was not the man for the job, it succeeded. Krauss advised Strauss to get rid of Gregor by telling him that he had decided to write it himself as he did *Intermezzo*. On 28 October Strauss thanked Gregor for his efforts as 'I now intend to try my luck myself.'

In Strauss's synopsis the castle was to be owned by a young Count and Countess, perhaps twins. In the first scene the poet would recite his offering for the Countess's birthday; in the second, the theatre director (to be like Reinhardt) would bring along two Italian opera singers. In the third of five scenes, the director, the Italian singers, a string quartet, an actress and the young Count, and the Countess with her poet and musician suitors, would all feature. All would give their views on words and music and the musician would improvise a setting of the poet's verses. It would be decided that poet and musician should collaborate on an opera to be performed on the Countess's birthday. The end would be the Countess alone with the musician's song. To this outline Strauss added details. The opera would begin with a string quartet playing an *andante*. Tea is served and a theatrical discussion follows: the Countess is stirred by music but perturbed by emotions she cannot understand. The Count praises the spoken word. The Countess likes the poem but is not wholly satisfied. The theatre director says poet and musician are unimportant compared with décor, pretty girls and costumes; the poet and musician should provide hits people can whistle on leaving the theatre. The five servants (representing the public) should discuss what they have overheard. There should be a great quarrel ensemble, from which comes the decision that poet and composer should collaborate on an opera. 'In the end, conciliatory resolutions . . . the Countess will give the ultimate judgment.'

Here, in broad outline, is the plot of what became *Capriccio*. Strauss now began to turn 'intellectual' symbols into flesh and blood. The location was to be a French château near Paris in the period 1770–89, just before the Revolution. The Countess was to be 'an enlightened 27-year-old Frenchwoman with a correspondingly liberal outlook in matters of love and

23 With Clemens Krauss and Horst Taubmann (the first Flamand)
at a *Capriccio* rehearsal, Munich, 1942

more serious aesthetic concepts than her brother, the *philosophical* friend of
the theatre and dilettante. Here, too, springs the inner meaning of the little
piece's action and the content which will interest the public to such an extent
that they willingly follow the theoretical discussion ... that is to say, the *love
issue* concerning the Countess must run side by side with the artistic question of Words *and* Music, Words *or* Music so that she experiences the same
sympathetic feelings for the poet as for the musician but in a different way.'
The time was now ripe for Krauss, closely aided by Strauss, to begin to write

the libretto for what was still optimistically conceived as a forty-five-minute curtain-raiser to another opera, probably *Daphne*.

But there was also *Die Liebe der Danae* to be completed. Strauss was at a Swiss spa in Baden when Hitler invaded Poland on 1 September 1939 and Britain declared war on Germany on the 3rd. He completed the full score of Act 1 on the 7th and of Act 2 on 20 November. This was a complete reversal of his usual routine. He always said he could compose only in the summer, in warmth. He kept the 'chore' of orchestrating for winter. Now he was so anxious to escape into his world of creativity at any possible moment that he overcame his dislike of winter work. A brief illness preceded his next compositional labour. He laid aside *Danae* to fulfil a commission – reluctantly accepted at first – from the Japanese Government for a work to mark the 2,600th anniversary of the Japanese Empire (a bogus date, as it happens). Composers in France, Italy, Britain (Benjamin Britten) and Hungary were also approached and Strauss knew it would do no harm to his efforts to protect Alice and her children if he agreed to this request from a power known to be friendly to Hitler's Germany. The fee was 10,000 Reichsmarks, not a big sum. He wrote a one-movement piece, subdivided into sections called Seascape, Cherry Blossom Festival, Volcanic Eruption, Attack of the Samurai and Hymn of the Emperor. Local colour was provided by the use of Japanese temple-gongs. Volcanic eruptions presented no problem to the composer of Alpine thunderstorms. A huge orchestra is employed. Written with the left hand, but without much effort beyond application of an expertise that was second nature to him, he completed the work, his Op. 84, at Meran on 22 April 1940. Its first performance was in the Kabukiza Theatre, Tokyo, on 14 December 1940, conducted by Helmut Fellmer, who had been chorus master at Hamburg Opera. The concert, which also contained the commissions written by Pizzetti, Ibert and Sándor Veress, was repeated next day. The first European performance was in Stuttgart on 27 October 1941, conducted by Hermann Albert. With this task behind him, Strauss finished *Die Liebe der Danae* on 28 June 1940. He 'relaxed' by orchestrating five of his Op. 68 Brentano songs – *Amor, Ich wollt ein Sträusslein binden, Als mir dein Lied erklang, An die Nacht* and *Säusle, liebe Myrthe!* – between 3 July and 2 August. He dedicated this version of *Amor* to Adele Kern, who was the successor to Elisabeth Schumann in the lighter Strauss roles. Schumann no longer had any place in Strauss's life. After her divorce from Carl Alwin in 1933, she was shunned by the Strausses, who took Alwin's side. She passed Strauss once while walking in the mountains near Garmisch. He greeted her curtly and politely, no more. While still working on *Capriccio*, he was reminded by Krauss of the Couperin *Tanzsuite* which Krauss had conducted as a ballet in Vienna in February 1923. Could he not add some more for a new ballet, *Verklungene Feste* (*Bygone Festivities*)? Strauss arranged six more pieces in September and December 1940 and the ballet was performed in Munich on 5 April 1941. In September 1941 Strauss selected seventeen of the Couperin pieces in eight movements as the *Divertimento*, Op. 86.

Strauss regarded *Capriccio* at this stage as a short epilogue to his operatic career. He intended that *Die Liebe der Danae* should be his last big opera and that it should not be performed until at least two years after the end of the war. 'That is to say', he wrote to Gregor, 'after my death. So that's how long you will have to preserve your soul in patience.' But he promised the first performance, whenever it might be, to Krauss; and he allowed Johannes Oertel, who had replaced the Jewish Fürstner as his publisher, to print the score. When he received a proof copy, he sent it to Krauss to check for mistakes. Krauss immediately asked to be allowed to stage it at the Salzburg Festival. 'Do you really think', Strauss asked him, 'that *Danae*, which is so hard and so demanding, could be at all adequately presented scenically or acoustically in that riding-school barn of a Festspielhaus?' He insisted still on his 'two years after the war' date, adding '*Die Frau ohne Schatten* still suffers today from having to be put on in German theatres too soon after the last war. Even the second Dresden performance (at that time) was a disaster.' However, during the autumn of 1942 Strauss gave way and agreed to a Salzburg première. Krauss told him he would conduct it there in 1944 'in celebration of your eightieth birthday'.

Throughout the last months of 1939, throughout 1940 and the first eight months of 1941 Strauss worked on *Capriccio*, as it was still not called. Krauss wrote a scenario which is almost the opera as we know it and then, with Strauss, began detailed work on the libretto, which was finally delivered in January 1941. A crucial point was the sonnet by the poet which the composer sets to music, much to the poet's fury. Now, the poet says, he no longer knows whether the sonnet belongs to him or the composer. It belongs to *me*, says the Countess and, like it or not, you are joined for all time in it. Strauss and Krauss wanted an 'authentic' sonnet of the period and delegated the task of finding one to a young conductor, Hans Swarowsky, who worked for Krauss in Munich as a *Dramaturg*. He discovered that French poets were not writing love-sonnets in 1774 and instead found one by Pierre de Ronsard (1524–85), *Je ne sçaurois aimer que vous*, which he translated into German. The delighted Strauss set it at once (2 November 1939) for voice and piano as a song which differs substantially from the opera version.

By now the characters, originally mere symbols, had acquired names – all except the Count, whose name we never discover. The Countess is Madeleine, the theatre director La Roche, the musician Flamand, the poet Olivier, the actress Clairon (she really existed, Claire Legris de Latude, known as Mme Clairon). She now becomes an old flame of Olivier. More erotic tensions! And the rehearsal of the play Olivier has written, which ends with the sonnet, is jeopardised because the prompter – M. Taupe, which is French for mole – falls asleep. The music at the opening became a quintet then a sextet. La Roche has brought along his protégé, a ballet dancer, and two comic Italians, soprano and tenor, who sing an aria to words by Metastasio. Strauss was thus enabled to repeat the success of his *Bourgeois gentilhomme* and Couperin dances and his *Rosenkavalier* Italian aria. Between the dancing and the singing, the collaborators inserted Strauss's 'theatrical fugue', as the chief characters discuss the 'words and music' theme. La Roche then discloses his ornate plans for honouring the Countess's forthcoming birthday. But the others laugh it to scorn. Old-fashioned rubbish, Flamand says, sparking off the quarrelling ensemble.

La Roche then sings his great exposition of the producer's role. In it we hear the voice of Strauss himself. 'The art of our fathers lies in my trust. I guard the old, patiently awaiting the fruitful new, expecting the works of genius of our time! Where are the works which speak to the heart of the people? which mirror their soul? where are they? I cannot find them, however hard I seek. Only pale aesthetes look me in the face; they ridicule the old and create nothing new.' And was he not saying something to the Munich audience with these words: 'Your loud veto will never deter me. . . Although the masks are discarded, grimaces greet you, not human dignity!

You despise these lewd doings, yet you suffer them. You share the guilt because of your silence. Do not aim your indignant shouting at me.' La Roche's speech impels the Countess to commission an opera from her rival suitors. She has already told Flamand she will reveal to him her choice between him and Olivier in the library at eleven the following morning. Now, as the house-party breaks up and returns to Paris, her major-domo, or butler, gives her a message from Olivier: he too will be in the library the next day at eleven to learn how she wishes the opera to end.

By the time he had finished plot and libretto to his exact requirements, Strauss had provided himself with a flawless vehicle for a display of his genius at its ripest, wittiest and most lyrical. Throughout the opera we can sense that he is not indulging but enjoying himself. Like *Till Eulenspiegel*, *Capriccio* is suffused with a comparable blend of poetry and humour in ideal symphonic equipoise. Never was his scoring more felicitous, and the score itself is a masterpiece of close-knit allusions, quotations and subtleties. In it, Strauss celebrated the muse of opera by surrounding its symbol, his wonderful soprano creation the Countess, with an allusive history of the genre. No composer excelled him in quotation and self-quotation and in this score are embedded references to Gluck, Rameau, Piccinni, Couperin, Mozart, Wagner (*Tristan* and *Meistersinger*), Verdi and himself. It resounds with echoes of his previous operas and is a virtual compendium of operatic styles and *aperçus*, yet nothing is second-hand, the invention never limp. He designed the opera in thirteen scenes, each flowing into the next, and one is reminded of *Don Quixote* by the richness of fancy and invention. From first to last, the phrases and melodies proliferate and intertwine in a seamless texture, insinuating themselves into our consciousness.

Strauss devised the work's finest *coup de théâtre*. When the Countess commands an opera, the original idea was that the result should be *Daphne*. But Krauss pointed out that their work was now much more than a curtain-raiser. So, instead, Strauss suggested that the Count should propose an opera 'about the happenings of this afternoon' – a play within a play, a mirror-effect. Could it have been the word 'mirror' that gave Strauss the idea for the most inspired self-quotation in all his works? Of all the melodies in *Capriccio*, the best had to be that representing Opera itself. And over twenty years earlier, in 1918, in the satirical song-cycle *Krämerspiegel* (*Shopkeeper's*

Mirror) he had written a long, enfolding melody for the piano as prelude to the eighth song (it returns at the end of the last, twelfth, song). The story goes that Strauss had forgotten the melody and that his son Franz reminded him of it, saying it was too beautiful to be buried in a privately-printed song-cycle. It is hard to believe Strauss had forgotten it, since his memory for music, whether his own or others', was phenomenal. The melody first unwinds from the orchestral texture when the Countess says that 'the theatre unveils for us the secrets of reality. In its magic mirror (*Zauberspiegel*) we discover ourselves.' At the word 'mirror', the 1918 melody occurs. It does not flower fully until a few pages later – on Strauss's favourite instrument, the horn – when the Count sings 'An opera is an absurdity' and goes on to mock operatic conventions – 'a murder plot is hatched in song . . . a suicide takes place to music'. Strauss uses the melody, therefore, for the dual purpose of underlining opera's magic power to disclose reality and its absurdity. This ambivalence was present, too, in *Krämerspiegel*. In the eighth song of the cycle, it precedes and follows the words 'Art is threatened by businessmen, that's the trouble. They bring death to music and transfiguration to themselves.' In the last song it is reintroduced at the word 'Eulenspiegel' ('Owl-mirror') when the singer asks who will stop merchants' evil ways and answers 'One man found a jester's way to do it – Till Eulenspiegel.' The melody, we discover, is a sublimated variant of Till's principal motif.

It is this melody, on horns, strings and harps, which floods the theatre with its wondrous sounds when the Countess makes her final entrance in the moonlight. For his loveliest and most appealing heroine – captivating alike in her banter with her brother and her gentle mocking of her suitors – Strauss found music that, as he himself said, was a testament he could not repeat. He prepares us for this magical scene first by the servants' scherzo-like octet in which they give their views on the day's events and then by a muted shadowy encounter with the prompter, M. Taupe, who has woken up and is given hospitality by the major-domo: 'Can this merely be a dream? Am I really awake?' At this point, dusk is enveloping the sounds from the pit. In the last scene, the Countess looks into the mirror as she tries to solve her dilemma: 'What says your heart?. . . You, mirror, showing me a lovelorn Madeleine – ah, please advise me. Help me to find the ending for our opera

– can I find one that is not trivial?' Strauss, music's incomparable jester-poet, then shows beyond any argument where his sympathies lay. For the last words in the opera could not be more trivial: 'My lady, your supper is served.' But they are set to an unforgettably touching, lyrical phrase, prolonged by the orchestra, which is a variant of a motif from the Sextet 'written' by the composer Flamand. The magic mirror has given its reply.

So the opera is a mirror-image of itself. Are we watching Strauss's opera or Flamand's, both at once? Would the Countess ever give an answer or is it likely, as Rodney Milnes once wittily suggested, that 'she will not be in the library at eleven o'clock tomorrow, she will be down at the bottom of the garden cutting back a rampaging viburnum'?[2]

25   After *Capriccio*

By July 1940, Strauss had composed the Sextet and the first scene of *Capriccio* as far as the first words by La Roche. The full score was completed on 3 August 1941. He told Krauss that he was 'concerned with making the instrumentation of the last scene especially beautiful for our dear friend [Ursuleac]'. All kinds of title had been bandied between Strauss and Krauss. *Wort oder Ton?* subtitled *Theatralische Fuge* was one of Strauss's ideas. *Capriccio* was suggested on 6 December 1940 by Krauss. Strauss was not too keen but eventually agreed. The subtitle was duly settled as *Theoretische Komödie* (*Theoretical Comedy*) until Krauss had another brainwave – 'ein Konversationsstück für Musik' ('a conversation-piece for music'). This was adopted. Krauss said it would 'disarm all possible objections that the piece had little apparent action . . . for it attests that there was the intention to write just such a piece'. Strauss this time put up no embargo on the performance of the opera as he had on *Die Liebe der Danae*, but he had his misgivings about it. 'Never forget', he told Krauss, 'that our *Capriccio* is no piece for the broad public, any more than it should be played in a big house where only a third of the text can be understood.' He described the opera as 'a dainty morsel for cultural gourmets, not very substantial musically – at all events, not so succulent that the music will compensate for it if the general public does not take a liking to the libretto. . . I have no faith in its theatrical effectiveness in the usual sense.' Krauss was so delighted by the finished opera that he began suggesting ideas to Strauss for their next collaboration. Ordinarily this was what Strauss would always have wanted – 'have you something new for me?' was his constant request to his librettists as he was finishing an opera – but this time he took a different view. On 28 July, six days before he completed *Capriccio*, he wrote to Krauss: 'As for a new opera, it can of course be agreeable to "think about it". But do you really believe that after *Capriccio*, or 'Fuge' or the 'Muse' or the 'Muse Madeleine' or 'Erato' or . . . something better or even just as good could follow? Is this D flat major not the best conclusion to my life's work for the theatre? After all, one can leave only one testament!'

They enjoyed working together. At Garmisch once, Strauss played him some of the music he had recently composed. Krauss suggested a change at one point and they argued about it, each playing his preferred version. Pauline walked through the room and casually remarked 'The way Krauss played it is better.' Strauss conceded.

Strauss undoubtedly admired Krauss as man and musician, although one wonders if he was not sometimes irritated by the conductor's obsessive desire to persuade him to revise his works – he wanted *Daphne* made into a full-length opera, he wanted changes in *Intermezzo*, he obtained major revisions of *Arabella* and *Die ägyptische Helena*. Was there just a tinge of malice when Strauss pointed out to Willi Schuh, his chosen biographer, in 1942: 'Krauss is so proud of his libretto that up until now I was quite happy to ascribe the authorship to him, or at least I said nothing if he claimed it all to be his. I shall continue to say nothing, for the sake of his other great efforts on my behalf and for my work – however in the biography a few minor discreet statements must be made, in particular that the main ideas came for the most part from me, the very deft formulations in the text (some entire scenes) were mainly by Krauss'? (The title-page of the score ascribes it to 'Clemens Krauss and Richard Strauss'.)

A significant phrase occurs above – 'his other great efforts on my behalf', separate from his music. Krauss was at this time in high favour in Germany. Hitler had wanted him to take over in Munich in 1937. But he was never a Nazi member and helped very many Jewish victims of persecution to escape. Rosenberg reported to Hitler on Krauss's 'ideological unreliability'. Krauss's devotion to Strauss's music ensured its continued performance in Germany and Austria even though the composer was out of favour. Strauss's remark to Schuh undoubtedly refers to the fact that Krauss was another element in the protection of the Strauss family from the wrath of the party hierarchy. Strauss's precarious position was emphasised to him in February 1942 when he and other composers were summoned to Goebbels's office in Berlin because of something Strauss had written to his colleagues in which he disparaged Lehár and added 'it is not for Dr Goebbels to interfere'. Werner Egk, one of the other composers present, described how Strauss was called in alone to see Goebbels. The others heard Goebbels shouting abuse at him. They were then called in. Goebbels read aloud the letter Strauss had written to them and yelled at him: 'Be quiet! You have no conception of who you are, or of who I am. You dare to refer to Lehár as a street musician. Lehár has the masses and you haven't. Stop your claptrap about the importance of serious music, once and for all. You, Herr Strauss, belong to yesterday!' Ashen-faced, Strauss left the room. He was heard to mutter: 'I should have listened to my wife and stayed in Garmisch.' This was the culmination of a period when Goebbels had been irritated by other written expressions of Strauss's views on Germany's musical life. 'I whisper a few sweet nothings into Strauss's ear on the subject of his insolent letters', he wrote in his diary in 1941. 'Next time I shall give him something to think about.'

It is not surprising, therefore, that Strauss went whenever he could to Vienna, where Franz, Alice and the two boys were living in the Belvedere house. He conducted his version of *Idomeneo* there in December 1941. (Some extracts from this performance have been issued on CD in Koch International's Wiener Staatsoper Live Edition, Volume 3.) He was there also immediately before the Berlin incident for the centenary of the Vienna Philharmonic on 18 February. He had intended to compose a tone-poem, *Die Danau*, with a choral finale but, as he explained in a letter to the orchestra, 'emotion is not as easily turned into music as in the days of the great old masters. . . I should like to put my praise today into one short [perhaps double-edged?] sentence: "Only he who has *conducted* the Vienna Philharmonic players knows what they are!" But that will remain our very own secret!' On 15 February he conducted *Salome* at the State Opera, mentioned here because extracts from it were recorded on CD, also in Koch International's Wiener Staatsoper Live, Volume 3. They support Strauss's admiration for the singing of Else Schulz in the title-role. On 16 April he conducted the Philharmonic in the *Festliches Präludium* and his *Eine Alpensinfonie*. While in Vienna this February he composed the song *Sankt Michael* (o.Op. 129) for the bass Alfred Poell, and *Blick vom oberen Belvedere* (o.Op. 130), for Ursuleac, although it was Hilde Konetzni who gave the first performance. Both songs were settings of poems by the Austrian poet (and Nazi supporter) Josef Weinheber, whose

24 With Viorica Ursuleac after the première of *Capriccio*,
Munich 1942

fiftieth birthday was marked by a concert in the Palais Lobkowitz on 9 March,
when they had their first performances.

At the end of 1941, Strauss had had to face the unpleasant task of telling
Karl Böhm that he had awarded the first performances of *Die Liebe der
Danae* and *Capriccio* to Krauss. In view of Strauss's long association with
Dresden and because Böhm had conducted the premières of *Die
schweigsame Frau* and *Daphne*, Böhm had every reason to be disappointed.
On 12 December 1941 Strauss wrote to Krauss: 'In a very painful conversation, Dr Böhm finally swallowed the bitter pill of *Danae* and *Capriccio* and
digested it! Because he is a dear good fellow, he did not even break off our
friendship (as so many of his worthy colleagues would have done). Thank

God these will be the last premières of my life: they could really put a man off composing altogether.' Strauss favoured a Salzburg première for *Capriccio*, Krauss having just been appointed the festival's artistic director, but Krauss had other plans. He wanted the *Capriccio* première as the climax of a big Strauss Festival in Munich in the autumn of 1942. Not without some difficulty, he gained Goebbels's approval. According to Rudolf Hartmann, this took a week and the negotiations were conducted through 'secret and tortuous channels'.[1] Krauss conducted *Arabella* at the 1942 Salzburg Festival (and Strauss conducted the Vienna Philharmonic in Mozart) and scheduled *Capriccio* for 28 October in Munich at the Nationaltheater.

Hartmann was the producer and he has written of how in the rehearsal period 'I learnt how intense concentration could make me forget the war completely and how a very special work like *Capriccio* could take shape and life from its librettist and composer. I can still recall the excitement.'[2] At one of the rehearsals, Krauss admonished the singers: 'Clarity! If no one can understand a word, the opera is meaningless.' Strauss was heard to mutter: 'Well, if a little bit of my music is heard now and again I shall raise no objection.' *Also sprach* Olivier and Flamand! Munich was having almost nightly air raids. *Capriccio* had been planned with an interval, but Krauss suggested it should be played without a break so that the audience could be out of the opera house by about 9.30 p.m. – the Allied bombers usually arrived between ten and eleven. Hartmann again: 'Who among the younger generation can really imagine a great city like Munich in total darkness, or theatregoers picking their way through the blacked-out city with the aid of small torches giving off a dim blue light through a narrow slit? All this for the experience of the *Capriccio* première. They risked being caught in a heavy air raid, yet their yearning to hear Strauss's music, their desire to be part of a festive occasion and to experience a world of beauty beyond the dangers of war led them to overcome all these material problems.'

The opera was received with tumultuous enthusiasm and on the following evening Strauss conducted *Daphne*, the last time he would appear at the desk of this theatre. He was no longer so sure that *Capriccio* would remain the province of connoisseurs. 'Will it not really "speak to the heart of the people"?' he asked Krauss, quoting La Roche. The Countess was sung by Ursuleac, Flamand and Olivier by Horst Taubmann and Hans Hotter, La

Roche by Georg Hann, Clairon by Hildegarde Ranczak. A further fifteen performances were given up to 17 June 1943, sometimes with different casts. The new opera was also performed in Hanover, Darmstadt, Bielefeld and Dresden. The first Vienna performance was on 1 March 1944 conducted by Karl Böhm. Two days after the Munich première, Montgomery's Desert Army launched its assault on Rommel's forces at El Alamein. Within five days the German army was in full retreat – the first reverse for the Germans since 1939 except on the Russian Front where their armies were being crushed at Stalingrad. One can hardly imagine an opera more out of key with the world in which it came to birth. But does that matter?

It has been asked many times how Strauss could write such a work when Dachau was only a few miles outside Munich. Let those who ask this glib question ponder Strauss's domestic situation at this period. In 1941 Alice's octogenarian grandmother, Paula Neumann, was in the Prague ghetto, having been stripped of her possessions. Her daughter, Marie von Grab (Alice's mother) was in Lucerne and willing to give a home to her mother. But although the Swiss had granted a visa, the Germans would not let her leave. She stayed in Prague until 1943 when she was sent to the concentration camp at Theresienstadt, where she died. Meanwhile, in the summer of 1942, some of her children were sent from Prague to Theresienstadt. Strauss wrote to the SS in Prague pleading for them, but was ignored. He and Alice thought Theresienstadt was a labour camp where Jews were collected together before being resettled elsewhere. 'We knew nothing of the extermination and wouldn't have believed it', Alice said. 'Now and then we received postcards with a few words of greeting.' Driving between Vienna and Dresden, Strauss stopped his car at Theresienstadt, went to the gate and announced: 'My name is Richard Strauss, I want to see Frau Neumann.' The guards thought he was a madman and told him to clear off. Others of Alice's relatives were taken to the Lodz ghetto and thence to extermination camps. By 1945, the Neumann family had lost twenty-six members in this way.

Another answer is that, even if one does not accept that Strauss was engaged in a policy of 'inward retreat', he was continuing to uphold what he felt to be the true civilised German tradition in the only way he knew. The choice of subject is immaterial – the idea of *Capriccio* had been in his mind for years and the time was ripe for him to realise it fully, irrespective of what was happening outside his study in Garmisch. Would the world have been any different or any better if Strauss had refrained from composing *Capriccio* in 1940–1? No, it would have been worse. He was a reader of Schopenhauer and could well have quoted: 'At the side of world history walks the history of philosophy, of learning and of the arts, without guilt and unspotted by blood.' Or there are the appropriate words of Ernst Jünger: 'Art as the hot-house of past times – one wanders as if in a water garden or in salons where palms bloom. This cannot be blamed, for the horrors of destruction are too powerful, too awful, therefore the will to rescue even a shadow is perfectly understandable.' Strauss's greatest opera needs no further vindication.

The Sextet which opens *Capriccio* had had its first performance five months earlier on 7 May in the house of Baldur von Schirach. The former leader of the Hitler Youth from 1933 to 1940 was appointed Governor of Vienna in August 1940. Always disliked by Martin Bormann, Hitler's deputy since 1941, Schirach aroused Hitler's distrust by his unorthodox cultural policies in Austria. But he was left unmolested. Son of an opera intendant who composed, he determined to restore Vienna to its place as Europe's cultural centre. He offered a kind of asylum there to Strauss, the playwright Gerhart Hauptmann and others. He ignored any boycott of their works emanating from Berlin. Strauss co-operated with him – and the deal was that Alice and her sons should be unmolested while Strauss and Pauline for their part were on a type of parole. Pauline told Schirach: 'When the war has been lost, we will give you refuge in Garmisch, but as for the rest of that gang. . .'. In September 1942 Strauss set one of Goethe's *Zahme Xenien I (Peaceable Epigrams)* as a six-bar song *Xenion* (o.Op. 131) for Hauptmann on his eightieth birthday, and he worked on the first of the series of instrumental works which followed *Capriccio*, a second horn concerto (o.Op. 132), completed in Vienna on 28 November. Writing to Viorica Ursuleac, he said that the third movement, a 6/8 rondo, had 'come out particularly well'.

The concerto was a substitute for the aborted *Danau* tone-poem. He had planned an equivalent of Smetana's *Vltava*, with an introduction describing the castle at Donauschingen, a G major section for the river in full flow, Pauline's theme from *Domestica* for her birthplace of Ingolstadt, a wine festival at Wachau and a finale in which the chorus sang a Weinheber poem about Vienna. He could not find the music for it, but the concerto flowed easily from his pen and he miraculously seemed to recapture the fluency of his youth and the mood of the concerto, also in the key of E flat, he had written for his father sixty years before. It was almost as if he was being reconciled to his father's conservatism. But with the experience of old age he now manipulated the form of the new work with ease and originality. The themes coalesce effortlessly, there are echoes of many facets of his style, the solo part is intensely demanding. And the work is not a note too long. It belongs to a bygone era, a demonstration that Strauss was no longer interested in being a man of his time but a man for all time. As he told Willi Schuh: 'My life's work is at an end with *Capriccio* and the music that I go on scribbling for the benefit of my heirs, exercises for my wrists (as Hermann Bahr used to say of his daily stints of dictation), has no significance whatever from the standpoint of musical history, any more than the scores of all the other symphonists and variationists. I only do it to dispel the boredom of idle hours, since one can't spend the entire day reading Wieland and playing Skat.' The concerto had its first performance at the Salzburg Festival on 11 August 1943. Karl Böhm conducted the Vienna Philharmonic whose principal horn, Gottfried Freiberg, was the soloist.

The benevolence, the lightness of spirit, in the concerto are all the more amazing when one considers the outer circumstances of Strauss's life at this time. Pauline had painful attacks of shingles and her eyes were giving her trouble. He was prone to bouts of influenza. Life at Garmisch was becoming beset with irritants imposed by Nazi bureaucracy. Strauss had to make petty requests to government offices, involving hours of sitting in waiting-rooms until attended to by a jack-in-office who was often rude and usually arrogant to the old man. Most of these requests were concerned with deferment of the call-up of the chauffeur, Theodor Martin, who was indispensable to Strauss's routine, and with obtaining a petrol ration. Once when Martin told Strauss that something he had requested had been refused, it brought on one of Strauss's red-faced rages. Rudolf Hartmann was present and heard Martin try to calm Strauss and to explain that it was the same for all Germans these days. 'I do not want to understand', the old man shouted. 'I must be able to move around for my commitments. Tell that to those

brown blockheads as they drive about in their limousines in their uniforms.'
Martin quietly replied: 'Herr Doktor, I can't say that.'

Strauss spent the winter of 1942–3 in Vienna. He finished the concerto
there. He attended many concerts and operas and listened attentively to new
works. Strauss disliked most contemporary music after 1920 but he listened
to it even though he confessed he did not understand it. But he remarked of
Werner Egk's *Columbus* after its stage performance in 1942 (it was originally
written for radio in 1933): 'He could have been a 20th century Meyerbeer.'
He admired Carl Orff's *Carmina burana*, writing to the composer in
February 1942: 'The purity of style and the unaffected musical language, free
from any posing and any digressions to left or right, make me certain that
you will give the stage a valuable work when you find a subject to suit your
nature. It is only in the theatre that I can see the future development of
which you speak to be possible.'[3] His suggestion of new ways in which opera
might revert to the mimetic origins of theatre was followed up by Orff in
Der Mond and *Die Kluge*. At the end of 1942 Strauss was awarded the City of
Vienna Beethoven Prize and in gratitude in January 1943 he wrote his
Festmusik der Stadt Wien (o.Op. 133) for ten trumpets, seven trombones, two
bass tubas and timpani. It is one of Strauss's most effective ceremonial
pieces. He conducted the first performance on 9 April and eight days later
made a very much shorter version (under two minutes) for the same forces.
Another pleasing task early in January 1943 was to write down a waltz
Schubert had composed in 1826 for the wedding of his friend Leopold
Kupelwieser. Schubert never wrote it down but the tune survived in the
Kupelwieser family, passed down like a folk-song. Manfred Mautner
Markhof's wife Marie was a Kupelwieser and she played it to Strauss. It is a
wistful piece, for apparently Schubert was himself in love with the bride.

Writing for the Vienna state trumpeters stirred memories for Strauss of
his youth when he had composed the *Serenade* for thirteen wind instruments and followed it with the *Suite* commissioned by Bülow. He had often
felt he had miscalculated the balance of woodwind and horns so in February
1943 he wrote a Romance and Minuet for sixteen wind instruments including basset-horn and bass clarinet but only two horns. The following month
he added an *allegro moderato* and in May an *allegro* finale. Composed during
bouts of 'flu, it became the First Sonatina in F (o.Op. 135) and was sub-titled

25 With Alice in Vienna, 1943

'From the Workshop of an Invalid'. It is another remarkable example of fluency, of revisiting the past, of time-travelling to youth from the perspective of age. There is a certain gorgeous garrulity, but the invention generally is fresh and the technique impeccable. Remembering that it was the Dresden Tonkünstlerverein which first performed his *Serenade* in 1882, he awarded them the first performance of the Sonatina, which Karl Elmendorff conducted on 18 June 1944 as part of Strauss's eightieth birthday celebration. But he forbade a broadcast of the work. Writing to Arthur Tröber, director of the Staatskapelle Dresden, from Garmisch on 10 January 1945, Strauss said:

I sincerely regret I cannot agree to your request for a radio broadcast of the Wind Sonatina. I do not want to depart from my intention to keep these last products of my workshop from the broader public before my death. Out of friendship for Elmendorff I have again made an exception of the Second Horn Concerto, but must ask you to forbear with the Sonatina. I have not heard it myself, and so cannot judge whether it would not make a bad impression in the inadequate reproduction of a broadcast. . . I must ask you once and for all to restrict the Sonatina to private performance in the distinguished Tonkünstler-Verein.

The Sonatina was fully scored back at Garmisch in July 1943. Around this time he was consulted by Krauss about the conductor's plan to give six performances of *Die Liebe der Danae* at Salzburg in August 1944 as part of the observation of Strauss's eightieth birthday. Strauss was at first reluctant, but he was secretly anxious to hear the work before he died and he agreed. Krauss obtained materials and fabrics for sets and costumes. If he could not find them in Germany, he went to Italy. He also assembled a cast, with Hotter as Jupiter. (Hotter was warned by Pauline: 'Don't let him write too many high passages into your part. He expects too much. He knows nothing about voices!') Then, in 1943, a fire at the printers in Leipzig destroyed the orchestral parts and they had to be done again.

As the Allies took the war into the heart of Germany, they bombed cities almost nightly. On 2 October 1943, during the raid on Munich, the Nationaltheater was reduced to ruins. Strauss, who had last visited the theatre for a performance of *Die ägyptische Helena*, was devastated. He wrote next day to his widowed sister Johanna: 'I can't write any more today.

I am beside myself.' (In one of the later air raids on Munich, Johanna's home was bombed. She took refuge in the Garmisch villa where she stayed until the end of the war even though she and Pauline had never got on.) To Willi Schuh on 8 October Strauss wrote:

I am disconsolate. Poor Krauss. Years of most valuable cultural effort in ashes. Grief and despair make one talkative. But the destruction of the Munich Court Theatre, where *Tristan* and *Meistersinger* were first performed, where 73 years ago I first heard *Freischütz*, where my dear father was first horn player for 49 years, where, at the end of my life, Krauss fulfilled my dreams as an author with ten new productions, is the greatest catastrophe of my life. There is no consolation and, at my age, no hope.

As the German armies experienced defeats in Russia and North Africa, the Nazi hierarchy had more to worry about than its bargains with an old composer whom they despised. The pressure on Strauss began to be increased. His only work at Garmisch in the summer of 1943 was an orchestration of the song *Ich liebe dich* (Op. 37/2) composed in 1898. In the light of the ever-present threat to Alice and her sons, Liliencron's words acquired a hideous new meaning: 'Our hands may bleed, / Our feet be sore, / Four pitiless walls, / No dog recognises us . . . / Whether you die in need, / My dagger drawn from its sheath, / I will follow you in death.' In the autumn, the district commander (*Kreisleiter*) of Garmisch, named Schiele, called at the Strauss villa to say that there could be no further deferment of the chauffeur Martin's call-up and that Strauss must accommodate evacuees and other homeless. Pauline, unwell, was already an octogenarian and Strauss was seventy-nine. He protested vehemently, annoying Schiele by referring to 'Herr Hitler'. 'Say "the Führer".' 'I call people by their names', Strauss retorted. 'I say Herr Hitler.' Schiele called on the old man to make sacrifices for the people's heroic struggle – 'Even you must think of the front, where thousands of Germans are falling.' Strauss's reply was 'No one needs to die on my account. I did not want the war, it is nothing to do with me.' Schiele was beside himself with rage: 'Other heads than yours have already rolled, Herr Doktor Strauss.' (*Es sind schon andere Köpfe gerollt als der Ihre, Herr Dr Strauss.*)

The encounter left Strauss both angry and fearful. Had he gone too far? He was saved by the intervention of Hans Frank who, as a young lawyer in Munich, had defended Hitler in several actions before 1933 and later became

Bavarian Minister of Justice. But he was never in Hitler's inner circle. He was made Governor of Poland in 1940. His brutal policy and his part in the extermination of thousands of Jews led to the death sentence at Nuremberg, where he pleaded guilty, became a Catholic and attacked Hitler. But in 1942 he had given lectures in German universities in which he called for a return to constitutional rule. This resulted in his being stripped of all his party honours and legal posts, although he was left in Poland. He had been an admirer of Strauss's music since his student days and had first met the composer in Munich in the 1920s. Coincidentally he was in Munich shortly after the incident at Garmisch and happened to telephone Strauss, inviting himself to tea. Strauss saw his chance and told Frank about Schiele's threats. As a result, Martin's call-up was deferred and the matter of billeting evacuees was dropped. But Frank's action did not pass unnoticed. He was not much in favour and had obviously run some risk in defending Strauss (he also had helped Hauptmann and Pfitzner). Hitler's deputy, Martin Bormann, was furious. He circulated a report on Schiele's fracas with Strauss to heads of all official Nazi organisations in which he said: 'Strauss even peremptorily refused the politely voiced plea of the district official to put two of the rooms in the lodge [which contained the porter's dwelling and two rooms with kitchen and bath] at the disposal of the engineers who were working for the armaments industry. The whole question is being widely discussed by the citizens of Garmisch and is being quite properly criticised. The Führer . . . has decided immediately to appropriate the entire lodge . . . and to billet within it evacuees and persons who have suffered from the bombing.' A further result was an edict from party headquarters on 16 January 1944, issued eight days later and signed by Bormann: 'The personal association of our leading men with Dr Richard Strauss shall cease. However, the Führer, to whom Reichsminister Dr Goebbels referred the question, decided today that no obstacles should be put in the way of the performances of his works.' The Nazis' first inclination had been to ban any celebration of Strauss's eightieth birthday, but Furtwängler, although never a particular admirer of Strauss, told Goebbels that he was still regarded as the greatest living composer and that to ignore his birthday would turn him into a martyr.

Strauss thanked Frank for his help by setting (on 3 November) six lines he had written himself beginning *Wer tritt herein so fesch und schlank? Es ist der Freund Minister Frank* (o.Op. 136). It is for unaccompanied voice and can have cost little exertion. He would have thought it well worth the price of inviolability for the Garmisch villa. The six lines are:

Who steps here so smart and slender?
It is our friend, Minister Frank.
Like Lohengrin as an envoy from God,
He saved us from misfortune
Therefore I shout praise and a thousand thanks
To our dear friend Minister Frank.

Strauss would never have contemplated publication of such a trifle. But the manuscript, or a copy of it, surfaced in Los Angeles where, on 1 July 1945, K. Louis Flatau quoted it in an article in the *Los Angeles Times* headed 'Richard Strauss's Shame'. Over twenty years later, on 31 August 1966, Martin Bernstein, professor of music at New York University, wrote to Dr Alfons Ott, joint editor with Franz Trenner (after the death of Dr Erich Müller von Asow) of the Strauss thematic catalogue:

According to an article in the *Los Angeles Times*, July 1, 1945, an American soldier then in Germany gave to Adolph Stern, whose address at that time was 809 S. Mansfield Ave., Los Angeles, a copy of a Strauss letter to Reichsminister Hans Frank containing a song in the latter's honour. While the effusive praising of the brutal Nazi Governor certainly does Strauss no credit, I assume that you will have to include it in the Thematisches Verzeichnis [Thematic Catalogue] and hence am sending you a mechanical copy of the newspaper illustration.

The 1945 article contributed to anti-Strauss feeling in the United States, as will be seen.

Immediately after the Garmisch incident, Strauss returned to Vienna where on 15 November he went to the Burgtheater for the première of Hauptmann's play *Iphigenie in Aulis* and sat with the playwright and Schirach. Two days earlier, in Garmisch, he had completed a peace-offering to Gregor, an epilogue to *Daphne* in the form of a nine-part unaccompanied motet for mixed choir, *An den Baum Daphne* (o.Op. 137). He had been asked in June by Viktor Mainwald, director of the Vienna Opera Chorus Concerts Society, for an unaccompanied work and remembered the abandoned

26 With Baldur von Schirach and Gerhart Hauptmann at the première
of Hauptmann's *Iphigenie in Aulis* in the Burgtheater, Vienna,
15 November 1943

choral finale to *Daphne*. He asked Gregor to re-shape it for him, which he
did after the usual prodding and pinpricks. To the normal double chorus
Strauss added an upper part for the Vienna Boys' Choir. Themes from the
opera are 're-cycled' in this rapturous work, which is shaped as an introduction, several sections and an extended coda in F sharp minor in the second
part of which the voices are wordless as the metamorphosis occurs and a boy
and a solo soprano alternate as did the voice of Daphne and an oboe in the
opera. The ending is not a fade-out, as in the opera, but a full-blooded
return to the work's opening theme – *Geliebter Baum* ('Beloved Tree') – and
a song of love and of eternity. *An den Baum Daphne* ranks with the *Deutsche
Motette* and the Op. 34 *Der Abend* and *Hymne* as supreme examples of
Strauss's *a cappella* writing. The first performance was given in Vienna on 5
January 1947 conducted by Felix Prohaska. This is the place to mention one
more sprig from the *Daphne* tree, the *Daphne Etude* in G (o.Op. 141), composed in grandfatherly affection on 27 February 1945 and dedicated 'to my
dear violin-pupil Christian on his 13th birthday'.

A few days before the Bormann edict was issued, on 9 January 1944, Strauss began another composition for wind instruments which he called *Introduction and Allegro*. Two months later he added an *Allegro con brio*. These were to become, respectively, the last and first movements of a Second Sonatina, but it was not to be completed for another year.

26   Eightieth birthday

One of the first results of Bormann's edict suggests that even Schirach in Vienna momentarily lowered his guard. On an evening when Franz and Alice Strauss left the Jacquingasse house in Vienna to play cards with friends, eight Gestapo men searched their rooms for an hour without telling the servants why. At 2 a.m. they were arrested and taken to Gestapo headquarters where they were questioned but not told what offences they were supposed to have committed. On hearing of this, Strauss tackled Schirach and others and obtained his family's release after two days. It was a frightening experience. How it affected him can be gauged from the tone of a letter he wrote on 3 March to his grandson Christian, one of Strauss's most personal and affecting utterances:

Your twelfth birthday coincides with the grievous event of the almost complete destruction of the beautiful imperial city [Vienna]. One hundred and sixty-five years ago people regarded the Lisbon earthquake as a turning-point in history, ignoring the greater significance of the first performance of Gluck's *Iphigenie in Aulis* which marked the conclusion of a process of musical development that had lasted for 3000 years and called down from heaven the melody of Mozart, revealing the secrets of the human spirit to a greater extent than thinkers have been able to over the course of thousands of years. Likewise when you remember your last birthday you should always think with loathing of the barbarians whose dreadful deeds are reducing our lovely Germany to ruin and ashes. Perhaps you will understand what I am saying as little as your brother does. If you read these sad lines again in 30 years' time, think of your grandfather who exerted himself for nearly 70 years on behalf of German culture and the honour and renown of his fatherland.

The whole family gathered in Vienna in the spring preparing to celebrate Strauss's eightieth birthday on 11 June. A cycle of his operas was to be given from 1 to 15 June. One of his biographers, Roland Tenschert, has left a

```
Reichspropagandaamt Baden        Strassburg, den 8. Juni 1944

Referat : Musik
Aktenzeichen : 1oooo/2

An alle Städtischen Musikbeauftragten des Gaues Baden - Elsass !

     Aus gegebener Veranlassung wird ausdrücklich darauf
hingewiesen, dass die Werke von Richard  S t r a u s s
uneingeschränkt aufgeführt werden können.

                    H e i l   H i t l e r !
                     gez. Müllenberg
                       Referent        Beglaubigt :


                                       Angestellte.
```

27 A Nazi 'Diktat' issued in Strassburg for Strauss's eightieth birthday,
    11 June 1944:

To all municipal music commissioners in the state of Baden-Alsace! It is
agreed for this particular occasion that the works of Richard Strauss can be
performed without restriction.

delightful picture of calling on Strauss and Pauline for tea in the garden on
1 June. A hose was watering the lawn while they ate. Pauline called to the
maid: 'Anna, tell them to put the hose somewhere else.' 'In other words, I
must do it', Anna replied. Strauss explained that this was 'the famous Anna
of *Intermezzo*. She has been with us for 38 years [since she was thirteen].'
Tenschert commented 'That's rare nowadays.' 'Yes', said Strauss, 'and my
wife can be a little irritable!' Later Tenschert was a witness of negotiations
with Anna about going to the opera in the car. Anna assumed she would go
with Strauss and Pauline, but he had assumed the grandchildren would
accompany him. Anna began to sulk. 'No, no', Strauss conceded, 'you come
along, the boys can walk.'[1]

On 8 June – two days after the Allied invasion of Europe on D-day – there
was a performance of *Josephs Legende* – 'still somewhat underrated' was its

composer's verdict. But he added: 'I'm so music-starved in Garmisch even my own works please me!' On the 9th and 10th there were rehearsals for the Vienna Philharmonic's concert for the birthday itself, while at 1 p.m. on the 10th the orchestra gave a 'breakfast' at the Hotel Bristol in Strauss's honour at which the guests included the young soprano Irmgard Seefried, who was to sing the Composer in *Ariadne auf Naxos*. It was here that Pauline caused some surprised comment by raising her glass to the violinist Wolfgang Schneiderhan and saying: 'Well, when are we going to America?' The concert on the 11th began in the Grosser Musikvereinssaal at 11.30 a.m. Karl Böhm conducted the Prelude to Act 1 of *Die Meistersinger*, the chairman of the orchestra made a speech, and Böhm conducted the *Rosenkavalier* waltzes after which he presented Strauss with a baton of ebony and ivory set with diamonds (worth 80,000 Reichsmarks) donated by the City of Vienna. (Schirach had already decided to ignore Bormann's decree that Strauss the man should not be honoured.) Strauss conducted *Till Eulenspiegel* with it, but said to Böhm in the interval: 'It's damned heavy, I shouldn't like to conduct *Götterdämmerung* with it. Give me another for the *Domestica*.'[2]

That evening the family went to the State Opera, where Böhm conducted *Ariadne auf Naxos* with Seefried as the Composer, Maria Reining as Ariadne, Max Lorenz as Bacchus and Alda Noni as Zerbinetta. (This great performance was broadcast and has been issued on LP and CD.) At the end of the evening, Strauss presented Böhm with a score of *Ariadne* and a sketchbook containing the Prelude and Final Scene. The audience was not allowed to leave the opera house until Schirach had departed. Siegfried Melchinger, as quoted by Ernst Krause, was 'hemmed in by a solid wall of people behind the barrier blocking the doorway. Once I turned round and saw a tall man standing behind me, holding a young boy by each hand. It was Richard Strauss with his grandsons.'[3] During the next four days Strauss recorded several of his own works with the Philharmonic – the *Bourgeois gentilhomme* suite and *Don Juan* on 12 June, *Also sprach Zarathustra* and *Tod und Verklärung* on the 13th, *Till Eulenspiegel* and *Ein Heldenleben* on the 15th. (He had recorded *Symphonia Domestica* with the Vienna Philharmonic the previous February.) These have all been reissued on CDs. In addition, on the evening of 12 June he attended a chamber concert at which his early Piano Quartet was played. The next evening he went to the Opera for the start of

Die Frau ohne Schatten, left for the Konzerthaus to hear a congratulatory address by Gregor and returned to the Opera! On the evening of the 14th he heard Böhm conduct *Ein Heldenleben*. (He told Tenschert he disapproved of the conductor's *ritardandi* in the tone-poem – 'I thought it would never end' – and in *Die Frau ohne Schatten*.) It was an incredible schedule for an octogenarian. And he had found time on 5 June to compose (or complete) a suite from *Capriccio*, with concert ending, for harpsichord. This comprised the three ballet movements – *Passepied, Gigue, Gavotte*. The suite was written for and dedicated to Isolde Ahlgrimm, who had played the harpsichord in the first Vienna performance of *Capriccio* on 1 March 1944. Strauss was so pleased with her performance that he asked her to play the ballet music in her recitals. She thought it was difficult enough with the two string players let alone without them. 'You'll manage', Strauss replied. In April she asked him for a concert ending and he asked if she would like a loud or soft coda. She received a loud one. She gave the first performance in Vienna on 7 November 1946.

With the birthday celebrations behind him, Strauss now looked forward to the Salzburg première of *Die Liebe der Danae* planned for August. But the problems of its production continued. Some of the scenery and costume material had been destroyed in air raids on Munich in the early part of the summer. Krauss wrote to Strauss on 28 June: 'The artists' work for the three sets of Act 3 was done in Prague and arrived on schedule last week. The entire wardrobe department, who had to cease work in Munich because there were so many days without electricity or light, moved into temporary workshops in Salzburg last week, bringing with them all the costumes that had been started and the fabrics for the rest.' It was a repetition of the days in Munich before *Capriccio*. Everyone connected with the première was totally dedicated to it. The world of Jupiter, Midas and Danae was all that mattered. But the real world could not be ignored. The Allies were advancing deep into France: the fighting was fierce. The Red Army was sweeping through Poland towards Warsaw. On 20 July a bomb exploded in Hitler's headquarters in East Prussia, killing three officers but not the Führer.

The original Salzburg programme was for three operas, *Così fan tutte, Die Zauberflöte* and the première of *Die Liebe der Danae* on 5 August. Krauss informed Strauss that *Danae* had been postponed until 15 August, with a dress rehearsal two days earlier. On 29 July Goebbels, having earlier in the month ordered the closure of all festivals in Germany so that there could be concentration on 'total war', specifically decreed cancellation of the Salzburg 'Theatre and Music Summer', as he called it. The *Gauleiter* of Salzburg, Dr Gustav Scheel, made a special appeal to Goebbels's Propaganda Ministry to allow the Strauss première to proceed. The Ministry allowed only a dress rehearsal of *Danae* on 16 August and a concert by the Berlin Philharmonic under Furtwängler (Bruckner's Eighth Symphony). Strauss on 6 August wrote from Garmisch to Dr Heinz Drewes, the Culture Minister, asking him to thank Goebbels for giving him 'the joy' of hearing his work. He travelled next day to Salzburg to attend the rehearsals. His mood throughout the ten days he spent there was sombre and gloomy: he knew this would be his last opera première, he had left Pauline at home and he was only too aware of the circumstances surrounding the occasion.

Rudolf Hartmann, who produced the opera, memorably described an occurrence at one of the last orchestral rehearsals:

Towards the end of the second scene [Act 3] Strauss stood up and went down to the front row of the stalls. His unmistakable head stood out in lonely silhouette against the light rising from the pit. The Viennese were playing the wonderful interlude before the last scene ('Jupiter's renunciation', Strauss once called it) with an unsurpassably beautiful sound. Quite immobile, totally oblivious to all else, he stood listening.

Hartmann then described how, as the last scene progressed, all present,

profoundly moved and stirred to our depths, sensed the almost physical presence of our divinity, art. . . Several moments of profound silence followed after the last notes died away. . . Krauss spoke a few sentences outlining the significance of these last days in Salzburg. Strauss looked over the rail of the pit, raised his hands in a gesture of gratitude and spoke to the orchestra in a voice choked with tears: 'Perhaps we shall meet again in a better world'. He was unable to say any more. . . Silent and deeply moved, everyone present remained still as he left the auditorium, carefully guided by myself.

Outside the Festspielhaus, Strauss took Hartmann's arm and said: 'Come on, let's go round by my beloved Mozart!'

After the performance itself on the 16th, Strauss was called on to the stage many times, but made no speech. In the artists' room he studied the full score and pointing heavenwards remarked: 'When I make my way up there, I hope I'll be forgiven if I bring this along too.' On 25 September he wrote a long letter – a 'factual report' – to Willi Schuh describing the performance enthusiastically and giving a *critique* of his own music:

The beginning: very lively, supple choral scenes in grey-brown colouring, leading with strong contrast to the Magic Gold with Jupiter's shining trumpet and trombone. . . Very happy duet for the two women flowing into the highly original 5-in-a-bar march-like entrance of the four queens and their consorts in which the oscillating rhythm of the horns hardly allows the listener to come to his senses until the appearance of the ship – all very well constructed dramatically and with nice contrast, fresh in tempo and expression. Then something of a recession after Midas's entry – perhaps the scene is necessary for the action and as an exposition of new themes later to become important, but with the exception of the passage where the gold dress is introduced, I myself did not feel very pleased with it. Perhaps the rather dry text was to blame, Hofmannsthal would most probably have given me a more exciting basis. The end of the act, almost contrary to my worst fears, once again works very well.

He regarded the third act as among the best music he had ever written ('something for a 75-year-old to be really proud of') particularly the orchestral prelude and the duet between Danae and Jupiter. Writing to the opera's dedicatee, Heinz Tietjen, who had not been allowed to attend the performances, Strauss described the third act as 'really moving, my last acknowledgment to Greece, and the final meeting of German music with the Grecian spirit'.

As even Strauss admitted, the opera has its weak passages, but it is a far better work than many commentators have conceded. The treatment of the many themes and motifs is amazingly inventive, the orchestral colours glow and shine – with Greek gold and Mediterranean sunlight. There is even a Kurt Weill-ish touch in the opening scene of the creditors and the *Belle Hélène* operetta style, especially in the music for the four queens, is more pronounced than in *Die ägyptische Helena*. But the mood is ambivalent throughout and changes in Act 3 to melancholic resignation where Jupiter-Strauss becomes a benevolent Wotan and Danae-Pauline recalls the end of *Intermezzo*. Also in this scene one cannot but be aware of Strauss's depression about the state of Germany's soul and that he was delivering another coded message. *Die Liebe der Danae* does not deserve its neglect. Its third act alone lifts it into the category of first-rank Strauss.

What happened next? When Strauss left Salzburg he promised the administrators of the festival that they could have the première for 1945. 'But', as he wrote on 8 December 1946 in his private *History of the opera Die Liebe der Danae*, 'they did not even take advantage of this offer for the 1946 festival.' Late in 1945 the Zürich Stadttheater, Amsterdam Opera and Stockholm Opera asked Strauss for the première. He considered the possibility of simultaneous premières at all three, but abandoned the idea because of 'the major technical difficulties involved' (finding three casts at that date being not the least!). 'In the meantime Schmid-Bloss, director at Zürich, repeatedly implored me to let the Stadttheater there have the première, but I could not make up my mind. The memory of the wonderful dress rehearsal at Salzburg renewed my desire to leave the performance to the administration of the Salzburg Festival in the same form and with the same director as for the dress rehearsal and I let Clemens Krauss know this.' But he had second thoughts and returned to his resolve that the première should be delayed until at least two years after the end of the war 'when the festival is restored to its previous style... I promise that until such a time I will not give the première to any other theatre without reaching an understanding with Salzburg.' To Krauss he was emphatic: 'The *Danae* première postponed to the Greek Calends. Perhaps in five or ten years the new Vienna Opera can open with it. Mercury can then personally deliver my greetings telegram.' The official première was at the 1952 Salzburg Festival on 14 August. Krauss conducted four performances; Jupiter was sung by Paul Schöffler and Danae by Anneliese Kupper. It has never been performed there since.

27   Metamorphosen

After the *Danae* rehearsal in August 1944, Strauss returned to Garmisch. He wrote to Hartmann: 'Since the 1st September my life is at an end; it would have been best if the great geniuses of Olympus had called me to them on the 17th August!' The significance of 1 September was that it was the day Goebbels closed all theatres and opera houses. Paris was already liberated; the Russian advance was relentless. The Germans had lost the war, even if they would not yet admit it. It occurred to Strauss that now, perhaps, the Nazis would no longer care about any bargains they might have made with him and would move against Alice and the children and indeed against Franz, for they were all *Mischlinge 1. Klasse* (half-breeds, first class). As usual in moments of despair, he turned to Goethe. He re-read the whole of Goethe, which he possessed in the Propyläen edition, except for the *Farbenlehre*. 'I am reading him as he developed and as he finally became, not tasting here and there', he told a visitor. 'Now that I am old myself I will be young again with Goethe and then once again old with him – in his way, with his eyes. For he was a man of the eye – he saw what I heard.' He found two of the *Zahme Xenien* and copied them into one of his pocket sketchbooks. They read (with a free translation):

Niemand wird sich selber kennen   No one can really know himself,
Sich von seinem Selbst-Ich trennen;   detach himself from his inner being
Doch probier'er jeden Tag   [lit. self-I]; yet he must daily put to
Was nach aussen endlich, klar,   the test what is objectively finally clear:
Was er ist und was er war   What he is and what he was, what he
Was er kann und was er mag.   can and what he may.

Wie's aber in der Welt zugeht,   But what goes on in the world, no one
Eigentlich niemand recht versteht,   really understands rightly, and also up to
Und auch bis auf den heutigen Tag   the present day no one gladly wishes

Niemand gerne verstehen mag.	to understand it. Conduct yourself with
Gehabe du dich mit Verstand.	discernment, just as the day offers itself
Wie dir eben der Tag zur Hand;	to you; always think: 'It's gone all
Denk immer: 'Ist's gegangen bis jetzt,	right till now, so it may well go
So wird es auch wohl gehen zuletzt.'	on to the end.'

Strauss set the first poem, probably for male voice choir, in August 1944. At that moment he was asked for a work for strings by the Swiss musician and philanthropist Paul Sacher for Sacher's Zürich Collegium Musicum. The commission was arranged at a meeting between Sacher, Karl Böhm and Willi Schuh. It seems certain that Strauss converted the Goethe setting into the Sacher commission on which he worked through August and September. He wrote to Böhm on 30 September: 'I have been working for some time . . . on an Adagio for some 11 solo strings, which will probably develop into an Allegro so that I do not drag it out too long in Brucknerian fashion.'[1] The work progressed well until early October when he encountered an impasse and laid it aside. He and Pauline were at Garmisch while Franz and Alice looked after the Vienna house. Thus it was that there was no family celebration of the golden wedding on 10 September. Strauss wrote to Franz and Alice on the 9th:

We shall celebrate with tears and sorrow after weeks of worry and troubles. Early on Tuesday our poor dear Anna left us (probably for ever!). Mama gave her a last farewell kiss in the kitchen at 5 in the morning, has cried every day since then and I usually join in and weep too. . . So far as we know she is now with her sister in Windsheim because there was still no bed free in the hospital in Erlangen. Neumaier [doctor] gave her another jab on Sunday which gave her so much relief that on Monday she was able to hand over the entire housekeeping to Mama, keys and all, which was very moving. We have had no news since then, but Neumaier holds out scarcely any hope. The poor loyal soul, fifty-one years old, we are inconsolable. For poor Mama it was a catastrophe.

Anna Glossner died of cancer two months later. She was succeeded by Anni Nitzl and her sister Resi.

With the Sacher commission at a standstill, Strauss found other projects to occupy him. The first seems incredible. He wrote to his grandson Richard on 3 October: 'The day before yesterday I began to make a new copy of the score of *Eulenspiegel*. It is more sensible than continuing to turn out senile new works. *Don Juan* and *Tod und Verklärung* shall follow and ought to make a valuable Christmas present for you all. The work is giving me a lot of fun and at least it stops me thinking about other things, now that I don't have even an occasional game of Skat to divert me and poor Mama needs a lot of comforting.' It is touching to think of the octogenarian composer copying out his youthful masterpieces so that they could be sold by his grandsons in a financial emergency. All Strauss's autographs are extraordinarily neat – a conductor could safely use one of his full scores for a performance.

To Heinz Tietjen, he wrote on 25 November:

This 16 August, with your Bayreuth *Meistersinger*, marked the last flickering of the flame of German operatic culture. Since 1 September the flower of German music, which had bloomed for 200 years, has been withering away, its spirit has been caught up in the machine, and its crowning glory, German opera, cut off for ever. Most of its homes are reduced to rubble and ashes, and some of those not destroyed are already degraded as cinemas (Wien Städtische Oper). My life's work is in ruins. I shall never again hear my operas, which have attained a high level of artistic maturity in the past decades and which I have been privileged to see performed with a rare degree of perfection by fine artistic ensembles, great conductors and producers, and masterly orchestras. . . In poor Munich the house in which I was born by the lovely Court Church of St Michael has been bombed [17 December 1944]. In short, my life is at an end, and I can only wait with resignation until my blessed namesake calls me to him in the waltz heaven. During the past weeks, in order to pass the time without brooding on the worries and tribulations of these days, I have carried out a task which I long had in mind: I have taken the *Rosenkavalier* Waltzes, which have been so unjustly vulgarised and whose poor arrangement by [Otto] Singer always displeased me, and by adding the Introduction to the opera I have made a new piece for full orchestra with a longer, brilliant conclusion. It is to be my farewell to this beautiful world.

The *Einleitung und Walzer aus Der Rosenkavalier, I and II Akt* had been finished in short score on 26 October and in full score on 15 November.

Around this time, too, he returned to the waltz he had composed in 1939 for the suppressed film about Munich. He changed the sub-title to *Gedächtniswalzer* (*Memorial Waltz*) (o.Op. 140) and inserted a new middle section in the minor key, again using themes from *Feuersnot*. The reference to fire now had a tragically topical significance. The short score was finished on 23 January 1945, the full on 24 February. He did not offer the work for performance and it was not heard until 31 March 1951, in Vienna. It was in January 1945, too, that Strauss wrote to Joseph Gregor to tell him he had had a dream in which he had breakfasted with Hofmannsthal who said: 'I have a one-act opera text for you. Very delicate, with nymphs.' He had vainly searched Greek mythology for an explanation. So would Gregor like to sketch a masque-like ballet-pantomime involving Diana and Endymion, with Venus and Adonis too. Gregor got to work but Strauss, as usual, found his efforts impossible. Go and look at some Titians, Strauss advised. In October 1946 Strauss asked the wretched librettist to show the libretto to Clemens Krauss. Some sketches for the music exist, but *Die Rache der Aphrodite* was abandoned by the start of 1947.

The Allied bombers were reaching Vienna almost nightly in 1944. Strauss urged his family to return to Garmisch. They arrived in December 1944. Franz worked in the local hospital. Richard, now seventeen, stayed in Vienna where he was sent to work at the factory at Schwechat owned by Manfred Mautner Markhof. (The house in Jacquingasse was now occupied by the exiled Serbian government.) No sooner had she returned to Garmisch than an order for the arrest of Alice arrived at the local Gestapo office. She was warned by the sister of the tenor Franz Klarwein. Friends suggested she should try to reach Switzerland through the Bregenz forest but she refused. A certain Herr Haas who worked in the district office ensured that the warrant was never served. Food and fuel were now scarce in Garmisch, as everywhere else. In the cold winter Pauline spent months in bed with a succession of ailments, from pneumonia to infection of her eyes. It was in these circumstances that Strauss returned to his sketches for the Sacher work for strings, working on them intensively from late January until the short score was completed on 8 March 1945. He then wrote another short score, completing it on 31 March, which he entitled *Andante* for two violins, two violas, two cellos and double bass. This septet version was discovered in Switzerland, bought by the Bavarian State Library in Munich, and first performed in Garmisch in 1994. Just why he wrote this version is unclear, since on 13 March he had already begun to write out the full score of the version for twenty-three solo strings which we now know as

Metamorphosen, although this title was still not in existence. The Septet version has a different modulation in the closing bars. The work was completed on 12 April, for ten violins, five each of violas and cellos and three double basses.

It is significant that Strauss began work on the full score the day after the destruction of the Vienna State Opera House. While working on the short score in January and February, he had received news of the destruction of the Lindenoper in Berlin and of Dresden State Opera House. To Joseph Gregor he wrote on 2 March: 'I am inconsolable. The Goethe House [Frankfurt], the most sacred place on earth, destroyed! My lovely Dresden – Weimar – Munich, all gone!'

Strauss's comments in his private diary during the last months of the Third Reich reveal the extent of his disillusionment: 'In 1939 I wrote: The Mark of Brandenburg has been returned to the Reich. In the meantime, the puffed-up frog Prussia, also known as Greater Germany, has been burst and Germany's political role is played out. The parallel with the destruction of Athens by Sulla is incredible. I have read today that even Luther said "Germany is a thing of the past!" He had not seen the ruins of modern Germany.' Later: 'On 12 March the glorious Vienna Opera became one more victim of the bombs. But from 1 May onwards the most terrible period of human history came to an end, the twelve-year reign of bestiality, ignorance and anti-culture under the greatest criminals, during which Germany's 2000 years of cultural evolution met its doom and irreplaceable monuments of architecture and works of art were destroyed by a criminal soldiery. Accursed be technology!' Strauss's sister Johanna was with him when the end of the war in Europe was announced and a recording of the *Eroica* Symphony was played. 'And *yet* Beethoven was a German', he said.

How forcibly the *Eroica* must have struck him, for the main theme of *Metamorphosen* (o.Op. 142) is a reminiscence of that symphony's funeral march. This was an unconscious quotation on Strauss's part – it 'escaped from my pen', he maintained. He quoted Beethoven's theme note for note in the bass at the end of the work and wrote 'In Memoriam' beneath the notes. *Metamorphosen* is an elegy for German culture as exemplified by the nineteenth-century composers and Strauss himself. A long *adagio* with a faster middle section, it is a complex texture of rich polyphony, marvellously written for the strings. There seem to be allusions to Wagner (*Tristan*) and Brahms, but nothing is directly quoted. The work is conceived in a great arch of melody, the themes undergoing symphonic development. It is the most deeply felt, the most spiritual, of Strauss's works, a masterpiece of the art of composition and at the same time an emotional catharsis, a confession and an atonement. The title does not refer to the musical structure, for there is no metamorphosis of themes in the way of variations; it was taken from Goethe, who used the term in old age when he contemplated works which had occupied his mind for a long period of time and compared them with the evolution of plant life, with seed growing into full flower, dying and reverting to seed.

When the score was completed Strauss wrote to Sacher: 'I now have finished *Metamorphosen*, study for 23 solo strings, *Adagio-Allegro-Adagio*, ca. 30 minutes.' He planned to send it to the Red Cross to be photographed and 'performed whenever convenient'. He did not send it, but took it with him to Switzerland in October 1945 when he handed it to Willi Schuh. Sacher conducted the first performance in Zürich on 25 January 1946. Strauss attended the final rehearsal the previous evening. He took the baton from Sacher, conducted magnificently, thanked the players and left. He did not attend the performance the following evening. This fact alone tells us how personal the work was to Strauss and how painful were the emotions enshrined in it.

28   'I am Richard Strauss . . .'

Garmisch, April 1945. Strauss's grandson Richard had been refused permission to leave Vienna, which was likely to fall to the Red Army. But he left on his bicycle, riding at night, and reached Garmisch a week later. A family with two children was billeted in the porter's lodge. Strauss's sister Johanna was in the villa. On the 30th, the day Hitler committed suicide, the American Army entered Garmisch. Jeeps drove up the drive of Zöppritzstrasse 42. The American soldiers were commandeering villas for their use and giving the residents fifteen minutes to leave. No. 42 looked ideal for their headquarters. Strauss had just risen, Pauline was ill and stayed in bed. Anni and grandson Richard told Strauss what was happening. Alice began to pack up valuables and some food. Strauss insisted on going to the front door. He said to the officer, Milton Weiss, 'I am Richard Strauss, the composer of *Rosenkavalier* and *Salome*.' Weiss had at once recognised him and ordered his men to show respect. Strauss invited them in, showed them his Morgantown freedom scroll, offered them wine and something to eat. Weiss recalled in 1997: 'Strauss told me at once that his son was married to a Jewish woman and that he had protected his grandchildren. . . I directed my sergeant to take over another house.'[1] An 'Off Limits' sign was erected to prevent any further attempt at requisitioning. In the following weeks many American soldiers were welcomed to the villa and shown round and given autographs. Some of them pointed to a bust of Beethoven and asked 'Who's that guy?' 'If they ask once more', Strauss told Alice, 'tell them it's Hitler's father.'

One of the visitors was John de Lancie, oboist in the Pittsburgh Symphony Orchestra and later to be director of the Curtis Institute, Philadelphia. He was shocked by the conditions in which Strauss was living: little to eat, no soap, no fuel. He and his G.I. friends offered help. De Lancie and Strauss spoke together (in French) about music, literature and world affairs. The American plucked up courage to ask if Strauss had ever thought of writing something for oboe. 'No', was the curt reply and the matter was dropped. But a seed had been sown. A few weeks later he began to sketch a concerto and completed the short score on 14 September.

Two other visitors were less friendly. Two German-speaking young men arrived at the villa saying they were journalists. One was 'Mr Brown', the other Curt Riess. Strauss received them 'most heartily', not realising that 'Mr Brown' was Klaus Mann (son of Thomas Mann) who was writing for the American Army newspaper *Stars and Stripes*. His hostile article about his visit to Garmisch was widely circulated and did more than almost anything else to create the picture of a Nazi Strauss. 'He was communicative and without shame', Mann wrote. 'Shame is not the point. His naiveté, his wicked, completely amoral egotism could be, almost, disarming. . . Frightening is the word. An artist of such sensitivity yet silent when it comes to questions of conscience. . . A great man yet without greatness. I cannot but be frightened of such a phenomenon and find it somewhat distasteful.'

Strauss, as has already been said, felt he had nothing for which to apologise and thought it beneath his dignity to do so. His Olympian detachment obviously jarred on Klaus Mann. He spoke of his annoyance over Bormann's attempt to billet people in the villa, about the affair of Stefan Zweig, about his fears for his opera royalties. He said that he was grateful for help from Hans Frank and Schirach. Mann reserved his most vitriolic invective for Alice. 'I was not allowed to go hunting, I was even prohibited from riding', she apparently said at one point, although the actual context is left vague. 'I swear those were her actual words', Mann wrote. 'There were the Nuremberg racial laws, there was Auschwitz . . . the most infamous government in the world reduced Jews to the level of hunted beasts, yet the daughter-in-law of Richard Strauss complains because she was not allowed to go hunting.' When the article appeared, Strauss wrote an angry letter to Thomas Mann, but did not send it. Perhaps he realised that the best reply was *Metamorphosen*. It is impossible to know now how accurate the article is and whether it truly reflected the mood of the interview. But one would read it with less disdain if Mann had had the guts and the decency to reveal his identity.

28 Idea for an oboe concerto: talking to John de Lancie, Garmisch, 1945

When *Metamorphosen* was finished, Strauss in June added two more movements to the second wind Sonatina (o.Op. 143) he had begun in the early part of 1944. He completed it on 22 June and subtitled it 'Merry Workshop', adding at the end of the score 'To the Manes of the divine Mozart at the end of a life full of thankfulness' [*Der Manen des göttlichen Mozart am Ende eines dankerfüllten Lebens.* Richard Strauss]. It had grown into a big score, forty minutes in duration, and apart from its slow, quiet introduction, it bubbles with wit, gaiety and Straussian reminiscences. In particular, the two middle movements, composed last, suggest that Strauss was celebrating the weight that had been lifted from his life with the end of the Third Reich. Only in the outer movements does one detect an elegiac vein running through the endlessly proliferating counterpoint. Undoubtedly writing the middle movements in June, a graceful *andantino* and a Mozartian minuet, suggested to him that it might be worth following up John de Lancie's suggestion. He wrote to Schuh on 6 July: 'In the studio of my old age, a concerto for oboe and small orchestra is being "concocted". The idea for this was given to me by an oboe player from Chicago.' Five autograph scores for the concerto exist. A sketchbook which was lost until 1980 and is now in the Austrian National Library is of special interest. It belongs between the first sketches and the short score. Entire passages correspond with the final version but are not arranged in their ultimate sequence – almost as if thrown together haphazardly.

Musically, therefore, 1945 showed Strauss returning to rich activity after the relatively fallow year of 1944. In April, after completing *Metamorphosen*, his thoughts turned to the future of German operatic life. On the 27th he wrote to Karl Böhm to give him 'a kind of testament; my artistic legacy in writing at least'. There followed a memorandum 'which I wrote down some time ago [in a letter to Roland Tenschert on 1 June 1944] on the significance of opera and the future I hope it has in Vienna, the cultural centre of Europe'. He urged two theatres of different sizes, one for 'serious opera', the other for lighter fare, in cities such as Vienna, Berlin, Munich, Hamburg and Dresden. In the larger house there should be 'a quasi-permanent exhibition of the greatest works of operatic literature in first-class productions with constant rehearsals to maintain standards'.

He then added a list of the works to be performed in this 'opera museum'. They should include five by Gluck, five by Mozart (the da Ponte works, *Die Zauberflöte*, and *Idomeneo* arr. Strauss), *Fidelio*, three Weber, two Berlioz (*Les Troyens* and *Benvenuto Cellini*), *Carmen*, three Verdi (*Aida*, *Simon Boccanegra* and *Falstaff*), all Wagner from *Rienzi* to *Götterdämmerung*, and eight heavyweights of his own plus *Josephs Legende*. He then gave a selection of operas by forty-two composers suitable for the second theatre. There are some eccentric surprises here – five by Auber, two by Chabrier, Dvořák's *Jacobin*, Dittersdorf's *Doktor und Apotheker*, two by Ritter, and works by Leo Blech, Kienzl and Méhul. *Die Fledermaus* is specified as 'in the original!'.

29 A good joke: snapped by John de Lancie, Garmisch, 1945

The four Verdi are *Rigoletto*, *La traviata*, *Il trovatore* and *Un ballo in maschera*. Seven of his own are included, making him the only composer to be represented by his complete operatic output! He thought that 'since in many earlier operas which are unbearable for us today such as *Macbeth*, *Luisa Miller*, *Vespri Siciliani*, there are parts of genius, I recommend a kind of pot-pourri of single scenes, for example Lady Macbeth's mad scene . . . I condemn *Otello* entirely, as I do all libretti from classical dramas distorted into opera libretti like Gounod's *Faust*, Rossini's *Tell*, Verdi's *Don Carlos*! They do not belong on the German stage.' Well, great geniuses can have a blinkered outlook – and one wonders where that final condemnation left *Elektra*![2]

29   The exile

The prospect of the 1945–6 winter in Garmisch was grim. There was no coal for heating. Food and medicine were short. For Strauss there were financial worries. His royalties were appropriated by the Allied Property Control. And because of his presidency of the Reich Music Chamber, he was told he would have to face a tribunal which would decide the extent of his guilt (what became known as 'deNazification') – he was automatically categorised as 'Class I – Guilty'. Each year he was accustomed to go for a cure at a Swiss spa and his applications for permission to leave Germany had been refused by the Nazis in 1943 and 1944. Now his application was blocked by American bureaucracy, but after American and Swiss friends had given certain guarantees, he and Pauline, who was still far from well, were given permission to live in Switzerland and they departed in early October.

Strauss took with him the newly-copied scores of four tone-poems, the manuscripts of the sonatinas, the Munich waltz, the *Rosenkavalier* waltz suite, *An den Baum Daphne, Die Göttin im Putzzimmer*, the second horn concerto and the unfinished oboe concerto. All were put into the safe of the Hotel Verenahof in Baden as securities against payment of the bill. He gave the French the manuscript of *Eine Alpensinfonie*, which is now in the Bibliothèque Nationale, in gratitude for help they gave to Alice when she took some of his scores to the Hämmerle family in Dornbirn. He gave the manuscripts of his two Weinheber songs – *Sankt Michael* and *Blick vom oberen Belvedere* – to the French commandant in Saxony, Comte d'Audibert, and his aide Major Moreau for their assistance on the journey to Baden. (Both scores are now in the Austrian National Library.) They arrived there on 11 October and were met by Schuh.

In his diary Strauss called the hotel 'an earthly paradise'. They had good rooms and good food. 'For us two sad Germans, who have lived only for art, and have fled from chaos, misery, slavery and the shortage of coal, this is heaven; driven by the destruction of our poor ravaged homeland to leave our dear children and grandchildren and the beautiful things we have owned for decades, to come far away from the ruins of our burnt-out theatres and other seats of the Muses – we can pass the rest of our days in peace and quiet, in the company of good people and friends.' A fortnight later, on 25 October, he finished the oboe concerto. One of his benefactors at this time, Werner Reinhart of Winterthur, was rewarded with the dedication of the Second Sonatina and was given the autograph score.

Another benefactor arrived in December 1945 in the person of Ernst Roth, an Austrian once employed in Vienna by Universal Edition but who had gone to London and become manager of Boosey & Hawkes. Unknown to Strauss, Boosey's had acquired the rights to his works from Otto Fürstner in 1942. Roth promised to help Strauss, but a £20,000 offer from Sir Alexander Korda for the film rights to *Salome* and *Der Rosenkavalier* was rejected because of the lack of a guarantee that there would be no cuts or changes. It was at this point that the manager of the Verenahof became worried and had the scores in his safe valued by the Swiss composer Heinrich Sutermeister. Strauss was not amused.

The 'earthly paradise' could not last. His presence in Switzerland was attacked in the Basle *National Zeitung*. A Swiss soprano protested at the guest appearance of Maria Cebotari in *Arabella* in Zürich because she had sung in Germany during the war. 'Another glorious achievement of the Nazi régime', Strauss wrote in his diary on 5 January 1946, 'that artists are no longer judged by their abilities but by what Americans think of their political opinions.' Later in the year, when a planned performance of *Ariadne auf Naxos* in Zürich was abandoned, he wrote to Schuh: 'Why? Because I am a German? Wagner is another German. Lehár is Hungarian. The Hungarians also shot at the Russians and two of his operettas are being performed. The Italians fired on the Allies and they're doing three operas by Verdi. Must all the chauvinistic German-hatred of the entire Swiss nation come down on my head alone?'[1]

But at least 1946 had begun with a series of first performances – of *Metamorphosen* in Zürich on 25 January, of the Oboe Concerto on 26 February in Zürich (Marcel Saillet the soloist, Volkmar Andreae conduct-

30 Discussing *Metamorphosen* with Willi Schuh (left) and Paul Sacher in
Zürich, 1945

ing) and the Second Sonatina in Winterthur on 25 March, conducted by
Hermann Scherchen. The Oboe Concerto quickly became a favourite with
oboists even though the soloist's first entry involves fifty-six bars of unin-
terrupted playing. It is one of those works which sound as if they had always
existed and had come fully formed into the creator's mind. The themes flow
rhapsodically, entwined with each other. The long cantabile melody belongs
to another age of sublime beauty. There are the harmonic sideslips so typical
of Strauss and a gentle rhythmical phrase which binds the three movements
together. Before the concerto was published Strauss extended the coda of
the finale on 1 February 1948. Those who wish to hear the original ending
can hear it on a recording made by Léon Goossens in 1947.

Despite these performances, Strauss became increasingly bitter and
depressed. His morale was not helped by his having no big work in hand.
But he kept up his voluminous correspondence. Among the most touching
of his letters at this time are those to his grandsons. In one to Richard on 20

January 1946, he wrote: 'Art is the finest gift of God that exalts over all earthly suffering and our beloved music is the most delightful. Your grandfather has worked conscientiously for over sixty years and you and your dear brother will share in this inheritance only if you pursue and persist in this work. Your letter tells me you are on the right track and my blessings accompany you as long as life is given me.'[2] Richard Jr., in a contribution to Kurt Wilhelm's superb 'personal portrait' of Strauss, has described how keen the old man was to educate the two boys in the humanities – educated Europeans must know Latin and Greek, read Goethe and Wieland and Homer and Sophocles (in the original). Although he told the boys stories (mainly opera plots) and occasionally played football with them, his main concern was that they should work on serious topics. His own life was entirely dedicated to his work except for card-playing and he expected others to be similarly diligent, although he once admitted that he always demanded or expected too much from other people.

At some time in 1946 Strauss read the poem *Im Abendrot* (*In the Sunset*) by Eichendorff. It described an old couple who had gone hand in hand in need and joy and now knew it was time to sleep 'so that we do not lose ourselves in this loneliness. . . How tired we are of wandering. Is that perhaps death?' This was so close a parallel with him and Pauline that he began to sketch a setting, altering 'that' in the last line to 'this' – *Ist dies etwa der Tod?* instead of Eichendorff's *Ist das etwa der Tod?*

The old couple may have been tired of wandering, but Pauline ensured that the wandering continued. Hotel life was uncongenial to her. She complained about the food and the staff. It was all right for Richard, if he had a table and some music paper, he was at home. But she had nothing. 'Nothing belongs to me', she told Ernst Roth. 'I have nothing to do all day. So I quarrel with people.' In March 1946 they left the Verenahof and went to Ouchy-Lausanne, Beau-Rivage. The following month Strauss underwent an appendix operation from which he quickly recovered. His mood of depression was now tinged with cynicism, as is evident from a letter to Schuh on 20 May:

All the historians of culture, the university professors, the Jewish press, as well as all the German patriots who look forward, following another war between America and Russia, to the resurgence of Germany as a 'world power' and the re-emergence of Barbarossa from the Kyffhäuser and of Hitler from the bunker of the Reich

Chancellery – there is a danger that all these will tear the author [i.e. Strauss] to pieces, quarter him, break him on the wheel, if he has the courage to write that political Germany had to be destroyed after it had fulfilled its mission to the world: the creation and the perfection of German music.[3]

He missed Garmisch, Franz and Alice and the grandsons. He tried to send them food parcels but it was not easy. Alice visited him in 1946, having illegally crossed into Switzerland where she was reunited with her mother and sister in Lucerne. She told Strauss of her journeys to Vienna to the Jacquingasse house to recover manuscripts and documents. The house had been occupied by Russians, with police dogs and horses, and the garage used as a slaughter-house. Furniture had been damaged, possessions had disappeared. After June 1945 it had been a British officers' mess. Strauss was so distressed that he compiled a detailed inventory of what had been in each room, where furniture and pictures had been placed and how he had bought them. At Ouchy on 30 May he completed a 'symphonic fantasy' on themes from *Die Frau ohne Schatten* in which he omitted any of the music associated with the Emperor, perhaps because (as I suggested earlier) it exposed Strauss's inner nerves too painfully. The fantasy had its first performance under Böhm in Vienna on 26 June 1947. The new (1944) arrangement of the *Rosenkavalier* waltzes was first performed on 4 August 1946 in London, conducted by Erich Leinsdorf.

On 13 September 1946 the Strausses moved to the Park Hotel, Vitznau, and a few weeks later returned to the Verenahof in Baden. Strauss was buoyed up by the chance of a *Danae* production at Salzburg in 1947, but his favourite conductor, Krauss, was still under a ban while being investigated for his activities during the Nazi régime. This was not lifted until 1947. Strauss was now at work on another orchestral fantasy, from *Josephs Legende*, and on a Duett-Concertino for clarinet and bassoon, with strings and harp, which he had promised to Hugo Burghauser, former principal bassoonist of the Vienna Philharmonic who had emigrated to America in 1938. In a letter written in October 1946, Strauss reported that he was 'busy with an idea for the work . . . thinking especially of your beautiful tone'. America had been on Strauss's mind in the autumn of 1946 since he and Pauline had been invited by the actor Lionel Barrymore to stay in his home in Hollywood. A few weeks later Barrymore wrote to say that, much as he himself wished for the visit, there had been so many allegations in the American Press about Strauss's role in Nazi Germany – beginning in July 1945 with the Los Angeles article about the song for Hans Frank – that it would not be in Strauss's interest to make the journey. Strauss replied on 1 January 1947, saying that he had given Barrymore's letter to Willi Schuh to show to the American consul 'together with the necessary explanations about the malicious lies and libellous reports which have appeared in the press and on the radio since spring 1945 by the Americans, first of all through the son of the author Thomas Mann. I know the clique that surrounds this patriot very well . . . I have a clear conscience and I have never been afraid of my adversaries. . . You certainly do not need to apologise. As you were unaware of the lies of big city reporters and the intrigues of the clique of envious musicians, you had the noblest intentions.'

To another New York correspondent who had accused him of making propaganda for Nazism by conducting he replied:

My commitments all occurred without influence by the authorities: for instance, especially in the past 12 years I conducted concerts by the Philharmonic orchestras of Berlin, Vienna and the Staatskapelle of Munich on a voluntary basis, by private mutual agreement and as a favour for my *artistic friends*. . . Apart from the fact that performances of my opera *Die schweigsame Frau* were absolutely prohibited and my operas based on texts by Hugo von Hofmannsthal were repeatedly sabotaged by the Reich Theatre Chamber, and apart from constantly harassing me, the Nazi government did not cause me any major difficulties particularly worth mentioning. It was a totally different matter as regards my son's family. He was regarded as being Jewish by his marriage and his wife and children were subjugated to the Nuremberg race laws. My intention to leave Germany for Switzerland could not be realised because I only managed with great difficulty to rescue my family from being exterminated by the Nazis, and my various applications to leave Germany were always rejected by the Gestapo. It is widely known that I was not a member of the Nazi party or any of its organisations. It is equally well known that I did not conduct at party political events or in the occupied territories (apart from my second homeland, Austria, of course).

This document is, so far as I know, the only written evidence that Strauss wanted to leave Germany during the war.

From 29 March 1947 to 13 June, the Strausses were in the Sanatorium

Sanrocco at Lugano. On 25 July he conducted the orchestra of Lugano Radio in his early wind Serenade, four of his songs sung by the soprano Annette Brun, and the suite from *Le bourgeois gentilhomme*. The sketchbooks for 1945–8 show Strauss at work on several projects. In addition to *Die Rache der Aphrodite*, he contemplated a second violin concerto, making notes for a minuet, *adagio* and *allegro*. Early in 1947 he had a letter from Stephen Schaller, monastic head of the Benedictine Gymnasium in Ettal, near Garmisch. His grandson Christian was at this school, which his son Franz had also attended. Schaller asked for a work which the boys could perform. Strauss again involved Gregor, who produced drafts of a libretto based on a story by Goethe's contemporary Christoph Martin Wieland.

This was about a dentist who rides into town on a hired donkey. The day is so hot that he dismounts to rest in the donkey's shadow. The donkey's owner sues him on the grounds that the donkey was hired, not his shadow. The whole town becomes obsessed with the case, which ends because the donkey dies from neglect during the legal wranglings. The townspeople then have to leave their homes because of a plague of frogs. Strauss approved, but soon the usual arguments began and he transferred the project to a Viennese writer, Hans Adler. Strauss planned six scenes of eighteen numbers, but only a few were sketched. He lost interest during 1948 when Christian transferred to a Swiss boarding-school at St Gallen. After Strauss's death, his family allowed the Ettal music master, Karl Haussner, to make a performing version of *Das Esels Schatten* from the fragmentary sketches. This was performed at Ettal on 7 and 14 June 1964 to mark the composer's centenary. But never mind the donkey's shadow, it remains only a Strauss shadow too.

30   London

During his Swiss exile, Strauss grew to trust, and accept as a friend, his London publisher Ernst Roth, whom he showered with letters, many of them on business matters such as negotiations for payments for his new works (which he insisted should not be published until after his death, although *Metamorphosen* appeared in 1946 and the Oboe Concerto in 1948).[1] The payment of royalties to Hofmannsthal's widow Gerty for *Der Rosenkavalier*, *Ariadne auf Naxos* and *Arabella* was raised ('I can only repeat: 5% and even that is too much'). He answered Roth's questions on whether Gregor and Ursuleac were Nazis. Of Gregor: 'One can't accuse him of being a Nazi merely because, out of necessity, he had to associate himself with the party label. I am certain he was an opponent even though under that administration he was responsible for theatre productions in the National Library and an exhibition about Alfred Roller . . . with an introduction by me!' Of Ursuleac: 'Her voice was not perfect any more in the middle range but absolutely perfect and secure in the upper range and with a fine *piano* – an outstanding artist, but cautious in relation to the Nazis.' Of Cebotari he said that she was 'feeble against the *Elektra* orchestra', but he recommended Irmgard Seefried as Chrysothemis in *Elektra* for the Vienna State Opera. He also kept Roth informed of the progress of his 'deNazification'. 'Mr Sommerlich [one of the American investigators] left me a few days ago', he wrote. 'He again tormented me for written evidence. In the end I became quite annoyed and declared that the interdict signed by Bormann should be sufficient, even for Americans. They don't seem to know what every decent and well educated European knows, that I was never a party member but always an opponent of the Nazis – and "impossible" according to Goebbels. A written note of dismissal [from the Reich Music Chamber presidency], which Sommerlich wants, does not exist. Some affidavits from, for instance,

Lotte Lehmann and God knows which other small people, I have dismissed as unworthy of me.'

There are other revealing requests in this correspondence. Could Roth please send cigarettes to his son Franz, hair-colouring ('No. 8 bright ash blonde') for Pauline, penicillin for his grandchildren, sugar for Alice and the drug AT10 for himself. Could he approach Winston Churchill or Ernest Bevin (British Foreign Secretary) to enable his grandsons to visit him before he died. Many letters referred to a plan for Strauss to visit London. First came a request from Walter Legge for him to conduct the recently formed Philharmonia Orchestra in the Royal Albert Hall in April or May. ('The fee is not sufficient, I would prefer £500.') The Oboe Concerto was out of the question in the vast Albert Hall (at that date London's only concert-hall), he ruled. The visit gradually took on larger proportions as Roth and Sir Thomas Beecham became involved and was put back until October 1947. After moving from Lugano to Pontresina in June, the Strausses settled in their last Swiss 'home', the Palace Hotel, Montreux, on 22 September. On 4 October Strauss flew to Northolt Airport, London. Pauline decided to stay behind but Willi Schuh joined him from 11 to 16 October. Like Elgar, who had made his first flight, to Paris, at the age of seventy-five in 1933, Strauss made his at the age of eighty-three. He stayed at the Savoy Hotel and enjoyed re-visiting St James's Park and, most of all, the National Gallery and the Wallace Collection. He told Schuh he ranked Titian with Wagner; he himself was like Tintoretto and Correggio. Standing before Veronese's Santa Helena he told Schuh that shortly after the turn of the century he had planned a 'symphony of paintings', with an *adagio* on Veronese's Helen of Troy and a *scherzo* on Hogarth. The Royal Philharmonic Society gave a reception and dinner for him. He was made to feel welcome and there was no comment about 'deNazification'. He attended the rehearsals and performances of Beecham's two concerts with the Royal Philharmonic Orchestra at the Theatre Royal, Drury Lane. On 5 October, Beecham conducted the *Bourgeois gentilhomme* suite, the Closing Scene from *Feuersnot*, *Don Quixote* (cellist Paul Tortelier in his English début) and the London première of the fantasy on *Die Frau ohne Schatten*. The last work was conducted by one of Beecham's horn-players, Norman Del Mar, who was beginning his conducting career. The programme of the second concert was *Macbeth*, an interlude from

31 In the Theatre Royal, Drury Lane, October 1947, listening to the
Royal Philharmonic Orchestra conducted by Sir Thomas Beecham

Intermezzo, Ein Heldenleben and the Closing Scene from *Ariadne auf Naxos*,
with Cebotari as Ariadne and Karl Friedrich as Bacchus. A visitor during the
interval of this concert was the Earl of Harewood at the invitation of Roth
who 'beckoned me inside, where I saw the great man standing at the other
end of the little ante-room with his overcoat over his shoulders . . . I was
taken up to him, presented, and stammered out in my best German how
much I enjoyed the music and the other programme I had heard. "Wo haben
sie ihre Deutsch gelernt?", he asked ['Where did you learn your German?']
. . . I said truthfully but irrelevantly "Ich war Kriegsgefangener" ['I was a
prisoner of war'], whereupon Strauss turned on his heel and walked away. I
was hurried out of the box and remembered that the old man was said to be
sensitive about any reminders of his much discussed and I suspect much-
exaggerated Nazi connections, but I thought at the time that this was, to put
it mildly, over-reacting.'[2] Among those he met during the visit to London
was the American composer Bernard Herrmann, who told me that Strauss

spoke to him for half an hour about the music of Raff. Herrmann had an encyclopaedic knowledge of obscure composers and always maintained that *Eine Alpensinfonie* was influenced by a work by Raff.

On 19 October, in an Albert Hall containing over 6,500 people, Strauss conducted the Philharmonia in *Don Juan*, the *Burleske* (pianist, Alfred Blumen), the *Rosenkavalier* Waltzes and *Symphonia Domestica* (Strauss had wanted *Eine Alpensinfonie* because of the hall's organ). Schuh had a memory of that day: 'In the afternoon he retired to bed and when it began to go dark, I went to sit with him. The lamp was dazzling, so I asked if I should turn it out. But he said no: "I do not like to be in semi-darkness, I like light". The casual nature of the occasion cannot obscure the deeper meaning of these words. It was easy to sense that the approaching concert weighed on him – he hadn't conducted for years [actually not since 25 July!] and was now in his eighty-fourth year. When he had lain still for a while, he said with a soft sigh: "These afternoons before a concert away from home! [*in der Fremde*]. Ah well, it won't last much longer now". How many hundred such afternoons must he have spent during his long life, alone, waiting!'[3] Like the Emperor in *Die Frau ohne Schatten*, isolated from home and wife. That evening, before going on to the platform, he said to Roth: 'So the old horse wanders out of the stables once more.' It was at one of the Drury Lane rehearsals that he told the orchestra: 'I know what I want and I know what I meant when I wrote this. After all, I may not be a first-rate composer, but I *am* a first-class second-rate composer.'[4] He will have said it in German, so some over-hearer must have been able to translate. The catch is that we do not know how many composers Strauss admitted into the first rank. Not many, I suspect. Those who were at the concert could not fathom how this old man, making hardly any movement with his baton, could obtain such powerful, searing and intense climaxes. There were emotional encounters in the Green Room afterwards. Elisabeth Schumann, who had not seen him since 1933, was not recognised. 'Who are you?' he asked. 'Elisabeth', she replied. They chatted and she left, wishing she had never gone. But his eyes filled with tears when he saw Gerty von Hofmannsthal, the poet's widow.

On 24 October he attended the first of two BBC Third Programme performances of *Elektra* conducted by Beecham at the Maida Vale studio. Erna Schlüter and Elisabeth Höngen sang Elektra and Klytämnestra. He also attended Beecham's *Don Quixote* recording sessions with the Royal Philharmonic Orchestra. Finally, on the 29th, he conducted *Till Eulenspiegel* at the Albert Hall in a BBC Symphony Orchestra concert, the remainder of which was directed by Sir Adrian Boult. Before he left he gave a press conference. To the reporter who asked what his plans were, he replied: 'Well, just to die, I suppose.' When he returned to Switzerland two days later he took with him all the earnings of his stay, slightly under £1,000 after tax. In addition, by the recent treaty with Austria, he recovered royalties due since September 1946. One pleasing aftermath of the London visit was renewal of contact with Bernard Shaw. Strauss had lost his copy of Shaw's 'Wagner Brevier' commentary on *Der Ring des Nibelungen* and the playwright sent him one at Christmas 1947 with an inscription reading: 'I have at last found this copy of the Brevier to replace the lost one. Our meetings in London and Brioni [in 1929] are very specially cherished in my remembrance. I am very very old (91½) but I have not forgotten. One of my chief pleasures is to hear *Till* and *Don Juan* on the wireless, conducted by yourself. What a difference!' Strauss replied warmly and told Shaw about the operas he had written since 1935.

Strauss's opinion of the London visit, including his reaction to the austerity of English life under the Labour Government, was expressed in a letter written on 11 November to his grandson Christian:

The flight was so quiet that one only realised one was flying when looking down. The tables enabled one to write which is more than one could achieve in a rattling train. If it were not for the bombers, one could praise this latest invention. I'm suffering from a slight stomach upset due to the shocking and disgusting food in England, which is short of all necessities. Frozen beef, no veal, no ham, no eggs, no sugar, no butter, no oil. Everything cooked in disgusting margarine. Unbelievable! Anyway, many friends looked after me and presented me with the necessities. The two-hour concert in the Albert Hall, attended by 7,500, did not tire me in the least. The applause was incredible and there was no unfriendly remark in the press, only admiration and recognition. The orchestra was excellent and delighted with my calm style of conducting. In short, a universal success in every way. While in London

I received five invitations to tour America, which I refused with thanks. Before that, Krauss presented *Salome* with the Viennese ensemble to great acclaim. Queen Mary was in the theatre. On 1 November Covent Garden presented *Rosenkavalier*, in English. That I didn't hear but preferred to return to dear Grandma in lovely Montreux. There we look forward to receiving you and your dear parents for Christmas. . . It will be nice to have you here in this beautiful hotel and warm climate, which will be very good for your father. We will also feed you up a bit and thus hope to improve the old grey matter to help with Latin. . . How do you like studying harmony and do you still play the piano?

Strauss's return to Switzerland coincided with more controversy. Rudolph Mengelberg had conducted the Amsterdam première of *Metamorphosen* after which Matthijs Vermeulen wrote in *De Groene Amsterdammer* on 11 October connecting the 'In memoriam' quotation with Hitler (in the way that Beethoven's *Eroica* was connected with Napoléon). 'All those who listen to *Metamorphosen*', he wrote, 'also the relatives of those uncountable many who were murdered and sacrificed to the warlords, will be forced by this music to witness a memorial service to "this great man"'.[5] The article was reprinted on 15 October in the Basel *National Zeitung*. Schuh and others sprang to Strauss's defence and the newspaper published a half-hearted retraction on 8 November in which its arts editor wrote that he awaited the revelation that Strauss was a hero of the resistance. To his credit, Bruno Walter declared in an interview that Vermeulen's opinions were laughable and that he looked forward to conducting *Metamorphosen* ('a noble work') in New York. Yet Vermeulen's theory has been given some credence by the Canadian musicologist Timothy L. Jackson, who wrote that 'the caption "In memoriam" could refer to Hitler, not as a true hero but as a false hero who aspired to greatness but descended to bestiality'.[6] After reading the preceding chapters of this book, I hope that no one will feel able to believe for a fraction of a second that Strauss commemorated Hitler in his most tragic work.

31   Last songs

Strauss's first task on return from London was to complete the Duett Concertino (o.Op. 147). The full score was ready on 16 December and it was first performed in Lugano on 4 April 1948 by the Radio Lugano Orchestra conducted by Otmar Nussio, with Armando Basile (clarinet) and Bruno Bergomaschi (bassoon). Strauss told Krauss that he originally had a 'programme' in mind based on Hans Andersen's 'The Swineherd' in which a prince woos a princess by posing as a swineherd. Strauss visualised a dancing princess (clarinet) alarmed by the grotesque gestures of a bear (bassoon). But when she dances with it, it becomes a prince. Two short movements precede a long and rambling rondo finale. The work begins with a prelude for strings which resurrects the vein of the *Capriccio* Sextet. Writing about this effervescent work to its dedicatee, Burghauser, Strauss said: 'My father always used to say it was Mozart who wrote most beautifully for the bassoon. But then he was also the one to have *all* the most beautiful thoughts, coming straight down from the skies! Please give Kapellmeister [Georg] Szell my greetings! Does he still play *Eulenspiegel* from memory?'

Burghauser visited Strauss in Montreux in 1948. He found him depressed. 'His publisher had paid the Palace Hotel', the bassoonist wrote, 'but he said to me "I don't even have a cent to give a tip, and my grandson Christian is studying here. I don't know how I will manage it, my royalties have been confiscated, I'm not allowed to draw anything". He then said: "You are a diplomat". I said: "Yes, sort of, but I don't know how much". He said: "Every head of an orchestra is also a diplomat, my father was also. At any rate I have here three scores, handwritten, clean, of *Don Juan*, *Eulenspiegel* and *Tod und Verklärung*. Take them with you. In peacetime I would get 1,000 dollars for each of them, but this time I'll sell all three for 1,000 dollars – gold dollars". He gave me a written authorization written on hotel paper. I demanded it as otherwise one could question how I came to be selling such scores. After two or three weeks I was able to send him 10,000 dollars – he was very happy.'[1] His re-copying of his manuscripts led to a contretemps for Paul Sacher, who had bought the autograph score of *Metamorphosen* when it was delivered. Some time later he was approached by a third party, who offered him an autograph score of *Metamorphosen*. 'But I already have it.' He bought the second one also.

In spite of the London triumph, of requests for him to tour the United States, and the increasing frequency of performances of his operas, he was still depressed and despondent. He wrote dozens of letters (remembering, for example, the 400th anniversary of the Staatskapelle Dresden on 25 July 1948, calling it 'the first opera orchestra of the world'). He had long discussions with Schuh. Sometimes they argued because Schuh made out a case for some modern music. Strauss could not bear it. Atonality was tantamount to crime. Schoenberg, Krenek and Hindemith were just 'placers of notes'. He studied scores of Beethoven and Haydn string quartets and especially he studied Mozart – 'the G minor quintet, that comes directly from above!' On one occasion his eyes filled with tears, he clasped Schuh's hand and said 'Forgive me, let's not quarrel ever again. It's my eternal obstinacy.' Franz visited him and said: 'Papa, stop writing letters and brooding, it doesn't do any good. Write a few nice songs instead.'

And that is what he did. On 27 April 1948 in Montreux he completed the short score of the setting of Eichendorff's *Im Abendrot* which he had begun to sketch in late 1946 or early 1947. He fully scored it on 6 May. Then on 9 June he orchestrated *Ruhe, meine Seele!*, the first of the Opus 27 songs he had given to Pauline as a wedding present in September 1894. This was no accident, for two days earlier the Garmisch Court of Arbitration's verdict on his contacts with the Nazis – the deNazification tribunal – delivered its verdict which then became legally effective. The three members, Dr Karl Piper (chairman), Franz Heiss and Anton Paulus found that Strauss was not incriminated, the proceedings were to be suspended and the costs were to be borne by the State Treasury. The words of Henckell's poem which he had set fifty-four years earlier must have seemed apposite: 'Rest, rest my soul/ Your storms were wild/ You have raged and you have trembled/ Like the breakers when they swell./ These times are momentous,/ They place heart and mind in need -/ Rest, rest my soul/ And forget what threatens you.' In its orchestral version the wonderful song is darkened, intensified and lengthened by several bars. It becomes even greater.

The deNazification tribunal's report, running to eight closely typed pages, contains much that has already been detailed in preceding chapters of this book. But some passages are worth quotation here:

He rejected any form of racist policies in art and therefore distanced himself increasingly from influential members of the party who sought to influence art in the sense of Nazi ideology. For instance, even the request of the Schlieffen Library, dating from 30.1.1934, which was preparing a work about the Reich Culture Chamber as an expression of thanks for Dr Goebbels and had asked Strauss for a contribution, only met with a refusal, despite the fact that all other presidents had consented to participate. Even the request for a few lines as Introduction or only a personal statement fell on deaf ears . . .

He always rejected the repeated invitations by Frank as Governor General of Cracow. All the travel comfort and luxury and convenience in the palace in Cracow were offered in vain. Despite all the enticing offers Strauss did not accept the invitation and Frank, in his last letter of July 11, 1943, even condescended to leave out *Heil Hitler* by his signature, something which certainly did not come easy to him . . .

The head of the main security office of the Reichsfachwerkes SS wrote to the Ministry of Propaganda: 'It is well known of Strauss that even in the year 1935 he avoided the German greeting in public and had contacts with Jewish circles at home and abroad.'

The findings of the tribunal were registered in Garmisch on 11 June, Strauss's eighty-fourth birthday. As a gift for that occasion Schuh sent him an advance copy of the periodical he edited, *Schweizerische Musikzeitung*. This contained Rudolf Hartmann's article 'Principles of Strauss Production' (*Grundsätzliches zur Strauss Regie*). The composer was delighted. 'A thousand thanks also', he wrote, 'in the names of the poor destroyed theatres of Germany. . . Could you perhaps arrange for 50 or 100 reprints, at my expense, of course. Is it not a crime against culture that such a clever chap as Hartmann should be sentenced to three years' inactivity? We must not speak about that. . . At the same time as your gift I am daily in receipt of touching congratulations regarding the deNazification, even from old ladies from the furthest corner of Germany. It is ironic that by such a farce one achieves "fame". Your journal, however, was a bright beam of light.'

At some date in 1947 Strauss was introduced to the poetry of Hermann Hesse, who lived in Switzerland. He was now seventy. The two men once met briefly in an hotel. Hesse had won the Nobel Prize for Literature in 1946. Strauss marked some of the poems as suitable for setting. On 20 June he wrote the short score of *Frühling*, scoring it on 18 July. From 25 to 30 June he stayed at the Zürich home of Dr Adolf Jöhr, his Swiss banker, where on the 28th as he left his room for lunch he was carrying a folio of music paper. He told Jöhr: 'Here I have a new song on a text by Hermann Hesse which I have dedicated to you and your wife.' This was *Beim Schlafengehen*. He and Pauline went from Zürich to Pontresina, where they spent the summer in the Hotel Saretz. There he orchestrated the new song on 4 August. He contemplated two other Hesse poems, *Nacht* (*Night*) and *Höhe des Sommers* (*High Summer*), but they duplicated poems already set. Ten days later he composed another Hesse poem, *September*, in short score, orchestrating it on 20 September in Montreux, to which they had returned on 1 September. When Franz and Alice next visited Montreux, Strauss went into their room, placed some scores on the table and said to Alice: 'Here are the songs your husband ordered.' *September* was dedicated to Mr and Mme Seery, in other words Maria Jeritza and her husband who had been loyal and helpful to Strauss in America. There was one more song to come. On 23 November he composed *Malven* (AV 304), a poem by Betty Knobel, for voice and piano. The dedication was 'to beloved Maria (Jeritza), this last rose'. In March 1949 he sent the manuscript to Jeritza, who kept it a secret until her death in 1982. (It was first sung (by Kiri te Kanawa) in New York on 10 January 1985.) Jeritza's letter to Strauss, written from Newark, New Jersey, on 16 March, merits full quotation. She was by then sixty years old:

Dear friend and honoured Master.

Hans Sachs, in *Meistersinger*, says: For you it is easy, for me it is difficult. This is the case with me. How should and how could I thank you for that magnificent song. People can cry from pain but also from joy. The latter is the case with me. I cried from joy. We thank you with all our hearts for the happiness which those two wonderful songs have given us. I am delighted that you are getting better daily, which is only what is to be expected from the attention and care of the dear Pauline. May God bless and protect you both. I have a very strong premonition that I will very soon be singing again under the Master Richard Strauss. I believe that on the evening after *Salome*, with you conducting, I will have to be carried from the theatre because I shall be overcome with happiness after the performance. That will be the crown of my career. I am sure I will never have sung better nor with more feeling than on such an evening. What do you think of that, can I talk you into it to appear with me in Vienna? I can guarantee that all Austria, and from even further afield, will be at your feet. "I will give you the cloak of the high priest", thus promises Herod. I, as Salome, promise that I shall sing and dance as never before in my whole life. Do you really think, dear Master, that I was as good as Salome as you always claim? I love that opera with all my heart and hate anyone who does not sing or dance as I have learnt from you. I will now close so as not to tire you with my scribbling. Greetings to you and our lovely Pauline, your devoted and sincere Mariandel triandel.

Might we not imagine Strauss's wry smile as he read this artistic love-letter from his first Ariadne and Empress?

The song-settings of Eichendorff and Hesse were published after Strauss's death as o.Op. 150 under the title *Vier letzte Lieder* (*Four Last Songs*) given them by Ernst Roth (inaccurately, as it happens, but he did not know of *Malven*). No one knows if Strauss intended them as a cycle. Timothy L. Jackson thinks that it was intended to include *Ruhe, meine Seele!* as a fifth song. There is no documentary evidence. But Edwin McArthur, accompanist to and friend of the soprano Kirsten Flagstad, has written that Strauss had chosen her 'to give the world première of his now famous *Four Last Songs*, the only condition being that there be a first-class conductor. The "first-class conductor" was none other than Wilhelm Furtwängler, her favourite of all.'[2] But not Strauss's favourite. According to McArthur, Flagstad sang in Zürich in January and May 1947 and April 1948. Timothy L. Jackson speculates that she and Strauss may have discussed the performance of the songs then. Strauss makes no reference to meeting Flagstad in any of his many letters to Schuh and Roth and in April 1948 he had in any case not written any of the Hesse songs (*Im Abendrot* was in short score on 27 April). Flagstad gave the first performance in London on 22 May 1950 with

Furtwängler conducting the Philharmonia Orchestra in the Albert Hall. It is more likely that she was chosen by Furtwängler. The songs were first sung in the order *Beim Schlafengehen, September, Frühling* and *Im Abendrot*, which is the order in which they were sung by Sena Jurinac, with Fritz Busch conducting, in Stockholm in May 1951 and recorded by Lisa Della Casa and Karl Böhm a year later. But they were published by Roth in 1950 in the order *Frühling, September, Beim Schlafengehen* and *Im Abendrot*. This is how they are usually heard today.

Since they were first sung, the *Four Last Songs* have become one of the most beloved works not only of Strauss but of any composer. One or other of them has been taken by distinguished people innumerable times to Roy Plomley's mythical Desert Island. They are Strauss's farewell to the world, but were not designed as such. They are songs about death, but death is accepted resignedly. Although each is dedicated to people who helped Strauss in his Swiss exile (*Frühling* is inscribed to Schuh and his wife), they are really a final homage to Pauline, his marital and artistic partner for over fifty years. 'Your blessed presence trembles through all my limbs', is the end of *Frühling*. His long love affair with the soprano voice, her voice, is consummated in this final masterpiece. It is often said they could have been written at any time in his career, but I believe they could only have been written at the end. They are the music of old age and wisdom and serenity, of death and transfiguration. Like all the late works especially, they are a reaffirmation of the glories of tonality, a demonstration of how much new music could still be found in the traditional diatonic and chromatic styles. They are contrived with superb artifice. Just as in his orchestration of *Morgen!* the solo violin depicts the lovers' souls in bliss, so in *Beim Schlafengehen* it illustrates 'the unfettered soul soaring in free flight in the magic circle of night'. The larks trill in *Im Abendrot* like the birdsong in *Der Rosenkavalier*. At the words *Ist dies etwa der Tod?* the Idealism theme from *Tod und Verklärung* is quoted. *September* ends with a valedictory solo by the horn, his father's instrument which haunts all his music. The great orchestral exordium which opens *Im Abendrot* is Strauss at his richest, ripest and most consoling. This is no winter of discontent, but an autumn harvest of fulfilment.

32   Return to Garmisch

On 15 December 1948 Strauss had a major operation in the Clinique Cécile, Lausanne, for the removal of a large stone from his bladder. On the 26th he wrote to Schuh: 'I ask myself why they have brought me back into an existence in which I have actually outlived myself.' He dictated his letters, which are in the handwriting of a nurse or of Franz when he was there. By 13 January 1949, however, he was asking Schuh to bring him miniature scores of *Tristan*, the Second Symphony and Op. 127 string quartet of Beethoven and Haydn's 'Emperor' quartet. Schuh thanked him on 28 January for the dedication of *Frühling*. Interestingly, he referred to it as 'the first' of the Hesse songs (*des ersten Hesseliedes*). By mid-April Strauss was in the Clinique Florimont, Montreux, before returning to the Palace Hotel. He was planning to fly to Paris in mid-May, but was not well enough. He hoped to attend a Strauss festival there organised by his friend Gustave Samazeuilh at which there was a concert performance of *Friedenstag* (*Jour de Paix*) as well as the French premières of some other works. Strauss wrote to Samazeuilh: 'The fact that the broadcast of *Friedenstag* coincides with the Foreign Ministers' conference is a sign of fate and I would like to see it as a happy premonition that my vision as an artist in 1938 . . . could now radiate over all the earth from the enlightened city that is Paris.' In the same week, *Friedenstag* was staged at the Théâtre de la Monnaie in Brussels. On 9 May he and Pauline stayed in the Hotel Central, Zürich, and next morning left by train to return to Garmisch after an absence of three years and seven months. Schuh and the conductor Erich Kleiber were at the station to bid them godspeed.

The friendship with Schuh had warmed Strauss's stay in Switzerland. He wrote to him the next day, 11 May:

We had a pleasant journey and were met at Innsbruck by Mr Garlock, the American Commandant of Garmisch, in his car. We travelled in a wild snowstorm and arrived at our villa which Alice had polished like a splendid exhibit. We slept well and are very happy and, thanks to dear Switzerland, restored to good health. Enclosed is a snap, the latest, taken by my son.

He had appointed Schuh his biographer and had given him a free hand selecting material for a collection of autobiographical essays. This appeared during 1949 under the title *Betrachtungen und Erinnerungen* (*Recollections and Reflections*). Strauss was 'not too happy' with the book when he saw it. He wrote to Schuh on 11 July:

I regret that you did not give me the manuscript to correct. I was not prepared that my carefree and uncorrected jottings in the blue diaries should be accepted uncritically, which I would, most likely, have amended or excluded. For instance, Richard Wagner's remark about the old Strauss [his father] being an 'impossible chap' could be interpreted that he is an opponent, or the item about the pickled cucumbers and some of the stories about Bülow could give the gutter press an opportunity to beat the great masters should they wish to do so. Also the letter to Karpath with the 10,000 servants I would never have entertained. It appears that even as distinguished a writer as you can fall into the trap of journalistic sensationalism. Is it possible, but certainly if there is a second edition [1957], that certain excisions and corrections be made which I will send in a special copy? In any case, these items must be considered in the English translation which Dr Roth is completing. Can you imagine the slaughter if the remarks about universal franchise should fall into the hands of an American *Revolverhelden*?

Among the letters he received congratulating him on his return was one from Krauss suggesting that he should compose an oratorio on the subject of Noah's Flood – 'you too have made an Ark with your music in which we can save all the good spirits of our art from the flood of atonality.'

Already plans were well advanced for celebrations of his eighty-fifth birthday on 11 June. He had to refuse several invitations. 'All my life I've been used to my body obeying me and now I have to obey it', he told Schuh. There were many callers at the villa, glad to welcome him home. On 10 June he travelled down to Munich for a dress rehearsal of *Der Rosenkavalier* in the Prinzregententheater and asked to be allowed to conduct the finales of Acts 2 and 3. This was filmed and included in a documentary being made about

him, *A Life for Music*, together with later film of his conducting the
Presentation of the Silver Rose. The conductor of the Bavarian State Opera
from October 1946 was the Hungarian-born Georg Solti. He accompanied
Strauss into the pit at the rehearsal on 10 June. Strauss asked him: 'Where
are the horns sitting?' On the left, trumpets on the right, Solti told him. 'I
can no longer see or hear very well', Strauss explained. Solti wrote in his
memoirs: 'As soon as he began to conduct, the feebleness of old age was
replaced with power and control. He began with the waltz at the end of the
second act, and just before Ochs's musical entrance, Strauss, though nearly
blind, automatically looked up at the stage and gave a cue with the instinc-
tive assurance of a seasoned Kapellmeister.'[1]

On the morning of the birthday, the Bavarian government and Garmisch
municipal authority combined to sponsor a concert in Garmisch town hall
at which his early Violin Sonata and Piano Quartet were performed. Solti
was the pianist in the sonata. Strauss was made an honorary citizen of
Garmisch and the University of Munich conferred an honorary doctorate
of law on him (not before time, one would say). The deputy mayor of
Munich announced the establishment of a Strauss scholarship at the
University of Munich. Strauss's speech in reply was recorded. He spoke
movingly of his early days in Munich, of how he initiated a Mozart renais-
sance there with *Così fan tutte*, and of his father's career. He presented the
manuscript of the first (1939) version of the *München* waltz to the Bavarian
State Library.[2] On 13 June he went to the Gärtnerplatz Theater in Munich
for a new production of *Der Bürger als Edelmann*. He had been asked by the
Bavarian government which of his works he would most like to see and had
chosen this, the final result of the long engagement with Molière's play
through which he and Hofmannsthal had struggled and quarrelled. 'It's a
pity Hofmannsthal couldn't have seen it too', he commented. Perhaps it was
an atonement. A month later, on 13 July, he returned to Munich to conduct
the radio orchestra in the Moonlight Music from *Capriccio*. (Fortunately, a
recording exists.) He never conducted again. He drove home afterwards
with Rudolf Hartmann through the Isar valley to call at Hartmann's home
where they talked about the post-war plans for opera in Munich.[3] They continued the conversation ten days later in Garmisch, together with Alois
Johannes Lippl, Intendant of the Bavarian State Theatre. 'Strauss gave new

32 Speaking at Garmisch on his eighty-fifth birthday, 11 June 1949

evidence of the unbroken intellectual capacity and clarity of his mind. With heartfelt joy he observed that the construction plans incorporated a number of suggestions that he had often expressed in the past to no avail.' Later they walked in the garden. 'He stood there in contemplative enjoyment, looking down at the blooming summer splendour and then said, as if talking to himself, in an aside: "They'll still be blooming when I am gone"'.

Solti was invited to visit the villa in Garmisch.[4] When he rang the bell he was surprised that the door was opened by Strauss himself. He was put at ease by the old man asking to hear 'all the gossip at the opera'. Solti asked about certain tempi in *Der Rosenkavalier*. 'It's very easy', Strauss replied. 'I set Hofmannsthal's text at the pace at which I would speak it, with a natural speed and in a natural rhythm. Just recite the text and you will find the right tempi.' He told him to conduct the Act 2 waltz in one beat to a bar, not three. 'Don't do what Clemens Krauss often does. He beats it in three. Try to stay in one – this makes the phrasing more natural.' Strauss also advised him to leave the pit when rehearsing 'because what you hear from your place in the pit is totally different from what the audience hears'. After lunch Solti was asked to leave by Pauline. 'Richard must take a nap.' Strauss said to his family later, 'This young man gives me a little hope.'

On 12 August he worked at his desk for several hours. The last music he composed was a projected choral setting of another Hesse poem, *Besinnung* (*Reflection*), but he had told Roth that a sixteen-part fugal section had become too complex. Perhaps he was still trying to solve the problems. Next day he took to his bed and became increasingly ill and weak. The catheter had been giving him pain for weeks. Uraemia set in and he was given oxygen. But in lucid moments he told Alice: 'I hear so much music.' She offered to bring him some music paper. 'No. I wrote it 60 years ago in *Tod und Verklärung*. This is just like that.' On the 27th he had several severe bouts of angina. Pauline, too, was ill and was in a clinic. On the 29th Strauss rallied and asked to see Hartmann. Next day Franz and Christian picked him up in Eberhausen and during the drive to Garmisch Franz said the doctors believed Strauss could live only a few more days, perhaps hours. In October 1949 Hartmann wrote a long and moving account of his visit, from which quotation is essential. He was shown into Strauss's room by Alice:

Then he says 'Death has dealt me the first heavy blow, given me the first signal . . .' Gradually his thoughts turn to the things that always interest him . . . I hear the deep, somewhat hoarse voice speaking of the constantly recurring concern for the future of European theatre; then after a short pause he says 'Imagine, 140 years ago Goethe and Napoleon shook hands in Erfurt! What a development that would have been: Napoleon as the ruler of a united Europe and Goethe his first minister of culture . . .'

33 At Garmisch, 1949, one of the last photographs

He tells me that he is working on composing a letter to an important political figure in present-day France, François-Poncet; the dictated draft is half finished.

In this letter, dictated but not signed, Strauss wrote:

Honoured and dear Mr Messenger! Please let me express my deeply-felt satisfaction that you, one of the most deserving Europeans, have accepted the position of Senior Commissioner in Germany. You have devoted a large part of your working life to German-French understanding. Therefore it is a great satisfaction, in the evening of my life, to know that it is you who holds this responsible position. With this in mind, I send my heartiest good wishes. Thoughts which were always closely associated with your person were what I hoped for in those catastrophic years. I would like to speak to you in greater detail and hope that your path will cross Garmisch one day.

In his conversation with Hartmann, Strauss again outlined the plans for an opera repertory he had sent to Böhm, spoke warmly of Krauss's era in Munich and of his wishes for a Salzburg première of *Die Liebe der Danae*. Hartmann's narrative continues:

A hasty movement has caused a button to come loose from my jacket; irritated, I look around for it. Strauss asks 'What's the matter?' and when he hears the cause of the little disturbance responds with 'Stand up, and it will fall on the floor so you can find it.' This happens just as he says it will.

He then spoke about difficulties of conducting Wagner, particularly the duet which ends *Siegfried*.

'You know the passage I mean . . .' Without waiting for an answer, he raises his arms, conducts and sings the orchestra melody in a loud voice, demonstrating with his arms. The face is slightly flushed; his shining eyes are gazing far, far beyond the walls of the room. . . He leaned back on his pillows, his eyes moist with tears. 'You must forgive me', he says, 'but when you lie here so alone and there is so much to think about, you become a little sentimental.'

They talked about contemporary opera singers, the rebuilding of destroyed theatres and who should rightly have which jobs. Strauss smiled.

'With that, we would seem to have divided the world up quite nicely – our world . . .' Quite changed, softly, his voice sounds again after a while: '*Grüss mir die Welt* – where does that come from?' I think fleetingly of the similar words from *Die Walküre* and say so, but he shakes his head. 'No, no, that's not it; this passage occurs some-where else.' [It is sung by Isolde to Brangäne in Act 1, Scene 4, of *Tristan und Isolde*.]

A short while later Hartmann rose to leave.

He gives me his hand and thanks me for the visit, in a perceptible attempt to deprive this parting of its all-too-palpable weight and significance. Then he grasps my right hand once more in both his and holds me fast: 'Perhaps we will see each other again; if not, you know everything.' A final squeeze, his hands release me, and quickly I leave the room. As I leave I hear Richard Strauss give a muffled sob and then call loudly for his son.[5]

He lived another nine days, often in much pain. But the end came peacefully at 2.12 p.m. on Thursday, 8 September. Pauline was holding his hand and also at his bedside were Franz and Alice, Christian (Richard was working in Munich), Anni Nitzl and the doctor.

His funeral was in Munich on 12 September. There was no Christian symbolism of any kind. The weather was mild, so the ceremony was held outside the crematorium at the Munich Ostfriedhof. Various speakers paid their tributes. The Jewish Georg Solti conducted the Bavarian State Opera Orchestra in the *Marcia funebre* from Beethoven's *Eroica* Symphony ('it can't have been very good', he recalled, 'as I'd never performed it before'). At the end, in accordance with Strauss's request, the Trio from Act 3 of *Der Rosenkavalier* was performed by Marianne Schech (the Marschallin), Maud Cunitz (Octavian) and Gerda Sommerschuh (Sophie), who had sung it under his baton three months earlier. 'One after the other', Solti wrote, 'each singer broke down in tears and dropped out of the ensemble, but they recov-ered themselves and we all ended together.'[6] The conductor and composer Alois Melichar described how, as the Trio began, 'an expression of unbear-able pain' could be seen on Pauline's face. 'At the entry of the first soprano, she fell, as if struck by lightning, on to her knees on the gravel, tightly grasp-ing her chair as if it was a prayer-stool. As the Trio blossomed and the famil-iar sounds and harmonies unfolded, the small figure was convulsed with sobs. At the climax, she extended her hands ecstatically towards the coffin, clasping and unclasping them fiercely as if she was seeking supreme power to retrieve and halt something. As the final chords sounded, she spread out her hands as if to say "Must the man who has written this die?"'[7] She then cried out 'Richard, Richard.' Still weeping, a broken old woman, she went to Solti to thank him.

Pauline's life, too, was over. 'I never realised anyone could weep so much', Alice said. Just before he died Strauss had urged Pauline to return to Montreux and from October 1949 until March 1950 she stayed at the Palace Hotel, attended by Resi Nitzl. She scarcely went out. Her eyesight worsened. Back at Garmisch she stumbled about in the garden and one night was found half-conscious, cold and weeping in the room where Richard had died. On 13 May 1950 death came as a relief. Nine days later, the *Vier letzte Lieder* were performed for the first time.

In many cases after the death of a composer, there is a dip in his reputation for about twenty years. This did not occur with Strauss, for it had occurred during his lifetime. For years he had been written off as one who was composing by ear, who had said anything of significance by 1911 and was irrelevant to the development of twentieth-century music. He was not merely ignored but shunned in academic circles. He was not to be taken seriously. Compared with Stravinsky and Schoenberg, he was of no account. How different today when dissertations and theses on many aspects of Strauss abound. Suddenly the climate changed. The works which had been regarded as mere note-spinning were re-evaluated. The truth dawned: that here was a composer with an almost Bach-like ability to turn his hand to anything, a composer whose relevance to contemporary trends was unimportant because he had served only one god and that was Music.

The critical estimation of Strauss never had any effect on his standing with the musical public. No orchestra could exist without his tone-poems, written to celebrate the glories of the post-Wagnerian symphony orchestra. His early chamber works and concertos, although immature, have held their place in the repertory. His late instrumental works were at once regarded as masterpieces. He wrote over 200 songs in virtually all of which the beauty of melody and the dramatic imagination of the word-setting make them equally rewarding for singer and listener, as do the works for unaccompanied chorus. Of his operas, at least seven are indispensable to the world's opera houses and this number is being increased as conductors and singers explore those once regarded as desert territory. Like all prolific composers,

34 Pauline at the cremation service in Munich, 12 September 1949, with
Franz (right) and Professor Dr Friedrich (Fritz) Lönne. The grandsons
Richard and Christian are in the background

Strauss was not invariably at the top of his form. But every work, after the *Burleske* at least, is indelibly stamped with his musical personality. His music is strong, positive and human. As I wrote earlier, it lacks a spiritual or religious element. He was a sorcerer but a dealer in white magic. His art could conjure up a mountain-range of human feeling and experience, from domestic bliss to the hothouse emotionalism of Oscar Wilde, from Greek tragedy to the *commedia dell'arte*, from Viennese charm and shallowness to the mystery of creation. Beware when he is accused of note-spinning, for the notes are spun into intricate and fascinating webs; if he spoke of 'wrist exercises' when writing his last works, they are the exercises of an Olympic athlete. Even inferior Strauss, such as *Josephs Legende* and the *Japanese Festival Music*, casts a malign spell on the Strauss-receptive listener – one should not be enjoying this music, but perversely one is!

As he admitted, he thought music all day. He had too complicated a mind, he complained, and this sometimes led him into prolixity. But it is not too much to compare him with his beloved Mozart, not in quality – for he would protest vehemently against such a judgment – but in sheer musicality. It was this protean creativity which earned him so much enmity and envy in his lifetime. He was better at almost everything than his contemporaries and rivals. They knew it, but did not like to admit it. He knew it and did not always conceal it.

But there was an enigma, a disparity between the musician and the man. There was almost nothing he could not do in music. He had the technique for anything. But was his inner being strong and pliant enough to cope with the ferocious demands of his technique? Was he fearful of how much his demon – the demon Stefan Zweig perceived in him – would demand of him? Was this why the Emperor's aria is so unnerving? Was this why he did not like the semi-darkness, why he said he could compose only in the summer? Was this why he escaped into conducting, into playing Skat, into domestic isolation in Garmisch? It is a possible solution.

As with all mighty creative artists, there are unanswerable questions. Was he right to continue so long with Hofmannsthal? Did Hofmannsthal impose unviable plots and librettos on him? The documentary evidence quoted in this book does not support this theory. It is true that one could say that his most successful operas were those where he chose the subject and bent the libretto to his requirements: *Salome, Elektra, Intermezzo, Capriccio*. But this does not explain *Der Rosenkavalier, Die Frau ohne Schatten, Ariadne auf Naxos* and *Daphne*. He admired and enjoyed the librettos of *Die Frau ohne Schatten* and *Die ägyptische Helena*. He was thrilled with Zweig's *Die schweigsame Frau*. Was he right to go back to Munich in 1894? Was he right to accept the Vienna Opera co-directorship in 1919? Maybe not, but he needed these outside stimuli to his restless nature just as he needed the constant turmoil of marriage to Pauline. We may laugh at the stories which make Strauss seem the henpecked husband – 'Do we have to eat goulash yet again, Pauxerl?' 'Eat what's put before you, Richard' – but there can be no doubt that we owe it to Pauline that she created a home with the sole aim that Strauss should have the time and energy and health to compose as much as possible. She too was a musician and she became a housewife of genius, in spite of her pre-marital fears that she would not cope. His music earned them a lot of money – although twice they lost everything – but they lived comfortably rather than luxuriously. The constant denigration of Strauss for his interest in royalties is another aspect of the jealousy and envy of his genius. It ignores his work on behalf of other composers, it ignores his help to many colleagues, it ignores his generosity in giving away manuscripts and sketchbooks.

And, of course, was it a mistake to have any kind of truck with the Nazi régime? Viewed from the post-1945 world, undoubtedly it was. But the world looked very different in 1933 and, as was said by one of those who gave evidence to his deNazification investigators, 'it is not possible to demand of someone who is a master of his subject masterly achievements in another field. It is therefore unseemly to accuse the musician and non-politician Richard Strauss of not appearing to be a political hero. As a composer he created an oeuvre that belongs to the great world achievements of the human spirit and for which humanity owes him simply respect and thanks.' A telling example of other musicians' attitude is that of Otto Klemperer. Conducting in Germany in the autumn of 1945, he refused to work with a soloist who had defended Furtwängler. He was reminded that he planned to conduct *Metamorphosen* in Germany. 'Furtwängler didn't compose *Rosenkavalier*', he retorted.[8]

This book will have failed if it has not shown that, whatever occurred in 1933, Strauss paid for his misjudgment with ten years of subtle and sometimes not-so-subtle persecution. In that dark period, he upheld the highest standard of German culture in which he had been nurtured. Amid evil, the light of true art shone brightly. One must regard it as a perverse tribute to Strauss's eminence that his conduct in the Third Reich period should arouse so much inquiry and controversy and that so little, comparatively, is said about the pro-Fascist and pro-Hitler views of Stravinsky and Webern. Could it be that composers regarded as progressive or *avant-garde* are somehow exempt from censure of their moral conduct?

It may be asked if, in spite of the passionate nature of so much of his music, Strauss was a cold man. He was certainly reserved, aloof, sometimes boorishly arrogant. He was not what the English would call 'clubbable'. He had a select circle of close friends, but they were few (as Hofmannsthal once commented) and he was only really relaxed with his family. 'Laid back' would be the contemporary term to describe his general attitude, but Mahler recognised that beneath the calm exterior, volcanic passions were raging. Strauss belonged to a generation which buttoned up its feelings in public – and he always remembered that in his own nature raged a conflict inherited from the quick temper and obstinacy of his father and the gentleness and supine attitude of his highly-strung mother. The clues to the familial warmth of his nature can be found in the dedications of his works – to his parents (his only religious song, *Die heiligen drei Könige aus Morgenland*, was dedicated to his mother, perhaps because he felt guilty that she was devout and he was an unbeliever), his uncles and aunts, his wife, his son. He dedicated works to musicians and to friends who had helped him at a time of crisis. But Ernst von Schuch, who conducted four great premières at Dresden between 1901 and 1911, missed out, possibly because Strauss was angered by the cuts he made. He composed nothing in memory of the dead. If there is dismay that he seemed more concerned about the destruction of buildings in Germany than about the millions who died, this should not be taken as an indication of heartlessness. He was a self-centred artist: his life was art and its temples. Their destruction was a personal wound. He was by no means impervious to the human tragedy but he viewed it through historical perspective. 'History', he wrote at the end of his life, 'consists almost entirely of a succession of stupid and wicked deeds, vulgarity, greed, deception, murder and destruction.'

In any case, he turned away from tragedy. 'I want to create joy', he told Hofmannsthal. After Salome and Elektra, there is only one death (Leukippos) in his operas. In that respect, too, he was Mozartian – and just as there are shadows across Mozart's joy, we find them too across Strauss's. He took us into the hearts of a gallery of immortal creations, into the amorousness of Don Juan, the roguishness and wit of Till Eulenspiegel, the harmless delusions of Don Quixote, the home life of a not-so-heroic Hero, the salacious sensuality of a teenage princess, the vengeful malice of the single-minded Elektra, the nostalgic resignation of the Marschallin, the level-headed opportunism of flirtatious Zerbinetta, the nobility of the Empress and sheer goodness of Barak, the wise head on young shoulders of Arabella, the conversion of Danae from gold-digger to a final emanation of Pauline, and the consummation of all the glory he found in the female voice in the *Capriccio* Countess. And he found the right music for every one of them, a continuous progression from youthful ardour to the wisdom of age and experience, expressed with an emotional range from violence to tenderness, from charm to kitsch, in music which remained faithful to the tenets of traditional tonality, manipulated with an acute responsiveness to the colour and significance of certain keys – E major, D flat especially – which meant much to him and stimulated his fertile musical mind.

The glory of music is that it has been created by so many diverse geniuses, each in his own way unique and inimitable. We go to them to satisfy our diverse and insatiable needs. We may discern their flaws, accept their deficiencies, recognise their limitations, but still cherish them for their special contribution to the enrichment of the human spirit. Strauss has as many flaws and limitations as any other composer, but they seem to me to fade into insignificance compared with the overwhelming greatness of his life's work. It was not a Beethovenian greatness. He did not seek to give mankind spiritual consolation. He did not believe he would alter mankind's destiny through his art. But he could look into the human heart, sometimes through a glass darkly. Intimations of immortality or of mortality did not concern him as they did Mahler. He was, like Mozart, a slave to music. 'Music is a holy art', the Composer sings in the Prologue to *Ariadne auf Naxos*. That was Richard Strauss's religion and his demon.

Appendix 1
Strauss as conductor and pianist

Strauss's conducting career stretched from the 1880s to within three months of his death. He divided it more or less equally between the concert-hall and the opera house. In his youth he was extremely demonstrative on the rostrum. Arthur Johnstone of the *Manchester Guardian* described him conducting Liszt's *Faust Symphony* at Düsseldorf in May 1902: 'A sphinx-like person who as his abnormally big head sways on the top of his tall and bulky figure, to the accompaniment of fantastic gestures, works up his audience with a sort of phosphorescent fever.' He put so much energy into his conducting that his doctors warned him he could damage his heart (a non-sensical medical prognosis!). He went to the opposite extreme, reserving extravagant gestures for only the most extravagant passages and obtaining extraordinarily intense and exciting playing by minimum movements of the baton – 'conducting with one's tie' was Strauss's description of his method. His *Tristan* was said by those who heard it to be the most erotic of all. In *Così fan tutte* he would improvise the keyboard continuo, often introducing quotations from his own works. This was done so lightly and with such wit that nobody was ever offended, rather the reverse, by the mixture of Mozart and Strauss.

He found conducting his own works 'boring'. He said that for many years he did not want to conduct *Der Rosenkavalier*. 'It tires me out too much and it gives me little pleasure as I have conducted it too often.' But his interpretations were not boring, as can be heard from recordings. Nobody else makes *Don Juan* so exciting; no one else sprinkles acid so effectively on the genial humour and sharp wit of *Till Eulenspiegel*. When one hears him conduct *Ein Heldenleben*, one remembers how much humour and wit there are in that score. The only fragment we have of his conducting of *Salome* shows how he could extract all the salaciousness from the score without lingering or causing it to sound in any way over-indulgent. There is a story of his telling a soprano singing Salome in Berlin with an excess of vocal and physical mannerisms: 'No, no, my dear. The music is disgusting enough already.' His tempi in his own works are generally fast: he believed that conductors should not dawdle over the juicy bits. He was not keen on rehearsing and if he thought an orchestra knew a work, he would let it go. He always had a score in front of him but only as a precaution – he did not know the rehearsal-cue numbers. At Weimar in his youth, the Commendatore in *Don Giovanni* came in much too early. Strauss tried to help by jumping ahead, shouting 'D minor chord'. The orchestra did not know what had happened, nor understand what Strauss was doing. It stopped playing. 'Since then', he told Roth, 'I have never conducted without the score.' On another occasion, in 1942 in Munich, he was conducting *Daphne* and came to a part marked 'three in a bar' where Krauss usually beat four. Strauss beat three and threw everybody.

Roth described Strauss's beat as like the pendulum of a metronome. From the first note the tempo of every piece was firmly established. 'One can conduct the prelude to *Tristan*', Strauss once said, 'only if one has the tempo of the last bar exactly in one's head.' The crucial part of conducting, he said, 'is a rhythmically precise upbeat in which the tempo to come is already clearly signalled, followed by a precise downbeat. The second half of the bar is not important, I very often do it *alla breve*.' Otto Strasser of the Vienna Philharmonic, described how 'nothing was more alien to Strauss than adopting poses. . . Frequent changes of tempo, as in *Salome* and *Elektra*, caused him no trouble. . . At rallentandos he used to raise both elbows, a characteristic gesture. His facial expression usually remained relaxed and yet there was an extraordinary tension in his whole demeanour. At climaxes he would rise to his feet [in later years he used a chair] and usually his face got very red. . . I often thought to myself during performances of *Rosenkavalier*, when other conductors lingered over some beautiful passages, extracting every last drop from them, how much more lightly the composer took them.'

This is supported by a memory of Arthur Tröber, a violinist in the Staatskapelle Dresden whose first experience of Strauss as a conductor was in *Der Rosenkavalier* in December 1919. He recalled (in some memoirs published in the *Richard Strauss-Blätter* No. 11 in May 1978) how 'Strauss conducted the performance with a minimum of gestures and without any visible expression of emotion. Just a few times he raised himself slightly at his desk and the orchestra automatically grew louder. But for all his calm and superiority and despite the dryness and precision of his gestures, he conjured up a tension in us that was difficult to account for. I shall never forget the fascinating way he lifted his eyebrows when he glanced up from the score at the stage or at a group of instruments. Rehearsals were rather more easy-going, as on one occasion for *Salome*. With rapid steps he hurried up to the rostrum on this morning but put down his baton after only ten minutes. "You know the piece, and so do I. Good morning, gentlemen", and he stepped agilely down from the podium and hurried to the Hotel Bellevue where his Skat companions from breakfast were still waiting.' Tröber also remembered a *Tristan* in 1933 when catastrophe was only narrowly avoided. 'A cut marked in the music had not been discussed beforehand and proved to be a trap. For once Strauss lost his calm for a minute until we found our feet again on firm ground and he could breathe with us once more.'

Herbert von Karajan (in *Conversations with Karajan* by Richard Osborne, Oxford 1989, pp. 112–13) said Strauss had an impeccable sense of rhythm, 'not in the metronomic, military sense of the term but in his feel for the real inner rhythm of the music. . . With Strauss you always had the sense of the music moving forward. In Mozart this was wonderful. He could be negligent at times. . . With him the slightest gesture would produce positive results. And he showed no emotion when conducting. His upbeat – you know how with many conductors this is a great upwards gesture and then a dreadful flop back down – with him there was none of this. The emotion came through the music. He knew in each piece exactly where the climaxes were.' After a performance of *Elektra* Karajan conducted in 1939, Strauss complimented him and added: 'You conduct it without the score in front of you, which I couldn't do any more as I am far away from the work! But don't forget that in five years' time you will have changed again.'

Some vivid memories of Strauss concerts in London came from Sir Adrian Boult. When he was fifteen, but already an acute critic, Boult heard Strauss conduct a Berlioz centenary concert in Queen's Hall on 11 December 1903. He was thrilled by the music but made no comment on the conducting. But on

26 June 1914 Strauss conducted *Don Juan, Till Eulenspiegel, Tod und Verklärung* and Mozart's 40th Symphony in the same hall. Boult wrote to me sixty years later: 'I was told that [at rehearsal] he polished off his three in an hour and spent the remaining five hours on the Mozart. It sounded like it – the end movements were amazing: for 10 bars you thought it was slow; it was, but you forgot it after 10 bars because the rhythm and the accentuation were so astonishingly light and lively.' When Strauss returned to London in January 1922, he conducted the same three tone-poems and some of his songs in the Royal Albert Hall. Boult noticed how Strauss 'had a wonderful knack of *just* giving people time to play things, while during the war we had all been rushing them'.

As a pianist, Strauss was good enough to play a Mozart concerto with Bülow and he was a fine, if erratic, accompanist in *Lieder*, not only to Pauline but to many other singers. Recordings of his accompanying made during the Second World War when he was nearly eighty give an idea of his extraordinary facility but also show that the years had taken much away – listen to *Kling!* for example. A famous description of him in his prime in the 1920s is given by Alfred Orel who turned the pages for Strauss at a Vienna recital with Elisabeth Schumann. Strauss whispered to him at the start: 'You mustn't follow the music, because I play it quite differently.' Orel said he then observed

such freedom and at the same time the highest degree of accuracy in suiting the music to the singer, and then again such guiding of her delivery, such support, in addition to knowing to a hairsbreadth where she would need assistance, whether in giving her time to breathe, or in helping her to avoid straining her own breath support, in short there has probably never been so perfect a unity between singer and accompanist.

The printed notes were often admittedly no more than aids to the composer's memory, a vocal score as it were. . . He went far beyond the printed accompaniment and exploited all the possibilities of the piano in a quite inimitable fashion. . . In *Heimliche Aufforderung* the rising run for piano began far lower, and therefore was played much more quickly, than it is notated. . . Countless times Strauss doubled the bass line and enriched the chords. Yet he could also, in *Morgen!* for example, follow the written notes punctiliously. In *Cäcilie*, certainly, it was as though one was hearing the surge of a full orchestra. . . While he left the singer to acknowledge the applause between numbers on her own, and while I was placing the music for the next song in front of him, he fingered the keys apparently at random. Great was my amazement when I realised it was always passages from his operas with which he made the transition to the new song, and specifically passages which were musically closely related to the song in question, but revealed that close relationship only now in the way he played them. Thus before *Du meines Herzens Krönelein* he played very softly – apparently entirely for himself – the closing duet from *Der Rosenkavalier*. . . It was an irrefutable demonstration of the great unity which encompasses Strauss's total *oeuvre* and of which the composer himself was also deeply aware, down to the smallest details.[1]

Strauss and the gramophone

Strauss, like Elgar, was one of the first great composers to appreciate the importance and significance of the gramophone. Late in 1905 he went into a recording studio in Freiburg to make a piano roll for the Welte Company who had developed a reproducing mechanism in Freiburg about five years earlier. He played extracts from *Salome* (which only had its première in December 1905), *Feuersnot, Ein Heldenleben*, four of the *Stimmungsbilder*, Op. 9, and *Heimliche Aufforderung*. In about 1914 he played two excerpts from *Ariadne auf Naxos*, the love scene from *Ein Heldenleben* and an excerpt from *Josephs Legende* for Hupfeld's 'Animatic' piano rolls.

He made his first records with an orchestra, the Berlin State Opera Orchestra, in 1917 – three movements from *Le bourgeois gentilhomme*, the overture to *Ariadne auf Naxos, Don Juan* (sides one and two of the 78 rpm discs were conducted by Georg Szell because Strauss was late arriving), *Till Eulenspiegel* and the *Rosenkavalier* waltzes. In 1921 he accompanied the tenor Robert Hutt in two of his songs, *Morgen!* and *Breit über mein Haupt* and the baritone Heinrich Schlusnus in *Heimkehr, Ich liebe dich, Ruhe, meine Seele!, Zueignung, Die Nacht* and *Das Geheimnis*.

While in America in 1921 he conducted an anonymous orchestra (probably members of the Chicago Symphony) in Chicago in Salome's Dance and two movements from *Le bourgeois gentilhomme*. On the same tour, in New York he made Ampico piano rolls of the second of the *Stimmungsbilder*, a transcription of *Zueignung* and the accompaniments only of *Zueignung, Allerseelen* and *Traum durch die Dämmerung*. Each of the accompaniments was played twice in different keys for different voices. In England in 1922 he recorded *Don Juan* (cut) and the *Rosenkavalier* Waltzes with the London Symphony Orchestra.

With the invention of electric recording, Strauss in 1926 conducted the

Berlin State Opera Orchestra in records of Beethoven's Seventh Symphony (the *finale* much cut), Mozart's 39th Symphony and *Ein Heldenleben*. In the same year he recorded the *Rosenkavalier* film music (including the Presentation March), in Queen's Hall, London, with the 'Augmented Tivoli Orchestra'. This has been re-issued on CD (EMI Classics 7 54610 2). Later in the same year, in Berlin, he recorded Mozart's Symphony No. 40, *Tod und Verklärung*, some interludes from *Intermezzo* and waltzes from *Der Rosenkavalier* with the Berlin State Opera Orchestra, returning to the studio early in 1927 to re-record the same works with a different recording technique. All except the Mozart were re-issued on CD (DG 429 925-2). He re-recorded the Mozart Symphony with this orchestra early in 1928 (both recordings are of the first version, without clarinets) and a few months later added Beethoven's Fifth Symphony and the overture to *Die Zauberflöte*. At the end of the year he recorded the overtures to Cornelius's *Der Barbier von Bagdad*, Wagner's *Der fliegende Holländer*, Weber's *Euryanthe* and Gluck's *Iphigenie in Aulis*, the Prelude to Act I of *Tristan und Isolde* and Salome's Dance (which has been re-issued on CD on DG 429 925-2).

In 1929, with the same orchestra, he recorded *Till Eulenspiegel* and *Don Juan*, following them in 1930 with the complete (nine movements) suite from *Le bourgeois gentilhomme*. His next recording was in mid-1933, again with the Berlin State Opera Orchestra. This was *Don Quixote*, with Enrico Mainardi as cellist (*Don Juan*, *Don Quixote* and *Le bourgeois gentilhomme* were re-issued on CD on DG 429 925-2).

He then made no more recordings until late in 1940 when, in Munich, he conducted the Bavarian State Opera Orchestra in the *Japanese Festival Music* (re-issued on CD on Preiser 90205 and DG 429 925-2). It is even possible that this was the world première, recorded before the Tokyo première. A year later, with the same orchestra, he recorded *Ein Heldenleben*, *Don Quixote* (cellist Oswald Uhl) and the *Rosenkavalier* Waltzes (all re-issued on CD on Preiser 90205. *Ein Heldenleben* and the Act 3 Waltz from *Der Rosenkavalier* were re-issued on CD on DG 429 925-2). Later in the year *Eine Alpensinfonie* was recorded (re-issued on CD on Preiser 90205). During 1942 and 1943 in Vienna he accompanied Maria Reining in *Meinem Kinde*, *Freundliche Vision*, *Cäcilie*, *Traum durch die Dämmerung*, *Zueignung* and *Wiegenlied*; Lea Piltti in *Heimkehr*, *Ständchen*, *Ich schwebe*, *Kling! All' mein Gedanken*,

Waldseligkeit and *Schlagende Herzen*; Anton Dermota in *Heimliche Aufforderung, Die Nacht, Zueignung, Ich liebe dich, Seitdem dein Aug' in meines Schaute* (twice), *Breit über mein Haupt, Ich trage meine Minne, Du meines Herzens Krönelein, Heimkehr, All' mein Gedanken, Glückes genug, In goldener Fülle* and *Sehnsucht*; Hilde Konetzni in *Schlechtes Wetter, Blick vom oberen Belvedere, Du meines Herzens Krönelein* and *Ach, Lieb, ich muss nun scheiden*; and Alfred Poell in *Ach weh mir unglückhaftem Mann, Wozu noch, Mädchen? Das Rosenband, Winterliebe, Ruhe, meine Seele!* and *Heimliche Aufforderung*. All these songs have been re-issued on two CDs by Preiser Records on 93261/2.

In February 1944 he recorded *Symphonia Domestica* on tape with the Vienna Philharmonic (re-issued on CD on Preiser 90216 and on DG 435 333-2). In June, during his eightieth birthday celebrations, came recordings of his tone-poems with the same orchestra: *Also sprach Zarathustra, Don Juan, Till Eulenspiegel, Ein Heldenleben, Tod und Verklärung* and the suite from *Le bourgeois gentilhomme* (all reissued on CD on Preiser 90216, *Till Eulenspiegel* also re-issued on CD on DG 435 333-2). Also in 1944, with the Berlin Radio Symphony Orchestra, he recorded a waltz from *Schlagobers*. In September 1944, in Munich, Strauss recorded four of his *Lieder* with orchestral accompaniment with the tenor Julius Patzak. They are *Ich trage meine Minne, Heimliche Aufforderung, Morgen!* and *Ständchen*. The orchestra is probably the Bavarian State Opera. On an unknown date in 1944 the Prelude to Act 1 of *Die Meistersinger* was recorded at a public concert with the Vienna Philharmonic (re-issued on CD on DG 435 333-2).

Other Strauss recordings known to exist include the *Festliches Präludium* (Berlin 1930); a complete *Don Quixote* and part of *Till Eulenspiegel* recorded off the air in November 1936 when he conducted the Staatskapelle Dresden in London; the complete Radio Lugano broadcast of 25 July 1947 of the *Serenade, Op. 7, Morgen!, Allerseelen, Ich trage meine Minne* and *Das Rosenband* (soprano Annette Brun), and the *Bourgeois gentilhomme* suite; the *Burleske* recorded on 19 October, 1947, with Alfred Blumen (piano) and the Philharmonia Orchestra, taken off the air.

A recording of Strauss's Symphony in F minor, Op. 12, in which the composer conducted the Great Orchestra of the Federal Radio on 5 November 1935 no longer exists.

NOTES

1 The family

1 G. Gould, 'An Argument for Richard Strauss', *High Fidelity*, March 1962, reprinted in *The Glenn Gould Reader*, ed. T. Page (New York, 1984; London, 1987), 84–92.
2 *Ibid.*, 86.
3 R. Strauss, *Betrachtungen und Erinnerungen*, ed. Willi Schuh (Zürich, 1949 and 1981), *Letzte Aufzeichnung*, 19 June 1949 (p. 182). This item is not included in the English version of this book, *Recollections and Reflections*, tr. L. J. Lawrence (London, 1953).
4 Johanna von Rauchenberger-Strauss, *Jugenderinnerungen*, in *Richard-Strauss-Jahrbuch* 1959–60 (Bonn, 1960).
5 Strauss, 'Recollections of My Youth and Years of Apprenticeship' (date unknown) in *Recollections and Reflections*, 134.
6 Strauss, 'Reminiscences of My Father' (date unknown) in *Recollections and Reflections*, 127–33.
7 C. Fifield, *True Artist and True Friend: a Biography of Hans Richter* (Oxford, 1993), 27.
8 Strauss, 'Reminiscences of My Father', 129–30.
9 R. Rolland, *Richard Strauss et Romain Rolland, Correspondance, Fragments de Journal* (Paris, 1951); English version *Richard Strauss & Romain Rolland, Correspondence, Diary & Essays*, ed. Rollo H. Myers (London, 1968), 134.
10 Strauss, 'Reminiscences of My Father', 131.
11 Quoted in W. Schuh, *Richard Strauss: Jugend und frühe Meisterjahre. Lebenschronik 1864–1898* (Zürich, 1976); English version *Richard Strauss: a Chronicle of the Early Years, 1864–1898*, tr. Mary Whittall, (Cambridge, 1982), 84–5.

2 Wunderkind

1 Strauss, 'Recollections of My Youth and Years of Apprenticeship', 134.
2 von Rauchenberger-Strauss, *Jugenderinnerungen*, 7–30.
3 Letter from Florence, 10 June 1893. R. Strauss, *Briefe an die Eltern 1882–1906*, ed. W. Schuh (Zürich, 1954), 181.

4 Schuh, *Richard Strauss: a Chronicle*, 26.

5 *Ibid.*, 26–7.

6 Rolland, *Richard Strauss & Romain Rolland* (diary, 25 March 1906), 140.

7 F. Trenner (ed.), *Richard Strauss-Ludwig Thuille: ein Briefwechsel* (Tutzing, 1980). First extracts in English, tr. Susan Gillespie, appeared in B. Gilliam (ed.), *Richard Strauss and his World* (Princeton, 1992), 193–236.

8 A facsimile of the original publication was published in 1985 by Hans Schneider, Tutzing, under the editorship of Stephan Kohler, director of the Richard-Strauss-Institut, Munich.

9 Strauss, 'Reminiscences of My Father', 129–30, 132.

10 The conductor Rudolf Moralt (1902–58) was related to Strauss through this branch of the family.

11 *Overture* in A minor (o.Op. 62), completed 16 July 1879 and dedicated to Strauss's teacher Meyer on his silver jubilee as a conductor.

12 *3 Lieder* to texts by Emanuel Geibel (o.Op. 55/AV 159/AV 160): *Die Liebe sass als Nachtigall; O schneller mein Ross; Die Lilien glühn in Düften*. Composed 9, 10 and 12 April 1879. First performed in Museumssaal, Munich, 16 March 1881 by Cornelia Meysenheim.

13 *Skizzen: fünf kleine Klavierstücke* (o.Op. 59): I *Allegro*; II *Andante*; III *Gavotte II*; IV *Gavotte III*; V *Gavotte IV* [*Gavotte I* is *Aus alter Zeit* (o.Op. 57)]. Completed 20, 21, 22/23 April, 1 May, 16 July 1879. Strauss orchestrated V on 16 July and it was performed by his father's Wilde Gung'l on 29 May 1880.

14 *Introduktion, Thema und Variationen* (o.Op. 56), completed 28–30 April 1879.

15 Sonata No. 2 in C minor (o.Op. 60). Completed 10 June 1879. Dedicated to his uncle Carl Hörburger.

16 *Romanze* in E flat (o.Op. 61). Completed 25 June 1879. First performed at the Ludwigsgymnasium, Munich, in the summer of 1879. Next known performance was on 14 July 1991 at Garmisch by Sabine Meyer and Michael Helmrath.

17 This was the fifth movement of *Skizzen* (see note 13).

18 *Quartettsatz* in E♭, *allegro moderato* (AV 211).

19 *Introduktion, Thema und Variationen* (o.Op. 52). Completed 4 October 1878. Written for 'dear Papa on his birthday'.

20 Johanna von Rauchenberger-Strauss, *Jugenderinnerungen*, 7–30.

21 Strauss, 'Reminiscences of My Father', 132.

3 Growing up

1 A. Holde, 'Unbekannte Briefe und Lieder von Richard Strauss' in *Internationale Richard-Strauss-Gesellschaft*, 19 November 1958, 2–6.

2 Strauss, *Briefe an die Eltern*, 24–5. Letter dated 12 December 1883.

3 Schuh, *Richard Strauss: a Chronicle*, 65.

4 Letter to Hofmannsthal 25 May 1916. F. and A. Strauss (eds.), *Richard Strauss und Hugo von Hofmannsthal: Briefwechsel* (Zürich, 1952). English version, *The Correspondence Between Richard Strauss and Hugo von Hofmannsthal*, tr. H. Hammelmann and E. Osers (London, 1961; Cambridge, 1980), 248–9.

5 Letter to Hofmannsthal, 2 August 1928, *ibid.*, 499.

6 Letter to Strauss, 5 August 1928, *ibid.*

7 Strauss told his father, letter dated 7 February 1884, that he had written two piano pieces *Heidebild* and *Nocturno* to add to the three previously composed, *Auf stillem Waldespfad*, *An einsamer Quelle*, and *Träumerei*. In the published work, *Intermezzo* replaces *Nocturno*.

8 Strauss, *Briefe an die Eltern*, 42. Letter dated 11 February 1884.

9 *Ibid.*, 46–9. Letter dated 29 February 1884.

10 Edmund Spitzweg died in 1884 and Eugen and his brother Otto were directors of the firm until 1904, when they were bought out by Universal Edition of Vienna.

11 R. Strauss, *Reminiscences of Hans von Bülow* (1909) in *Recollections and Reflections*, 119–20.

12 Strauss, *Briefe an die Eltern*, 54. Letter dated 12 January 1885.

4 Meiningen

1 Strauss, 'Recollections of My Youth and Years of Apprenticeship', 138.

2 Strauss, *Briefe an die Eltern*, 84–6. Letter dated 31 January 1886.

3 *Ibid.*, 90–1. Letter dated 4 April 1886.

4 Strauss, 'Reminiscences of Hans von Bülow', 120.

5 Third conductor

1 Strauss, 'Recollections of My Youth and Years of Apprenticeship', 138–9.

2 *Ibid.*, 140.

3 F. Trenner (ed.), *Cosima Wagner – Richard Strauss: Ein Briefwechsel* (Tutzing, 1978), 11. Letter dated 26 November 1889.

4 M. A. DeWolfe Howe, *The Boston Symphony Orchestra 1881–1931* (Cambridge, Mass., 1931), 73.

5 During rehearsals, Strauss grew more enthusiastic. In May 1888 he told Otto Lessmann that it was 'extremely interesting and full of capital things. The opera is very dashing, has colossal drive, the Wagner of *Holländer* and *Rienzi* already expresses himself in it to a quite significant extent.' To his uncle Carl Hörburger he wrote on 11 June: 'The ghost of Beethoven haunts the finales, elsewhere you can detect Weber and Marschner too, and Wagner's lion's paw is already quite strong.' Quoted in Schuh, *Richard Strauss: a Chronicle*, 127.

6 Dora and Weimar

1 'Master, 'tis not that dangerous', *Die Meistersinger von Nürnberg*, Act III, Scene 4, Eva's reply to Sachs when he says how lovely she looks.
2 Felix Mottl was conductor at Karlsruhe.
3 Strauss, *Briefe an die Eltern*, 135–6. Letter dated 9 December 1890.
4 This letter (dated 15 August 1890) is quoted in Schuh, *Richard Strauss: a Chronicle*, 208, but no letter to Cosima from Strauss on that date is included in Trenner (ed.), *Cosima Wagner – Richard Strauss: Ein Briefwechsel*.

7 First failure

1 Trenner (ed.), *Cosima Wagner – Richard Strauss: Ein Briefwechsel*, 66. Letter dated 23 January 1892.
2 Strauss, 'Recollections of My Youth and Years of Apprenticeship', 141.
3 Letter to Johanna, 11 February 1892. Brahms also regarded Richter as lazy.
4 Strauss, 'Recollections of My Youth and Years of Apprenticeship', 142.
5 Strauss, *Briefe an die Eltern*, 152. Letter dated 18 March 1892.
6 Reinhard Gerlach, *Richard Strauss: Prinzipien seiner Kompositionstechnik* (Archiv für Musikwissenschaft, 23:4, Wiesbaden, December 1966).
7 Strauss, *Briefe an die Eltern*, 163. Letter dated 13 February 1893.
8 Letter to Humperdinck, Weimar, 30 October 1893.
9 R. Strauss, 'Reminiscences of the First Performances of My Operas' (1942) in *Recollections and Reflections*, 147.
10 R. Strauss, 'Erinnerungen an die ersten Aufführungen meiner Opern' (1942), in *Betrachtungen und Erinnerungen*, 222. This essay appears in revised form only in the German edition.

8 Engagement

1 Extracts from Strauss's Egypt diary.
2 Strauss diary. Garmisch archive.
3 Strauss, 'Reminiscences of the First Performances of My Operas', 147.
4 These letters are given more fully in Schuh, *Richard Strauss: a Chronicle*, 353–7.

9 Pauline

1 N. Del Mar, *Richard Strauss: a Critical Commentary on His Life and Works* (London, 1969), Vol. II, 239.
2 A. Mahler, *Gustav Mahler: Erinnerungen und Briefe* (Amsterdam, 1940); in English as *Gustav Mahler: Memories and Letters*, ed. Donald Mitchell, tr. Basil Creighton, 3rd edn. (London, 1973).

3 H. Blaukopf (ed.), *Gustav Mahler – Richard Strauss Briefwechsel, 1888–1911* (Munich, 1980); in English as *Gustav Mahler–Richard Strauss Correspondence 1888–1911*, tr. E. Jephcott (London, 1984), 65. Letter dated early or mid-January 1902.

4 K. Wilhelm, *Richard Strauss persönlich* (Munich, 1984); in English as *Richard Strauss: an Intimate Portrait*, tr. Mary Whittall (London, 1989), 66.

5 *Ibid.*

6 J. A. Stargadt, *Autographen Auktionkatalog 597* (Marburg, 1971).

7 A. Orel, 'Richard Strauss als Begleiter seiner Lieder. Eine Erinnerung', *Schweizerische Musikzeitung* 92:1 (1952), 12f.

8 Rolland, *Richard Strauss & Romain Rolland*, 133.

9 L. Lehmann, *Singing With Richard Strauss* (London, 1964), 25–7.

10 K. Böhm, *Ich erinnere mich ganz genau* (Vienna, 1970); in English as *A Life Remembered*, tr. J Kehoe (London, 1992), 88.

11 G. Puritz, *Elisabeth Schumann*, tr. J. Puritz (London, 1993), 142.

12 F. Grasberger (ed.), *Eine Welt in Briefen* (Tutzing, 1967), 519.

13 *Ibid.*, 141–2.

14 F. and A. Strauss (eds.), *The Correspondence Between Richard Strauss and Hugo von Hofmannsthal*, 426.

15 Wilhelm, *Richard Strauss*, 177–8.

16 Translation by Andrew Porter.

17 F. and A. Strauss (eds.), *Correspondence Between Richard Strauss and Hugo von Hofmannsthal*, 76. Letter dated 20 March 1911.

10 The tone-poet

1 Schuh, *Richard Strauss: a Chronicle*, 428.

2 Strauss's reply to Hausegger was included in *Gedanken eines Schauenden* (Munich, 1903), a posthumous collection of Hausegger's essays edited by his brother Siegmund, the conductor.

3 Schuh, *Richard Strauss: a Chronicle*, 428.

4 P. Heyworth (ed.), *Conversations with Klemperer* (London, 1985), 47.

5 R. Strauss, 'On the Munich Opera' (1928) in *Recollections and Reflections*, 82.

6 Letter dated 14 June 1898 to Georges Khnopff.

7 Readers may be interested by other fees (in Deutschmarks) for which Strauss sold his works at this stage of his career: *Don Juan*, 800; *Tod und Verklärung*, 1,600; *Till Eulenspiegel*, 1,000; *Also sprach Zarathustra*, 3,000; *Zwei Gesänge*, for mixed chorus, Op. 34, 2,000; *Symphonia Domestica*, 35,000; *Eine Alpensinfonie*, 50,000. See Barbara Petersen, 'Richard Strauss as Composer's Advocate', in B. Gilliam (ed.), *Richard Strauss: New Perspectives on the Composer and his Work* (Durham and London, 1992), 115–32.

8 For a detailed examination of this question, see J. Hepokoski, 'Fiery-Pulsed Libertine or Domestic Hero? Strauss's Don Juan Reinvestigated', in Gilliam (ed.), *Richard Strauss: New Perspectives*, 135–75.

9 Böhm, *A Life Remembered*, 80.

10 J. Williamson: *Strauss: Also sprach Zarathustra* (Cambridge, 1993), 23. This excellent monograph is recommended to all who wish to delve deeply into every aspect of the tone-poem.

11 Rolland, *Richard Strauss & Romain Rolland*, 134.

12 H. Lohberger (ed.), *Richard Strauss in the Diaries of Anton Berger* (*Richard Strauss-Blätter* 11, Vienna, May 1978), 6.

13 Rolland, *Richard Strauss & Romain Rolland*, 134.

14 *Ibid.*, 112.

15 *Ibid.*, 122–3.

16 *Ibid.*, 133.

17 Schuh, *Richard Strauss, a Chronicle*, 478.

18 Rolland, *Richard Strauss & Romain Rolland*, 121.

19 Strauss, *Briefe an die Eltern*, 283–4. Letter dated 26 November 1903.

11 At the Kaiser's court

1 Blaukopf (ed.), *Gustav Mahler–Richard Strauss Correspondence*, 47.

2 Strauss conducted three of Mahler's songs with orchestra, soloist Emilie Herzog, in Berlin on 9 April 1900.

3 Rolland, *Richard Strauss & Romain Rolland*, 132.

4 F. and A. Strauss (eds.), *Correspondence Between Richard Strauss and Hugo von Hofmannsthal*, 1. Letter dated 30 November 1900.

5 Strauss, *Briefe an die Eltern*, 232.

6 Rolland, *Richard Strauss & Romain Rolland*, 114.

7 Strauss, 'Reminiscences of the First Performances of My Operas', 149.

8 Friedrich von Schuch, *Richard Strauss, Ernst von Schuch und Dresdens Oper* (Leipzig, 1953), 61.

9 *Ibid.*, 61–2.

10 The London Strauss Festival of 3, 4, 5 and 9 June 1903 was given by the Concertgebouw Orchestra of Amsterdam conducted by Willem Mengelberg and Strauss.

11 Blaukopf (ed.), *Gustav Mahler–Richard Strauss Correspondence*, 93.

12 Mahler: *Gustav Mahler: Memories and Letters*, 97–8.

13 A. Gide, *Journal*, 22 May 1907 (Bibliothèque de la Pléiade, Tours, Gallimard, 1965), 245–6.

14 *Bibliothèque de l'Opéra*, Acq. 26444–Dossier V (III, 73).

15 J. Caullier, *La Belle et la Bête: L'Allemagne des Kapellmeister dans l'imaginaire français (1890–1914)* ('Transferts', Lérot, Tusson, Charente, 1993), 56–7.

16 H. Jourdan-Morhange, *Ravel et nous* (Geneva, 1945), 89.

17 W. Schuh, *Richard Strauss, Stefan Zweig: Briefwechsel* (Frankfurt, 1957); in English as *A Confidential Matter: the Letters of Richard Strauss and Stefan Zweig, 1931–1935* tr. Max Knight (University of California Press, 1977), 90.

18 *Ibid.*, 103.

19 R. Osborne, *Conversations with Karajan* (Oxford, 1989), 114.

20 R. Craft, *Chronicle of a Friendship* (New York, 1973), 215.

21 Rolland, *Richard Strauss & Romain Rolland*, 83. Letter dated 14 May 1907.

22 *Ibid.*, 156.

12 Enter Hofmannsthal

1 Strauss, 'Reminiscences of the First Performances of My Operas', 154–7.

2 K. Pringsheim, 'Zur Aufführung von Mahlers Sechster Symphonie', *Musikblätter des Anbruch*, Vol.2, No. 14, 1920, 497.

3 K. Pringsheim, 'Erinnerungen an Gustav Mahler', *Neue Zürcher Zeitung*, 7 July 1960.

4 Strauss, 'Reminiscences of the First Performances of My Operas', 154.

5 F. and A. Strauss (eds.), *Correspondence Between Richard Strauss and Hugo von Hofmannsthal*, 12–13.

6 von Schuch, *Richard Strauss, Ernst von Schuch und Dresdens Oper*, 82.

7 Strauss, 'Reminiscences of the First Performances of My Operas', 154–7.

8 G. Gould, 'Strauss and the Electronic Future', *Saturday Review*, 30 May 1964, 59.

9 F. and A. Strauss (eds.), *Correspondence Between Richard Strauss and Hugo von Hofmannsthal*, 3. All the subsequent quotations in this chapter are taken from this correspondence.

10 von Schuch, 95.

11 F. and A. Strauss (eds.), *Correspondence Between Richard Strauss and Hugo von Hofmannsthal*, 252.

12 H. Moldenhauer, *Anton von Webern, a Chronicle of His Life and Work* (London, 1978), 148.

13 G. Brosche, *Richard Strauss und Arnold Schoenberg* (*Richard Strauss-Blätter*, Neue Folge, Heft 2, December 1979), 21.

14 E. Stein (ed.), *Arnold Schoenberg Letters* (Faber, 1964), 50–1.

15 *Ibid.*, 50–1.

13 The *Ariadne* crisis

1 F. and A. Strauss (eds.), *Correspondence Between Richard Strauss and Hugo von Hofmannsthal*, 106–11.

2 This letter is dated 27 February 1911 in Grasberger (ed.), *Eine Welt in Briefen*, 194, but this is impossible. It must have been written in December 1911 or early in January 1912.

3 I. Stravinsky and R. Craft, *Conversations with Igor Stravinsky* (Faber, 1959), 75.

4 L. Sokolova, *Dancing with Diaghilev* (John Murray, 1960).

5 T. Beecham, *A Mingled Chime* (London, 1944), 128.

6 Wilhelm, *Richard Strauss*, 147.

14 Twentieth-century Offenbach

1 Strauss, 'Reminiscences of the First Performances of My Operas', 166. Strauss's memory let him down in 1942. Franz Strauss had volunteered.

2 E. Schumann, article in a music magazine 1920, quoted in G. Puritz, *Elisabeth Schumann*, 76–7.

15 Vienna

1 F. and A. Strauss (eds.), *Correspondence Between Richard Strauss and Hugo von Hofmannsthal*, 308–9.

2 *Ibid.*, 310–11.

3 R. Tenschert, *Memories of Richard Strauss from the Period of the Commemorative Events for his 80th Birthday in Vienna* (*Richard Strauss-Blätter* No. 10 Vienna, December 1977), 13–14.

4 Strauss, 'Reminiscences of the First Performances of My Operas', 166.

5 A. Tröber, 'Strauss-Erinnerungen eines Dresdener Kammermusikers' in *Richard Strauss-Blätter* No. 11 (Vienna, May 1978), 2.

6 Götz Klaus Konde, 'Alterations to the Instrumentation of the Third Act of *Die Frau ohne Schatten*,' *Richard Strauss-Blätter* No. 2 (Vienna, November 1971), 30–3.

7 Between 1919 and 1924 Strauss conducted sixteen performances of *Salome*, thirteen of *Der Rosenkavalier* and thirteen of *Ariadne auf Naxos*. There were seven performances of *Feuersnot*, twelve of *Die Frau ohne Schatten* and nineteen of *Josephs Legende*.

8 K. Kraus, *Die Fackel*, June 1924, 52–6.

9 *Ibid.*

16 *Intermezzo*

1 B. Gilliam, 'Strauss's *Intermezzo*: Innovation and Tradition' in Gilliam (ed.), *Richard Strauss–New Perspectives*, 259–83.

2 P. Turing, *Hans Hotter, Man and Artist* (John Calder, London, 1983), 217.

3 The Rules were first published in the *Allgemeine Musikzeitung*, Jg.55, No. 17, 27 April 1928. Strauss included them in his memoirs (1949), published in English as *Recollections and Reflections*, 38.

4 N. Del Mar, *Richard Strauss: a Critical Commentary on His Life and Works*, Vol. II, 221.

17 Helena

1 F. and A. Strauss (eds.), *Correspondence Between Richard Strauss and Hugo von Hofmannsthal*, 435–6.

2 R. Strauss, 'Interview on *Die ägyptische Helena*' (1928) in *Recollections and Reflections*, 103–5.

3 F. and A. Strauss (eds.), *Correspondence Between Richard Strauss and Hugo von Hofmannsthal*, 447.

4 *Ibid.*, 451.

5 Blaukopf, *Gustav Mahler–Richard Strauss Correspondence*, 75.

6 L. Wurmser, 'Richard Strauss as an Opera Conductor', *Music and Letters*, Vol. XLV (January 1964), 4–15.

7 Letter to Rychner, 19 February 1929.

18 Arabella

1 F. and A. Strauss (eds.), *Correspondence Between Richard Strauss and Hugo von Hofmannsthal*, 442.

2 *Ibid.*, 459.

3 *Ibid.*, 512–4.

4 *Ibid.*, 533–4.

19 The gathering storm

1 *Richard Strauss-Ludwig Karpath Briefwechsel*, 21 September 1929, in *Richard Strauss-Blätter No. 7* (May 1976), 8.

2 Strauss to B. von Niessen, 27 February 1932, in Grasberger (ed.), *Eine Welt in Briefen*, 338.

3 *Ibid.*

4 An extract from this performance, including the numbers Strauss composed, was recorded and has been issued on CD by Koch Schwann in Vol.3 of its Wiener-Staatsoper Live edition (3–1453–2).

5 S. Zweig, *Die Welt von gestern* (Stockholm, 1942); English version, *The World of Yesterday* (London, 1943), 280.

6 F. Busch, *Aus dem Leben, eines Musikers* (Zürich, 1949); English version, *Pages from a Musical Life*, tr. M. Strachey (London 1953), 169ff.

7 M. H. Kater, *The Twisted Muse: Musicians and their Music in the Third Reich* (New York, 1997), 122.

8 R. Schlötterer, *Ursuleac, singen für Richard Strauss* (Vienna, 1986), 15.

9 *Das schöne Sachsen* (Dresden, 1933), 162–3.

10 Schlötterer, *Ursuleac, singen für Richard Strauss*, 15.

11 *Sunday Times*, London, 20 September 1953.

20 Taking Walter's place

1 Lord Esher, *Journals and Letters*, 4 vols. (London, 1934–8).

2 Heyworth (ed.), *Conversations with Klemperer*, 45–6.

3 H. H. Stuckenschmidt, *Arnold Schoenberg, His Life, World and Work* (London, 1977), 544–5.

4 Osborne, *Conversations with Karajan*, 113.

5 Friedrich Ebert was first president of the Weimar republic, elected in 1919.

6 Internationale Richard-Strauss-Gesellschaft, Berlin, *Mitteilungsblätter*, May 1955, Vol.7.

7 R. Strauss–A. Kippenberg, *Briefwechsel*, in *Richard Strauss Jahrbuch* 1959/60, 120.

21 The Reich Chamber

1 G. Splitt, *Richard Strauss 1933–1935: Aesthetik und Musikpolitik zu Beginn der nationalsozialistischen Herrschaft* (Centaurus Verlagsgesellschaft, Pfaffenweiler, 1987), 81.

2 H.-H. Schönzeler, *Furtwängler* (London, 1990), 61.

3 L. Foreman, *From Parry to Britten: British Music in Letters 1900–1945* (London, 1987), 239.

4 Sir Morosus, the principal character in *Die schweigsame Frau*. Strauss and Zweig always referred to the opera by this name.

5 Kater, *The Twisted Muse: Musicians and their Music in the Third Reich*, 209.

6 Information supplied to the author by Dr Christian Strauss in writing and in conversation.

22 Dismissal

1 Schuh (ed.), *A Confidential Matter*, 67.

2 *Ibid.*, 67–8.

3 *Ibid.*, 68–9.

4 *Ibid.*, 71.

5 *Ibid.*, 73–4.

6 *Ibid.*, 75–6.

7 *Ibid.*, 79–80.

8 *Ibid.*, 90.

9 *Ibid.*, 91–2.

10 *Ibid.*, 93.

11 *Ibid.*, 94.

12 Böhm, *A Life Remembered*, 80.

13 Schuh (ed.), *A Confidential Matter*, 99–100.

14 K. Birkin, *Friedenstag and Daphne: an Interpretative Study of the Literary and Dramatic Sources of Two Operas by Richard Strauss* (New York and London, 1989), 77.

15 von Schuch, *Richard Strauss, Ernst von Schuch und Dresdens Oper*, 134.

16 Böhm, *A Life Remembered*, 87.

17 H. G. Alsberg (ed.), *Stefan and Friderike Zweig: Their Correspondence 1912–1942*, tr. Alsberg (New York, 1954).

18 P. H. Láng, *Critic at the Opera* (New York, 1971), 261–2.

23 Working with Gregor

1 Strauss's letters to Pauline from Milan on 8 March and Dijon on 17 March make no reference to the crisis, as they would have done if he had known of it – an extraordinary reminder of the lack in 1936 of radio news and an indication that Strauss did not bother to buy a newspaper when away from home.

2 E. Krause, 'The Singing Laurel Tree' in *Richard Strauss-Blätter* No. 3 (Vienna, 1972), 43.

3 Tröber, 'Strauss-Erinnerungen eines Dresdener Kammermusikers', 1–6.

4 B. Geissmar, *The Baton and the Jackboot* (London, 1944), 230.

24 Danae and Madeleine

1 Böhm, *A Life Remembered*, 81.

2 R. Milnes, 'A Comedy of Mirrors' (Glyndebourne programme book, 1990), 160.

25 After *Capriccio*

1 R. Hartmann, *Die Bühnenwerke von der Uraufführung bis heute* (Fribourg, 1980); in English, *Richard Strauss: the Staging of his Operas and Ballets*, tr. G. Davies (Oxford, 1982), 261.

2 *Ibid.*, 253.

3 Grasberger (ed.), *Eine Welt in Briefen*, 408–10.

26 Eightieth birthday

1 R. Tenschert, *Memories of Richard Strauss*, 12–18.
2 Böhm, *A Life Remembered*, 89.
3 E. Krause, *Richard Strauss: Gestalt und Werk* (Leipzig, 1955); English version, *Richard Strauss: the Man and his Work*, tr. J. Coombs (London, 1964), 57.

27 *Metamorphosen*

1 In German, Strauss wrote *Brucknerscher Orgelruhe*. Although Strauss conducted Bruckner's Ninth Symphony in Salzburg in 1906 and the Seventh in Buenos Aires in 1923, he did not like the music. Bruckner's mystical religiosity was an anathema to a man of Strauss's non-beliefs (which makes it all the more surprising that he praised Elgar's *The Dream of Gerontius*). Writing in 1904 to an author who wished to write a book about Bruckner in a series Strauss edited, Strauss said: 'I admit that every form of piety is so disagreeable to me that I cannot be fair even to its most naive expression. Since I sincerely admire the melodist Bruckner, I am willing to be quiet and retain an unbelieving smile when one crowns his primitive counterpoint stutterings with the title of mastership.' In a letter to Reznićek in March 1935 he wrote: 'The boring farmer's music of the good old Anton seems to me to be completely superfluous: Te Deum, wenn aus ist, benamst! (called: Te Deum, *praise God* when it's over!).' See G. Brosche, 'Richard Strauss und Anton Bruckner' in *Richard Strauss-Blätter* No. 12 (Vienna, December 1978), 27–9.

28 'I am Richard Strauss. . .'

1 M. Weiss, 'Remembering Strauss', letter in *New Yorker*, 25 August & 1 September 1997.
2 The full list, and the full text of Strauss's letter, is given as an appendix in Böhm, *A Life Remembered*, 157–63.

29 The exile

1 R. Strauss, *Briefwechsel mit Willi Schuh*, ed. W. Schuh (Zürich, 1969), 101–2.
2 Grasberger (ed.), *Eine Welt in Briefen*, 449–50.
3 Strauss, *Briefwechsel mit Willi Schuh*, 89.

30 London

1 Over ninety letters from Strauss to Roth are now in the Bavarian State Library, Munich.

2 Lord Harewood, *The Tongs and the Bones* (London, 1981), 93–4.

3 W. Schuh, *Ein paar Erinnerungen an Richard Strauss* (Zürich, 1964), 15.

4 N. Del Mar, *Richard Strauss: a Critical Commentary on his Life and Works*, Vol.I (London, 1962), xii.

5 M. Vermeulen, 'Een dubbed schandaal: Het Concertgebouw herdenkt Hitler', *De Groene Amsterdammer*, 11 October 1947, 7.

6 T. L. Jackson, 'The Metamorphosis of the *Metamorphosen: New Analytical and Source-Critical Discoveries*' in B. Gilliam (ed.), *Richard Strauss: New Perspectives*, 193–241.

31 Last songs

1 H. Burghauser, 'Richard Strauss als Wiener Operndirektor. Erinnerungen von Hugo Burghauser', ed. P. Dusek *Richard Strauss-Blätter* No. 12 (Vienna, December 1978), 8–23.

2 E. McArthur, *Kirsten Flagstad* (New York, 1965), 289–90.

32 Return to Garmisch

1 G. Solti, *Solti on Solti, a Memoir* (London, 1997), 79–80.

2 The text of Strauss's speech is reprinted in Schuh, *Betrachtungen und Erinnerungen*, 250–2, but not in the English version of the book.

3 R. Hartmann, 'The Last Visit to Richard Strauss' in R. Schlötterer (ed.), *Richard Strauss – Rudolf Hartmann: Ein Briefwechsel* (Tutzing, 1984), 91–6.

4 Solti, *Solti on Solti*, 80–2.

5 Hartmann, 'The Last Visit', 91–6.

6 Solti, *Solti on Solti*, 83.

7 Grasberger (ed.), *Eine Welt in Briefen*, 479–80.

8 P. Heyworth, *Otto Klemperer, His Life and Times, Vol.2, 1933–1973* (Cambridge, 1996), 142.

Appendix 1

1 A. Orel, 'Richard Strauss als Begleiter seiner Lieder. Eine Erinnerung', *Schweizerische Musikzeitung* 92:1 (1952), 12ff.

SELECT BIBLIOGRAPHY

Armstrong, Thomas, *Strauss's Tone-Poems* (Oxford, 1931).

Asow, Mueller von, *Richard Strauss: Thematisches Verzeichnis* (Vienna, 1954–68).

Beecham, Thomas, *A Mingled Chime* (London, 1944).

Birkin, Kenneth, *Friedenstag and Daphne: an Interpretative Study of the Literary and Dramatic Sources of Two Operas by Richard Strauss* (New York and London, 1989).

Arabella (Cambridge, 1989).

(ed.) *Stefan Zweig-Joseph Gregor Correspondence 1921–1938* (Dunedin, 1991).

Blaukopf, Herta, (ed.) *Gustav Mahler-Richard Strauss Briefwechsel 1888–1911* (Munich, 1980); English version *Gustav Mahler-Richard Strauss Correspondence 1888–1911*, tr. Edmund Jephcott (London, 1984).

Böhm, Karl, *Ich erinnere mich ganz genau* (Vienna, 1970); English version *A Life Remembered*, tr. J. Kehoe (London, 1992).

Brosche, Günter, 'The Concerto for Oboe and Small Orchestra (1945): Remarks about the Origin of the Work' in Gilliam, (ed.) *Richard Strauss: New Perspectives* (Durham and London, 1992).

Richard Strauss: Bibliographie (Vienna, 1973).

Brosche, Günter, and Karl Dachs, *Richard Strauss: Autographen in München und Wien: Verzeichnis* (Tutzing, 1979).

Busch, Fritz, *Aus dem Leben eines Musikers* (Zürich, 1949); English version *Pages from a Musical Life*, tr. M. Strachey (London, 1953).

Caullier, Joëlle, *La Belle et la Bête: L'Allemagne des Kapellmeister dans l'imaginaire français (1890– 1914)* (Charente, 1993).

Del Mar, Norman, *Richard Strauss: a Critical Commentary on His Life and Works*. Three volumes (London, 1962, 1969, 1972; rev. 1978).

English National Opera Guide No.8, *Der Rosenkavalier*, ed. N. John (essays by P. Branscombe, M. Kennedy and D. Puffett) (London, 1981).

English National Opera Guide No.30, *Arabella*, ed. N. John (essays by K. Forsyth, W. Mann, M. Ratcliffe and P. J. Smith) (London, 1985).

English National Opera Guide No.37, *Salome/Elektra*, ed. N. John (essays by P. Banks, J. Burton, K. Segar and C. Wintle) (London, 1988).

Erhardt, Otto, *Richard Strauss* (Olten, 1953).

Forsyth, Karen, *Ariadne auf Naxos by Hugo von Hofmannsthal and Richard Strauss, Its Genesis and Meaning* (London, 1982).

Gilliam, Bryan, *Music and Performance During the Weimar Republic* (Cambridge, 1994).

(ed.) *Richard Strauss and His World* (essays by L. Botstein, B. Gilliam, J. Hepokoski, T. L. Jackson, D. Puffett, M. P. Steinberg, and reprints of various articles) (Princeton, 1992).

(ed.) *Richard Strauss: New Perspectives on the Composer and his Work* (essays by K. Agawu, G. Brosche, B. Gilliam, S. E. Hefling, J. Hepokoski, T. L. Jackson, L. Lockwood, B. A. Petersen, P. M. Potter, R. Schlötterer, R. L. Todd) (Durham and London, 1992, 2nd edition 1997 with introduction by M. Kennedy).

Richard Strauss's Elektra (Oxford, 1991).

Gould, Glenn, 'An Argument for Richard Strauss' and 'Strauss and the Electronic Future' in *The Glenn Gould Reader*, ed. T. Page (New York, 1984; London, 1987).

Grasberger, Franz, *Eine Welt in Briefen* (Tutzing, 1967).

(ed.) *Richard Strauss und die Wiener Oper* (Munich, 1969).

Gray, Cecil, 'Richard Strauss' in *Survey of Contemporary Music* (London, 1924).

Gregor, Joseph, *Richard Strauss, die Meister der Oper* (Munich, 1939; 2nd edition 1943).

Hartmann, Rudolf, *Die Bühnenwerke von der Uraufführung bis heute* (Fribourg, 1980); English version *Richard Strauss: the Staging of his Operas and Ballets*, tr. Graham Davis (Oxford, 1982).

Hofmannsthal, Hugo von, *Briefe der Freundschaft*, correspondence with Eberhard von Bodenhausen (Frankfurt, 1953).

Jaacks, Gisela, and Jahnke, A.W., (eds.) *Richard Strauss, Musik des Lichts in dunkler Zeit* (essays by K. Böhm, G. Brunner, W. Geierhos, R. Hartmann, G. Jaacks, S. Kohler, E. Krause, W. Schuh, F. Trenner) (Mainz, 1980).

Jackson, Timothy L., 'The Metamorphosis of the *Metamorphosen*: New Analytical and Source-Critical Discoveries', in Gilliam, (ed.) *Richard Strauss: New Perspectives* (Durham and London, 1992).

'*Ruhe, meine Seele!* and the *Letzte Orchesterlieder*, in Gilliam, (ed.) *Richard Strauss and His World* (Princeton, 1992).

Jameux, Dominique, *Richard Strauss* (Paris, 1986).

Jefferson, Alan, *The Lieder of Richard Strauss* (London, 1971).

The Life of Richard Strauss (Newton Abbot, 1973).

The Operas of Richard Strauss in Britain, 1910–63 (London, 1963).

Richard Strauss (London, 1975).

Der Rosenkavalier (Cambridge, 1985).

Kaminiarz, Irina, *Richard Strauss Briefe aus dem Archiv des Allgemeinen Deutschen Musikvereins 1888–1909* (Weimar, 1995).

Kämper, D., *Richard Strauss und Franz Wüllner im Briefwechsel* (Cologne, 1963).

Tuchman, Barbara W., *The Proud Tower* (London, 1966).

Ursuleac, Viorica, and Roswitha Schlötterer, *Singen für Richard Strauss* (Vienna, 1987).

Wanless, Susan, *Vier letzte Lieder* (Leeds, 1984).

Wellesz, Egon, 'Hofmannsthal and Strauss' in *Music and Letters*, Vol. xxxiii (1952).

Wilhelm, Kurt, *Fürs Wort brauche ich Hilfe: die Geburt der Oper Capriccio* (Munich, 1988).

Richard Strauss persönlich (Munich, 1984); English version *Richard Strauss: an Intimate Portrait*, tr. Mary Whittall (London, 1989).

Williamson, John, *Strauss: Also sprach Zarathustra* (Cambridge, 1993).

Wurmser, Leo, 'Richard Strauss as an Opera Conductor', in *Music and Letters*, Vol.xlv, January 1964.

Zweig, Stefan, *Die Welt von gestern* (Stockholm, 1942); English version *The World of Yesterday* (no translator named) (London, 1943).

INDEX

Aagard-Oestvig, Karl, 196, 212
Abendroth, Walther, 290–1
Adam, Adolphe, 105
Adler, Guido, 295
Adler, Hans, 374
Adolph, Dr Paul, 262, 285, 298, 299
Adorno, Theodor, on R.S., 224
Ahlgrimm, Isolde, 353
Ahna, Major General Adolf de (father-in-law), 58, 81–3
Ahna, Mädi de (sister-in-law), 81–2
Ahna, Maria de (mother-in-law), 58
Ahna, Pauline de. See *Strauss, Pauline*
Aibl, Joseph, 34, 109
Albert, Eugen d', 32, 56
Albert, Hermann, 328
Allen, Sir Hugh, 312
Allgemeiner Deutscher Musikverein, 73, 108, 153, 306
Allgemeine Musikzeitung, 33, 62, 290
Altenberg, Peter (Richard Englander), 148
Alvary, Max, 68
Alwin, Carl, 94, 212, 222, 224, 238, 255, 256, 329
Ampico (piano rolls, Chicago 1921), 406
Amsterdam. See *Concertgebouw Orchestra*
Anders, Peter, 318
Andersen, Hans, 381
Andreae, Volkmar, 369
Andrian-Werburg, Baron Leopold von, 205

Annunzio, Gabriele d', 175, 187
Arnim, Achim von, 103, 202
Artôt de Padilla, Lola, 193
Aschenbrenner, Carl, 19, 27
Asow, Dr Erich Müller von, 18, 347
Astruc, Gabriel, 144
Auber, Daniel, 16–17, 32, 48, 130, 316, 366
Audibert, Comte d', 368

Bach, Johann Sebastian, 4, 128, 395; *Well-Tempered Clavier*, 15
Baden-Baden, 28
Bahr, Hermann, 96, 199, 231, 341; works on R.S. libretto, 196
Bakst, Léon, 186
Bantock, Sir Granville, 284
Bärmann, Carl, 20
Barrymore, Lionel, invites R.S. to Hollywood, 372–3
Basile, Armando, 381
Bayreuth, 8, 26, 47, 54, 55, 57, 60, 61, 68, 83, 85, 86, 143, 281, 287; R.S. first conducts at, 78; R.S. conducts *Parsifal* at, 276–7; Pauline sings at, 66, 78
Beardsley, Aubrey, 148
Becker, Carl, 33
Beecham, Sir Thomas, 133, 143, 182, 314, 376, 379; on *Josephs Legende*, 187
Beethoven, Ludwig van, 4, 5, 7, 8, 14, 15, 16, 17, 32, 40, 45, 46, 47, 49, 62, 101, 129, 184,191, 270, 318, 325, 361, 363, 387, 394,

Beethoven, Ludwig van (*cont.*)
407; *Fidelio*, 66, 106–07, 211, 286, 318–19, 366; R.S. conducts *Leonore*, 130; *Die Ruinen von Athen*, 228; Symphony No. 5 as 'Götz', 236–7; Violin Concerto, 15
Begas, Grethe, 34
Bekker, Paul, 220
Berg, Alban, 201, 210, 224, 231
Berger, Dr Anton, 112, 236
Berger, Elly Félicie, 239
Bergomaschi, Bruno, 381
Berlin, 29, 38, 56, 69, 74, 90, 95, 96, 105, 112, 126, 136, 139, 150, 152, 173, 177, 179, 184, 191, 193, 201, 229, 239, 244, 258, 262, 271, 275, 286, 324; first visit by R.S., 31–4; Court Opera, 106, 134, 135, 143, 154, 164, 170; R.S. becomes conductor of, 106, 127–9; first *Rosenkavalier* in, 170; R.S. work-load at, 196; R.S. leaves, 207; Philharmonic Orchestra, 32, 79, 202, 247, 274, 289, 354, R.S. conductor of, 101–2; Tonkünstler-Orchester concerts, 130–31
Berlioz, Hector, 16, 101, 366, 403; R.S. views on, 61, 145
Bernhardt, Sarah, 104
Bernstein, Martin, 347
Bethge, Hans, 255
Bierbaum, Otto Julius, 20, 119–20, 125
Bilse, Benjamin, 33
Bischoff, Hermann, 132
Bismarck, Otto, Prince von, 106, 117, 205, 272
Bispham, David, 138
Bittner, Julius, 211, 223
Bizet, Georges, 101, 366
Blech, Leo, 164, 192, 366
Blumen, Alfred, 378, 408
Böckmann, Ferdinand, 28, 30, 31
Böckmann, Helene, 30, 31
Bodman, Emanuel von, 120

Böhm, Karl, 92, 111, 235, 275, 297, 298, 299, 302, 303, 309, 324, 337–8, 339, 341, 352, 353, 358, 366, 372, 386, 393; dedicatee of *Daphne*, 319
Bohnen, Michael, 239, 240
Boieldieu, François, 17, 48, 215
Boosey & Hawkes, 201, 369
Bormann, Martin, 340, 349, 350, 352, 364; edict against R.S., 346
Bote & Bock, 33, 200, 201
Boulez, Pierre, 4, 278
Boult, Sir Adrian, 312, 379; on R.S.'s conducting, 403–4
Brahms, Johannes, 4, 30, 42, 47, 79, 101, 184, 291; advice to R.S., 35, 41, Symphony No. 4, première, 41
Brain, Dennis, 28
Brandenburg, Dr Lili, 272
Brecher, Gustav, 132, 210
Breitkopf & Härtel, 18, 201
Brentano, Clemens, 198
Briand, Aristide, 259
Britten, Benjamin, 247, 328
Bronsart, Hans, 53, 54, 64, 66–7, 68, 75; conflicts with R.S., 59–60
Bruckner, Anton, 4, 116, 132, 222, 280, 289, 354; R.S.'s opinion of, 420
Brüll, Ignaz, 101
Brun, Annette, 408
Brüning, Dr Heinrich, 261
Bülow, Hans von, 7, 18, 31, 32, 33, 40, 41, 43, 46, 47, 49, 50, 52–3, 55, 56, 59, 67, 342, 404; on R.S., 34, 40–1; R.S. début, 35; appoints R.S. at Meiningen, 38; leaves Meiningen, 42; rejects *Burleske*, 44; on *Aus Italien*, 51; on *Macbeth*, 56, 79; death, 79
Bülow, Maria von, 43
Burghauser, Hugo, 372; sells MSS for R.S., 381–2
Busch, Fritz, 26, 105, 229, 235, 244, 247,

260, 262, 263–4, 276, 386; removed by
    Nazis, 262
Busoni, Ferruccio, 181
Busse, Carl, 120
Buths, Julius, 51

Carmu, Maria, 187
Carré, Albert, 144
Caruso, Enrico, 322
Cassirer, Paul, 201
Casti, Abbé Giambattista, 287, 325
Catelain, Jaque, 239
Caullier, Joëlle, 144
Cebotari, Maria, 146, 147, 297, 298, 301,
    369, 375, 377
Cervantes, Miguel de, 135
Chabrier, Emmanuel, 62–3, 130, 132, 366
Chamisso, Adelbert von, 22
Cherubini, Luigi, 48, 66
Chicago Symphony Orchestra, 36, 406
Cologne, 28, 50, 51, 69, 84, 150, 169, 261;
    Gürzenich concerts, 36
Concertgebouw Orchestra of
    Amsterdam, 104
Corinth, Lovis, 151
Cornelius, Peter, 48, 105, 407
Correck, Josef, 229
Couperin, François, 215, 329, 331
Couvray, Louvet de, 163
Cox, John, 229, 303
Cunitz, Maud, 394
Czerny, Carl, *Schule der Fingerfertigkeit*,
    15

Dahn, Felix, 51, 68
d'Annunzio, Gabriele. See *Annunzio,
    Gabriele d'*
Debussy, Achille-Claude, 145, 285
Dehmel, Ida, 99
Dehmel, Richard, 23, 99, 119–20, 125, 126,
    148

De Lancie, John, 363, 366; suggests Oboe
    Concerto, 364
Delibes, Léo, 48
Della Casa, Lisa, 386
Del Mar, Norman, 28, 87, 99, 230, 236,
    252, 376
Denza, Luigi, 51
Dermota, Anton, 408
Destinn, Emmy, 130, 135, 143, 181
Diaghilev, Serge, 182–3, 186, 187, 208
Diepenbrock, Alphons, 104
Dillmann, Alexander, 90
D'Indy, Vincent, 132
Dittersdorf, Karl Ditters von, 366
Döhring, Dr Theodor, 116
Donizetti, Gaetano, 48, 322
Dresden, 27, 29, 57, 69, 98, 134, 139, 181,
    193, 199, 200, 201, 228, 239, 247, 324;
    first visit by R.S., 30–1; R.S. freeman of,
    286; Court Orchestra (Staatskapelle),
    28, 31, 32, 36, 69, 177, 344, 382; R.S.
    conducts in London, 312, 314, 408;
    Semperoper, 28, 212–13, first
    performances of *Feuersnot*, 135, *Salome*,
    142, *Der Rosenkavalier*, 162, 166–7,
    Intermezzo, 229, *Die ägyptische Helena*,
    242–4, *Arabella*, 262–4, *Die
    schweigsame Frau*, 297–9, *Daphne*, 319;
    Tonkünstlerverein, 27, 30, 344
Dresdner Nachrichten, 258
Drewes, Dr Heinz, 317, 354
Droescher, Dr Georg, 207
Duflos, Huguette, 239
Dukas, Paul, 145; R.S. conducts *Ariane et
    Barbe-Bleue*, 307
Dux, Claire, 199
Dvořák, Antonin, 101, 148, 366

Eberlein, Gustav, 33
Egk, Werner, 336, 342
Ehrenberg, Carl, 323

Eichendorff, Joseph, 248, 371, 382
Einstein, Alfred, 258
Elgar, Sir Edward, 5, 111, 132, 219, 376, 406
Elman, Mischa, 15
Elmendorff, Karl, 344
Engel, Erich, 146
Erdmannsdörfer, Max, 102
Erhardt, Otto, 244, 259, 261
Erlanger, Camille, 144
Esher, Lord, 269
Eysoldt, Gertrud, 136, 152

Fallersleben, August Heinrich Hoffmann
     von, 23
Fallières, Armand, 144
Fanto, Leonhard, 262, 263, 298, 299
Farrar, Geraldine, 130
Fauré, Gabriel, 144
Fellmer, Helmut, 328
Field, John, *Nocturnes*, 15
Fingesten, Michael, 201
Fischer, Franz, 52, 55, 113
Fitzwilliam Virginal Book, 303
Flagstad, Kirsten, 385
Flatau, K. Louis, 347
Flotow, Friedrich von, 48
Fokine, Michael, 186
François-Poncet, R.S. letter to, 393
Franckenstein, Baron Clemens von, 191
Frankfurt, 29, 38, 50, 51, 69, 74, 86, 105,
     113, 135, 190, 244, 256, 316
Frank, Dr Hans, 281, 364, 373, 383;
     protects R.S., 345–6; R.S. song for,
     346–7
Franz Ferdinand, Archduke, 221
Franz Josef, Emperor, 142, 250
Franz, Oscar, 31, 36
Freiberg, Gottfried, 341
Freud, Sigmund, 151
Fried, Oskar, 120
Friedel, Rudolf, 224

Friedrich, Karl, 377
Fuchs, Robert, 295
Funk, Walther, 301
Fürstner, Adolph, 51, 64, 157, 202, 329
Fürstner, Otto, 369
Furtwängler, Wilhelm, 94, 95, 207, 233,
     262, 264, 271, 274, 278, 281, 282, 285,
     288, 314, 346, 354, 385–6, 398; defends
     Hindemith, 289

Garden, Mary, 142
Garmisch, 75, 88, 91, 92, 93, 99, 136, 154,
     174, 178, 185, 187, 196, 197, 200, 207, 208,
     221, 222, 230, 235, 240, 248, 258, 259,
     270, 286, 296, 307, 309, 311, 316, 326, 336,
     340, 344, 346, 357, 368, 372, 395; R.S.
     builds villa in, 150–1, moves into villa,
     157, in wartime, 341–2, R.S. refuses
     evacuees, 346, Americans in, 363–4,
     R.S. leaves, 368, R.S. returns to, 387–8,
     85th birthday celebrations, 389
Geibel, Emanuel, 24
Geissmar, Berta, 314
Gerhardt, Elena, 90, 199
Gerhäuser, Emil, 72
Gericke, Wilhelm, 51
Geyer, Stefi, 261
Gide, André, 144
Gielen, Josef, 262, 298
Giessen, Hans, 88
Gilliam, Bryan, 231–2
Gilm, Hermann von, 23, 43
Glossner, Anna, 97–9, 283, 351; death,
     358
Gluck, Christoph Willibald von, 64, 105,
     331, 350, 366, 407; R.S. version of
     Iphigénie en Tauride, 64
Glyndebourne Opera, 105, 229, 264, 303
Goebbels, Dr Josef, 272, 274, 285, 286, 287,
     288, 289, 298, 300, 302, 306, 311, 323, 335,
     338, 346, 383; sets up Reich Culture

Chamber, 280–1; R.S. dedicates song to; 282, R.S. 'decadent', 293; shouts abuse at R.S., 336; closes theatres, 354

Goering, Hermann, 261, 264, 293

Goethe, Johann Wolfgang von, 23, 27, 35, 68, 71, 77, 78, 111, 118, 162, 201, 216, 234, 236, 240, 255, 270, 282, 290, 309, 311, 340, 391; and *Metamorphosen*, 357–8, 362

Goldmark, Károly, 48

Goossens, Léon, 370

Gorky, Maxim, 147

Gould, Glenn, 3, 4, 160

Gounod, Charles, 58, 62, 118, 366

Grab, Alice von. See *Strauss, Alice*

Grab, Emanuel von, 221, 235

Grab, Marie von, 339

Grab, Mizzi von, 202

Graf, Max, 135, 212

Grasberger, Franz, 212

Grasenick, Mary, 199, 201

Gravina, Count Biagio, 78

Gravina, Countess Blandine, *née* Bülow, 78

Gregor, Hans, attacks R.S. Vienna appointment, 211

Gregor, Joseph, 67, 118, 283, 298, 301, 317, 319, 329, 347–8, 353, 360, 375; Zweig recommends to R.S., 294–5; R.S. agrees to set 3 librettos, 306–7; R.S. dissatisfaction, 307–8; R.S. critical of *Daphne*, 308, 309–12; fear for his job, 317; revisions of *Danae* libretto, 321–3; excluded from *Capriccio*, 326

Grey, Sir Edward, 269

Gropius-Mahler, Alma. See *Mahler, Alma*

Grünfeld, Heinrich, 136

Gung'l, Joseph, 14

Gutheil, Gustav, 80

Gutheil-Schoder, Marie, 76, 146, 190, 196

Hafiz (Shams-ud-den Mohammed), 255

Halíř, Carl, 106, 130

Halíř Quartet, 35

Hallé Orchestra, R.S. conducts, 219, 239

Hammerstein, Oscar, 142

Hanfstaengel, Ernst, 299

Hann, Georg, 316, 339

Hanslick, Eduard, 47, 64, 84, 89, 135

Harbni Orchestra, 13, 19

Harewood, Earl of, 377

Hart, Heinrich, 119

Hartleben, Otto Erich, 119

Hartmann, Rudolf, 94, 230, 253, 275, 326, 338, 341, 383–4, 389–90; describes *Danae* rehearsal, 354; last visit to R.S., 391–4

Hasse, Max, 74

Hauptmann, Gerhart, 224, 340, 347

Hausegger, Friedrich von, 46, 102–3

Hausegger, Siegmund von, 48, 105, 132

Haussner, Karl, 374

Haydn, Franz Joseph, 7, 14, 15, 24, 101, 387; *The Creation*, 15

Heckmann, Robert, 51

Heger, Robert, 74

Heilbrunn, 29

Heine, Heinrich, 23, 202

Heiss, Franz, 382

Hempel, Frieda, 177

Henckell, Karl, 119, 120, 382

Herrmann, Bernard, 377–8

Hertz, Alfred, 169

Herzogenberg, Heinrich von, 30, 32

Hesse, Hermann, 384, 391

Heyse, Paul, 40

Hindemith, Paul, 210, 216, 231, 306, 382; proscribed by Nazis, 288–9

Hindenburg, President Paul von, 261–2, 286

Hinkel, Hans, 300, 305

Hitler, Adolf, 143, 258–9, 264, 269, 272, 276–7, 280, 281, 286, 287, 288, 289, 298, 299, 300, 301, 308, 316, 319, 323, 335, 340, 345, 346, 363, 380; path to power, 261–2; R.S. letter to, 305; bomb plot against, 353

Hochberg, Count von, 135

Hofmannsthal, Gerty von, 256, 375, 378

Hofmannsthal, Hugo von, 31, 96, 99, 118, 187, 211, 213, 215, 219–20, 238, 240, 241–2, 255, 256, 257, 260, 270, 274, 275, 310, 315, 321, 360, 389, 397; meets R.S. 126, war service, 189, 190, opposes R.S. Vienna post, 205–6, fiftieth birthday, 225–6, tribute to R.S., 227, on *Intermezzo*, 233–4, death, 251; collaboration with R.S. on: *Elektra*, 151–3, 155–8, *Der Rosenkavalier*, 161–72, *Ariadne I*, 174, 177–82, *Ariadne II*, 184–5, 191–5, *Die Frau ohne Schatten*, 174–5, 185–6, 188, 189–90, 191, 194–5, 199–200, *Josephs Legende*, 182–3, 185, *Le bourgeois gentilhomme*, 199–200, *Die ägyptische Helena*, 221, 222–3, 240–1, 242, 245–6, *Arabella*, 248, 250–2

Hölderlin, Johann Friedrich, 210, 240

Höngen, Elisabeth, 379

Hörburger, Bertha (*née* Pschorr), 13

Hörburger, Carl, 13, 56, 61

Hotter, Hans, 118, 235, 240, 316, 318, 319, 338, 344

Hoyer, Bruno, 28

Huber, Hans, 132

Hülsen, Botho von, 31, 143, 170, 186, 205, 206, 207

Hummel, Johann Nepomuk, 17

Humperdinck, Engelbert, 79, 101, 127, 130, 133; R.S. conducts première of *Hänsel und Gretel*, 72

Hupfeld's "Animatic" piano rolls, 406

Hutt, Robert, 198, 406

Huysmans, Camille, 308–09

Ibert, Jacques, 328

Iffland, Wilhelm, 69

Ireland, John, 284

Italy, 47, 50, 56, 143, 260, 308, 311, 316, 344

Jackson, Timothy L., 380, 385

Jacquingasse, R.S. house in, 228; wartime damage to, 372

Jahn, Wilhelm, 27

Janáček, Leoš, 224

Jerger, Alfred, 209, 229, 263

Jeritza, Maria (Mizzi), 94, 146, 181, 193, 196, 207, 212, 245, 248, 314; crisis over *Helena*, 242–4; letter to R.S. about *Malven*, 384–5

Joachim, Joseph, 32, 79

Joachim Quartet, 32

Johanson, Sigrid, 201

Johnstone, Arthur, on R.S. conducting, 62, 401; on R.S. as composer, 136–7

Jöhr, Dr Adolf, 384

Jonson, Ben, 260, 299, 303

Jünger, Ernst, 340

Jurinac, Sena, 386

Kabasta, Oswald, 324

Kahn, Otto H., 144,

Kalbeck, Max, 27, 211

Karajan, Herbert von, 147, 256, 271, 324; on R.S.'s Mozart, 403

Karpath, Ludwig, 211, 228, 254, 257, 264, 388

Karsavina, Tamara, 187

Keilberth, Joseph, 304

Keldorfer, Viktor, 247–8

Keller, Hans, 148

Kemp, Barbara, 98, 146, 198, 207, 210

Kern, Adele, 275, 316, 328

Kerr, Alfred, 201, 210
Kessler, Count Harry, 99, 126, 162, 183, 270; and *Rosenkavalier*, 163–4
Keudell, Otto von, 301
Kienzl, Wilhelm, 366
Kipnis, Alexander, 277
Kippenberg, Anton, 260, 275
Kirchhoff, Anton, 40
Klarwein, Franz, 235, 360
Kleiber, Erich, 387
Kleist, Heinrich von, 44
Klemperer, Otto, 105, 209, 270, 272, 398
Klimt, Gustav, 148, 151
Klopstock, Friedrich Gottlieb, 44
Klose, Hermann, 33
Knappertsbusch, Hans, 229, 235, 262, 275, 278, 296
Knaus, Ludwig, 33
Kniese, Julius, 55
Knobel, Betty, 384
Knözinger, Amalie von, 19, 28
Knözinger, Anton von, 19
Knözinger, Ludwig von, 19
Knüpfer, Paul, 130, 198, 231
Konetzni, Anny, 275
Konetzni, Hilde, 275, 336, 408
Königsthal, Hildegard von, 29
Kopsch, Dr Julius, 272–3, 286
Korda, Sir Alexander, 369
Körner, Theodor, 23
Korngold, Erich, 209, 222, 247; clash with R.S. and Schalk, 220–1
Korngold, Julius, 220, 223
Kosak, Dr Ernst, 228
Krasselt, Alfred, 28
Kraus, Ernst, 202
Kraus, Karl, 227–8; on *Schlagobers*, 226
Krause, Ernst, 352
Krauss, Clemens, 214, 229–30, 253, 257, 262, 275, 278, 283, 286, 291, 312, 325, 329, 337, 345, 356, 360, 372, 388, 391, 393, 402;

becomes Vienna Opera director, 256; conducts *Arabella* première, 263–4; R.S. consults him on *Daphne*, 311–12; suggests ending of *Daphne*, 314; becomes Munich Opera director, 316; conducts *Friedenstag* première, 318; intervenes in *Danae* libretto, 322; collaborates on *Capriccio* libretto, 327–8, 334–5; helps protect R.S., 335; conducts *Capriccio* première, 338–9; conducts *Danae* première, 353–4
Krenek, Ernst, 382
Krenn, Fritz, 275
Kreutzer, Conradin, 48, 101
Krzyzanowski, Rudolf, 64
Kubrick, Stanley, 113
Kuhač, Franjo Z., 248
Kupelwieser, Leopold, 342
Kupelwieser, Marie. See *Mautner Markhof, Marie*
Kupper, Anneliese, 356
Kurz, Selma, 177, 211, 215
Kutzschbach, Hermann, 262
Kuznetsova, Marie, 186

Lachmann, Hedwig, 135–6, 142, 147
Lachner, Franz, 7, 43
Lambert, Constant, 284
Lancie, John de. See *De Lancie, John*
Láng, Paul Henry, 304
Lassen, Eduard, 53, 55, 61, 66, 68, 75
Le Borne, Fernand, 130
Legge, Walter, 376
Legris de Latude, Claire (Mme Clairon), 330
Lehár, Ferencz [Franz], 168, 283, 336, 369
Lehmann, Lotte, 92, 98, 193, 212, 229, 230, 265, 275, 376
Leinhos, Gustav, 35, 36, 38, 40
Leinsdorf, Erich, 372

Leipzig, 28, 30, 37, 49, 50, 69, 105, 108, 193, 239, 344; Gewandhaus Orchestra, 41, 272

Lenau, Nikolaus, 23, 69

Lenbach, Franz von, 47

Lessmann, Otto, 33

Levi, Hermann, 7–8, 18, 24, 26, 29, 31, 42, 47, 49, 52, 53, 67, 68, 72, 78, 86, 106, 270, 278

Levin, Willy, 231, 235

Liliencron, Detlev von, 119, 345

Lindner, Anton, 135

Lindner, Eugen, 70

Lippl, Alois Johannes, 389

List, Emanuel, 277

Liszt, Ferencz, 43, 46, 49, 66, 79, 85, 86, 105, 140; R.S. influenced by, 46–7; R.S. views on, 61–2; R.S. conducts *Faust Symphony*, 62, 101

London, 137, 139, 169, 187, 193, 219, 239, 265, 286, 372, 404; R.S.'s first visit, 105; R.S. conducts Dresden Opera in, 312; R.S. last visit, 376–80

Lönner, Professor Dr Friedrich (Fritz), 316

Lorenz, Max, 352

Lortzing, (Gustav) Albert, 48, 101, 284

Losch, Tilly, 215

Löwe, Ferdinand, 211

Lubahn, Robert, 288

Lubin, Germaine, 239

Ludwig I of Bavaria, King, 6, 12

Ludwig II of Bavaria, King, 12, 43

Lully, Jean-Baptiste, 199

McArthur, Edwin, 385

Mackay, John Henry, 69, 111, 119

Maeterlinck, Maurice, 145

Mahler, Alma, 87–8, 125, 154, 173, 211, 218

Mahler, Gustav, 5, 76, 88, 93, 96, 105, 110, 125, 132, 138, 139, 140, 148, 149, 166, 173, 175, 177, 196, 211, 218, 222, 244, 255, 285, 289, 318, 400; R.S. and *Die drei Pintos*, 49, 62; Symphony No. 6, first performance of, 153–4; and *Feuersnot*, 87–8, 135; and *Salome*, 142–3

Maillart, Aimé, 101

Mainardi, Enrico, 407

Mainwald, Viktor, 347

Makart, Hans, 250

Manchester Guardian, 62, 136, 401

Mandyczewski, Eusebius, 211

Mann, Klaus, 373; interview with R.S., 364

Mann, Thomas, 272, 364, 373; on *Rosenkavalier*, 170, 172; row over Wagner lecture, 278–9

Mann, William, 252

Mannstädt, Franz, 33, 38, 42

Marnold, Jean, 145

Marquartstein, 58, 71, 78, 82, 83, 86, 93, 106, 117, 136, 137, 153

Marschalk, Max, 23, 103, 202

Marschner, Heinrich, 66

Martin, Theodor (chauffeur), 98, 235, 285, 341–2, 345, 346

Martucci, Giuseppe, 52

Mascagni, Pietro, 62, 132

Massenet, Jules, 38, 66

Massine, Leonide, 186

Maugham, W. Somerset, 187

Mautner Markhof, Manfred, 88, 235, 319, 342, 360

Mautner Markhof, Marie (*née* Kupelwieser), 342

Mayr, Richard, 166, 209, 212, 275

Meader, George, 199

Meggendorfer, Lothar, 18

Méhul, Étienne-Nicolas, 366

Meiningen, 22, 36, 43, 44, 46, 47, 55, 56, 78; R.S. at, 38–44; Duke and Duchess of, 38, 40, 42, 44, 189, 190; Princess

Marie of, 38, 42; Meiningen Orchestra, 33, 34, 35, 38, 42, 46, 189, 190
Melchinger, Siegfried, 352
Melichar, Alois, describes R.S. funeral, 394–5
Mendelssohn, Felix, 7, 14, 15, 24, 25, 50, 101, 161, 285
Mengelberg, Rudolph, 380
Mengelberg, Willem, 154
Merian-Genast, Emilie, 64
Merz, Oskar, 73, 275
Messiaen, Olivier, 4
Meyer, Friedrich Wilhelm, 14
Meyerbeer, Giacomo, 130
Meysenheim, Cornelia, 24
Michelangelo, 47, 51
Mikorey, Max, 73
Mildenburg, Anna von, 196
Milnes, Rodney, 3, 333
Mitropoulos, Dimitri, 110
Molière (Jean Baptiste Poquelin), 163, 174, 177, 179, 184–5, 187, 199, 200, 389
Monteux, Pierre, 186
Monteverdi, Claudio, 303
Moralt, Linda, 19
Moralt, Rudolf, 143
Moreau, Major, 368
Morgan, J. Pierpont, 143
Mottl, Felix, 47, 55, 61, 66, 68, 72, 85–6, 102, 106, 125, 143, 170, 171
Mozart, Leopold, 25
Mozart, Wolfgang Amadeus, 4, 7, 8, 13, 14, 15, 24, 40, 41, 105, 108, 148, 161, 168, 196, 198, 256, 270, 283, 303, 331, 365, 366, 397, 400, 401, 407; 41st Symphony (*Jupiter*), 16; *Die Entführung aus dem Serail*, 105, *Die Zauberflöte*, 13, 32, 64, 101, 146, 198, 211, *Don Giovanni*, 66, 105, 146, 198, 209, *Le nozze di Figaro*, 66, 215; R.S. conducts *Così fan tutte*, 48, 105, 130, 209, 215, 389, 401; R.S. version of

Idomeneo, 257–8; R.S. soloist in concerto, 40
Muck, Karl, 106
Mücke, Mieze, 95–6, 100, 137, 196, 229
Mühlfeld, Richard, 40
Münchner Neueste Nachrichten, 24, 73, 74, 275, 278; reviews *Guntram*, 73–4
Munich, 6, 7, 12, 15, 19, 22, 27, 28, 29, 31, 35, 36, 38, 42, 46, 47, 53, 54, 57, 61, 69, 83, 85, 90, 93, 119, 121, 132–4, 169, 170, 185, 191, 214, 229, 235, 260, 262, 275, 296, 310, 316, 329, 335, 346; R.S. composes Munich waltz, 323–4; Nationaltheater bombed, 344–5; R.S.'s 85th birthday celebrations, 388–9; R.S. conducts for last time, 389; R.S. funeral in, 394–5; Centralsäle, 18; Court Opera: 52, 389, R.S. appointed 3rd conductor, 43, R.S. début at, 47–8, R.S. leaves, 53, R.S. offered post, 72, *Guntram* fiasco, 73–5, conductor, 78, chief conductor, 86, R.S. leaves, 106–7, Krauss music director, 316; *Friedenstag* première, 318; *Capriccio* première, 338–9; Court Orchestra, 6, 8, 12, 13, 14, 23, 24, 46, 50, 75; Ludwigsgymnasium, 13, 22, 26; Museumssaal, 23; Musical Academy concerts, 24, 78, 101, 113, R.S. dismissed from, 102; Odeonssaal, 13, 24, 29, 34; Philharmonic Association, 13; Residenztheater, 105; Royal School of Music, 15, 20, 22, 58; University, R.S. attends, 27; Wilde Gung'l, 14, 18, 24, 35, R.S. plays in, 27
Musical Times, The, 220
Mutschmann, Martin, 298, 301
Muzio, Claudia, 216

Napoléon I, Emperor, 5, 198, 391
Naumann-Gungl, Virginia, 67
Neue Freie Presse, Vienna, 56, 220

Neumann, Angelo, 109
Neumann, Paula, 339
Newman, Ernest, 4, 265, 277, 278
New York, 30, 35, 69, 96, 106, 142, 143, 169, 218, 244, 265, 347, 406; Strausses' visits to, 138–9, 218; Philharmonic Society, 35–6
Nicodé, Jean Louis, 49
Nicolai, Otto, 48
Niessen, Bruno von, 257, 258
Niest, Carl, 17
Nietzsche, Friedrich Wilhelm, 71, 103, 111–12, 128, 175, 311
Nijinsky, Vaclav, 183, 186, 187
Nikisch, Arthur, 102
Nikisch, Grete, 229
Nitzl, Anni, 358, 363, 394
Nitzl, Resi, 358, 395
Noni, Alda, 352
Nussio, Otmar, 381

Oestvig, Karl. See Aagard-Oestvig, Karl
Offenbach, Jacques, 167, 194
Oertel, Johannes, 329
Orel, Alfred, 90; on R.S. as accompanist, 404–05
Orff, Carl, R.S. likes Carmina burana, 342
Osten, Eva von der, 263
Ott, Dr Alfons, 347

Papen, Count Franz von, 261
Papst, Eugen, 306
Paris, 8, 15, 31, 105, 169–70, 265, 278, 319; R.S. visits to, 129–30, 140, 258–9; Salome première in, 143–5; Josephs Legende première in, 186–7
Pataky, Koloman von, 255
Pattiera, Tino, 299
Patzak, Julius, 316, 408
Paulus, Anton, 382

Perfall, Baron Carl von, 35, 42–3, 52, 55, 73, 106, 113, 275
Pester Lloyd, 189
Pfitzner, Hans, 132, 172, 209–10, 222, 223, 241; Palestrina, 209, 290
Piccinni, Niccolò, 331
Pierné, Gabriel, 239
Pierson, Georg Henry, 106, 134
Piltti, Lea, 407
Piper, Dr Karl, 382
Pizzetti, Ildebrando, 328
Plaschke, Friedrich, 263, 298
Poell, Alfred, 336, 408
Pollak, Fräulein, 34
Pollini, Bernhard, 81, 93
Possart, Ernest von, 85, 90, 93, 105, 106
Preetorius, Emil, 278
Prey, Hermann, 229
Pringsheim, Klaus, 153–4
Prohaska, Felix, 348
Prokofiev, Sergei, 174, 247
Pschorr, Georg (1), 6
Pschorr, Georg (2) (uncle), 6, 10, 13, 18, 26; death, 78
Pschorr, Johanna (aunt), 13, 19, 23, 43, 58, 198
Pschorr, Joseph, 6
Pschorr, Josepha. See Strauss, Josepha
Pschorr, Robert, 51
Puccini, Giacomo, 5, 134, 142, 211, 220, 230, 241, 284; R. S. on, 283

Raabe, Peter, 290, 305–06
Radecke, Robert, 33
Raff, (Joseph) Joachim, 32, 378
Ralf, Torsten, 316, 320
Rameau, Jean-Philippe, 101, 331
Ranke, Leopold von, 175
Ranczak, Hildegarde, 316, 339
Rasch, Hugo, 274
Raucheisen, Michael, 201

Rauchenberger, Lt. Otto, 10

Rauchenberger-Strauss, Johanna (sister), 5–6, 10, 11, 19, 23, 24, 28, 37, 57, 58, 81, 82, 344–5, 361, 363

Ravel, Maurice, 144, 160, 187, 247

Reger, Max, 132, 172, 189

Reich Music Chamber, 288, 298, 305, 306, 368, 383; established, 281; R.S. as president, 281–3, 284–5; R.S. disenchanted with, 285–6; R.S. dismissed from presidency, 301–02

Reinhardt, Max, 136, 152, 177, 178, 179, 180, 181, 190, 191, 196, 208, 295; produces *Rosenkavalier*, 166

Reinhart, Werner, 369

Reinicke, Karl, 30

Reining, Maria, 352, 407

Reszke, Jean de, 144

Rethberg, Elisabeth, 243, 244, 275

Reucker, Alfred, 262, 263

Rezniček, Emil Nikolaus von, 104, 132

Rheinberger, Joseph, 20, 43, 48

Ribbentrop, Joachim von, 312

Richter, Hans, 8, 27, 32, 55, 64, 68

Riess, Curt, 364

Rimsky-Korsakov, Nicolai, 186

Ritter, Alexander, 48–9, 51, 56, 62, 66, 70, 74, 78, 91, 104, 132, 366; influences R.S., 46; rift over *Guntram*, 71

Ritter, Franziska, 46, 58, 64

Rolland, Clotilde, 130

Rolland, Romain, 5, 8, 15, 92, 112, 115, 118, 126, 141, 150, 169, 186–7, 196–8, 271, 272; meets R.S., 66; on R.S. in Berlin and Paris, 128–30; on *Domestica*, 140; Paris *Salome*, 144–5; on R.S.'s music, 148–9; on R.S. in Vienna, 226–7; sixtieth birthday, 240

Roller, Alfred, 166, 181, 208, 211, 212, 213, 215, 239, 278, 375

Ronsard, Pierre de, 330

Rosbaud, Hans, 74, 286

Rösch, Friedrich, 70, 95, 108, 117, 201, 207

Rosenauer, Michael, 241

Rosenberg, Alfred, 280, 289, 297, 335

Rossini, Gioachino, 47, 366

Roth, Ernst, 88, 369, 371, 375, 376, 377, 378, 385, 388, 391, 402; on R.S.'s business sense, 218

Rothschild, Alphonse, 283

Rothschild, Baron Henri de, 144

Royal Philharmonic Society, 376; Gold Medal for R.S., 312

Rubinstein, Anton, 14, 101

Rubinstein, Arthur, 144

Rubinstein, Ida, 187

Rückert, Friedrich, 178, 184, 257, 291, 306, 317

Rüdel, Hugo, 184

Sacher, Paul, 358, 360, 362, 382

Saillet, Marcel, 369

Saint-Saëns, Camille, 16, 145

Salieri, Antonio, 325

Salzburg Festival, 229, 253, 256, 260, 275, 329, 338, 341, 344, 356, 393; R.S. joins artists' council, 208; R.S. first conducts at, 209; R.S. operas at, 275; ban on R.S., 285–6; première of *Danae*, 353–5

Samazeuilh, Gustave, 387

Sardou, Victorien, 31, 32, 151

Sawallisch, Wolfgang, 28

Schack, Count Adolf Friedrich von, 51

Schalk, Franz, 170, 193, 207, 208, 209, 211, 212, 215, 223, 227–8; on *Die Frau ohne Schatten*, 214; clashes with R.S., 216–17, 219–20; dismissed from Vienna, 256

Schaller, Stephen, 374

Scharwenka, Franz X., 32

Schech, Marianne, 394

Scheerbart, Paul, 125, 126

Scheel, Dr Gustav, 354

Schéhafzoff, Sonja von, 78

Schellendorf, Hans Bronsart von. See
Bronsart, Hans

Scherchen, Hermann, 370

Schiele, Egon, 148

Schiele (Kreisleiter), 345–6

Schiller, Johann Christoph Friedrich von,
68, 178, 270, 290

Schillings, Max von, 101, 104, 105, 128, 130,
132, 181, 207, 222

Schirach, Baldur von, 132, 319, 347, 350,
352, 364; protects R.S. in Vienna, 340

Schirach, Carl von, 132

Schleicher, General Kurt von, 261–2

Schlusnus, Heinrich, 406

Schlüter, Erna, 379

Schmid-Bloss, Karl, 356

Schmidt, Franz, 222, 247

Schneiderhan, Franz, 255

Schneiderhan, Wolfgang, 352

Schnitzler, Arthur, 185, 211

Schoenberg, Arnold, 119, 140, 174, 210,
224, 231, 382, 395; relationship with
R.S., 172–3; praise for Intermezzo, 233;
defends R.S. on Nazism, 271

Schöffler, Paul, 356

Scholz, Bernhard, 130

Schöne, Lotte, 209, 242

Schopenhauer, Arthur, 46, 71, 77, 103, 111,
175, 340

Schreker, Franz, 209, 223, 231

Schubart, Christian Friedrich Daniel, 13

Schubert, Franz, 7, 14, 16, 32, 41, 101, 108,
270, 283

Schuch, Ernst von, 29, 30, 31, 128, 134, 299,
399; conducts Feuersnot, 135, Salome,
142, Elektra, 158, Der Rosenkavalier, 166,
170; R.S. anger with, 170

Schuch, Friedrich von, 235, 299

Schuh, Willi, 117, 284–5, 315, 335, 341, 355,
358, 362, 366, 368, 371, 373, 382, 383, 385,

386, 387; in London with R.S., 376, 378;
R.S. appoints him official biographer,
388

Schulz, Else, 336

Schumann, Clara, 17

Schumann, Elisabeth, 90, 94, 146, 209,
255, 256–7, 314, 328–9, 404; first works
with R.S., 198–9; Vienna controversy,
212; USA tour with R.S., 218; sings
Helena aria, 240; meets R.S. in
London, 378

Schumann, Robert, 7, 17, 50, 101, 186; R.S.
on Piano Concerto, 14

Schumann-Heink, Ernestine, 156

Schwarzkopf, Dame Elisabeth, 30

Scribe, Eugène, 32, 164

Seebach, Count Nikolaus von, 166, 177,
185

Seefried, Irmgard, 352, 375

Seidl, Arthur, 67

Seiff, Elise, 6

Serafin, Tullio, 170

Sert, José-Maria, 186

Shakespeare, William, 27, 31, 111, 149,
190

Shaw, George Bernard, 219, 250, 379

Shostakovich, Dimitri, 272

Sibelius, Jean, 130

Singer, Otto, 238, 359

Sixt, Paul, 74, 286

Smetana, Bedřich, 101

Smyth, Dame Ethel, 284

Sokolova, Lydia, 186

Solti, Sir Georg, 265, 389, 394; visits R.S.
in Garmisch, 391; conducts at R.S.'s
funeral, 394

Sommer, Hans. See Zincke, H. F. A.

Sommerschuh, Gerda, 394

Sophocles, 151

Specht, Richard, 189, 211, 241

Speyer, Sir Edgar, 144, 208

Speyer, Lotti, 33, 50, 51; romance with R.S., 29–30

Spielhagen, Friedrich, 34

Spitzweg, Edmund, 34

Spitzweg, Eugen, 34, 38, 40, 51, 52, 79, 109

Spohr, Ludwig, 7, 14; Violin Concerto No. 8, 15

Stanford, Sir Charles Villiers, 132

Staram, Walter, 142

Stargardt-Wolff, Edith, 274

Stauffer-Bern, Karl, 127, 175

Stefan, Paul, 211

Steffek, Hanni, 229

Stein, Fritz, 202

Steinbach, Fritz, 38, 55

Steiner, Franz, 199, 218

Steinitzer, Max, 23, 24, 49, 58, 125

Stern, Ernst, 181

Stieler, Karl, 29

Stirner, Max, 69, 71

Stransky, Josef, 96

Strasser, Otto, 80, 324, 402

Straus, Oscar, 95

Strauss, Alice (née von Grab), 94, 202, 221, 222, 228, 247, 259, 270, 286, 290, 305, 316, 328, 336, 345, 357, 363, 384, 391, 394, 395; marriage, 224; isolation as Jew in Nazi Germany, 271–2; meets Hitler, 277; evades arrest, 316; family victims of Nazis, 339; arrested by Vienna Gestapo, 350; order for arrest in Garmisch, 360; attack by Klaus Mann, 364; recovers MSS from Vienna house, 372

Strauss, Dr med. Christian (grandson), 93, 271, 290, 336, 340, 345, 348, 357, 374, 394; beaten up at school, 316; R.S. letters to, 350, 379–80

Strauss, Edmund von, 95

Strauss, Franz (father), 11, 12, 13, 14, 15, 17, 18, 19, 20, 22, 24, 25, 26, 27, 28, 31, 33, 35, 36, 41, 42, 43, 44, 48, 49, 50, 59, 61, 66, 67, 70–1, 72, 116, 127, 345; early life, 6; R.S.'s view of, 7; on Wagner, 8; at home, 8, 10; advice on Dora Wihan, 38; dismissal, 53; on Macbeth, 56; on Salome, 140; death, 140

Strauss, Franz (son), 88, 93, 94, 137, 146, 208, 215, 221, 228, 235, 247, 256, 259, 289, 309, 332, 336, 360, 374, 382, 384, 391, 394; born, 90–1; excused war service, 191, 194; accompanies R.S. to America, 218; engaged, 222; marriage and illness, 224–5; attitude to Nazis, 290; arrested by Gestapo, 350

Strauss II, Johann, 101, 130, 168, 283

Strauss, Johann Urban, 6

Strauss, Johanna (sister). See Rauchenberger-Strauss, Johanna

Strauss, Josef, 283

Strauss, Josepha (née Pschorr) (mother), 6, 13, 15, 17, 37, 38, 69, 100, 106, 399; mental illness, 10–11, 36, 113–14

Strauss, Pauline Maria (née de Ahna) (wife), 57–8, 68, 69, 76, 79, 104, 105, 106, 107, 108, 117, 119, 132, 137, 138, 143, 150, 157, 174, 178, 188, 191, 196, 199, 200, 205, 207, 216, 218, 235, 251, 270, 286, 297, 307, 308–09, 335, 340, 344, 345, 351, 352, 354, 371, 376, 382, 386, 391, 398, 400, 404; R.S.'s pupil, 58; sings with R.S. at Weimar, 64–8; sings at Bayreuth, 66, 78; engaged to R.S., 73; doubts about marriage, 80–3; wedding, 83; character, 84–100; Munich contract, 85–6; as a singer, 89–90; tour of USA, 89–90; birth of son, 90–1; divorce threat, 95–6; Dyer's Wife modelled on, 99; Munich début, 101; remarks in Paris, 144; and Trio of Rosenkavalier, 169; on Ariadne I venue, 181; on Die Frau ohne Schatten, 195; in Vienna controversy, 212; on R.S.

Strauss, Pauline Maria (*cont.*)
  quitting Vienna post, 228; as
  'Christine' in *Intermezzo*, 229–30; at
  Helena rehearsals, 244; Hofmannsthal
  death, 256; operation, 287; liking for
  Daphne, 319; remark to Schirach, 340;
  ill at Garmisch, 360, 363, 368, 391;
  bored in Switzerland, 371; at R.S.'s
  death-bed, 394; at R.S. funeral, 394–5;
  death, 395; R.S. letters to quoted: 66,
  86, 86–7, 93–4, 95–6, 99, 100, 104, 106,
  107, 108, 113, 200, 205, 207, 216, 218, 244,
  259, 297, 307, 308, 309
Strauss, Richard (grandson), 24, 94, 248,
  290, 324, 336, 340, 345, 357, 358, 360,
  363, 395; beaten up at school, 316; on
  R.S. as grandfather, 371
Strauss, Richard Georg, LIFE: birth, 6;
  mother's illness, 10–11; schooldays, 13;
  first compositions, 13–14; hears first
  operas, 13; first *Lieder*, 13–14;
  composition lessons, 14; youthful
  enthusiasms, 16–17; illnesses, 17–18, 66,
  68, 143–4, 150, 196, 257, 316, 328, 371,
  387; first publication, 18; youthful
  works composed, 19–20, 22–3; early
  performances, 23–4; conversion to
  Wagner, 26; leaves school, 26; at
  university, 27; visits Vienna, 27–8;
  romance with Lotti Speyer, 29–30;
  visits Dresden and Berlin, 30–4; learns
  Skat, 33; conducting début, 35;
  romance with Dora Wihan, 37–8, 54–5,
  56–8; Meiningen appointment, 38; at
  Meiningen, 38–44; 3rd conductor in
  Munich, 43, 47–53; meets Ritter, 46;
  Liszt influence, 46–7; opera-
  conducting début, 47–8; Ritter's
  influence, 48–9; meets Mahler, 49;
  Weimar appointment, 53; invited to
  Bayreuth, 55; meets Pauline, 58;
  friendship with Cosima Wagner,
  58–60; conflict with Bronsart, 59–61;
  with Pauline de Ahna at Weimar, 64–8;
  at Bayreuth, 66; meets Rolland, 66;
  first *Tristan*, 67; *Guntram* libretto, 70–1;
  trip to Egypt, 71; completes *Guntram*,
  71; offered Munich post, 72; leaves
  Weimar, 75–6; visits Greece, 77;
  negotiates Munich post, 78; conducts
  at Bayreuth, 78; engaged to Pauline, 73,
  79–83; wedding, 83; composes *Till*, 84;
  rift with Bayreuth, 85; chief conductor
  of Munich Opera, 86; first tour of
  USA, 89–90, 138–9; birth of son, 90–1;
  divorce threat, 95–6; conductor of
  Berlin Philharmonic, 101–02;
  conducting in Munich, 103–06; loses
  Munich Academy post, 104; becomes
  Berlin Opera conductor, 106; leaves
  Munich, 106–07; work on copyright,
  107–10; knowledge of literature, 111;
  works on ballets, 125–6; meets
  Hofmannsthal, 126; moves to Berlin
  Opera, 127–8; conducting described by
  Rolland, 129–30; repertoire in Berlin,
  130, 131; composes *Feuersnot*, 132–4;
  composes *Salome*, 135; begins
  Domestica, 137; honorary doctorate,
  137–8; French version of *Salome*, 141–2;
  Salome premières, 142–5; heart trouble,
  150; composing *Elektra*, 151–3;
  completes *Elektra*, 154–8; composes
  Rosenkavalier, 161–6; relationship with
  Hofmannsthal, 161–2; success of
  Rosenkavalier, 162–3, 166, 169–70; anger
  over cuts, 170; relationship with
  Schoenberg, 172–3; completes
  Alpensinfonie, 175–6; composes *Ariadne
  I*, 177–81; *Ariadne I* performed, 181–2;
  works on *Josephs Legende*, 182–3, 185;
  uninterested by *Ariadne II*, 184–5;

Josephs Legende performed, 186–7; begins *Die Frau ohne Schatten*, 185–6; *Josephs Legende* in London, 187; Oxford hon. degree, 187; works on *Die Frau*, 188, 191, 194–5, 199–200; First World War begins, 188–90; works on *Ariadne II*, 191–5; *Ariadne II* first performed, 193; first considers *Intermezzo*, 196; returns to song-writing, 198–9; works on revision of *Bourgeois gentilhomme*, 199–200; composes *Krämerspiegel*, 201–02; approached by Vienna Opera, 205–06; leaves Berlin Opera, 207; riots in Berlin, 207–08; co-founder of Salzburg Festival, 208–09; position in early 1920s, 209–210; accepts Vienna Opera post, 211–12; première of *Die Frau*, 212–13; visit to S. America, 215–16; clashes with Schalk, 216–17, 219–20; second USA tour, 218–19; buys Vienna plot of land, 221–2; second tour of S. America, 222; son engaged, 222; crisis in Vienna, 223; sixtieth birthday, 224; son's marriage and illness, 224–5; *Schlagobers* flop, 226–7; dismissed from Vienna post, 227–8; première of *Intermezzo*, 229; passion for Skat, 234–5; '10 Golden Rules', 235–6; *Rosenkavalier* film, 238–9; London visits, 239, 376–80; reconciliation with France, 239–40; plan for Greek theatre, 241; '*Meistersinger* project', 241–2; annoyance with Hofmannsthal, 243; writes left-hand piano works, 247; works on *Arabella*, 248, 250–2; first grandson born, 248; Hofmannsthal dies, 251; grief over Hofmannsthal, 256–7; version of *Idomeneo*, 257–8; visit to Paris, 258–9; visits to Italy and Switzerland, 260–1; impressed by Zweig libretto, 262; crises over *Arabella*

première, 262–5; and anti-Semitism, 270–2; takes Walter's place, 272–4; revises *Helena*, 275; substitutes for Toscanini at Bayreuth, 276–7; 'fast' *Parsifal*, 277–8; president of Reich Music Chamber, 281–3, 284–5; disenchantment, 285–6; seventieth birthday, 286; composes *Olympic Hymn*, 288; Hindemith affair, 288–9; plans secret collaboration with Zweig, 292–6; unimpressed by Gregor, 295–7; anti-Nazi letter confiscated, 297–8; demands reinstatement of Zweig's name, 299; dismissed from presidency of Reich Music Chamber, 301; writes to Hitler, 305; accepts Gregor librettos, 306–07; conducts Jewish composers, 307; diplomatic success in Belgium, 308–09; works on *Friedenstag* and *Daphne*, 309–12; conducts Dresden Opera in London, 312, 314; interest in *Danae* scenario, 315; grandsons beaten up, 316; Gregor's plea to, 317; *Friedenstag* in Vienna, 319; works on *Die Liebe der Danae*, 321–3; composes Munich waltz, 323–4; 75th birthday, 324; works on *Capriccio*, 325–8, 329–32; composes *Japanische Festmusik*, 328; lives in Vienna, 336–7; *Capriccio* première, 338–9; calls at Theresienstadt, 339; writes 2nd horn concerto, 340–1; wartime life in Garmisch, 341–2; in Vienna, 342; awarded Vienna Beethoven Prize, 342; writes 1st Sonatina, 342, 344; distress over Munich bombing, 344–5; defiance of Garmisch *Kreisleiter*, 345–6; refuses evacuees, 346; returns to Vienna, 347; obtains family's release, 350; 80th birthday celebrations, 350–3; première of *Danae*, 353–5; re-reads all Goethe,

Strauss, Richard Georg, LIFE (*cont.*)
357; begins *Metamorphosen*, 358; golden wedding, 358; copies out tone-poems, 358–9; mourning for Munich, 359–60; grief over bombing, 361; Americans in Garmisch, 363–4; scurrilous Mann interview, 364; artistic testament, 366–7; faces deNazification, 368; exile in Switzerland, 368–74; sketches *Im Abendrot*, 371; defence of conduct after 1933, 373; deNazification process, 375–6; cleared by deNazification tribunal, 382–3; composes *Vier letzte Lieder*, 384–5; major operation, 387; returns to Garmisch, 387–8; rebukes Schuh over memoirs, 388; 85th birthday celebrations, 388–9; honorary citizen of Garmisch, 389; conducts for last time, 389; talk with Solti, 391; last illness, 391–4; death, 394; funeral, 394–5; collaborations with: Hofmannsthal on *Elektra*, 151–3, 155–8, *Der Rosenkavalier*, 161–72, *Ariadne I*, 174, 177–82, *Ariadne II*, 184–5, 191–5, *Die Frau ohne Schatten*, 174–5, 188, 189–90, *Josephs Legende*, 182–3, 185, *Le bourgeois gentilhomme* (1917), 199–200, *Die ägyptische Helena*, 221, 222–3, 240–1, 242, *Arabella*, 248, 250–2; Zweig on *Die schweigsame Frau*, 260, 262, 280, 286; Gregor on *Friedenstag*, 307–08, *Daphne*, 307, 308, 309–12, 314, 317, *Die Liebe der Danae*, 315–16, 321–3, 324, 325, 328; Krauss on *Capriccio*, 325–8, 329–32; opinions on: Alma Mahler, 88, 154; America, 218; Auber, 16–17; Beethoven, 15–16; Berlin, 128; Berlioz, 61, 145; Brahms, 32, 41, 49–50; Bruckner, 420; Bülow, 32, 33, 42, 44–5; Chabrier's *Briséis*, 62–3; Clara Schumann, 17;

Debussy's *Pelléas*, 145; himself, 70, 102–03; his father, 8–9, 10; Hitler and Nazis, 259, 274–5, 286, 361, 369, 371–2, 373; Lehár, 283; Liszt, 61–2; Mahler's Fifth Symphony, 244; Massenet's *Hérodiade*, 38; melodic form, 23; modernity, 4, 132, 382; Mozart, 16, 105, 365, 381, 382; Pauline, 92, 94, 96–7, 100, 259; Pauline's singing, 89; Puccini, 283; religion, 17, 111, 145–6, 296; Richter, 68; Ritter, 46; Rossini, 47; Saint-Saëns, 16, 145; Salzburg Festival, 209; Sardou, 31; Schopenhauer, 46; Schuch, 170; song-writing, 118; tempi in *Rosenkavalier*, 391; Thuille, 20–2; *Tristan*, 26, 67–8; Verdi, 47; Wagner, 16–17, 26, 302–03; Weimar years, 75–6; words and music, 232–3; World War I, 189–90, 197–8, 200, 205; **WORKS:**
BALLETS:
Der Kometentanz AV 228, 125–6
Die Flöhe oder der Schmerzenstanz (abandoned), AV 222, 125
Die Insel Kythere, AV 230, 126
Die Rache der Aphrodite (abandoned), AV 296, 360, 374
Josephs Legende, Op. 63, 126, 208, 227, 351–2, 366, 397, 406; composed 182–3, 185; produced and discussed, 186–8; Vienna première, 221
Kythere (*Die Insel Kythere*), AV 230, 126
Lila (AV 221) (ballet sketched for Singspiel), 85
Schlagobers, Op. 70, 228; begun, 216; completed, 221; première, 226–7
Tanzsuite, o.Op. 107, 215, 238, 329
Verklungene Feste, o.Op. 128, 329
CHAMBER MUSIC:
Arabian Dance in D minor, piano quartet, AV 182, No. 1, 79
Cello Sonata, Op. 6, 29, 30, 31, 33, 37

Concertante in C, piano, 2 violins, cello, AV 157, 14

Daphne-Etude, violin, o.Op. 141, 348

Etudes, o.Op. 12, 14

Hochzeitmusik, piano, toy instruments, AV 163, 19

Hochzeitpräludium, two harmoniums, o.Op. 108, 224

Introduktion, Thema und Variationen, horn, piano, o.Op. 52, 20, 410

Introduktion, Thema und Variationen, flute, piano, o.Op. 56, 19, 410

Little Love Song (*Liebesliedchen*) in G, piano quartet, AV 182, No. 2, 79

Piano Quartet in C minor, Op. 13, 35, 44, 352, 389

Quartettsatz in E flat (string quartet), AV 211, 20, 410

Romanze in F, cello, piano, o.Op. 75, 28–9

String Quartet in A, Op. 2, 23, 34

Suite from *Capriccio*, harpsichord, o.Op. 138, 353

Variationen über 'Das Dirndl is harb auf mi', violin, viola, cello, 19

Violin Sonata in E flat, Op. 18, 51, 261, 389

Wedding Music (*Hochzeitmusik*), piano, toy instruments, AV 163, 19

CHORAL:

An den Baum Daphne, o.Op. 137, 347–8, 368

Austria (*Wildgans*), Op. 78, 257

Bardengesang (Kleist), AV 181, 44

Bardengesang (Klopstock), Op. 55, 44

Besinnung (abandoned), AV 306, 391

Cantate (Hofmannsthal), o.Op. 104, 185

Der Abend, Op. 34, No. 1, 110, 120, 348

Deutsche Motette, Op. 62, 184, 348

Die Tageszeiten, Op. 76, 247–8, 255

Die Göttin im Putzzimmer, o.Op. 120, 291, 320, 368

Drei Männerchöre, o.Op. 123, 306

Durch Einsamkeiten, durch waldwild Gehig, o.Op. 124, 317

Electra, o.Op. 74, 22

2 *Gesänge*, Op. 34, 109, 110, 120

Hymne, Op. 34, No. 2, 100, 120, 348

Hymne, 120–1

Olympische Hymne, o.Op. 119, 288, 312

Skatkanon, o.Op. 95A, 235

Taillefer, Op. 52, 20, 120, 137–8, 173

Utan svafvel och fosfor, o.Op. 88, 68

Wandrers Sturmlied, Op. 14, 35, 50

INCIDENTAL MUSIC:

Le bourgeois gentilhomme (*Der Bürger als Edelmann*) (*Ariadne auf Naxos*, 1st version), Op. 60, 126, 178, 185, 192

Le bourgeois gentilhomme (1917 revision), Op. 60 (III), 126, 199–200, 228; R.S. chooses for 85th birthday, 389

Fanfare, o.Op. 88A (*Die Jäger*), 69

Musik zu 'Lebende Bilder', o.Op. 89, 69, 238

JUVENILIA:

Etudes, o.Op. 12,

Lila (3 songs for Goethe Setting) (AV 206/o.Op. 44/5), 85

Mass in D, o.Op. 31, 5

Panzenburg-Polka, o.Op. 10, 13

Schneider-Polka, o.Op. 1, 13

Weihnachtslied, o.Op. 2, 13

LIEDER:

Ach, Lieb, ich muss nun scheiden, Op. 2, No. 3, 408

Ach weh mir unglückhaftem Mann, Op. 21, No. 4, 408

Allerseelen, Op. 10, No. 8, 43, 406, 408

All' mein Gedanken, Op. 21, No. 1, 218–19, 407, 408

Strauss, Richard Georg, LIEDER (cont.)

Als mir dein Lied erklang, Op. 68, No. 4, 199, 328

Amor, Op. 68, No. 5, 328

An die Nacht, Op. 68, No. 1, 328

Befreit, Op. 39, No. 4, 88, 119, 276

Begegnung, o.Op. 72, 29

Beim schlafengehen (Vier letzte Lieder, No. 3), 384, 386

Blauer Sommer, Op. 31, No. 1, 198

Blick vom oberen Belvedere, o.Op. 130, 336–7, 368, 408

Breit über mein Haupt, Op. 19, No. 2, 406, 408

Cäcilie, Op. 27, No. 2, 83, 404, 407

Das Bächlein, o.Op. 118, 282

Das Geheimnis, Op. 17, No. 3, 406

Das Lied des Steinklopfers, Op. 49, No. 4, 119, 120, 138

Das Rosenband, Op. 36, No. 1, 408

Der Arbeitsmann, Op. 39, No. 3, 119, 202

Der Fischer, o.Op. 33, 23

Der Stern, Op. 69, No. 1, 103, 202

Des Dichters Abendgang, Op. 47, No. 2, 202

Die Drossel, o.Op. 34, 22–3

Die erwachte Rose, o.Op. 66, 29

Die Frauen sind oft fromm und still, Op. 21, No. 5, 68–9

Die Georgine, Op. 10, No. 4, 43

Die heilige drei Könige, Op. 56, No. 6, 399

Die Liebe sass als Nachtigal, o.Op. 55, 19, 24, 410

Die Lilien glühn in Düften, AV 160, 19, 24, 410

Die Nacht, Op. 10, No. 3, 43, 406, 408

Die Ulme zu Hirsau, Op. 43, No. 3, 138

Die Verschwiegenen, Op. 10, No. 6, 43

Die Zeitlose, Op. 10, No. 7, 43

Drei Hymnen (Hölderlin), Op. 71, 210, 240

Drei Mutterlieder, 89

Du meines Herzens Krönelein, Op. 21, No. 2, 404, 408

Durch allen Schall und Klang, o.Op. 111, 240

Einerlei, Op. 69, No. 3, 202

Einkehr, o.Op. 3, 14

Erschaffen und Beleben, o.Op. 106, 240

Four Last Songs (Vier letzte Lieder), o.Op. 150, 384–6

Freundliche Vision, Op. 48, No. 1, 89, 119, 202, 407

Frühling (Vier letzte Lieder, No. 1), 384, 386, 387

Frühlingsfeier, Op. 56, No. 5, 276

Gesang der Apollopriesterin, Op. 33, No. 2, 120

Gesänge des Orients, Op. 77, 255

Glückes genug, Op. 37, No. 1, 408

Heimkehr, Op. 15, No. 5, 406, 407, 408

Heimliche Aufforderung, Op. 27, No. 3, 83, 404, 406, 408

Hochzeitlich Lied, Op. 37, No. 6, 135

Ich liebe dich, Op. 37, No. 2, 345, 406, 408

Ich schwebe, Op. 48, No. 2, 407

Ich trage meine Minne, Op. 32, No. 1, 120, 408

Ich wollt ein Sträusslein binden, Op. 68, No. 2, 199, 328

Im Abendrot (Vier letzte Lieder, No. 4), 385, 386; sketched, 371; completed, 382

In goldener Fülle, Op. 49, No. 2, 408

In Vaters Garten, o.Op. 64, 23

Jung Hexenlied, Op. 39, No. 2, 119

Kling!, Op. 48, No. 3, 120, 407

Krämerspiegel, Op. 66, 201–2, 210, 237; quoted in Capriccio, 331–2

Lass ruh'n die Toten, o.Op. 35, 22

Liebeshymnus, Op. 32, No. 3, 120

Lied der Frauen wenn die Männer im Krieg sind, Op. 68, No. 6, 199, 276

8 Lieder (Gilm), Op. 10, 43

5 Lieder, Op. 15, 51

6 Lieder (Schack), Op. 17, 51

6 Lieder (Schack), Op. 19, 51

2 Lieder (Lenau), Op. 26, 69

4 Lieder, Op. 27, 69, 83, 382

6 Lieder, Op. 67, 201

6 Brentano Lieder, Op. 68, 198–9, 255, 328

5 Lieder, Op. 69, 202

Mädchenblumen, Op. 22, 51

Malven, AV 304, 94, 384, 385

Mein Auge, Op. 37, No. 4, 119, 276

Meinem Kinde, Op. 37, No. 3, 89, 407

Morgen!, Op. 27, No. 4, 23, 83, 89, 386, 404, 406, 408

Muttertänderlei, Op. 43, No. 2, 89

Nachtgang, Op. 29, No. 3, 119, 138

Nebel, o.Op. 47, 23

Nichts, Op. 10, No. 2, 43

Notturno, Op. 44, No. 1, 119

Ophelia Lieder, Op. 67, Nos. 1–3, 201

O Schneller mein Ross, AV 159, 19, 24, 410

Rote Rosen, o.Op. 76, 23, 29–30

Ruhe, meine Seele! Op. 27, No. 1, 22, 83, 120, 382, 385, 406, 408

Sankt Michael, o.Op. 129, 336–7, 368

Säusle, Liebe Myrthe! Op. 68, No. 3, 199, 328

Schlagende Herzen, Op. 29, No. 2, 408

Schlechtes Wetter, Op. 69, No. 5, 202, 408

Schlichte Weisen (*5 Dahn Lieder*), Op. 21, 68

Sehnsucht, Op. 32, No. 2, 408

Seitdem dein Aug' in meines Schaute, Op. 17, No. 1, 408

September (*Vier letzte Lieder*, No. 2), 3, 384

Spielmann und Zither, o.Op. 40, 23

Ständchen, Op. 17, No. 2, 407, 408

Stiller Gang, Op. 31, No. 4, 119

Three Hymns (Hölderlin), Op. 71, 210, 240

Traum durch die Dämmerung, Op. 29, No. 1, 89, 92, 103, 119, 406, 407

Und dann nicht mehr (Rückert), o.Op. 114, 257

Vier letzte Lieder, o.Op. 150, 210, 395; composed, 384; discussed, 386; order of songs, 386; first performed, 386

Vom künftigen Alter (Rückert), o.Op. 115, 257

Waldgesang, o.Op. 55, 19, 24, 410

Waldseligkeit, Op. 49, No. 1, 119, 202, 408

Wenn . . ., Op. 31, No. 2, 120

Wer hat's getan? o.Op. 84A, 43

Wer tritt herein so fesch und schlank?, o.Op. 136, 346–7

Wiegenlied, Op. 41, No. 1, 89, 119, 407

Winterliebe, Op. 48, No. 5, 120, 202, 408

Winterreise, o.Op. 4, 13

Winterweihe, Op. 48, No. 4, 120, 202

Wozu noch, Mädchen, Op. 19, No. 1, 408

Xenion, o.Op. 131, 340

Zueignung, Op. 10, No. 1, 43, 406, 407, 408

Zugemessne Rhythmen reizen freilich, o.Op. 122, 291

MELODRAMA:

Enoch Arden, Op. 38, 90, 106

OPERAS:

Arabella, Op. 79, 94, 113, 137, 140, 230, 246, 256, 257, 264, 286, 288, 296, 308, 311, 324, 335, 338, 369; work begins on, 248; libretto constructed, 248,

Strauss, Richard Georg, OPERAS (*cont.*)
250–1; composition begun, 251–2,
257; discussed, 252–4; Munich
revision, 253; Hofmannsthal dies,
251; progress continues, 259–61;
crises over première, 262–3;
rehearsals and première, 264–5
Ariadne auf Naxos, Op. 60 (first
version), 104, 126, 174, 187;
composed, 177–81; first performed,
181–2; discussed, 182
Ariadne auf Naxos (second version,
with Prologue), 126, 182, 196, 209,
211, 213, 221, 226, 230, 231, 232, 233,
239, 252, 256, 275, 291, 308, 312, 320,
369, 377, 400; planned, 184–5; work
on, 191–5; first performed, 193; on
80th birthday, 352
Capriccio, Op. 85, 137, 140, 160, 201, 232,
235, 291, 329, 337, 339, 341; scenario
planned, 325–6; libretto fashioned,
329–31; Moonlight music, 332–3;
Sextet composed, 334; opera
completed, 334; première, 338–9;
Sextet première, 340; R.S. conducts
Moonlight music for last time, 389
Celestina (abandoned), AV 274, 293, 315
Danae, oder die Vernunftheirat, AV 256,
216, 315
Daphne, Op. 82, 232, 291, 306, 335, 337,
338, 402; libretto drafted, 307; R.S.
dissatisfied, 308, work begun on,
309; R.S. critical of libretto, 309–12;
music begun, 311; R.S. involves
Krauss, 311–12; orchestral ending,
314; full score completed, 317;
première, 319; discussed, 320
Das erhabenes Lied der Könige
(abandoned), 77
Der Reichstag zu Mainz (abandoned),
77–8

Der Rosenkavalier, Op. 59, 4, 57, 94, 137,
140, 152, 158, 159, 160, 174, 177, 180,
187, 193, 194, 195, 196, 209, 211, 216,
221, 232, 239, 250, 264, 275, 284, 369,
406, 407; composed, 162–6; success
of, 166, 170–2; discussed, 167–9; score
given to Vienna, 221; Paris première,
240; R.S. conducts dress rehearsal,
388–9; Trio at R.S. funeral, 394; R.S.
'bored' by it, 401
Der Rosenkavalier (film), o.Op. 112,
238–9, 407
Des Esels Schatten, AV 300, 374
Die ägyptische Helena, Op. 75, 214, 230,
247, 252, 255, 335, 344; score given to
Vienna, 221; Act 1 play-through,
240–1; completed, 242; trouble over
première, 242–3; première, 244;
discussed, 245–6; revisions, 275–6
Die Frau ohne Schatten, Op. 65, 134,
180, 183, 187, 191, 193, 200, 230, 232,
246, 252, 261, 275, 296, 329, 352–3;
origin of, 174–5; begun, 185–6; work
on, 188, 189–90, 191, 194–5, 199–200;
first performances, 212–13;
discussed, 213–15; revisions, 214–15
Die Liebe der Danae, Op. 83, 306, 334,
344, 393; Hofmannsthal origin, 216,
315; work begins on, 315–16; libretto
fashioned, 321–3; short score Act 2
finished, 324; full score completed,
328; Salzburg première, 353–5; R.S.
describes, 355; discussed, 355–6;
official première, 356
Die schweigsame Frau, Op. 80, 146, 289,
294, 308; draft synopsis, 262; work
proceeds, 280, 286; completed, 294;
rehearsals and première, 297–9, 301;
banned, 302; discussed, 303–4
Don Juan (abandoned), 69
Ekke und Schnittlein (abandoned), 127

Elektra, Op. 58, 4, 23, 88, 94, 112, 115, 141, 147, 162, 169, 174, 187, 196, 222, 231, 232, 233, 240, 256, 260, 272, 286, 320, 324, 379; begun, 151–3; completed, 154–8; discussed, 158–61

Feuersnot, Op. 50, 78, 84, 87–8, 126, 152, 172, 187, 241, 296, 406; composed, 132–4; first performed, 135

Friedenstag, Op. 81, 306; Zweig suggests, 287; libretto drafted, 307; R.S. dissatisfied with, 307–08; completed, 308; première, 318, discussed, 318–19; Paris première, 387

Guntram, Op. 25, 55, 56, 64, 67, 69, 78, 80, 84, 85, 86, 101, 105, 109,111, 117, 125, 152, 227; completed, 70–2; first performed, 72–3; Munich failure, 73–5; revised, 286

Intermezzo, Op. 72, 78, 80, 89, 94, 104, 113, 137, 140, 210, 227, 230, 233, 235, 238, 246, 256, 335, 407; origin of, 95–6; libretto quoted, 97–8; first stirrings, 196; R.S. works on, 200, 221; completed, 222; first performances, 229; discussed, 230–4

Peregrinus Proteus (abandoned), AV 257, 210

Salome, Op. 54, 63, 104, 112, 115, 147, 150, 152, 154, 158, 159, 169, 187, 193, 207, 222, 232, 233, 240, 280, 369, 401, 406; French version, 141–2; first performances and censorship troubles, 142–5; discussed, 147–9

Semiramis (abandoned), AV 239, 174, 294, 295, 296, 297, 306, 315

Till Eulenspiegel bei den Schildenbürgen (abandoned), AV 219, 84

ORCHESTRAL:

Also sprach Zarathustra, Op. 30, 85, 100, 104, 105, 133, 138, 152, 177, 218, 312, 352, 408; discussed, 111–13

Aus Italien, Op. 16, 20, 46, 50–1, 53; first performed, 50

Bildersinfonie, AV 233, 376

Brandenburgsche Mars (*Der Rosenkavalier* film), o.Op. 99, 238

Concert Overture in C minor, o.Op. 80, 29, 30, 33

Der Antichrist (abandoned), AV 247, 175–6

Die Donau (abandoned), AV 291, 336, 340–1

Divertimento, Op. 86, 329

Don Juan, Op. 20, 3, 55, 59, 69, 105, 110, 112, 139, 352, 359, 381, 401, 406, 407, 408; first performed, 56

Don Quixote, Op. 35, 11, 102, 103–04, 116, 135, 139, 201, 218, 227, 230, 232, 376, 379, 407, 408; completed, 106; discussed, 113–14

Ein Heldenleben, Op. 40, 78, 89, 92, 94, 103–04, 109, 129, 135, 138, 230, 352, 353, 377, 401, 406, 407, 408; completed, 106, discussed, 114–18

Eine Alpensinfonie, Op. 64, 112, 127, 184, 187, 190, 239, 336, 368, 407; composed and discussed, 175–7; first performed, 191

Einleitung und Walzer aus Der Rosenkavalier, I. und II. Akt, o.Op. 139, 359, 368, 372

Fanfare (Wiener Philharmoniker), o.Op. 109, 226

Festliches Präludium, Op. 61, 183–4, 281, 336, 408

Festmarsch in D, o.Op. 84, 35

Festmarsch in E, Op. 1, 18, 24

Festmusik der Stadt Wien, o.Op. 133, 342

Japanische Festmusik, Op. 84, 328, 397, 407

Strauss, Richard Georg, ORCHESTRAL (*cont.*)

Kampf und Sieg, o.Op. 89, No. 3, 69

Künstler-Tragödie (abandoned), AV 231, 127, 175

Macbeth, Op. 23, 51, 55, 69, 79, 110, 112, 376; first performed, 56

Metamorphosen, o.Op. 142, 365, 366, 369, 375; begun, 358; completed, 360–01, Septet version, 360–01; discussed, 361–2; controversy over, 380

Military March in F (*Der Rosenkavalier* film), o.Op. 112, 238

München (*Gedächtniswalzer*), o.Op. 140, 359–60

München (*Gelegenheitswalzer*), o.Op. 125, 323–4; MS given to Bavarian State Library, 389

Overture in A minor, o.Op. 62, 19, 20, 410

Serenade in E flat, Op. 7, 27, 33, 34, 342, 344, 374, 408

Serenade in G, o.Op. 32, 14

Sextet from *Capriccio*, 334, 340

Sonatina No. 1 in F, o.Op. 135, 342, 344, 368

Sonatina No. 2 in E, o.Op. 143, 349, 365–6, 368, 369, 370

'Spring Symphony' (abandoned), 127

Suite in B flat, Op. 4, 34–5, 342

Suite, *Le bourgeois gentilhomme*, Op. 60 (IIIA), 200, 352, 374, 406, 407, 408

Suite, *Schlagobers*, Op. 70, 262, 408

Symphonia Domestica, Op. 53, 4, 15, 78, 94, 113, 129, 152, 218, 227, 230, 352, 378, 408; first performed, 139–40; discussed, 139–40; R.S. conducts on 75th birthday, 324

Symphonic Fantasy on *Die Frau ohne Schatten*, o.Op. 146, 372, 376

Symphonic Fantasy on *Josephs Legende*, o.Op. 148, 372

Symphony No. 1 in D minor, o.Op. 69, 18, 24–5

Symphony No. 2 in F minor, Op. 12, 28, 30, 33, 40–1, 49, 50, 408; first performed, 35–6

Till Eulenspiegels lustige Streiche, Op. 28, 85, 100, 110–11, 112, 139, 152, 331, 352, 358, 381, 401, 406, 407, 408; composed, 84–5

Tod und Verklärung, Op. 24, 55, 64, 69, 75, 104, 105, 110, 116, 139, 140, 291, 252, 359, 379, 381, 407, 408; first performed, 56; quoted in *Im Abendrot*, 386; reference on deathbed, 391

PIANOFORTE:

Aus alter Zeit (Little Gavotte), o.Op. 57, 18, 410

De Brandenburgsche Mars, o.Op. 99, 238

Five Pieces, Op. 3, 34

14 Improvisationen und Fuge über ein Originalthema (2 hands), o.Op. 81/AV 177, 31, 38

Little Gavotte (*Aus alter Zeit*), o.Op. 57, 18, 410

Skizzen, o.Op. 59, 19, 20, 410

Sonata No. 1 in E, o.Op. 38, 20

Sonata No. 2 in C minor, o.Op. 60, 19, 410

Stimmungsbilder, Op. 9, 26, 33, 406

Waltz in G minor (*Kupelwieser Walzer* by Schubert), AV 192, 342

SOLO INSTRUMENT & ORCHESTRA:

Burleske in D minor, piano, o.Op. 85, 44, 50, 378, 397, 408; first performed, 56

Duett Concertino in F, clarinet, bassoon, o.Op. 147, 381; begun, 372

Horn Concerto No. 1 in E flat, Op. 11, 26, 36; first performed, 28

Horn Concerto No. 2 in E flat, o. Op. 132, 340, 341, 344, 368

Oboe Concerto in D, o.Op. 144, 366, 368, 375; suggested, 364; discussed, 369–70

Panathenäenzug, piano left-hand, Op. 74, 247

Parergon zur Symphonia Domestica, piano left-hand, Op. 73 (I) 247

Rhapsody in C minor, piano, AV 213, 44

Romanze in E flat, clarinet, o.Op. 61, 20, 410

Romanze in F, cello, o.Op. 75, 28–9

Violin Concerto, Op. 8, 26; first performed, 27–8

Violin Concerto No. 2 (sketches), AV 299, 374

VERSIONS OF OTHER COMPOSERS' WORKS:

BEETHOVEN: *Die Ruinen von Athen*, AV 190, 228

GLUCK: *Iphigénie en Tauride*, AV 186, 64, 69

MOZART: *Idomeneo*, AV 191, 257–8, 259, 336

Stravinsky, Igor, 148, 174, 187, 210, 224, 395, 399; on R.S. at rehearsal, 186

Streicher, Julius, 274, 285

Strindberg, August, 119, 224

Suitner, Oskar, 320

Sutermeister, Heinrich, 369

Swarowsky, Hans, 330

Szell, Georg, 211, 229, 381

Tauber, Richard, 209, 242

Taubmann, Horst, 338

Tchaikovsky, Pyotr, 43, 101

te Kanawa, Dame Kiri, 384

Tenschert, Roland, 139, 211, 350–1, 353, 366

Ternina, Milka, 73

Terrasse, Claude, 163

Teschemacher, Margarete, creates Daphne, 320

Teschendorff, Emil, 33

Tetrazzini, Luisa, 177

Theodor, Karl, 241

Thode, Daniela (*née* Bülow), 79, 278

Thomas, Ambroise, 66

Thomas, Theodor, 35–6

Thuille, Ludwig, 23, 26, 32, 34, 40, 46, 48, 61, 62, 70, 105, 132, 235; boyhood letters to R.S., 15–22; R.S.'s opinion of, 20–2

Thumann, Paul, 33

Tietjen, Heinz, 235, 262, 276, 278, 355; R.S. letter to, 359

Toller, Georg, 166

Tombo, August, 13

Tortelier, Paul, 376

Toscanini, Arturo, 143, 278, 287–8, 298; R.S. substitutes for at Bayreuth, 276–7

Treitschke, Heinrich von, 86

Tröber, Arthur, 214, 344; on R.S. conducting, 402–3

Tuchman, Barbara W., 115, 127

Turecek, Emilie, 250

Turgenev, Ivan, 241

Uhl, Oswald, 407

Uhland, Ludwig, 22, 120, 137

Ursuleac, Viorica, 94, 95, 263, 265, 275, 276, 282, 283, 312, 314, 316, 323, 334, 336, 340, 375; creates Arabella, 264; creates Maria, 318; creates Countess Madeleine, 338

Vaughan Williams, Ralph, 111, 137, 174, 284

Verdi, Giuseppe, 6, 47, 48, 101, 134, 148, 161, 283, 303, 331, 366, 367, 369; on *Guntram*, 75; *Falstaff*, 75, 128, 303, 325

Veress, Sándor, 328

Vermeulen, Matthijs, 380

Vienna, 27, 32, 64, 89, 99, 152, 170, 172, 173, 183, 191, 193, 199, 200; R.S. house in, 221–2; R.S. 75th birthday in, 319; R.S. wartime refuge in, 336–7, 342, 347–8; R.S. 80th birthday in, 350–3; Opera House destroyed, 361; *Wiener Allgemeine Zeitung*, 27; Philharmonic Orchestra, 27, 80, 222, 226, 324, 336, 338, 341, 352, 372, 402, 408, R.S. centenary tribute, 336; Vienna Opera, 27, 76, 88, 125, 135, 139, 142, 143, 166, 229, 255, 262, 263, 307, 339, 372, R.S. début at, 164, approach to R.S., 205–06, R.S. accepts post, 211–12, tour to raise money for, 215–16, R.S. controversies, 219–21, R.S. dismissed, 227–8, *Helena* première, 244–5, Krauss appointed, 256

Vogl, Heinrich, 47, 73

Wagner, Cosima, 54, 66, 67, 68, 79, 85, 133, 196, 276; R.S. meets, 55; friendship with R.S., 58–60

Wagner, Eva, 85, 278

Wagner, Richard, 4, 7, 16, 17, 19, 22, 26, 35, 45, 46, 49, 62, 67, 71, 79, 84, 88, 101, 105, 130, 133, 138, 149, 168, 172, 175, 270, 276, 284, 302, 303, 366, 369; *Das Rheingold*, 27; *Der fliegende Holländer*, 41–2; *Der Ring des Nibelungen*, 19, 67; *Die Feen*, R.S. rehearses, 52; *Die Meistersinger von Nürnberg*, 7, 55, 66, 68, 78, 79, 101, 133, 150, 285, 291, 331, 345, 408; *Die Walküre*, 17, 27, 38, 66, 393; *Götterdämmerung*, 352, 366; *Lohengrin*, 7, 55, 58, 66, 67, 158, 253, 300, R.S. conducts, 58–9; *Parsifal*, 5, 8, 26, 47, 55, 68, 71, 133, 207, 215, 278, 282, R.S. conducts at Bayreuth, 276–7; *Rienzi*, 101, 366; *Siegfried*, 16, 393;

Tannhäuser, 7, 26, 55, 59, 66, 71, 78, 100, 101, 158; *Tristan und Isolde*, 7, 26, 47, 52, 55, 59, 68, 78, 79, 101, 127, 133, 168, 211, 331, 345, 387, 394, 401, 402, 403, R.S. conducts, 67

Wagner, Siegfried, 61, 270, 276; rift with R.S., 75, 85

Wagner, Winifred, 276, 277, 278

Wallerstein, Lothar, 256, 257, 275, 311

Walter, Benno, 13, 23, 28, 73

Walter, Bruno, 185, 191, 247, 276, 286, 298, 380; R.S. substitutes for, 272–4

Walter, Maria Kunigunda, 6

Wanamaker's department store, NY, 139

Wassermann, Jakob, 211

Weber, Carl Maria von, 7, 13, 14, 24, 48, 49, 52, 66, 101, 130, 184, 303, 366, 407

Weber, Ludwig, 316, 318

Webern, Anton von, 173, 210, 233, 399; on *Rosenkavalier*, 172

Wedekind, Frank, 125, 147

Weidt, Lucie, 212

Weill, Kurt, 210, 355

Weimar, 35, 46, 54, 62, 64, 67, 71, 74, 79, 82, 83, 84, 106, 108, 271, 402; Weimar Opera, R.S. appointed conductor, 53; conducts *Lohengrin*, 58–9; *Guntram* première, 72–3

Weingartner, Felix von, 72, 106, 256

Weinheber, Josef, 337, 341

Weis family, 30

Weiss, Milton, 363

Welitsch, Ljuba, 146

Wellesz, Egon, 211

Welte Company, 406

Welti, Emil, 127

Welti, Lydia, 127

Werner, Anton von, 33

Wetzler, Hermann Hans, 138–9

Wiborg, Elisa, 66, 68

Wieland, Christoph Martin, 341, 374

Wiene, Robert, 238

Wihan, Dora, 42, 43, 47; romance with R.S., 37–8, 54–5, 56–8

Wihan, Hanuš, 23, 28, 29, 30, 37, 38

Wilde, Oscar, 135–6, 147, 148, 151, 397

Wildgans, Anton, 257, 317

Wilhelm II, Kaiser, 115, 117, 127–8, 150, 170, 175, 189, 190, 216, 269, 271, 293

Wilhelm, Kurt, 31, 371

Williamson, John, 111

Wittgenstein, Paul, 247

Wittich, Marie, 142, 243

Wolf-Ferrari, Ermanno, 185

Wolfes, Felix, 298

Wolff, Louise, 272, 274

Wolzogen, Ernst von, 132–3, 135, 172

Wöpke, Peter, 28

Wüllner, Franz, 27, 28, 31, 36, 41, 84

Wüllner, Ludwig, 88

Wurmser, Leo, 244

Zeller, Heinrich, 60, 67, 68, 69, 73, 79, 80

Zincke, H. F. A. (Hans Sommer), 108, 130

Zola, Émile, 148

Zöllner, Heinrich, 52, 105

Zweig, Stefan, 145, 146, 210, 211, 264, 276, 280, 286, 288, 289, 297, 300, 301, 305, 306, 307, 310, 314, 318, 397, 398; first meets R.S., 260; impressions of R.S., 260, 302–03; draft synopsis of *Die schweigsame Frau*, 262; *Friedenstag* planned, 287; denies Toscanini anecdote, 287–8; R.S. plans secret collaboration, 292–6; Nazis and *Die schweigsame Frau*, 285, 298; R.S. demands reinstatement of S.Z.'s name, 299; critical of opera, 302; suicide, 304; origin of *Capriccio*, 325